Civic Center Reference
299
Wheeler Post, 1869-1956
The sacred scriptures of
the Japanese, with all
authoritative variants,
chronologically arranged,

D1775364

THE SACRED SCRIPTURES
OF THE JAPANESE

WITH ALL AUTHORITATIVE VARIANTS, CHRONOLOGICALLY ARRANGED, SETTING FORTH THE NARRATIVE OF THE CREATION OF THE COSMOS, THE DIVINE DESCENT OF THE SKY-ANCESTOR OF THE IMPERIAL HOUSE AND THE LINEAGE OF THE EARTHLY EMPERORS, TO WHOM THE SUN-DEITY HAS GIVEN THE RULE OF THE WORLD UNTO AGES ETERNAL

NEW YORK

THE SACRED SCRIPTURES OF THE JAPANESE

BY

POST WHEELER, Ph.D., LL.D., Litt.D.
Sometime American *Chargé d'Affaires* at Tok'yo

HENRY SCHUMAN, INC.
Marin County Free Library
Civic Center Administration Building
San Rafael, California

COPYRIGHT, 1952, BY POST WHEELER
MANUFACTURED IN THE UNITED STATES OF AMERICA
BY H. WOLFF, NEW YORK
DESIGNED BY MARSHALL LEE

To
James Henry Dunham, Ph.D., LL.D.
Dean Emeritus of the College of Liberal Arts and Sciences
of Temple University
in recognition of his distinguished scholarship
and with personal gratitude for his
interest in this work.

CONTENTS

AUTHOR'S FOREWORD   v

INTRODUCTION
ix

SOURCES: xviii

    1. Records-of-Wind-and-Earth (Fudoki)   xviii
    2. Narration-of-Ancient-Things (Kujiki)   xx
    3. Records-of-Ancient-Matters (Kojiki)   xxi
    4. Written-Chronicles-of-Nippon (Nihongi)   xxiii
    5. Collection-of-Omitted-Ancient-Sayings (Kogo-Shui)   xxiv
    6. Records-of-Family-Titles-and-Names (Shojiroku)   xxv
    7. Institutes-of-the-Engi-Era (Engi-Shiki)   xxvi
    8. Other Myth-Material   xxvii

THE TEXT   xxviii

THE ARGUMENT   xxxvii

THE MYTH NARRATIVE
1

KAMI LIST
(Deities and Personages)
361

ANALYSIS OF THE NARRATIVE
385

I   MYTH PARALLELS   387

II   PRIMEVAL CULTS   393

    1. The Cult of the Sun   393
    2. The Cult of the Sword   395
    3. The Cult of the Phallus   399
    4. The Cult of the Serpent   402

      5. Tree Worship   406
      6. Living Entombment and Human Sacrifice   409
      7. Matriarchy   411

III   WESTERN ELEMENTS   **416**

IV   SOUTHERN ELEMENTS   **424**

V   LOCAL (ABORIGINAL) ELEMENTS   **429**

VI   THE RATIONALE OF THE NARRATIVE   **439**

NOTES   **445**

AUTHOR'S FOREWORD

The better part of a century has flown since Matthew Perry, commodore of the American Navy, nosed his flagship *Mississippi* into Edo (present-day Tok'yo) Bay and by his unwelcome midwifery brought to birth the *enfant prodige* of the modern nations, the Japan of Prince Ito and the Imperial Constitution, of Admiral Togo and Tsushima Strait, of General Araki and Manchukuo, of Premier Tojo and Pearl Harbor.

The miracle of its reorganization along the lines of modern government began to dawn on the Western world even before the China War of the '90s, and with the Russo-Japanese conflict a decade later the portent of its stark militarism struck deep into Occidental consciousness. Since then an army of books, in a dozen languages, have been written of Japan and its people, whose readers today know little of the Japanese mind. The West, in peace and in war, has concerned itself with the surface of its civilization, with its borrowed Western overlay rather than the subsoil beneath. That subsoil is the myth-mass which the race, from its remotest beginnings, has made its own, it is to that one must look to find the Japanese formula.

This body of legend, folklore to us but credible history to the people of the archipelago, is tangled in the roots of everything Japanese. Behind its painting, its music, the symbolism of the gorgeous mimes called the Nō, behind temple ceremonial and festival, or strange demoniac "curtain-raiser" at the theatre, or children's game, or folk-superstition—always this mass of myth is there, at the back of the beyond, the subsoil of modern Japanese thought. From it spring the inspirations of the national art, the national poetry, the national dance and religious drama of the empire.

In no other land do we find a people's sacred legend so interknit with the individual's daily thought and life. Its episodes peer at one from every nook and byway. The primal myth of the slaughter of the Eight-Forked-Serpent by the deity Brave-Swift-Impetuous-Male, brother of Bright-Sky-

Shiner the Sun-Goddess, is pictured on Japan's paper currency. I have seen it produced *au grand sérieux* at Tok'yo's Imperial Theatre in the same week with one of Ibsen's tragedies and a Viennese light opera. The scene of the presentation to the first Earthly Emperor Jimmu-*Tenno* with whose reign the Japanese begin their chronology, of the divine crosssword fallen from the Sky, is engraved on an issue of bank notes, and the opening chapter of the history which the Japanese urchin dog-ears in the public schools relates the formation of the first island of the archipelago from the spear-point of the creative deity standing on the "Floating Sky-Bridge," whose rock-ruin (since it fell to earth after that divine service) the modern guide is at pains to point out to the tourist.

It is not difficult to see how this extraordinary familiarity with the race's sacred myth and its reverence for it came about. It is only in the last century that the Japanese mind has come to concern itself with world-movements. For the mass of the people the history of the world has been almost literally the history of the archipelago. Thus confined the racial imagination has naturally developed along national lines. The physical isolation that produced such a profound unity in the material life of the race fostered in its mental life an unparalleled knowledge and appreciation of its own national history. And this history has its roots deep in the legends surrounding its deities, its origin, and its primeval adventures.

For this reason the myth-mass is the inevitable introduction to a knowledge of the Japanese people. He who would understand them has first to acquaint himself with this background, as the Oriental who would comprehend our West of the twentieth century must know first of all the Christian Bible. The more so as Japan, religiously speaking, has not yet emerged from the era of fundamentalism. The chronology of its sacred texts is as true to the Japanese peasant as the chronology of the Hebrew Genesis was to the crusader of the Middle Ages. The Japanese counterparts of the miracle-plays and the churchly buffooneries of the Europe of that era are still very much alive.

The myths by which Japan lives today are embalmed in its sacred Scriptures, the most ancient of which, handed down by verbal repetition from a time long antedating the beginning of history (as were the epics of Homer and the metaphysical speculations of the Brahman Sanscritists) attained written form about the time the Venerable Bede was biting his quill over the *Historia Ecclesiastica*. In their entirety they constitute the Japanese Bible, though the Shinto, the native and State system of worship, has never boasted a canon. They are to the race what the Old Testament—the sacred narrative of the creation and the early history of the Jewish race—would be to the races of Christendom, if there were added thereto the so-called Apocryphal Books, with a fair quantity of the Talmud, and the resultant whole invested with the authority of inspiration.

In the tapestry of this omnium gatherum are woven unmistakably the traits and qualities we recognize as characteristically Japanese. But it holds much more. It pictures the primal faiths and loyalties and ambitions that in fusion have created the national urge that has prompted the Japan of today to run amok through the jungle-turmoil of global war, and at end to fling itself in suicidal frenzy at the throat of the West. The pattern it holds is as distinct as the Nazi blueprint of *Mein Kampf*.

In the Japanese Scriptures two greater writings stand above the rest. And these are supplemented and amplified by a large number of lesser manuscripts that have been preserved from time immemorial in certain temples and a few in the secret archives of certain great families, as some of the Epistles and Apocryphal Books were preserved in churches in Asia Minor and Egypt in the first two centuries of our era. With the exception of the two greater Scriptures these have not been translated, except fragmentarily, into any European tongue, and such renditions as exist in English and German are primarily for the scholar, and have remained coffined in dusty leather on the shelves of learned societies.

In this volume these scattered Scriptures, greater and lesser, with all known variants, are collated and combined in a connected narrative, as far as possible chronological, the race-story proceeding from the emergence of deity from the primordial chaos, through the descent from the sky of the Imperial Ancestor and the conquest of the realm by the earthly emperors, whom the Sun-Deity has divinely invested with the rule of the World "unto fine-dust ages."

This, the doctrine of the Divine Descent, with its corollary, the apotheosis of the Imperial Succession, is the key to the riddle of the new militaristic Japan. It runs through all the weave of shadowy colors like a sharp bright thread, marking the texture over and over with the key *motif* of the whole design, Japan's divine right to the over-rule of this unruly planet we call The Earth.

INTRODUCTION

Japan's oldest Scripture extant, whose authenticity is unquestioned, is the *Kojiki* (Records of Ancient Matters), which achieved written form in the early part of the eighth century, and which recites the stories and genealogies of the ancient deities of the archipelago and of their descendants who people and rule the Japan of the present. It is a bald narrative, grotesque, *sauvage*, throwing the imagination back to primeval, uncouth dawns. The *Nihongi* (Written Chronicles of Japan), the second of the two "Greater Scriptures," contemporaneous in compilation but centuries later in method and feeling, supplementing and amplifying the *Kojiki*, with its classified variants of the myths, humanizes the story.

There are other writings of great antiquity, which, though modern scholarship accounts them of lesser value and authority, contain further material of scarcely less interest and value—such as the *Kujiki* (Narration of Ancient Things), the *Kogo-Shui* (Collection of Omitted Ancient Sayings), the *Shojiroku* (Records of Family Titles and Names), and the *Engi-Shiki* (Institutes of the Engi Era). And to these is to be added the mythic material in the *Fudoki* (Records of Wind and Earth), in large part most ancient of all, those local and provincial writings the great mass of which have come down to us in the merest fragments and these, like the Sapphic poems, mainly as they have been quoted by later commentators. This material is of value for mythic detail surrounding deities or heroic personages identified with the particular localities of which these writings form record. There remain only a small number of legends of undisputed age and widespread distribution. Such are the main sources from which the myth-story of the Japanese race is to be constructed.

In the preparation of this myth-narrative I have incurred much more obligation for every kind and degree of assistance than could be adequately acknowledged in many pages. The invaluable translations of Chamberlain and Aston, together with the elaborate notes of Motoöri's *Kojiki-Den*

(1823), throw a flood of light upon the older texts. The latter author's treatise on the *Kujiki* is of especial value. The earlier work of Mabuchi has furnished his pupils with a thousand quotations and citations. I have had access to the *Teïseï-Kokun-Kojiki* Text (1803). I am under deep obligation, in connection with the *Shojiroku*, to Dr. Kurida Hiroshi, whose *Shin-Shojiroku* I count the best of all the commentaries, and for some translated fragments of the *Engi-Shiki* I am indebted to Sir Ernest Satow. As for the *Fudoki*, I have made most use of the *Izumo-Fudoki-Kaï* of Uchiya Shinr'yo (1782). Dr. Kurida's collation of the fragments (the *Santeï-Kofudoki-Ichibun*) and his treatise on the *Kujiki* (the *Kunimiya-Tsuko-Hongi-Ko*) have been of inestimable service.

For critical notes I have made free use of all procurable commentaries of both Japanese and European scholars, and of the transactions and proceedings of learned societies, historical, geographical, ethnographical, and anthropological; and their scope has been enlarged by study of various manuscripts, such as the *Koro-Kojitsu-Den* (1300) of Enseï, the most complete treatise I have found on animal messengers of deity, and the *Kwaï-Kitsudan*, of unknown authorship, dealing with historical localities and vulgar tales of Izumo Province. For the former I am beholden to Masayoshi Ozaki's invaluable compilation, the *Gunsho-Ichiran* (Complete View of a Collection of Army Writings) (1801), a collection of synopses that was the result of thirty years labor. The Imperial Library in Tok'yo contains also an anonymous copy of the *Gunsho-Ichiran-Betsuroku* (-Classified Statement), which is based upon Ozaki's work. It contains some thirty-four divisions of classified classical Japanese literature.

These annals are not peculiar in their assertion of the race's celestial origin; indeed, the concept is a hallmark of the early myths of many peoples. It becomes remarkable, however, in the light of the fact that the Japanese alone have brought it down into modern times as an undebatable and guiding tenet, a primal axiom upon which the national philosophy is based. The race denies celestial descent to all others—it moves alone, estranged by its very nature from all other earthly stocks, the unique exception in human creation, the one crystal current in an ocean of turbidities. In the *Heïke-Monogatari* (late twelfth centry) one of the priestly characters declares Buddha and the Emperor to be of equal authority.

The fact that the Western mind finds it difficult to take seriously this specious claim per se is no measure of the seriousness of its appeal to the race that puts it forward. The Western historian of Japan finds this evidenced in the insistence with which the doctrine has been taught in every era. The priesthood through many centuries, drawing inspiration and authority from regent and shogun, have jealously employed it to foster the national loyalty by developing what Professor de Benneville has characterized as "the propaganda of the imperial apotheosis."

Up to the close of the recent world-war the growth of democratic ideas among the urban population, and the progressive individualism that sprang from it, ran parallel with the conservative nationalism of the ruling class, which has sternly upheld the traditional sanctity surrounding the Sovereign, the nation's spiritual as well as its temporal head. "The Emperor," wrote Prince Ito in his commentaries on the constitution, "is Sky-descended, divine and sacred. He is pre-eminent above all His subjects. He must be reverenced and is inviolable. . . . Not only shall there be no irreverence toward the Emperor's person, but also He shall not be made a topic of derogatory comment, nor of discussion." This conception was the keystone of the arch of Japanese national solidarity, and there was seldom need to invoke the official prohibition against vernacular publication of any critical treatise on the imperial origin and genealogy. Social readjustment in accordance with the thought of the modern world must be well established before this fortress may be considered wholly abandoned. "He [the Emperor]," wrote Uëhara, in his *Political Development of Japan*, "is to the Japanese mind the Supreme Being in the cosmos of Japan, as God is in the universe to the pantheistic philosopher. From him everything emanates; in him everything subsists; there is nothing on the soil of Japan existent independent of him. He is the sole owner of the empire, the author of law, justice, privilege and honor, and the symbol of the unity of the Japanese. . . . He is supreme in all temporal affairs of state as well as in spiritual matters, and he is the foundation of Japanese social and civic morality." *

---

* Necessarily this supremacy carries with it in popular thought the attributes of the supernatural. "The hallowed Scion of Divine Descent," wrote Yaë-Kichi Yabè, in "The Philosophy of the Serious-Minded" (*Japan*, December, 1915), "our Emperor represents on earth all the celestial virtues, wisdom and might. He comes among us in unruptured lineage from the remotest ancestral Deity, the Heavenly God, who laid the foundation of the empire destined to be so mighty and so lasting. In his veins runs the very blood of the God, and in him we behold the glory and effulgence of the Supreme Being, self-existent and eternal." Conformably to this doctrine the acts of evil emperors are variously explained. The excesses of Muretsu (Buretsu)-*Tenno* (reigned 499-506) of whom the *Nihongi* records, "he worked much evil and accomplished no good thing," are even claimed by some modern historians to have been confused with the annals of a Kudaran contemporary, King Multa.

Twenty-five years ago Japanese journals were apt to state the logical conclusion of the reasoning with sufficient clearness. "Is it possible," asked one Buddhist organ, "to reconcile the idea of the sacredness of the Japanese Emperor with the doctrine of Christianity? . . . Is it not against the very constitution of Japan to recognize supreme beings such as a God, a Jesus, a

To the Japanese bred in this teaching his gods are still on earth; in a very real sense their celestial ichor glows in the veins of Hirohito, the one hundred and twenty-third Sovereign after the deified Jimmu-*Tenno*. Small wonder if the legend of the sun-descent tallies the genealogies of the Emperors after the manner of the Gospel of Saint Mark—"which was the son of Enos, which was the son of Seth, which was the son of Adam, which was the son of God."

Moreover, the subject as well as his Sovereign was the lineal offspring of the deities, for this living chain of uninterrupted continuity links not alone the ruling line but likewise the commoner of the sun empire to the ancestral deities of his populous pantheon. Religious teaching inculcated the lesson at every hand—how certainly may be seen from the *Catechism of the Great Way* (Shinto).*

Question: "In what manner was human life first produced?"

Answer: "Their Augustnesses He-Who-Invites and She-Who-Invites, in obedience to the divine will of the Sky Deity, first trod the path of spouses and produced deity-men, deigning to lay the foundation for all enterprises. Hence it was that all mankind (i.e., the Japanese) breathe and have their being. For this reason the present writer's flesh and blood have been inherited from these deities and they are the first parents of the human race."

Thus to the Japanese—in far greater measure than to the Greek of the classical period, to whom all outer peoples, lacking the Olympian culture, were barbarians—all other of the earth's races have formed but a *hoi polloi* from which the Sun-Race stood apart, unique and supreme. He alone had blood kinship with the High-Sky, as well as with every superman that towers above legend and real history. The legends of the primal Kami merge into the heroic epic, and the hero *epos* is the vestibule of the drama of aristocracy. Deity and demigod, godling and hero, the chain links, without a break, the spirits of all who have passed before fusing to form the vast ancestral soul of the race.

Here and there, to be sure, have been lifted voices. Araï Hakuseki,

pope, a church, or a bible, other than the sovereign of the country? Do Christians mean to regard Jesus as a faithful subject of the Japanese Emperor, or do they mean to bring down the latter under the rule of the former, so that he might offer the prayer, saying, 'Jesus, the Son of God, have mercy upon me'?"

---

* Composed by Baron Sengè Takatomi (*Sompuku*), founder of the *Taïsha* sect. Published 1890. It has been translated by W. L. Schwartz. (See *Transactions of the Asiatic Society of Japan*, vol. XLI, pt. IV, "The Great Shrine of Idzumo.")

early in the eighteenth century, proved to his own satisfaction that the miraculous portions of the legends were allegorical, and the Sky-Kami mere men deified after death. Hirata Atsutanè (1776-1843) also thought that "what we call Kami were all men," but in the early dawn of science and philosophy example was not made of a heterodoxy so unique. There is too the well-known poem of the *R'yojin-Hisho*:

> O myriad-mighty Kami!
> If so be Kami ye || Veritably are,
> I pray you, look on me with pity.
> E'en the ancient Kami once || Were men, as we are.

> *Chihayaburu Kami!*
> *Kami-ni mashimasu* || *Mono naraba,*
> *Awarè-to oboshimesè.*
> *Kami mo mukashi-wa* || *Hito zo kashi.*

It is not so many years, however, since the learned Professor Kumi, of the Imperial University of Tok'yo, published his study in comparative religion that brought about his retirement.* The face of officialdom remained sternly set against the "dangerous thought" (*kiken-shiso*) of the scholarly iconoclast. Even among the great commentators there have been few who have possessed both the temperament and the courage to approve the rationalizing process through which myth is nowadays called upon to pass.

With the masses the modern skepticism has made little progress. The worship of the old Kami will be long in decaying. The great shrines of Izumo and of Isè will still look down upon their venerating millions, and the wayside altar, cheek by jowl with the country schoolhouse where the Japanese youth of this twentieth century has pored over his integral calculus and Herbert Spencer, will have no dearth of offerings. For a period that cannot now be computed, the *Kancho* of the *Taïsha K'yoha* —true echo of sermons of a thousand years ago—will preach that Prince Tokugawa Keïki, the last shogun of the last shogunate, was inspired by the Great Deity (Great-Land-Master) when he resolved to resign his office to the needs of the new time and at the call of the revitalized throne.†

---

* The official *History of the Empire of Nippon*, while admitting that "strange and difficult-to-be-believed legends have been transmitted from that era (the Deity-Age)," adds that "in order to understand the history of the empire's beginnings, the traditional incidents of the time, however singular, must be studied."

† W. L. Schwartz (*The Great Shrine of Idzumo*, p. 577) states that the *Kancho* (Sengè Takayoshi) in an interview, September 2, 1912, told him that he often preached this doctrine.

Thus reiterated precept and preachment have gifted the Japanese with an exultant sense of his own racial dignity. It is the extremest individualism extended to the consciousness of a people, a mass ultra-egoism such as the world has never before seen thus perpetuated. The only approach to a parallel is in Judaism, and the relationship of the Jew to Yahweh is only a spiritual one. To the Japanese his Sovereigns are *de jure* if not *de facto*, lords of the planet. On this specific ground the great test of the later literati, quoted above, justifies Hideyoshi's expedition against Korea. "Because," says the Grand *Norito* [Liturgy], "the Great Deity [the Sun-Goddess] has bestowed on Him [the Emperor] the lands of the four quarters over which her glance extends: as far as the rising of the Sky-wall, as far as the standing-up of the earth-boundaries: as far as the blue clouds are suffused, as far as the place where the white clouds settle down opposite: by the blue sea-plain as far as the prows of ship go without the drying of their poles and sculls, by land as far as the hoofs of horses go, with tight pack-cords treading among the roots of rocks and trees—where the long road extends, continuously widening the narrow regions and making the steep regions level, *drawing together, as it were, the distant countries by throwing over them a net of many ropes.*"

De jure lordship, however, was not the goal. Japan's lordship must be *de facto* as well. Her imperial house must be the supreme arbiter of the nations, and the Japanese race the over-race of the world. After World War I each month heard this proclaimed anew:

"To preserve the world's peace," declared the *Niroku* (magazine), "and promote the welfare of mankind, is the mission of the imperial house. . . . It is as worthy of respect as God, and the embodiment of benevolence and justice. . . . It is above all racial considerations. All human disputes, therefore, may be settled in accordance with its immaculate justice. Only by placing the imperial house of Japan at its head can the League of Nations, which was proposed to save mankind from the horrors of war, attain its objective. For this it must have a strong punitive force of supernatural and superracial character, and only in the imperial house of Japan can this be found."

As for the race, it must, in the words of Dr. Uzawa Someï, "act as mediator between the East and West. . . . We possess the faculty of universal sympathy and progress. . . . As Japan has a special civilization of her own, she must believe that she has a special mission to mankind." The national concept was more directly stated by Count Okuma, writing in 1914, when he was premier: "It becomes Japan's duty to represent both East and West, and bring about harmony between their peoples and civilizations. The mission of Japan is to bring about an international civilization." And the logical sequitur—the headship of the Earth—was pronounced by Mr. Hogi Oshikawa, at a meeting of the *Dokaï* (Society of the Right Path) in 1916: "With these loveliest virtues, which are the heritage of our ancestors, and traditions more glorious than any other of the world's nations has ever enjoyed, I unhesitatingly declare that the task of instructing the rest of the world devolves upon us and upon our nation, and that it is the destiny of us Japanese *to become its dominating factor*."

For good measure Matsuoka Yosukè, Japanese delegate to the League of Nations in Geneva in 1933, declared: "In a few years we shall be understood by the world as Jesus of Nazareth was. . . . Japan's mission is to lead the world, spiritually and intellectually. . . . Japan will be the cradle of a new Messiah."

This, the doctrine of the Divine Descent, is the key to Japanese character and motive. From this lofty Pisgah the militarist Japan of the past has looked across the turbulent Jordan of international strife, to that shrouded distance that has wrapped the Promised Land of Japanese Supremacy. In this faith its trust has been fixed.

POST WHEELER

駐日米國代理大使
ポースト、ウイラー

SOURCES

The Myth-Narrative which follows has been derived from the following:

I. RECORDS-OF-WIND-AND-EARTH *
(Fudoki)

From very early times there existed at the Japanese court a corps of historiographers, such as were maintained by the kings of ancient Greece. These, known as the *Fumi-no Obito*, were a corps of officials whose function it was "to record words and events," that is, to write the history and geography of the several provinces. According to their special occupations they were divided into *kuni-fubito, funa-fubito, tsu-fubito, gwa-fubito*, etc. In A.D. 403, according to the *Nihongi*, "provincial recorders were first appointed throughout the provinces who wrote down words, and sent their records to the four directions (or, communicated the records of the four directions)." The *Kogo-Shui*, under the same reign, records that "Achi-no Omi [Magnate of Omi] and Wang-in (or Wani), learned men of Pekchè [Kudara], were made to record the ingoings and outcomings (of treasury property)." This is perhaps too early a date to assign in fact to this step,† but shortly after the middle of the century we have a date that can be substantiated—461. It was not, however, till the reign of the Empress Gemmeï, in the early part of the eighth century, that an imperial decree compelled an orderly compilation of such data for submission to the court,‡ and some volumes were not completed until 930.

---

* Except for isolated fragments, these have not been translated into a European tongue.
† Murdoch suggests that Korean scribes may have been assigned to this duty in the course of this or the following generation.
‡ These were the beginnings of the mass of topographical literature now called *Meïsho*.

SOURCES

Of these productions, which were given the generic name of *Fudoki*, only five remain, those of Izumo (c. 733), *Hitachi* (782?), Harima (?), Bungo (?), and Hizen (?)* provinces. Of these the first named is the best known, but all of them contain valuable local traditions and legendary passages. The other *Fudoki* are now lost, being known only by fragments, preserved in quotations by later authors in whose time they were still extant. In this way have been preserved material portions of the *Fudoki* of Yamashiro, Yamato, Settsu, Iga, Isè, Owari, Izu, Mino, Mutsu, Tango,† Hoki, Mimasaka, Bitchu, Awa, Iyo, Tosa, Chikugo, Chikuzen, Tsukushi (K'yushu), Buzen, Higo, H'yuga, and Osumi provinces.

TEXTS

The *Izumo-Fudoki*. The version of Izumo-no Sukunè Toshinobu is the preferable one. Other texts are those of Shirobè Chitatè, the *Izumo-Fudoki-Ka* of Nita Harumitsu, and the Sakakibara copy, transcribed in 1729. For notes the student should consult the *Izumo-Fudoki-Kaï* of Uchiya Shinr'yo (1782) and the *Izumo-Fudoki-Sho* of Kishizaki Tokiteru.

The *Hitachi-Fudoki*. The chief text is known as the "Old Printed Text," which was corrected and printed during the Era of *Tempo* (1830-1844) by Nishino Nobuaki, with notes by Ban Nobutomo. That next in value is the so-called Kaga Text, made by the Maëda family in 1677. There are three other reliable texts—one bearing corrections by Isè Sadatakè, a copy made by Oyamado Tomokiyo (with notes), which is contained in the *Gunsho-Ruiju*, and one which was found in the Kagoshima Collection. Notes are in the *Shimpen-Hitachi-Kokushi* of Nakayama Nobuna, the *Hitachi-K'yujiko* of Omisawa Oümi, and the *Gunk'yoko* of Miyamoto Mototama.

The *Harima-Fudoki*. The best text available is a copy made in 1852 by one Tanimo, or Tanimori, presumably a scribe, from a roll preserved in the library of the west palace of Sanjo. Notes of value are to be found in the *Meïsekisho*, written in the Era of *Gembun* (1736-1741) by one Usui, and in the *Wamyosho*.

The *Bungo-Fudoki*. The authoritative text is that of Arakida Hisaoï (1746-1804), pupil of the learned Kamo Mabuchi, and author of the famous commentary on the *Manyoshu*. The Shokokan text is next in value, and a third is contained in the *Gunsho*. Notes have been contributed by Karahashi Seïsaï.

The *Hizen-Fudoki*. The "Old Printed Text," so called, is the most valuable. Arakida Hisaoï has written a commentary (1800). The *Hizen-Fudoki-Sanchu* of Itoya Sadamiki contains valuable notes.

---

* One authority alleges that the *Bungo-* and the *Hizen-Fudoki* date from as late as the Era of *Empo* (1673-1681), but internal evidence points to a far greater antiquity.
† Until A.D. 713 Tango was a part of Tamba Province.

These five *Fudoki* have been printed, in combined form, with valuable annotations, by Dr. Kurida Hiroshi (*H'yochu-Kofudoki*, 1899).

The fragments of the lost *Fudoki* were collected during the Era of Genroku (1688-1703) by the Shokokan, and collections were also made by Imaï Jikan, Ban Nobutomo, and Yoshida Reïseï. These collections have in large part been combined and published, with copious notes, by Dr. Kurida Hiroshi (*Santeï-Kofudoki-Itsubun*, 1897).

II. NARRATION-OF-ANCIENT-THINGS *
(Kujiki)

The Narrative (see Suiko's reign) states that "The heir to the throne [Uë-no Miya-No Umayado-no Toyoto-Mimi-No Shotoku-no Miko-no Mikoto, known to history as Shotoku-*Taïshi*] with the Great-Magnate [Soga-no Umako-no Sukunè] (the prime minister) set down a History of the Sovereigns, a History of the Land, and the first Annals of the Magnates [*Omi*], Tribe-Masters [*Muraji*], Rulers of the Guard [*Tomo-no Miyatsuko (Miyakko)*] the Land-Rulers [*Kuni-Miyatsuko (-Miyakko)*], the one hundred and eighty Clans [*be*] and of the citizens (nonslave subjects)." This was in the year 620. Twenty-five years later, in Kog'yoku's reign, the *Nihongi*, relating the destruction of the Soga family by Prince Hirakasu-Wakè (or more popularly, Naka-no Ohoë, who later became the Emperor Tenchi) records: "Emishi, Magnate of Soga, and his folk, whilst waiting to be put to death, burned the History of the Sovereigns, the History of the Land, and other valuable things. Esaka, Scribe-of-Ships, straightway snatched up the burning History of the Land and gave it to Ohoë-of-Naka."

The volume that bears the name *Kujiki*, known less commonly as the "Principal-Narrative-of-Ancient-Things-of-Former-Ages" [*Sendaï-Kujiki*], purports to be this compilation. Its authenticity was never called in question before the day of Mabuchi, since which time best Japanese authorities, including Motoöri and Hirata, have regarded it as a forgery, either compiled from the *Kojiki* and the *Nihongi*, or written in imitation of the original,† and produced probably early in the ninth century. It contains an account of the death of *Shotoku-Taïshi*, one of its alleged authors,

---

* Styled by some *Kuji-Honki*.
† Bakin (see his *Nimazè-no Kizenshu*) says it was compiled by a Buddhist abbot, Cho-on, who, says the *Nihon-Kodaï-Monjiko* of Ochiaï Naozumi (1839-1891), wrote it in the Era of *Tenwa* (1681-1684). According to the latter authority, the fraud was discovered before its completion, and its editor banished, while Cho-on himself escaped exile only through the interposition

SOURCES

quotes passages from the *Kogo-Shui*, which purports to date back only to the year 807, and makes mention of the Emperor Saga, who reigned from 810 to 823; but these portions may, I think, be regarded as later incorporations.

Although this document, when judged by the standards of the *Kojiki* and *Nihongi*, is for the most part a clumsy and inconsistent jumble, it nevertheless contains versions of the more popular myths whose antiquity cannot be doubted. It is written in Chinese, and carries the tale to 621.

TEXTS

There are many ancient manuscript texts, the most celebrated being one in the possession of the Maëda family and known by this name, and two that are preserved in the libraries of the Isè Naïgu and Gegu (Inner and Outer Shrines).

The earliest printed text is the Kaneï Text, so-called, which dates to the Era of *Kwaneï* (1624-1644). It was followed by the Enka Text, which is a revision by Wataraï Enka, and the Goto-H'yochu Text, also a revision, with notes by Nakayama Shigeki.

There are only two valuable commentaries on the work as a whole, the *Kujiki-Kogi* (MS.) a product of the Urabè family, and the *Kujiki-Sekisho* (MS.) of Wakada Masatoshi, but there are many manuscript commentaries on the various volumes. Most notable of these are the *Kunimiyatsuko-Hongi-Ko* of Ban Nobutomo (vol. X), the *Kokugo-Ko* of Uchiyama Shinr'yo (Land-Names), the *Owari-Uji-Mononobè-Uji-Keïzu-Kakirè* of Wono Takakiyo (vol. I), and the *Sendaï-Kujiki-Rekiko* of Ando Arimasu. There is also the printed *Kunimiyatsuko-Hongi-Ko* of Dr. Kurida Hiroshi, which is contained in the *Sonsaï-Sosho*. He has given extended labor to the preparation of commentaries on the genealogies contained in the work.

III. RECORDS-OF-ANCIENT-MATTERS *
(*Kojiki*)

In 682 Ama-no Nunahara Oki-no Mabito, known under his canonical name of Temmu-*Tenno*, fortieth Sovereign (reigned 673-686), issued an imperial decree:

---

of the shogun's mother. It seems more likely, however (as has been suggested by deVisser), that Cho-on's work was a second counterfeit of the same original, and is not to be confounded with the *Kujiki* now extant.

---

* Portions of this work were first translated into English by Aston (*Grammar of the Japanese Written Language. Crestomathy*) and by Satow (*Shinto Rituals*). A complete translation has been made by Chamberlain. (*Transactions of the Asiatic Society of Japan*, 1882, vol. X, sup.)

"I learn that the annals of the Emperors and also the original words possessed by various families differ from the truth and have been added to by valueless inventions. Unless now these faults be corrected, before many years the meaning of this warp and woof of the country and prime foundation of the empire will be lost. I therefore now desire that the annals of the Emperors be taken and recorded and the ancient words examined and certified, inventions stricken out and the truth ascertained, for handing down to future ages."

For this work of collection and expurgation he appointed Prince Kawashima and eleven other court officials.

At that time there was in the imperial household a retainer named Hiyeda-no Arè, a young man * of twenty-eight, a professional "Reciter" † of such extraordinary memory that he could "repeat with his mouth whatsoever his eyes saw, and remember in his heart whatsoever struck his ears." He was chosen by the imperial commission and commanded to commit to memory the genealogies of the Emperors and the true traditions as they were ascertained. The Emperor died, however, before these could be written out,‡ and the project rested for twenty-five years. The Empress Yamato-neko-Amatsu-Mihiro-Toyokuni-nari-Himè (Gemmeï) then issued a decree commanding one Ono-Yasumaro Futo-no-Ason, a court noble and officer of the upper division of the fifth rank, to write down such of the ancient lore as had been memorized by Hiyeda-no Arè. The manuscript was completed probably in the year 712.

This is what is known as the *Kojiki* or *Furu-Koto-Bumi* § (Records-of-Ancient-Matters), and it is the prime scripture of the Shinto. Its authenticity has never been called in question by either native or foreign scholars. It is written in quasi-Chinese, but largely phonetically, Chinese ideographs being used to represent the Japanese sounds, and was first printed, from manuscript copies preserved by the Shinto priesthood, in 1644. It brings the story of the race down to the year 628.

---

* Hirata gives slender reasons for supposing Arè to have been a woman. Papinot follows him in this, calling her *une veille femme,* and adding that she was a descendant of the deity Sky-Frightening-Female.

† *Katari-be.* These raconteurs formed a hereditary class and exercised their function before the Emperors on State occasions. They flourished in Izumo Province down to the fifteenth century.

‡ Some authorities (among them Hirata—see his *Koshi-Chiyu,* vol. I) hold that a compilation was made at this time which was afterward lost.

§ Motoöri's pronunciation of the characters.

TEXTS

The oldest existing text (a copy dating from 1266) is that known as the *Shimpukuji* or *Ohosu* Text, which was preserved at the Shimpuku-Ji (-Temple) at Nagoya, Owari Province. It is one of the national treasures. It is inaccessible to the student. Motoöri himself had access only to a copy, made probably in the fourteenth century.

The "Old Printed Text" (printed in K'yoto in 1644 by Maëkawa Moëmon and issued in facsimile in the same year) is too rare to be available to most students, and the *Goto-Kojiki* Text of the Shinto priest Enka of Wataraï (1687) has no notes of value.

The *Teïseï-Kokun-Kojiki* Text, published by Nagata Shobeï, in K'yoto, with government aid, was issued in 1803 and reproduced in 1870. Another text based upon this, but containing essential differences, was published in the same year by Hakuetsudo, in Tok'yo. The first text to intersperse the Chinese characters with the *kana* syllabary is the *Kana-Kojiki* of 1874. This era was prolific of new editions based upon, or combinations of, those already mentioned.

The text par excellence for the student is that of Motoöri's *Kojiki-Den* (1789-1823), in forty-four volumes, including exposition and elaborate notes, together with a general discussion of the old manuscript texts, and treatises on the *Nihongi* and the *Kujiki*. It has had many adaptations and imitations.

The only textual notes of great value outside of Motoöri's are to be found in the older treatise of Kamo-no Mabuchi, which is so rare that I have never met a man who has seen it, although the Imperial Palace Library, it is believed, possesses a copy.

IV. WRITTEN-CHRONICLES-OF-NIPPON *
(*Nihongi*)

Meantime the compilation begun under the Emperor Temmu remained, except for the portion used in the *Kojiki*, unutilized. During the reign of the Empress Jito (687-696), further material had been collected, and in the reign of the Empress Gemmeï, who assisted the work of the commission by the appointment of additional literary editors, the resultant accumulation was compiled in the so-called *Kana-Nihongi* (Syllabled-Chronicles-of-Japan). The compilation was then submitted to Prince Toneri, seventh son of the Emperor Temmu and father of the Emperor Junnin, and to Ono Yasumaro (who had transcribed the *Kojiki*). Their joint revision, which was completed in 720, is known as

---

* Some earlier writers style it *Nihon-Shoki*. It has been translated into English by Aston (*Transactions of the Asiatic Society of Japan*, 1896, vol. I, sup. 1. *Nihongi*), and books 1, 2, 22 and 30 have been translated into German by Florenz.

the *Nihongi* (Written-Chronicles-of-Japan). It consisted of thirty-one volumes, thirty of which are extant.

This work is written not in the ancient Japanese character but in Chinese, then the classic tongue, and the legends have unmistakably been tampered with, presumably to make them conform more nearly to the newer standard of culture that had been introduced with the Chinese language and literature. While the subject matter of this compilation is the same as that of the *Kojiki*, the older material is amplified and reclassified, and the whole recital is perceptibly tinctured with Chinese philosophy.* Some few legends are omitted and others added, while variants are given of the main episodes.†

It continues the story down to the year 697.

TEXTS

Anciently there were many texts, of whose material differences record has been made by various scholars. The first printed text dates back only to the Era of *Keïcho* (1596-1615).

The text called the Collected-Interpretations (*Shugè* [*Shukaï*]) is to be preferred. It includes notes and a copious commentary, written in Chinese, which is enriched by many quotations from other writings, some no doubt of great antiquity.

The student of the text should consult Florenz's monograph.

V. COLLECTION-OF-OMITTED-ANCIENT-SAYINGS ‡

(*Kogo-Shui*)

This work, which gives eleven ancient legends not included in the myths of the *Kojiki* and *Nihongi*, was compiled by Imibè-no Hironari, in 807 or 808.

It is asserted by some Japanese commentators § that it was produced in order to glorify the ancestry of the author, and was presented in the form of a petition to the imperial court, being intended as an argument substantiating the claim of the Imibè families (to which line Hironari

---

* Entire passages, and even fragments of dialogue in this work, are strongly reminiscent of Chinese works written at a date later than the period assigned to the mythical events related.
† Aston holds that these have been added by subsequent copyists. Japanese scholarship, however, prefers to believe them a part of the original text.
‡ This has been translated into English by Professors Genchi Kato of the Tok'yo Imperial University and Hikoshiro Hoshino of the Hoseï College.
§ Notably Tada Yoshitoki.

belonged) to equal court rank with the Nakatomi. The latter counted descent from the Kami Sky-Beckoning-Ancestor-Lord (Amè-no Koyanè), and the former from the Kami Great-Jewel (Futo-Tama), which two, these legends go to show, were on an equality in the deity age.

It is written in Chinese and brings the narrative down to the year 807.

The student is referred to the modern translation by Kengi Kato.

TEXTS

There are various texts, falling under the two classifications of Isè and Urabè, the latter being the more favored by scholars. The best is that of the *Gunsho-Ruiji*, a revision belonging to the Urabè group.

Commentaries have been written by Fujiwara Narinobu (the *Kogo-Shui-Kukaï*) and R'yoshokwa (the *Kogo-Shui-Genyosho*).

VI. RECORDS-OF-FAMILY-TITLES-AND-NAMES
(*Shojiroku*)

The full name of this work is *Shinsenseïshi-Roku* (Newly-Selected-Records-of-Family-Titles-and-Names), from which it is popularly called *Seïshi-Roku*. It constitutes a peerage list, tracing the descent from the Kami of one thousand and seventy-seven noble houses.

In the latter years of the era of *Temp'yo-Hoji* (757-765) quarrels among noble families over their genealogies became very frequent. "There are those," says the preface of the book, "who speak falsely concerning their descent and appropriate the ancestors of others. They falsify documents as they please, naming Kami and Emperors in order to pretend to be of families who wear court robes and head-dresses" To correct this license the Emperor Junnin assigned a group of famous scholars of the time to begin the preparation of the so-called *Shizokushi*, but before its completion he was forced to abdicate and was banished to the island of Awaji. In 800 the Emperor Kwammu revived the project and ordered the Magnates and chief men of the empire to record the main lineage of each family of rank. The completed portion of the *Shizokushi* was revised and formed the basis of the new compilation. The task was carried on by Junnin's successor, the Emperor Saga, who entrusted it to Prince Manta, Fujiwara Sonohito (*Udaïjin*), Sangi Fujiwara Wotsugu, and a corps of assistants, who are said to have spent ten years on the undertaking. The work is in thirty volumes and was presented to the Emperor in 815.

It divides the families listed into three main classes, namely: *Kobetsu*

(335), who were cadet families of princely houses, *Shimbetsu* (404), who were descended from the original Kami who opened the country, and *Bambetsu* (326), who were naturalized foreigners. Beside these there were one hundred and seventeen families not classified; forty-eight of these, however, were later added to the *Bambetsu*. It had been intended in the *Shojiroku* to enumerate all the family names in Japan, but in fact only those in the Gokinaï (the five provinces adjoining K'yoto) were given, and the work was never completed.

In addition to the genealogies this work contains some ancient legends not found in other manuscripts.

TEXTS

The first text published with commentary of value is that of 1664, with notes by Shirawi Soïn. A text of the following year has a preface by Matsushita Kenrin. These, however, are not free from errors.

The text most practicable for the student is the revision by Minamoto Inehiko, issued in 1821. The best commentary is the *Shinsen-Seïshroku-Kosho* of Dr. Kurida Hiroshi.

VII. INSTITUTES-OF-THE-ENGI-ERA *

(*Engi-Shiki*)

In 905, in the reign of the Emperor Daïgo, a commission consisting of twelve court functionaries and scholars was appointed to revise the ceremonial laws. The first portion of the name given to the resulting compilation is that of the era (*Engi*, 901-923) in which the work was done. The code thus revised was promulgated in 927. It is of value chiefly in that it preserves the *Norito*, or ancient rituals of the Shinto, which contain fragments of mythical narrative. The ceremonies in which these liturgies were used antedate historical records, and it may be assumed that some of them are of extreme antiquity.† The *Engi-Shiki* names seventy-five *Norito*, giving the texts of twenty-seven, and enumerates 3,132 shrines that were, at the time of its compilation, officially recognized.

---

* Portions have been translated by Aston, Florenz, and Sir Ernest Satow (see *Sacred Books and Early Literature of the East*, vol. XIII).

† Mabuchi attributes two (the Ceremony of General purification (*Ohobarahi*) and the Izumo Kami-Invocation (*Izumo Kuni-no Miyatsuko Kamu-Yogoto*) to the seventh century, but they are probably much older. The older Japanese commentators claim that the former originated in the time of the first creative deity pair.

TEXT

The *Gunsho-Ruiju* copy is the most practicable for the purposes of the student.

VIII. OTHER MYTH MATERIAL

The crystallization of the ancient myths in these permanent forms gives the essential cosmogonic legends current at the present time. There has always been, of course, a further mass of legendary material containing elements of great antiquity; this, while not dignified by a place in the compilations above named, was handed down by oral transmission till it found later embodiment in written form.

THE TEXT

The ideograph has nowhere been used in the explanatory notes of the text. The student of the character will have recourse to the original, and except for the meager handful of European scholars who have acquaintance with the written language, the *romaji* (the representation of the Japanese syllabary by Roman letters) must for long be the bridge over which Western scholarship must pass to a knowledge of Japanese texts.

Any attempt to select and collate the *Fudoki* fragments leaves at best much to be desired. A great part of the material, whatever its interest per se, is purely local and, so far as concerns the Narrative, extraneous and irrelevant. As a rule only those fragments are incorporated which associate themselves with deities and personages named in the "sun list" of the Greater Scriptures; where others are utilized it is because of their connection with localities that play a large part in the story. A few that throw light upon the text without properly belonging to its episodes are cited in notes *in loco*.

The earlier legends are related in full, with citation of conflicting variants. Only in the later Narrative has some omission seemed justified. In the chronologies only such Kami are included as are manifestly principal deities, play a significant part in the Narrative, or are designated as ancestors of Clans or families. Burdensome detail is here and there omitted. For example, the full text of the moral maxims (sometimes incorrectly called "laws") promulgated by Shotoku-Taïshi, the famous crown prince of Suiko's reign, is not given, but only the content of each section.* I have passed over also the citations of the Korean records and the constant bickerings with the San-Kan: only those episodes of trouble with Korea have been included which have direct bearing on the main

---

* These are to be found *in extenso* in Aston's translation of the *Nihongi*.

thread of the story of the Sun Folk or are themselves the basis of persisting legend.

In the interest of clarity, the headings given to the various episodes of the deity age by Motoöri, and since his time very generally adopted by Japanese commentators, have been used, the later Narrative, however, being permitted to flow on, as in the original texts, without break, save for the natural division of the story into separate reigns.

Where the detail of one or another version is palpably Chinese (as often occurs in the *Nihongi*) I have preferred the native version as, for example, in using the "holly-wood spear, eight *hiro* long" of the *Kojiki* in preference to the "battle-ax" of the *Nihongi*. With the same object of keeping the text as pure as possible, quotations from the histories of the Han, Wei, Sung, Liang, and Wu dynasties of China have been omitted, and the partly (or wholly) Chinese decrees and observations with which the compilers of the *Nihongi* plentifully sprinkled their rolls, have been eliminated. The less important citations of omens also have been omitted, with records of confirmations of rank, the creation and wearing of insignia and uniform, entries of deaths, the weather, earthquakes, conventional prayers for rain, bestowals of posthumous honors, and court practices (such, for example, as the periodic excursions to gather medicinal herbs) that seem to have been mere conventional junketings decreed by an ever elaborating etiquette of the seasons.

In the interest of simplicity the more elaborate honorifics, adjectival or titular, in such phrases as "His Augustness" (*no-Mikoto*), "augustly," "great august," etc., have been dropped as unnecessarily burdensome. The words "addressed," "proceeded," etc., when used in connection with the Sovereign, are in the text expressed by characters that have no exact equivalent in English, containing the imperial essence or significance of the act or attitude involved. The meaning might be approximated by "imperially addressed," "made an imperial progress," etc. These redundant trappings have been sparsely used. In connection with the later reigns, too, references to imperial consorts employ characters that distinguish between different grades or ranks of concubines, whereas in relation to earlier reigns distinction of this sort is made only in the case of the Empress. These distinctions, which have purely a court etiquette value, have not been indicated in the translation, all consorts being alike referred to as wives. The "prince" and "king" of the *Kojiki* are practically interchangeable terms.

It may be noted in passing that the recurrent phrases Ama-no (Amè-no), coupled so continually in the texts with names of deities or allusions to them, which is commonly rendered "heavenly," is best translated, throughout all but the last portion of the Narrative at least, as "Sky."

that is belonging to the upper firmament, the empyrean. The Japanese, like the Greek, took no account of the sixth orientation point (nadir) before the advent of Buddhism developed his conception of space and lent to his "sky" the further paradisiacal significance.

In the translation of songs the original syllabic rhythms have been reproduced. To say that Japanese verse has no rhythm is as misleading as to say that French verse has none, because to the Anglo-Saxon ear it is of feebler ictus. Consider, for example, a half-dozen lines, chosen at random, from Princess-Lagoon-River's second song to Great-Land-Master (p. 65). The Japanese runs as follows:

> Awo-yama-ni || Hi-ga Kakuraba
> Nuba-tama-no || Yo-ha idè-namu
> Asa-hi-no || Emi-sakaë-kitè.

Given their natural rhythm, slightly exaggerated, the lines read thus:

> When the sun doth hide || Back of the mountains green,
> Then within the night || That is black as berries
> Plucked on the moor, || Straightway to thee I'll hasten.

By this method there may be loss in grace of phrasing, but I count this more than compensated by the gain in metrical effect.

The songs are so rendered, moreover, that corresponding syllable groups of the original and of the translation not only have the same number of syllables but as a general rule correspond in sense. The difficulties of such transliteration are not lessened by the peculiar inversion of idea and of form to which Japanese thought and language structure lend themselves.

As a rule the songs occupy the places assigned to them (it would seem more naturally) in the *Kojiki*, rather than the somewhat arbitrary order given in the *Nihongi*. Where, however, the older text shows a clear tendency to credit an Emperor *in persona* with sayings and doings that logically belong to others and are so attributed in later variants, they are given in what are presumably their rightful places. Thus one song attributed by the *Kojiki* to Mountain-Gate-Brave (Yamato-Dakè) has been assigned to the Emperor Prince-Great-Perfect-Ruling-Lord (Keïko), as attributed in the *Nihongi*. The breaking of the song into three fragments, however, as it appears in the *Kojiki*, seems distinctly preferable.

One characteristic of later classic Japanese verse occasionally appearing in these Scripture songs is the so-called "pillow word" (*makura-kotoba*), an epithetic phrase conventionally used, as in "Great Kami *of eight thousand spear shafts*," or "Isè *the divine winded*." This is a mere stock decoration that has become so welded with the expression it once supplemented as to be, for purposes of poetry at least, inseparable from it. Wherever possible these ancient pillow words have been rendered, but occasionally, except for the most indefatigably ingenious of Japanese root-hunters, they defy translation.

Occasional puns in the verse have been found in most cases impossible to render, as for example in the song sung to Sujin-*Tenno* by the brewer to the Great Kami, where "how long ago" (*ikuhisa*) is a play upon the singer's name, Ikui.

The footnotes necessarily will not be without some difficulties for the student. Many of the older works quoted from, brush-copied in Chinese and Japanese script, lack complete pagination, and only chapter-numbers have been noted. As I am writing essentially for Japanese texts, and my work addresses itself first and foremost to students of the Japanese rather than the Chinese, I have elected to spell Chinese words as they are written in Japan (Sino-Japanese). For example, I refer (p. 421) to the Chinese Emperor known in Japan as Buwo and his dynasty as Shu, rather than as Wu Wang and his dynasty as Chou (Wade transcription). Some Japanese works well-known to native scholarship are referred to under different titles. In my own quotation from Japanese commentators, I have thought it best to retain the credit as given, even at the risk of sending the student, on occasion, to his bibliography.

A word as to pronunciation. There are no diphthongs or triphthongs in Japanese, hence the frequent occurrence of the diaeresis. In the *romaji* * both vowels and consonants are pronounced as in Italian. Final *e* is always pronounced. G, except in some local dialects, such as that of modern Tok'yo, is invariably hard, and *ch* never plays the part of *k*. A, *o*, and *u* are sometimes "long," that is to say, the single vowel sometimes represents a crasis of two short ones, long ō, for example, standing for what was originally *oö* and receiving double time. Final *n* is prolonged in verse (because it has taken the place of an archaic *nu*), as is *m* in words like *ambaï*. Some vowel sounds ordinarily are either elided or so faintly touched by the voice that the Western ear distinguishes them no more than, for example, the *e* in the French *Samedi*. Aside from the *i* in words like *furoshiki* (*furosh'ki*), the *u* sound oftenest disappears. Sukeshigè becomes S'keshigè and *futari* becomes *f'tari*. At word-ends *bu-* and *mu* as a rule lose the vowel sound when immediately following a stressed syllable, as in such names as Harunób', but retain it otherwise, as in Shíkibu. The written text need take no account of pronunciational

---

* See p. XXVIII.

variations, however, and except for the diaeresis and the accent of the terminal *e,* diacritical marks have been omitted.

Spelling has been simplified, *z,* for example, taking the place of the ancient *dz* in such names as *Izumo* (*Idzumo*) and wherever practicable a modern recognizable form is substituted for one that has become obsolete. Thus Tsutsuki becomes Tsuzuki; Yeshinu, Yoshino; Ahaji, Awaji; Toho-tsu-Afumi, Totomi; Afumi, Omi; Hiyè, Hiyeï; Himuka, H'yuga; Yamanobè, Yamabè; Wohari, Owari; Shinanu, Shinano; Sagamu, Sagami; Agi, Aki; Kuruda, Kuroda; Sanugi, Sanuki; Kamitsukenu, Kozukè; Mimoro, Mimuro; Taniha, Tamba; Tsukuha, Tsukuba; Kuhimata, Kumata; Naniha, Naniwa; Shiragi, Silla, etc.* In proper names, also, the connective *-no* is used only where ancient usage has made the syllable indispensable.

Throughout the Narrative the literal rendering has been used (wherever it has not been forgotten) of all proper † and place names, and not solely with a view to picturesqueness. Some few names perhaps have so changed in form that they convey no more of their onetime suggestion than does the name of Manchester, or resemble their original forms no more than the modern "Snooks" resembles its stately forebear "Sevenoaks," but these are exceptions. The average name, such is the tonal simplicity of the Japanese syllabary, has no more lost its concrete suggestion to the modern Japanese ear than have such names as Chief Sitting-Bull or Annie-Lost-Her-Name to the American Indian, or Broadway, Big Salmon River, Bright Angel Trail, Threadneedle Street, or Bubbling Well Road to the Anglo-Saxon globe-trotter.‡ The syllables "Yokimori" to the English ear are merely a succession of meaningless sounds: substitute their exact equivalent, "Goodwood" (*yoki* = good; *mori* = forest), and the original suggestion is preserved.

When a deity has several alternative names, the various forms of the myth refer to the possessor sometimes by one, sometimes by another, the

---

* Shiragi is believed by some to be the corrupted Sinico-Japanese form of Shinra (Korean Shin-la), otherwise Silla. But E. H. Parker has pointed out that the Sinico-Korean "Shinra" was not adopted till the end of the fourth century. Previously it was called *Kerin* (*Kirin*) or Sulofa.

† Japanese surnames were originally derived from avocations, circumstances of birth, names of places or objects, or presumed qualities. This, however, is probably true of all nations. "Crab's-Eye-Fierce," as a name, might be matched by that of Heaven-Be-Praised-For-Jones, of the Barebones Parliament.

‡ With all its original picturesqueness of nomenclature, the English tongue is rapidly losing even its old inn names. Germany has shown the opposite tendency. Berlin's cafes used to boast a "Thirsty Pelican" and a "Lame Louse," and Leipzig has (or had, a few years ago) its "Old Straw Bag."

result, except to the experienced student of the genealogies, being misleading. Sometimes too the use of alternative names in the original is merely to distinguish the status of the character, as heir apparent or as reigning Sovereign, a verbal distinction unnecessary and impeding. In the Narrative the most usual and popular name is used wherever practicable, the alternative names being given in the notes in connection with their owner's first appearance.

In some few cases the ancient and authoritative signification of a name of place or of personage has been laid aside in favor of a later image that has become the popular one. Thus, in the earlier pages of the Narrative, Japan is referred to (with various syllabic permutations) as the "Dragonfly Island" (Akitsushima). When the *Kojiki* and *Nihongi* were written, Akitsu-Shima meant "Island of Great Harvests," and the name came very early to bear the later meaning to the historian, and bears only that meaning to the Japanese of today. It is probable that the names of the deities Izanagi (He-Who-Invites) and Izanami (She-Who-Invites) originally meant no more than He-of-Isè and She-of-Isè, and that the popular rendition is a *volks-etymologie*. The same is true of the name of the deity Brave-Swift-Impetuous-Male (Takè-Haya-Susa-no Wo); though the popular fancy refers the syllables Susa to *susamu* (to be impetuous), there seems little doubt that the name originally signified no more than He-of-Susa,* Susa being a place in Izumo Province. So the scholar may quarrel with some renditions. It must be borne in mind, however, that the translations adopted are the popular ones rather than those consistently approved by Japanese erudition and commentary. As to place-names, when popular fancy has not emphasized a particular translation, I prefer, as a rule, the older commentators, choosing, for example, for Minu (Mino) the simpler interpretation of "Three Moors" rather than the "True Moor" (*ma-nu*) of the moderners. In deity names, for reasons as obvious, the doubtful syllables themselves have been preferred to a too hazardous translation.

Some verbal distinctions that are without modern values have been dispensed with—as, for instance, that between the words *sato* † and *mura* (village), where the distinction is between like units differently

---

* Aston has pointed out that the syllables Susa occur also in some versions in the name of Impetuous-Male's mother-in-law (Susa-no Yatsu-Mimi), where they would seem more naturally to be the name of a place.

† The *Koreï* says: "Fifty houses make a *sato*. The *Nihonshoki-Gikäi* says: "When there are sixty houses, ten of them are set apart and make a *sato*, for which a chief is appointed. But when there are less than ten, they are added to a large *mura*, and there is no need of a separated *sato*." A *mura* can be larger or smaller than a *sato*.

organized for purposes of government.

Some difficulties of the text are due to imperfect concepts or deficiencies in the language itself. The peculiar disregard of the language structure for *number* is a familiar pitfall. A deity is sometimes single, sometimes a pair or a trio, as in the case of the deity of the wind, and the three sea deities, who are often grouped together as one. Occasionally a whole group of deities—as for example the deities of thunder—are referred to as if they are to be considered a single personality. Thus what seems likely to have been an original vagueness in the concept is still further clouded by a loose grammatical form.

In some cases too the Japanese word has no English equivalent, notably the word Kami, which occurs on well-nigh every page of the Narrative, and for which neither "god," "deity," nor "being" has a signification sufficiently broad to do service.

The root meaning of Kami is "excellence," and the word indicates primarily nothing more than upper or superior, being properly written not with the Chinese character *shin* (divinity) but with the character *jo* (superior). It is applied indiscriminately to beings clearly supernatural and beings evidently earthly, to the primal deities, the later divinities, the Emperors and their descendants in all generations, to animals and in a lesser degree even to inanimate things—a peach, a great tree, a gem, a white stone, or a sword—to anything and everything, in short, that from the human standpoint is mysterious and hence awe-inspiring. In the beginning the Sky-Kami were descendants of the primal uncreated deities and projected themselves to the archipelago in the lineage of the Sun-Goddess. But the Kami of the land also had, many of them, celestial descent. There were good Kami and evil Kami, even in the High-Sky. There were incorporeal Kami and Kami with bodies, who might be slain, and some that were able to assume flesh at will. The distinction increases with the tally of the Emperors, till the line of the Sun-Descent distinguish between the divine (which is invisible) and visible human Kami like themselves.* But the distinction goes no further.† The term otherwise is applied in all gradations—even to evil or "violent" human Kami that

---

* When the *Emishi* chieftains Kami-of-Island and Kami-of-Land submit to Mountain-Gate-Brave (Yamato-Dakè) in the Land of Michi-no-Oku, the latter awes them with the declaration that he is "the child of a Kami of visible men" (see p. 257).

† The legends contain only a single record that at first glance seems to dispute this. Of Kenzo's reign it is recorded, "At this time Noble-of-Oïha-of-Tree, resting upon Mimana, entered into relations with Koma. Purposing to govern the three Han on the western side, he set up a government *and called himself a Kami*." But the meaning of this is only that he represented himself to be a viceroy when he was without authority.

can be classed only with the autochthons—till it comes at length to be used as a mere title of respect bestowed upon high rank.*

When all has been said, however, the Narrative presents huge difficulties. There is great confusion, here and there, in the genealogies, which sometimes flatly contradict one another. In such cases the names selected have the weight of older or more numerous authority. Many of the deities named possess no shrines and have bequeathed nothing to later ceremonial or myth. There are frequent lacunae, and alternate versions are often in dire conflict. In the latter case, where the detail is irreconcilable, as a rule the older version is given place in the Narrative and the more recent one is noted parenthetically. Even a deity cannot well have had two fathers.

In a few instances, where relative *age* in conflicting variants is not to be determined, main place has been given to the most likely version. A larger instance of this may be seen in the distribution by He-Who-Invites, among his favored children, of their several realms. In the *Kojiki* the Sun-Goddess is made to rule the Sky, the Moon-Deity the Night, and the Impetuous-Male-Deity the Sea; but in the *Nihongi* and the *Kujiki* it is the Moon-Deity who finally receives as his portion, with the night, "the eight-hundred-fold tides of the ocean-plane," while to the Impetuous-Male is given the rule of the World. This latter is the logical division (the Sky, the Earth, and the Sea) and who so likely to govern the sea tides as the Moon-Deity? As to the murder of the Food-Deity by the Moon-Deity instead of by Impetuous-Male, the *Nihongi* and *Kujiki* versions have been followed, as they furnish the explanation why sun and moon are not seen together in the firmament, which has, besides, parallels in the myths of other countries.

Finally there has been no attempt at adjustment. That may be left to the Japanese commentators—who, from Motoöri to Bakin, have wasted much India ink and worn out many brushes in a vain attempt to force consistency upon a fanciful chronology. Nor has there been expurgation. License in this regard in the past has done much to give Japanese myth a reputation for obscenity that is undeserved. Père Papinot calls the *Kojiki* "a tissue of vulgar fables," even Chamberlain refers to it as "a collection of fantastic and often filthy stories," and still another Western critic stamps it "an extraordinary farrago of feeble and filthy

---

* In this case, however, it is not, as Hodgson thought, like the assumption of the French *de* or the German *von*, a mere attempt to ennoble the bearer. The Japanese framers of Admiral Stirling's Convention of 1854 and of Lord Elgin's Treaty of 1858 so signed themselves, and without impropriety, as did also the three chief members of the first Japanese embassy to the United States, in 1860. So did the governors of Nagasaki and Hakodatè.

myths and legends." Yet I cannot believe that serious students will find these more fantastic than the older myths of the Greeks, as they are not more lacking in the element of the poetic, nor their *chronique scandaleuse* a whit filthier than is to be found in the Vedic poems, the "Sacred Chapters" of Hesiod or the earlier Persian nature fictions. Nor are their allusions coarser than those of the Talmud or the Koran, not to mention some portions of Jewish scripture.*

With this prologue there is set before the reader, as it has been handed down to our own time (until the opening of the eighth century in greater part by oral transmission), the Myth-Story of the Sun-Folk, whose fabric hangs, a many-colored curtain woven of myriad threads, the background of Japanese national and individual life today.

---

* Chamberlain thought it "not objectionable, however, to translate some portions of the *Kojiki* text in *Latin*," and in his *Nihongi* Aston has followed his example. Fancy a learned Japanese dishing up the Old Testament to the Japanese scholarly world, in the vernacular, with the smug "aside" that he had felt obliged to render some parts of it in Sanskrit!

THE ARGUMENT

The Myth-Narrative, as it is told in the co-ordinate Japanese legends, follows this outline:

From the primordial chaos, sky and earth gradually separate and there spontaneously appear the five primal deities, with only two of which the later story at all concerns itself. The first to appear is Mid-Sky-Master, of whom it is told only that he "stood motionless in the center of the cosmos." The five are followed by a series of mated deities, closing with the creative pair, He-Who-Invites and She-Who-Invites. These, standing on the "floating-sky-bridge," thrust down a spear into the sea brine and stir it, and thereby the first land (a small islet) is created. To this they descend, and learning the art of cohabitation from observing a wagtail, they procreate a child. This first offspring they abandon as unsatisfactory, after which are brought forth various islands of the archipelago, the deity of food, and deities of land and sea, of river, mountain, moor, tree, and plant. Next is born the deity of fire, and in giving him birth She-Who-Invites is burned and made ill. From her vomit, feces, and urine spring earth and water deities, and the deity of metals. She dies and betakes herself to the underworld of Yomi (Hades), and He-Who-Invites, in grief at losing her, slays the fire deity, from whose spattered blood and from portions of whose body, other deities, now unknown save for their names, come into being.

He-Who-Invites, longing to see his dead wife, follows after her to Yomi. She comes out of the Palace of the Dead to speak to him, and he begs her to return to the upper world. Replying that she has already eaten of the food of the underworld, but will consult the deity of the place (of whom the Narrative tells nothing), she warns him not to look upon her, and re-enters. She is long in returning, however, and He-Who-Invites, disregarding the prohibition, strikes a light and goes in, to find her a mass of putrefaction, on which sit eight thunder deities. He flees and she, angered at his disobedience, sends in pursuit the Ugly-Females-of-the-Land-of-Night and the thunder deities. He casts behind him his head-dress and his comb, which become grapes and bamboo shoots; these the Ugly-Females stop to devour, and, again hard pressed by them, he urinates, the water becoming a great river that they cannot quickly cross. He frightens away the thunder deities by hurling at them three peaches which he plucks from a tree. She-Who-Invites takes up the pursuit and he blocks the Level-Pass-of-the-Land-of-Night with a "thousand-man-lift" rock, across which they divorce each other. She-Who-Invites hereupon vanishes from the Narrative.

Regaining the upper world, He-Who-Invites performs lustration. Various deities are born from the articles of clothing he casts off and from the filth he has gathered on his person. As he washes his left eye there is born Great-Sky-Shiner, the Sun-Goddess, the head-to-be of the Japanese hierarchy; as he washes his right eye the Moon-Deity (concerning whom the Narrative recounts only one episode, and that of no particular significance); and as he washes his nose, the Impetuous-Male-Deity is born. The first two are resplendent and he sends them to the Sky, the Sun-Deity to rule there (though by what authority he decrees this is not stated), and the Moon-Deity to serve as her consort. To the Impetuous-Male-Deity he assigns the rule of the Earth.

On her arrival in the Sky the Sun-Deity assumes the celestial government, which at times she appears to carry on jointly with High-Producer, one of the primal deities. Her first act is to send the Moon-Deity to Earth to attend the female Food-Deity, who affronts him by offering him food taken from her mouth, her nose, and her anus. In anger he slays her, and from various portions of her body are born the silkworm, ox and horse, the five grains, and the mulberry tree. Enraged at the Moon-Deity's overt act, however, Great-Sky-Shiner sends him to rule the night. From this point the Moon-Deity disappears from the story.

The Impetuous-Male-Deity is wicked and of fierce and destructive character, spending his time in fuming and wailing, to the neglect of his earthly rule, so that He-Who-Invites condemns him to govern the underworld, presumably taking precedence over the deity of that realm. The Impetuous-Male-Deity asks permission to visit the Sky to bid farewell to Great-Sky-Shiner, his sister, and after being granted this, He-Who-Invites vanishes in his turn from the scene.

The Impetuous-Male-Deity, ascending to the Sky, gives his evil nature free rein. He persecutes the Sun-Deity with malicious mischief, and as a climax breaks a hole in the roof of her weaving house and hurls through it a flayed piebald colt, so startling her that she wounds herself with her shuttle. At this outrage she shuts herself within the Sky-Rock-Cave, the Sky and Earth being darkened in consequence—although presumably there had been light in both before her birth—and the Sky-Deities gather to devise a plan to tempt her back. In accordance with this plan various articles, including a mirror, are made, and after divination are displayed on the branches of an uprooted tree before the Rock-Cave, while a Grand Liturgy is recited and the deity Sky-Frightening-Female dances lewdly, exciting the laughter of the rest.

Thus Great-Sky-Shiner is tempted from her seclusion, and the deities, rejoicing in the returned radiance, make the cavern *tabu*, the Hand-Strength-Deity hurling its door to the Earth. The Impetuous-Male-Deity is fined and punished, after which he is driven downward to his banishment in the nether world. Before he departs he again ascends to the Sky, to the alarm of the Sun-Goddess, to whom, however, he declares his peaceful intent, and proposes a contest by the terms of which each is to produce deities, his own production of males to constitute proof that he speaks truth. After this test he descends with his son, Fifty-Brave, to Korea, from which he crosses in a clay boat to Sacred-Quarter (Izumo) Province, in Japan, which he plants with trees.

Here he comes upon an earth deity (a child of the Mountain-Deity, a grandson of the creative pair) who, with his wife, is bewailing the approaching fate of their daughter, whom the Eight-Forked-Serpent-of-Koshi is to devour. The Impetuous-Male-Deity bids them brew *sakè*, with which the monster is made drunk, and slaying it, he finds in its tail a sword, which he subsequently sends to the Sky. He weds the maiden Kami whom he has thus rescued, their descendant in the sixth generation being Great-Land-Master, the Earth-Ruler. Finding the land too small, the Impetuous-Male-Deity tows across and sews to it projecting portions of the adjoining Korean coast, and finally departs to take up his rule in the nether world.

The Narrative for a time now leaves celestial affairs, to follow the career of the Land-Master, which opens with his conquest of his eighty brothers. The Hare-Deity, having been flayed of his fur by a vengeful *wani* (a sea animal) whom he has tricked, in his plight has been mistreated by the eighty, and the Land-Master shows him how to regain his natural covering. In the outcome the Land-Master is enabled to wed the Princess-Yakami-in-Rice-Leaves, whom they desire, and they plot his murder. First they heat red hot a great boulder shaped like a boar, and roll it down a mountain; when he seizes this, he is burned to death. In answer to his mother's entreaties, however, one of the primal deities sends his daughters, the Cockle-Deity and the Clam-Deity, who anoint him with a milky trituration which restores him to life. Next the eighty fell a great tree, split it with a wedge, and make him stand in the cleft, then they withdraw the wedge and thus slay him a second time. His mother again brings him to life, after which he flees to the nether world to take refuge with the Impetuous-Male-Deity.

The latter exposes him to snakes, centipedes, and wasps (from which he is protected by the deity's daughter, Princess-Forward, whom he has wedded) and lastly, sending him to fetch an arrow that he has shot into a grass moor, fires the moor on all sides. From this peril the Land-Master is rescued by a speaking mouse, and returns in safety. While the Impetuous-Male-Deity sleeps, he ties his host's hair to the rafters of his palace, possesses himself of the other's weapons and lute, and flees with the daughter on his back to the upper world, where he exterminates his eighty brothers and assumes the rule of the land.

In the making of the land he is aided for a time by a midget deity from oversea, who comes riding in a boat made of a berry, and who is identified, by the aid of a speaking frog and the Scarecrow-Deity, as a vagabond child of one of the primal deities. Together the pair bestow on men and animals the hot bath and medicines, and subdue the deities of evil. The midget deity, however, soon departs and is heard of no more.

The story now returns to the Sky, where Great-Sky-Shiner bids her son Truly-Conqueror-I-Conquer-Swift-Sun-Sky-Great-Great-Ears (one of the children produced in her contest with the Impetuous-Male-Deity) descend to take over the earth-rule. From the "Floating-Sky-Bridge" (on which the earlier creative pair had stood when they thrust down the Sky-spear to produce the first island) he discerns great confusion, and concludes that the land is unfit for his advent, whereon the deities, in conference, choose Sky-Great-Sun, his younger brother, to pacify it. This envoy departs, but ingratiates himself with the Land-Master, and for three years brings back no report. His son, sent after him, does likewise. Next there is sent down a third deity, Prince-Sky-Young, who weds the Land-Master's daughter, and planning to seize the rule himself, for eight years sends no word to the Sky. The cock pheasant and the dove are then dispatched, and when these do not return, the hen pheasant, who delivers her message to Prince-Sky-Young, but is shot by him. The arrow that pierces her reaches the Sky, and, flung back by the primal deity, who appears throughout to occupy the position of adviser to the Sun-Goddess, kills the recreant prince. The latter's body is borne to the Sky, where a mortuary is built, and various birds (not spoken of as deities) officiate in the ceremonies of mourning.

Again there is celestial conference and two more deities are sent down, one being the son of the sword with which the deity He-Who-Invites had slain his son, the Fire-Deity, and the other the boat in which the creative pair had abandoned the first, unsatisfactory child. The pair demand of the Land-Master that he abdicate in favor of the Sky-Ruler-to-come, and he refuses. On returning to the Sky to report, they are sent again to offer him the promise that he shall be made the head of religious affairs, that a palace shall be built for him, and festivals be instituted in his honor. The Land-Master submits the decision to his two sons, who accept the proposal. Accordingly the two Sky-deities erect the palace as agreed, install the abdicated monarch in it, and proceed to pacify the evil deities of the land, a star-deity (the only star-deity of whom mention is made in the Narrative) being the last to submit.

The pacification completed, the abdication is confirmed in the Sky, and the Sun-Deity again bids her son descend. He, however, has meanwhile wed, and has begotten two sons, the younger of whom he proposes be sent in his place. While the celestial descent is accordingly preparing, however, the elder son, Plenty-Swift-Sun, descends, takes to wife the sister of one of the earth princes, and dies, transmitting to his own son his weapons as symbols of his Sky origin.

The imperial heir, Ruddy-Plenty, now descends with a numerous company of attendant deities, Great-Sky-Shiner investing him on his departure with the mirror with which the deities had lured her from the rock-cave, the sword which the Impetuous-Male-Deity had found in the tail of the serpent, and her jewels—these being symbols of his divine authority, the mirror representing the giver's own presence upon earth. The cavalcade descends upon a mountain in the island of Tsukushi, and thus the rule of the imperial line begins.

The Sky-descended one weds a lady of the land, Princess-Blooming-Tree-Blossom (a daughter of the Mountain-Deity), who bears him three sons at a single birth. As he has given to her but one night, he suspects the parentage, and in anger she shuts herself with them in a doorless hall which she sets afire. All are unhurt, and the imperial heir accepts this fact as proof of his paternity.

Of the three sons one, Fire-Fade, is a hunter and another, Fire-Glow, a fisherman. To better their luck they exchange weapons, Fire-Glow taking Fire-Fade's bow and arrows, and Fire-Fade taking the other's fish-hook, which he loses in the sea. On Fire-Glow's demanding its return, Fire-Fade wanders on the seashore lamenting, when he meets the Salt-Deity, who, hearing his story, sets him in a basket and lowers him into the sea, by which means he reaches the palace of the Sea-Deity. Following the Salt-Deity's instructions previously given, he climbs a tree at its gate, and, when the maidservants of the Sea-Deity's daughter come to draw water from a well there, he drops his neck-jewel into their urn, to which it adheres, and it is thus carried to the princess, who goes to look and informs her father of the stranger's presence.

The Sea-Deity welcomes the newcomer and gives him his daughter in marriage, and for three years Fire-Fade dwells there content. One day, however, she finds him sighing, and he reveals the original cause of his coming. The Sea-Deity thereupon calls together all the fishes, and the lost hook being found in the mouth of the red *taï*-fish, it is returned to Fire-Fade. The Sea-Deity sends him back to his own land on the back of a *wani*, his wife promising to come to him when her pregnancy is fulfilled, in order that his child may be born there. On his departure the Sea-Deity, giving him two jewels, of which one, cast from him, will cause the tide to flow and the other to ebb, instructs him to employ these to vanquish his brother, Fire-Glow.

Accordingly, Fire-Fade overwhelms his brother with the jewel of tide-flow and when he makes submission, recalls the water with the jewel of tide-ebb. Fire-Glow covenants that he and his descendants shall be the other's "falcon men," and constitute his bodyguard. The victor has meanwhile built a "bringing-forth-house" thatched with cormorants' feathers, and his sea wife, coming on tortoise-back from the sea realm, enters it to bring forth her babe, warning him against looking at her while she is in travail. Just as He-Who-Invites disobeyed his wife's similar prohibition in the nether world, so Fire-Fade is disobedient, and, making a light with a comb, peeps in, to find her changed into a *wani*. He flees from the sight aghast, and she in anger leaves the newborn boy babe on the seashore, and goes down again to the sea realm, closing the boundary so that there may no more be open communication between his land and hers. She sends back, however, her younger sister to nurse the babe, and her—his maternal aunt—the child in due time takes to wife. From this union springs Young-Three-Hairs-Moor (Jimmu-*Tenno*), who is accounted the first earthly emperor.

From this point the Narrative relates the gradual conquest of the archipelago by the imperial line.

Young-Three-Hairs-Moor, having heard of the land to the eastward, which had earlier been taken possession of by Plenty-Swift-Sun, the elder brother of Ruddy-Plenty, his Sky ancestor, proposes to invade it and establish his capital there. Accordingly, after preparing ships and supplies, he sets out with his forces, absorbing or exterminating as he proceeds various earth deities, some of whom are tailed, and vanquishing others by means of a cross-sword which had been used in pacifying the land by one of the two Sky-deities, this cross-sword (itself a deity) being now thrown down from the Sky to assist his conquest. Great-Sky-Shiner dispatches also an eight-footed crow which acts as his guide, and later a gold-colored fish-hawk, whose radiance dazzles the eyes of the enemy so that they are unable to fight. He thus overcomes all disposed to offer resistance, including the powerful Land-Deity Prince-of-Isè, and the descendant of Plenty-Swift-Sun, who exhibits as proof of his Sky origin the weapons left by his ancestor and whom Young-Three-Hairs-Moor makes chief of his army. He overcomes also hordes of "ground-spiders," savage and untamable pit-dwellers, and having made good his title by force of arms, establishes his capital and erects his palace. He then dispenses rewards, inaugurates a system of public purification and worship, and develops his machinery of government.

From time to time Sky-deities enter the Narrative in various forms. One flies as a bird maiden who, leaving her feather robe on the shore as she bathes in the bay, is captured by a mortal. The Land-Master (who has last been seen installed by the celestial conqueror as spiritual head of the earthly realm) transforms himself into a red arrow to further a human liaison, whose fruit becomes the Empress of Young-Three-Hairs-Moor; later he visits a damsel by night, in the guise of a lovely youth, his identity being finally discovered through the fastening to his garment of a thread which in the morning is found to lead through the hook-hole of the door of his shrine. To an ex-Empress whom he "weds," he reveals himself as a small snake in her toilet box.

Succeeding reigns, however, though rich in like mythical episodes, are uneventful, and the Narrative is little more than a record of genealogies, of lesser conquests, and of the gradual elaboration of the distinctive worship, till the time of the Emperor Great-Perfect-Ruling-Lord (Keïko-Tenno) whose reign is marked by a revolt of the *Kuma-So* folk in Tsukushi (modern K'yushu), the southernmost island of the archipelago. He dispatches his son, Little-Pestle, later known as Mountain-Gate-Brave (Yamato-Dakè), to subdue them. The latter, who is but a youth, penetrates one of their strongholds in the disguise of a girl, and with his own hand slays two of the *Kuma-So* leaders, after which he puts down recalcitrant elements and pacifies the region. He is next sent against the revolting aborigines (*Emishi*) in the eastern provinces. For this task he borrows from the shrine where it has been worshiped the sword that had originally been found by the Impetuous-Male-Deity in the tail of the Eight-Forked-Serpent. When one of the local rulers fires the moor grass against him, with his blade he mows down the grass and escaping, destroys the recreant chiefs. The deity of a sea-ford raises a tempest so that he cannot cross, but his consort throws herself into the waves as a sacrifice, after which his vessel is able to proceed. He slays an earth deity appearing in the guise of a white deer (or, according to some legends, a great serpent) but is vanquished by another in the form of a white boar which brings an illness upon him, and from this he dies. From his burial mound he soars to the Sky as a white swan, leaving in the tomb only his clothing.

The Emperor Prince-Perfect-Middle (Chuaï-*Tenno*) prepares to carry on the campaign against the *Kuma-So*, when a deity, through the mouth of his Empress, Jingu, instructs him to proceed against the land of Silla (a country of Korea) which, with all its treasures, it is promised shall become the prize of the Sun-Folk. He distrusts the oracle and as penalty is stricken with death. The Empress, with the assistance of the prime minister, conceals the fact of his death and after making a religious purification of the land, herself prepares to lead the expedition. She is at this time pregnant, and to postpone childbirth binds a stone in her girdle. Her sister she sends to the sea realm where Fire-Fade had made his sojourn, and obtains, to assist her in the enterprise, the two jewels of flood-tide and ebb-tide (which presumably had come again into the possession of the Sea-deity when Fire-Fade cast them from him in subjugating his brother Fire-Glow).

Aided by various deites, Jingu's fleet reaches the Korean coast. There she casts down the jewel of ebb-tide so that the vessels are stranded and the folk of Silla hasten across the shallows to the attack, whereon she casts down the jewel of flood-tide and they are overwhelmed. The Sillan king at this makes submission and declares himself her vassal, and receiving also the submission of the two neighboring countries (Kudara and Koma) she leaves an imperial viceroy behind her and with hostages and tribute, returns to Nippon, where she permits herself to give birth to her child, whom, after crushing a revolt of her two stepsons, she seats firmly in the seat of power.

This son is Ojin-*Tenno*, whose reign brings us, according to Japanese chronology, into the opening of the fourth century of the Christian era. From this point the Narrative recounts the slow process of the government's development as an organism, the unending feuds of the Korean monarchs and the struggles of the Sun-Folk to retain an ever weakening suzerainty, the undertaking of public works, the imperial chronologies, and at length the opening of the realm to Buddhism, the new gospel from the mainland.

This, in its salient features, is an interwoven sequence, beginning in primal chaos and progressing by successive episodic chapters whose alternating scenes are laid in the Sky, on the Earth, and in the Underworld Thus:

Chaos	The Separation of the Sky and the Earth
The Sky	⎧ The Appearance of the Primal Deities ⎨ The Appearance of the Lesser Deities ⎩ The Appearance of the Creative Deity-Pair

THE ARGUMENT

The Earth
- The Formation of the first Land by the Creative Pair
- The first House (architecture)
- The first Marriage (ceremony)
- Cohabitation
- Trial Birth (unsuccessful)
- The Birth of Lands
- The Birth of Elemental Deities:
  - (Food, trees, mountains, rivers, etc.)
- The Birth of the Fire-Deity
- The first Death
- The first Murder

The Under-World
- The first Divorce
- The Creation of Phallic Deities
  - (Thunder, disease, etc.)

The Earth
- The Creation of the Three Ruling-Deities:
  - The Sun-Deity (good)
  - The Moon-Deity
  - The Rebellious-Deity (evil)
- The Distribution among these three of the All-Rule
- The Withdrawal of the Earlier Creator
- The Murder of the Food-Deity
  - Creation of grains, silk, and beasts of burden

The Sky
- The Struggle Between the Good Deity and the Rebellious Deity
  - Weaving (the loom)
- The Self-Sequestration of the Good Deity
  - Sky and Earth Eclipsed
- The Return of the Good Deity Invoked (divination)
  - Invention of
    - Sculpture
    - Metal-working (the forge)
    - Feminine Adornment
    - Music (wind- and string-instruments)
    - Liturgy
    - Dance
    - Song (incantation)
- The Return of the Good Deity
- The Birth of the Sky-Ancestor of the Imperial Line
- The Expulsion of the Rebellious Deity
- Religious Purification

The Earth
- The Peopling of the Earth by the Rebellious Deity
  - Distribution of trees and seeds
  - Cultivation of the Land
- The Slaying of the Earth-Serpent
  - Poetry (the first poem)
- Multiplication of Earth-Deities
- The Birth of the Land-Master
- The Withdrawal of the Rebellious Deity to the Under-World
- The Persecution of the Land-Master by his Brethren

The Under-World	{ The Rape of the Rebellious Deity's Daughter and Property by the Land-Master
The Earth	{ The Land-Master Vanquishes his Brethren Improvement of the Land The Coming of the Southern Ovea-Sea Deity 　His Assistance 　　Medicine 　　The Hot-Bath 　His Departure
The Sky	{ The Decision of the Good Deity to assume Earth-Rule The First Embassies to Earth (unsuccessful)
The Earth	{ The Land-Master Submits to the Sky-Ancestor 　The first Temple (ritual)
The Sky	{ His Abdication Confirmed by the Good Deity The Descent of the Deity-Ancestor
The Earth	{ The First Earthly Emperor 　His Conquest of the Realm

THE MYTH-NARRATIVE

NOTE

The two greater scriptures, the *Kojiki* and the *Nihongi*, on account of their unquestioned antiquity and authority, must always be the foundation of any legendary structure, other writings serving to supplement and verify.

In order that legend materials drawn from lesser sources may be distinguished at a glance, those portions of the narrative which embody them are printed in italics, and the sources are indicated in the footnotes.

MEASURES

Cho (area) : About 2½ acres
Hiro (linear) : About 6 feet.

The Japanese Fathom

Jo (linear) : About 10 feet
Ken (linear) : About 6 feet
Kin (weight) : About 1⅓ pounds
Ri (linear) : About 2½ miles
Shaku (linear) : About 1 foot
Shiro (area) : About 30 square feet
Sun (linear) : About 1⅕ inches
Tsubo (area) : About 16 square yards.

THE DEITY AGE

THE BEGINNING OF THE SKY AND THE EARTH

Of old time the Sky and the Earth were not yet set apart the one from the other, nor were the female and male principles [1] separated. All was a mass, formless and egg-shaped, the extent whereof is not known, which held the life principle. *Thereafter* the purer tenuous essence, *ascending gradually*, formed the Sky; the heavier portion sank and became the Earth. The lighter element merged readily, but the heavier was united with difficulty. Thus the Sky was formed first, the Earth next, and later Kami were produced in the space between them.

When the Sky and the Earth began, there was a something in the very midst of the emptiness whose shape cannot be described. At the first a thing like a white cloud appeared, *which floated between Sky and Earth,* and from it three Kami came into being in the High-Sky-Plain. These three Kami, appearing earliest, were born without progenitors and later hid their bodies.[2] They were

MID-SKY-MASTER [3]
HIGH-PRODUCER
DIVINE-PRODUCER.[4]

(*Some hold that the last two did not appear till after He-Who-Invites and She-Who-Invites, and that High-Producer was their child.*)
These first three were called the Three-Creator-Kami. High-Producer produced the Kami

SKY-DIVINE-STANDER.[5]

Now while the soil of the young Earth which made the Lands drifted

---
[5] *Ancestor of the Governors of Kuga in Yamashiro.*

about as floating oil, like a jelly-fish sporting on the water-surface, or a cloud floating over the sea without root or attachment, a something *clear and bright like crystal* sprouted up, *like a horn*, like a reed shoot when it first emerges from the mud. This became transformed into Kami of human shape, and there appeared, *springing out of the buds of the reed-shoot,* two more Kami

PLEASANT-REED-SPROUT-PRINCE-ELDER

ETERNAL-SKY-STANDER.

(Some say the latter preceded the former. *Others, also, count Mid-Sky-Master and Pleasant-Reed-Sprout-Prince-Elder Companion-born Kami.*)

These likewise were born without progenitors and later hid their bodies. *The Three-Creator-Kami and these two are called the Sky-Kami.* Pleasant-Reed-Sprout-Prince-Elder was a divine man.

THE SEVEN-SKY-GENERATIONS

There next appeared, spontaneously, through the action of the Sky-Principle, the following male Companion-Kami, which later hid their bodies:

ETERNAL EARTH STANDER [6]

EARTH-SOIL [7]

FRUITFUL-SHAPE-MOOR. [8]

Eternal-Earth-Stander and Fruitful-Shape-Moor were Companion-born Kami. *From the last was produced the Kami*

SKY-EIGHT-DESCEND.

Next after these appeared the following mated Kami:

LORD-MUD-EARTH | LADY-MUD-EARTH

GERM-INTEGRATOR | LIFE-INTEGRATOR

GREAT-PLACE-ELDER [9] | GREAT-PLACE-ELDER-LADY [10]

PERFECT-FACE [11] | AWFUL-LADY [12]

HE-WHO-INVITES [13] | SHE-WHO-INVITES.[14]

(*As to these five mated pairs, some say that Germ-Integrator and Life-Integrator preceded Lord-Mud-Earth and Lady-Mud-Earth.* Some hold that He-Who-Invites and She-Who-Invites were children of Awful Lady. *Others count them descendants, in the seventh or the sixteenth generation, of Mid-Sky-Master.* Still others say that He-Who-Invites was produced later by the Kami Foam-Calm.[15])

Lord-Mud-Earth and Lady-Mud-Earth, his younger sister (wife),[16] together produced the Kami

SKY-MEET.

Germ-Integrator and Life-Integrator, his younger sister (wife), together produced the Kami

SKY-THREE-DESCEND.

Great-Place-Elder and Great-Place-Elder-Lady, his younger sister (wife), together produced the Kami

SKY-EIGHT-HUNDRED-DAYS.

Perfect-Face and Awful-Lady, his younger sister (wife), together produced the Kami

SKY-EIGHTY-MYRIAD-JEWEL.

The two Companion-born Kami [17] and five generations of mated Kami are called the Seven-Generations-of-the-Deity-Age.

(Some, however, count these as beginning with Mid-Sky-Master.)

The next to appear were the two Kami

SHAKE-JEWEL
TEN-THOUSAND-JEWEL.

The former of whom produced the two Kami

LUCK-JEWEL
SKY-EAGLE-STANDER

and the latter of whom produced the single Kami

SKY-HARD-RIVER.[A]

THE ISLAND SELF-CURDLING

Now all the Sky-Kami (*some say* High-Producer) deigned to bid He-Who-Invites and She-Who-Invites to make and consolidate the drifting earth, saying, "There is the Fruitful-Reed-Plain-Land-of-Fresh-Rice-Ears-of-Thousand-Autumns. Go and set it in order." So, a Sky-Jewel-Spear [18] *whose staff was of coral* having been granted them, the pair took stand upon the Floating-Sky-Bridge [19] (or, as some say, in the midst of the Sky-Mist).

At some later time, while He-Who-Invites slept, this bridge fell down, and it is now the great stony cape northeast of the village of Gukè, in Yosa, Tango Province. It was named, at its upper part, Wondrous-Beach.[B]

(*Some say otherwise that the stone ledge at Village-of-House, in Kako District, Harima Province, was this Sky-Reaching-Bridge. In ancient times, it is said, eighty persons passed along it up and down betwixt the Earth and Sky, wherefore it was called Eighty-Bridge.*[20] °

On the Bridge the two Kami held counsel, after which, saying, "Lo, there is something here like floating oil; perhaps there is an island in its midst," they dipped down the Sky-Jewel-Spear and moved it about till they found the sea plain, and searching for a land, they stirred the briny silt till it was all *kowaro-kowaro*, saying, "Surely there must be a land!" When they drew the spear up, the drippings from its point piled up and formed the Island Self-Curdling.[21] At that they rejoiced and drew up the spear, saying, "Good! There is a land!"

THE WOOING OF THE KAMI HE-WHO-INVITES AND SHE-WHO-INVITES

They descended and dwelt in this island and erected a palace eight *hiro*[22] long, *of which they made the jewel spear the central pillar*,[23] and they set up a Sky-Pillar and made the Island Self-Curdling the Pillar of the Land's center. Now they desired to become husband and wife and to produce countries, and would have cohabited, but knew not how. However, *while they were thus embarrassed*, there came to them a wagtail[24] which beat together its head and its tail, and the two, imitating it, obtained knowledge of the manner of sexual intercourse. He-Who-Invites then asked his younger sister She-Who-Invites, "In what fashion is your body formed?" She replied, "In the growing of my body there is one part which grew not joined together, which is the female source-spot." Then said He-Who-Invites, "In the growing of my body there is one part which grew superfluous, which is the male source-spot. Would it not be well, therefore, that I insert that part of my body which grew superfluous, the male source-spot, into the part of your body which grew not joined together, the female source-spot, and procreate territories?" She-Who-Invites replied, "It would be well." Then said He-Who-Invites, "To this end let us go around about this Sky-Pillar[25] and mutually meeting, join together our august parts in cohabitation." Having thus agreed, He-Who-Invites said, "Do you go around to the right; I will go to the left." So, the male Kami going to the left and the female Kami to the right, when they had gone around separately and met on the same side, She-Who-Invites speaking first, said, "O comely and lovable youth!" At that He-Who-Invites said, "O comely and lovable maiden!" When they had thus spoken, he was displeased and said, "I am the man and of right should have been the first to speak. How is it that you, on the contrary, spoke first? This was unlucky. We should go around again." Nevertheless, the female Kami took the hand of the male Kami and they became united as husband and wife and began to cohabit,[26] and begot a son named

LEECH [27]

(Who, some say, was not born until after Great-Sky-Shiner and Moon-Darkness-Possessor.[28])

This child did not please them, since even at the age of three years it could not stand upright; so, having next given birth to

BIRD-ROCK-CAMPHOR-TREE-BOAT [29]

they took this boat, and laying the child Leech in it, set it adrift, abandoning it to the winds and the currents. *The boat in which he drifted arrived at Ebisu Shore, below the present West-Palace, wherefore the Kami is called Ebisu Saburo.*[A]

(Some hold that this Kami was set adrift in a boat made of reeds, and that Bird-Rock-Camphor-Tree-Boat was not born till just before the Kami Fire-Shining-Swift-Male.)

Next they procreated Foam-Island,[30] which is not reckoned among their offspring.

(There are those, however, who say that this island was not brought forth at this time, but later, next after Great-Mountain-Gate-Fertile-Dragon-Fly-Island.)

THE PROCREATION OF THE GREAT-EIGHT-ISLANDS

They then took counsel together, saying, "These children to whom we gave birth are not good," and reascending to the Sky-Kami, they announced this fact in the august place. Thereon the Sky-*Ancestor*-Kami, having made grand divination, decreed, "How can one think of the woman speaking first!" and *determining the day and hour by divination*, bade them descend and make the trial again. So, descending, they again went around the pillar as before (*some saying that He-Who-Invites this time went around it from the left and She-Who-Invites from the right*) when, *having met face to face*, He-Who-Invites spoke first, saying, "Ah, what a fair and lovely maiden!" Then She-Who-Invites said, "Ah, what a fair and lovely youth!" When they had thus spoken they cohabited and gave birth to islands as follows:

MY-SHAME-ISLAND [31]

(Some hold that this Kami was born after Great-Mountain-Gate-Fertile-Dragon-Fly-Island, others that it was born before Leech. Some say that Foam-Island was, with it, reckoned as the afterbirth with which Great-Mountain-Gate-Fertile-Dragon-Fly-Island was born, and some reckon the Island Self-Curdling as the afterbirth with which My-Shame-Island was born. Others, also, count My-Shame-Island elder brother [32] to Great-Mountain-Gate-Fertile-Dragon-Fly-Island.)

In this their minds took no pleasure. Therefore it was so named, *because they were not satisfied with the offspring.*

GREAT-MOUNTAIN-GATE-FERTILE-DRAGON-FLY-ISLAND [33]

(Which some say [34] was the eighth, rather than the third, to be born.)

DOUBLE-NAME-ISLAND [35]

This is of Iyo and it has one body and four faces, each face having a name. Thus, Iyo is called Princess-Lovely, Sanuki is called Prince-Good-Boiled-Rice, Awa is called Princess-Great-Food, and Tosa is called Brave-Good-Lord.

THREE-CHILDREN-ISLAND [36]

This also has one body and four faces, each face having a name. Thus, Tsukushi [37] is called White-Sun-Lord, Fertile is called Fertile-Sun-Lord, Fire is called Brave-Sun-Facing-Fertile-Wondrous-Prince-Lord, and Kuma-So is called Brave-Sun-Lord.

IKI-ISLAND [38]

(Which, according to some, was born later than Small-Island.)

PORT-ISLAND [39]

(Which some say was born next after Small-Island, and others say last of all.)

SADO-ISLAND
OKI-ISLAND

(Which some count triplets and some a twin of Sado-Island.)

Of these eight, two were born as twins, which was the beginning of the twin births that take place among mankind. The name "Great-Eight-Island-Land" originated in these eight [40] islands having been born first. Next they procreated

ISLAND-OF-KOSHI [41]
GREAT-ISLAND [42]
SMALL-ISLAND [43]

(Which some hold was born before Sado-Island.)

THE DEITY AGE

AZUKI-ISLAND [44]
PRINCESS-ISLAND [45]
DEER-BLOOD-ISLAND [46]
TWO-CHILDREN-ISLAND.[47]

The smaller islands *and foreign countries* in various parts were produced from the *bubbles and* coagulation of the salt-water (or as some say the fresh-water) foam. *All the islands when first born were small and feeble and attained their present size gradually, by growing, like human beings.*

THE BIRTH OF THE VARIOUS KAMI

When they had finished giving birth to land, He-Who-Invites said, "This land is the Land of Favorable-Bays, the Land of Thousand-Good-Slender-Spears, the Land True-of-Rock-Ring-Superior-Kami." Also he said, "Nothing is over the country we have produced save morning-mists which everywhere shed their perfume. So he blew these away with his breath which produced the Kami

PRINCE-LONG-WIND [48]
LADY-LONG-WIND [49]

Kami of the Wind.[50] Also, when they hungered they procreated the Kami

JEWEL-OF-STOREHOUSE-RICE.[51]

(*Some say this Kami was a child of Divine-Producer and others that she was a child of Brave-Swift-Impetuous-Male* [52] *by the Kami Princess-Divine-Great Ichi.*[53])

This is the Kami who rules the five grains.[A] *The child of famine-time, born later, was the Kami*

AKANO-JEWEL.[54]

After this they gave birth to Kami as follows:

GREAT-MALE-OF-GREAT-THING
PRINCE-ROCK-EARTH
PRINCESS-ROCK-NEST
GREAT-DOOR-SUN-LORD
SKY-BLOWING-MALE
PRINCE-GREAT-HOUSE
YOUTH-OF-WIND-GREAT-MALE [55]
GREAT-OCEAN-POSSESSOR [56]
PRINCE-SWIFT-AUTUMN [57]
PRINCESS-SWIFT-AUTUMN.[57]

The last two were Kami of river mouths. *They govern harbors, one taking in charge the seaside and the other the riverside. The last-named dwells in the myriad tide-meetings of the myriad brine-ways of the myriad paths of the currents of the boisterous sea.*

Prince-Swift-Autumn and Princess-Swift-Autumn governed separate realms of river and sea, and bore the following Kami:

FOAM-CALM

(Who some say was the father of He-Who-Invites. Others hold that he was the child of the Kami

SKY-TEN-THOUSAND,

that Sky-Ten-Thousand was procreated by the Kami

SKY-MIRROR [58]

and that Sky-Mirror was produced by Eternal-Earth-Stander.)

FOAM-WAVE
BUBBLE-CALM
BUBBLE-WAVE
SKY-WATER-DIVIDER
EARTH-WATER-DIVIDER
SKY-WATER-DRAWING-GOURD-POSSESSOR
EARTH-WATER-DRAWING-GOURD-POSSESSOR
TREE-ELDER
GREAT-MOUNTAIN-POSSESSOR [59]

(who according to some was born from the head of Fire-Shining-Swift-Male, when that one's father, He-Who-Invites, cut him to pieces,[60] *and according to others, came from the Land of Kudara, at a later time*).

PRINCESS-REED-MOOR.[61]

Tree-Elder was a Tree-Kami, the ancestor of the trees, and Princess-Reed-Moor was the ancestress of the plants. The two latter governed separate realms of mountain and moor, and brought forth the Kami

SKY-HILL-PASS-ELDER
EARTH-HILL-PASS-ELDER
SKY-MIST [62]
EARTH-MIST [62]
SKY-DARK-DOOR
EARTH-DARK-DOOR

THE DEITY AGE

PRINCE-GREAT-VALE
PRINCESS-GREAT-VALE.

He-Who-Invites and She-Who-Invites, *having become united as husband and wife,* thus procreated the eighty countries, the eighty islands, and the eight hundred myriad deities, with the Great-Eight-Island-Land, the sea, the rivers, the mountains, the ancestor of the trees, and the ancestress of the plants.

They then procreated the Kami

FIRE-SHINING-SWIFT-MALE.[63]

THE WITHDRAWAL OF SHE-WHO-INVITES

In giving birth to this child the vagina of She-Who-Invites was burned, and she sickened with fever and lay down. From her vomit were produced the two Kami

PRINCE-METAL-MOUNTAIN [64]
PRINCESS-METAL-MOUNTAIN.[64]

From her feces were produced the two earth-Kami

PRINCE-CLAY-EASY
PRINCESS-CLAY-EASY.[65]

From her urine were produced the two water Kami

PRINCESS-WATER-HANOMÈ
YOUNG-PRODUCER

and there were born to these two the Kami

PRINCESS-FRUITFUL-FOOD.[66]

(*It is said by some, however, that Fire-Shining-Swift-Male took to wife Princess-Clay-Easy, and that the two begot Young-Producer, a female child, on the crown of whose head were produced the silkworm and the mulberry tree and in her navel millet, corn, rice, hemp, and beans.*[A] Others say this latter Kami was a male Kami, the child of Prince-Clay-Easy and Princess-Water-Hanomè, and that Princess-Water-Hanomè was born from the blood of Fire-Shining-Swift-Male, when he was later slain.)

She-Who-Invites also brought forth the Kami

SKY-GOURD.

This was to hold water with which to subdue Fire-Shining-Swift-Male when he should become violent.

> (Some say that the Water-Kami, the Clay-Kami, and the Gourd-Kami were not born until later than this, relating that She-Who-Invites, after the birth of Fire-Shining-Swift-Male, died and started for the Land-of-Night. But when she reached the Level-Pass-of-the-Land-of-Night, she said to herself, "I have brought forth an evil-hearted child and have left him behind in the world ruled by my august husband." And so saying, she returned and brought forth Princess-Water-Hanomè, Sky-Gourd, Princess-Clay-Easy, and
>
> RIVER-WEED.[67]
>
> counseling He-Who-Invites thus: "When this evil-hearted child becomes violent, calm it with these four Kami.") ▲

So She-Who-Invites, through giving birth to the Kami of fire, was burned, and at length suffered change and divinely ceased to be, and He-Who-Invites buried her at the village of Arima, in Bear-Moor,[68] in the Land of Tree.

> (Some say, however, that her body was buried on Hiba Mountain, on the boundary between Sacred-Quarter Province and Broom [69] Province.)

Now, in the time of blossoms, the folk worship her spirit by offering flowers, and with drums, flutes, and flags, *men and women all* singing and dancing.

Then He-Who-Invites was angered and said, "Oh, my lovely younger sister! Alas, that I should have exchanged you for this one child!" And as he crept *on his belly* weeping about her head and her feet, there was born from the tears he shed as they fell the Kami that dwells at the foot of the trees on the slopes of Mount Fragrant [70]

CRYING-WEEPING-FEMALE.

THE SLAYING OF FIRE-SHINING-SWIFT-MALE

Afterward, drawing his ten-hand-lengths sword, He-Who-Invites cut off the head of his child, Fire-Shining-Swift-Male, whose birth had caused her death. Now the blood of Fire-Shining-Swift-Male *flowed to the village of Cave-of-Yuzu and* brought forth the following: From that which adhered to the sword point and spattered the crowded rock masses in the bed of the Sky-River,[71] were born the Kami

ROCK-SPLITTER
ROOT-SPLITTER.

From the blood that adhered to the knob of the sword guard and spattered the crowded rock masses were born the Kami

AWFUL-SWIFT-SUN
SUN'S-SWIFT-SUN
BRAVE-AWFUL-POSSESSING-MALE.[72]

(Some, however, hold that Awful-Swift-Sun was the child of

SACRED-MALE-PILLAR.[73]

Others have it that Sun's-Swift-Sun did not appear at this time, but later, being one of the male Kami [74] *born from the mist of Brave-Swift-Impetuous-Male's breath when he had his contest with Great-Sky-Shiner.* Some say, moreover, that these three Kami made three generations rather than one, and some that Brave-Awful-Possessing-Male was the child of Awful-Swift-Sun.)

These three Kami have their seat in the Sky-Cave, on the upper course of the Sky-River-of-Eight-Currents.

From the blood that collected on the sword-hilt and dripped between the fingers of He-Who-Invites were born the Kami

DARK-OKAMI [75]
DARK-MOUNTAIN-BODY [75]
DARK-WATER.[75]

Of the Kami thus produced, Rock-Splitter and Root-Splitter begot the Kami

SNAP-MASTER.[76]

(Some say, however, that the blood that dripped from the sword-edge became the myriad rocks in the Sky-River-of-Eight-Currents, and that this Kami was born from them.)

Now the blood from the wounds spurted out and stained the rocks, trees, and herbage. It is for this reason that herbs, trees, and pebbles contain, naturally, the elements of fire. From the dead body [77] of Fire-Shining-Swift-Male were born Kami as follows: From his head (or, as some say, from his loins) and from his breast

TRUE-PASS-MOUNTAIN-POSSESSOR
MOUNTAIN-DESCENT-POSSESSOR.

From his belly and from his penis were born the Kami

INMOST-MOUNTAIN-POSSESSOR
DARK-MOUNTAIN-POSSESSOR.

From his left arm (or, as some say, from his leg and his right arm) were born the Kami

DENSE-MOUNTAIN-POSSESSOR
MOUNTAIN-SPUR-POSSESSOR.

From his left leg and his right leg were born the Kami

MOUNTAIN-PLAIN-POSSESSOR
MOUNTAIN-GATE-POSSESSOR.

(Some say that He-Who-Invites with his sword cut Fire-Shining-Swift-Male into three pieces, one of which became the Thunder-Kami,[78] one Great-Mountain-Possessor, and one Brave-Awful-Possessing-Male. Others say that he cut him into five pieces, which became five Mountain-Kami, that from his head sprang the Kami Great-Mountain-Possessor, and from his trunk the Kami

MIDDLE-MOUNTAIN-POSSESSOR.[79])

The name of the sword that He-Who-Invites wielded was

SKY-POINT-BLADE-EXTENDED.[80]

THE-LAND-OF-NIGHT

Then He-Who-Invites, longing to see his dead wife, followed after her [81] to the Land-of-the-Yellow-Spring [82] and when, appearing like one alive, she lifted the door of the palace and came out to meet him, he said, "O lovely younger sister! I have come because I sorrowed for you. The lands I and you made are not finished. Therefore come back." Then she, *who had been yearning for him as in her lifetime,* answered, "Alas, my august lord and husband, that you did not come sooner, for I have eaten food within the cooking-place of the Yellow Spring and I would *sleep and* rest. Nevertheless, as I am beholden to you for your coming [83] and am wishful to return, *tomorrow* I will discuss the matter with the Kami of the place. We are of the same house.[84] I beseech you, look not upon me!" And so saying, she re-entered the palace and became invisible.

It was then dark, and as she tarried there exceeding long, he did not heed, and *breaking his promise,* secretly broke off one of the large end-teeth of the close-toothed comb he wore stuck in his left hair-bunch for a torch, and making a single light, entered. When he looked, however, he saw that *she was much swollen,* rotten matter was flowing from her, and maggots were swarming in her. (This is why at night people now avoid the use of a single light and do not throw away a comb.) Eight Thunder-Kami [85] sat on her: [86]

GREAT-THUNDER

dwelt on her hand; on her breast and on her belly sat

FIRE-THUNDER
EARTH-THUNDER.

On her back, her buttocks, her arm, and her leg, sat

YOUNG-THUNDER
BLACK-THUNDER
MOUNTAIN-THUNDER
MOOR-THUNDER

and on her vagina—eight Thunder-Kami in all—sat

CLEAVING-THUNDER.

He-Who-Invites, dismayed at the sight, shrank back; whereon She-Who-Invites was angered and cried, "Why did you not obey my warning? Now I am shamed. You have seen my nakedness. I will in turn see yours!" At that He-Who-Invites was deeply ashamed and would have gone back, *but he remained silent and did not at once take his departure*, at which She-Who-Invites sent to pursue him, and to compel him to remain, the eight

UGLY-FEMALES-OF-THE-LAND-OF-NIGHT.[87]

(It is said by some that when the vagina of She-Who-Invites was burned by bringing forth Fire-Shining-Swift-Male, she said to He-Who-Invites, "Oh my husband, for seven nights and seven days forbear to look upon me," and so saying she became concealed. Before this time was up, however, he, wondering at her concealment, looked upon her and saw that her vagina had been burned. Then she was angered and said, "You, my august husband, have done me wrong in looking upon me now, when I begged you to forbear. For this reason you shall govern the upper world and I the lower world." So saying, she became concealed.) ▲ *(Others say that after her death, She-Who-Invites was placed in a temporary burial place and that He-Who-Invites went there to see her. Thereon she, coming forth as she had been when alive, spoke to him, saying, "I pray you, look not upon me." Having said this, she vanished, and as it was at the time dark, he lit a light and looked at her. Then seeing her swollen and festering, he was shocked and ran away, when the eight Thunder-Kami who rested on her arose and pursued him.)*

As He-Who-Invites swiftly fled back he took his black headdress and cast it behind him, and it instantly turned into grapes,[88] and while the Ugly-Females stopped to devour these, he fled on. When they, having finished eating these, pressed him, he broke the close-toothed comb in his right hair bunch and cast it behind him, and the teeth straightway became bamboo shoots, and while they pulled these up and ate them, he fled on. When having finished eating these they again pressed him, he urinated against a large tree, and the water instantly became a great river, and while the Ugly-Females were preparing to cross this river, he fled on. Then She-Who-Invites sent in pursuit the eight Thunder-Kami, with fifteen hundred

WARRIORS-OF-THE-LAND-OF-NIGHT [89]

but he drew his ten-hand-lengths sword and fled on, brandishing it behind him. Now there grew by the roadside a great peach tree at whose foot he concealed himself, and he plucked three peaches [90] that grew on it and with them he smote the Thunder-Kami so that they all fled back. (This was the origin of the custom of keeping off evil spirits by means of peaches.) Then he said to the peaches, "As you have helped me, so shall you help all living folk in the Land-Amid-Reed-Plains when they shall be harassed." And he gave these Kami the name of

GREAT-DIVINE-FRUIT.[91]

Lastly She-Who-Invites came herself in pursuit. But by this time He-Who-Invites had reached the Level-Pass-of-the-Land-of-Night. So he took up a thousand-man-lift rock and set it in the middle of the Level-Pass, blocking it up. The rock is called the great Kami

LAND-OF-NIGHT-GATE-BLOCK.[92]

What was called the Level-Pass-of-the-Land-of-Night is now called Pass-of-Evening-Darkness [93] in the Land of Sacred-Quarter.[94]

> (By some, however, it is said that this pass is not any special place, but means only the instant when the breath fails at the coming of death.)

So from opposite sides of the rock He-Who-Invites and She-Who-Invites divorced each other. "If you do thus," said she, "my lovely elder brother, I will in one day strangle to death a thousand of the people of your land!" He-Who-Invites replied, "If you do that, then will I in one day cause fifteen hundred bringing-forth houses to be built. Thus each day, though a thousand people will surely die, fifteen hundred will surely be born." (*For this reason it befalls that one thousand men die and fifteen hundred men are born each day.*) [A] Then said he, "Our relationship is severed; nor will I submit to be worsted by a relative, for whom it was weakness in me at first to sorrow and mourn." And he spat out spittle,[95] whose Kami was called

THE DEITY AGE

SWIFT-JEWEL-MALE.

He also threw down his staff, which became the Kami

GREAT-ELDER-OF-COME-NOT-PLACE [96]

saying, "Come no further!" Then the

ROAD-KEEPERS-OF-THE-LAND-OF-NIGHT

said, "We have a message for you, and it is this: 'I and you have produced countries. Why should we wish to produce more? I shall remain in this land, nor will I depart with you.' " (By reason of this She-Who-Invites is called the Great-Kami-of-the-Land-of-Night, and as she pursued and caught up with He-Who-Invites, she is called Road-Reaching-Great-Kami.) Then

PRINCESS-LISTEN [97]

daughter of He-Who-Invites and She-Who-Invites,[98] spoke, and He-Who-Invites, listening to her words, praised them *and they parted from each other.* After this She-Who-Invites vanished away. (*It is perhaps by reason of this occurrence that a man whose wife dies before him avoids a burying place.*) Thus did He-Who-Invites see in person the Land-of-Night, a most inauspicious thing.

THE PURIFICATION OF HE-WHO-INVITES

Then in regret said he, "Truly, in coming to an abominable and corrupted land, I have brought upon myself ill luck, and must purify my person of its filth!" And *repenting,* he returned to the upper world, where he visited the Naruto Passage [99] and the Quick-Sucking-Passage.[1] The tide in these two passages, however, was exceeding strong, so he went to a small river mouth near Orange [2] in Sun-Facing [3] in the Island of Tsukushi, and on a plain covered with bush-clover, cleansed himself. When he threw down his girdle and skirt there were born from them the Kami

LONG-ROAD-SPACE

LOOSEN-PUT.

From his upper garment (*or as some say from his foot-coverings*) was born the Kami

TROUBLE-MASTER.

This Kami is the Kami of torture. From his trousers, his hat, and his sandals were born the Kami

OPEN-MOUTH

OPEN-MOUTH-MASTER

ROAD-SPREAD-OUT.

From his left bracelet there were born the two Kami

SEA-HORIZON-DISTANT
WAVE-EDGE-SEA-HORIZON-PRINCE.

And from his right bracelet were born the three Kami

SHORE-DISTANT
WAVE-EDGE-SHORE-PRINCE
INTERMEDIATE-SHORE-DIRECTION.

(Some accounts, however, say that his throwing down of these articles occurred earlier, when he threw down his staff, in forbidding She-Who-Invites to come further.)

When at length he was about to wash away the impurities of his body, he made a prayer, saying, *"The male Kami has come to the bush-clover plain of Orange to exorcize the filth of the Land-of-Night and make his body clean."* Then he lifted his voice, saying, "The water in the upper current is swift and that in the lower current is sluggish." So he plunged into the middle current, and as he bathed there the following **Kami were born** from the filth he had acquired:

BODY-OF-EIGHTY-EVILS
BODY-OF-GREAT-EVILS
DIVINE-RECTIFYING-BODY
GREAT-RECTIFYING-BODY
FEMALE OF IZU.[4]

The last three were produced to root out the first two (which pair some account a single Kami). As he bathed in the water's bottom current were born the Kami

OCEAN-BOTTOM-POSSESSOR
MALE-BOTTOM-POSSESSOR.[5]

As he bathed in the mid-water there were born

OCEAN-MIDDLE-POSESSOR
MALE-MIDDLE-POSSESSOR.[6]

As he bathed at the water's surface there were born

OCEAN-SURFACE-POSSESSOR
MALE-SURFACE-POSSESSOR.[7]

These three ocean-possessing Kami [8] had as son

LIVING-HIKANA-SAKU.[9]

Male-Bottom-Possessor, Male-Middle-Possessor and Male-Surface-Possessor are the Great Kami of the three shrines of Pleasant-to-Dwell-In.[10]

> (Some say that He-Who-Invites entered and issued from the water three times. When he entered the first time he blew forth the Kami
>
> ### ROCK-POSSESSOR
>
> and on coming forth, the Kami Great-Rectifying-Body. When he entered the second time he blew forth the Kami Male-Bottom-Possessor, and on coming forth the Kami
>
> ### GREAT-PATTERN-BODY.
>
> When he entered the third time he blew forth the Kami
>
> ### RED-POSSESSOR [11]
>
> and on coming forth, the various Kami of the Sky, the Earth, and the Sea-Plain.)

There was next born, as He-Who-Invites washed his left eye, the female Kami

GREAT-SKY-SHINER [12]

and as he washed his right eye there was born the male Kami

MOON-DARKNESS-POSSESSOR.[13]

> (It is said by some, however, that this Kami was a female. Others too say that this Kami was produced when he washed his right hand.) ᴬ

These two were of a shining and beautiful nature, made to shine upon the sky and the earth. *They have their seat on the upper reach of the River Fifty-Bells, being called The-Great-Kami-Whose-Shrines-Are-Dedicated-at-Isè.*[14] Thirdly, as He-Who-Invites washed his nose, there was born the male Kami

BRAVE-SWIFT-IMPETUOUS-MALE.[15]

> (By some it is said that He-Who-Invites, saying, "I desire to create a precious child who shall govern the earth," took in each

---

[9] ***Ancestor of the Tribe-Masters of Azumi.****

---

* Moribè derives this word from *Ama-tsu-mochi* (Fisherman-Possessor).

hand a mirror of white copper, upon which there came from the mirror in his left hand the Kami Great-Sky-Shiner, and from the mirror in his right hand the Kami Moon-Darkness-Possessor; and that when he turned his gaze sidewise there was produced the Kami Brave-Swift-Impetuous-Male.)

(Other accounts [16] say that after He-Who-Invites and She-Who-Invites had given birth to all the lesser Kami, they consulted together, saying, "It is now time to bring forth the Sovereign of the Sky-Under, and that thereupon Great-Sky-Shiner, Moon-Darkness-Possessor, and Brave-Swift-Impetuous-Male were born *in the natural way*.)

(Still others say that the Kami Leech was born after these—imperfect children appearing both at the beginning and ending of the procreation, for the reason that the rule of the male's priority had been broken—and that they then gave birth to the Kami Bird-Rock-Camphor-Tree-Boat, in which they set the Kami Leech adrift.)

Then He-Who-Invites rejoiced greatly, saying, "In my continued begetting I have at last begotten three illustrious children."

THE INVESTITURE OF THE THREE CHILDREN-KAMI

Now the resplendent luster of Great-Sky-Shiner shone throughout all the six directions,[17] and He-Who-Invites said, "Though I have had many children none has been the peer of this wondrous child. She should not be kept long in this land, but I should send her straightway to the Sky, with whose affairs she should be invested." So, jinglingly taking off and shaking his jewel-string necklace, whose name was

STOREHOUSE-SHELF-KAMI

he bestowed it upon Great-Sky-Shiner, charging her to rule the Plain-of-the-High-Sky.[18] Now at this time the Sky and the Earth were still not far separated and were connected by the Sky-Pillar,[19] by which he sent her up. The refulgence of Moon-Darkness-Possessor was next to that of Great-Sky-Shiner in splendor and he was to be her consort and share in her government, so he was likewise sent up to the Sky.

Now after these two had come there, Great-Sky-Shiner said to Moon-Darkness-Possessor, "I hear that in the Central-Land-of-Reed-Plains is a Kami called Jewel-of-Storehouse-Rice. Do you go and attend upon her." Moon-Darkness-Possessor descended and going to the place where Jewel-of-Storehouse-Rice dwelt, begged food of her. *There was there a cassia tree of five hundred branches against which he leaned (for which reason the place was called Cassia Village)*.ᴬ Then, turning her head toward the land, she took from her mouth boiled rice; she faced the sea and there came from her mouth broad-finned and narrow-finned things; she faced the mountains and there came from her mouth rough-haired and soft-haired things. Also she took from her nose and her anus all sorts of dainty things, and preparing various dishes, set them on a hundred tables and offered them to him for his entertainment. At that Moon-Darkness-Possessor reddened with anger. Said he, "Filthy! Do you dare to feed me with such mouth-disgorged things?" Then plucking forth his sword, he slew her, and returning, made report, detailing all the circumstances.

> (Some say, to the contrary, that Jewel-of-Storehouse-Rice was not slain then in this manner, but later by Brave-Swift-Impetuous-Male, who begged food from her after his expulsion from the Sky.)

Great-Sky-Shiner was enraged at this, and exclaimed, "You are a wicked Kami. It is not fitting that I should see you face to face." So she and Moon-Darkness-Possessor were from that time separated by a day and a night [20] and dwelt apart from each other, and Moon-Darkness-Possessor was made to rule the Realm of the Night [21] and the eight hundred fold tides of the Sea-Plain.[22] Later Great-Sky-Shiner sent

SKY-CLOUD-MAN [23]

who found Jewel-of-Storehouse-Rice dead. From her body, however, the following articles had been born: From the crown of her head (*or, as some say, her eyes*), the ox and horse *and the mulberry tree*; from the top of her forehead (or, as some say, her ears) millet; [24] from her eyebrows, silkworms; [25] from her eyes, panic; from her nose, small beans; [26] from her belly, rice; from her vagina, barley, wheat (and, according to some, small beans and large beans); [27] from her buttocks, large beans. All these things Sky-Cloud-Man carried to Great-Sky-Shiner, who rejoiced, saying, "These are the things the race of visible beings will eat in order to live." *So she appointed Head-Men of the Sky-Villages,* and the panic, the wheat, and the beans she (or, as some say, Divine-Producer) made seed for the dry fields, and the rice she made seed for the flooded fields, and for the first time sowed the rice seed in the narrow fields and the long fields of the Sky, so that in the Autumn the *yellow* ears drooped down, eight hand-lengths long, exceedingly pleasant to the eye. Also she took the silkworm cocoons in her mouth and reeled thread from them. (This was the origin of the art of silkworm rearing *and weaving.*)

THE HAVOC OF BRAVE-SWIFT-IMPETUOUS-MALE

Brave-Swift-Impetuous-Male was now of adult age, and had an eight-hand-lengths beard. He was of a fierce temper and a wicked disposition, prone to wailing and anger. His character was to love destruction, and he caused many people to die in their youth. Him He-Who-Invites gave to rule the Earth, but while the other two Kami assumed rule over their dominions, Brave-Swift-Impetuous-Male was dissatisfied. He neglected his rule and wailed and wept and fumed with rage till his eight-hand-lengths beard reached to his midriff. His bewailing was such that it withered the green mountains into withered mountains and dried up all the rivers and seas *so that speedy calamity fell upon all things* and the noise of the evil Kami *who visited him* was like the buzzing flies in the fifth moon, and myriad woeful portents arose.

Then He-Who-Invites asked Brave-Swift-Impetuous-Male, "Why, instead of ruling the Land I gave you, do you always wail and weep thus?" He answered, "I wail for no other reason than because I wish to depart to my dead mother's land,[28] to the Nether-Distant-Land." At this He-Who-Invites was filled with loathing of him, and said, "If you were to rule this country, much destruction of life would surely result. Since this is so, you shall not dwell in the land I gave you. Go, even as your heart's wish is, and rule over the Land-of-Roots." [29] And forthwith he divinely expelled him.

Then Brave-Swift-Impetuous-Male made petition, saying, "I will obey your command and proceed to the Nether-Land. I desire, however, for a short time, to go to the High-Sky-Plain to take leave of my elder sister, Great-Sky-Shiner, after which I will depart forever." This permission being granted him, He-Who-Invites, his divine task having been accomplished his power being great, and his spirit about to undergo a change, built himself a dwelling of darkness in the Island of My-Shame, where he abode forever in silence, unseen.

> (*By some, however, it is said that He-Who-Invites now dwells at Taga* [30] *in Fresh-Sea.*[A] *And by others it is said that, being about to die,* he ascended to the Sky and made report of his mission, after which he dwelt in the smaller Palace of the Sun.)

So Brave-Swift-Impetuous-Male ascended to the Sky. Now there Great-Sky-Shiner had made three inclosed ricefields of Sky-narrow shape and of Sky-long shape, which she made her imperial ricefields, and which were called the Sky-Eight-Fold-Ricefield, the Sky-Level-Ricefield, and the Sky-Village-Join-Ricefield. All these were good ricefields, nor suffered they even in drought or after prolonged rain. Brave-Swift-Impetuous-Male, however, planted three ricefields, called the Sky-Stump-Field, the Sky-River-Side-Field and the Sky-Sharp-Mouth-Field, which were all barren places, whose soil was swept away by the rains and parched by droughts. Brave-Swift-Impetuous-Male, in jealousy, destroyed the ricefields of his elder sister, in spring knocking away the troughs and pipes, filling up the ditches, and breaking down the divisions. Also he resowed the seed and in the autumn, when the grain was formed, *going secretly to her ricefields*, set up *troublesome* skewers with incantations, stretched ropes around the ricefields, and made *piebald* horses lie down in them. When the time was come for Great-Sky-Shiner to celebrate the Feast of First Fruits,[31] he secretly voided excrement beneath her seat in her new palace *and smeared the doors with it*,[B] so that when she went there and took her seat, she was greatly sickened. In all these various matters his conduct was rude in the last degree. Nevertheless, though these things went on incessantly, out of her friendliness for him she was not indignant nor resentful, but took all calmly and with forbearance, saying, "What looks like excrement must be my brother's drunken vomit, and surely he has broken down the field divisions and filled up the ditches because he thinks the land they occupy is thus wasted."

In spite of these apologies for him, however, he continued his evil deeds in greater and greater measure, and as she sat in her hallowed garment-house, weaving the august robes of the Kami, he broke a hole in its roof tiles and flung inside a piebald colt that he had flayed alive with a backward flaying,[32] at which sight Great-Sky-Shiner started with alarm, wounding herself with the shuttle and her younger sister

YOUNG-SUN-FEMALE [33]

was so frightened that she fell from the loom and pierced her vagina with the sharp shuttle she held in her hand, and divinely died.[34]

THE DOOR OF THE SKY-ROCK-CAVE

Then Great-Sky-Shiner said, "You have evil intentions, I will no more see you face to face." And, enraged, she retired into the Sky-Rock-Cave and closed and made fast the door and dwelt there in seclusion, so that the whole Plain-of-the-High-Sky was darkened and all the Central-Land-of-Reed-Plains unilluminated, from which unchanging night befell and the alternation of day and night was unknown.[35] *The Kami had no place to set their hands or feet and all their affairs were carried on by means of lights*. So that all the myriad Kami were grieved and their noise was like the buzzing flies in the fifth moon and ten thousand woeful calamities befell.

So, *when there was no light but candlelight*, the eighty myriad Kami assembled in a divine company in the dry bed of the Sky-River-of-Eight-Currents [36] (or, as some say, in the Sky-High-Market-Place) to consider how they should beseech her, and bade the Kami

THOUGHT-INCLUDER

child of High-Producer, who was of deep plan and far-reaching thought, conceive a plan. He considered the matter and said, "Let there be made an image of Great-Sky-Shiner and let prayer be offered to it." So they assembled the long-singing cocks [37] of the Eternal-Land [38] and made them utter their long-drawn cry to one another. *(It was at this time that the torii [39] originated, they being used as roosts for the Sky-cocks.)* And they took hard rocks from the Sky-River-Bed *for an anvil*, and iron (or, as some say, copper) from the Sky-Metal-Mountains, and calling in the one-eyed Kami, the smith

SKY-MARA [40]

bade him make from it a Sun-spear. Also he stripped off in a single piece the hide of a true stag and made of it a Sky-bellows. Now the female Kami which he fashioned by this means on the upper reach of the Sky-River-of-Eight-Currents is the Kami

SUN-MAË

who dwells in the Land of Tree. They then appointed the Kami

AGAIN-FORGING-OLD-WOMAN [41]

as artisan to make a Sky-Mirror [42] *in shape like the sun*. This she did, but the mirror did not give satisfaction, so that she forged it a second time. *The first mirror is the Kami at Hisaki in Tree Province.*

> *(Some say that at two trials the mirror was too small and did not please the Kami, but at the third time it was large and beautiful. Others say the second mirror was forged by the Kami*
>
> ## SKY-GATE
>
> *who was the son of Again-Forging-Old-Woman. Others, also, say that she took copper from Sky-Mount-Fragrant and made the Sun-spear and also the Sky-bellows.)*

Then they deigned to lay command upon the Kami

JEWEL-ANCESTOR [43]

a child of He-Who-Invites, to make a jewel-string of five hundred *very*

---

[40] **Ancestor of the Abstainer Clan of Tsukushi and Isè Provinces, and of the Warrior Clan. (Monono Be).**
[41] **Ancestress of the Chieftains of the Mirror-Makers Clan.**
[43] **Ancestor of the Chieftains of the Jewel-Makers of Izumo Province.**

splendid augustly-fastening-together jewels, eight shaku long. *They bade the Kami*

LONG-WHITE-LEAF [44]

plant hemp from which to make blue soft cloth (from which originated the cloth called Shiroha [45]*), and the Kami*

TSUKU-HI-MI [46]

they bade plant paper mulberry to make white soft cloth. Now these grew in a single night. They commanded also the Kami

SKY-SUN-EAGLE [47]

child of High-Producer, to make paper-mulberry cloth,[48] *and the weaver Kami*

BRAVE-LEAF-ELDER [49]

to weave cloth of divers designs. Moreover they deigned to bid

PRINCESS-SKY-HAND-LOOM [50]

to weave soft Kami-garments.^A *They also bade the Kami*

HAND-PLACING-SOIL-CARRIER [51]

make a hat of sedge, and laid the making of a shield upon

PRINCE-MEASURE-KNOWING.*[52]*

The Kami Sky-Mara they bade make various swords, axes, spears and iron bells. Also they caused Great-Mountain-Possessor [53] *to procure eighty precious bunches of a sakaki* [54] *tree of five hundred branches and Princess-Reed-Moor* [55] *to procure eighty precious bunches of suzuki-grass of five hundred branches. And they ordered Hand-Placing-Soil-Carrier and Prince-Measure-Knowing to cut down trees with Sky-tools in dales and dells and to erect a new and lovely palace. Now the Kami*

PORT-SWIFT-JEWEL

had begotten the kami

ONE-THOUSAND-JEWEL

---

[44] **Ancestor of the Hemp-Spinners of Isè Province.**
[47] **Ancestor of the Head-men of the Abstainer-Clan of Awa.**
[49] **Ancestor of the Figured-Cloth Weavers.**
[51] **Ancestor of the Abstainer Clan * of the Land of Kii and of Sanuki Province.**
[52] **Ancestor of the Abstainer Clan of Kii Province.**

---

* Imibè (Imu-Murè).

who was the father (or, as some say, the brother) of the Kami

KOGOTO-JEWEL

who was the father (or, as some say, the brother) of the Kami

SKY-BECKONING-ANCESTOR-LORD [56]

who had for son the Kami

BRAVE-UCHI-NOKORI.[57]

Sky-Beckoning-Ancestor-Lord, with the help of the Kami

GREAT-JEWEL [58]

child of High-Producer, was made to pull out the shoulder-blade of a stag [59] from the Sky-Mount-Fragrant and to take birch-bark and to make divination with it. When all these objects were assembled, they caused the Kami Mountain-Thunder to pull up by the roots a *sakaki* tree of five hundred branches from the Sky-Mount-Fragrant, hung upon its upper branches the Jewel-String, on its middle branch the eight-hand-length Mirror, and on its lower branches the offerings of blue hemp-cloth and of white paper-mulberry cloth,[60] *and the various other things mentioned*, and these different articles Great-Jewel held up before the door of the Rock-Cavern, while Sky-Beckoning-Ancestor-Lord *(some say Great-Jewel)* with lavish and earnest words of praise, prayerfully recited a grand ritual, *saying*, "The Mirror I have is bright and beauteous, like you. Will you not open the door and look upon it?"

Meanwhile there stood hidden beside the rock-door the Kami

SKY-HAND-STRENGTH-MALE.[61]

(*Some, however, hold his other names Wondrous-Rock-True-Gate and Fruitful-Rock-True-Gate to be the names of separate Kami, children of Great-Jewel, saying that the last dwells now at Wataraï.*[A])

He was a son of Thought-Includer (or, as some say, of Great-Jewel) and was father of the Kami

SKY-FEATHER-FEATHER [62]

to whom there is a shrine at Asakura-Village, in Tosa. Also the Kami

SKY-FRIGHTENING-FEMALE [63]

---

[56] **Ancestor of the Chieftains of the Intercessor Clan.** [57] See p. 92, n. 87.
[58] **Ancestor of the Head-Men and Nobles of the Abstainer Clan.**
[63] **Ancestress of the Clan-Chieftainesses of Sarumè.**

who was strong and fierce *(for which reason she was given this name, from which people now call strong women uzushi)*, tricing up her sleeves with a cord of club-moss, making a headdress of spindle-tree [64] leaves and a hand-boquet of bamboo-grass, *fastened bells to her hand*, took the spear wreathed with eulalia grass, kindled bonfires,[65] and setting a hollow tub before the door of the Sky-Rock-Cave, stamped upon it as though Kami-possessed until it resounded, playing meanwhile upon a bamboo flageolet to the accompaniment of a harp made of bows set together with strings uppermost,[66] while the Kami kept time with wooden clappers. Dancing skillfully a mime,[67] she gave forth a divine utterance,[68] *which was:* "One, two, three, four, five, six, seven, eight, nine, ten, hundred, thousand, myriad." [69], A

> *(Some say however, that these words were an incantation taught by Great-Sky-Shiner to the Kami Sky-Plenty-Earth-Plenty-High-as-Sky's-Sun-Fire-Ruddy-Plenty, her descendant, whom she later sent down from the Sky to rule the Central-Land-of-Reed-Plains.*[70]*)*

As Sky-Frightening-Female sang,[71] she pulled out the nipples of her breasts and pushed down her skirt-string to her mons veneris, at which the Plain-of-the-High-Sky shook and all the eight hundred myriad Kami laughed together.

When Great-Sky-Shiner heard this, she was astonished, and opening with her august hand the door of the Sky-Rock-Cave [72] for a little space, peeped out, and exclaimed: "Though of late many prayers have been offered me, none has been of such beautiful language as these. Moreover I thought that since I have withdrawn and shut myself in the Rock-Cave, the Plain of the High-Sky and the Central-Land-of-Reed-Plains would be in continued darkness. How is it that Sky-Frightening-Female makes merry and the eight hundred myriad Kami all laugh?" Sky-Frightening-Female answered, "We rejoice that a Kami has been found more shiningly lovely than you." While she spoke, Sky-Beckoning-Ancestor-Lord and Great-Jewel held up before her the Mirror, whereupon Great-Sky-Shiner, more and more amazed, little by little came outside the door to gaze into it.[73] At this time, when the Mirror was thus used, it struck against the door of the Sky-Rock-Cave and received a small scar which remains to this day. (This Mirror is the great Kami worshiped at Isè.) Then Sky-Hand-Strength-Male, who had been standing in hiding, seized the hand of Great-Sky-Shiner and drew her out, *and led her to the new palace, Sky-Beckoning-Ancestor-Lord and Great-Jewel surrounding it with an august bottom-tied Sun-rope, and beseeching her not to return.* Afterward Great-Jewel stretched the return-preventing rope across behind her,[74] saying, "You shall not go further back than this!" At this time Sky-Hand-Strength-Male leaned upon one leg and his foot touched the earth. His footprint is Saddle-Lake on Mount Door-Conceal. After this he seized the stone door, and tearing it from its place, threw it into the air. It flew for more than four hundred ri, coming to earth on the center of Mount Newly-Cultivated,[75] where it rests on a pinnacle. It is twenty shaku long and fifteen shaku wide.

> (Others, however, say that this rock-door is the present Mount-Door-Conceal,[76] in Lime-Tree-Moor Province.)

Now when Great-Sky-Shiner had come forth, her radiance filled the Sky-Under, and both the Plain-of-the-High-Sky and the Central-Land-of-Reed-Plains again became light, *so that all could see each other's faces distinctly*, at which the eight hundred myriad Kami rejoiced greatly, *and, stretching forth their hands, danced and sang together, shouting, "How pleasant! How delightful!" the sound being like the rustling of the leaves of the bamboo and the okè tree. "Now the universe for the first time is truly fair!"* The Kami

GREAT-PALACE-FEMALE

daughter of Great-Jewel, was ordered to attend the presence of the Great Kami. Thus came about the resemblance to the present court, where females bring into harmony the relations between lord and vassal and comfort the mind of the Sovereign with good and beautiful words.[A]

THE EXPULSION OF BRAVE-SWIFT-IMPETUOUS-MALE

Then the eight hundred myriad Kami took counsel together, and putting the blame on Brave-Swift-Impetuous-Male, convicted him *of all his sins and offenses* and imposed upon him a fine of a thousand tables of articles required for the Ceremony of Purification. To expiate his fault he had his beard cut off and his hair and the nails of his fingers and toes pulled out, and they made of his fingernails things that expel good luck and of his toenails things that expel evil luck. (This is why the people of the world to this day are careful in the cutting and the disposal of their nails.) Of his spittle white soft offerings and of the mucus from his nose blue soft offerings were made,[77] with which the Purification Service was performed; and they caused Sky-Beckoning-Ancestor-Lord to recite the Great Purification Liturgy. Thus they chastised Brave-Swift-Impetuous-Male, saying then, "Your conduct has been of the unseemliest. You shall dwell neither in the Sky nor in the Central-Land-of-Reed-Plains, but you shall go speedily to the bottom Nether-Land." So together they banished him according to the law of divine banishment, and divinely expelling him, drove him away downward.

Now this was in the period of continuous rains. So Brave-Swift-Impetuous-Male bound together green grass and made of it a broad hat and a raincoat, and thus clothed, begged the assembled Kami for lodging. But they answered, "Your behavior has been filthy and wicked, for which you have been banished. How can you ask lodging of us?" And one and all they repulsed him, so that he was unable to find a resting-place from the wind and rain, which were very violent, and went downward in great suffering. (Ever since which time everyone in the world has avoided entering the house of another wearing a broad hat and a grass raincoat, or bearing a bundle of grass on the back. For breaking this rule certain penance is imposed. This custom has come down to us from remote ages.)

THE OATH-SWEARING

Then said Brave-Swift-Impetuous-Male, "As all the Kami have banished me, and as I am now about to depart forever, why should I not see my elder sister again face to face, and why willingly depart thus without more ado?" So he straightway reascended to the Sky, disturbing the Sky and Earth, and by reason of the fierceness of his nature there was a commotion in the sea *which foamed and raged* and the mountains and rivers shook and the hills groaned aloud and every land and country quaked. At the uproar Sky-Frightening-Female reported the state of affairs to Great-Sky-Shiner, and the Great Kami, knowing the relentlessness and wickedness of her brother, was startled and changed countenance. "Surely," said she, "my elder brother [78] reascends here with no good heart. While our parent entrusted us with our respective domains, I think it must be his purpose to rob me of my Kingdom, the Sky-Plain. So he refuses to go to his proper realm and dares to come here to spy. But though I am a woman, why should I shrink?" And she unbound her hair and twisted it in two bunches, wound it with jewels, tied up her skirts in the form of trousers,[79] bejewelled her arms, donned a string of five hundred jewels eight shaku long, girded on three swords of ten-, nine-, and eight-hand-lengths, armed her lower arm with a dread loud-sounding elbow-pad [80] and slung on her back two quivers holding one a thousand and the other five hundred arrows, brandished her bow and set it upright with shaking top, grasped tight her sword-hilt and stamped her feet into the hard ground of the courtyard up to her thighs, kicking away the soil like bubble-snow. Then with the dread valor of a warrior, she uttered a loud cry of defiance and took posture of defense, demanding of him straightforwardly why he had ascended there.

And he, protesting his peaceful intent, replied, *"I harbor no malice.*

From the beginning my heart has not been black, but since in obedience to the stern command I am about to depart forever to the Nether-Land, how could I bear to go without seeing you, my elder sister, face to face? So I have fared afoot through clouds and mists and have come here from afar, only for a brief space. I am amazed, therefore, that you should wear so stern a look." Then Great-Sky-Shiner asked, "If this be so, how will you prove that your heart is red?" He answered, "Let us take an oath together and produce offspring. If the children I produce are females, it will be a sign that my heart is black, and they shall be sent down to the Central-Land-of-Reed-Plains. But if my heart is red, I shall produce male children, and let them be made to rule the Sky. The same oath shall hold as regards the children produced by you, my elder sister." So, placing between them the Sky-River-of-Eight-Currents (or, as others say, digging and placing between them three Sky-True-Wells) they made a covenant, and Great-Sky-Shiner, standing opposite him, swore an oath, saying, "If you have not a traitorous heart, and no purpose of relentless robbery, the children born to you will assuredly be males, and if they are males I will consider them my children and will cause them to govern the High-Sky-Plain."

Then, asking for his ten-hand-lengths sword, she broke it in three pieces, washed them in the Sky-True-Pool-Wells [81] (which are also called True-Wells-of-Isa), crunched them crunchingly in her teeth and blew the fragments away, from the mist of her breath being born the Kami

PRINCESS-TAGORI [82]

PRINCESS-LOVELY-ISLAND [83]

PRINCESS-TORRENT. [84]

(Some say the name Princess-Tagiri was that of one of the other two daughters. Others declare that Princess-Lovely-Island was born first and Princess-Torrent second of the three.)

On his part Brave-Swift-Impetuous-Male took the strings of five hundred jewels that were twisted in her left and right hair-bunches, in her headdress and on her left and right arms, jinglingly, washed them likewise in the Sky-True-Pool-Wells, crunchingly crunched them and blew away the fragments, from the mist of his breath being born the five male Kami

TRULY-CONQUEROR-I-CONQUER-SWIFT-SUN-SKY-GREAT-GREAT-EARS [85]

---

[85] **Ancestor of the Imperial Line.**

THE DEITY AGE

SKY-GREAT-SUN [86]
PRINCE-SKY-LORD [87]
PRINCE-LIFE-LORD
WONDROUS-OF-BEAR-MOOR.

These eight [88] Kami born of this contest are now worshiped under the name of The Eight-Princely-Ones.[89]

(As to these, some say that Truly-Conqueror-I-Conquer-Swift-Sun-Sky-Great-Great-Ears was the son of Great-Sky-Shiner and High-Producer,[90] and that Sky-Great-Sun was begotten also by High-Producer. Some hold that Sky-Great-Sun was born first of the five and others that he was the fourth to be born.)

(Some, also, relate otherwise that when Brave-Swift-Impetuous-Male was about to ascend to the Sky, the Kami

WONDROUS-SHINING-JEWEL [91]

meeting him, presented to him lovely curved jewels eight shaku long, and that he took these up to the Sky, protesting to his sister that his only intent was to offer to her these rare treasures. So he and Great-Sky-Shiner agreed and exchanged, he taking her girdle-sword and she taking his jewels, which she floated on the True-Sky-Well and bit off their heads, the Kami Princess-Lovely-Island being born from her breath. When she bit through the middle portions the Kami Princess-Tagori was born. When she bit through their tails the Kami Princess-Torrent was born.)

(Others hold that Great-Sky-Shiner ate her own three swords, which became transformed into the three female Kami, and that Brave-Swift-Impetuous-Male placed the string of five hundred jewels, which he wore twined in his left hair-bunch, in his mouth and on the palm of his left hand, and the jewels in his right

---

[86] **Ancestor of the Magnates and Rulers of the Land of Izumo, of the Rulers of the Lands of Musashi, Upper and Lower Unakami, Izhimi * and Tatomi; of the District-Governors of the Island of Tsu, of the Tribe-Masters of the Clay-Workers † and of the Rulers and Nobles of the Imperial-Guard.**

[87] **Ancestor of the Rulers and Governors of the Lands of Ohoshi-Kafuchi Ochi-Kochi) and Yamashiro, the Rulers of the Lands of Kii, Umaguta, Kinhè in Michi-No-Shiri (Echigo) and Suhaü; of the Tribe-Masters of the Nakada Clan (Nukatabè-No-Yuë), the Governors of Tanaka (in Yamato) the Rulers of Amuchi (in Yamato) of Mubaraki and of the Sakikusa ‡ Clan, the District-Governors of Takechi, the Country-Lords of Kamafu§ and the Army (Kumè) Governors.**

---

* Part of modern Kazusa.   † See p. 204, n. 6.
‡ Lit., luck-plant (Lycopodium).   § Part of Omi.

hair-bunch he placed in his mouth and on the palm of his right hand, and the jewels that hung on his neck he placed in his mouth and on his left fore-arm. From these and from his right fore-arm and his right leg were born the five male children named above, and from his left leg was born the male Kami Sun's-Swift-Sun.)

(Others, again, say that Brave-Swift-Impetuous-Male visited Great-Sky-Shiner but once, at which time of his arrival occurred this test of his sincerity, when she produced from his sword the three female Kami and he produced from her jewels the three male Kami. Then said she, "Since the seed of the five male Kami born last was from articles of mine, without doubt they are my children; and since the seed of the three female Kami born first was from an article of thine, so without doubt they are your children." Thus she declared the division. Brave-Swift-Impetuous-Male, however, declared, "Truly it is I who have produced these male children. The victory is mine." Then, on his becoming inordinately triumphant and acting violently, Great-Sky-Shiner withdrew into the Sky-Rock-Cave, and the assembled Kami, when she had again come forth, expelled Brave-Swift-Impetuous-Male to the Nether-Land.) ▲

Then said Brave-Swift-Impetuous-Male, "Truly I have won, and in begetting these male children have shown forth the sincerity of my intentions." So also Great-Sky-Shiner knew that his heart had been pure.

THE DIVISION OF THE MALE AND THE FEMALE CHILDREN

Then said Brave-Swift-Impetuous-Male, "Now that our interview is finished, I must depart to the Nether-Land, in obedience to the divine command of the assembled Kami. I beseech you, my elder sister, to illuminate the Plain-of-the-High-Sky, and may it enjoy tranquility. Moreover, I deliver to you the children which, with a pure heart, I have produced." Having done this, he departed downward. *There is now a shrine* [92] *dedicated to him at Retirement-Moor in Sacred-Quarter Province.* So, taking the five male children, Great-Sky-Shiner made them hers, and they were caused to govern the Plain-of-the-High-Sky. Of these, Sky-Great-Sun begot the Kami

MASTER-OF-MIKUMA-OF-GREAT-BOILED-RICE
SKY-AUGUST-BIRD.[93]

The latter Kami descended from the Sky at the village of Resistance-Calm in Sacred-Quarter Province (wherefore the place was so named). Truly-Conquer-I-Conquer-Swift-Sun-Sky-Great-Great-Ears Great-Sky-Shiner brought up, loving him in especial, always holding him in her arm-

*pit, and calling him Arm-Pit-Child.*⁹⁴ (*The modern vulgar name for a young child* ⁹⁵ *is a corruption of this.*) The three female children she sent down to Tsukushi, instructing them thus: "Do you go down and dwell in the center of the province, and there assist the Sky-descendants and receive their worship." So they descended *on Mount Cape-Gate* ⁹⁶ and dwelt at Usa-Island ⁹⁷ in the Central-Land-of-Reed-Plains. They are now in the center of the Northern-Sea-Province and are called Road-Master-Possessors. *Now when the great Kami came to Village-of-Inside-River, they took food there, and the many Kami who accompanied them spread straw which had been gathered by a certain one at this village and sat on it. At that the owner of the straw was offended and appealed to the Great Kami. So the latter said, "Your rice shall grow as well as it has grown, and without spreading of straw."* (*For this reason, the people of this village even now make their ricefields without spreading straw upon them.*) ᴬ Princess-Tagori, the first-born, dwells in the Sea-Horizon Temple (or, as some say, in the Middle Temple) of Body Form.⁹⁸ Princess-Lovely-Island dwells in the Middle Temple (or, as some say, in the Sea-Horizon Temple) of Body-Form, Princess-Torrent dwells in the Seashore Temple of Body-Form. These three Kami are reverenced by the Clan-Chiefs of Body-Form, in Tsukushi. *Princess-Torrent-Mist is represented by a blue jewel, Princess-Lovely-Island by a blue jewel and Princess-Torrent by an eightfold mirror. By these the forms of the Kami were represented and they were enshrined in the three shrines, wherefore the place is called Body-Form.*ᴮ

(*By others, however, the form of the Kami of Body-Form is said to be the eight-shaku string of five hundred jewels.*) ᶜ

THE EIGHT-FORKED SERPENT

So, having been expelled, Brave-Swift-Impetuous-Male, accompanied by his son

FIFTY-BRAVE ⁹⁹

(Who some say was the son of Great-Year by Princess-Dog) ¹

descended to the Land of Silla, where he dwelt at Mount Soshi.² But there he lifted up his voice and said, "I will not dwell in this land." So he took clay and made of it a boat, and embarking in it, crossed over eastward till he came to a place called Bird's-Hairs ³ at the head-waters of the River Fire ⁴ in the Land of Sacred-Quarter.⁵ Then said he, "In the region of the Land of Kara there are both gold and silver. It will not be well if the country which my son shall rule have not floating riches." So he plucked out his beard and scattered the hairs, which became cryptomeria. He plucked out the hairs of his breast, which became firs, and the hairs of his buttocks, which became maki,⁶ and the hairs of his eyebrows, which became camphor trees. This done he decreed their uses; the cryptomeria and the camphor trees to be made into ships, the firs to be timber for building shrines, the maki to make coffins in which men should be laid in secluded burial-places. And for food he sowed and made to grow all the eighty fruits.⁷

> (Some say that when Fifty-Brave descended from the Sky, he took down with him great quantities of the seeds of trees. He did not, however, plant these in the Land of Kara, but finally sowed them, every one, throughout the Land-of-the-Great-Eight-Islands, beginning with Tsukushi. Thus green mountains were produced. For this reason he is called Kami-of-Merit.)

Beside Fifty-Brave, Brave-Swift-Impetuous-Male begot also

PRINCESS-OF-GREAT-HOUSE
PRINCESS-OF-TSUMA.

These three Kami also scattered well the seeds of trees, and then crossed over to the Land of Tree. Fifty-Brave is the great Kami who dwells in that Land. *These three Kami are given divine worship by the governor of the Province of Tree.* Now while Brave-Swift-Impetuous-Male was in the Land of Sacred-Quarter, a chop-stick came floating down the River Fire. Considering that there must be people at the river's source, he followed upstream till he heard a sound of wailing, and searching it out, came on an old man and an old woman, with a young damsel placed between them whom they were caressing and weeping over. He asked, "Who are you?" The old man replied, "Your servant is a Kami of the land, child of Great-Mountain-Possessor,⁸ and my name is

FOOT-STROKE-ELDER.⁹

This my wife is named

HAND-STROKE-ELDER,¹⁰

and my daughter is named

PRINCESS-COMB-RICEFIELD.¹¹

Then he asked, "Why do you weep?" The other answered, "We had originally eight maiden daughters, but the

EIGHT-FORKED-SERPENT-OF-KOSHI ¹²

the man-devourer, coming each year, has devoured one, and we weep because it is now the time of its coming for this damsel. There is no means of escape for her. Therefore we grieve."

Asked Brave-Swift-Impetuous-Male, "What is it like?" The old man replied, "Its eyes are red as the winter-cherry,[13] its body is single, eight-headed and eight-tailed, rock firs grow on each of its heads, on each of its sides is a mountain, and on its back grow moss, pine-trees [14] and cryptomeria. Its length, as it crawls trails over eight valleys and eight hills, and its belly to the sight is always bloody and fomented. It is a very fearful beast." Said Brave-Swift-Impetuous-Male, "If this is your daughter, will you offer her to me?" The other replied, "With respect I will comply with your request, but I do not know your name." Answered Brave-Swift-Impetuous-Male, "I am elder brother [15] to Great-Sky-Shiner and have just descended from the Sky." Then Foot-Stroke-Elder and Hand-Stroke-Elder said, "This being so, we will respectfully offer her. We pray you first to slay the serpent and afterward it will be well to give her your favor."

So Brave-Swift-Impetuous-Male devised a plan and at once changed the damsel into a comb of many close-set teeth, which he stuck in his hair-bunch. (*Thus arose the superstition that one who picks up a comb which has been thrown away will be transformed into another person.*[A]) Then he commanded the two Kami, "Do you now take fruits of all kinds and distill some eightfold refined, poisonous spirit,[16] and build a circular fence. In the fence make eight gates, at the gates tie eight platforms, on each platform set a liquor tub and in each tub pour the eightfold refined spirit, and wait the serpent's coming, and I will slay it for you." And, truly, when everything had been made ready as he bade, the Eight-Forked-Serpent came as the old man had said, when it found the spirit, and straightway it dipped a head into each of the tubs and drank, and becoming drunken, laid down all its heads and slept. At that Brave-Swift-Impetuous-Male, drawing his ten-hand-lengths sword, severed its heads and belly, cutting it into *eight* small pieces,[17] *each of which became a Thunder-Kami and flew up to the Sky*, and the river flowed on, a river of blood.

> (It is said by some, however, that Brave-Swift-Impetuous-Male descended at the head-waters of the River E in the Province of Aki, and that the two Kami there had had many children, each of which, when born, the Eight-Headed-Serpent came to devour. The wife was then about to bring forth another. When the serpent came to the door, Brave-Swift-Impetuous-Male addressed it, saying, "You are an awful Kami. Shall I dare to neglect to feast you?" And so saying, he poured a jar of sakè into each of its mouths, on which the Serpent fell asleep and he slew it. The child which was afterward born was removed to the head-waters of the River Hi in the Land of Sacred-Quarter and was brought

up there, and later Brave-Swift-Impetuous-Male made her his consort.)

When Brave-Swift-Impetuous-Male cut the middle of the tail his sword-edge was slightly notched. Deeming this strange, with the point he thrust and slit the flesh of the tail and looked and in it was a keen sword. Now because clouds continually gathered over the place where the serpent was, this sword was originally called Sword-of-Sky-Gathering-Clouds.[18] This is the Sword-Kami which is now known as

HERB-QUELLER.[19]

It is now in the village of Ayuchi in the Province of Owari. It is this Kami which is in the charge of the Hafuri of Hot-Field.[20] It is now at Above-the-Rock.[21] (Others say it is in the charge of the Kami-Clan of the Land of Maise.[22])

After that Brave-Swift-Impetuous-Male sought for a place where he might celebrate his marriage with Princess-Comb-Ricefield, and at length came to Refreshment [23] in the Land of Sacred-Quarter. Arriving there, he said, "Coming here, my heart is refreshed," (from which the place is so called) and there he erected a dwelling-palace. When he began to build, clouds arose, so he made this song: [24]

> Eight clouds rise [25]—a screen || Eight-fold of Sacred-Quarter,
> Screening man and wife.[26]
> Eight-fold the screen they furnish || Lo, what a screen of eight folds! [27]

Summoning Foot-Stroke-Elder, he said, "I make thee head-man of my palace." And also he gave him the name Master-of-Rice-Temple-Eight-Eared-Kami-of-Refreshment.

THE DESCENDANTS OF THE KAMI BRAVE-SWIFT-IMPETUOUS-MALE

When he cohabited with Princess-Comb-Ricefield, Brave-Swift-Impetuous-Male begot

EIGHT-ISLAND-RULE-MASTER [28]

who took to wife the daughter of Great-Mountain-Possessor, the Kami

PRINCESS-FALLING-TREE-BLOSSOM,

by whom he begot the male Kami

MOJI-KU-MOOR-SU-MOOR-OF-FUWA

who took to wife the daughter of Dark-Okami, the Kami

PRINCESS-SUN-RIVER,

THE DEITY AGE

by whom he begot the male Kami

    WATER-SPOILED-DEEP-POOL-BLOSSOM

who took to wife the Kami

    SKY-ASSEMBLING-TOWN-LADY

by whom he begot the Kami

    GREAT-WATER-MASTER

who took to wife the Kami

    GRAND-EARS

by whom he begot

    SKY-WINTER-CLOTHING.[29]

Then said Brave-Swift-Impetuous-Male, "The sword which I took from the Serpent's tail is assuredly a divine sword. How shall I dare to keep it for myself?" And he straightway sent it respectfully up, by the hand of Sky-Winter-Clothing, to Great Sky-Shiner.

> (It is said, indeed, by some, that this sword had previously been stolen by the Eight-Headed-Serpent from Great-Sky-Shiner. Some, also, say that Brave-Swift-Impetuous-Male gave it to her in exchange for her jewels.[30])

Sky-Winter-Clothing took to wife the Kami

    PRINCESS-YOUNG-OF-SASU-LAND,

who was the daughter of

    GREAT-SASU-LAND-KAMI,

and there was born to the pair the Kami

    GREAT-LAND-MASTER [31]

> (who, some hold was the son, in the first generation, of Brave-Swift-Impetuous-Male, by Princess-Comb-Ricefield.)

    PRINCESS-AWAKA.[32]

The latter resided on Mount-Awaka, which thus received its name. Brave-Swift-Impetuous-Male also begot

---

[31] **Ancestor of the Clan-Chiefs of Kamo and Ohomiwa.***

---

* As August-Luck-Spirit-August-Wondrous-Spirit. (See n. 31.)

PRINCESS-ISHIKI-ISLAND [33]
PRINCE-TIDE-POSSESSOR.[34]

This son was resentful against his father and checked, pushed back and barred the sea-tide of Sacred-Quarter to the northward and caused his father to drift upon it. The tide reached to Tide-Village [35] (from which the place is so called). Also Brave-Swift-Impetuous-Male begot

PRINCE-BLUE-CLOTH-SA-GRASS.[A]

Brave-Swift-Impetuous-Male wedded also

PRINCESS-DIVINE-GREAT-ICHI

daughter of Great-Mountain-Possessor, by whom he begot

GREAT-YEAR.[36]

(By some, however, this Kami is held to be Brave-Swift-Impetuous-Male's descendant in the twelfth generation. By others, again, he is said to have been a son of

GREAT-MOUNT-SA,

a descendant, in the twenty-first generation, of Sky-Beckoning-Ancestor-Lord.)

The Kami Great-Year augustly took to wife the Kami

PRINCESS-DOG

who was the daughter of the Kami

DIVINE-LIFE-WONDER-PRODUCER

and by her he begot the following four male Kami:

SPIRIT-OF-GREAT-LAND
SOÖRI
WHITE-SUN
SUN-GOVERNING.

Next he augustly took to wife the Kami

PRINCESS-REFULGENT

---

[36] **Ancestor of the Arakida Family.***

---

* According to the *Jinno-Zatsuyo-Senki-Roku*, the name Arakida (Rough-Ricefield) was first given to Mogami, son of Kikori-no Mikoto. They were the chief priests of the shrine.

and by her he begot the two male Kami

GREAT-REFULGENT-MOUNTAIN-DWELLING-MAGNATE
AUGUST-YEAR.

He augustly wedded after that the Kami

PRINCESS-SKY-GOVERNING-FRESH-KARU

and by her he begot the following ten Kami:

PRINCE-OF-INSIDE
PRINCESS-OF-INSIDE [37]
GREAT-MOUNTAIN-INTEGRATOR [38]
YARD-FIRE-KAMI [39]
ASAHI
ENTRANCE-LIMIT
REFULGENT-MOUNTAIN-DWELLING-MAGNATE
SWIFT-MOUNTAIN-DWELLING
YARD-FIRE-HIGH-KAMI
GREAT-EARTH.[40]

Of these Prince-of-Inside and Princess-of-Inside are reverenced [41] by all people as the Kami of the Kitchen. Great-Mountain-Integrator dwells on Mount Hiyeï, in the Land of Close-Fresh-Sea,[42] and is the Kami residing at Pine-Tree-Declivity [43] in Mulberry-Moor [44] who was changed into an arrow.[45]

(*Some, however, say that Princess-Sky-Governing-Fresh-Karu was wedded by Fire-Shining-Swift-Male, by whom she gave birth to nine of these children.*[A])

Altogether Great-Year had sixteen sons and daughters. Swift-Mountain-Dwelling wedded Jewel-of-Storehouse-Rice,[46] and begot

YOUNG-MOUNTAIN-INTEGRATOR
YOUNG-YEAR
YOUNG-RICE-TRANSPLANTING-FEMALE
WATER-SPRINKLER
HIGH-SUMMER-SUN [47]
PRINCESS-AUTUMN
STEM-YEAR
LORD-STEM-TREE-YOUNG-HOUSE-ROPE.

THE DRAWING OF THE LANDS

Now Brave-Swift-Impetuous-Male said, "The Land of Eight-Clouds-Rising-Sacred-Quarter is a young Land as narrow as a cloth, since it was created small in the beginning; therefore I will sew land to it." Then regarding the promontory of Silla and perceiving that it had a portion in excess, he took up a spade, wide and flat like the breast of a maiden, and thrust it into the land, parting it asunder as one cuts the gills of a huge fish, and severed it. Then, binding to it a three-fold twisted rope, he drew it, swinging like a frost-vine, slowly, slowly like a river-boat, saying, "Land, be drawn! Land, be drawn!" [48] (The Land which was thus sewn is the Cape of Pound-Build.[49] Its boundary is at the end of Kozu. The stake which thus secured the land is Mount Princess-Sa,[50] on the boundary betwixt Rock-Sea [51] and Sacred-Quarter Provinces. The rope with which the Land was drawn is Long-Beach [52] of Garden.[53]) Wishing to serve the Great Kami who made the Land beneath the Sky, all the Kami gathered and built the Land by pounding it. (For which cause this portion was called Pound-Build.) [A]

> (Some say, however, otherwise, that this name was given it later, when all the Kami assembled to assist in the raising and building of the palace for Great-Land-Master.[54])

It is for this reason that all the Kami leave their various residences, to assemble in Sacred-Quarter Province in the tenth moon. (So this moon is there called Kami-Present-Moon, but in all other Provinces is called Kami-Without-Moon.[55]) [56]

Next Brave-Swift-Impetuous-Male regarded the Land-of-Saki [57] at the North, and perceiving that it had a portion in excess, took up the spade, wide and flat like the breast of a maiden, and thrust it into the Land, parting it asunder, as one cuts the gills of a huge fish, and severed it. Then, binding to it a three-fold twisted rope, he drew it, swinging like a frost-vine, slowly, slowly like a river-boat, saying, "Land, be drawn! Land, be drawn!" The Land which was thus sewn is the Land of Narrow-Ricefield,[58] whose boundary is at the end of Taku.

Then regarding the Land-of-Nunami at the North, and perceiving that it had a portion in excess, he cut it and sewed it similarly. (The Land which was thus sewn is the Land-of-Kurami, whose boundary is at the end of Sure).[59] Lastly, regarding the Promontory of Pipe, in Koshi,[60] perceiving that it had a portion in excess, he cut and sewed it also. (The Land which was thus sewn is Cape Miho.[61] The rope with which the Land was drawn is Bow-Island.[62] The stake which thus secured the Land is Mount-Great-Kami in Hahaki Province.) Then saying, "The drawing of Lands is now finished," he set up [63] his august staff at a forest, and exclaimed "Oü!" [64] (or, as some say, "Aha!" For this reason that forest and district were named Oü.) Also he said, "Though this Land is small, it is nevertheless a Land. I will not name stones or trees after my name." However, he made his spirit dwell at Village-of-Impetuous, and straightway fixed the Great-Impetuous-Ricefield and the Small-Impetuous-Ricefield. (Therefore the place was called Impetuous.) △

Now when the Kami Buto,[65] who formerly lived in the North-Sea, rested in the shrine of the Land of Plague-Corner,[66] he came forth to wed a daughter of the Kami of the South-Sea, and it was at the time of sunset. There were two brothers

SOMIN-SHORAÏ
K'YOTAN-SHORAÏ

the elder of whom was exceedingly poor, but the younger was rich, having a hundred dwellings and storehouses. Of the latter Buto asked a night's shelter, but K'yotan-Shoraï refused it.[67] The elder, however, granted it to him, making him a seat of millet-straw, and offering him boiled millet to eat. Many years after Buto had departed, he returned, bringing with him eight children, and said to the elder brother, "I will reward you; have you descendants in your dwelling?" Somin-Shoraï replied, "I have a daughter and this woman," [68] whereon Buto bade them put about their waists circlets of reeds. In the night he slew all save Somin-Shoraï and the two women, whereon he said, "I am the Kami Brave-Swift-Impetuous-Male. In after years, when the plague appears, if people shall say, 'We are descendants of Somin-Shoraï,' and shall wear about their waists circlets of reeds, those of that dwelling shall be excused." △

Village-of-Field, in the Land of Sacred-Quarter, is the place where the Kami

FIELD-POSSESSOR

descended from the Sky (therefore the place was so named).△

After this Brave-Swift-Impetuous-Male, having traveled about the limits of the Sky and the Earth, even to the Sky-Upright-Limiting-Wall,[69] dwelt on Mount Bear-Moor [70] and finally he departed to the Nether-Land.

THE WHITE HARE OF RICE-LEAVES

Great-Land-Master had eighty Kami-brothers, but these all left the Land to him. The reason for this was that each of the eighty desired in his heart to wed

PRINCESS-YAKAMI-IN-RICE-LEAVES.[71]

They set out together, therefore, to Rice-Leaves, putting their bag upon Great-Land-Master, whom they took with them as attendant. When they arrived thus at Cape Roof-Cross-Beams they came upon a furless hare lying prostrate. The eighty Kami said to the hare, "You should bathe in the sea-water and then lie on a high mountain's slope in the wind's blast." The hare followed their counsel, but as the sea-water dried, the wind's blast caused all the skin on its body to split, so that it lay in pain and weeping.

Last came Great-Land-Master, and beholding the hare, asked him, "Why do you lie and weep?" The hare replied, "*There was a great flood and the water overflowed the bamboo-forest and overthrew it, and I, floating on a bamboo-root, came to the Island of Oki.* From the Island of Oki, *after the waters had subsided,* I desired to cross *home* to this Land, but had no means to do so. So I deceived the sea-creatures which are called wani,[72] saying, 'How many kinsmen have you?' *They replied, 'We have so many kinsmen that they fill the sea.'* At that I said, 'I have so many that they fill the mountains and the moors.* Now do you compete with me, computing the numbers of our two tribes. Go and bring every member of your tribe and make them lie in a row across from this island to Cape Roof-Cross-Beams.'" (*Some say, from Cape Roof-Cross-Beams to Muro Island.*) "'Then I will tread on them, and running across, count their number; so we shall know whether your tribe or mine is the more numerous.' When I spoke thus, they were fooled and *their kindred, gathering,* lay down in a row, and I trod on them, counting them as I crossed *on their backs to Bamboo-Cape.*" (*From this incident arose the saying, "The hare trod on them and counted their number and crossed."*) "However, as I was about to step on land again *after I had gained my point,* I said, 'You have been fooled! *I had no desire, in truth, to know the number of your kindred.' When they heard this they were angry, and no sooner had I spoken than the wani who was last of all seized me and stripped off my raiment.*[A]

Whilst I was weeping and wailing for this, eighty Kami who passed by in advance of you counselled me to bathe in the sea-water and lie down exposed to the wind, and following their instruction, my whole body has been hurt."

Then Great-Land-Master counselled the hare, saying, "Go speedily to a river-mouth and bathe your body with the fresh water, then spread out sedge-pollen [73] and roll upon it and your body will truly regain its skin." So the hare followed the instruction, and its body became as it had been before. (Now this was

NAKED-HARE-OF-RICE-LEAVES.[74])

Then the Hare said to Great-Land-Master, "These eighty Kami of a surety shall not get Princess-Yakami-in-Rice-Leaves. Though you bear the bag, you shall have her."

THE PERSECUTION OF GREAT-LAND-MASTER ON MOUNT TEMA

Now Princess-Yakami-in-Rice-Leaves replied to the eighty Kami, "I will not hear you. I purpose to wed Great-Land-Master." At this the eighty were enraged, and desiring to slay him, took counsel together. So when they came to the foot of Mount Tema, in the Land of Hahaki, they said to him, "On this mountain is a boar. We will drive it down and do you wait and catch it. If you do not succeed, truly we will slay you." Having thus spoken, they took fire and heated a huge stone that was shaped like a boar and rolled it down, and Great-Land-Master laid hold on it, and clinging to it, was burned and died. At this his august parent wept and wailed, and going up to the Sky, besought Divine-Producer who straightway despatched *his two daughters*

PRINCESS-COCKLE [75]
PRINCESS-CLAM

to bring him to life. So Princess-Cockle burned and pulverized shell and Princess-Clam brought water, and they smeared him as with nurse's milk, when he became a comely youth and wandered away.

Now as for Princess-Cockle it is related that she gave birth to

GREAT-KAMI-OF-SODA

who was born at Kami-Cape-of-Sparkle.[76] At that time a bow and arrow were lost, so Princess-Cockle prayed, saying, "If my son is to be a brave Kami then may the lost bow and arrow be restored." Whereon a bow and arrow came floating on a stream, but the son said, "These are not mine," and threw them from him. Then there came floating a bow and arrow of metal. These he took, and going to a cavern a hundred shaku high, saying, "How dark is this cavern!" shot the arrow into it, and it sparkled in the darkness. (From this the place received its name.) There is a shrine there for Princess-Cockle, and when folk near the cavern they raise their voices, since if one approaches it stealthily, a Kami appears with a rising hurricane and his vessel fails not to broach-to.[A]

Princess-Clam became a bush-warbler [77] and, flying, settled at Bush-Warbler-Village (*from which it was so called*). Now seeing how Great-Land-Master had escaped, his eighty Kami brothers again hoodwinked him, taking him with them into the mountain, where they felled a great tree, inserted a wedge in it, and making him stand in the cleft, drew out the wedge and so slew him. When his august parent again sought him, she found him thus, and cleaving the tree, took him out and brought him to life, and saying, "If you remain here the eighty Kami eventually will destroy you," despatched him speedily to the august seat of the Kami

GREAT-HOUSE-PRINCE [78]

in the Land-of-Tree.[79] The eighty Kami pursued him and overtaking him, fixed their arrows, but he dodged under a tree-branch and fled away.

THE NETHER-DISTANT-LAND

Now the Kami Great-House-Prince said, "It is necessary for you to go to the Nether-Distant-Land where dwells Brave-Swift-Impetuous-Male, and that great Kami surely will counsel you." So he obeyed this command and came to the august seat of Brave-Swift-Impetuous-Male, when the latter's daughter

PRINCESS-FORWARD [80]

coming out, perceived him and they regarded each other and were wed. Then she went in again and said to her father, "A very lovely Kami has arrived."

The Great Kami went out to look also, and saying, "This is the Kami Ugly-Male-of-the-Reed-Plains," called him and compelled him to sleep in the snake-house. His wife, Princess-Forward, however, gave him a snake-scarf, saying, "When the snakes are about to bite you, wave this scarf three times to drive them off." This he did and the snakes became quiet, and he came forth after sleeping calmly. Again on the next night he was put into the centipede- and wasp-house,[81] when Princess-Forward gave him a centipede- and wasp-scarf and instructed him likewise, and he came forth without hurt. Then Brave-Swift-Impetuous-Male, having shot a humming-arrow [82] into the midst of a great grass-moor, sent him to fetch it and when he had entered the moor, set fire to it on all sides. But when Great-Land-Master found no place of exit, there came a rat [83] (mouse) which said, "The inside is hollowly hollow; the outside is narrowly narrow." [84] When it spoke thus, he trod on the spot, and falling into the hollow, hid himself until the fire had burned over, when the rat (mouse) brought him the humming-arrow in its mouth, and the arrow's feathers were brought in like manner by its young ones.

Now his wife, Princess-Forward, weeping, made preparation for the funeral, and her father, deeming Great-Land-Master dead, went out and took stand on the moor, when the other brought the arrow and gave it to him. Then the great Kami took him into the palace and into a great-spaced room, where he made Great-Land-Master pick the lice from his head, among which were many centipedes. His wife, however, gave him aphananth [85] berries and red earth, and he chewed up the berries and spat them out with the red earth which he held in his mouth, so that the great Kami, believing him to be chewing and spitting out the centipedes, began to feel a liking for him in his heart and fell asleep. Then Great-Land-Master bound Brave-Swift-Impetuous-Male's hair fast to the palace rafters, and blocking up the door with a five-hundred-man-lift rock, took his wife Princess-Forward on his back, possessed himself of the Kami's great life-preserving sword,[86] his bow-and-arrows and his Sky-speaking lute, and fled. But the Sky-speaking lute smote against a tree so that the earth resounded, and the great Kami started from sleep at the sound and pulled down the palace.

While he was freeing his hair from the rafters, however, Great-Land-Master fled a long way; so pursuing after him to the Level-Pass-of-the-Land-of-Night, and gazing on him from afar, Brave-Swift-Impetuous-Male called out to him, saying, "With the great, life-preserving sword and the bow-and-arrows which you carry, pursue your low-born brethren till they crouch on the hill-slopes and are swept into the river-currents! And do you, fellow! make good your name of Great-Land-Master, and your name of Spirit-of-the-Living-Land, and making my daughter Princess-Forward your chief wife, make strong the pillars of your palace at the foot of Mount Inquiry [87] in the lowest rock-bottom, and rear its crossbeams to the Plain-of-the-High-Sky, and dwell there!"

Then, bearing the great sword and book, Great-Land-Master pursued and scattered the eighty Kami, *saying, "They shall not be permitted within the circle of the blue fence of mountains."* He pursued them till they crouched on every hill-slope, he pursued them till they were swept into every river, and then he began to rule [88] the Land. (*Therefore the place where he overtook them was called Come-Overtake.*[A]) Then Princess-Yakami-in-Rice-Leaves, following their former agreement, cohabited with him. Her he brought with him, but fearing [89] his wife Princess-Forward, she thrust into a tree-fork the child she had borne and went back. (For this reason the child was called

TREE-FORK-KAMI.[90]

When Great-Land-Master came to the hill of Island-Village [91] *he made a stool and set a basket in a river for a fish-trap (from which the place was called Trap-Door).*[92] *No fish entered it, but there came a deer which he caught and roasted for food. As he was about to eat, however, the meat fell to the ground. So he left that place for another.*[B]

THE WOOING OF THE KAMI GREAT-LAND-MASTER

Now Great-Land-Master, when he went to make love to the Kami

PRINCESS-LAGOON-RIVER

of the Land of Koshi, *who was a daughter of the Kami*
WONDROUS-WELL-OF-OKI,
when he came to her house, sang to her,

    I the Kami great || Of Eight-Thousand-Spear-Shafts,
    Finding me wifeless || In the Great-Eight-Island-Realm,
    Since they have told me || That in far Koshi-Land
    Dwells a wise maiden: || Since this damsel they have said
    Is as beauteous too, || Here I stand to woo her true.
    Here in wooing her, || Back and forth pacing,
    Not yet have I || Loosened e'en my sword-cord;
    Even is my veil || As yet unloosed.
    I push the plank-door || Thus shut against me by her,
    And I pull it forward. || Whilst I stand the Nuë [93] sing
    On the green mountain, || And the pheasant, the true bird,
    Moor-haunter, warbles; || While the chanticleer doth crow
    From within the yard. || Ah, it is piteous
    That birds should sing so. || Alas those birds unkindly!
    Ah, if I only || Possessed the power
    Now to pummel them || Until they should leave it off!
    Oh, song of mine, || You who swiftly fly along,
    You Sky-messenger, || Even hence to tradition racing on,
    Shall carry forward now this event.

Then Princess-Lagoon-River, without opening the door, sang from within:

    You the Kami great || Of Eight-Thousand-Spear-Shafts!
    I am but a maid || Like a low-drooping plant
    And my timid heart || Just a bird upon a dune
    By the sandy shore. || Now it seems like a sand-piper,
    But anon it will be || A very tame bird.
    Die not therefore! || Oh you fleeting song of mine,
    You Sky-messenger, || Even hence to tradition racing on,
    Shall carry forward now this event.[94]

She sang also this second song to him

    When the sun doth hide || Back of the mountains green,
    Then within the night || That is black as berries
    Plucked on the moor, || Straightway to you I'll hasten.
    When I come all smiles, || Radiant like the morning,
    Then your arms, like white || Rope of paper-mulberry,
    Shall pat my breasts || As soft as melting snow-drifts.
    So interlaced, || One's arm the other's pillow,
    With our legs outstretched, || We shall lie slumbering.
    So speak not || Too lovingly to me,
    O you great Kami || Of eight thousand spear-shafts!
    Let this song || To far tradition bear this event.

On that night they did not cohabit, but on the night following they cohabited. *They begot*

BRAVE-MINA-KATA

who is worshiped at the Shrine of Suwa in Suwa District, Lime-Tree-Moor Province, and

MIHO-SUSU-MI

(The place where the latter settled is for this reason called Miho.) Great-Land-Master also took to wife

PRINCESS-YOUNG-EIGHT-MOORS [95]

daughter of Brave-Swift-Impetuous-Male, and for this marriage he built a palace at Eight-Moors (wherefore the place was so named).[A]

Now it befell that a daughter of Divine-Producer,[96] the Kami

PRINCESS-JEWEL-ORNAMENTED-WITH-CLUSTERS-OF-AUGUST-JEWELS [97]

settled at Meeting-Village, and a wani, coming up the river, yearned after her. So she checked the river with a rock, so that the wani could not come to her (for which cause the mountain there was called Yearn-For-Mountain).[98] Great-Land-Master was desirous of wedding her, but she was unwilling and hid herself and he searched for her at Inquiry-Village [99] (from which it received its name; now, however, it is called Uga). Afterward she settled at Morning-Mountain,[1] and Great-Land-Master wedded her and visited her each morning (from this the place was so called).[A]

Princess-Forward, Great-Land-Master's chief-wife, was exceedingly jealous, so, being distressed at this, he was about to leave Sacred-Quarter to go to the land of Mountain-Gate. And as he stood armed and attired, with his hand on the saddle of his horse and one foot in the stirrup, he sang,

> When I clothe myself || In garments of sable hue,
> Like the moor-berries, || At my breast gazing
> Like as the birds do || Of the sea-horizon,
> When I raise my sleeves [2] || Then they seem not good to me;
> To the wavelets || On the beach I cast them!
> When I clothe myself || Augustly in robes of green
> Like the king-fisher, || At my breast gazing
> Like as the birds do || Of the sea-horizon,
> When I raise my sleeves, || Then they seem not good to me;
> To the wavelets || On the beach I cast them!
> When I clothe myself || In raiment all dyed in color
> Either from dye-tree sap || Or the pounded madder
> Sought in mountain-fields, || At my breast gazing
> Like as the birds do || Of the sea-horizon
> When I raise my sleeves, || Then they seem goodly!
> Ah my dear revered, || My fair younger sister,

Though you tell me now || That you will not stand and weep
If like flocking birds || I too, with my flock, depart—
If like convoyed birds,³ || I too am led away
And so depart, || Surely you will hang your head
As on the mountain || Hangs a lonely pollinia.
As the morning mist || Comes from the shower,
Your tears will rise. || Oh, my august spouse
Like the tender grasses! || Let this song
To far tradition bear || this event.

Then Princess-Forward, his Empress, drawing near, and causing to be offered him a great liquor-cup, sang:

O you Kami great || Of Eight-Thousand-Spear-Shafts!
O my great Land-Master, || You who, verily,
Are a man, possessing, || I think likely,
Upon the promontories || Of the islands
Various that you gaze upon— || And no less I know
Every sea-side headland || You look upon—
Maidens like tender grass; || For my own part
I, unhappy! || Being woman,
Man have I never || Saving only you;
Spouse have I never save you. || Underneath the screen
That flutters its splendid hangings, || 'Neath the coverlid
So soft and warm to nest us, || 'Neath the quilt of cloth
Rustling when it covers us, || Then your arms like white
Rope of paper-mulberry || Shall pat my breasts
As soft as melting snow-drifts, || So interlaced,
One's arm the other's pillow, || With our legs outstretched,
So shall we slumber. || High do you, then,
Lift the august liquor!

Having sung thus, they pledged each other with the cup at their lips,⁴ and are at rest till the present time. (These are called divine words.)

THE DESCENDANTS OF GREAT-LAND-MASTER

He wedded Princess-Tagori,⁵ the Kami who dwells in the inner-temple of Body-Form. *When first he paid court to her, however, she would not listen, at which he was angered and with a rock checked the course of the Mountain-Forest River, so that it flowed three ways and had little water.*^A By her he begot

PRINCE-HIGH-LORD-OF-AJI-SPADES ⁶

PRINCESS-UNDER-SHINING.⁷

When the time of her bearing was over, she came to a mountain and said, "The time of my child-bearing is finished." (Therefore the mountain was named Finish-Mountain.⁸)

(*Some say otherwise that this occurred at Gone-Out-Hill,*[9] *which thus received its name.*[B])

Prince-High-Lord-of-Aji-Spades wept bitterly day and night, and his words were inarticulate, till his beard was eight hand-lengths long. A high house was built for him at High-Ladder [10] *to live in and a tall ladder was made by which to ascend and descend. (For this reason the place was so named.) His mother caused him to embark upon a vessel and made a tour of eighty islands to soothe* [11] *him, but his weeping did not cease. In a dream Great-Land-Master prayed that his son might speak, and in his dream this occurred. When he awoke he spoke to his son, who replied, saying, "A water-place." On Great-Land-Master's asking what he meant, he left the Great Kami and crossing Stony-river, proceeded to Kami-Slope,*[12] *and saying, "Here," he drew the water of the place and poured it over himself. (Therefore the place was named Water-Place.*[13] *This was the origin of the custom by which, when the Land-Rulers go to the imperial court to speak congratulatory words, they draw and use the water of the place. Even now pregnant women never eat rice of the village there, lest their children be born dumb.)* [A]

Great-Land-Master took to wife also the Kami

PRINCESS-DIVINE-HOUSE-SHIELD

and there were born to the two the Kami

EIGHT-FOLD-THING-SIGN-MASTER [14]
PRINCESS-OVER-SHINING.

(*Some hold, however, that these two Kami were his children by Princess-Tagori, and that Prince-High-Lord-of-Aji-Spades and Princess-Under-Shining were born of still another wife.*)

Eight-Fold-Thing-Sign-Master spent many an hour at Cape-Miho bird-hunting and fish-catching. The cock was his friend, upon whom the duty was laid to crow when it was time for the Kami to leave off his sport and return. On one occasion, however, the cock forgot his duty, and the Kami, hastening to return in his boat, lost his two oars, and being thus compelled to propel it with his hands, had them severely bitten by fishes.

(*Some say that he paid a nightly visit to*

PRINCESS-OF-MIHO [15]

who lived at Village-of-Koïya, *at the other side of the sea, remaining with her each night till cock-crow. One night the cock, in error, crowed at midnight, and as he forgot his oars in his haste, a wani bit his hands.*)

For this reason Eight-Fold-Thing-Sign-Master hates cocks and hens, and none is permitted at Cape-Miho.[A]

Great-Land-Master took to wife also the Kami

BIRD-EARS

who was the daughter of the Kami

EIGHT-ISLAND-POSSESSOR

and there was born to the two

BIRD-SOUNDING-SEA.

Beside these children he begot also

PRINCE-AGA [16]
PRINCESS-AGA [16]
PRINCE-PERFECT-JEWEL
PRINCESS-PERFECT-JEWEL

the two latter of whom gave birth to the Kami

GREAT-STONE [17]

who was especially loved by his father. (For this reason he was called Unu.) He also begot

YOUNG-SNAP-MASTER [18]

who served as the Kami of the Sky-August-Ricefield-Possessor and settled at Mitami[19]*-Village (which thus received its name).*

Great-Land-Master had, in all, as children, one-hundred and eighty-one Kami. Prince-High-Lord-of-Aji-Spades wedded the Kami

PRINCESS-SKY-MIKAJI [20]

who settled at Taku-Village, and there was born of the two

PRINCE-OF-TAKI.

There is a stone statue one hundred shaku high and ten shaku in circumference to his spirit at Mount Kami-Nabi, with some one hundred small stone statues beside it. If this statue be asked for rain, it is always sent.[A]

Bird-Sounding-Sea took to wife the Kami

IKOCHINI

who was a daughter of the Kami

RUSTIC-ILLUMINATOR-NUKATA-BICHI

and there was born to the two the Kami

LAND-GREAT-WEALTH.

Land-Great-Wealth took to wife the Kami

> ASHI-NADAKA [21]

and there was born to the two the Kami

> SWIFT-AWFUL-BRAVE-LAND-RULER-OF-SAHAYA

who took to wife the Kami

> PRINCESS-LUCK-SPIRIT

who was a daughter of the Kami

> SKY-AWFUL-MASTER

and there was born to the two the Kami

> PRINCE-AWFUL-MASTER.

Prince-Awful-Master took to wife the Kami

> PRINCESS-PERFECT-OF-HINA

who was a daughter of the Kami

> OKAMI

and there was born to the two the Kami

> POSSESSOR-OF-TAHIRI-AND-KISHIMA.

Possessor-of-Tahiri-and-Kishima took to wife the Kami

> PRINCESS-LIFE-SPIRIT-LUCK-SPIRIT

who was a daughter of the Kami

> WAITING-TO-SEE-HOLLY-FLOWERS [22]

and there was born to the two the Kami

> MIRO-NA-MI.

Miro-Na-Mi took to wife the Kami

> PRINCESS-AWO-NUMA-OSHI

who was a daughter of the Kami

> SHIKI-MOUNTAIN-MASTER

and there was born to the two the Kami

> NUNOSHI-WEALTH-BIRD-GROWING-EARS.

He took to wife the Kami

YOUNG-DAY-FEMALE

and there was born to the two the Kami

SKY-HIBARA-GREAT-LONG-WIND-WEALTH.

Sky-Hibara-Great-Long-Wind-Wealth took to wife the Kami

AUGUSTLY-DISTANT

daughter of the Kami Sky-Mist,[23] and begot

PERFECT-DISTANT-MOUNTAIN-CAPE.

It came to pass that Great-Land-Master's younger sister,

PRINCESS-OF-JEWEL [24]

strove with him in securing land, and catching a deer alive, she severed its belly and planted rice-seeds in the blood. The rice plants grew in one night and she set them out. Then said Great-Land-Master, "You have planted rice on a May night." And he departed to another place. (Therefore that place was called May-Night.[25]*) Also Great-Land-Master had a son and a daughter, named*

PRINCE-OF-ROCK-RICEFIELD
PRINCESS-OF-ROCK-RICEFIELD

and the two quarreled concerning the water of a stream, he the elder desiring to cause it to flow northward to Pass-Over-Clan [26] *Village, and she desiring it to flow to the southward to Spring-Water-Village.*[27] *And when he caused it to flow down from the east,*[28] *she stopped the stream with her comb and digging a canal about a peak, led it to Spring-Water-Village. Thereon he would have caused it to flow to Mulberry-Plain-Village* [29] *to the westward, and to this end went to the river-bed and stole the water; but she would not permit this, and by an underground conduit caused it to flow to the end of the ricefield of Spring-Water-Village, so that the water of the river dried up and did not flow. (Therefore this river was named Waterless-River.)* [30] *Also there was a Kami whose name was*

PRINCE-SANUKI

and it came to pass that he wooed the Kami

PRINCESS-HIKAMI

who said no to him. When he would have taken her by force she was angered, and saying, "Why do you thus force me?" she employed

BRAVE-STONE,[31]

a son of Great-Land-Master, and they fought with Prince-Sanuki, who, retreating in defeat, exclaimed, "Wretched that I am!" (Therefore that place was called Wretched.[32]) Fleeing, he crawled upon his hands, and Brave-Stone pursued him as far as the slope of Crawling-Ricefield (from which came the village's name). There he said, "In future you shall not cross this border," and he left there his head-ornament.[33] Later, when the boundary was fixed between Rice-Leaves Province and Harima Province, great jars were buried at this place, for which cause it was called Jar-Slope. (The District of Kami-Cape is so called because Brave-Stone there resided.) ᴬ

Now Wondrous-of-Bear-Moor,[34] grandchild of He-Who-Invites, and Great-Land-Master, taking up the spades, the five hundred spades, were entrusted with them (the place where this occurred being called therefrom Kami-Clan-of-Sacred-Quarter.) [35] Also Great-Land-Master and Great-Mountain-Integrator [36] took the spades and did meritorious deeds, and the latter, rending mountains in two and causing rivers to flow, parted the water-courses and made ricefields. Also Prince-High-Lord-of-Aji-Spades, taking the five hundred divine spades of his father, Great-Land-Master, labored to improve the Land. (It is for this reason that the word Spades enters into his name.) ᴮ

THE KAMI PRINCE-LITTLE-RENOWNED

When Great-Land-Master was subduing the land, he went to Wobama in Isasa (or, as some say, to Cape Miho),[37] in the Land of Sacred-Quarter, and while he was eating and drinking, on a sudden there was heard a human voice from the sea-surface. Seeing nothing, he was astonished. Presently, however, he beheld coming riding on the spray-tips of the waves in a boat made of Sky-kaganu,[38] a midget *Kami* dressed in *white* wren-skin (or, as others say, goose-skin) [39] *bearing a Sky-spear ornamented with jewels*. He came floating on the tide, and Great-Land-Master, taking him up, set him on the palm of his hand. While he was thus diverting himself with him the midget leaped up and bit him on the cheek. When he asked his name, the newcomer made no reply, and the Kami who attended him declared they did not know it. Then exclaimed a frog

"CRUMBLING-PRINCE [40]

certainly will know it." Now this Kami is the scare-crow in the mountain-fields.[41] Though he has legs which will not walk, he is a Kami who knows the Sky-Under.[42] (*He is still worshiped at Mountain-Ricefield under the name Soödo.*) Said he, when he was summoned, "This is the Kami

PRINCE-LITTLE-RENOWNED [43]

child of Divine-Producer."

So Great-Land-Master sent a messenger respectfully to report the matter to the Sky-Kami; and Divine-Producer said, "This is truly a child of mine. The children I have produced number in all fifteen hundred. Among them was one *who was born from my hand*, who was exceeding wicked and would not obey my commands, but slipped betwixt the fork of my hand [44] and ran away. This must be that child; let him be loved and nurtured. Do you and he become brothers and continue the making of the Lands. So, from that time on, Great-Land-Master and Prince-Little-Renowned made the Land together. Then said Great-Land-Master to Prince-Little-Renowned, "Can we declare the Land we have made to be a well-made Land?" Prince-Little-Renowned replied, "In some portions it is complete, but in others incomplete." Doubtless this conversation had a mysterious meaning.

After the making and establishment of the Land, Great-Land-Master made a boundary of the end of a river valley, when he met a great deer which thrust out its tongue, and he perceived that an arrow was in it. (Therefore the district was named Meet-Much [45] *and the village there was called Arrow-Ricefield-Village.*[46]*) Now Great-Land-Master and Prince-Little-Renowned disputed as to which is the more irksome, to go a long way bearing a burden of clay, or to go a long way without evacuating. Said Great-Land-Master, "I will choose to go without evacuating," whilst Prince-Little-Renowned said, "I will go bearing the burden of clay." Thus they fared several days, when Great-Land-Master said, "I can bear to go no further," and sat down and evacuated. Then said Prince-Little-Renowned, smiling, "Aye, it is irksome!" and threw down the burden of clay upon a hill in Harima Province. (For this reason the place is called Clay-Hill.*[47]*)*

> (By some, it is said, otherwise, that the Sovereign Great-Elbow-Pad-Lord, while passing through the Land, built a palace on this hill, when he said, "This soil is only clay." So the hill was thus named.)

When Great-Land-Master evacuated, dung sprang up from a bamboo-bush and ruined his robe (so the place was named Springing-Village [48]). The clay and dung turned to stone and remain to this day. Also when these two Kami were at the Peak-of-Life-Field, at Village-of-Clay, Kami-Cape District, they looked upon the mountain and said, "Rice-seeds should be preserved at this mountain." So the seeds were heaped up there.

The shape of the mountain, too, is like a heap of rice-plants (so it is called Mount-Rice-Plant-Heap).^A

Now Prince-Little-Renowned fell sick, and Great-Land-Master, seeing him on his pallet, was desirous of restoring him, so he led the hot water of the Hot-Spring-of-Great-Ricefield, of Hayami, through an underground pipe and immersed Prince-Little-Renowned in it, by which means he presently recovered. Then Prince-Little-Renowned said, "I have slept awhile," and he trod in the water, the prints of his feet remaining in the spring to the present time.^B

Also, compassionating the early death of the people of the Island-of-the-Dragon-fly, Great-Land-Master and Prince-Little-Renowned gave them this art of charm-medicine and of hot-spring bathing. Moto-Hot-Spring of Hakonè is one that was begun by them and Hot-Spring-of-Kami, of Izu Province, is another.^A *With united strength and single heart the two constructed this Under-Sky-World. For the visible race of men, and for wild beasts, they laid down the methods of curing diseases. Also, to prevent calamities of birds, beasts and creeping things, they decreed means by spells for their prevention and control. Up to the present folk everywhere enjoy the protection of these. Savage Kami were called to a divine account and expelled with a divine expulsion. Moreover the rocks, trees and smallest leaves of grass which had power of speech were put to silence.*^B Later, however, Prince-Little-Renowned went to Cape Bear-Moor [49] and at last crossed over to the Eternal-Land.[50]

(Some say that he went to Foam-Island, or, *as others have it, to Millet-Island, where he planted millet-seed which bore a good crop, and that there he climbed a millet-stalk, from which he was snapped off, and that his present whereabouts is unknown*.)

After that, whenever there appeared a part of the Land which was imperfect, Great-Land-Master visited it alone and repaired it. At length he came to the Land of Sacred-Quarter, when he said, "This Central-Land-of-Reed-Plains was always a wild desert, whose rocks, trees and herbs were all unruly. These are now reduced to submission and all are compliant."

THE KAMI AUGUST-LUCK-SPIRIT-AUGUST-WONDROUS-SPIRIT

Great-Land-Master lamented the departure of Prince-Little-Renowned, saying, "I alone now govern this Land. But how, alone, shall I govern it? Is there, perhaps, any Kami who can join with me in its government?" On a sudden, then, a divine radiance illumined the sea and a being floated towards him, who said, "Were I not here, how could you subdue this Land? It is because I am here that you have been able to accomplish this mighty enterprise." Great-Land-Master asked, "Who are you?" The being replied, "I am the Kami August-Luck-Spirit-August-Wondrous-Spirit.[51] If you will cause me to rest well, I will assist you." Said Great-Land-Master, "Truly, I know that you were my guardian spirit and a wondrous one. How shall you be made to rest?" He replied, "Worship me on Mount August-House,[52] which stands like a green fence in the eastern part of Mountain-Gate." So Great-Land-Master built a Shrine at that place and made the spirit go and dwell there. This is the Kami that dwells on the top of Mount August-House.

(*Some, however, say that the Kami of this mountain is Eight-Fold-Thing-Sign-Master,[53] and others that it is*

SUMI-ZAKA-OF-UDA.)

On a day when Great-Land-Master cultivated the ricefields, he made his field-folk eat the flesh of an ox, and a child of the Kami Great-Year,[54] going thither, spat on the food, and returning, reported the occurrence to his father. Thereat Great-Year was angered and freed many rice-insects in the ricefield, so that the leaves of the young rice-plants suddenly withered till they looked like dwarf-bamboo. Then Great-Land-Master, to discover the cause, made augury by the Shitoto-bird and by the rice-kettle ring,[55] and the augur declared that Great-Year caused the curse and that his anger might be placated by offerings of white boars, white horses and white pheasants. Amend was made according to this instruction, when the august Kami answered, "Truly it was by reason of my will. Do you, now, make reels of stripped hemp-stalks and reel with them. Take the leaves and sweep with them. Take Sky-push-grass and push with it, and crow-fan [56] and fan with it.[57] If the insects do not depart, take the flesh of an ox and place it in the mouths of the runnels, adding to it images of the male-stem.[58] Then scatter on the partitions of the ricefields seeds of Job's-tears [59] and of ginger, with walnut-leaves and salt." These directions having been followed, the leaves of the young plants grew again and the year's harvest was abundant. (For this reason at present the festival for Great-Year is celebrated by the Department-of-Worship with white boars, white horses and white pheasants.[60]) Then, when he had pacified eight Provinces of the Land-of-Koshi, Great-Land-Master settled at Mount-Long-Bay, saying, "The Land which I have constructed shall be ruled by the imperial grandson forever,[61] but this Land of Eight-Cloud-Rising-Sacred-Quarter, where I have settled, shall be guarded by me, surrounded by the fences of the blue-mountains, and I shall leave beads in it." [62] (Therefore the place was called Guarding.[63]) ᴀ

He named Mountain-Gate, also, Land-Within-Jewel-Fence.

THE AUGUST COUNCIL FOR PACIFYING THE LAND

Now Great-Sky-Shiner commanded, saying, "The Fruitful-Reed-Plain-Land-of-Fresh-Rice-Ears-of-Thousand-Autumns-of-Long-Five-Hundred-Autumns is the Land which my child Truly-Conqueror-I-Conquer-Swift-Sun-Sky-Great-Great-Ears shall rule." Thus charging him, she sent him down from the Sky. In the Land, however, were many Kami who shone with a luster like fire-flies and at night made a clamor like fire-flames, and evil Kami who swarmed like flies in the fifth moon, and where rocks, tree-stems and herbs *and blue water-foam* had power of speech.[64] Therefore, when he descended to the Floating-Sky-Bridge,[65] he said, "This Land truly is painfully uproarious, a tumbledown Land, hideous to look upon." And reascending, he informed Great-Sky-Shiner why he had not gone down. At that Great-Sky-Shiner, with High-Producer, calling the eight hundred myriad Kami to a divine assembly in the bed of the Sky-River-of-Eight-Currents, bade the Kami Thought-Includer consider. Said she, "This Central-Land-of-Reed-Plains is the realm we have deigned to charge our august child to rule. As he believes there are many violent and savage Kami of the Land there, I desire to have them subdued and expelled. Which Kami is it fitting that we despatch for this purpose?[66] I pray you, all you Kami, do not conceal your opinions."

Thought-Includer and the eight hundred myriad Kami conferred and said, "Sky-Great-Sun[67] is the most heroic among the Kami; he should be sent." So, complying with the general counsel, they sent Sky-Great-Sun, but he straightway ingratiated himself with Great-Land-Master, and during three years[68] brought back no report. Therefore his son, Master-of-Mikuma-of-Great-Boiled-Rice, was sent after him, but he was compliant to his father and made no report.

> (*By some it is said that Sky-Great-Sun was not disobedient to the command of the Sky-Kami, but, forcing his way through the eight-fold clouds of the Sky, and soaring over the Earth, he surveyed the under-sky on all sides and was about to return when Brave-Awful-Possessing-Male and Bird's-Rock-Camphor-Tree-Boat were later sent down.*) ᴬ

THE GOING OF PRINCE-SKY-YOUNG

Then High-Producer and Great-Sky-Shiner said to all the Kami, "Sky-Great-Sun, whom we sent down to the Central-Land-of-Reed-Plains, is long in reporting. It may be that he is detained by force by some of the Kami of the Land. Which Kami is it well to send anew?" Thought-Includer replied,

"PRINCE-SKY-YOUNG

should be sent, for he is a valorous one." Now he was a son of

SKY-COUNTRY-JEWEL.

On him, accordingly, they bestowed a wax-tree bow and broad-feathered arrows and sent him, and he descended to the Land.
There he was joined by a Kami of the Land,

SKY-SPYING-FEMALE [69]

who came in a ship of hard camphor-wood. (Therefore the place where the hard camphor-wood Sky-ship anchored was named Sky-Harbor.[70]) B

Prince-Sky-Young, however, proved disloyal and immediately taking to wife Princess-Under-Shining,[71] daughter of Great-Land-Master, and many daughters of Kami of the Land, said, "I, too, wish to govern the Central-Land-of-Reed-Plains," and planning to seize the realm, during eight years brought no report. So High-Producer and Great-Sky-Shiner again said to all the Kami, "Prince-Sky-Young is long in reporting. Which Kami shall we send anew to inquire the cause of his long tarrying?" And all the Kami and Thought-Includer replied, "The

COCK-PHEASANT

should be sent." So the two charged the Cock-Pheasant, *and a dove,* saying, "Go and observe, and say to Prince-Sky-Young, 'You were sent to the Central-Land-of-Reed-Plains to overcome and pacify the savage Kami of the Land. Why during eight years have you brought back no report?'" So the Cock-Pheasant *and the dove* departed, but seeing the fields of millet and pulse, remained also and did not return. (This was the origin of the sayings, "the pheasant as a single messenger," *and "the dove which, alighting, stays to peck the beans.")* Afterward there was sent down from the Sky the hen-pheasant,

NAMELESS-FEMALE

and she, instructed likewise, descended and perching on a many-branched katsura tree [72] at Prince-Sky-Young's gate, told him all the command of the Sky-*Kami*. But Sky-Spying-Female, hearing the bird's words, said to Prince-Sky-Young, "A strange bird has come and perched on the top of the katsura tree. Its cry is evil. Shoot it down." And thus urged by her, he took the Sky-wax-tree bow and the Sky-deer-arrows that had been given him and shot the pheasant dead.

Now the arrow, shot straight upward from beneath through the hen-pheasant's breast, reached the bed of the Sky-River-of-Eight-Currents, where sat Great-Sky-Shiner and High-Producer, and the latter, taking up the arrow, perceived blood on its feathers. Said he, "This arrow is the one given to Prince-Sky-Young. Perhaps it is stained with blood because he has been fighting with the Earth Kami. Why has it come here?" And exhibiting it to all the Kami, he pronounced this curse over it: "If this arrow was shot at the evil Kami of the Land by Prince-Sky-Young, in obedience to our bidding, may it not strike him. But if he has a wicked heart, let him come to crookedness by it." So saying, he flung the arrow down through the hole it had made.

(Some say, however, that the hen-pheasant did not expire till she reached the Sky, when Great-Sky-Shiner drew out the arrow from her breast and threw it back to Earth.)

When it fell, it hit Prince-Sky-Young, who was lying down after the Feast of First-Fruits, on the high mount of his breast, so that he at once died. (From this arose the saying, "Beware a returning arrow." And from the fact that the pheasant did not return, comes the modern saying as to the hasty message-carrying of the pheasant.) [73]

Now the sound of the weeping and wailing of Princess-Under-Shining, Prince-Sky-Young's wife, echoing in the wind, reached the Sky, and Sky-Country-Jewel, the father of Prince-Sky-Young, hearing, knew that he was dead, and sent down the Kami

SWIFT-FATHER [74]

with Prince-Sky-Young's wife and children, to bring the coffined corpse up to the Sky.[75] So they bore it upward and built a mortuary there in which they placed it, and made the wild river-goose the head-hanging-bearer,[76] the heron the broom-bearer,[77] the king-fisher the food-preparer, the fish-hawk the carder of tree-fibre,[78] the crow the flesher,[79] the sparrow the rice-pounding-woman,[80] and the pheasant and wren the wailing-women. Altogether the assembled birds were entrusted with the matter. And they wept and wailed and sang dirges while others made merry,[81] for eight days and eight nights.[82]

(Some say otherwise that the relatives of Prince-Sky-Young descended from the Sky to the Earth and built the mourning-house.)

In the Central-Land-of-Reed-Plains Prince-Sky-Young had dwelt in friendship with Prince-High-Lord-of-Aji-Spades, brother to Princess-Under-Shining, and the latter ascended to the Sky to offer condolences in the mourning. It so happened that this Kami greatly resembled the dead Kami in feature, so that the father and wife, with all his relations, cried out, "Our lord is not dead, no! Our lord is not dead, no!" and so crying, clung to his hands and his girdle and garments, rejoiced and distracted. But at that Prince-High-Lord-of-Aji-Spades waxed red with anger, and said, "It is but a friendly act to bear condolence, so that I shrank not from pollution but came from afar to mourn. Why then should I be likened to an unclean dead person?" And so saying, he drew his ten-hand-lengths sword from his girdle and cut down and kicked away the mortuary, which fell to earth and became Mourning-Mountain, at the head-waters of Knot-Grass-Seeing-River,[83] in the Land of Three-Moors.[84] (This is why people shrink from mistaking a living person for a dead person.) The great sword he used was called Great-Leaf-Mower, and also Divine-Sharp-Sword. When Prince-High-Lord-of-Aji-Spades flew away in anger, his effulgence was so bright that it illumined two hills and two valleys, and those who had gathered for the mourning made a song:

> With the Sky-splendor || Of the Weaving-Maiden's [85] gems
> Augustly gathered, || Marshalled to make her necklace,
> Bright as hole-drilled gems || Shiningly assembled,
> Thus does he traverse valleys two—
> Prince-High-Lord-of-Aji-Spades. 'Tis he,
> The Kami Great!

(*It is said by some, however, that Prince-High-Lord-of-Aji-Spade's younger sister, Princess-Under-Shining, wife of Prince-Sky-Young, when he flew back in anger, made the song, wishing to reveal his name.*)

Also they sang another song which said

> Where the Sky-distant || Country-side women
> Cross over the narrow strait || Of the rocky river's eddy—
> There at the eddy || Bring you and spread out your nets!
> Fair are the wenches, || Fair are they, so draw near,
> To the rocky river's eddy!

(These two songs are in what is now called a country style.)

THE ABDICATION OF THE KAMI GREAT-LAND-MASTER

Afterward High-Producer again assembled all the Kami and asked, "Which Kami would it be best to send anew to the Central-Land-of-Reed-Plains?" And Thought-Includer and all the Kami said, "He who is named Sky-Point-Blade-Extended [86] and dwells in the Sky-Rock-Dwelling at the head of the Sky-River-of-Eight-Currents. If not he, then his son, Brave-Awful-Possessing-Male. However, since Sky-Point-Blade-Extended has dammed up and turned back the waters of the river, other Kami cannot go to his dwelling. So let the Kami

SKY-DEER

be sent to ask him." Sky-Deer was sent and Sky-Point-Blade-Extended replied, "I will obey and will respectfully serve you. On this road, however, you should send your servant's child, Brave-Awful-Possessing-Male." And he made offer of him. So the Kami Bird-Rock-Camphor-Tree-Boat [87] was attached to Brave-Awful-Possessing-Male and the two were sent.

(Some say, however, that the Kami Snap-Master [88] was chosen for this errand and that Brave-Awful-Possessing-Male came forward of his own accord, saying, "Is Snap-Master alone to be accounted a hero? Am I not a hero also?" So, as his words were indignant, he was sent down with Snap-Master.)

(According to others it was neither Bird-Rock-Camphor-Tree-Boat nor Snap-Master that was sent, but Sky-August-Bird.)

It was at this time that the Kami

WORSHIP-MASTER [89]

received the name Ushi-of-Worship. This is the Kami who now dwells in the Land of Kabori in Ah-my-wife.[90] So Brave-Awful-Possessing-Male and Bird-Rock-Camphor-Tree-Boat, descending to the little beach of Yes-or-No,[91] in the Land of Sacred-Quarter, drew their ten-hand-lengths swords, set them hilt-down on the wave-crest, and squatting on their points, said to Great-Land-Master, "High-Producer and Great-Sky-Shiner have sent us to say to you: 'We have deigned to give Our august child your realm, the Central-Land-of-Reed-Plains, for him to preside over as its lord.) We two Kami have been sent to clear and pacify it. How, now, is your heart? Will you stand aside, or no?" (*The place was for this cause named Yes-or-No.*) He replied, "I expected the arrival of you two Kami, and as for what you ask, I will not concede it." So the two returned to the Sky and made report, when High-Producer sent them back again, bidding Brave-Awful-Possessing-Male say as follows: "I find deep reason in your reply. Therefore now I issue my commands to you more particularly, thus: Let My grandchild conduct the public affairs with which you are charged, and you shall rule divine affairs. I will build for you a palace in the Sky-Sun-Corner *that shall remain for a hundred myriad years, and will measure it with a Sky-measure,*[A] and will take a rope made of paper-mulberry-bark a thousand hiro long and tie in it one hundred and eighty knots, and as for the dimensions of the palace, its pillars shall be high and massive and its beams wide and thick. Also I will *furnish and till wide ricefields for you, and prayers shall be offered that full harvests may continue for you.* And that you may take pleasure on the sea I will make for you a high bridge, a floating bridge and a Sky-bird-boat. Moreover I will make a flying bridge over the Sky-River-of-Eight-Currents. I will also make for you white shields of one hundred and eighty stitchings and Sky-Great-Sun shall be director of the festivals in your honor."

This message was given to Great-Land-Master, who replied, "I myself cannot answer. My son, Eight-Fold-Thing-Sign-Master,[92] will tell you. But he is gone to Cape Miho [93] bird-hunting and fish-catching, and has not yet returned." He sent then as messenger

YES-OR-NO-SHINS [94]

in Bird-Rock-Camphor-Tree-Boat, who announced to Eight-Fold-Thing-Sign-Master the declaration of the Sky Kami, and asked in what words reply should be made. Then Eight-Fold-Thing-Sign-Master, being graciously asked, said to the messenger, "I will obey. My father should respectfully give this Land to the august son of the Sky Kami. Nor will I make any opposition." And he trod on his boat so as to overturn it, made in the sea an eightfold fence of green branches, clapped his Sky-departing hands, and disappeared.[95] *Eight-Fold-Thing-Sign-Master thereon retired to an island, where he built a rude dwelling for his abode. (So to this day the people of Cape Miho celebrate this event by two festivals, one in honor of the dwelling this Kami erected and the other in honor of the boat in which Yes-or-No-Shins came to him.[96])* Then the messenger returned to Great-Land-Master and said, "This your son has thus spoken. Have you other sons who should speak?" He replied, "I have one other, the Kami

BRAVE-AUGUST-NAME-FIRM.[97]

There is none beside." Now while he spoke, Brave-August-Name-Firm came to them, carrying on his finger-tips a thousand-man-lift rock (*which rock is said to be the Pebble-Rock,[98] off the shore of Yes-or-No Beach*). Said he, "Who comes to our land and talks thus in secret? Come, I propose a test of strength. I will first take your hand." So Brave-Awful-Possessing-Male let him take his hand, but when Brave-August-Name-Firm touched it, it turned into an icicle and then into a sword-blade, so that he drew back in alarm. Then Brave-Awful-Possessing-Male, in his turn, asked permission to take the hand of Brave-August-Name-Firm, and grasping it, crushed it as if it were a young reed and cast it aside, whereon the other fled. But Brave-Awful-Possessing-Male pursued and overtook him at Suwa Lake in the Land of Lime-Tree-Moor,[99] *when, in his surprise, he exclaimed "Suwa!"* ᴬ Then, at the point of being slain, he said, "I will obey. Slay me not. I will go nowhere else, nor will I disobey the command of my father, Great-Land-Master, nor oppose the words of the

---

[97] **Ancestor of the Chief Priests* of Suwa**

---

* *Oho-hafuri.*

Kami Eight-Fold-Thing-Sign-Master. I will give up this Central-Land-of-Reed-Plains according to the bidding of the child of the Sky-Kami."

So they returned and asked Great-Land-Master, saying, "Your two sons have said that they will follow and not oppose the commands of the child of the Sky-Kami. Now, how is your heart?" He replied, "The instructions of the Sky-Kami are so courteous that I may not presume to disobey. As my two children, on whom I rely, have said thus, I will not oppose them. In accordance with the command I will at once give up this Central-Land-of-Reed-Plains and depart. If I were to offer resistance, all the Kami of this Land would surely resist also. But as I now respectfully withdraw, who will be so bold as to deny you submission?"

He gave to the two Kami the broad-spear he had used to pacify the Land, and said, "By means of this spear I was in the end successful. If the Sky-Grandchild uses this to rule the Land, he will no doubt tranquilize it. Let him control the public affairs with which I have been charged, and I will retire and direct secret matters. As for the one hundred and eighty Kami who are my children, if Eight-Fold-Thing-Sign-Master be made the Sky-Kami's protection both before and behind, they will not be disobedient." He summoned the Kami of Roads, Great-Elder-of-Come-Not-Place,[1] and investing him with jewels, said, "This one will take my place and give respectful obedience."

Then said Great-Land-Master, *"In the Land to be governed by the Sovereign-Grandchild, the Land of Great-Mountain-Gate, I will make my own gentle-spirit*[2] *to be attached to an eight-hand-lengths mirror and enshrined at Three-Threads, under the title of Great-Thing-Master-Wondrous-Dread-Spirit-of-Mountain-Gate. The spirit of my son Prince-High-Lord-of-Aji-Spades I will cause to be enshrined at Kamo in Mulberry-Castle, the spirit of my son Eight-Fold-Thing-Sign-Master at Unadè and the spirit of*

KAYANARUMI

at Asuka, setting them apart to dwell there divinely as near guardian Kami of the Sovereign-Grandchild.[A]

Brave-Awful-Possessing-Male and Bird-Rock-Camphor-Tree-Boat built a Sky-dwelling[3] for Great-Land-Master's worship on the little beach of Tagishi in the Land of Sacred-Quarter, *and Sky-August-Bird*[4] *was sent down from the Sky as Shield Clan, and he descended at Shield-Sew*[5] *and began to make shields to ornament the palace of the great Kami. (From this cause the place is so named.)*

(Some, however, say that it was so-called because Snap-Master mended Sky hard-shields there.)

Even now shields and spears are made as offerings to the great Kami.[A]

(By some it is said that Great-Land-Master did not refuse at first, but submitted with his sons, saying to the two Kami, "I will not withdraw to the concealment of the eighty road-windings,[6] there to be his servant. But do you, for my dwelling, make me a Palace whose pillars are set in the deepest rock-bottom, and rear its cross-beams to the Plain-of-the-High-Sky, like the rich lattice in which the child of the Sky-Kami will rule the descendants of the Sky-Sun, and establish my worship there.")

The grandson of Prince-Swift-Autumn,[7] the Kami

WONDROUS-EIGHT-FOLD-JEWEL [8]

was made victualer, to offer the Sky-banquet. So, having prayed, he transformed himself into a cormorant, and diving to the sea-bottom, took in his mouth red-earth from thence and made eighty Sky-platters, and cutting the stalks of seaweed made a mortar, and making a pestle out of hondahara,[9] he drilled fire,[10] and said, "I will burn this fire till the soot on the new Sky-lattice of the gable of Divine-Producer, on the Plain-of-the-High-Sky, hangs down eight hand-lengths. And as for what is underneath the earth, I will bake it to the lowest rock-bottom, and stretching a thousand-hiro rope of paper-mulberry-bark and with many shouts, drawing in the fishermen-sailors' large-mouthed, small-finned perch, will offer to him the Sky-fish-food till the split-bamboo hampers sag beneath the offerings."

Afterward Great-Elder-of-Come-Not-Place besought the messengers of the Sky-Kami to permit him to act as substitute messenger, and they, appointing him their guide, made a circuit of pacification, inspecting all beneath the Sky, and this Kami united his strength to theirs. They put to death all the rebellious and malignant Kami and the tribes of herbs, trees and rocks. All who were rebellious to their authority they put to death and those who rendered obedience were rewarded. *Brave-Awful-Possessing-Male employed for this purpose an army of deer.* (So, now, when the imperial troops win a battle, the deer go to the sea-beach, but when they lose a battle, the deer creep with drooping ears into the houses of the people.)[11] At length all were subdued save the Star-Kami,

KAGASÈ-MALE [12]

who refused to submit, whereon they sent the Weaving-Kami Brave-Leaf-Elder,[13] and he rendered submission.

---

[8] **Ancestor of the District Chiefs of Kamo. (But see p. 69, n. 34.)**

(By some it is said that Kagasè-Male resided in the Sky, and that these two Kami, before they were sent down, said, "In the Sky there is an evil Kami named Kagasè-Male, and we pray that he be put to death before we depart to clear the Central-Land-of-Reed-Plains.")

Now the two chiefs of all who had rendered obedience were Great-Land-Master and Eight-Fold-Thing-Sign-Master, so Brave-Awful-Possessing-Male and Bird-Rock-Camphor-Tree-Boat took these two with them to the Sky, *Great-Land-Master leading eight hundred Kami.*[14] *Thus ascending, riding on the white clouds, his mission being completed, Brave-Awful-Possessing-Male threw off and left behind him his staff on which he leaned, his helmet, spear, shield and sword, and the bead-ornaments he wore.*[A]

The eighty myriad Kami being assembled in the Sky-Market-Place, Great-Land-Master and Eight-Fold-Thing-Sign-Master declared their full loyalty. And High-Producer said to Great-Land-Master, "If you take to wife one of the Kami of the Land, I shall deem your heart still disloyal. Therefore I will now give you to wife my daughter, Princess-of-Miho (*who, some say, was the wife of Eight-Fold-Thing-Sign-Master* [15]) *and you shall command* eighty myriad Kami to be the guards of my august grandchild to all ages. *As for Great-Jewel, he shall lead all the tribes of the Kami and fill offices as in a Sky-rite.*" So saying, he sent them down again. Thus the subduing and pacification of the Central-Land-of-Reed-Plains was accomplished.

(By some, however, it is said that Great-Land-Master, after he had thus given over the land to be governed by the Sovereign-Grandchild, became concealed forever. *Others say that he retired to rest at the Shrine of Kizuki.*)

THE SKY-DESCENT OF THE AUGUST GRANDCHILD

Great-Sky-Shiner and High-Producer commanded Truly-Conqueror-I-Conquer-Swift-Sun-Sky-Great-Great-Ears, saying, "The pacification of the Central-Land-of-Reed-Plains is now completed. Do you, as We have graciously bidden, descend to dwell in and reign over it." Now Truly-Conqueror-I-Conquer-Swift-Sun-Sky-Great-Great-Ears had wedded

PRINCESS-MYRIAD-LOOMS-FRUITFUL-DRAGON-
FLY-ISLAND

sister of Thought-Includer [16] (who was a child of High-Producer) and had begot

SKY-SHINING-EARTH-SHINING-SKY'S-FIRE-RUDDY-COMB-JEWEL-PLENTY-SWIFT-SUN [17]

and the latter, while in the Sky, had taken to wife the Kami

SKY-ROAD-SUN

by whom he had begot the Kami

SKY-MOUNT-FRAGRANT.

Also, by Princess-Myriad-Looms-Fruitful-Dragon-Fly-Island, Truly-Conqueror-I-Conquer-Swift-Sun-Sky-Great-Great-Ears had begot

PRINCE-SKY-PLENTY-EARTH-PLENTY-HIGH-AS-SKY'S-SUN-FIRE-RUDDY-PLENTY.

So he replied, "While your servant has been preparing to descend, I have begot a child, Prince-Sky-Plenty-Earth-Plenty-High-As-Sky's-Sun-Fire-Ruddy-Plenty. Let him be sent down.

First, however (some say by command of the Sky Kami) Plenty-Swift-Sun, the elder brother, entering the Sky-Rock-Boat, descended to the summit of Mount-Howling, on the upper course of a river in Kawachi. In the Sky-Rock-Boat he soared through the Sky, and after many days of inspection, came to Mount-White-Garden at Fish-Hawk, in Mountain-Gate. (For this reason it was called Mount Land-of-Mountain-Gate-Sky-Looking.) There he took to wife

PRINCESS-THREE-COOK-HOUSE [18]

who was the younger sister of the Kami

PRINCE-LONG-MARROW.

Afterward High-Producer said to Swift-Father, "Previously I despatched Plenty-Swift-Sun to the Land-of-Fruitful-Reed-Plains. My mind has question concerning him. Go therefore, observe his circumstances, and bring me report." Obedient to this command, Swift-Father descended, and learning the facts, reported that Plenty-Swift-Sun had died before his wife had been delivered of his son. Pitying him, then, High-Wonder-Producer sent Swift-Father to bring his body to the Sky, where, after sacred rites had been held before it during seven days and nights, it was given burial.[A]

---

[17] **Ancestor of the Tribe-Masters of Owari.***

---

* But see p. 123, n. 78.

(Others say that Plenty-Swift-Sun is buried at the village of White-Garden, at Fish-Hawk.)

Now Swift-Father, when he later came from the Sky, settled in the eight-forked branches of a tree at Pine-Swamp, where he severely punished the people, visiting sickness upon any who evacuated or urinated in his direction, so that the people of the neighborhood who were thus harassed, reported it to the Sovereign of that time. Then the Great-Tribe-Master of One-Half-Hill,[19] with others, was sent to the place, and he prayed to the Kami, saying, "You have people near by, and uncleanliness by morning and evening, and it is not fitting for you to settle here. Therefore it is hoped that you will remove to the clear vantage of a high mountain." The Kami yielded to this request and removed to the peak of Kabirè.[20] The Shrine there has a stone fence, and the Kami having many kin, even now many sorts of tools and implements, such as bows, spears, kettles, and other articles, remain there, turned to stone. All passing birds avoid flying over it and never pass above the mountain's topmost peak. From ancient time it has been so.[B]

Now the son whom Plenty-Swift-Sun had begot was the Kami

SWEET-TRUE-HAND [21]

he having told his wife, when she was pregnant, that if a son should be born it should be so named, and if a daughter, she should be named Ugly-Mami. After he died Plenty-Swift-Sun appeared to Princess-Three-Cook-House in a dream and bade her cherish the son in memory of him, and gave to her divine treasures which were token of his Sky-origin, with Sky-bow-and-arrows, Kami-dress and girdle and rings for the hand. Also Sky-Mount-Fragrant, the son which had been born to Plenty-Swift-Sun in the Sky, following his father, had descended to the earth at the village of Retirement-Moor, in Retirement-Moor Province. He wedded

PRINCESS-FRAGRANT

who was his sister by a different mother, and their son was the Kami

SKY-GATHERING-CLOUDS.[22]

---

[21] *Ancestor of the Tribe-Masters of the Warrior Clan; of the Magnates of Hozumi and of the Neck Clan.**
[22] *Ancestor of the High Priests † of Watarai.*

---

* Unebè (*unemè*). This clan waited on the imperial table, wearing a peculiar veil over the neck.
† Kannushi (*Kamu-nushi: Kami*-owner).

(*Some say, however, that this Kami was one of those sent down later from the Sky, as a guard for Prince-Sky-Plenty-Earth-Plenty-High-As-Sky's-Sun-Fire-Ruddy-Plenty.*)

Sky-Gathering-Clouds took to wife the Kami

>PRINCESS-AHIRA-GOOD

and there were born to the two

>PRINCE-SKY-GREAT-MAN [23]
>SKY-GREAT-MALE
>PRINCESS-GREAT-SUN.

Of these, Prince-Sky-Great-Man took to wife the Kami

>PRINCESS-HORN-HOUSE [24]

and there was born to the two the Kami

>SKY-DOOR-EYE

who took to wife the Kami

>PRINCESS-AVOIDING-OF-MULBERRY-CASTLE

and there were born to the pair two sons. Sky-Great-Male wedded the Kami

>PRINCESS-KANARACHI

who was a daughter of

>TSURUGINÈ

a Kami of the Land at Mulberry-Castle, and the two begot

>PRINCE-MULBERRY-CASTLE [25]
>PRINCE-BRAVE-RED-BROW.

The former served the Sovereign, Prince-Lord-Shinè-of-Mima, as Great-Tribe-Master. The latter wedded

>PRINCESS-OKI-OF-OWARI

---

[23] **Ancestor of the Tribe-Masters of the Kanimori.***

---

* These had charge of a portion of the imperial palace. The guild finally grew into the Kanimori-Zukasa, which were attached to the Department of the Treasury and the imperial household, the latter group being known as Uchi-Kanimori. In 820 they were reunited to form the Department of the Imperial Household (*Kunai-Sho*). The name Kanimori became corrupted to *Kamon*, in which form it has come down to modern times.

and there were born to the two a son and a daughter

PRINCE-BRAVE-TUBE-GRASS [26]
PRINCESS-PERFECTLY-ORNAMENTED [27]

who became the consort of the Sovereign, Prince-Lord-Shinè-of-Mima.[28] There was also sent down from the Sky beforehand

BRAVE-HORN-BODY

a grandson of Divine-Producer, who, dividing the eight-fold clouds, came to Mount High-Thousand-Rice-Ears [29] (or, as others say, to Sono-Peak) in Sun-Facing, where he erected a palace, setting its pillars deep, and remained for a long time. He then came to the Province of Behind-The-Mountains, and proceeded down the Behind-The-Mountains River to the place where the Katsura [30]-Moor River and the Kamo River meet. He followed up the latter stream and settled at the base of the northern mountain of Kuga District. (From that time the place has been named Kamo.) He wedded

PRINCESS-IKAKOYA [31]

of Kami-Moor of Ricefield-Place [32] Province, by whom he begot

PRINCESS-JEWEL-GOOD [33]
PRINCE-JEWEL-GOOD.[34, A]

It happened that when Princess-Jewel-Good was playing by Small-Shallow-Looking-River-of-Pebble River, there came floating down from the upper stream an arrow lacquered red and feathered with a wild duck's white feather, which adhered to her water-jar.

(Some say that she was washing clothing in the stream, and others that she came there every morning and evening to draw water to offer to the Kami of the place in worship.)

The arrow she took up and put on the eave of her dwelling. (According to others, by her bedside.) Soon she conceived and gave birth to a boy, without knowing who was his father.

(Others say that at night the arrow became transformed into a lovely youth who lay with her.[35])

---

[26] *Ancestor of the Tribe-Masters of Tachihi, Tsumori, and the Young-Mountain-Gate Clan (Wakayamatobè) and of the Governors of Mitsushi in Katsuragi.*
[34] *Ancestor of the District-Chiefs of Kamo.**

Her parents asked her, but she replied that the child had no father, and they supposed she desired to keep her secret and hence did not speak the truth.

So when her child was three years old, her parents said, "How can there be a child without a father in the world? Probably he is one of the villagers." Then the grandfather, Brave-Horn-Body, built a house each side of which was eight hiro long, and whose eight doors would fasten firmly, and mixed eight-fold refined sakè, and gathering there many Kami and inviting the villagers, held a merry-making for seven days and nights. When they had drunk, he put a cup of the sakè into the child's hands, saying, "Give to him whom you regard as your father this sakè to drink." At that the child went outside the house and set the cup before the arrow with the wild duck feather which was on the eave, and saying, "I am a child of a Sky-Kami!" he ascended to the Sky.

(Others say that, without leaving the house, he held the cup high in air and made of it a festival-offering, facing the Sky, whereon he became a Thunder-Kami and, breaking through the roof, ascended to the Sky.)

His mother, Princess-Jewel-Good, also, at the same time ascended to the Sky. His grandparents and all the people wondered, saying, "The child should be named after this wild duck-feathered arrow and should be called Wild-Duck." [36] The red arrow was the Kami Fire-Thunder [37] and the child is the Kami

WAKI [38]-THUNDER-OF-KAMO.

Now there was a ricefield where the middle shrine of Kamo now stands, and its owner planted a young rice plant which suddenly was transformed into a keyaki tree, under which the Kami Princess-Jewel-Good descended.[A] This is the present middle shrine.[39]

The ancestral Kami [40] yearned after the child and dreamed a dream in which the son of the Sky-Kami said, "If you desire to see me, make a Sky-feather-robe and Sky-feather-trousers and kindle a fire and offer spears. Decorate a running-horse [41] and take a sakaki tree from the depths of a mountain and set it up, hanging upon it various colors. Also make head-ornaments of hollyhock and maple, and wait. Then I will come." So they bade that a festival be made for the child of the Kami, according to the advice of the dream. (Thus originated the use of the running-horse and of head-ornaments of hollyhock and maple.[42]) Then he descended from the Sky at Mount August-Shadow-Hill in Small-Moor [43]-Village. This spot is the upper shrine of Kamo.[44, A]

The Red-Arrow is worshiped at the shrine of Pine-Tree-Declivity.[45]

*The three Kami, Brave-Horn-Body, Princess-Ikakoya and Princess-Jewel-Good, settle at the Three-Body-Shrine of Waterwort-Storehouse.*⁴⁶· ▲

Great-Sky-Shiner and High-Wonder-Producer charged Prince-Sky-Plenty-Earth-Plenty-High-As-Sky's-Sun-Fire-Ruddy-Plenty, saying: "This Fruitful-Reed-Plain-Land-of-Fresh-Rice-Ears you shall rule," and he answered, "I will descend accordingly."

(*According to some, however, his father, Truly-Conqueror-I-Conquer-Swift-Sky-Great-Great-Ears descended with his consort, and the child was born while she was still in the void between the Sky and the Earth, whereon they returned to the Sky and the child was then sent in his place.*)

When he was about to descend, Great-Sky-Shiner bade Sky-Great-Sun [47] conduct

SKY-ROUND-EYE [48]

whom she bade carry weapons, as a forerunner. Descending in advance to clear the road, he returned, saying: "There has appeared at the Sky's Eight-Road-Fork a Kami whose nose is seven hands [49] long and the length of whose back is seven hiro. A light shines from his mouth and from his buttocks, and his eyeballs are like eight-hand-long mirrors and glow red like the winter cherry."

Thereon it was commanded that his attendant Kami go and make inquiry, but among all the eighty myriad Kami there was not one who could confront the stranger, for his radiance reached upward to the Plain-of-the-High-Sky and downward to the Central-Land-of-Reed-Plains. So Great-Sky-Shiner and High-Producer said to Sky-Frightening-Female, "You are but a weak female, yet you are superior to others in the power of your looks, and can face Kami successfully. Do you go and ask, 'Who is there upon the road by which our child is about to descend from the Sky?'"

So Sky-Frightening-Female bared the nipples of her breasts [50] and pushed down the band of her trousers below her navel and confronted the Kami, laughing in mockery. Then said he, "O Sky-Frightening-Female! What do you mean by these actions?" She asked in reply, "Who are you who wait in the road by which the child of Great-Sky-Shiner is to make his imperial way?" To which the unknown Kami answered, "I am a Kami of the Land,

PRINCE-MONKEY-RICEFIELD [51]

---

[48] ***Ancestor of the Army-Clan [Kumè-Be].***
[51] ***Ancestor of the Abstainer Clan of the Land of Ki.***

who, having heard of the descent of the child of the Sky-Kami, am come in humbleness to meet him, to offer myself respectfully as his guide." She again inquired of him, "Will you go before me, or shall I go before you?" He replied, "I will go before you and be his forerunner." [52] Again she asked, "Where will you go and where shall the august Grandchild go?" He answered, "He shall go to a wondrous peak of High-Thousand-Rice-Ears [53] in H'yuga in the Land of Tsukushi, and I will go to the upper waters of the River Fifty-Bells [54] at Sanada in Isè. You are the one who discovered me. Therefore you should escort me and complete your task."

Sky-Frightening-Female returned and made report. Then High-Producer took the coverlet that was on his true couch and cast it over his august grandchild, and attaching to him Sky-Beckoning-Ancestor-Lord, Great-Jewel, Sky-Frightening-Female, Again-Forging-Old-Woman and Jewel-Ancestor, in all five chiefs of companies, they bade Sky-Plenty-Earth-Plenty-High-As-Sky's-Sun-Fire-Ruddy-Plenty go down from the Sky.

> (*By some it is said that the five Kami who especially accompanied him in his descent were: Hand-Placing-Soil-Carrier as broad-hat-sewer; Prince-Measure-Knowing as shield-sewer; Sky-Mara* [55] *as metal-worker; Sky-Sun-Eagle as tree-fibre-maker, and Wondrous-Shining-Jewel,*[56] *as jewel-maker.*)

Also High-Producer said, "I will erect a Sky-divine fence [57] and rock-boundary, *and will set up the Sky-mirrored sakaki* [58] *in the Fruitful-Reed-Plain-Land,* and you, Sky-Beckoning-Ancestor-Lord, *who have administered the greater part of divine affairs,* and Great-Jewel, *and Sky-Frightening-Female,* shall take it with you to the Central-Land-of-Reed-Plains, *where you shall institute a festival for my grandchild,* and within the fence you shall practice abstinence on behalf of my descendants." (It was when Great-Jewel was thus sent that the custom first began of worshiping him with stout straps flung over weak shoulders [59] when taking the place of the imperial hand. From that, too, arose the custom by which Sky-Beckoning-Ancestor-Lord had in charge divine matters. Hence he was made to divine by means of the Greater Divination.

Also Great-Sky-Shiner took in his hand the precious Mirror, and giving it to Prince-Sky-Plenty-Earth-Plenty-High-as-Sky's-Sun-Fire-Ruddy-Plenty, prayed, saying, "My child, when you look upon this Mirror, let it be as if you were looking at Me. Regard it as if it were Our august spirit and reverence it *daily, with purification,* as if reverencing before Us. Let it be with you on your couch and in your hall, and let it be to you a sacred Mirror. *Thus shall the glory of your reign be as boundless as the*

Sky and the Earth." She gave him, too, the great sword Herb-Queller [60] and the alluring eight-hand-lengths string of curved jewels,[61] *these three Sacred Treasures* [62] *being a perpetual evidence of the rule. The Mirror was of the first significance, the Necklace and the Sword being naturally subordinate.* Furthermore she said to Sky-Beckoning-Ancestor-Lord and to Great-Jewel, "Attend to me, you two Kami: Do you also remain in attendance in the palace hall to guard it well. *You, Great-Jewel, shall command many companies of Kami, performing your duty as in the High Sky.*" Thereon the Kami of all companies were bade to follow him.

> (Some say that the Kami Great-Land-Master [63] was also put in command of eight-hundred Kami and commanded to protect the Sky-Grandchild forever.)

Also she said, "I will give over to my child the rice-ears of the sacred enclosure, of which I partake in the Plain-of-the-High-Sky." *Giving him also a jeweled spear,* she sent with him likewise the Kami of Eternal Night, Thought-Includer, Sky-Hand-Strength-Male [64] (*whom she ordered to guard the gate of the palace*), Sky-Sun-Eagle [65] and Princess-Fruitful-Food, and bade them thus: "Go! And may prosperity attend your dynasty, and may it, like the Sky and the Earth, endure forever! Let Thought-Includer manage Our affairs and carry on the government." [66] (Now the Mirror and Thought-Includer are worshiped at the Temple of Fifty-Bells of the broken-bracelet.[67] Princess-Fruitful-Food is the Kami dwelling in the outer temple of Crossing-Meeting.[68] Sky-Hand-Strength-Male is the Kami of the Gate of the imperial palace and dwells in Sanagata.)

There were given also to Prince-Sky-Plenty-Earth-Plenty-High-as-Sky's-Sun-Fire-Ruddy-Plenty ten august treasures: *One mirror-of-the-sea-horizon, one mirror-of-the-shore, one eight-hand-lengths sword, one birth jewel, one returning-from-death jewel, one jewel of satisfaction, one road-returning jewel, one snake-scarf, one bee-scarf, and one scarf of various uses,* with this command: "When illness occurs do you shake these treasures danglingly and repeat before them these words: 'One, two, three, four, five, six, seven, eight, nine, ten, hundred, thousand myriad.' [69] If you do this, the dead will without fail return to life."

> (There are some, however, which allege that these words were not an incantation given at this time to Prince-Sky-Plenty-Earth-Plenty-High-as-Sky's-Sun-Fire-Ruddy-Plenty, but were, in fact, the divine words that had been given forth by the Kami Sky-Frightening-Female, when she danced before the Rock-Cave into which Great-Sky-Shiner had retired.)

In addition to those mentioned, there were sent down as a guard to attend the Sky-Grandchild

SKY-ROAD [70]

SKY-KAMI-JEWEL [71]

(*who were the children of the Kami Divine-Producer*)

SKY-KUNONO [72]

SKY-RICE-BRAN-DOOR [73]

SKY-DIVINE-STANDER [74]

SKY-AUGUST-SHADE [75]

PRINCESS-SKY-AUGUST-SERVANT [76]

SUN-PLACE-TRUE-SEEING [77]

SKY-ELDER-BROTHER [78]

PRINCE-SKY-JEWEL-WONDROUS [79]

PRINCE-SKY-FIVE-HUNDRED [80]

SKY-TREE-FALLING [81]

SKY-SUN-SPIRIT [82]

SKY-MILK-SWIFT-SUN [83]

PRINCE-SKY-YASAKA [84]

SKY-ISAFU-JEWEL [85]

SKY-IKISHINIHO [86]

SKY-LIFE-JEWEL [87]

(*which latter was a child of the Kami Divine-Producer*)

---

[70] Ancestor of the Rulers of Kawasè.
[71] Ancestor of the District-Governors of Mishima and of Kano in Kazunu.
[72] Ancestor of the Governors of Nakato.
[73] Ancestor of the Tribe-Masters of the Mirror-Makers.
[74] Ancestor of the Governors of Kuga in Yamashiro.
[75] Ancestor of the Governors of Ohoshi-Kafuchi [Oshi-Kochi].
[76] Ancestress of the Tribe-Masters of Azumi.
[77] Ancestor of the Tribe-Masters of Yuza in Nukatabè.
[78] Ancestor of the Governors of Amabè in Nakajima, Owari.
[79] Ancestor of the Tribe-Masters of Hashihito.
[80] Ancestor of the Rulers of the Land of Agi (Aki).
[81] Ancestor of the Rulers of the Land of Usa in Toyokuni.
[82] Ancestor of the District-Governors of Tsushima.
[83] Ancestor of the Tribe-Masters of Kanomi, in Hirosè.
[84] Ancestor of the Tribe-Masters of Kanomi, in Isè.
[85] Ancestor of the Tribe-Masters of Shitori.
[86] Ancestor of the Rulers of the Land of Yamashiro*
[87] Ancestor of the Governors of Niitabè.

---

* See p. 31, n. 87. Presumably a descendant of Prince-Sky-Lord.

THE DEITY AGE

PRINCE-SKY-LITTLE-RENOWNED [88]
SKY-THING-FIVE-HUNDRED [89]
SKY-UPPER-SPRING [90]
SKY-LOWER-SPRING [91]

(*the two latter being sons of Thought-Includer*)

SKY-MOON-SPIRIT.[92]

In all two-and-thirty commanders of companies were sent down thus. And to these were added

SKY-SOSO [93]
SKY-AKAÜRA [94]
HOHORO [95]
SKY-RED-STAR.[96]

Accompanying them were five companies of rulers, leading Sky-warrior clans: The rulers of Two-Ricefields, Great-Garden, Retainer, Yusè, and Sakato. Following these were twenty-five Sky-warrior clans, leading armed men: the warrior clans of Two-Ricefields, Boiling-Hemp, Parsley-Field, Bird-Looking, Yoko-Ricefield, Bird-Door, Floating-Ricefield, Town-Well, Log-Ricefield, Sakè-Folk, Ricefield-End, Red-Space, Old-Rice, Narrow-Bamboo, Ohomamè, Shoulder-Field, Feather-Kashi, Hirotsu, Futsuru, Sumito, Three-Fields-of-Sanuki, Aïtsuki, Kiku-of-Tsukushi, Harima, and Sacrifice-Field-of-Tsukushi. Also there descended from the Sky

SKY-FEATHER-FIELD [97]
SKY-MARA [98]

as Masters-of-Ships, accompanied by the Kami

SKY-MAÜRA [99]

---

[88] *Ancestor of the Tribe-Masters of Totori.*
[89] *Ancestor of the Tribe-Masters of Toriwo.*
[90] *Ancestor of the Under-Priests* * of Achi, in Shinano.*
[91] *Ancestor of the Land-Rulers of Chichifu in Musashi.†*
[92] *Ancestor of the District-Chiefs of Iki.*
[93] *Ancestor of the Broad-Hat-Sewer Clan.*
[94] *Ancestor of the Inabè.*
[95] *Ancestor of the Head-Men of Toïchibè.*
[96] *Ancestor of the Warrior Clan of Tsuruda, in Tsukushi.*
[97] *Ancestor of the Head-Men of Atobè.*
[98] *Ancestor of the Tribe-Masters of Ato.*
[99] *Ancestor of the Smiths of Yamato.*

---

* *Hafuri.*
† See p. 31. Presumably a descendant of Sky-Great-Sun.

who served as helmsman, and as boatmen the Kami

SKY-MAÜRA ¹
SKY-RED-MARA ²
SKY-RED-STAR.³, ᴬ

THE AUGUST REIGN IN SUN-FACING

Thus was Prince-Sky-Plenty-Earth-Plenty-High-as-Sky's-Sun-Fire-Ruddy-Plenty commanded. So, leaving the Sky-Rock-Seat, pushing asunder the eight-fold, Sky-spreading Sky-clouds, and opening the road with a sacred road-opening, he set out, floating on the Floating-Sky-Bridge, and descended onto the wondrous *Two-Kami* Peak ⁴ of High-Thousand-Rice-Ears in So,⁵ of Sun-Facing, in Tsukushi.

When he descended darkness covered the sky, so that there was no difference between day and night, and men and animals lost their way and the colors of things could not be distinguished. And there were two Ground-Spiders ⁶ *of Great-Suwa and Little-Suwa, who said to him, "If you pull off a thousand ears of rice and scatter the unhulled grains, casting them in every direction, there will surely be light." So the Kami took the ears of rice and scattered them, and by this means the sun and moon shone brightly.*⁷ *(For this reason the place is called High-Thousand-Rice-Ears, and it is for this cause that wild rice still grows on Peak-Wondrous.)* ᴬ

The Kami Sky-Great-Sun and Sky-Round-Eye, putting on their forearms dread, loud-speaking elbow-pads, taking on their backs Sky-Rock-Quivers and at their sides great broad-tempered swords, with the Sky-wax-tree bows in their hands, and clasping under their arms the true Sky-deer-arrows and eight-eyed humming-arrows, stood before him as Tribe-Masters of the imperial guard, in respectful attendance.

There followed him from the Sky also the Kami

PRINCESS-KAMI-CLOTH ⁸

*to weave his clothing. From Two-Kami Peak, of Sun-Facing in Tsukushi, she went to Hikitsu-ne-Hill in Three-Moors Province.*ᴮ

First in his search for a country to dwell in, Prince-Sky-Plenty-Earth-Plenty-High-as-Sky's-Sun-Fire-Ruddy-Plenty traversed the waste land of Sojishi from the Hill of Hitawo till he came to the Cape of Kasasa,⁹ in

---

¹ *Ancestor of the Broad-Hat-Sewers.*
² *Ancestor of the Broad-Hat-Sewers of Soso.*
³ *Ancestor of the Ina Clan.*
⁸ *Ancestress of the Long-Loom Clan [Nagahata-be].*

Ata-no Nagaya, where he stood on a level part of the floating sand-bank. There appeared to him the Lord of the Land, the Kami

SALT-POSSESSOR [10]

a child of He-Who-Invites, of whom he asked, "Is there a country here, or is there not?" The other replied, "There is. Deign to go through it at your pleasure. I will obey your commands." At which Prince-Sky-Plenty-Earth-Plenty-High-as-Sky's-Sun-Fire-Ruddy-Plenty said, "This place is over against [11] the Land of Kara coming straight across to this august cape, and it is a Land on which the morning sun shines straight and which the evening sunlight makes bright. This place is exceedingly good." So saying, he made strong the pillars of his palace on the lowest rock-bottom and reared its cross-beams to the Plain-of-the-High-Sky, and dwelt there.

After this Prince-Monkey-Ricefield proceeded to the upper waters of the River Fifty-Bells at Sanada in Isè, when Prince-Sky-Plenty-Earth-Plenty-High-as-Sky's-Sun-Fire-Ruddy-Plenty said to Sky-Frightening-Female, "Do you, who discovered this great Kami, Prince-Monkey-Ricefield who served as my guide, bear him company [12] and let his name be made your title." (For this reason the Clan-Chieftainesses of Monkey, like the Clan-Chiefs, bear the name of the male Kami, Prince-Monkey-Ricefield, though they are women.)

So Prince-Monkey-Ricefield named the country the Land of Swift-Wind-Isè and governed it.

He had a daughter

PRINCESS-OF-AGA

who had in her charge a metal bell [13] which had been thrown from the Sky by the august Kami

FOUR-KAMI.[14]

The bell was enshrined at Kashi-no Wazuka-no, which at present is called, mistakenly, Hand-Oak-Field.[15] Since the country was governed by Princess-of-Aga, it was called Aga, which name was later changed to Iga.^A

Now this Kami Prince-Monkey-Ricefield dwelt at Azaka, and while fishing, had his hand seized by a *sarubo-yahi* [16] shell-fish and was drowned in the sea-water. (Thus the name by which he was called, from his sinking to the bottom, was Bottom-Touching-August-Spirit and his name from the formation of the bubbles was Bubble-Flowering-August-Spirit.) When Sky-Frightening-Female, who had escorted him, arrived there, driving together all broad-finned and narrow-finned fishes, she asked them, "Will you respectfully serve the son of the Sky-Kami?" And all the fishes answered that they would do so, only the bêche-de-mer [17] did not reply. So Sky-Frightening-Female said to the bêche-de-mer, "This mouth, then, is a mouth that does not reply!" and slit its mouth with her short sword. (So now the bêche-de-mer has a slit mouth. Therefore, also, up to this august reign, when the first island-fruits are presented as offerings, a portion of them is granted to the Clan-Chieftainesses of Monkey.)

THE CURSE OF THE KAMI GREAT-MOUNTAIN-POSSESSOR

There was in that Land a fair damsel whose name was

PRINCESS-BLOOMING-TREE-BLOSSOM [18]

and Prince-Sky-Plenty-Earth-Plenty-High-as-Sky's-Sun-Fire-Ruddy-Plenty, meeting her as he walked on the seashore at the Cape of Kasasa, asked her, "Whose daughter are you?" She answered, "Your handmaid is a daughter of the Kami Great-Mountain-Possessor." [19] Then he asked, "Have you any brothers?" She replied, "I have a sister

PRINCESS-ROCK-LONG.[20]

We have built a palace eight hiro long on the highest crest of the waves, and tend the loom with jingling wrist-jewels." [21]

Then said he, "I am desirous of cohabiting with you. How do you regard this?" She answered, "Your handmaid is unable to say. My father, the Kami Great-Mountain-Possessor, will answer." So the august grandchild said to Great-Mountain-Possessor, "I have seen your daughter and desire her." And Great-Mountain-Possessor, greatly pleased, respectfully sent her, with her elder sister Princess-Rock-Long, and with gift-tables holding a hundred sorts of food and drink. But as the elder sister was exceedingly ugly, Prince-Sky-Plenty-Earth-Plenty-High-as-Sky's-Sun-Fire-Ruddy-Plenty was alarmed at the sight and sent her back, retaining the younger, Princess-Blooming-Tree-Blossom, whom he wedded for one night.[22]

Great-Mountain-Possessor was greatly ashamed at the sending back of Princess-Rock-Long, and sent a message saying, "I presented both my daughters together, in order that your august child, though the snow and rain fall and the wind blow, might be perpetually permanent as lasting rock (for that reason I sent Princess-Rock-Long) and might live flourishingly like the blooming of the tree-blossom (for that reason I sent Princess-Blooming-Tree-Blossom) and as a pledge of this I presented them as tribute. But since you have sent back Princess-Rock-Long and kept only Princess-Blooming-Tree-Blossom, your children shall fade and fall like tree-blossoms." (This is why, up to the present time, the lives of the Sky-Sovereigns are not long.)

(Others have it, however, that when she was sent back, Princess-Rock-Long, in her shame and resentment, spat and wept, and cursed the children of Prince-Sky-Plenty-Earth-Plenty-High-As-Sky's-Sun-Fire-Ruddy-Plenty with short lives, saying, "The race of invisible mankind shall hereafter change swiftly like tree-blossoms, and shall decay and pass away!" This is why the life of man is so short.)

Princess-Blooming-Tree-Blossom chose by divination a ricefield which she named Sana-Ricefield, and from the rice grown there she brewed sweet Sky-sakè for her husband's entertainment. And with rice from the ricefield named Nuna-Ricefield she made boiled rice and entertained him with it.

THE BIRTH-GIVING OF PRINCESS-BLOOMING-TREE-BLOSSOM

Princess-Blooming-Tree-Blossom became pregnant and at length gave birth [23] to three (or, as others say, four) boys, when she took them in her arms and respectfully approaching Prince-Sky-Plenty-Earth-Plenty-High-As-Sky's-Sun-Fire-Ruddy-Plenty, said, "Your handmaid has given birth to these. It is not fitting that children of the Sky be privately brought up; therefore I bring them to you for your information."

But the Sky-Grandchild was slow to believe, and looked upon the children and laughing in mockery said, "What! These are Princes of mine? How delightful is the news of their birth!" Angered, Princess-Blooming-Tree-Blossom said, "Why do you mock your handmaid?" Said he, "Surely there is doubt of this, and for that reason I mock. How can I, Sky Kami though I be, cause one to become pregnant in the course of one night? I suspect the children cannot be mine. They must be the children of a Kami of the Land."

At that she was still angrier, and building a doorless hall eight hiro long, she entered it with her children and plastered it up with earth, and made a vow, saying, "If these children which I have conceived are not the offspring of the Sky-Grandchild, let them surely perish! But if they are his offspring, let them suffer no hurt!" So saying, she set fire to the hall. But when the fire was first burning, one child sprang out, announcing, "Here am I, a child of the Sky-Kami, and my name is

FIRE-GLOW.[24]

> [24] Ancestor of the Clan-Chiefs of Little-Bridge in Ata (in Satsuma Province) and of the Falcon-Men.*

* *Haya* (Swift, clever)-*hito* (person): *Haya-bito* (*hayato* or *hāito*). The latter formed the imperial-guard. They were called, also, "dog-men" (see p. 87, n. 46).

Where is my father?"

(*Some say, otherwise, that Princess-Blooming-Tree-Blossom wedded Great-Land-Master, whose son Fire-Glow was.*) ᴬ

When the fire was burning fiercest and she drew back from the heat, the second child sprang out, announcing, "Here am I, a child of the Sky-Kami, and my name is

FIRE-CLIMAX.

Where are my father and my elder brother?" Also, when the flames were beginning to be extinguished, the third child sprang out, announcing, "Here am I, a child of the Sky-Kami, and my name is

FIRE-FADE.[25]

Where are my father and my elder brothers?"

(*Some say that the first child to spring out was Sky-Shining-Earth-Shining-Sky's-Fire-Ruddy-Comb-Jewel-Plenty-Swift-Sun,[26] and that Fire-Fade was a fourth who sprang out when Princess-Blooming-Tree-Blossom shrank back from the heat.*)

Their mother, then, Princess-Blooming-Tree-Blossom, came forth from amid the embers and approaching Prince-Sky-Plenty-Earth-Plenty-High-As-Sky's-Sun-Fire-Ruddy-Plenty, said, "The children which your handmaid has brought forth, and your handmaid herself, have undergone the danger of fire and yet have suffered no hurt. Will you not look on them?" He replied, "From the first I knew them to be my children. Yet as they were conceived in one night, I supposed suspicions would arise, and I desired to demonstrate to all that they are my children and that a Sky-Kami can cause pregnancy in one night. Moreover I desired to demonstrate your own wondrous dignity and the surpassing spirit of our children. Thus it was that formerly I used mocking words."

(*Others say that Princess-Blooming-Tree-Blossom announced her pregnancy to the Sky-Grandchild and when he mocked her, built the hall and gave birth to the three children in the midst of the flames, which failed to harm them. She cut their navel-strings with a bamboo knife,[27] which she threw away, when there sprang up from it a grove of bamboo. Therefore the place was called Bamboo-House.[28] The bamboo-knife which she used is said still to exist.*)ᴬ

In spite of his words, however, Princess-Blooming-Tree-Blossom was incensed and would not speak to him. Grieved at this, then, Prince-Sky-Plenty-Earth-Plenty-High-As-Sky's-Sun-Fire-Ruddy-Plenty composed a song:

Though the seaweed come || To shore from the far horizon,
Yet for me, alas!
(Hear ye, snipe of the beaches!) || Never henceforth is your bed!

Long after this Prince-Sky-Plenty-Earth-Plenty-High-As-Sky's-Sun-Fire-Ruddy-Plenty died and was buried in the mound of H'yuga-no E,²⁹ in K'yushu.

His spirit is enshrined at Peak-of-Sun-Gold,³⁰ in Izu Province.ᴬ

(Those who say that Fire-Glow was a son of Great-Land-Master relate that he was violent in his actions, at which his father grieved and would have cast him off. So he sent Fire-Glow to draw water, and before the son returned, he launched his vessel and departed. But when Fire-Glow returned from drawing the water and saw the vessel departing, he was angered and raised the wind and waves and made them pursue it, so that the vessel could not advance and was finally broken. (Therefore the place was called Ship-Hill, and also Wave-Hill.³¹) Then Great-Land Master said to his wife

PRINCESS NUTSU

"In endeavoring to escape from a wicked son I have encountered the wind and waves, by which I have been much distressed." For this cause the place was called Angry-Tide and also Telling-Ford.³²) ᴮ

THE AUGUST-LUCK-EXCHANGE

Now Fire-Glow was a prince who had by nature a sea-gift and got his luck from the sea and caught broad-finned fish and narrow-finned fish, while Fire-Fade had by nature a mountain-gift and got his luck on the mountains and took rough-haired beasts and soft-haired beasts. (From which Fire-Glow is called also Prince-Sea-Gift and Fire-Fade is called also Prince-Mountain-Gift.) When the wind blew and the rain fell the elder brother got no gain, but in wind and rain the younger brother's gain did not lack. So the two brothers, the elder and the younger, conversed together, and Fire-Glow said to Fire-Fade, "Let us for a trial exchange our gifts with one another and use each other's luck." Three times he proposed this vainly but at length with difficulty the exchange was made. So the elder brother, Fire-Glow, took the bow and arrows that were the gift of the younger brother, and trying the mountain-luck, went to the mountains in quest of wild animals, but never a trace of one did he come upon. The younger, Fire-Fade, took the fish-hook which was the other's gift, and trying the sea-luck, angled in the sea, but got no fish, and moreover he lost the fish-hook in the sea. Then, since neither of them gained anything but both returned empty-handed, Fire-Glow, repenting of the bargain, said, "A mountain-luck is its own luck and a sea-luck is its own luck. Let each of us restore to the other his own luck." So saying, he returned to his brother the other's bow and arrows, asking that his fish-hook be given back to him.

The younger, Fire-Fade, replied, however, "I got no fish by angling with your fish-hook, and in the end lost it in the sea and there is no means of finding it." Then, his elder brother demanding it urgently, he made another new hook which he offered him, but the other refused to accept it and demanded the old one. So Fire-Fade took his ten-hand-lengths cross-sword, and forged from it five hundred fish-hooks, and heaping them on a winnowing-tray made offer of them, but the other would not take them. Again he made a thousand, but Fire-Glow was angered and would not receive them, saying, "Though they are many, I will not take them. I will have my own fish-hook and no other." And he continued repeatedly to demand it vehemently.

THE PALACE OF THE KAMI GREAT-OCEAN-POSSESSOR

By reason of this Fire-Fade's grief was profound, and he went to the seashore and wandered about grieving and moaning. There, as he was weeping and lamenting, he came upon a wild river-goose which was caught in a snare, and taking pity on its distress, he released it and let it go. Presently there approached him the Kami Salt-Possessor [33] who asked, "What is the cause of your weeping and lamentation?" So he told the matter from first to last. Then said Salt-Possessor, "Grieve no more. I will well advise you, and will arrange the matter for you." And taking from a bag a black comb, he flung it on the ground, and it straightway became a five-hundred-fold clump of bamboo. He took the bamboo and made of it a strong small basket without meshes, set Fire-Fade in it and attaching him to it with a cord, instructed him, saying, "When I have sunk the basket, go on ahead and you will find a pleasant path which is called the Little-Shore-of-Delight. Go along this till you see a palace built like fish-scales. This is the palace of the Kami Great-Ocean-Possessor.[34] When you come to that Kami's gate, you will see a many-branched katsura tree above the wall at its side. Sit in the top of that tree and the Sea-Kami's daughter will see and advise you." So, being sunk in the sea, Fire-Fade found himself in the pleasant strand, where he left the basket and proceeded on his way for a short distance till he arrived at the palace of the Sea-Kami.

(It is told otherwise that Salt-Possessor said to Fire-Fade, "The charger on which the Sea-Kami rides is a wani [35] eight hiro in length who waits with fins erect, in the small orange-tree house. I will consult with him." So together they went to the wani,

who said, "I will carry the Sky-Grandchild to the sea-palace, but the journey will take eight days. The Sea-Kami, however, has another charger, a wani of one hiro, who can assuredly carry him there in a single day. I will return and make him come to you. Mount him and enter the sea and he will carry you to the palace of the Sea-Kami." Accordingly Fire-Fade remained there waiting during eight days, when the wani of one hiro arrived and carried him to the sea-realm.)

The palace of the Sea-Kami, Great-Ocean-Possessor, had turrets and tall towers of exceeding beauty. Before the gate was a well, and over the well grew a many-branched katsura tree with wide-spreading branches. All happened as had been said. Fire-Fade climbed the katsura tree and when the maidservants of the Sea-Kami's daughter,

PRINCESS-FRUITFUL-JEWEL

came with jeweled utensils to draw water, there was a shadow in the well, and looking up they saw to their amazement a lovely youth.

(Some say that he stood at the foot of the tree. Others say one attendant came to draw the water, but could not fill the utensil. She looked down into the well and saw there, upside down, the face of a man smiling. She then looked up and saw the lovely Kami leaning against the tree, and went inside and informed her mistress.)

Fire-Fade asked the maidservants to give him some water, and they drew some and presented it to him in a jeweled urn, and without drinking, he took his neck jewel in his mouth, and spat it into the urn. The Jewel clung to the urn and as it could not be removed, they took the urn with the clinging jewel and gave it to Princess-Fruitful-Jewel. Asked she, "Is there someone outside the gate?" They replied, "One sits in the top of the katsura tree above our well—a very lovely youth, even more splendid than our king. When he asked for water we gave him some, but without drinking he spat this jewel here. As it could not be moved, we bring the urn with the jewel in it to you."

Wondering, Princess-Fruitful-Jewel went out with a jewel-urn to see, and looking up, was so startled with pleasure at his comeliness that she let fall the urn, which was broken to pieces. Now she was a damsel the like of whose face, for beauty, is nowhere to be seen. So they regarded each other, and she went in and said to her father, "There is a lovely stranger of no ordinary appearance in the tree at our gate. If he had come down from the Sky he would have on him Sky-filth; if he had come from the Earth, he would have on him Earth-filth. Does his loveliness mark him a prince of the Sky?" Said the sea-Kami, "I will try him and see," and he sent one to ask, "What stranger are you and why have you come here?" To which Fire-Fade replied, "I am the Grandchild of the Sky-Kami," and in the end told the reason of his coming. Then the Sea-Kami himself went out to look, and made obeisance, and inquiring courteously as to his welfare, invited him inside and spread eight layers of rugs made of sea-asses' skins,[36] and set on them eight more layers of silk rugs for a three-fold dais. Thereon the Sky-Grandchild at the first step of the dais wiped both his feet, at the second step he put both his hands to the ground; at the inner portion he sat down at his ease on the cushion that covered the couch. When the Sea-Kami beheld this, he said, "This is the august child of Prince-Sky-Plenty-Earth-Plenty-High-As-Sky's-Sun-Fire-Ruddy-Plenty," and he treated him with all respect, and arranging a table holding a hundred sorts of merchandise, fulfilled the rites of hospitality and made a great banquet, and straightway gave him his daughter, Princess-Fruitful-Jewel, in marriage.

Fire-Fade dwelt in that land for three years, in close and warm affection, but then, thinking of former things, he heaved a single deep sigh. Hearing the sigh, Princess-Fruitful-Jewel spoke to her father, saying, "During the three years he has dwelt here he has never sighed, but tonight he heaved a sigh as if in grief. Perhaps it is sorrow due to longing for his country." So the great Kami said familiarly to his son-in-law, "What is the cause of your sighing? And why did you come here? Some time ago it was told me you were mourning on the seashore. Whether this is true I do not know. If you desire to return to your country, I will send you back." So Fire-Fade told the great Kami the circumstances of his coming and how his elder brother had importuned him for the lost fish-hook, and the Sea-Kami, in pity for him, called together all the sea-fishes, broad of fin and narrow of fin, great and small, and asked, "Has any fish taken this fish-hook?" And the fishes answered, "We do not know, but the red taï-fish [37] has for long complained of a sore throat which prevents her from eating, and she has not come." The taï-fish was summoned and when her mouth was examined, the fish-hook was found.

> (*Some say that the fish in whose mouth the fish-hook was found was the mullet,*[38] *and that Great-Ocean-Possessor chided her, saying, "Henceforth you shall not be able to swallow bait, nor shall you be given a place at the table of the Sky-Grandchild!" These say that this is the reason why the mullet is not among the articles of food set before the Emperor.*)

The fish-hook was straightway taken and washed and respectfully presented to Fire-Fade. Then said Great-Ocean-Possessor, "My inmost heart is rejoiced that you, the Sky-Grandchild, have been graciously pleased to visit me. When shall I ever forget it? Though you may be separated from me by eight-fold road windings, I hope we shall from time to time think of one another."

Then he counselled Fire-Fade, saying, "When you are about to give this fish-hook to your elder brother, invoke it privately, saying, 'O fish-hook, be to all his descendants of whatever degree of relationship, a big hook, a striving hook, a poor hook, a silly hook!' Use also this imprecation: 'Root of poverty, beginning of ruin, well-spring of wretchedness!' Give it not to him till you have said this, nor face to face, but spit three times [39] and fling it to him with your hand behind your back. Then, if he plant the upland fields, do you plant the lowland fields, and if he plant the lowland fields, do you plant the upland fields. When he goes fishing, take your stand on the sea-beach and do whatever raises the wind. (Now that which raises the wind is whistling.) [40] When you do this I will overwhelm and harass him with the hurrying waves. If you do this, since I rule the waters, in three years your elder brother most certainly will be made poor." Also he presented to him the tide-flow-jewel and the tide-ebb-jewel, which, when thought of, made the tide flow and ebb, instructing him thus: Do not throw these away. If your brother in anger attacks you with intent to do you hurt, throw down this tide-flow-jewel, and the tide will straightway flow and thus you shall drown him. But if he repent and beg forgiveness, if you throw down the tide-ebb-jewel, the tide will straightway ebb and you shall permit him to live. Thus you shall vex him till he renders you submission and becomes your vassal." In such manner did the Sea-Kami, with a sincere heart, counsel him. Great-Ocean-Possessor called to him all the wani of the sea, and said, "Fire-Fade, august child of Prince-Sky-Plenty-Earth-Plenty-High-As-Sky's-Sun-Fire-Ruddy-Plenty, is about to go out to the upper land. Who will conduct him and bring back report, and in how many days?" At which each spoke, according to the length of his body in hiro, fixing the days, one of them, a wani of one hiro, saying, "Your servant will conduct him and come back in one day." Said Great-Ocean-Possessor then, "Do you respectfully conduct him, but while crossing the sea's expanse let him not be alarmed."

When Fire-Fade was about to set out, Princess-Fruitful-Jewel addressed him intimately, saying, "Your slave is pregnant and the time of her delivery is not far distant. The child of a Sky-Kami should not be brought forth in the sea-plain. On a day of raging wind and wave, then, when my pregnancy is fulfilled, I will truly come to the seashore to my lord's abode. I pray you therefore to erect for me a bringing-forth house [41] and wait for me there." [42] Then Great-Ocean-Possessor seated Fire-Fade on the wani's head and saw him go, and the wani respectfully conducted him home in one day as had been promised. When the wani was about to return, Fire-Fade undid the short-sword he wore and putting it on the wani's neck, sent it back. So the wani of one hiro is now called

BLADE-POSSESSOR.[43]

(Some say, to the contrary, that the Kami thus named is rather Rice-Boiled-Rice, grandchild of Fire-Fade, who later plunged into the sea, when the Emperor Young-Three-Hairs-Moor led the army eastward to possess the Land.)

THE SUBMISSION OF FIRE-GLOW

Fire-Fade gave the fish-hook to his elder brother, even as the Sea-Kami had instructed, and the other became poorer and poorer and, with new plans of violence, came attacking him. But when he was about to attack, Fire-Fade threw down the tide-flow-jewel to drown him, at which the tide rose with a mighty overflow so that Fire-Glow fled to a high mountain. The tide, however, submerged the mountain, so that Fire-Glow climbed a high tree, when the tide submerged also the tree. Then the elder brother, finding himself in utmost straits and extremity, and not knowing where to flee, showed sorrow and admitted his offense, saying from afar, "I have been at fault. You have dwelt long in the sea-plain and have manifestly gained excellent knowledge. I beseech you have pity on me and thereby save my life." So Fire-Fade granted the petition and left off whistling and threw down the tide-ebb-jewel to permit the other to live, on which the wind again rested and the tide ebbed and his elder brother was restored to tranquility.[44]

(By some it is said that Fire-Glow refused to receive the fish-hook, at which Fire-Fade, with the tide-flow-jewel, produced the mighty tide. Fire-Glow then besought him, saying, "Spare my life and I will be your slave." The other then, with the tide-ebb-jewel, made the tide recede, when Fire-Glow altered his former words, saying, "I am your elder brother. How shall the elder serve the younger?" At this Fire-Fade again produced the mighty tide, on which Fire-Glow saw that the younger possessed marvelous powers and submitted to him.)

(Others relate that Fire-Fade, on a day when his elder brother went fishing, took his stand on the shore of the sea and whistled, and at once there arose a sudden tempest and Fire-Glow was overwhelmed, on which he admitted his fault.)

(Still others say that after Fire-Glow had been relieved by the tide-ebb-jewel, he pined away from day to day and became impoverished until finally he yielded his submission.)

When Fire-Glow had been thus harassed, he reflected and said, "Henceforth your slave and my descendants for eighty generations and for all degrees of relationship will be your subjects and will abide in the place which is your precinct, as your guard by day and night, and your mimes and dog-men. (On this account the various Falcon-Men descended from Fire-Glow to this day do not leave the neighborhood of the enclosure of the imperial palace, and render the service of barking dogs.)

Fire-Fade, however, was still angered and would not converse with him, at which his elder brother, clad only in his loincloth, smeared his face and his palms with red clay, and saying, "Thus do I defile my body and make myself your mime forever!" he kicked with his feet and danced and postured in the manner of his drowning struggles. When the tide reached his feet, he did the foot-divination; [45] when it reached his knees, he lifted his feet; when it reached his hips, he ran in circles; when it reached the middle of his body he rubbed his loins; when it reached his sides, he put his hands on his breast; when it reached his neck, he threw up his hands and waved them. (So, to this present, Fire-Glow's different postures while he was drowning are augustly shown forth without ceasing.[46] Moreover this was the origin of the present custom of not pressing one for the return of a lost needle.[47]

THE BRINGING-FORTH-HOUSE OF CORMORANTS' FEATHERS

Now Fire-Fade, so soon as he returned home, had taken cormorants' feathers and building a bringing-forth-house on the wave-marge of the sea-beach, had thatched it with them. (*From this arose the belief that a cormorant's feather, held in the hand, eases the pains of childbirth.*) Before the tiling of the house was finished, however, the Sea-Kami's daughter, Princess-Fruitful-Jewel, fulfilling her promise, bravely fronted wind and wave and arrived at the seashore, riding on a great tortoise and throwing a splendor over the sea-plain. So she respectfully came to Fire-Fade and said she, "The time for your handmaid's child-bearing is come," and unable to restrain the urgency of her womb, she did not wait for the completion of the house, but entered at once and remained in it.

Now Prince-Sky-Great-Man [48] *was in attendance upon them and having in his care the matting, made a broom with which he swept away the crabs. (For which cause he was invested with this office, which was called Crab-Guard.*[49, A]

When she was about to be delivered, Princess-Fruitful-Jewel said to her husband, "When an outlander is about to give birth, she assumes the shape common to her native land. So now I am about to assume the shape common to my own country. Look not upon me, I pray you, while I am in travail!" Thinking these words strange, however, he could not restrain himself, and went stealthily and made a light with a comb and peeped in at the very moment she was delivered, when she turned into a wani [50] of eight hiro (or, as some say, a dragon), crawling and writhing about on her belly; so that in terror at the sight, he straightway fled.

Now she was aware that he had looked, and was ashamed, and said she, "I had always desired to come and go across the sea-path, and had you not disgraced me I would have made the sea and land communicate, the one with the other, and prevented them from being sundered forever. But your peeping was an outrageous act. With what now shall friendliness be knit together? Therefore, from this time forward, do not send back again any servants of your handmaid who may come to this place, and I will not send back again any of your servants who may come to my place." And so saying she swaddled the infant in a coverlet of rushes and abandoning it on the seashore, closed the sea-boundary and went down again to the sea realm. (This is the reason there is now no communication between the land and the sea.)

The name of the child she had borne was

PRINCE-HIGH-AS-SKY'S-SUN-WAVE-MARGE-BRAVE-CORMORANT-THATCH-MAKING-TO-MEET-INCOMPLETELY.[51]

(He was so named because the bringing-forth-house by the seashore was thatched with cormorants' feathers, and he was born before the tiles had met.) When Princess-Fruitful-Jewel took her departure Fire-Fade made a song:

> Love, with whom I slept || There on the Isle-of-Wild-Ducks—
> Sea-horizon birds—
> While one night links to another || Her I can never forget!

And he chose women to be wet-nurses, hot-water providers, chewers-of-boiled-rice, and bathing women. All these various clans he provided for the respectful bringing up of the infant. (This provision for milk from other women was the origin of the present employment of wet-nurses.)

Later, when Princess-Fruitful-Jewel heard tidings of the august infant, she could not overcome the love in her heart, and she was desirous to return to nurse him herself, but could not appropriately do so. So she sent her younger sister,

PRINCESS-JEWEL-GOOD [52]

to nurture him, sending by her a song in reply to Fire-Fade's:

> More than gems of red || That lend to their string bright lustre,
> Does my loved lord shine,
> Sending abroad his radiance || Like jewels of blinding white.

(These two stanzas, one sent and one received in reply, are what are called exalting-songs.⁵³)

> (Some say, however, that she sent her song to him first and that his was sung in reply.)

> (By some, also, it is said that she did not abandon the child on the beach, but departed with it in her arms, and that many days after this, saying, "It is not meet that the child of the Sky-Grandchild be left in the sea, sent it back by her sister, Princess-Jewel-Good.)

> (According to others, Princess-Jewel-Good accompanied her elder sister from the sea realm in the first place and remained there when the other went back.)

Fire-Fade dwelt in the Palace of High-Thousand-Rice-Ears ⁵⁴ for five hundred and eighty years.⁵⁵ His imperial grave also is on the west of Mount High-Thousand-Rice-Ears.

> (Some say, however, that he was buried in the mound on the summit of Mount Bamboo-House, in Sun-Facing.)

Prince-High-As Sky's-Sun-Wave-Marge-Brave-Cormorant-Thatch-Making-to-Meet-Incompletely wedded his maternal aunt, Princess-Jewel-Good, and begot

FIVE-RIVER-CURRENTS
RICE-BOILED-RICE ⁵⁶
THREE-HAIRS-MOOR.⁵⁷
YOUNG-THREE-HAIRS-MOOR ⁵⁸
BRAVE-KURA-OKI.⁵⁹

Long afterward he died ⁶⁰ in the Palace of the western country and was buried in the mound on the top of Mount Ahira in Sun-Facing.

---

⁵⁹ **Ancestor of the Land-Rulers of Yamato.**

THE EARTHLY SOVEREIGNS

THE EMPEROR YOUNG-THREE-HAIRS-MOOR [61]
(VALOROUS DEITY [62])

Young-Three-Hairs-Moor, the fourth child, when young, was called Sano. From his birth he was of clear intelligence and strong will, and at the age of fifteen was made heir apparent. When he reached adult age and dwelt in Sun-Facing, he wedded

PRINCESS-AHIRA

younger sister of the Clan-Chief of Little-Bridge in Ata [63] and begot

RUDDER-EARS
KISU-EARS

In the first year of his reign [64] he built a Shrine at Deer-Island,[65] nigh to Sawaru, in Soaking [66] Province, and enshrined therein the Kami Brave-Awful-Possessing-Male,[67] Snap-Master [68] and Sky-Beckoning-Ancestor-Lord.[69] There was a plain called Takara-Mountain-Plain which was covered with a good forest, and its people refused to contribute timber, at which the Kami was angered and he sunk the plain in a single night. It is now a desert.[70] The place now called Pool-of-Kami is a part of it from which the soil was removed.[A]

Now beneath the Fertile-Land-of-Reed-Plains lay a Kami in the form of a great cat-fish,[71] and by its movement it caused the earth to quake, till the Great Deity of Deer-Island thrust his sword [72] deep into the earth and transfixed the Kami's head. So, now, when the evil Kami is violent, he puts forth his hand and lays it upon the sword till the Kami becomes quiet.

In the eighteenth year of his reign, also, Young-Three-Hairs-Moor founded at Katori, in Shimosa Province, the Shrine of Katori,[73] in which he enshrined the Kami Snap-Master, Sky-Beckoning-Ancestor-Lord, and

PRINCESS-GREAT-KAMI.[74]

(Some, however, have it that this last Kami was enshrined here later, holding her to be the daughter of the Sea-Kami, wedded by the Sovereign Great-Elbow-Pad-Lord,[75] in accordance with a promise made by the Empress Princess-Long-Life-Perfect when she borrowed from the Sea-Kami the jewels of flood-tide and ebb-tide.) [76]

Now the two [77] Kami of Kashima and Katori went upon the sea to fish, when a storm broke a mast and the rudder of their vessel, and they hardly reached the shore. There they found two cryptomeria-trees of which to make masts, but when they cut one, red blood came from the cut. Astonished at this the Kami brought a huge stone and put it in the cut, and thus stopping the blood's flow, safely returned. These two trees are still to be seen.[A]

When Young-Three-Hairs-Moor was forty-five years old, he addressed his elder brothers and his children who dwelt in the Palace of High-Thousand-Rice-Ears, saying, "Of old time, when the world was everywhere desolate and the time was one of gloom and violence, our Sky Kami, High-Producer and Great-Sky-Shiner gave all this Fertile-Reed-Plain-Land-of-Lovely-Rice-Ears to our Sky-Ancestor, Prince-Sky-Plenty-Earth-Plenty-High-As-Sky's-Sun-Fire-Ruddy-Plenty. And he, opening the Sky-barrier and clearing a cloud-way, made his divine progress until he rested, and in this darkness established justice and ruled the western border. Thus our ancestors and imperial parent, with divine wisdom heaped up pleasure and glory. Many years have elapsed, till now it is one million, seven hundred and ninety-two thousand, four hundred and seventy years since the Sky-Kami descended.[78] Still there are distant territories which do not enjoy the blessings of imperial rule. Each city, by sufferance, has always had its lord and each hamlet its chief, and these, each of his own will, parcel the Land and promote invasion and discord. Where shall We dwell in order tranquilly to govern the Sky-Under? Probably We would better go to the eastward. Now I have learned from the Kami Salt-Possessor [79] that to the eastward lies a lovely country surrounded on every side by blue mountains, where dwells the Kami Plenty-Swift-Sun,[80] who flew down to it in a Sky-Rock-Boat. I am of opinion that it is in that Land that the Sky-task should be carried on, so that its glory shall fill the universe. That Land is no doubt the world's center. Let Us therefore proceed there and set up there Our capital." All the Princes replied, "This is true. We constantly think as you do. Let us go there at once."

THE IMPERIAL EASTWARD-JOURNEYING

So in the winter they left Sun-Facing and made their imperial way to Tsukushi. (*Now this Land was so named for the reason that in ancient times Chikugo and Chikuzen Provinces formed a single province, and between was a steep slope along which travelers had their saddles and under-saddles worn off. Therefore the folk called it Saddles-Under-Saddles-Worn-Off Land.*[81]) ᴬ

(*Some say, however, that there was on this slope a very violent Kami who slew half of all wayfarers, till*

HINO

Clan-Chief of Tsukushi, made an augury and

PRINCESS-MIKA-YORI

made a festival, after which travelers suffered no calamity. Therefore it was called Human-Life-Exhausting [82] *Province. Others, again, say that in order to inter the slain travelers trees were felled to make coffins, by which the trees of the mountain were like to be exhausted. Wherefore it was called Exhausting* [83] *Province.*) [84]

When they came to Usa [85] in the land of Fertile, two of the natives

PRINCE-OF-USA [86]
PRINCESS-OF-USA

built a palace standing on a single pillar on the bank of the River Usa, and made them a great banquet, and Young-Three-Hairs-Moor gave Princess-of-Usa in marriage to his attendant minister,

SKY-SEED.[87]

From there they proceeded to the Harbor of Oka [88] in the Land of Tsukushi, where Young-Three-Hairs-Moor dwelt for a year in the Palace of Hillock-Ricefield. After this they made their imperial way to the Land of Aki,[89] where he dwelt seven years at the Palace of Takeri. Again removing, they fared to the Land of Maise [90] where he dwelt in the Palace of High-Island for eight years, preparing oars and ships and collecting store of provisions, minded in a single campaign to subdue the empire.

From that place they sailed eastward, the prow of one vessel touching the stern of another, till they came to the Quick-Sucking-Passage,[91]

---

[86] **Ancestor of the Land-Rulers of Usa.**
[87] **Ancestor of the Nakatomi Family.***

* See p. 26, n. 56.

where they encountered one riding toward them on the carapace of a turtle and waving his sleeves as he fished. *The Sovereign asked one who stood by him, "Who is it that floats on the sea?" Thereon he sent Sky-Sun-Eagle* ⁹² *to see, who reported and was bidden to bring him to the Sovereign.* Young-Three-Hairs-Moor bade the fisher come near and asked him, "Who are you?" He replied, "Your slave is a Kami of the Land, *a grandson of the imperial ancestor, Fire-Fade*,ᴬ and my name is Prince-Rare. I angle for fish in the ocean-bays. Hearing that the child of the Sky-Kami was coming, I came to receive him." It was asked him, "Do you know the sea-way?" He answered, "I know it well." Then Young-Three-Hairs-Moor asked, "Will you act as guide?" And he replied, "I will respectfully serve you." So Young-Three-Hairs-Moor ordered a pole of oak wood ⁹³ to be extended to him, and he laid hold of it and was hoisted into the imperial vessel. And he was straightway made pilot and was given the name

PRINCE-OF-OAK-ROOT.⁹⁴

In this land there was a great Kami called by the people

SKY-WANI

who had descended upon a mountain, and of ten wayfarers who came there he let five pass, but the other five he held; until one named

KUWA-MALE

made a tunnel which led near to where the Kami was, and passing through it, offered prayer to him. (Therefore the mountain was called Mount-Under-Ground.) ᴮ

When they came up from that Land, at Wave-Swift-Crossing ⁹⁵ they encountered a mighty swift current and proceeding upward against it, reached the harbor of White-Sand-Bank, at the village of Kusaka, in the Province of Kawachi, where shortly after, arrayed for battle, they marched on to Tatsuta. Here the way was narrow and steep and the men were unable to march abreast, so they turned about and again journeyed eastward, crossing over by way of Mount Ikoma, desirous thus to enter the inner-land. There Prince-Long-Marrow of Fish-Hawk,⁹⁶ hearing of his coming, said, "Truly the children of the Sky-Kami come hither to rob me of my Land!" And he summoned all the forces under his rule and

---

⁹⁴ **Ancestor of the Rulers of the Land of Yamato and the Head-Men of Awoümi.***

---

* According to the *Shojiroku*.

with this army waited to attack them. So the battle began and the imperial troops were unable to advance.

When they ran out of weapons Prince-of-Oak-Root drew from his quiver a quantity of arrows that could not be exhausted, and the troops, gaining fresh courage, put the enemy to flight. Their provision then failed and Prince-of-Oak-Root drew from his quiver such a store of food that all the troops had a sufficiency. Afterward he drew from it such a quantity of precious things that every man of the imperial army was made rich. The Sovereign, marveling, asked him, "How is it that you have the power of the Kami?" He replied, "I am a Kami of the highest descent. More I shall tell you later, but for the present do not press me with questions." [A]

Now, while Five-River-Currents fought, Prince-Long-Marrow's baleful arrow wounded him in the hand, whereon Young-Three-Hairs-Moor said, "It is not meet that a child of the Sun-Kami should proceed against the sun to attack an enemy. Indeed, this is to act contrary to the way of the Sky. For this reason Five-River-Currents has been smitten and wounded by the hand of this villainous slave. It is better to retreat and pretend weakness. Then, having offered sacrifice to the Kami of Sky and Earth, and setting behind us the power of Great-Sky-Shiner, we shall follow her rays and trample the enemy underfoot. Thus they will be routed without our swords being stained with blood." All the rest cried, "Good!" and he bade the army wait and go no further forward, and the imperial force withdrew, the enemy also not daring to attack them. After that, retiring to the harbor, they set up their shields and presented a martial front. (For this reason they called that place Shield-Harbor. It is now called Smart-Wood-Harbor [97] of Kusaka.) Now in the battle there had been one who hid himself in a huge tree and thus escaped harm. So he said, "I am as grateful to this tree as to my mother." (Hence the people called the place Mother-Tree-Village.) From there they made their way around about from the southern side, and reaching the Sea of Blood-Lagoon, Five-River-Currents washed the blood from his hand. (From this that sea received its name.) Coming then to the river-mouth of Man [98] in the Land of Tree, finding his wound exceedingly painful, he grasped his sword and taking the posture of a warrior, said he, "Alas! How exasperating that I, a man, should die wounded by the hand of that villain, nor be able to avenge it!" (For this reason that river-mouth was so called.) Reaching Mount-Furnace, in the Land of Ki, he died, and his imperial tomb is on that mountain. From there they proceeded to the village of Nagusa, where they slew its ruler, and crossing the moor of Sano, in Bear-Moor, reëmbarked in their vessels.

There, in the midst of the sea, a violent wind arose and buffeted the imperial vessel, when Rice-Boiled-Rice exclaimed, "Were not my ancestors Sky-Kami, and my mother a Kami of the Sea? Yet I am harassed both by land and sea!" And so saying, he drew his sword and plunged into the sea-plain, which was his mother's Land.

> (*Some say that he straightway became transformed into the Kami Blade-Possessor and that the latter is not the one-hiro wani who bore back Fire-Fade from the Sea-Realm.*)[99]

Then said Three-Hairs-Moor, equally indignant, "Both my mother and my aunt are Sea-Kami. Why do they raise great waves to overwhelm us?" So he too plunged into the Sea-Plain, and treading on the wave-crests, crossed over to the Eternal Land.

After that Young-Three-Hairs-Moor, the Emperor, was alone with the imperial prince Rudder-Ears. And he, leading the army forward, came to Arazaka Harbor (called also Nishiki Bay) where he slew the Ruler of Nashiki.

THE CROSS-SWORD THAT WAS SENT DOWN FROM THE SKY

Now when Young-Three-Hairs-Moor made his imperial way around from there and came to the village of Bear-Moor, a great bear came from the mountain and immediately vanished in it, whereupon Young-Three-Hairs-Moor and his army all swooned and fell prone.

> (*It is said otherwise that the cause of the army's ailment was not a bear, but rather a poisonous vapor belched up by the Kami, from which everyone suffered and was unable to raise himself, and that Young-Three-Hairs-Moor at the time was asleep.*)

There came, however, to where the august child of the Kami lay, one of Bear-Moor named

UNDER-HIGH-STOREHOUSE

bringing a single cross-sword, which he presented to him, on which Young-Three-Hairs-Moor straightway rose up, saying, "I have slept long!" And when he took the cross-sword in his hand, the savage mountain-Kami of Bear-Moor all instantly fell down, cut asunder, while the whole army that had been bewildered and prostrate came to and arose to their feet. The child of the Sky-Kami asked Under-High-Storehouse how he had obtained the cross-sword, and he replied, "I dreamed a dream in which Great-Sky-Shiner spoke to Brave-Awful-Possessing-Male, saying, 'I hear still a sound of uproar from the Central-Land-of-Reed-Plains. Our august children no doubt are disturbed. Since that Land is one that you particularly pacified,[1] do you descend and pacify it.' He, however, replied, 'Though your servant himself will not descend, I have the cross-sword with which I subdued it, and if I send it down, the Land will become tranquil.' To this Great-Sky-Shiner assented, whereon Brave-Awful-Possessing-Male addressed me, saying, 'I will send my sword down by piercing a hole in the roof-ridge of your storehouse and dropping it through. Do you, counting it lucky to see it in the morning, take it and present it to the child of the Sky-Kami.' Thus was I instructed, and replying, 'I will do so,' I straightway awoke. When I looked in my storehouse early next morning, there indeed was a cross-sword standing point upward on its plank floor. I took it and now present it to you." The name by which this sword-Kami is called is

THRUST-SNAP.[2]

It dwells in the Temple of the Kami of Above-the-Rock.[3]

THE EIGHT-FOOTED CROW

After this Young-Three-Hairs-Moor started to advance into the interior, but the mountains were so steep that the troops lacked a way by which to go and they were held back, and wandered about ignorant how to proceed. Then Great-Sky-Shiner (or, as others say, High-Wonder-Producer) instructed the Emperor in a dream of the night, saying, "August son of the Sky-Kami! Take not your imperial way from here into the interior, for the savage Kami are very many. I will send from the Sky an Eight-Footed-Crow, to guide you and make your imperial way behind it as it proceeds through the Land." And there did indeed appear the

EIGHT-FOOTED-CROW [4]

flying down through the Sky-void.

> (*By some it is said that this was the Kami Brave-Horn-Body,[5] grandson of Divine-Producer, who transformed himself into a great Crow and flew to conduct the Sovereign.*)▲

Said Young-Three-Hairs-Moor, "The coming of this Crow accords with my auspicious dream. O glorious! My imperial ancestor, Great-Sky-Shiner, wishes with it to aid me in establishing the imperial rule." Then

SUN-MINISTER [6]

commander of the van, looked up to the Eight-Footed-Crow, and lead-

---

[4] **Ancestor of the District-Chiefs of Kadono and the Palace-Guardian Clan.**
[6] **Ancestor of the Tribe-Masters of the Imperial Guard.***

---

* Sun-Minister presumably derived his own ancestry from the Kami Sky-Great-Sun (see p. 31).

ing a great force struck out a path across the mountains, following its guidance, *and the wicked air was cleared away and there was neither wind nor dust.*ᴬ Young-Three-Hairs-Moor praised him, saying, "You are brave and loyal and guide us successfully. Therefore I give you the new name of Road-Minister." Thus following the Eight-Footed-Crow, Young-Three-Hairs-Moor proceeded westward till he reached the lower portion of the river Good-Moor ⁷ where was one catching fish in a bamboo-trap. The child of the Sky-Kami asked, "Who are you?" He answered, "Your servant's name is

CHILD-OF-OFFERING-HOLDER ⁸

and I am a Kami of the Land." Also, when Young-Three-Hairs-Moor proceeded a little further, a tailed person came out of a radiant well. He was asked, "Who are you?" And he responded, "Your servant's name is

WELL-SHINE ⁹

and I am a Kami of the Land." Then, when he entered the mountains, Young-Three-Hairs-Moor again met a tailed person who came forth, cleaving the rocks. He was asked, "Who are you?" And he replied, "My name is

CHILD-OF-ROCK-PUSH-DIVIDE ¹⁰

and I am a Kami of the Land. I have heard that the son of the Sky-Kami makes his Imperial way through here and have come out to meet you."

THE BROTHERS UKASHI

From there Young-Three-Hairs-Moor proceeded on foot to the District of Uda, to the village of Ukashi. (Therefore people speak of "Ukashi of Uda.") Now there were in Uda two brothers, Chiefs of the District,

UKASHI-ELDER-BROTHER
UKASHI-YOUNGER-BROTHER ¹¹

---

⁸ **Ancestor of the Cormorant Fishers of Ada (Ata).**
⁹ **Ancestor of the Head-men of Yoshino.**
¹⁰ **Ancestor of the Kuzu Tribe of Yoshino***
¹¹ **Ancestor of the Water-Caterers of Uda†**

---

* This was a local tribe of *Emishi* which persisted for centuries. Aston translates the word as "local chiefs," and Chamberlain supposes the word *Kuzu* to be a contraction of *Kuni-nushi* (Land-Chief) which comes to the same thing. When they appear later in the Narrative, however (see pp. 251 and 316), it is as an uncouth rustic tribe with outlandish customs of their own. The name perhaps means "moor men."

† *Mohitori* (*Mondo*). These had in charge the ice and water used on the imperial table.

and the Eight-Footed-Crow was sent in advance to ask them, saying, "The Child of the Sky-Kami proceeds here. Will you serve him?" But Ukashi-Elder-Brother waited for the messenger and sped a humming-arrow at him to compel him to turn back. (From which the place where the arrow fell is called Cape-Barb.) Then, purposing to wait for Young-Three-Hairs-Moor and smite him, he went about to raise an army. But having seen from far off the strength of the imperial forces, he feared to oppose them. So he declared deceitfully that he would offer service, and secretly placing his troops in ambush, built a hall and set a trap in it and waited patiently. But Ukashi-Younger-Brother came respectfully to the gate of the imperial camp, and making obeisance, said, "Your servant's elder brother offers resistance. He has built a hall and devised a snare in it, purposing to invite you to a banquet and thus to injure you. So I have come to give you information. Knowing his treachery, do you take means against it."

So Young-Three-Hairs-Moor sent Sun-Minister and Sky-Round-Eye [12] to reconnoiter, and the latter, verifying the hostile intent, summoned Ukashi-Elder-Brother and cursed him, overwhelmed by rage, shouting violently, "Enter first, miscreant, into the hall which you built to serve Young-Three-Hairs-Moor, and show clearly how you intended to serve him." At which, grasping the hilt of his cross-sword, couching his spear and fixing his arrow, he drove him in. And Ukashi-Elder-Brother, being guilty before the Sky, and the matter not allowing excuse, trod upon the trap which he himself had fixed, and died. Then, dragging him out, they cut him to pieces, and the blood which flowed from his body was ankle-deep. (For this reason the place is called Blood-Plain-of-Uda.) Afterward Ukashi-Younger-Brother gave a great banquet of beef and sakè which Young-Three-Hairs-Moor bestowed upon his army. At this banquet Young-Three-Hairs-Moor sang:

> In the tree of Uda high || For the woodcock fashioned,
> I contrived a snare || Set it up and waited there.
> Yet the wild woodcock || Never comes striking it.
> But against it || Strikes a brave whale.
> (If your elder wife || Ask you for sea-food,
> Then slice her off a bit || Small as soba [13] berries;
> But your younger wife, || If she demand the sea-food,
> Give a piece as big || As sasaki [14] berries!)

At which jest the soldiers shouted "Ah! Ho! The villain! Ah! Ho!" And they laughed the dead man to scorn. (This is called an army song. At present, when it is rendered by the Department of Music, the measurement of great and small is still indicated by means of the hand and the contrast between coarse and fine by the tones of the voice.[15] This rule has been handed down from ancient times.)

Now Young-Three-Hairs-Moor ascended the Peak of Mount High-Storehouse in Uda, from where he could view the whole land, and on the Hill of Land-View were to be seen eighty bandits, at Female-Slope was stationed an army of women, and at Male-Slope an army of men. At Charcoal-Slope was a barrier of burning charcoal. (For these reasons the three slopes were thus named.) He saw also the army of Shiki-Elder-Brother which covered the village of Iharè, and these bandits and slaves held all the strong places and barred the roads against passage. Young-Three-Hairs-Moor was angered and prayed and then slept, when the Sky-Kami came to him in a dream, saying, "Take clay from inside the Shrine of Mount Fragrant [16] and make of it eighty Sky-Platters and sacred urns with which to make sacrifice to the Kami of Sky and Earth. If you then pronounce a solemn curse, the enemy will submit."

(*Now Mount Fragrant was a part of a Mountain in the Sky which had been divided and had fallen upon the Earth. One portion of it is Mount Sky in Iyo Province to which the Kumè Shrine was dedicated. The other is Mount Fragrant of Mountain-Gate Province.*) [A]

(*By some, however, it is said that one fragment fell in Awa Province, in Shikoku, and is now Mount Sky-Norito.*) [B]

When Young-Three-Hairs-Moor awoke, Ukashi-Younger-Brother respectfully said to him, "There are in the Province of Mountain-Gate,[17] in the village of Shiki, eighty bandits, and in the village of Mulberry-Castle are other eighty bandits of copper.[18] As all these are minded to oppose you, your servant is fearful. It would be well to take clay from the Sky-Mount-Fragrant and to make Sky-platters of it and with these to offer sacrifices to the Kami of the Sky- and earth-shrines. Afterward, if you move against the enemy, they will easily be dispersed." Young-Three-Hairs-Moor, having already received the dream as an omen of success, was pleased at Ukashi-Younger-Brother's words and he caused Prince-of-Oak-Root to don the dress of an aged man, with tattered garments and a grass-woven rain-coat and hat, and caused Ukashi-Younger-Brother to don the dress of an old crone and carry a winnowing-tray, and bade them journey to the summit of the Sky-Mount-Fragrant and privately to fetch clay from there, saying to them, "Thus shall I divine whether I shall succeed in founding the empire. Do all watchfully."

Now since the enemy army covered the way it was impossible to pass, and Prince-of-Oak-Root made a prayer, saying, "If the Emperor is to overcome this Land, let our travel be unopposed, but if not, let the bandits bar our way." When he had thus prayed, they went forward, and the enemy, beholding them, laughed uproariously, saying, "Ho, the wretched old man and woman!" And they let them pass, so that they reached the mountain and returned with the clay. (Hence the place from where they took the clay was named Clay-Easy.)

And Young-Three-Hairs-Moor joyfully made eighty platters, eighty Sky-urns, and eighty small urns, and going to the upper waters of the River Nifu, offered sacrifice to the Kami of Sky and Earth. And lo, the reed-plain by the river of Uda became covered with water-foam, by reason of the curse which clung to it. Then he made divinement, saying, "I will mix sweetmeat in these eighty platters without water. If I make sweetmeat thus, I shall be certain that I will pacify the empire without the use of weapons." So he mixed the sweetmeat, which came into being of its own accord. A second time he made divinement, saying, "I will plunge these Sky-urns into the river Nifu. If the fishes, great and small, become drunken and float downstream like fir tree [19] leaves, then I shall not fail to establish this Land, but if not, my effort will come to nothing." At that he plunged the urns in the river, mouth down, and presently the fish came up gasping and floated down with the current. So Prince-of-Oak-Root, observing this, told Young-Three-Hairs-Moor, who rejoiced greatly, and tearing up a spindle tree of five hundred branches, worshiped all the Kami. (This was the beginning of the custom of setting up sacred urns.) And he commanded Sun-Minister, saying, "I am about to celebrate a visible festival to High-Producer, and I appoint you ruler of the festival with the title Princess [20]-Sacred. The urns which are set up shall be the food of the festival." Then he drew up his army and marched forth.

THE GROUND-SPIDER OF OSAKA AND THE BROTHERS SHIKI AND KURAJI [21]

First Young-Three-Hairs-Moor overcame and slew eighty bandits at Mount Kunimi; whereon, having won the victory, he sang:

Like as the shell-fish [22] || Go creeping round about
The huge rock || In the sea of Isè where
Blows the wind divine, || Like as the shell-fish,
O, our sons! O, our sons! || Like as the shell-fish,
So will we, creeping round them, || Smite and utterly end them.

(By the great-rock is meant the Hill of Kunimi.) Since there were many of the enemy still remaining whose whereabouts was not known, Young-Three-Hairs-Moor said privately to Sun-Minister, "Do you take with you a large force and make a great roofed-pit [23] at the village of Osaka.[24] Then we shall prepare a great banquet and invite the enemy and capture them." And Sun-Minister, as he was bade, dug the roofed-pit at Osaka and selecting the bravest of his soldiers, waited in it, mingling with the enemy. So when Young-Three-Hairs-Moor made his imperial way there, some eighty bandits, tailed Ground-Spiders,[25] were there awaiting him. The child of the Sky-Kami gave the banquet to the eighty bandits, appointing eighty victualers, one for each of them, and these he girded with swords, and commanded the serving-men, saying: "When you have made all of them drunk with sakè, I will stand up and sing, and when you hear the sound of my song, cut them all down."

So arranged, they took their seats and the drinking proceeded, while the Ground-Spiders, unaware of the plot, became drunk without reserve. Seeing this, Young-Three-Hairs-Moor sang the song by which he gave the signal to cut them down:

> Unto the huge || Roofed-pit of Osaka
> Many folk have come || And wait within it.
> But though many folk || In it are waiting,
> We, of warriors born, || Augustly mighty,
> Will with broad-tempered, || Our true hard-tempered, weapons,
> Smite and utterly end them. || We of warriors born,
> Augustly mighty, || Wielding broad-tempered,
> Our true hard-tempered, sabres, || Let us wait not to cut them down!

(*It is said by some, however, that Sun-Minister stood up and sang this song, and not the Emperor, and by others that he sang it at the Emperor's private behest.*)

And when the troops heard the song, they drew their broad-tempered swords and put the bandits to death, all of them, so that no mouth [26] was left. Then the soldiers were overjoyed, and looking up to the Sky, laughed. And Sun-Minister sang:

> Ha! It is now! || Ha! It is now!
> Ah! Ah! || Now to act!
> It is even now, O our sons! [27] || It is even now, O our sons!

(Thus arose the custom soldiers have of singing this song and afterward laughing boisterously.) Again he sang thus:

> But a single Emishi [28] || To one hundred men.
> So the saying goes, and yet || These do not even struggle.

Said Young-Three-Hairs-Moor, then, "Though the chiefs of the bandits have now been slain, there are yet more than ten companies of such miscreants who resist. Their whereabouts cannot be learned if we remain in one place. Therefore let us move our army." So they made their way against the Princess of Shiki. First the Eight-Footed-Crow was sent as a messenger, and flying to the camp of

SHIKI-ELDER

it cried, "The child of the Sky-Kami desires you. Make haste!" But Shiki-Elder was angered and said, "I have heard of the coming of the Sky-Kami and am resentful. Therefore, O Crow, your voice is a hateful one!" And he discharged an arrow from his bow against it. So the Crow flew to the dwelling of

SHIKI-YOUNGER [29]

and cried, "The child of the Sky-Kami summons you. Make haste!" Shiki-Younger was filled with fear, and wove eight oak-leaf trays, and put food upon them, and offered them to the Crow, saying, "O Crow, well have you summoned me. Hearing of the coming of the Sky-Kami, your slave has been fearful by morning and by evening." And he came before Young-Three-Hairs-Moor and said, "My elder brother has gathered eighty bandits to oppose you. It will be well to go against him at once." So Young-Three-Hairs-Moor consulted with his leaders and said, "What is to be done?" They answered, "It will be well to send Shiki-Younger ahead to convince him and also to give counsel to the brothers

KURAJI-ELDER
KURAJI-YOUNGER.

If they still refuse submission, then battle should be given." Shiki-Younger was therefore sent, but nevertheless Shiki-Elder remained evil-minded and would not submit. Then said Prince-of-Oak-Root, "It will be well to despatch a small force by the Osaka road, so that, seeing them, the robber-slaves will go against them with their main army. We can then hasten with our strongest force to Charcoal-Slope, sprinkle water on the burning charcoal,[30] and taking them unawares, put them to rout." This plan Young-Three-Hairs-Moor approved and it was carried out. Now from the attacking, with its captures, and the battling with its victories, the warriors were wearied, so Young-Three-Hairs-Moor heartened his leaders and soldiers with this song:

> Here in the battle, || Our shields in a linkèd line,
> As we forward go, || Watching between the tree boles
> On Inasa's hill, || We are nigh famishing.
> Ho! then ye keepers || Of island cormorants,
> Come ye now to our rescue!

Then the strongest force crossed Charcoal-Slope and fell upon the robber-slaves' rear, so that, attacked on both sides, they fled in rout and Shiki-Elder was slain. Also they slew the two chieftains Kuraji-Elder and Kuraji-Younger.

THE PRINCE- AND PRINCESS-OF-ISÈ

Now it befell that Young-Three-Hairs-Moor laid his command upon

SKY-SUN-LORD [31]

saying, "There is a Land toward the east which you may subjugate," and he gave him a sword as a token. So Sky-Sun-Lord obeyed the command and proceeded several hundred ri to where was a Kami named

PRINCE-OF-ISÈ [32]

who was a son of the Kami Great-Land-Master,[33] and a brother of

PRINCESS-OF-ISÈ.

Him he asked whether he would offer the Land to the descendant of the Sky-Kami, and Prince-of-Isè replied, "It was I who found this Land and through long years I have ruled it, therefore I will not obey your order." But when Sky-Sun-Lord would have sent an army to slay him, the Kami feared and said, "I will offer my entire Land to the Sky-descendant, nor will I remain here."

Then Sky-Sun-Lord bade another ask Prince-of-Isè, "By what sign will you show when you depart?" And Prince-of-Isè answered, "This night I will raise an eight-fold wind and will cause the sea-water to rise, and I will ride on the waves to the eastward. This shall be the sign of my departure." So Sky-Sun-Lord armed his host and watched, and in the middle of the night a hurricane arose from every side and raised great billows, and land and sea shone as bright as in the daytime, and at length Prince-of-Isè went riding on the waves to the eastward. (From this came the ancient name Swift-Wind-Isè Province.) Prince-of-Isè was commanded to reside in Lime-Tree-Moor Province: he now settles at the Shrine of Hole-Stone [34] in Iga Province.[A]

When the ancestors of

BOAR-HAND-OF-CLOTHES-SEWING

settled in the Land of Harima, together with the ancestors of

GOOD-SWORD-OF-HAN-MAN [35]

the houses they built would not remain quiet, so they erected a shrine at the foot of the mountain and dedicated it to Prince-of-Isè and Princess-of-Isè, after which all their houses remained quiet. The place was called Isè-Moor and their village was called Isè. As to the Land of Isè, Sky-Sun-Lord pacified it, and Young-Three-Hairs-Moor was greatly pleased, and named the Land after the name of that Kami and gave it to Sky-Sun-Lord to govern. He gave him also an estate at the village of Without-Ears [36] in Mountain-Gate Province. In Isè Province Sky-Sun-Lord slew rebellious Kami and chastised such as withheld their obedience, made boundaries with mountains and rivers, and fixed districts and villages.[A]

Now smoke arose at the mountain ridge of Garisa,[37] in Cross-Meet,[38] and Sky-Sun-Lord, looking, said, "There a chief of the people may reside," and sent a messenger to observe. The messenger, returning, reported that at the place was a female Kami named

GREAT-LAND-JEWEL

who had made the fire. Sky-Sun-Lord went there and she sent a messenger to receive him, bidding the messenger build a bridge. Sky-Sun-Lord, however, arrived there before the bridge was completed, and the messenger laid down bows of azusa [39] wood on which he crossed. So Great-Land-Jewel came, with her daughter

PRINCESS-WATER-SASARA [40]

and they received Sky-Sun-Lord at the village of Hill-Foot in Soil-Bridge,[41] at which he was pleased, saying, "I have crossed and met a Princess." (From this the place was called Cross-Meet.) Sky-Sun-Lord wedded Princess-Water-Sasara and begot

BRAVE-YOTSUKA.[B]

PRINCE-LONG-MARROW OF FISH-HAWK

After this Young-Three-Hairs-Moor made a campaign against Prince-Long-Marrow [42] of Fish-Hawk, and many times the Imperial army fought him but did not gain the victory. But suddenly there miraculously appeared a Fish-Hawk [43] of the color of gold, which came flying and perched on the end of Young-Three-Hairs-Moor's bow. The bird was of a radiance like to lightning and its brilliance dazzled the troops of Prince-Long-Marrow so that they could not fight. (For this reason the village there, which was named Long-Marrow, was renamed Village-of-Fish-Hawk.) [44] Now ever since the smiting of Five-River-Currents in the battle at Kusaka by the arrow from which he died, Young-Three-Hairs-Moor had been resentful, and he desired to slay all this folk. So he sang:

> Born of an army || Augustly powerful,
> We will smite and end || The one-stemmed stinking garlic
> In the millet-field, || Stem of root, root and sproutings,
> Smite and utterly end them!

And also he sang this song:

> Born of an army || Augustly powerful,
> We beneath the hedge || Planted ginger, which ever
> In my mouth rankles. || I shall never forget it.
> Smite and utterly end them!

(These songs are called army songs, inasmuch as they were sung by the army.)

After this he made the attack. Then Prince-Long-Marrow sent a messenger on foot to Young-Three-Hairs-Moor, saying, "There was of old a child of the *Sky-Shining, Earth-Shining* Sky-Kami, named *Comb-Jewel-Plenty-Swift-Sun*,[45] who descended through the void from the Sky, riding in a Sky-Rock-Boat, and seeing this Land, gave it the name of Sky-Sun-Mountain-Gate and dwelt here, wedding my younger sister Princess-Three-Cook-House,[46] to whom was born the Kami Sweet-True-Hand. Therefore I served Plenty-Swift-Sun as my lord. Are there two descendants of the children of the Sky-Kami? Why should another call himself thus and come to rob people of their Land? I have pondered this, but cannot accept it." Young-Three-Hairs-Moor responded, "The Sky-Kami has many children. If your lord is truly his child, then assuredly he possesses something that may be shown as evidence." So Prince-Long-Marrow brought one of Plenty-Swift-Sun's Sky-feathered arrows and a quiver and exhibited them. Then Young-Three-Hairs-Moor showed him one of his own Sky-feathered arrows and his quiver, and at the sight Prince-Long-Marrow was taken aback; but nevertheless he clung to his intention. Sweet-True-Hand, however, proved that the Sky-Kami had bestowed the realm on Young-Three-Hairs-Moor, and that Prince-Long-Marrow was of a disposition which did not comprehend the right relation of vassal to lord, and Young-Three-Hairs-Moor slew him and Sweet-True-Hand surrendered with his army.

> (*Some accounts* [47] *say that Plenty-Swift-Sun was not dead at this time and that it was he himself and his son, Sweet-True-Hand, who slew Prince-Long-Marrow.*)

So Young-Three-Hairs-Moor, knowing that Plenty-Swift-Sun had descended from the Sky, praised Sweet-True-Hand's loyal service, *saying*, "*Inasmuch as Prince-Long-Marrow was of a violent disposition though of clouded intelligence, and had great strength, none was able to vanquish him. Without joining him, however, you have submitted to the imperial arms. Receive Our praise for your loyalty.*" And he presented him with a divine sword, as reward of his great merit. (*This sword is called Sword-of-Spirit-of-Snap, Sashi-Snap, Brave-Snap, or Fruitful-Snap.*)[48]

On his part, Sweet-True-Hand offered to Young-Three-Hairs-Moor the ten sorts of divine treasures which Plenty-Swift-Sun had received from the ancestors of the Sky-Kami. Thus the favor of Young-Three-Hairs-Moor was given him more increasingly, and Sweet-True-Hand subdued the riotous, leading the Sky-guard, and as head of the army, pacified the whole country.[A]

At this time there were in various places treacherous people who lived *always in holes in the ground, whom, for this reason, Young-Three-Hairs-Moor called Ground-Spiders.*[49] (*It was at this time that the name was first used.*)[A]

There were Ground-Spiders in three places: there was Chief-of-Nihiki at Hill-Spur of Hata in Sofu District, Kosè-Hofuri [50] at Bottom-Slope of Wani, and Wi-Hofuri at Hill-Spur of Nagara in Hosomi. These, vaunting their strength, were unsubmissive, and Young-Three-Hairs-Moor sent against them separate companies and slew all of them. Other Ground-Spiders at the village of Taka-Owari had short bodies and long arms and legs, like pigmies, and the troops wove nets of mulberry-fiber [51] which they threw over them and so slew them. (For this cause the village was after that called Mulberry-Castle.[52] Its name of old time was Kataru or Katatachi. Also, because of the many evil-disposed gathered there, and the great army that filled the land, it was called Assembling. The place where he built a castle was called Castle-Field, the field where the enemy fell prostrate and dead in the fight, pillowed on their forearms, was called Face-Pillow-Field, and the field where the imperial army had battled was called Brave-Field.)

THE AUGUST INSTITUTION OF THE SKY-RULE

Then said Young-Three-Hairs-Moor, "For six years our expedition has gone eastward. While the unsubmissive people of the borders are not yet rooted out, in the land's center are no longer wind and dust, so let us build here an august capital. And since things are still unfinished and the people ignorant, dwelling in nests or in pits, it is well to lay down laws and uphold justice. So, throwing open the mountain-ways and clearing the forest, let us rear a palace, that I may take on the imperial dignity and carry on the line of the Sky's sons. Afterward the capital shall be extended on all sides. The plain to the southwest of Mount Unebi is the land's center." From this the place which he chose was called Oak-Planted-Place.[53] So there Young-Three-Hairs-Moor founded his palace pillars stoutly on the rock-bottom and reared its cross-beams to the Plain-of-the-High-Sky, and dwelt in the Palace of Oak-Planted-Place and ruled the Sky-Under.

SKY-TOMI

a descendant of Great-Jewel, was ordered to take command of the descendants of the Kami Hand-Placing-Soil-Carrier and Prince-Measure-Knowing and to erect this palace with timber from the mountain, using for the first time sacred axes and mattocks. And he built a wondrous palace and threw open its imperial doors. (His descendants now reside in the two villages of August-Wood and Araka in Name-Grass District in

Tree Province, the place in which settled the Abstainer Clan who worked the timber being called August-Wood, and that in which settled the Abstainer Clan who erected the palace being called Araka.) Also Sky-Tomi was commanded to take in charge many families of the Abstainer Clan and to make various kinds of Kami treasures, such as mirrors, jewels, spears, shields, and cloth of mulberry and of hemp. A descendant of Hand-Placing-Soil-Carrier made spears. (His descendants are now separated and in Sanuki Province. Each year they offer, beside tribute, eight hundred spears.) A descendant of Feather-Shining-Jewel made prayer jewels.[54] (His descendants now reside in Sacred-Quarter Province and each year offer jewels as tribute.) Also a descendant of Sky-Sun-Eagle made cloth of mulberry and of hemp, as well as rough cloth.[55] Sky-Tomi was moreover commanded to take in charge the descendants of Sky-Sun-Eagle, and having searched out a fertile Land, to send them to Millet-Province to plant the seeds of grain and of hemp. (Their descendants now reside in that province and in the year of a Taïsensaï[56] they offer mulberry cloth, rough cloth, and various kinds of articles. It is from this cause that one district is named Hemp-Planting District.) Again Sky-Tomi searched out a fertile Land and dividing the Abstainer Clan, led them into the Land of Ah-My-Wife, where they planted hemp and grain. (The place where good hemp grew is called Land-of-Hemp,[57] and the place where grew the trees for mulberry cloth is called Yuki District. The place where the Abstainer Clan of Millet settled was named Millet District. It is the present Millet Province.) There Sky-Tomi built a shrine for Great-Jewel, which is now called Millet-Shrine. Also, by the command of High-Producer and Great-Sky-Shiner, shrines were erected to the Kami High-Producer, and to the following Kami:

JEWEL-PILE-WONDROUS-PRODUCER
LIFE-WONDROUS-PRODUCER
SUFFICIENT-WONDROUS-PRODUCER

(who, some [58] say, is Great-Land-Master), Great-Palace-Female,[59] Eight-Fold-Thing-Sign-Master, Jewel-of-Storehouse-Rice [60] (all of whom are now worshiped by priestesses), Sky-Hand-Strength-Male (who is worshiped by the priestesses of the imperial-gate), and to

LIFE-ISLAND

(who is the spirit of the Great-Eight-Islands and is worshiped by the priestesses of Life-Island), and

SIT-PLACE [61]

(who is the spirit of the site of the imperial palace, and is now worshiped *by the priestesses of Sit-Place.)*

MAGNATE-OF-SUN

had command of the Warrior-Clan and guarded the imperial gate, directing its opening and closing.

> *(Those who hold that Plenty-Swift-Sun was not dead at this time, say he had command of the Army Clan of the house and had in his charge the making and disposition of swords and shields.)*

Sky-Tomi, in command of many of the Abstainer Clan, lifted up the Sky-tokens, the Mirror and the Sword, and set them up in the palace, and hung the Jewels, making offerings to them, and he made a prayer for the palace festival and a festival for the imperial gate. After that the Army Clan placed at hand their spears and shields, the imperial guard and the warriors placed at hand their weapons and opened the gate, making the people of Lands on every side attend to observe how venerable was the Sky-rule. Now at this time the distance between the Sovereign and the Kami was not yet great: they were in the same palace and on the same floor, and there was no distinction between the affairs of the Kami and of the government. A storehouse was erected in the palace, which was called Sacred-Storehouse, and the Abstainer Clan had permanent charge of it. Sky-Tomi was put in command of many families who made articles for the Grand Offerings.

SKY-TANEKO

a descendant of Sky-Beckoning-Ancestor-Lord, was commanded to purge away Sky-offenses and Earth-offenses. Now Sky-offenses are those which had already been committed;[62] Earth-offenses are those which were committed by the people. The festival enclosure[63] was erected on Mount Tomi. Sky-Tomi arranged offerings and made a prayer, with a festival for the Sky-Kami and for many Land-Kami, requiting their favor. Thus the Intercessor Clan and the Abstainer Clan had the management of the festivals, the Clan-Chieftainesses of Monkey[64] were charged with the Kami-Music, and other families held other offices.[A]

After he had thus cleared and subdued the realm and had control of the Great-Eight-Islands, Young-Three-Hairs-Moor was called also Prince-Assembling-of-Divine-Mountain-Gate. *(At this time, when he assumed the imperial dignity, the era of Nippon began.)* On the day he first began the Sky-institution he transmitted to Sun-Minister, with the Army Clan, secret cogent verses and upside-down words[65] to ward off evil influences. *(From this arose the custom of using upside-down words.)* Afterward he dispensed rewards, granting to the army a place on the river-bank west of Unebi, named Army-village. (Thus it received its name.) Also he made Prince-of-Oak-Root Ruler of the Land of Mountain-Gate.

Later Young-Three-Hairs-Moor inquired of Prince-of-Oak-Root what was his high descent, and he replied, "I am the great Kami Leech,[66] child of your divine ancestors, and came to defend your rule. I have in my sway all the products of the land. Taking the ricefields under my protection they become fruitful, taking merchandise under my protection I cause trade to flourish.[67] When I guard the sowing of seed abundant harvests are given. When I aid troops in battle I bring victory. When I direct the Imperial concerns the Government prospers. I am the Kami who has in charge all the precious things of the Land." Having made this declaration he withdrew to his abode in the Land of Hiroba.[A]

Young-Three-Hairs-Moor made Ukashi-Younger-Brother District-Chief of Takeda. Shiki-Younger he made District-Chief of Shiki, and he made a certain one named

TSUNÈ

Ruler of the Land of Mulberry-Castle. The Eight-Footed-Crow also received recompense. Then the Sky-Sovereign, saying, "All enemies have now been made submissive and the seas are at peace," established sacred terraces on Fish-Hawk Hill, which were called Persimmon-Plain-of-Upper-Little-Moor and Persimmon-Plain-of-Lower-Little-Moor, on which is worshiped his imperial ancestors, the Sky-Kami.

THE SKY FEATHER-ROBE DAMSEL

Now Sky-Beckoning-Ancestor-Lord [68] had as son the Kami

SKY-PUSH-MAN

whose descendant in the fourth generation abode in the District of Ikako, in the Province of Omi, and was named

IKATOMI [69]

From the western slope of a mountain he beheld eight celestial beings descend from the Sky in the form of white birds, to bathe at Minamitsu on the bay of Yako. By reason of their remarkable appearance thinking them Kami, Ikatomi went to observe them. He was then unable to leave them, and sent a white dog to steal the feather-garment of one. The dog stole that of the youngest and Ikatomi hid it. The celestial ones, becoming aware of him, soared up to the Sky; only the youngest could not fly

---

[69] **Ancestor of the Tribe-Masters of Iga.**

away, her return to the Sky being for long postponed, and she became an inhabitant of the earth. (The spot where they bathed is now called Kami-Shore.) Ikatomi lay with her and she gave birth to two sons and two daughters

MISHIRU-MALE
NASHITOMI
PRINCESS-ISERI
PRINCESS-NASERI.

Afterward she found the Sky-feather-robe which she had worn, and donning it, departed up to the Sky, so that Ikatomi lived alone and in sorrow in his dwelling.[A]

(By some it is said, however, that, discovering that he had stolen the feather-robe, the celestial being wept and besought him to return it, and that he, pitying her, did so, requesting in return that she dance for him a celestial dance. This she did, after which she soared up to the Sky.) [B]

(Others, again, say that these eight celestial beings came to bathe in a well called True-Well [70] at the top of Mount-Land,[71] in Yosa District, Tango Province, where there is now a morass. There lived there an old couple whose names were

WANASA-OKINA
WANASA-OÖMA

who, going to the well, stole the robes of one of them. So when those who had their robes soared up to the Sky, the one who had none remained there, concealing her body in the water, alone and ashamed. Then the old man said to her, "I beseech you to dwell with us as our daughter." She replied, "How can I help but obey you, since I alone remain among mankind. But I ask you to return to me my robe." Said he, "Would you then deceive me?" She answered, "The chief virtue of celestial beings is sincerity. Why do you disbelieve me and refuse to allow me to wear my robe?" Said the old man, "It is a common thing in this world to have doubt and to lack faith. For this reason only I did not permit you to wear your robe." So he brought her to his dwelling, where she lived for ten years. She was skilful at mixing sakè, one cup of which would cure every kind of ailment, and in payment for this sakè, articles sufficient to fill a wagon were sent to the house, through which means the couple became rich and the land productive. (Therefore the place was called Village-of-Land-Shape.[72]) Today it is called Village-of-Soil-Swamp.[73] Then the old couple said to her, "You are not our daughter:

we did but borrow you for a time. Depart, therefore, quickly." At that the celestial being wept and lamented, gazing to the Sky and stooping to the Earth. Said she, "I came not here of my own will, but of yours. Why have you begun to hate me? Why do you bid me depart thus suddenly?" At this the old couple, angered, bade her depart, and she went out from their gate sadly and with tears. Then she said to the people of the village, "For a long while I have degraded myself among mankind and now I cannot go to the Sky, neither have I kin to depend upon. What shall I do?" So, gazing up to the sky, she sang

>Now toward the sky || Lift I mine eyes, but only
>Mist is before them.
>Lost is my home-way, I bide || Knowing not whither to go.

There on she departed and coming to Rough-Sea-Village,[74] she said to the people, "When I consider the wish of that old couple, my heart is like a rough sea." (For this reason the place is so named.) From there she went to the village of Weep-Tree [75] in Tamba Province, where she leaned against a keyaki tree [76] and wept. (For this reason the place is so named.) From there she went to the Village of Comfort [77] in Ship-Wood, in Bamboo-Moor District, where she said to the people, "Here my heart has become comforted." At this village she remained. She is the Kami

FEMALE-OF-FRUITFUL-FOOD [78]

who dwells in the Shrine of Nagu, in Bamboo-Moor-District.[A]

THE WEDDING OF YOUNG-THREE-HAIRS-MOOR AND PRINCESS-TATARA-STARTLED-GOOD-PRINCESS

When he dwelt in Sun-Facing, the Sky-Sovereign had wedded Princess-Ahira as consort. Now as he sought afresh for a beautiful damsel whom he should make his Empress, Sun-Minister said to him, "The Kami

DITCH-STAKE-OF-THREE-ISLANDS [79]

has a daughter who is of a beauty admired by Great-Land-Master, the Great Kami of Three-Threads,[80] and whose name is

PRINCESS-JEWEL-COMB." [81]

So the Great Kami transformed himself into an arrow painted red, and when the lovely damsel evacuated in the privy, he transfixed her vagina from the rear. At that she was frightened and rose up and fled, trembling. At once she took the arrow and placed it by her bed, and on a sudden it became a comely youth who quickly joined her in wedlock and begot a daughter who was named

PRINCESS-VAGINA-TATARA-FLEEING.[82]

(Her name was changed to Princess-Tatara-Startled-Good-Princess because it is unseemly to make mention of the vagina.) By reason of her birth she is called the child of a Kami.

(*By some, however, Princess-Tatara-Startled-Good-Princess is said to have been a daughter of the Kami August-Luck-Spirit-August-Wondrous-Spirit. Again, others say that Eight-Fold-Thing-Sign-Master, son of the Kami Great-Land-Master, having transformed himself into a bear-wani eight hiro long, had intercourse with Princess-Jewel-Comb and begot a son named*

SKY-SOUTHWEST-WIND-WONDROUS-SOUTHWEST-WIND

and Princess-Vagina-Tatara-Fleeing.)

At the time seven lovely damsels were playing on the Takasazhi Moor, this same Princess-Tatara-Startled-Good-Princess being one of them, and Sun-Minister spoke to the Sovereign in a song:

Seven maidens || On Takasazhi Moor
Of Mountain-Gate. || Which shall sleep, her limbs
Interlacing with your own?

Now Princess-Tatara-Startled-Good-Princess was standing first amid the damsels, and at once the Sovereign, gazing on them, knew in his heart that it was she standing there at the front, and sang in reply:

Ah, then I will choose || With that one to interlace
(Lovely!) who stands at the front.

So Sun-Minister informed her of the Sky-Sovereign's decree, at which she, looking into Sun-Minister's eyes, that were long and sharp,[83] sang in her surprise:

* * *
* * * * [84]
Wherefore are the long, sharp eyes?

And Sun-Minister sang in reply:

My long sharp eyes || They are thus to discover
Thee, O maiden, instantly.

At which she declared that she would offer respectful service. Now the dwelling of the princess was upon the bank of the River Mountain-Lily, which was so called because the mountain-lily grew there abundantly, and the Sky-Sovereign made his imperial way there and slept there one sojourn.[85] Afterward, when she came to enter the palace as Empress, he sang:

On the reed moorland, || Within a humid cabin,
Spreading mats sedge-wove || The one atop its fellow,
So we two took our slumber.[86]

The names of the august children he begot by her were

PRINCE-EIGHT-WELLS [87]
DIVINE-EIGHT-WELLS-EARS [88]
DIVINE-LAGOON-RIVER-EARS [89]

Now on a time the Sky-Sovereign ascended the Hill of Hotsuma in Young-Divine, and gazing on the shape of the Land, said, "Of what a lovely Land are we the lords! Though a Land of paper-mulberry bark, yet it resembles a dragonfly licking its hinder parts." (From this the Land received its name of Dragonfly Island.)

Altogether the years of the Sky-Sovereign, Prince-Assembling-of-Divine-Mountain-Gate, were one hundred and thirty-seven (or, as some say, one hundred and twenty-seven). He died in the Palace of Oak-Planted-Place and his grave is on the top of Oak-Ridge on the northern side of Mount-Unebi,[90] in Mountain-Gate Province.

THE EMPEROR DIVINE-LAGOON-RIVER-EARS (TRANQUILLITY) [91]

Divine-Lagoon-River-Ears was of lovely appearance and as a child possessed a man's strength. As a man he was of great size, accomplished in knowledge of war and of firm will. He was, moreover, of a filial mind and at the death of the Sky-Sovereign he himself conducted the funeral ritual. The elder half-brother, Rudder-Ears,[92] wedded the Empress, Princess-Tatara-Startled-Good-Princess. He was now of mature age [93] and of experience in high matters, so that affairs were put into his hands, and Divine-Lagoon-River-Ears made him his comrade. He was, however, evil-minded, and his authority becoming potent during the time of the imperial mourning, he plotted secretly to slay his three younger brothers. Their parent, Princess-Tatara-Startled-Good-Princess, learning of this, lamented and apprised them in a song which said:

---

[87] **Ancestor of the Tribe-Masters of Mamuta (in Kawachi Province) and Teshima (in Settsu Province).**

[88] **Ancestor of the Magnates of Oho (in Yamato Province), of Niwa and of Shimada (in Owari Province): of the Magnates and Rulers of the Sazaki-Clan; of the Tribe-Masters of the Chihisaka *- and Sakahi †-Clans and of the Tsukushi granaries; of the Clan-Chiefs of Hi ‡ (in Tsukushi), Okida (in Toyo Province) and Aso (in Higo); of the Governors of Tsukè (in Yamato Province) and Funaki (in Isè); of the Rulers of Wohasè and of the Lands of Iyo (in Shikoku), Shinano and Naka (in Hitachi Province), Nagasa (in Kazusa Province) and Iwaki in Michinoku (northern Japan).**

---

* *Chihisaka*: little child (see p. 279, n. 12).
† Boundary.   ‡ Yet see p. 128, n. 6.

> From Sawi's river || Cross-wise clouds have arisen;
> Rustle the tree-leaves || On Unabi's mountain side.
> Soon the wind will rise and blow.

And again she sang:

> On Unabi's Mount || What repose as daylight clouds,
> When the night has come
> Surely will be blowing wind. || List the rustling of the leaves!

At this her children, hearing and understanding, took alarm and purposing to slay Rudder-Ears, they caused

PRINCE-YOUNG

of the Bow-Makers-Clan to make a bow, and the smith of Mountain-Gate,

SKY-MARA [94]

to make true deer arrowheads, and the Arrow-Clan to make an arrow. Now when the bow and arrows were prepared, Rudder-Ears was lying alone on a great couch in a hall in Side-Mound.[95] So Divine-Lagoon-River-Ears said to his elder brother, Divine-Eight-Wells-Ears, "It is a favorable time. We have no partner in this plan, which is yours and mine also. While I open the door of the hall, do you enter with the weapons and slay him." Accordingly Divine-Eight-Wells-Ears took the weapons and went in, but his arms and legs shook so that he could not shoot the arrow. Then the younger brother took the bow and arrows from the elder brother and shot two shafts, the first of which struck Rudder-Ears in the breast and the second in the back, and so slew him. (From which, in praise, he was called also Brave-Lagoon-River-Ears.)

Divine-Eight-Wells-Ears resigned the supremacy to the younger Divine-Lagoon-River-Ears, saying, "I could not slay our enemy, but you have shown divine courage and were able to slay him. Therefore, though I am the elder brother, it is not fitting that I should be the higher. It is better that you should make the Sky-estate radiant and assume the rule of our imperial ancestors. So do you be the higher and rule beneath the Sky, while I become a priest, assisting and serving you in attendance on the worship of the Sky- and Earth-Kami." Later Divine-Eight-Wells-Ears died, and his grave is on the northern side of Mount Unebi.

So Divine-Lagoon-River-Ears dwelt in the Palace of High-Mound in Mulberry-Castle and ruled the empire. This Sky-Sovereign wedded

PRINCESS-RIVER-FORK [96]

---

[96] **Ancestress of the District-Chiefs of Shiki.***

---

* But see p. 116, n. 8.

who was daughter of the District-Chief of Shiki, and begot

PRINCE-OF-SHIKI-TAMADÈ-EARS.

His august years were forty-five (or, as some say, eighty-four). His grave is on the mound of Ibis-Ricefield,[97] in Mountain-Gate.

THE EMPEROR PRINCE-OF-SHIKI-TAMADÈ-EARS (PEACE) [98]

Prince-of-Shiki-Tamadè-Ears was twenty-nine years of age when he assumed the imperial rule, and removing the capital to Hard-Rock,[99] dwelt in the Palace of Floating-Hole. He wedded

PRINCESS-AKUTO [1]

and the two begot

PRINCE-ELDER-BROTHER-OF-TOKONÈ
PRINCE-GREAT-MOUNTAIN-GATE-SUKI-FRIEND
PRINCE-OF-SHIKI.[2]

There were born to Prince-of-Shiki two kings [3]

(UNNAMED) [4]
WA-CHI-TSU-MI.

The latter had two daughters,

ELDER-SISTER-HAË [5]
YOUNGER-SISTER-HAË.

This Sky-Sovereign's august years were forty-nine (or, as others say, fifty-seven) and his grave is in the private precincts of Mount Unebi.

THE EMPEROR PRINCE-GREAT-MOUNTAIN-GATE-SUKI-FRIEND (WARM-VIRTUE) [6]

Prince-Great-Mountain-Gate-Suki-Friend was forty-five years of age when he assumed the imperial rule, and removing the capital to Karu,[7] dwelt in the Palace of Boundary-Mound. He wedded

---

[2] Ancestor of the Tribe-Masters of Itsukahi.
[4] Ancestor of the Country-Lords of Suchi, of Nabari and of Minu (all of these in Iga).*

---

* A portion of Isè.

PRINCESS-VAST-TRUE-YOUNG [8]

and there were born to the two

PRINCE-LORD-SHINÈ-OF-MIMA
PRINCE-RUDDER.[9]

His august years were five and forty and his grave is above the valley of Sandy-Waste [10] by Mount Unebi.

THE EMPEROR PRINCE-LORD-SHINÈ-OF-MIMA
(FILIAL-PIETY-BRIGHT [11])

Prince-Lord-Shinè-of-Mima, removing the capital to Mulberry-Castle, dwelt in the Palace of Ikegokoro at Kami-of-Waki. He wedded Princess-Perfectly-Ornamented,[12] and there were born to the two

PRINCE-SKY-GREAT-PERFECT [13]

PRINCE-PERFECT-GREAT-MOUNTAIN-GATE-COUNTRY-GREAT-MAN.

Now when he had built a palace in the land of Harima, a great stag belled, whereon he said, "A stag bells!" So the place was named District-of-Stag-Ma.

His august years were ninety-three, and his grave is on Mount Hakata [14] at Waki-no-Kami.

THE EMPEROR PRINCE-PERFECT-GREAT-MOUNTAIN-
GATE-COUNTRY-GREAT-MAN
(FILIAL-PIETY-PEACE)[15]

Prince-Perfect-Great-Mountain-Gate-Country-Great-Man, removing the capital to Cave, in Mulberry-Castle, dwelt in the Palace of Dragonfly-Island. He wedded his brother's daughter

PRINCESS-GREAT [16]

and there were born to the two

---

[8] **Ancestress of the District-Chiefs of Shiki.***

[9] **Ancestor of the Lords of Shinu and of Takè in Tajima, and of the Country-Lords of Ashiwi.**

[13] **Ancestor of the Magnates of Kasuga, Ichihiwi and Ohoyakè (in Yamato Province), Ahata (in Yamashiro), Wonu (in Omi), Kaki-No-Moto, Ohosaka, and Ana (in Bingo), Taki (in Tamba), Haguri and Chita (Districts in Owari), Muza (a District in Kagusa) and Tsunuyama: of the Clan-Chiefs of Ihitaka and of Ichishi (in Isè); and of the Rulers of the Land of Chika-Tsu-Omi.**

---

* But see p. 114, n. 96.

COMPLETE-ADVANCER-OF-GREAT-MAISE
PRINCE-VAST-JEWEL-GREAT-MOUNTAIN-GATE-LORD.

His august years were one hundred and twenty-three, and his grave is on the mound of Tamadè Hill.[17]

THE EMPEROR PRINCE-VAST-JEWEL-GREAT-MOUNTAIN-GATE-LORD
(FILIAL-PIETY-SPIRIT)[18]

Prince-Vast-Jewel-Great-Mountain-Gate-Lord, removing the capital to Black-Ricefield,[19] dwelt in the Palace of Hut-Door. He wedded

PRINCESS-BEAUTIFUL[20]

who was the daughter of the Land-Chief of Shiki,

GREAT-EYES[21]

and there was born to the two

PRINCE-LAND-RULER-GREAT-MOUNTAIN-GATE-LORD.

Also he wedded Elder-Sister-Haë, by whom he begot

PRINCE-SASHI-KATA-LORD[22]
PRINCE-VALOROUS-ADVANCER-PRINCE[23]

Also he wedded Younger-Sister-Haë, younger sister of Elder-Sister-Haë, and begot

PRINCE-SAMEMA[24]
YOUNG-PRINCE-BRAVE-PRINCE-OF-MAISE[25]

Among the children of this Sky-Sovereign were five kings and three queens.[26] He had in all eleven children. Prince Valorous-Advancer-Prince and Young-Prince-Brave-Prince-of-Maise together set sacred jars at the mouth of the River Ice in Harima, and making Harima the opening of their journey, subdued and pacified the Land of Maise.

In this Land of Harima it is related that the Kami

FRESH-WATER,

---

[21] Ancestor of the District-Chiefs of Tohochi, in Yamato Province.
[22] Ancestor of the Magnates of Tonami (a District in Etchu Province) and Kunisaki (a District in Bungo Province); of the Clan-Chiefs of Ihobara (a District in Suruga); and of the Governors of Ama in Tsunaga.
[23] Ancestor of the Magnates of Kamu-Tsu-Michi (Bizen Province).
[24] Ancestor of the Magnates of Uzhika (in Harima Province).
[25] Ancestor of the Magnates of Shimo-Tsu-Michi (Bitchu Province) and the Magnates of Kasa.

when she was in pursuit of her husband, the Kami

FLOWER-WAVES,

overcome by anger, cut open her belly with her own hand and plunged into a marsh. (Hence the marsh is named Belly-Cut-Marsh. The carp in it to this day are without bellies.) A

It is said to have been in the fifth year of this Sovereign's reign that Fuji Mountain rose from the plain in a single night, and at the same time Biwa Lake was formed in Omi Province.B

The Sky-Sovereign's august years were one hundred and six, and his grave is at Horse-Slope, at Side-Mound.[27]

THE EMPEROR PRINCE-LAND-RULER-GREAT-MOUNTAIN-GATE-LORD
(FILIAL-PIETY-ORIGIN)[28]

Prince-Land-Ruler-Great-Mountain-Gate-Lord, removing the capital to Karu, dwelt in the Palace of Boundary-Moor. He wedded

BEAUTIFUL-UGLY-FEMALE [29]

who was the younger sister of

BEAUTIFUL-UGLY-MALE [30]

and there were born to the two

PRINCE-GREAT [31]
PRINCE-GREAT-EARS-YOUNG-MOUNTAIN-GATE-LORD
PRINCESS-MOUNTAIN-GATE-TO-TO-HI-MOMOSO.[32]

Secondly he took to wife

AUGUST-BRILLIANT-UGLY-FEMALE

daughter of Beautiful-Ugly-Male, whom he made Empress, and begot

PRINCE-VAST-GREAT-TRUTH.

Also he took to wife

PRINCESS-CLAY-EASY

and there was born to the two

---

[30] **Ancestor of the Magnates of Hozumi (unidentified).***
[31] **Ancestor of the Magnates of Abè, Iga, Kashiwadè and Ahè, the Clan-Chiefs of Sasaki-Yama, and the Rulers of Tsukushi and Koshi.**

---

* See p. 125, n. 88.

THE EARTHLY SOVEREIGNS

PRINCE-BRAVE-CLAY-EASY.

Prince-Great begot

BRAVE-LAGOON-RIVER-LORD
PRINCE-RICE-CHARIOT.[33]

Prince-Vast-Great-Truth took to wife

PRINCESS-UNDER-MOUNTAIN-GLOW [34]

who was the younger sister (or, as some say, the daughter) of

PRINCE-UZU [35]

and there was born to the two

NOBLE-OF-BRAVE-UCHI.[36]

(According to some, however, this latter was their grandson.) (Others say that at a later time, during the reign of the Sovereign Prince-Great-Perfect-Ruling-Lord,[37] divination was made to determine whether he should journey to the Land-of-Tree to worship the Sky- and the Earth-Kami. The time was found to be unpropitious, and accordingly the imperial carriage was sent back. Then

YA-NUSHI-OSHIHO-BRAVE-BOAR-HEART

went there, remaining at Oak-Plain in Abi, where he performed the worship. He lived there nine years, and wedded Princess-Under-Mountain-Glow,[38] by whom he begot Noble-of-Brave-Uchi.)

Prince-Vast-Great-Truth took to wife also

PRINCESS-TAKACHIMA-OF-MULBERRY-CASTLE

who was the younger sister of

PRINCE-GREAT-RICE [39]

and there was born to the two

NOBLE-OF-SWEET-UCHI.[40]

Noble-of-Brave-Uchi begot in all nine children:

---
[33] **Ancestor of the Magnates of the Victualers.**
[35] **Ancestor of the Rulers of the Land of Ki.**
[39] **Ancestor of the Tribe-Masters of Owari.**
[40] **Ancestor of the Magnates of Uchi (in Yamashiro).**

NOBLE-OF-HATA-SHRINE [41]
NOBLE-OF-OKARA-OF-KÒSÈ [42]
NOBLE-OF-SOGA-OF-STONE-RIVER [43]
NOBLE-OF-HEGURI'S-OWL [44]

(The origin of this last name was this: the child was born on the same day as the Emperor Great-Wren,[45] and on the day of their birth an owl flew into the bringing-forth-house of the palace and a wren into the bringing-forth-house of Noble-of-Brave-Uchi, for which reason the two children were named after the birds, and exchanged names.) [46]

NOBLE-OF-TSUNU-OF-TREE [47]
PRINCE-FIERCE-OF-LONG-INLET-OF-MULBERRY-CASTLE [48]
NOBLE-OF-YOUNG-CHILD.[49]

The Sky-Sovereign's august years were fifty-seven, and his grave is on the mound in the middle of the Pool-of-Sword.[50]

THE EMPEROR PRINCE-GREAT-EARS-YOUNG-MOUNTAIN-GATE-LORD
(CULTURE) [51]

Prince-Great-Ears-Young-Mountain-Gate-Lord, removing the capital to Kasuga, dwelt in the Palace of Izakawa and ruled the empire. He wedded his father's concubine, Beautiful-Ugly-Female, whom he made his Empress, and there were born to the two

PRINCE-INIYÈ-MIMA-KIRI.

Also he took to wife

PRINCESS-OF-OKÈ

who was the younger sister of

---

[41] **Ancestor of the Magnates of Hata, Hayashi (in Kawachi), Hami, Hoshi-Kawa (in Yamato Province), and Omi; and of the Clan-Chiefs of the Hase (Hatsusè) Clan.**
[42] **Ancestor of the Magnates of Kose, and of the Sazaki and Karu Clans.**
[43] **Ancestor of the Magnates of Soga, Kawanobè (in Settsu Province), Tanaka, Owarida, and Kishida (in Yamato Province), Takamuko (in Echizen Province), and Sakuraï (in Kawachi Province).**
[44] **Ancestor of the Magnates of Heguri and of Sawara (in Echizen Province) and of the Tribe-Masters of Uma-Mikuhi.**
[47] **Ancestor of the Magnates of Ki, Tsunu, and Sakamoto (in Izumi Province).**
[48] **Ancestor of the Magnates of Tamadè (unidentified), Ikuha, Ikuë (unidentified), and Agina (unidentified).**
[49] **Ancestor of the Magnates of Yenuma (a District in Kaga Province).**

PRINCE-LAND-OF-OKÈ [52]

and there was born to the two

KING-PRINCE-IMASU.

Likewise he took to wife

PRINCESS-EAGLE

and there was born to the two

KING-BRAVE-FRUITFUL-HAZURA-LORD.[53]

King-Prince-Imasu begot

KING-GREAT-MATA [54]
KING-NOBLE-OF-SHIBUMI [55]
KING-PRINCE-SAHO [56]
KING-LITTLE-SAHO [57]
PRINCESS-SAHO [58]

(who became consort of the Sky-Sovereign Prince-Ikumè-Iri-Isachi),

KING-PRINCE-CAVE.[59]

He took to wife also

PRINCESS-FLOURISHING-GOOD-OF-LONG-LIFE

daughter of the Sky-Kami

MIKAGÈ [60]

who is reverenced by the Hafuri of Mikami in Close-Fresh-Sea,[61] and begot

KING-TATATSU-ROAD-MASTER-PRINCE-OF-TAMBA

---

[52] Ancestor of the Magnates of Wani (in Yamato Province).
[53] Ancestor of the Magnates of the Road-Keepers (Chimori); of the Rulers of the Oshinumi Clans in Yamato and Inaba Provinces, and of the Mina Clan; of the Lords of Takanu in Tamba (in Tango Province); and of the Abiko (Family) of Yosami (in Kawachi Province).
[54] Ancestor of the Clan-Chiefs of Magari in Tagima (a District in Yamato Province).
[55] Ancestor of the Clan-Chiefs of Sasa (in Iga).
[56] Ancestor of the Tribe-Masters of the Kusaka Clan and of the Rulers of the Land of Kahi.
[57] Ancestor of the Lords of Kazumi (in Yamashiro Province) and Kanu in Chika-Tsu-Omi.
[59] Ancestor of the Lords of Mimi, in Wakasa.

> KING-TRUE-YOUNG-OF-NEW-RICE-EARS [62]
> KING-DIVINE-GREAT-LORD.[63]

Also he took to wife his mother's younger sister

> PRINCESS-OF-OKÈ [64]

and there was born to the two

> KING-TRUE-YOUNG-OF-GREAT-TSUZUKI-OF-BEHIND-THE-MOUNTAINS.

The elder son, King-Great-Mata, begot

> KING-DAWN-RISE [65]
> KING-UNAKAMI.[66]

King Tatatsu-Road-Master-Prince-of-Tamba begot

> PRINCESS-HIBASU
> PRINCESS-IRI-OF-NUBATA [67]
> PRINCESS-IRI-OF-AZAMI
> KING-LORD-AUGUST-GATE.[68]

King-True-Young-of-Great-Tsuzuki-of-Behind-the-Mountains had as descendant in the second generation

> KING-NOBLE-OF-LONG-LIFE

who took to wife

> PRINCESS-HIGH-BROW-OF-MULBERRY-CASTLE

by whom there were born to him three children:

> PRINCESS-LONG-LIFE-PERFECT [69]
> SKY-PRINCESS [70]
> KING-PRINCE-LONG-LIFE.[71]

Also King-True-Young-of-Great-Tsuzuki-of-Behind-the-Mountains begot

> KING-GREAT-WINDING-ASCENT.[72]

---

[62] Ancestor of the Governors of Yasu in Chika-Tsu-Omi.
[63] Ancestor of the Rulers of the Lands of Minu and Motosu (a District in Mino) and of the Tribe-Masters of the Nagahata Clan.
[65] Ancestor of the Clan-Chiefs of the Homuji Clan (in Isè) and of the Rulers of Sana (in Isè).
[66] Ancestor of the Clan-Chiefs of Himeda (in Omi Province).
[68] Ancestor of the Lords of Ho (in Mikawa Province).
[71] Ancestor of the Clan-Chiefs of Homuji in Kibi (Bingo Province) and of Aso in Harima.
[72] Ancestor of the Rulers of the Land of Tajima.

The august years of the Sky-Sovereign, Prince-Great-Ears-Young-Mountain-Gate-Lord, were sixty-three (*or, some say, one hundred and fifteen*) and his grave is in the mound on the upper slope (some say the lower slope) of Izakawa, in Kasuga.[73]

THE EMPEROR PRINCE-INIYÈ-MIMA-KIRI (HONORING-DEITY)[74]

Prince-Iniyè-Mima-Kiri was of active mind and as a child loved manly sports. In manhood he possessed broad knowledge and was of correct deportment, worshiping the Sky- and Earth-Kami, and continually mindful of the Sky-rule. Removing the capital to Stone-Castle,[75] he dwelt in the Palace of Fresh-Hedge. He wedded

PRINCESS-TROUT-EYED-BEAUTIFUL-EYES-OF-FAR-HARBOR

by whom he begot

PRINCE-FRUITFUL-KI-IRI [76]
PRINCESS-FRUITFUL-STONE-CASTLE-IRI.[77]

Likewise he took to wife

PRINCESS-GREAT-OF-AMA [78]

and there were born to the two

GREAT-IRI-KI [79]
PRINCE-YASAKA-IRI
PRINCESS-NUNAKI-IRI.

He also took to wife

PRINCESS-MIMA-KI

daughter of Prince-Great, whom he later made his Empress, and by her he begot

PRINCE-IKUMÈ-IRI-ISACHI
PRINCE-MOUNTAIN-GATE.

In this reign there arose a great pestilence, and more than half of the people died, as if the population was to be exhausted. Vagrancy flourished

---

[76] **Ancestor of the Rulers of Kozukè and the Clan-Chiefs of Shimotsukè.**
[78] **Ancestress of the Tribe-Masters of Owari.***
[79] **Ancestor of the Magnates of Noto.**

---

* But see p. 66, n. 17.

and there arose a rebellion that only virtue could subdue, so that the Sky-Sovereign grieved and lamented, rising early in the morning and worshiping until evening, asking for punishment from the Sky- and Earth-Kami. Up to this time Great-Sky-Shiner and Great-Land-Master [80] had been worshiped jointly within the great hall of the imperial palace. Now, however, the Sky-Sovereign feared their power to be disquieting by reason of their dwelling together, *so he caused the Intercessor-Clan to command the descendants of the Kami Again-Forging-Old-Woman, with*

SKY-LAND

of the District of Uda, in the Province of Mountain-Gate, who was a far-removed descendant of the One-Eyed-Kami,[81] *to forge, as august tokens for the imperial guard, duplicates of the Mirror and the Sword (which are the Mirror and Sword of the Kami-symbols offered now on the day of the Assumption of the Dignity).*[82, A]

He built the sacred wattle of Stone-Castle at the village of Broad-Hat-Sewing [83] in Mountain-Gate, and *placing the originals within it,* gave in charge the worship of Great-Sky-Shiner there to Princess-Fruitful-Stone-Castle-Iri, and with the worship of Great-Land-Master he charged Princess-Nunaki-Iri.[84] The latter, however, being bald and thin, was unfit for the service.

On the evening the Treasures were moved, the people of the court went there and made merry throughout the night. They sang:

Lo, the palace folk, || Whiling away the night hours
Merrily they pass.
Ah, how pleasant the snowfall, || Whiling away the night hours.

Popularly, by a change of the phrases, one now sings:

Lo, the palace folk || Wearing their noblest raiment
Hanging from the knee!
Ah, how pleasant the snowfall, || Wearing their noblest raiment.[B]

THE LORD-OF-GREAT-TATA

Afterward the Sovereign went to the plain of Kami-Asachi and there, calling together the eighty myriad Kami, *for whom he made festivals,* he made great divination and consulted them, when the Kami spoke through the mouth of Princess-Mountain-Gate-to-to-Hi-Momoso,[86] his aunt on his father's side, saying, "Why does the Sky-Sovereign sorrow because the Land is in disorder? If he but gave us due worship, it would become peaceful." Then Prince-Iniyè-Mima-Kiri asked, "What Kami speaks thus?" And the reply was, "I am the Kami dwelling in the Land of Mountain-Gate, and my name is Great-Land-Master." Thereon the Sky-

Sovereign worshiped, as he had been instructed, but vainly. So he bathed and abstained and purified the hall and prayed, saying, "Have we not yet fulfilled all the ceremonies due the Sky-Kami? As, cruelly, you do not accept our worship, we pray you to instruct us further in a dream, that we may gain the divine approval." So that night, as he dreamed on his divine couch, the Great Kami, Great-Land-Master, appeared to him as a man of noble mien, and standing opposite him in the door of the hall, said to him, "Grieve no longer by reason of the Land's disorder. What has happened is the wish of my heart. Now, if you will cause me to be worshiped by

LORD-OF-GREAT-TATA [87]

the divine spirit will not arise to your hurt and the Land will be made tranquil. Also, the Lands beyond the seas will submit themselves." Later, also,

PRINCESS-MOUNTAIN-GATE-TO-TO-KAMI-ASACHI-HARAMA-GUHASHI,
NOBLE-OF-GREAT-MINA-KUCHI [88]

and the Clan-Chief of Wo-Umi in Isè, had all three a like dream, which they reported to the Sovereign, saying, "Last night we dreamed that a man of noble mien appeared to us who counselled us, saying, "Lord-of-Great-Tata should be appointed Master-of-Worship of Great-Land-Master, and

NAGAŌCHI-OF-ICHISHI

Master-of-Worship of Great-Country-Jewel.[89] Then truly the empire shall have perfect peace." So when the Sovereign learned the words of the dream, greatly delighted, he made a proclamation, and couriers were sent in all four directions to search for the person called Lord-of-Great-Tata, who was at length found in the village of Three-Moors in Kawachi, (*or, according to some, in a village called Suwè, in the District of Chinu* [90]) and was dutifully sent to the capital. Whereon the Sky-Sovereign, going to the plain of Kami-Asachi, and calling together all the princes and ministers and the eighty clans, asked Lord-of-Great-Tata, "whose child are you?" He answered, "Your servant is the child of

BRAVE-AWFUL-POSSESSOR [91]

---

[87] **Ancestor of the Clan-Chiefs of Miwa and of Kamo.**
[88] **Ancestor of the Magnates of Hozumi.***

---

* Presumably a descendant of Beautiful-Ugly-Male (see p. 118).

who is the great-grandson of the Great Kami, Great-Land-Master, by his wife

PRINCESS-LIFE-JEWEL-GOOD [92]

who was the daughter of the Kami

EARS-OF-SUWÈ. [93]

(Others say that he declared these two Kami, Great-Land-Master and Princess-Life-Jewel-Good, themselves, to be his father and mother.)

Lord-of-Great-Tata was known to be a Kami's descendant for this reason: Princess-Life-Jewel-Good was exceedingly beautiful, and a youth who deemed her queenliness unmatched in all time came suddenly to her in the middle of the night. So they mutually loved and cohabited, and the maiden before long became pregnant. Her father and mother then, astonished at this, said to her, "You are pregnant by yourself. How comes it that you are with child without a man?" She answered, "I have conceived naturally by the coming here every night of a lovely youth whose surname and personal name I do not know, *who comes riding on a great eagle of Sky-feathers and* who has stayed with me."

The parents, wishing to know the man, instructed her, saying, "Do you scatter red earth before your couch and pass a winding of hemp thread through a needle and pierce the skirt of his garment with it." She did as they bade her, and when they looked in the morning, the hemp thread led out through the hole of the door-hook, and all that remained was three windings. Then, certain that he had gone out by the hook-hole, they followed the thread which, reaching Mount Three-Threads,[94] stopped at the shrine of the Kami there. So they knew that her child was the child of that Kami.[95] (Therefore the place was called by the name of Three-Threads, on account of the three windings of hemp thread that had remained over.)

(*Now by some it is said that the Kami who did this was the Kami August-Luck-Spirit-August-Wondrous-Spirit,*[96] *who dwelt on Mount-August-House.*[97] *Others, again, say that these two Kami are the same.*)

The Sovereign rejoiced exceedingly and said, "Now shall the empire be tranquilized and the people made to prosper." And ascertaining by divination that it would be lucky to send

REFULGENT-UGLY-MALE [98]

---

[98] **Ancestor of the Tribe-Masters of the Army Clan.**

to make offerings to these Kami, but unlucky at that time to worship other Kami, he appointed Lord-of-Great-Tata Kami-Owner to conduct the worship of Great-Land-Master, on Mount August-House, and the Nagaōchi-of-Ichishi to conduct the worship of Great-Country-Jewel-of-Mountain-Gate. Also he appointed one named.

IKUI

of the village of Takahashi, brewer to the Great Kami. Then, after divination, finding it would be lucky to worship other Kami, he gathered together and worshiped the eighty myriad Kami, made decrees declaring which shrines were Sky-shrines and which Earth-shrines, and set apart land and buildings for their service. Also he bade Refulgent-Ugly-Male take eighty Sky-platters, made by the eighty army clans, and worshipfully to found the shrines of the Kami of the Land. And being instructed by the divine person in a dream, he decreed worship with a red-colored shield and spear to the Kami of Charcoal-Slope at Uda [99] and with a black-colored shield and spear to the Kami of Great-Slope: [1] and also, he commanded offerings of cloth to be presented to all the Kami of the august hill slopes and river currents, without omitting any.

As a result the vapor of the pestilence entirely ceased, the land was tranquilized, the five grains sprang up, and the folk had plenty.

In this reign also there were offered at the shrine of Deer-Island [2] ten swords, two spears, two iron bows, two arrowheads, four helmets, a piece of iron plate, a piece of steel, a horse, a saddle, two eight-fold mirrors and a roll of rough silk of five colors.

On a day when the Sovereign caused Lord-of-Great-Tata to worship the Great Kami, Ikui, presenting to the Sky-Sovereign some sacred sakè, sang:

This sacred sakè || Is not my sacred sakè.
It by Mountain-Gate's || Great-Thing-Master [3] was mingled—
This sacred sakè || How long ago! [4] How long ago!

After they had feasted in the shrine of the Kami, the various officials sang:

Ah, sweet sakè || Of the Hall of Three-Threads!
The door, at morning,
We will thrust wide open || Door of the Hall of Three-Threads!

Then the Sky-Sovereign himself sang this song:

Ah, sweet sakè || Of the Hall of Three-Threads!
The door, at morning,
We will issue forth from || Door of the Hall of Three-Threads!

Whereon the door of the shrine was thrown open and the Sovereign departed.

Now on Mount Morning-Come-Name [5] there were Ground-Spiders whose two chiefs, Smite-Monkey and Neck-Monkey, commanding more than one hundred and eighty Ground-Spiders, lay hidden on the peak of the mountain, continually opposing the Sovereign's authority and refusing to surrender to him. So he sent to chastise them

BRAVE-MALE-KUMI [6]

who, obedient to the Sovereign's command, destroyed them all. In investigating the land, he came to Mount White-Hair, in Eight-Sign-District, where, when the sun went down, he spent the night. In the night there appeared in the sky a fire that slowly descended upon this mountain and burned there like a torch. Seeing this, Brave-Male-Kumi was astonished, and when his service was accomplished, he returned and reported the matter to the Sovereign, who said, "None can excel your merits in clearing out the bandits and pacifying the western country. That a fire came down from the sky and burned upon the mountain is strange, and therefore I will name the Land Land-of-Fire." [7] Brave-Male-Kumi, for his merit, was named Land-of-Fire-Brave-Male-Pure, and was bidden to rule the Land.[A]

Also, the Sovereign sent

BRAVE-DEER-ISLAND [8]

at the head of troops, to chastise the rough rebels of the eastern Emishi, and he, chastising them as he went, came to the island of Easily,[9] where he surveyed the sea beach to the eastward. Smoke rose there, by which he thought there might be inhabitants. Then, gazing up to the sky, he swore an oath, saying, "If the smoke is raised by the people of the Sky-descendants, may it cover me, and if it is raised by the Emishi, may it drift toward the sea. Then the smoke drifted toward the sea, so that he knew the people to be fierce Emishi, and he ordered his host to take food and to proceed there. They found there Kunisu led by two chiefs named Yasakashi and Yatsukushi,[10] who had dug pits and built a fortress there for a permanent habitation, and who, meeting the imperial troops, de-

---

[6] **Ancestor of the Clan-Chiefs of Hi.***
[8] **Ancestor of the Land-Rulers of Naka (in Hitachi Province)** †

---

* Yet see p. 128, n. 6. Presumably Brave-Male-Kumi counted himself a descendant of Divine-Eight-Wells-Ears.
† That is, a descendant of Divine-Eight-Wells-Ears (see p. 113, n. 88). According to the *Kunimiyatsuko-Hongi*, he was appointed Land-Ruler (*Kunimiyatsuko*) in the reign of Seïmu-*Tenno* (131-190).

fended themselves. Brave-Deer-Island bade his troops pursue them, as they fled, and closing their fortress, guarded it stoutly. So he resorted to a stratagem and choosing a number of brave warriors, bade them hide in the shadow of a mountain, and made weapons with which to slay the Emishi. He ordered the troops then to go to the sea coast,[11] by vessels and rafts, waving silk covers [12] like clouds and flags like rainbows, and made them play Sky-bird harps and Sky-bird flageolets and sing Kishima songs,[13] floating on the waves and the tide for seven days and seven nights. Thus, dancing and singing, they made merry. The Emishi heard the music and came forth, leaving their fortress empty, and filled the beach with merriment, on which Brave-Deer-Island ordered his riders to close the fortress and, surprising them from the rear, caught them all and burned them to death. Some died bitterly (the place, because of this, is even to the present day named Village-of-Bitter), and some were cut down with a snapping sound (the place because of this is called Village-of-Snap), and some were slain easily (the place because of this, is called Village-of-Easily), and some were slain well (and the place, because of this, is called Village-of-Good-Slope.)[A]

In this reign Prince-Great was sent to the land of Koshi in the north, and his son, Brave-Lagoon-River-Lord, was sent to the twelve provinces on the eastern sea to quiet the rebellious people. The Sovereign sent

YOUNG-BRAVE-PRINCE-OF-MAISE [14]

to the west, and to Ricefield Place [15] he sent

CHI-NUSHI-OF-RICEFIELD-PLACE

Also, King-Prince-Imasu was sent there to slay one

MIKASA-OF-KUGAMIMI.

To these four he gave seals and ribbons and appointed them shogun, saying, "If you find any who are contumacious, battle with them and smite them."

THE REBELLION OF PRINCE-BRAVE-CLAY-EASY

Now when Prince-Great was departing to the Land of Koshi, when he arrived at the top of Wani-Slope (or, as some say, the Hira-Slope) in

---

[14] **Ancestor of the Magnates of Kibi (Maise) and of the Magnates of Marubè.***

---

* According to one text of the *Harima-Fudoki*. Some commentators, however, hold this to be an error.

Behind-the-Mountains,[16] a young girl wearing a loin-skirt, stood on the Hill of Hera and sang:

> Now oh-ho!
> O Prince Mima-Ki-Iri! Oh-ho!
> O Prince Mima-Ki-Iri! Oh-ho!
> Unaware that folk || In order to steal your life
> And put you to death || Cross backward and forward
> By the after gate, || Cross backward and forward
> By the forward gate, || Spyingly too—
> You, like a lady divert yourself! [17]

Prince-Great, thinking the occurrence strange, turned back his horse and asked the damsel: "What are these words you speak?" But she replied, "I said nothing. I was only singing a song!" And singing it a second time, she vanished.

Prince-Great returned and made report to the Sky-Sovereign. At that, Princess-Mountain-Gate-to-to-hi-Momoso, who was intelligent and far-seeing, understanding the meaning of the song, said to the Sovereign, "This is a sign that your half-brother, Prince-Brave-Clay-Easy,[18] who dwells in the Land of Behind-the-Mountains, is cherishing a bad heart." (Some, however, say the Sovereign said this, afterward bidding his uncle raise an army and proceed.) "For I have heard that his wife, coming secretly to Mount Fragrant in Mountain-Gate, took clay from there, wrapped it in her neckband and prayed, saying 'Let this clay stand for the Land of Mountain Gate.' And so saying, she turned the neckcloth upside-down.[19] This I know to be a sign of trouble. If you do not act quickly it will be too late."

The Sky-Sovereign recalled his shogun for conference, and presently Prince-Brave-Clay-Easy, conspiring with his wife,

PRINCESS-ATA,

raised an army and came by different roads, he by way of Behind-the-Mountains and she by way of Great-Slope, planning to join their forces in an assault upon the capital. The Sovereign, however, sent

PRINCE-ISASERI

who fell upon the force of Princess-Ata at Great-Slope and routed the troops and slew them and her. He despatched also Prince-Great, in company with

PRINCE-LAND-PACIFIER [20]

---

[20] **Ancestor of the Magnates of Wani.**

to attack Prince-Brave-Clay-Easy at Behind-the-Mountains. These set sacred urns on Wani Hill, and advancing with their forces, ascended Mount Level,[21] and held it, and in their encamping the imperial army trod down level the bushes and trees. (For this reason the mountain was so called.) From there they came to the Wakara River, in Behind-the-Mountains, where Prince-Brave-Clay-Easy was waiting to intercept them, and thus they stood facing and challenging each other on either side of the river. (Therefore the name of the river was changed to Challenging,[22] but now it is called Source.[23])

Then Prince-Brave-Clay-Easy, standing on the river bank, asked Prince-Land-Pacifier, "Why do you come here with an army?" Prince-Land-Pacifier replied, "Because you, opposing the Sky and contrary to right, purpose to overthrow the imperial hall; therefore I have come with loyal troops to put down your revolt." When he begged the phalanx of men on the other side to shoot the sacred arrow,[24] Prince-Brave-Clay-Easy by a little missed, and Prince-Land-Pacifier winged a shaft that struck him in the breast and killed him. So his whole army turned and fled in panic, and the others pursued the fleeing troops north of the river as far as a ford, where, harassed by the pursuers, their feces extruded and stuck to their trousers. (Because of this the name Dung-Trousers[25] was given to the place. It is now called Kusuba.) As they ran they took off their armor and, knowing there was no escape, put their foreheads to the ground saying, "Our Lord!" And they were intercepted and cut down till their bodies floated in the river like cormorants. (Therefore the river was called by the name of Cormorant-River. And because the warriors were there cut to pieces, the place was called Garden-of-Cutting-to-Pieces. The place where the armor was taken off was called Armor[26] and the place where they bowed their heads was called Our-Lord.)

Having thus finished the pacification, they went up to make report, after which Prince-Great departed to the Land of Koshi, in accordance with the earlier command, and Brave-Lagoon-River-Lord, who had been sent round by the eastward, and Prince-Great his father, met together in Meeting-Port. (For this reason the place was called by that name.) Then each of them, having put in order the government of the Land to which he had been sent, made his report, and later strange tribes came in great numbers, employing interpreters, and the empire was at peace and the people prosperous. The Sky- and Earth-Kami were in harmony, wind and rain came in their season, and the hundred grains grew. Moreover, families lacked not supplies and there was sufficient population. At this time taxes were first levied upon the arrow-toll of men and the handicraft[27] of women. (*From this it comes about that bear-fur, deer-fur, horn, and cloth are used in Kami-festivals.*)[A]

Every province was commanded to build ships, and in praise of this reign people called the Sovereign "the Sky-Mikami, founder of the first Land." In this reign the Pool of Yosami, the Pool of Karusaka, and the Pool of Sakawori were made. Also the Land of Kara [28] sent tribute.

In this reign the Kami Princess-Kami-Cloth,[29] who had descended from the Sky with Prince-Sky-Plenty-Earth-Plenty-High-as-Sky's-Sun-Fire-Ruddy-Plenty, removed to Whale,[30] where she built a weaving house, and

TATE [31]

removed to that place from Three-Moors. The cloth woven there became transformed into garments without being cut or sewn. This cloth was called uchi-cloth. When the Kami wove, she shut the doors, lest the people should readily observe, and as it was woven in the darkness, it was named crow-weave.[32] It could not be cut even with a sharp sword. At the present time it is offered each year to the imperial court as a divine woven cloth.[A]

GREAT-LAND-MASTER AND PRINCESS-MOUNTAIN-GATE-TO-TO-HI-MOMOSO

Later Princess-Mountain-Gate-to-to-hi-Momoso [33] was taken to wife by Great-Land-Master, who came to her at night and was never seen by day, so that she once said to him, "Since you, my lord, are never seen by day, I am unable to behold your august face. I beg you then to tarry awhile, so that in the morning I may gaze on your great loveliness." The Great Kami answered, "You speak rightly. Tomorrow morning I will go into your toilet-box and remain there. But be not alarmed at my form." She wondered at this, and at dawn, looking into her toilet-box, saw there a small and lovely serpent as long and thick as a garment-cord. And she was frightened and cried out, so that the Great Kami was embarrassed, and instantly transforming himself into human form, said, "Because you did not control yourself and have put me to shame, I will put you also to shame!" And he ascended through the void to Mount-August-House. Then she blamed herself, and sitting down, stabbed herself with a chopstick in her vagina and died, and was buried at Oho-chi. (For this reason people called her tomb the Chopstick-Tomb.) Men erected this tomb by day, and Kami by night, with stones carried from Mount Great-Slope, and men standing in a row passed the stones from one to another, thus transporting them to the tomb. And the people made a song concerning it:

> As upon Great Slope || Where they are up-builded,
> Passing on the rocks, || Hand from hand, how difficult
> Thus it is to transport them!

Now the Sovereign summoned Prince-Fruitful-Ki-Iri and Prince-Ikumè-Iri-Isachi and said, "You, Our two children, We love alike, and are unable to make choice between you for Our successor. Therefore dream and tell Us your dreams that We may divine them." So the pair, thus commanded, bathed and worshiped, after which each slept and dreamed. At daylight the elder, Prince-Fruitful-Ki-Iri, reported to the Sovereign thus: "In my dream I ascended Mount August-House, and facing eastward, shook a spear eight shaku long and smote with a sword eight shaku long. The younger, Prince-Ikumè-Iri-Isachi, said, "In my dream I ascended Mount August-House and stretched a cord in the four directions to drive away sparrows that were eating grain." The Sovereign divined the dreams, saying, "Since the elder child turned to the eastward, it is fitting that he should rule the eastern land; but as the younger surveyed the four directions, he should inherit the Sovereignty." Therefore Prince-Fruitful-Ki-Iri-Isachi was appointed heir apparent.

Later the Sky-Sovereign said to his ministers, "The divine treasures, when they were brought from the sky, were stored in the shrine [34] of Great-Land-Master at Sacred-Quarter. I desire to see them." Accordingly

TAKÈ-MORO-SUMI [35]

was sent to fetch them that they might be exhibited to him. Now

SACRED-QUARTER-ROOT-BRANDISHER [36]

who had the treasures in his keeping, was in the Land of Tsukushi and did not meet him, but his younger brother

IÏ-IRI-NE

when he received the imperial command, entrusted them to his brother and his son

UKATSU-KUNU [37]

and sent them.

When Sacred-Quarter-Root-Brandisher returned from the Land of Tsukushi and learned of it, he rebuked his younger brother, saying, "You should have waited. Were you in fear, that you sent away the divine treasures so readily?" And he harbored wrath against him for months and years and at length determined to slay him. To this end he misled his younger brother, saying, "The seaweed [38] grows luxuriantly in the Eight-Temples Pool. Let us go to see it." And they went together. Beforehand, however, he had secretly girded on a sham sword of oak, which resembled the real one that his younger brother wore. When they reached the head

---

[35] **Ancestor of the Rulers of the Yata Clan.**
[36] **Ancestor of the Magnates of Izumo.**

of the pool he said, "The water is clear and cool. Let us bathe in it." So they bathed, each taking off his sword and laying it down on the bank. Then Sacred-Quarter-Root-Brandisher came from the water first and took up and girded on the real sword of his younger brother, who, coming after him, girded on the sham sword. Then Sacred-Quarter-Root-Brandisher railed at him, saying, "Come, let us join our swords in combat." But on laying hold, the younger could not draw the sham sword and the elder struck and slew him. The people of that time made a song:

> So the warrior then, || Of cloud-wrapped Sacred-Quarter
> Girded on his sword.
> Many a creeper wound it, || But it had no blade, alas!

(Some say, however, that this song was not sung at this time, but later, by Mountain-Gate-Brave, when he had slain the Sacred-Quarter bandit [39] whom he deceived in the same manner, with a sham sword.)

The brother and son of Iï-Iri-Ne, however, went to the capital and made report, and the Sovereign caused Sacred-Quarter-Root-Brandisher to be put to death. For this reason the Magnates of Sacred-Quarter were stricken with fear and for a time left off worshiping Great-Land-Master.

Now there came to Prince-Ikumè-Iri-Isachi a man of Tamba, who said, "I have among my children a babe who recently spoke, saying, 'The people of Sacred-Quarter, who have the jewel-like waterweed and the bottom-stone, worship the following Kami:

TRUE-KIND-LOVELY-AUGUST-MIRROR
LOVELY-AUGUST-FEATHER-WAVER
BOTTOM-MASTER-TREASURE-AUGUST-TREASURE
AUGUST-SPIRIT-PLUNGED-IN-MOUNTAIN-STREAM-WATER
AUGUST-TRANQUIL-WAVER.'

This is not like the speech of a babe. Perhaps the saying was divinely inspired." Prince-Ikumè-Iri-Isachi made report of this, and the Sky-sovereign caused worship to be given to these Kami.

THE KAMI WHITE-STONE

In this reign there was in the Land of Great Kara a man named Tsu-noga-Arashito,[40] son of the king of that Land, who went one day into the country with an ox laden with farming implements. The ox disappearing, he followed its footprints to a village, where he met an old man who said, "The ox you seek did indeed enter this village. The headmen of the village, however, said among themselves, 'From the implements this ox carries it is most certainly meant to be killed and eaten.

If perhaps its owner should come in search of it, we can make its loss good in some way.' Then they killed and ate it. When they ask you what you desire as its price, demand instead of treasure the Kami worshiped in the village." So presently, when the head-men came and asked what he demanded, he answered as the old man had bidden him. Now the Kami worshiped by the village was a

WHITE-STONE [41]

and they gave this to Tsunoga-Arashito and he took it away with him and put it in his sleeping-room. There the divine stone became transformed into a lovely damsel, at which he rejoiced and desired to cohabit with her. But in his absence she vanished. In alarm he asked his wife where she had gone. She answered, "She went to the eastward." So he departed to find her, crossing, in the end, the farther sea in a ship, until he reached the bay of Kebi in the Land of Koshi. Now he had horns on his forehead (for which reason that place was called Horn-Forehead).[42] When Tsunoga-Arashito arrived at Horn-Forehead and people asked him from what Land he came, he said, "I am the son of the king of Great Kara, and learning that there is in the Land of Nippon a wise Sovereign, I desire to ally myself to him and so came to Hole-Door.[43] There was there, however, a man named Prince-of-Usa,[44] who said to your servant, 'I am the king of this land and there is no king save myself. Therefore go no farther.' But when I observed what sort of a man he was, I knew of a surety that he was no king. So I left there and visited various islands and harbors, passing around through the northern sea, by the Land of Sacred-Quarter, till I reached this place." So he was sent to the capital to serve the Sovereign, but at this time the latter died.

The Sky-Sovereign's august years were one hundred and sixty-eight (or, as some say, one hundred and twenty) and his grave is on the mound at the corner of the Mountain-Vicinity-Road.

THE EMPEROR PRINCE-IKUMÈ-IRI-ISACHI
(CONDESCENDING-BENEVOLENCE)[45]

Prince-Ikumè-Iri-Isachi from his birth was handsome and talented, a lover of truth and a foe of deceit, and was well beloved by his father. When he ruled the empire he removed the capital to Makimuku, where he dwelt in the Palace of Jewel-Hedge, and wedding Princess-Saho, youngest sister of King-Prince-Saho,[46] made her his Empress.

THE PLOT OF KING-PRINCE-SAHO AND THE EMPRESS

Now her elder brother, King-Prince-Saho, plotted to overthrow the rule. So, waiting for a time when she was unoccupied, he asked her,

"Which is the dearer to you, your elder brother or your husband?" She, knowing not why he asked her thus, replied, "My elder brother." So King-Prince-Saho enticed her, saying, "Man's love ceases when the beauty that served him wanes. This Land has many lovely women who will come one by one. You cannot put trust in your beauty. As for me, I desire to hold the rule. If I be in truth the one dearer to you, let us two rule the empire together for a hundred years." And he straightway made a short body-sword, and tempering it eight times, gave it to her, saying, "Fasten this sword under your garments and when the Sovereign sleeps, stab him in the neck and so slay him." At this the Empress was filled with secret fear and knew not what to do, and taking the short sword, fastened it beneath her garments. And while the Sovereign, ignorant of this conspiracy, was augustly taking his noontime rest in High-Palace at Kumè, sleeping with the Empress' knees as his pillow, she tried to slash his throat with the body-sword; but though she raised it three times she could not do the deed because of her unconquerable sadness, and she wept tears that, overflowing, dropped onto his face.

> (*Some say, however, that the Empress took the sword from her elder brother, knowing that for the time remonstrance would be useless and minded to turn him from his purpose, and that she wept from grief, never thinking to slay the Sovereign.*)

At that the Sky-Sovereign awoke, and said to her, "I have dreamed a strange dream. A small damask-colored serpent coiled about my neck and a heavy rain came from the direction of Saho and drenched my face. What can such a dream portend?" So she, deeming it bootless to conceal the plot, bowed herself in fear and told him, saying, "My elder brother, King-Prince-Saho, asked your handmaid, 'Which is the dearer, your husband or your elder brother?' And when, taken aback by the direct question, I replied, 'My elder brother,' he tempted me, saying, 'I and you together shall rule the empire, and to this end the Sky-Sovereign must be slain.' With these words he made a short body-sword and handed it to me. I could not oppose the purpose of my elder brother, yet I could not be false to my obligation to you. To confess would have been my elder brother's undoing; to be silent would have overturned the empire; so that on one side I feared and on the other I sorrowed. Above me and beneath me was grief, and before me and behind me was weeping. Night and day I was perplexed. Today when you were asleep with my knees as your pillow, I was minded to cut your august throat, but though I raised the sword three times, I could not do the deed, and though I wiped the tears with my sleeve, they fell and wet your face. This truly was what the dream portended. The small damask serpent is the sword that was given me, and the rain is my tears."

Said the Sky-Sovereign, "How narrowly have I escaped destruction!" And he straightway raised an army and commanded

YATSU-NADA [47]

to attack King-Prince-Saho, who erected a castle to await the combat. He built this castle hastily by piling up rice stalks;[48] nevertheless, it was so stout that it could not be breached, and after a month was still untaken. Then Princess-Saho, unable to forget her elder brother, fled out through a rear entrance of the palace and entered into the castle. At the time she was pregnant, and for this reason the Sky-Sovereign could not restrain his feeling for her, since he had loved her for three years past. So he diverted the attack and did not make haste and during this delay the child she had conceived was born. Then she exposed the babe to view outside the castle and sent a message to the Sovereign, saying, "Your handmaid fled into the castle hoping that for her sake and the sake of her child her elder brother might be forgiven his guilt. But he has not been forgiven, and I know that I am guilty. Nevertheless, though I die, I cannot forget your imperial favor. If you wish to consider this child as your own, deign to undertake its care." The Sovereign thereon, though he detested her brother, could not repress his love for the Empress, and at once planned to get possession of her. For this purpose he chose from among his warriors a number of the strongest and quickest and bade them, "When you take the child, steal also the queen, its mother, and grasping her by the hair or by the hands or how best you may, draw her forth."

But the Empress, guessing his intent, shaved off her hair and covered her head with it, and rotted her jewel-string and wound it three times about her arm, and rotted her garments with sakè and then donned them as if they were whole. Thus prepared she took the babe in her arms, and thrust it outside the castle. The strong men, seizing the babe, snatched at her; but when they grasped her hair, the hair came away; when they grasped her arm, the jewel-string broke; and when they grasped her garments, the garments at once tore. Thus they secured the child but not the parent. So they returned and made report, and the Sky-Sovereign, grieved and angered, hated the people who had made the jewel-string and deprived them of all their lands. (Thus the proverb says, "Jewel-makers without lands.")

Then he caused it to be proclaimed to the Empress, "A child's name must be given by the mother; by what name shall this babe be called?"

---

[47] **Ancestor of the Clan-Chiefs of Kozukè.**

She replied, "As he was born now at the time of this castle's burning by fire, it would be well to name him

PRINCE-FIRE-POSSESSING-LORD.

Also he had her asked, "How shall he be reared?" and she replied, "He must be reared by taking a foster mother and choosing women, old and young, to bathe him." So he was reared according to the Empress's instructions. Also the Sovereign asked her, "Who shall loose my youthful inner girdle that you fastened?" She replied, "It is best that the five [49] daughters of King-Tatatsu-Road-Master-Prince-of-Tamba [50] should serve you, for these queens are subjects of pure descent. They should be housed in the side-chambers, to fill the number of the imperial consorts."

> (Others say that the child Prince-Fire-Possessing-Lord was born before this, and that the Empress, after King-Prince-Saho's castle had held out for a month, saying within herself, "How can I, even though I am Empress, preside over the empire after bringing to ruin my elder brother?" took the child and fled into the castle, and that when it was set on fire she came out again with the child in her bosom and delivered it to the Sovereign, returning to die with King-Prince-Saho.)

So, at length, Yatsu-Nada, having increased his army further and invested the castle on all sides, set fire to it, and when the fire mounted, the troops all fled, and King-Prince-Saho and his younger sister Princess-Saho died together in the castle. Therefore the Sovereign praised Yatsu-Nada, granting to him the name of Prince-Mountain-Gate-Sun-Facing-Brave-Sun-Facing.

Now after Tsunoga-Arashito, the horned man of Kara, had served the Sky-Sovereign three years, the latter asked him, "Do you desire to return to your own Land?" He replied, "I greatly desire to do so and I ask your permission." The Sovereign answered, "Because you lost your way, you arrived here too late to serve the Sovereign Prince-Iniyè-Mima-Kiri. So do you therefore take his august name of Mima-Kiri and make it the name of your Land." (From which the name of that country became Mimana.)[51] He presented to him a hundred pieces of red silk cloth as a gift to the king of Great Kara and sent him back to his own country, where he stored it in a keep there. But the people of Silla,[52] learning of it, came with an army and stole the red silk away. Thus these two countries first became enemies.

> (Some say, however, that the Silla people waylaid him and robbed him of the silk before he reached his own land.)

SKY-SUN-SPEAR AND HIS DESCENDANTS

At this time there was in the Land of Silla a poor girl who one noontide fell asleep on the mud bank of a lagoon called the Lagoon of Agu. And the sun's rays, like Sky-arrows, struck upon her vulva. There was also a poor man who, wondering, ceased not to watch her. She conceived from that time, and at length was delivered of a red jewel that the man who had watched her begged of her and kept constantly tied to his loin. Having planted a ricefield in a mountain valley, he one day loaded an ox with food for the laborers and went down into the middle of the valley, when he met the son of the ruler of the land, who was named

SKY-SUN-SPEAR

and who said to him, "What is your purpose in entering the valley with this food-laden ox? Surely you intended to kill and eat it." And he would have thrown him into prison, but the man denied this absolutely, and when Sky-Sun-Spear still would not let him go, he unfastened the jewel at his loins and bribed him with it. At this Sky-Sun-Spear let the poor man go, and taking the jewel, set it beside his couch, and it became transformed into a lovely damsel whom he at once wedded and made his chief wife. She never ceased preparing and feeding him all kinds of dainties, but he was of a disdainful heart and reviled her, so that she said, "I am no woman to be wife to such as you. I will go to my ancestral Land." [53] And she secretly embarked in a vessel and fled away across the sea and landed at Wave-Swift. When he learned of his wife's flight, he pursued her across to Wave-Swift, but the Kami of that place prevented his entrance, so he left there and came ashore in the land of Harima.

Coming to the bed of the Whirlpool River [54] *he asked Great-Land-Master* [55] *for a place in which to pass the night, saying, "You are the owner of this Land, so I ask this of you." And Great-Land-Master permitted him to pass a night in the sea, and he stirred the sea water with his sword and passed the night there. But the Kami who was his host feared this powerful act of his guest and (minded, himself, to occupy a Land that was elsewhere) went round about to Grain-Hill, where he took food, and where grains dropped from his mouth. (From this the place was so named, this hill's gravel being like grain.) From a spot where he thrust in his staff, fresh water gushed out, flowing to the north and south, the northern water being cold and the southern water being warm.*[A]

Great-Land-Master and Sky-Sun-Spear both raised armies and fought together, and the rice bran from the army of Great-Land-Master accumulated till it made a hill. (Therefore that place was called Rice-Bran-Hill.[56]

And the valley, which each one in turn plundered, was called Plunder-Valley,⁵⁷ and since it was plundered by force, it is crooked like a bent vine.)

Sky-Sun-Spear dwelt in the village of Shisaha. The woman he sought, when she came to Wave-Swift, was called

PRINCESS-BRILLIANT.

She is the Kami who dwells in the Himegoso Shrine at Wave-Swift. Afterward she proceeded to the Land of Fertile. She is worshiped in both these places.

> (Some say that this Kami was not the woman who was the red jewel of Silla, but the woman who was the divine White-Stone of Great Kara.)⁵⁸ (Others say that she did not come at this time, but later, in the reign of the Emperor Great-Elbow-Pad-Lord, and that she at first dwelt at Princess-Island-of-Iwahi in Tsukushi, but saying that island was not far distant, and that her husband-Kami might come there to seek her, she removed to Princess-Island, in Settsu Province, which she named after the place of her previous residence.)ᴬ

In the Province of Hizen there is a river that is called Mountain-Gate-River. It has its source in the north and, flowing to the south of the mountains, meets the great River-of-Three-Wells. West of this place there was a violent Kami who attacked many wayfarers, half being killed and half spared. So by an augury she made inquiry why the Kami made this curse. To this answer was made: "If you will summon

KASEKO

who is a native of Body-Form District of Chikuzen Province, to make a festival for my shrine, my violence will cease." So Kaseko was summoned and ordered to make a Kami-festival, and he offered a flag to the Kami and prayed, saying, "If you have a desire to be supplicated, carry this flag to the place where you are." Then he hoisted the flag and let it fly away in the wind. It flew away and fell by the Himegoso Shrine of Three-Fields District, where it flew back and fell again at Tamura on this Mountain-Gate-River, by which Kaseko knew where the Kami was settled. In his dwelling by night he dreamed a dream in which there appeared a lady holding the cords of a weaving machine and a reeling stick. Startled at this, he made also a shrine ⁵⁹ for the weaving-woman Kami and worshiped her. After that the Kami slew no more people. The shrine is called Himegoso Shrine.ᴮ

Now the Sovereign sent to Sky-Sun-Spear the pair

HARIMA-GREAT-TRIBE-MASTER [60]
NAGAŌCHI [61]

to ask him who he was and to what Land he belonged. To this he replied, "I am the son of the king of Silla. Hearing that there was in the Land of Nippon a wise sovereign, I gave my country to my younger brother Chiko, and have come to offer allegiance." Now the things that Sky-Sun-Spear brought with him, which were called jewel-treasures and which he gave as tribute, were a leaf-slender gem, a leg-high gem, a red stone ukaka-gem, a sacred stone short-sword, a sacred stone spear, a sun-mirror, a bear-fence,[62] and an Isasa-sword—eight things altogether.

> (Others say the things he brought were two strings of jewels, a wave-raising scarf and a wave-stilling scarf, a wind-raising scarf and a wind-stilling scarf, a mirror of the sea horizon and a mirror of the beach.)

The Sovereign said to Sky-Sun-Spear, "You shall dwell either in the village of Shisaha in the Land of Harima or in the village of Idesa in the island of Foam-Way, as you choose." But he replied, "As to a place to dwell in, should your servant be so favored as to be granted the place of his choice, he will visit the several provinces in the hope that that place may be given him that is pleasing to him." This having been granted, he ascended the river Uji and went to the northward to the village of Hole in the Province of Omi. From there he went westward through the Province of Wakasa till he came to the Province of Tajima, which latter he chose as his dwelling place. Therefore the potters of Mirror-Valley in the Province of Omi became his servants. The jewel treasures he brought were stored in the Land of Tajima, and were made divine forever. This is the

EIGHT-FOLD-GREAT-KAMI-OF-SACRED-STONE.[63]

Now this Kami had a daughter who was named

MAIDEN-SACRED-STONE

and eighty Kami desired to wed her, but none succeeded. Then one of them,

YOUTH-UNDER-ICE-OF-AUTUMN-MOUNTAIN,

said to his younger brother

YOUTH-MIST-OF-SPRING-MOUNTAIN,

---

[60] **Ancestor of the Clan-Chiefs of Miwa.**
[61] **Ancestor of the Governors of Yamato.**

"Though I have asked for Maiden-Sacred-Stone, I cannot win her to wife. Can you?" The other replied, "Easily." At that the older made a wager with him, saying, "If you succeed, I will in payment doff my upper and lower garments and, measuring my height, will distill the fill of a liquor jar [64] and prepare for you all products of mountain and river." Then the younger repeated to his mother what the elder had said, and she took wistaria fiber and in one night wove and sewed an upper garment and trousers, with foot-covering and boots, and made a bow and arrows, and thus clothing him, made him carry the bow and arrows to the maiden's house, and the clothing and the weapons were transformed into wistaria flowers. There he hung up the bow and arrows in her privy and when she, thinking the blossoms remarkable, brought them out, he followed after her into her house and wedded her. Thus she begot one child, and he said to his elder brother, "I have won Maiden-Sacred-Stone."

When the other, chagrined that the younger had wedded her, did not pay his wager, he complained to his mother, who said, "While I augustly live, the Kami should be carefully patterned after; assuredly in not paying, he patterned himself after living people." And, angered at her elder child, she took a single joint of a bamboo from an island in the Sacred-Stone River, and made a rough basket with eight orifices, and soaking river stones in salt water, wrapped them in bamboo leaves and pronounced this curse: "Like the greening of these bamboo leaves, do you become green and wither! Like the flowing and ebbing of this salt water, do you flow and ebb! Like the sinking of these stones, do you sink and lie down!" Then she set the basket in smoke, and the elder brother dried up, shriveled, sickened, and withered during eight years.[65] At that the elder brother besought her, wailing and weeping, so that she caused the curse to be remitted, and his body was again restored to health. (From this arose the saying, "Payment of a divine wager.")

Sky-Sun-Spear remained in that land and his descendant in the fourth generation was

PRINCE-PURE

who begot

TAJIMA-MORI [66]

TAJIMA-SUN-HEIGHT

(which latter, some say, was father of Princess-High-Brow-of-Mulberry-Castle, who begot Princess-Long-Life-Perfect, who became the Empress [67] of the Emperor Prince-Perfect-Middle.)

---

[66] **Ancestor of the Tribe-Masters of the Granaries (Miyakè).**

Now it was reported to the Sovereign that in the village of Tajima [68] was one

KUEHAYA

who was so strong that he could break horns and bend hooks straight, and who was accustomed to say to his people, "Where throughout the four directions is there a match for my strength? I wish to find a man of might and have a test with him to live or die." So the Sovereign said to his ministers, "Kuehaya is said to be the first in strength in the empire. Is there anyone to equal him?" Said one of the ministers, "In the land of Sacred-Quarter is one named

NOBLE-OF-NOMI [69]

who should equal him." So the Sovereign sent Nagaōchi [70] to summon Noble-of-Nomi, who came from Sacred-Quarter, and he and Kuehaya were made to wrestle.[71] They faced each other and each lifting his foot kicked the other, and the kick of Noble-of-Nomi broke Kuehaya's ribs and his loins, so that he died. And all Kuehaya's land was taken and bestowed upon Noble-of-Nomi. (Therefore the place in that village is called Broken-Loin-Field.)

Now in accordance with the words [72] of the Empress, Princess Saho, the Sovereign summoned to be his wives the five daughters of King-Tatatsu-Road-Master-Prince-of-Tamba. Three he kept, but the two younger queens, on account of their extreme ugliness, he sent back to their native place. At this Princess-Motonu [73] was humiliated, and said she, "When it becomes known in the adjacent villages that we sisters of the same family have been sent back on account of our ugliness, it will be most mortifying," and at the place that is now called Hanging-Tree [74] in the Land of Beyond-the-Mountains, she sought death by hanging herself from a tree branch, but this attempt failed. (For this reason the place was so named.) And at the place that is now called Otokuni, she killed herself by throwing herself into a deep tarn (or, as some say, from her carriage). For this reason the place was named Falling-Country.[75]

PRINCESS-HIBASU

the Sky-Sovereign made his Empress, and by her he begot

PRINCE-INI-STONE-CASTLE-IRI
PRINCE-GREAT-PERFECT-RULING-LORD

---

[69] **Ancestor of the Tribe-Masters of the Clay-Workers.***

---

* Presumably reckoning his descent from Great-Sky-Sun (see p. 31).

PRINCE-OF-GREAT-MIDDLE [76]
PRINCESS-MOUNTAIN-GATE [77]
PRINCE-YOUNG-KI-NI-IRI. [78]

By Princess-Iri-of-Azami, younger sister of Princess-Hibasu, he begot

IKOBAYA-LORD. [79]

Prince-Ini-Stone-Castle-Iri made the pool of Blood-Lagoon.[80] Also he made the pools of Ravine [81] and of Takashi and the pool of Smart-Wood-Harbor at Kusaka, the pools of Saki in Mountain-Gate, and of Fish-Hawk. He dwelt in the Palace of River-Head at Bird-Catching [82] and caused to be made a thousand cross-swords, which he first deposited in the village of Osaka and later presented to the shrine of the Kami of Above-the-Rock. These swords were called the Naked-Companions. And the Sovereign, at the Kami's request, put them in charge of

ICHIKAWA [83]

of the family of the Magnate of Kasuga. There were also given to Prince-Ini-Stone-Castle-Iri the ten Clans of the Shield-Makers, the Figured-Cloth-Makers, the Sacred-Bow-Shavers, the Sacred-Arrow-Makers, the Great-Anashi, the Hatsu-Kashi, the Kami-Osaka, the Daily-Offering-Bearers and the Sword-Wearers.[84]

From this time Prince-Ini-Stone-Castle-Iri dwelt in the temple of Above-the-Rock. He established, moreover, the River-Head Clan. At length he said to his younger sister,

PRINCESS-OF-GREAT-MIDDLE [85]

"I am old and cannot have in charge these divine treasures. Do you take them in charge." But she answered, "I am a woman and feeble. How can I mount up to the divine Sky-storehouse?" He replied, "Though the storehouse is indeed high, I can make a ladder." (From which arose the saying, "One can mount up even to the divine storehouse of the Sky if one but place a ladder.") So Princess-of-Great-Middle transferred the charge of these sacred treasures to

GREAT-TRIBE-MASTER-OF-TOCHINÈ [86]

---

[76] Ancestor of the Lords of Yamabè (in Yamato Province), Sakikusa, Inaki, Ada, Minu in the Land of Owari, Ihanashi (in Bizen Province), Koromo (a Village in Mikaha), Takasuka and Murè (unidentified), and of the Clan-Chiefs of Asuka (unidentified).
[79] Ancestor of the Lords of Anahobè in Saho.
[83] Ancestor of the Head-Men of the Imperial Guard.

one of the imperial guard. (So the Tribe-Masters of the imperial guard at present have in charge these treasures of Above-the-Rock.)

PRINCE-FIRE-POSSESSING-LORD AND HIS FIRST SPEAKING

Now Prince-Fire-Possessing-Lord,[87] when he had reached the age of three times ten years, had spoken no word, but though his eight-hand-lengths beard reached to his midriff, he wept continually like an infant. Therefore the Sovereign had his ministers consider the matter. They led the child about and amused him by making a two-forked boat out of a two-forked cryptomeria from Meeting-Port in Owari, bringing it up and floating it on the pools of Ichisi and of Karu, in Mountain-Gate. It was on hearing the cry of a high-flying swan that he first spoke. The Sovereign was standing before the great hall with the prince when a swan crossed the great void uttering its note, and Prince-Fire-Possessing-Lord, hearing, looked up and asked, "What is that?" The Sovereign at this was overjoyed, and asked his attendants, "Which of you will catch that bird for me?" At which one named

GREAT-HAWK-OF-MOUNTAIN-NEIGHBORHOOD [88]

replied, "Your servant will assuredly catch it for you." Said the Sovereign, "If you do this, I will greatly recompense you." So, looking far out, in the direction to which the swan had flown, Great-Hawk-of-Mountain-Neighborhood pursued it from the Land of Tree to the Land of Harima, from which he crossed over to the Land of Rice-Leaves, from there reaching the Lands of Tamba and Tajima; and from that place pursuing it around to the eastward, he arrived at the Land of Fresh-Sea and crossed over into the Land of Three-Moors. From there he passed along by the Land of Owari, pursuing it into the Land of Lime-Tree-Moor, and at length, coming in his pursuit to the Land of Koshi, he spread a net in the estuary of Snare-Net,[89] and caught the bird.[90] (From this that estuary was so named.)

(Others say he caught the swan in the Land of Sacred-Quarter, and yet others say in the Land of Tajima.)

Returning, Great-Hawk-of-Mountain-Neighborhood presented the bird to the Sovereign, and was recompensed and given the title of Ruler-of-Bird-Catchers.[91] Also there were formed the Bird-Catcher-Clan, the Bird-Feeder Clan and the Fire-Possessor Clan. Now the swan was given to Prince-Fire-Possessing-Lord and he played with it, but, though it had been thought that on seeing the bird again he would speak, nevertheless

[88] **Ancestor of the Rulers of Tottori (unidentified).**

he did not. Thereon the Sky-Sovereign, grieving, fell asleep and in a dream was instructed thus: "If you will build me a shrine like your own palace,⁹² the child shall surely speak." Accordingly, he made grand divination to find what deity's heart's-wish this was, and it appeared that the infliction of muteness was the heart's-wish of Great-Land-Master, the Great Kami of Sacred-Quarter.

> (*By some it is said that when Prince-Fire-Possessing-Lord reached the age of seven years without being able to speak, the Sovereign asked of all his retainers the reason why, but there was none who could tell. Later the Empress dreamed, and in her dream a Kami revealed himself to her, saying, "I am the Kami of the Land of Cloth ⁹³ and my name is*
>
> ### PRINCESS-SKY-AWFUL.
>
> *As yet, however, no worship is paid me. If you will appoint one to give me worship, the prince shall speak perfectly and his life shall be long." So the Sovereign made augury to find one who could approach the Kami. Now the Clan-Chief of Brave-Hill ⁹⁴ seemed suited for the augury, and he was ordered to seek the Kami. So he went to Mount Flower-Deer ⁹⁵ in Three-Moor Province, where he climbed a sakaki tree, and taking his head ornament, he declared, "At the spot where this head ornament falls, there truly the Kami shall be present." So a shrine was built at the place. (For this reason, it was called Head-Ornament Village.)* ▲

Now when the child was about to be sent to worship at the shrine of the Great Kami, King-Dawn-Rise ⁹⁶ was chosen by lot to attend him. So he made an invocation, saying, "If there is to be a true answer to our worship of this Great Kami, may the heron that lives here on the tree by the Pool of Heron's-Nest, fall because of this invocation!" And when he thus spoke, the heron that had been invoked fell to the ground dead. Then by an invocation he bade it come to life, and it came to life again. Moreover, by two invocations he caused a broad-branched bear oak on Cape Sweet-Oak ⁹⁷ to wither and be brought to life again. For that reason there was granted to King-Dawn-Rise the name of Prince-Mountain-Gate-Old-Stone-Castle-Tomi-Tomi-Fruitful-Asakura-Dawn-Rise.

When the child was sent off attended by King-Dawn-Rise and King-Unakami, it was shown by divination that at the exit of Level they would

---

⁹⁴ **Ancestor of the Sun-Placing Clan.***

* *Hiyoki (Heki)-Be.*

meet a lame person and a blind person, and that only the side exit that led to the Land of Tree would be lucky. So they started, establishing the Fire-Possessor Clan in every stopping place. Having come to Sacred-Quarter, and having finished worshiping the Great Kami, on their return they erected in the middle of the river Hi a temporary palace for the child Prince-Fire-Possessing-Lord to dwell in, and plaited a bridge of bark-black boughs. The ancestor of the rulers of the Land of Sacred-Quarter,

KIHISA-POSSESSOR [98]

made an imitation green-leaved hill and set it in the lower current of the river, and was about to present the ceremonial food, when the child spoke, saying, "What seems a green-leaved hill here in the lower river, in spite of its resemblance, is not a hill. Is it perhaps the courtyard of the under-priests who worship the great Kami, Great-Land-Master, who dwells in the Shrine of So at Rock-Curve in Sacred-Quarter?" Thus he asked, and the attendant kings, hearing with joy and seeing with delight, established Prince-Fire-Possessing-Lord as a dweller in the Palace of Long-Rice-Ear at Palmetto,[99] and despatched a courier to inform the Sovereign.

Prince-Fire-Possessing-Lord wedded

PRINCESS-HINAGA

for one night. On looking secretly at the beautiful damsel, however, she turned into a serpent, at which sight he fled away in alarm. At this Princess-Hinaga was angered and illuminating the sea plain, pursued them in a vessel, and they, in greater and greater alarm, dragged their vessel across the mountain valleys and fled up to the capital. There they made report, saying, "We have come up because your great and august child has become able to speak through his worship of the Great Kami." So the Sky-Sovereign in delight straightway sent King-Unakami back to erect a shrine to the Kami, and on the child's account established the Elder-Bather and Younger-Bather Clans.

THE SHRINE OF GREAT-SKY-SHINER IN ISÈ

After that the Kami Great-Sky-Shiner was taken from Princess-Fruitful-Stone-Castle-Iri [1] and put in charge of Princess-Mountain-Gate,[2] who searched for a spot where the great Kami might dwell. First she built her a shrine at Bottom-of-Sacred-Tree in Stone-Castle and made sacrifice to her there.

---

[98] **Ancestor of the Rulers of the Land of Izumo.**

From there she went to High-Hill at Boiled-Rice-Moor, where she built a weaving-house in which to weave the clothing [3] *of Great-Sky-Shiner. She went then to Village-of-Hemp-Tiers* [4] *in Isè,* [5] *where she built a shrine that was called Shrine-of-Kami-Cloth-Weaving, or Eight-Hiro-Loom-Palace.*[A]

(*Hemp-Tiers is so named for the reason that there is a Kami place in the northern part of the district where cloth offerings were made to the Great Deity. The Hemp-Tiers family, with others, had residence there, from which it received its name. Isè was so named because the Kami Prince-of-Isè* [6] *built a stone castle there in the ancient time, and*

PRINCE-OF-ABESHI [7]

came, together with others, to take the castle, but was not able to do so and returned.) [B]

In Iga District, while Princess-Mountain-Gate stayed there, the governor of the province appointed Kami-folk. From there she went to Palace-of-Wistaria-Kata in Ano District, where she remained three years, and the governor of the province offered to her six places as Kami-villages: these were Ano, Ichishi, Bell-Deer, River-Bend, Kuwana, and High-Boiled-Rice. From there she went to Middle-Island District, Owari Province, where the governor offered to her Long-Island as a Kami-village. From there she went to Azumi District, Three-Rivers Province, where the governor offered her Azumi as a Kami-village. From there she went to Hamana District of Far-Fresh-Sea [8] *Province, where the governor offered her Hamana as a Kami-village. From there she returned to Iitaka District, Isè Province, where she remained three months.*[A]

(Some say that she went to Sasahata in Uda, in the Province of Behind-the-Mountains, then to the Land of Omi, then eastward to Three-Moors, and from there to the Province of Isè.)

Great-Sky-Shiner instructed Princess-Mountain-Gate, saying, "The Province of divine-winded Isè is the Land where go the waves of the Eternal-Land. It is a withdrawn and pleasant Land, and here I will reside." So a shrine [9] was built for her in that province and a palace-of-abstaining at Fifty-Bells, which was called the Palace of Iso. It was in this place that Great-Sky-Shiner first descended from the Sky. In the beginning there had been made beforehand in the Sky a secret promise and agreement, and it was for a deep reason that Prince-Monkey-Rice-field had there descended.

(*Some say, however, that she first descended in Uda District, where the Kami-Clan of Uda* [10] *was formed, and that she later was moved to Fifty-Bells.*)

(Others say that she first descended on Mount-Newly-Tilled [11] in Soaking-Province.) ᴀ

Through an oracle she commanded that governors of all provinces should mark places where a radiance was found as shrine-places, and that the Sovereign should visit these places. There descended with her also the Kami

GREAT-RICEFIELD [12]

a descendant of Prince-Monkey-Ricefield.[13] The deities of this province are Sky-Beckoning-Ancestor-Lord, Great-Year,[14] and Great-Ricefield.

Now Great-Land-Master [15] spoke through the mouth of Noble-of-Great-Mina-Kuchi, saying, "In the Great Beginning it was promised that Great-Sky-Shiner should rule all the Plain-of-the-High-Sky and that her Sky-descendants should reign over the eighty spirits of the Central-Land-of-Reed-Plains, while I myself should carry on the government of the Great Earth. But my sway of the Great Land has come to an end. Such was the covenant made, but though the Sovereign Prince-Iniyè-Mima-Kiri kept up the worship of the Sky- and Earth-Kami, he did not search for the root of the matter, but stopped at the foliage. For this reason he died early. Do you, however, be watchful in the worship: so you will live long and the empire be tranquil." Hearing this, the Sovereign caused divination to be made and by this chose Princess-Nunaki-Iri [16] to make sacrifice, but she was so emaciated that she could not and Nagaōchi [17] was appointed in her stead. Also the Sovereign sent Great-Tribe-Master-of-Tochinè to Sacred-Quarter to examine and verify the Sky-treasures, and put him in charge of them. Furthermore the Department of Worship made divination by which bows, arrows and cross-swords were placed, as propitious offerings, in the shrines of all the Kami. (This was the origin of the practice of offering weapons to the Sky- and Earth-Kami.) At this time also granaries were built in the army villages.

THE ABOLITION OF DEAD-FOLLOWING

It befell that Prince-Mountain-Gate, the Sovereign's younger brother on his mother's side, died and was buried, and all his attendants were buried alive upright about the mound. For some days they did not die but wept and wailed day and night. Finally they died and rotted and were eaten by dogs and crows. The Sovereign heard this wailing and sorrowed at it, and said to his ministers, "It is painful to compel those

---

12 **Ancestor of the Rulers of the Land of Uji.***

---

* Fubosuekoko's *Kogo-Shui-Kogi* states that Tsuchi, ruler of Uji, was a descendant of Prince-Monkey-Ricefield.

whom one has loved during life to follow one when he dies. While it is an ancient custom, yet it is a bad one and should not be continued. Do you confer together now so that in future the custom of dead-following may be made to cease!"

> (*It is said by some, however, that this was the first time living men were thus buried with the dead.*)

At this time the Empress, Princess-Hibasu, died and for several days they prepared for the burying. Then the Sovereign said to his ministers, "We have known the evil of the practice of dead-following. What shall now be done?" Said Noble-of-Nomi,[18] then, "It is not good to bury men alive at the mound of a prince, and the custom should not be handed down. Grant me leave to propose a plan." This having been granted, he summoned from the Land of Sacred-Quarter a hundred men of the Clay-Workers Clan and made them take clay and shape from it men, horses, and various objects, and showed these to the Sovereign, saying, "In future let these things of clay by law be set up at mounds instead of living men." Then said the Sovereign, in delight, "Your plan pleases Our heart!" And he issued a decree that these clay shapes should in future be set up at mounds and that men should not be harmed. (These clay objects were called clay circles, or set-up things.) He also recompensed Noble-of-Nomi and gave him a kneading place and made him head of the Clay-Workers Clan. So after that he was called the Magnate-of-the-Clay-Workers. (This is why the Tribe-Masters of the Clay-Workers have in charge the burials of the Sovereign.) At this time the prayer-stone-makers also were established.

Now Noble-of-Nomi frequently visited Sacred-Quarter Province and at Black-Slope-Clan-Moor there he fell ill and died, and a man of that province came and hired people to carry gravel from a river bed to build a tomb. (So the place was named Set-up-Moor [19] *and the grave was called Tomb-House* [20]*-of-Sacred-Quarter.)* ᴀ

Princess-Hibasu was buried in the tomb of Buddhist-Temple-Place,[21] near Saki.

In this reign, in the Province of Soaking, white birds flew down from the Sky and transformed themselves into young damsels. They flew up in the morning and flew down in the evening and gathered stones to make a pool. Vainly they constructed the embankment through days and months, but as fast as they built it, it broke, and it was never finished. Then the damsels sang:

> *Though we white birds strove,* || *Bearing soil on our pinions*
> *To construct a dyke,*
> *Down it tumbles! Ah, too sad* || *To remain here* * * *[22]

So singing, all the white birds flew up to the Sky, nor did they ever return. (*Therefore the place was called White-Bird-Village.*²³)ᴬ

Now the Sovereign said to Prince-Iri-of-Ini-Stone-Castle and Prince-Great-Perfect-Ruling-Lord, "Tell me, each of you, what thing his heart most desires." Prince-Iri-of-Ini-Stone-Castle replied, "I desire a bow and arrows," and Prince-Great-Perfect-Ruling-Lord replied, "I desire the imperial rule." Then the Sovereign said, "The desire of each shall be given him." And a bow and arrows were given to Prince-Iri-of-Ini-Stone-Castle and Prince-Great-Perfect-Ruling-Lord was declared heir apparent.

While the Sovereign was making his imperial way to Behind-the-Mountains, it was told him that there was in that land a most lovely damsel named

KARIBATA-TOBE.

So he took his spear in his hand and vowed, saying, "If I am to possess this lovely one I shall meet a good omen." Proceeding to his traveling palace, there came from the river a great turtle, which, when he thrust at it with the spear, turned into a white stone. Then said his attendants, "This is an omen, if one could but divine its meaning." Karibata-Tobè was brought and lodged in the after palace, and by her he begot

KING-OCHI-LORD ²⁴
KING-PRINCE-SEVERE-PERFECT ²⁵
KING-ITOSHI-LORD.²⁶

Also he took to wife her sister, and begot

KING-IWA-TSUKU-LORD ²⁷
PRINCESS-IWA-TSUKU.²⁸

In the Land of Ricefield-Place, in the village of Kuwada, there was a man named Mikaso, who had a dog named Ayuki. The dog attacked and killed a wild animal called a mujina,²⁹ in whose belly was a yasaka-gem that was presented to the Sovereign. It is now in the Shrine of Above-the-Rocks.

Now the Sovereign said to his ministers, "The divine treasures brought by Sky-Sun-Spear are at present in the Land of Tajima. We desire to

---

²⁴ Ancestor of the Clan-Chiefs of Mount Wotsuki (in Omi Province) and of Koromo.
²⁵ Ancestor of the Clan-Chiefs of Mount Kasuga (in Yamato Province), Ikè in Koshi (unidentified), Kasuga-Be, and Ishida.
²⁶ Ancestor, by adoption, of the Itoshi Clan.
²⁷ Ancestor of the Clan-Chiefs of Haguchi (in Noto Province).

see them." So Prince-Pure,[30] great-grandson of Sky-Sun-Spear, was bidden to fetch them, and he brought and presented all but the sacred stone short-sword, which he hid in his clothing. The Sovereign, not missing it, sent for Prince-Pure to come to the palace and offered him sakè, when the sword issued from his garments and was seen. When the Sovereign asked what sword it was, Prince-Pure replied that it belonged to the sacred treasures. The Sovereign, saying, "How can this remain apart from the others?" had it placed in the sacred treasury. But afterward, when the treasury was opened for examination, it had disappeared. So a messenger was sent to inquire of Prince-Pure if it had come to him. He replied, "Last night, of its own accord, it came indeed to the house of your servant. Today, however, it has again vanished." So the Sovereign, awe-struck, gave up the search. The short-sword went of itself to the Island of My-Shame, where the people, counting it a Kami, built it a shrine, in which it is now worshiped.

The years of the Sovereign, Prince-Ikumè-Iri-Isachi, when he died, were one hundred and fifty-three (or, as some say, one hundred and forty), and he was buried in the mound of Fushimi in the middle of the moor of Mitachi at Sedge-Plain.[31]

TAJIMA-MORI FETCHES THE ORANGE FROM THE ETERNAL-LAND

Now before his death he had bidden Tajima Mori [32] depart to the Eternal-Land to fetch the fruit of the fragrant everlasting tree, called the orange.[33] Tajima-Mori at length reached that country, plucked the fruit of the tree, and brought back eight of the fruit growing on leaved branches and eight on the bare twig. Meanwhile, however, the Sky-Sovereign had died.

Then Tajima-Mori, setting apart four of each sort, which he presented at the tomb of the Great Empress, Princess-Hibasu, took the other four as an offering to the door of the Sovereign's imperial tomb, and raising on high the tree-fruit, wailed and wept, saying: "At the Sky-bidding I departed to a far land across the thousand ri of waves, passing beyond the weak-water,[34] to a land that is the strange abode of Kami and spirits, which common mortals cannot reach. In going and returning, ten years have passed. Daring, of myself, the mountainous waves, I did not expect to return again to my native land, but trusting in the spirit of the Sovereign, with difficulty I have returned, bearing the fruit of the fragrant everlasting tree from the Eternal-Land! But the Sovereign is dead and I cannot make report. Why then should I remain alive?" So, turning his face toward the imperial mound, he wailed and wept himself to death. When the Ministers heard this they all wept.

THE EMPEROR PRINCE-GREAT-PERFECT-RULING-LORD
(LUMINOUS-CONDUCT [35])

Prince-Great-Perfect-Ruling-Lord removed the capital to Makimuku,[36] where he dwelt in the Palace of Pine-Tree-Enclosure and ruled the empire. His stature was ten shaku, two sun, and the length of his shin four shaku, one sun.

Now the beauty of

PRINCESS-ELDER-LADY-OF-WAVE-HIDING-OF-HARIMA

who was the daughter of Young-Brave-Prince-of-Maise,[37] was at the time unequalled, and he went to pay court to her, fastening eight-shaku curved jewels to the upper cord of his sword and a perfect large mirror [38] to its lower cord.

> (Some say, however, that in the reign of the Emperor Prince-Young-Perfect,
> ### PRINCE-SACHI [39]
> being sent with others to fix the borders of the provinces, there came to meet him Young-Brave-Prince-of-Maise and
> ### PRINCESS-OF-MAISE
> and that he wedded the latter and begot Princess-Elder-Lady-of-Wave-Hiding-of-Harima.) ᴀ

LONG-LIFE [40]

with others, acted as go-between.[41] When they were about to cross the ford of High-Shallow, in Settsu Province, the ferryman, who was

SMALL-PERSON-JEWEL

of Tree-Province, asked, "O my Sovereign, will you make me your victualer? [42] The Sovereign answered, "First set us across the river." Small-Person-Jewel obeyed but asked pay for it, when the Sovereign threw into the boat a younger-headdress [43] that he had brought for use as a reward on the way. It shone brightly in the boat. Since the ferryman received his pay and permitted them to cross the river in his boat, the place was named Crossing-of-Our-Clan-Chief. When they arrived at August-Well-of-Table-Server,[44] in Red-Stone District, the Sovereign dined (so the place was thus named). Princess-Elder-Lady-of-Wave-Hiding-of-Harima, hearing of his coming, was surprised, and went away to a certain island.

---

[39] *Ancestor of the Magnates of the Wani Clan.*
[40] *Ancestor of the Governors of Kamo-no Kori-no Yama.*

The Sovereign, going to the pine field of Small-Deer searching for her, beheld a white dog which looked toward the sea with prolonged barking. On his asking whose dog this was, the headman of Bell-Village replied that it belonged to the damsel. At which the Sovereign, saying, "How delightful is your news!" gave him the name of

HEAD-MAN-OF-TELLING.

Knowing that she was upon that little island, he crossed the sea to Repast-Harbor and took a meal there. (Therefore the place was called Village-of-Repast.) Fish were caught in the bay for this meal. (Therefore it was called August-Added-Bay.) A wharf having been built of new timbers at the place of the boat's departure, they proceeded to the place, and the Sovereign met her, saying, "Here my dear wife hid herself." (Therefore the place was named Decline-Wife-Island.) When his boat and hers had been lashed together, they came to the mainland. The name of the helmsman was

GREAT-MIDDLE-ISHIJI.

Returning to Six-Join-Village,[45] *of Wave-Hiding, he for the first time cohabited with her. (Therefore the place was thus named.) Now the Sovereign said, "The sound of the waves and fowls is irksome to me," and removed to High-Palace. (Thus the Village-of-High-Palace received its name.) Also a sakè-house was built (the place being named Sakè-House-Village), and a house built for flesh (the place being named Flesh-Village.)* [46]

Also a palace was built at Mansion-Village [47] *(which thus received its name). After this the Sovereign removed to Castle-Palace-Ricefield-Village, where he wedded Princess-Elder-Lady-of-Wave-Hiding-of-Harima, and made her his Empress. Later her attendant*

PRINCESS-HISURA

Magnate of Sacred-Quarter, was given to Long-Life. Her tomb is to the west of Small-Deer Station.[A]

By Princess-Elder-Lady-of-Wave-Hiding-of-Harima the Sovereign begot

KING-WONDROUS-TSUNU-LORD [48]
GREAT-PESTLE [49]
LITTLE-PESTLE [50]

---

[48] **Ancestor of the Tribe-Masters of Mamuta (in Kawachi Province).**
[49] **Ancestor of the Clan-Chiefs of Mori (unidentified) Ohota (in Mino Province), Shimada (in Owari Province), and Muketsu.**

(the latter two being twins, born with one caul, so that the Sovereign, marveling, informed the mortar [51] and gave them these names)

PRINCE-MOUNTAIN-GATE [52]

(who, some say, was his son by Princess-Yasaka-Iri.)

KING-DIVINE-WONDROUS.[53]

Now when the Sovereign made a journey to Mino it was told him that there was in that province a lovely damsel named

PRINCESS-YOUNGER

daughter of Prince-Yasaka-Iri,[54] and desiring to wed her, he went to her house. She, however, learning that he was coming in his carriage, hid herself in a bamboo glade. So the Sovereign gave her residence in his palace and amused himself morning and evening by watching carp that he had placed in a pool. She also, desiring to see the playing of the fish, came out and stood by the pool, when he kept her there and cohabited with her. Then she reflected, and thinking, "The habit of husband and wife, though it has always been the custom, does not suit me," said to the Sovereign, "Your handmaid is of a frame of mind which shrinks from cohabitation. She has obediently dwelt for a while within the curtain, but she takes no joy in it. She is moreover of an unlovely countenance and not worthy of a place in the side courts. She has, however, an elder sister named

PRINCESS-YASAKA-IRI

lovely in face and virtuous, and fit to occupy the after-palace." So the Sovereign wedded Princess-Yasaka-Iri and begot

PRINCE-YOUNG-PERFECT
PRINCE-IRI-OF-IHOKI.

Prince-Iri-of-Ihoki took to wife

OLD-WOMAN-SHIRITSUKI

who was the daughter of

NOBLE-OF-BRAVE-RICE-SEED [55]

and there was born to the two

KING-TRUE-YOUNG-OF-ELBOW-PAD.

---

[53] Ancestor of the Abiko (Family) and of the Sakè-Clans of the Land of Ki and of Uda.
[55] Ancestor of the Tribe-Masters of Owari.

Also the Sovereign wedded Princess-Quite-Black [56] and there was born to the two

KING-GREAT-ELDER-BROTHER

who begot

PRINCESS-OF-GREAT-MIDDLE [57]

whom the Sovereign Prince-Perfect-Middle took to wife. He wedded also

LADY-BEAUTIFUL-TEETH

of the Miho family, and there was born to them

PRINCESS-OF-IHO. [58]

By other wives also the Sovereign begot

PRINCE-DIVINE-COMB [59]
PRINCE-IRI-OF-INASÈ [60]
PRINCE-BRAVE-LAND-KORI-LORD [61]
PRINCE-SOTSU-OF-SUN-FACING [62]
PRINCE-KUNICHI-LORD. [63]

The children of the Sovereign numbered in all eighty. All of these, except Little-Pestle, Prince-Young-Perfect, and Prince-Iri-of-Ihoki, were made rulers of Lands, lords, country-lords, or district-chiefs, and went to their own places, and the present lords of the various provinces are their descendants.

Now the Sky-Sovereign, that he might be more certain as to reports of the beauty of the two damsels

PRINCESS-ELDER
PRINCESS-YOUNGER [64]

daughters of King-Divine-Great-Lord, ruler of Three-Moors, sent his son Great-Pestle to examine their faces and to summon them to the capital. Great-Pestle, however, instead of summoning them, straightway had secret intercourse with both the damsels himself, and choosing other women, gave them falsely the damsels' names and sent them. On this, the Sovereign, knowing these to be other women, frequently

---

[59] **Ancestor of the Rulers of Sanuki.**
[60] **Ancestor of the Lords of Harima.**
[61] **Ancestor of the Lords of Mimuro (in Iyo Province).**
[62] **Ancestor of the Clan-Chiefs of Amu (in Nagato Province).**
[63] **Ancestor of the Lords of Minuma.**

gave them long glances but lay not with them, at which they grieved, and he was angered at Great-Pestle. By Princess-Elder, Great-Pestle begot

KING-PRINCE-ELDER-OF-GREAT-KURO [65]

and by Princess-Younger he begot

KING-PRINCE-YOUNGER-OF-GREAT-KURO.[66]

At this time the Kuma-So [67] folk revolted and refused to give tribute. Therefore the Sovereign made his imperial way to Tsukushi. When he came to the port of Saba [68] in Suwa [69] he gazed to the southward and said to his Ministers, "From over there much smoke arises. There must be outlaws there." Accordingly he bade the three,

BRAVE-MOROGI [70]

UNADÈ [71]

NATSUBANA [72]

go in advance. The ruler of the land was a woman named

PRINCESS-DIVINE-NASHI

and she ruled many folk. When she heard of the arrival of the Sovereign's messengers, she broke off a sakaki tree of Mount Shitsu, and hanging on its top branch an eightfold mirror and on its bottom branch a yasaka-gem, put a white flag on her vessel's prow and came to meet them, saying, "Let us not take up arms. My people are not rebellious but will submit. There are, however, four wicked outlaws. One, named Competent-Nose, has made a camp of many men at Upper-River-Current [73] in Usa. Another, named Competent-Ears, dwells at Upper-River-Current in August-Tree [74] and robs the people. The third, named Asahagi, has secretly gathered men at Upper-River-Current in Takaha. The fourth, named Earth-Break-Well-Break,[75] is hidden at Upper-River-Current in Midorino and robs the people, protected by mountains and rivers. All these camps are strong, and each of these outlaws has appointed his relatives as chiefs, and all declare that they will not submit to the imperial command. I beg you to fall upon them at once and conquer them."

---

[65] **Ancestor of the Lords of Unesu (unidentified) in Mino Province.**
[66] **Ancestor of the Clan-Chiefs of Mugetsu (Mugè) in Mino Province.**
[70] **Ancestor of the Magnates of Oho.**
[71] **Ancestor of the Magnates of Kusaki.**
[72] **Ancestor of the Clan-Chiefs of the Warrior-Clan.***

---

* See pp. 24, n. 40 and 67, n. 21. Natsubana was presumably a descendant of Sweet-True-Hand.

Then Brave-Morogi and the rest made gifts of red trousers and many strange things to the men of Asahagi and so decoyed them into bringing the four rebellious leaders with their followers, whereon they seized and slew all of them.

Unadè the Sovereign was sent to govern the land to the northward, and he proceeded to Magnate-of-Middle-Village [76] of Middle-District, when the sun set and he stopped there. Next morning there came flying from the north white birds, which flocked at this village. Unadè sent his servants to observe them. They changed first into rice-cakes and then into potato plants, whose leaves and blossoms grew even in winter. Beholding this, he exclaimed joyfully, "Never before have potato plants like these been seen. They are, indeed, a sign of the supreme virtues of the Sovereign and of Sky- and Earth-happiness." Straightway he presented himself at the imperial court and made report, at which the Sovereign was glad, and said, "Because of this good sign from the Sky and these rich plants of the earth, the province which you govern should be called Fruitful-Land.[77] Gazing from a great distance at Land-Cape District, he asked, "Is it a cape of a province that I see?" (So that land was named Land-Cape.) ▲

Then, continuing his way, the Sovereign came to the District of Nagawo [78] in the Province of Buzen, where he built a palace, wherefore the place was called Capital.[79]

(Some say, to the contrary, that this palace was at Nagawo-Beach, in Jewel-Name District, in Fire-Rear Province.)

While he resided there, he looked upon a certain mountain, and said, "The shape of that mountain is different from that of others. I wish to know whether it belongs to the main island or not." So he sent to examine it

NOBLE-OF-GREAT-MOOR-OF-THREE-THREADS

who proceeded there, when someone met him, saying, "I am

TAKUZU-WELL.[80]

Having heard that a messenger has arrived from the Sovereign, I have come to receive you." (So that place was called District-of-Taku.) Now at Hill-of-Koto-Tree there was at that time no elevation, the place being a plain. So the Sovereign, saying, "This place should have a hill," ordered the people of the district to build one. When it was completed, he ascended it and held a feast, in the midst of which he placed a koto which was transformed into a camphor tree. (For this reason the hill received its name.) ▲

Coming to Village-of-Taro and finding abundant produce, he said, "Though this place is small, its food is plenty. It should be called Abundant-Village." [81] (It is now corruptly called Village-of-Taro.) At a certain place, too, there was a well whose water was salty and that had seaweed growing at its bottom. When the Sovereign saw this, he named it Seaweed-Growing-Well.[82] (It is now corruptly called Meta-Well.)▲ In the winter the Sovereign proceeded to the district of Great-Ricefield, which is broad and lovely, and said he, "How broad it is! It should be named Great-Ricefield.[83] (Thus its name originated.) Also, at Village-of-Imi, he said, "This land is a distant one, of steep mountains and valleys, and it has few travelers." (So, as he viewed it, the place was called Village-of-Land-Seen.[84] It is now corruptly called Village-of-Imi.) There were two Ground-Spiders named Shinu-Kaoku and Shinu-Kaomi, who provided food for the Sovereign, and when the pair made a hunt on the ricefields their voices were exceedingly raucous, so that the Sovereign exclaimed, "How noisy!" (Wherefore that place was named Noisy-Moor.[85] It is now corruptly called Amishi-Moor.)▲

Now, it befell that he sent one of his attendants, who was governor of Kami-Sign,[86] to Quick-Arrive-Village,[87] of that province, to apprehend some of the Ground-Spider people. There he found a woman named

PRINCESS-OF-QUICK-ARRIVE

who said to him, "My younger brother,

BRAVE-OF-THREE-ROOMS

who dwells in the Village-of-Bamboo-Forest, has a lovely jewel that is called the Tree-Lotus-Jewel-of-Above-the-Rock. He keeps it jealously and will not show it to others." The governor of Kami-Sign sent for the man, but he fled over the mountains. However, falling at Stone-Peak, he was caught, and when direct inquiry was made of him he replied that he had two jewels, the Tree-Lotus-Jewel-of-Above-the-Rock and another called White-Jewel, saying, "They are like stones, and I will offer them to the Sovereign." Likewise he said, "There lives at the Village-of-River-Shore, one

MI-WISTARIA-WEIR [88]

who has a lovely jewel upon which he so dotes that it is not certain he will obey your command." Him also the governor of Kami-Sign caught and questioned. He then replied, "I have in truth a jewel, which I will offer to the Sovereign without regret at parting with it." So the governor of Kami-Sign brought the three jewels to the Sovereign, who said, "This land should be called the Land of Fully-Furnished-Jewels." [89] (It is now called, corruptly, District-of-Sonoki.)

It is said that of old time in this land, at the foot of Mount-Neck, there was a ricefield called House-Ricefield, where deer fed on the young rice plants. The owner of the field built a stockade around it, and when a deer came and thrust its head between the stakes of the stockade to crop the young rice plants, he caught it and would have cut off its head. Then the deer said, "Now I take oath, if by your great favor you will permit me to continue to live I will order my descendants never to eat the young rice plants." So the owner of the ricefield, wondering, did not kill the deer, but set it free. Since that time the rice plants bear their seed without being cropped by the deer. For this reason the place was called Neck-Ricefield and the mountain was called Mount-Neck.[A]

Now at the village of Hayami there was a chieftainess named

PRINCESS-OF-HAYA

who, hearing of the Sovereign's coming, went out to meet him in person and said, "In a mountain here is a huge cave named Rat's-Cave, and in it dwell two Ground-Spiders, one named White and the other Blue (-Green).[90] Also there are three other Ground-Spiders at Comfort-Moor[91] in the district of Nawori. The first is named Smite-Monkey,[92] the second Eighty-Fields, and the third Country-Fellow. These five are all huge men *of fierce nature*, with many followers, and all are recalcitrant and will resist." Hearing this, the Sovereign was angered and built a *temporary* palace dwelling at the village of Kutami and dwelt there. Then he said to his Ministers, "We must raise an army and slay these Ground-Spiders, who, if they take to hiding in the hills and moors through fear of us, will cause trouble." So they made mallet-weapons of camellia wood for the soldiers. Then the Sovereign went to a great oak-moor where was a stone six shaku long, three shaku wide, and one shaku five sun thick, and prayed to the Kami of Shiga, and the Kami of the Warrior-Clan and the Intercessor-Clan of Nawori, saying, "I desire to chastise these rebels. If I am to be successful, when I kick the stone let it rise like an oak leaf." Then he kicked the stone, and it rose into the great void like an oak leaf.[93] (Therefore the stone was called Kick-Stone and the place Kicked-Moor.)[94]

Afterward he chose the bravest of the troops and they crossed the hills, and clearing away the underbrush, fell upon the rock-dwelling Ground-Spiders and slew them at Upper-River-Current in Rice-Leaves. The entire company were slain and the blood ran ankle-deep. (So people called the place where the mallets were made Camellia-Market, and the place where the blood flowed Blood-Ricefield.) *The country was named Country-of-Princess-of-Haya,*[95] *but the people of a later time called it District of Haya-mi.* After this the Sovereign crossed Mount Comfort to battle with Smite-Monkey. The enemy's arrows, shot across from the mountain, fell like rain, so he retreated to Shirohara and made divination by the river. Then he sent his army against Eight-Fields on Comfort-Moor and routed him. On this Smite-Monkey, hopeless of victory, offered submission, and this being refused, his men threw themselves into a ravine and were killed. (As the Sovereign here gave comfort to a host, the moor was thus named.)

Now his vessel came to a place where fine seaweed grew abundantly on the sea-bottom; he bade them take the best, and it was offered to him at his meal. (Therefore the place was named Best-Seaweed-Passage.[96] It is now corruptly called Hoto.) Coming from Sabanotsu of Suwo Province, and gazing afar, he said, "Is it the cape of a province that I see yonder?" (Therefore the place at which he gazed was called Cape-of-Country.) Then the Sovereign, in his journey to the land of Sun-Facing,[97] came to the village of Hita. There was a Kami there whose name was

PRINCESS-OF-OLD-PORT

who took the form of a human being and received the Sovereign and reported to him the condition of the province. (Therefore the place was named District of Princess-Old-Port.[98] It is now corrupted to District-of-Hita.)[A]

In Sun-Facing he built the palace of Takaya and dwelt there.

THE KUMA-SO HERO AND HIS TWO DAUGHTERS

Now the Sovereign said to his ministers, "It has been told me that in the Land of the Kuma-So are two leaders named Atsukaya and Sakaya, who are called the Eighty [99] Kuma-So Heroes and who have many followers. Their spearheads are not to be equaled. With a small army we cannot destroy them, yet the movement of a large army would injure the people. Is there perhaps a way of conquering the land without battle?" Then one of the Ministers said, "One of the Kuma-So Heroes has two brave and lovely daughters, elder and younger, who are named

ICHI-FUKAYA
ICHI-KAYA.

Call them beneath your banner as if to present them with rich gifts, and thus gain information of the enemy, so that we may fall upon them unaware." The Sovereign bade that this be done, and when the gifts were given, the two damsels, deceived by it, entered the pavilion, where he had intercourse with Ichi-Fukaya and pretended love for her. Then said she, "Fear not that the Kuma-So will not make submission. In accordance with your handmaid's device, let a few soldiers follow me."

So she returned home and making strong sakè, gave her father some to drink, and he became drunken and fell asleep. Then having cut the string of his bow, she called one of the soldiers who had come with her, and he killed him. But the Sovereign was angered at this unfilial deed, and slew her, giving Ichi-Kaya as concubine to the ruler of the Land of Sun.

There was there also a beautiful woman named

PRINCESS-AUGUST-SWORD-OF-MIMUKU

whom he took as concubine and by whom he begot

KING-FRUITFUL-LAND-LORD.[1]

Afterward the Sovereign made his imperial way to the District of Child-Hot-Water,[2] where, at the little Moor of Nimo, he gazed to the eastward and said *to those who stood at his left and right*, "This land faces the Rising-Sun." (For this reason the Land of Sun-Facing was so named.) On that day he stood on a huge stone in the midst of the moor, and yearning for his own Land, sang:

> Ah, Mountain-Gate, || Of Lands the most secluded,
> Retiring behind || Awogaki Mountain,
> Folding it round! || Ah, Mountain-Gate,
> How delightful![3]

Moreover he sang a second song, which said,

> Let it be his || For whom life is unbroken,
> To wear for head-dress || The leafy foliage plucked
> From the branch of the bear-oak
> On Mount Heguri, || Oh! this child!

(This is a land-remembering song.) Also he sang:

> Ah, how enchanting! || From the homeward direction
> Clouds are rising and coming!

(This is an incomplete song.)

> (There are some who say that these three songs are but a single song and that it was sung not by the Sovereign, Prince-Great-Perfect-Ruling-Lord, but later, by his son, Mountain-Gate-Brave, when pacifying the twelve provinces of the east.)

Now when the Sovereign passed along to the capital, viewing the Land of Tsukushi, at Hinamori a crowd of people were gathered by the River

---

[1] **Ancestor of the Rulers of the Land of H'yuga and the Lords of the Province of Hi (Hizen and Higo Provinces).**

Ihasè. Beholding them from afar off, he sent

HINAMORI-ELDER
HINAMORI-YOUNGER

to inquire if they were evilly disposed. The latter returned, however, saying that

PRINCESS-IZUMI

Clan-Chieftainess of Murokata, desired only to offer the Sovereign a banquet, for which cause her tribe was gathered together. After that the Sovereign came to the District of Bear, where were two brothers named

PRINCE-BEAR.

He sent for the elder, who came, but the younger would not, so he sent soldiers who slew him. From there he departed by sea and came to a small island in Ashikita. Taking food there, he asked

LITTLE-LEFT [4]

for some cold water. Now there was no water on that island, but Little-Left lifted his gaze and besought the Sky- and Earth-Kami, and lo, a spring burst forth from the hillside and he drew a draught and offered it to the Sovereign. The spring still remains. (Therefore the island was called Water-Island.) [5]

Then he set sail for the Land of Fire, when the sun set, and in the dark night, knowing not where to go, they could not come to shore. Afar off, however, a fire [6] shone, *and the Sovereign bade his boatman go toward it,* so proceeding toward the place of its shining, they reached the shore, *which was a cliff.* The Sovereign asked, "What is the name of this place *where fire is burning, and what fire is it?*" The people answered, "This is Village-of-Fire (others call it Fruitful-Village) of Yatsushiro District, of the Land of Fire. *But the cause of the fire we have never discovered.*" So none could be found to have made the fire, and it was clear that no mortal had kindled it. *Therefore the Sovereign said, "This is no ordinary fire and I now understand why the country was named Land-of-Fire."* [A]

(Some say, however, that the name was first given to the land by him at this time.)

He anchored his vessel at the Beach of *Nagasu* in the District of *Jewel-Name.*[7] Many fish swam past the vessel's left side, and the helmsman,

---

[4] **Ancestor of the Princes of Yama.**

MORNING-KATSUMI

of Maise Province, hooked them with fishing hooks, getting many, which he offered to the Sovereign, who asked, "What are these fish called?" The man replied, "I do not know their name, but they are very like the trout." Then said the Sovereign, "You offered me very many, so the fish should be called many-fish.⁸ (From this that fish took its name.)ᴬ

After this, crossing over to Tamakina-Village, he slew a Ground-Spider called Tsuzura, and then proceeded to the Land of Wherefore.⁹ Now though this Land was flat and wide, it held no houses of men, so that the Sovereign asked, "Are there no people in this Land?" Then two Kami,

PRINCE-OF-WHEREFORE
PRINCESS-OF-WHEREFORE ¹⁰

having become transformed into human beings, and walking toward him, said, "We are two. Why do you say there are no people here?" (For this reason the land was called Why.)

His vessel stopped at Village-of-Rock-Ricefield-Pestle, where water gushed out of the hole of the lashing stake and formed an island. Seeing this, he summoned his attendants and said, "Let this land be called Lashing-Stake-Island.¹¹ (It is now corruptly called Pestle Island.)¹² From the southwest to the northeast of this district three mountain peaks stand side by side, called Pestle-Island. The southwestern one is named Prince-Kami, the middle one Princess-Kami, and the northeastern one Priestess ¹³-Kami. Each spring and autumn men and women of the neighboring villages climb the mountain hand in hand, with vessels of sakè hanging from their shoulders, and sometimes koto. There they enjoy the view and make merry with drinking, singing, and dancing, returning when they have had their fill of enjoyment. They sing this song:

> Where the hailstones fall, ‖ The peak of Pestle-Island,
> So steep it rises,
> Grasses I may not pluck there, ‖ But my loved one's hand I hold.ᴬ

When the Sovereign came to August-Tree in the Land of Tsukushi, he dwelt in the Palace of Takata. Now there was a prostrate tree there that was eight thousand seven hundred and thirty shaku long, and the one hundred officers walked back and forth on it. So the people made a song:

> The morning-frosted ‖ Sacred bridge of tree branches!
> They pass over it,
> The honorable lords! ‖ The sacred bridge of tree boughs!

The Sovereign asked concerning it and an old man answered, "This tree is an oak. Before it fell, in the morning sun it shaded Pestle-Island Hill, and in the evening it shaded Mount Why."

> (*By others it is said that the tree was a standing camphor tree, ninety-seven hundred shaku tall, its shadow in the morning sun covering Mount Abundant-Sufficient of Wistaria-Port District in Fire-Front Province and in the evening sun covering Mount Aratsunè in Mountain-Deep*¹⁴ *District in Fire-Rear*¹⁵ *Province.*)^B

Said the Sovereign, "This tree is a divine tree, and this land shall be called the Land-of-August-Tree." (*People now call it, corruptly, Mikè.*) When he came to the District of Yamè, he crossed Mount Mahe, and looking to the southward toward Sakè-of-Awa, he said, "The ridges and ravines of this Land lie fold on fold and are very lovely. Does a Kami dwell here?" Then

MONKEY-GREAT-SEA

District-Chief of Minuma, replied, "There is a Kami named

PRINCESS-OF-YAMÈ

who has dwelt forever on this mountain." (*This is the reason that Land is called the Land-of-Yamè.*) Later he came to a village where he took food, and his attendants left behind them there a drinking cup. (*Therefore the people called the place Drinking-Cup.*¹⁶)

*Now the ford of the August-Well River in Chikugo*¹⁷ *Province was wide, so that people and cattle could hardly cross. When he made a hunt, he built a vessel at Mount Drinking-Cup and a helm at Mount Treasure to guide it, by which means people and cattle could cross the ford.* (*Therefore it was named Village-of-Crossing.*)¹⁸ *In the District of Yafu*¹⁹ *all the magnates and distinguished persons*²⁰ *of the district gathered, so that the Sovereign's hounds barked, till a woman in childbed looked out at them, when they ceased barking.* (*Therefore the district was named Dog-Bark-Stop*²¹ *Land. It was corruptly called District of Yafu.*) *At Kami-Cape there was a violent Kami who slew many wayfarers, and while on the hunt the Sovereign pacified this Kami, who after that did no harm.* (*Therefore the place was called District-of-Kami-Cape.*) *All distinguished persons took ship and came to a port of the River August-Sleep, to pay the Sovereign homage.* (*For this reason the place was called Village-of-Ship-Sail.*)²² *There are four anchors near by; one is six shaku high and five shaku wide, and another four shaku high and five shaku wide. If a barren woman supplicates these, she becomes pregnant. The third anchor is four shaku high and five shaku wide, and the fourth three shaku high and four shaku wide. If one supplicates the* two in time of drought, rain will fall. Coming from Kawasè, the Sovereign's vessel stopped for the night at Village-of-August-Sleep, where he said, "It is calm. Let this village be called August-Sleep-Calm-Village." (Therefore it received that name.)

While the Sovereign stayed at the temporary Palace of Treasure, in August-Well District, of K'yushu, he made a tour of observation, and seeing how the fog covered Mount Kii, he said, "That province shall be called Land-of-Fogs." [23] (Later folk called it Kii, and now there is a district by that name.) When he returned from the Palace of Treasure, he passed by Spring-of-Sakè-Palace, where he took food. At that time his helmet and armor shone strangely, so he bade

PLANT-SLOPE

of the Augury-Clan to make augury, and it was reported that there was a Kami who desired the armor. Said the Sovereign, "If that is so, I will preserve this armor at a shrine, as a treasure of long ages. (Therefore the shrine was called Shrine-of-Long-Ages. Later people called it Shrine-of-Long-Hill.) The cords of the armor have now disappeared, but the helmet and plates still exist. While the Sovereign stayed at a temporary palace on Mount Sa, wandering about and gazing in every direction, he said, "It is light." [24] (Therefore the place was called Light-Village. At present it is corruptly called Village of Mount-Sa.) [A]

Now while he rested in the Palace of Shishiki-Island, the Sovereign gazed on the western sea, and there were islands there that were covered with dense smoke. Therefore he sent his attendant

HUNDRED-COMPLETE

Tribe-Master of Azumi, to investigate. There were eighty of these islands, upon two of which were people. One of these islands was called Little-Near, and on it dwelt a Ground-Spider named Great-Ear, and the other was called Great-Near, on which dwelt a Ground-Spider named Hang-Ear. Other inhabitants there were none. Hundred-Complete captured these and made report to the Sovereign, who bade him slay them. At that the Ground-Spiders prostrated themselves and said, "Our crimes are deserving of the extreme penalty, nor could even death requite them; if, however, the Sovereign of his favor permit us to live, we will always make some offering for the imperial repast." Then they took the bark of trees and cut out shapes of long ear-shell fish, whip [25] ear-shell fish, short ear-shell fish, shade ear-shell fish, and feather ear-shell fish, and offered them to his attendants. So the Sovereign had compassion and set them free. Then said he, "These islands, though far away, seem to be near, so they shall be called Near-Islands." [26] There are two ports there, one called

Port-of-Aïko, where more than twenty vessels can lie, and the other called Coast-of-Kahara, where more than ten can lie. Messengers to foreign lands started from these and came to Crossing-of-Minekura, from where they went toward the west. The fishermen of these islands are like falcon-men,* loving to ride and hunt. Their speech is different from that of ordinary people. In the westward part of Iki Province is Village-of-Whale Lying.[27] Of old time a wani pursued a whale, which fled and lay hidden there. (From this the place was thus named.) The wani and the whale were turned into stone. There is one ri between them.[A]

At Great-House-Island there was a Ground-Spider tribe called Great-Body, which resisted the Sovereign's command and would not yield, whereupon he bade his retainers chastise it. Since then fishermen have built dwellings on this island (from which it received its name). At the Village-of-Bowing three Ground-Spiders, one of whom was named Great-White, built a fortress for defense and would not obey, therefore he sent

PRINCE-YOUNG [28]

one of his attendants, to destroy them. Then Great-White and the others prostrated themselves and asked pardon for their offenses and permission to serve the Sovereign. (For this cause the place was called Village-of-Bowing.) There was another tribe that was called Lady-Seapine-Oak.[29] To destroy these he sent his attendant

GREAT-HOUSE-RICEFIELD-CHILD.

At this time fogs covered every side so that the place could not be seen. (So it was named Village-of-Fog. It is now corruptly called Village-of-Kasu.) Also while he rested at the temporary Palace of Usa-Beach,[30] he said to the Governor of Kami-Sign,[31] "I have made circuit of many Provinces and tranquilized them, and there is no rebel who does not obey my order." The other replied, "Yonder is a village, however, whence smoke rises, which is not yet subjugated." So the Sovereign sent him, with his commands, to that village. There was there a Ground-Spider whose name was Princess-Float-Hole-Foam, who dared to disobey the Sovereign's order, and she was slain. The place was named Village-of-Float-Hole.[A]

Later Noble-of-Brave-Uchi, who had been sent to explore the northern and central provinces, and inquire into the condition of the people, returned and reported to the Sovereign, saying, "To the eastward is a Land called High-as-the-Sun-Ears, whose people, male and female, tie their hair mallet-wise and ink [32] their bodies. They are savage and are

---

[28] **Ancestor of the Governors of Ki.**

called Emishi. Moreover, their land is broad and fruitful. Let us give them battle and seize it."

MOUNTAIN-GATE-BRAVE AND THE TWO KUMA-SO OUTLAWS

Now the Sovereign said to Little-Pestle, "Why does your elder brother not come forth to the great morning and evening repast? Let it be you who instructs him." Thus he commanded, but for five days after that Great-Pestle did not appear. So the Sovereign asked Little-Pestle, "Why is your elder brother so long in coming? Have you perhaps not yet instructed him?" He replied, "I have taken that trouble." The Sovereign then asked, "How did you do that?" And he answered, "In the early morning, when he entered the privy, I grasped him and crushed him, and pulling off his limbs, wrapped them in matting and threw them away." At this the Sovereign was alarmed at the valor and savageness of his son's character, and since at this time the Kuma-So people had again rebelled and were preying on the border, he commanded him, saying, "In the west at Kuma-So there are two outlaws, recalcitrant and disrespectful men. Do you capture them." And so saying, he sent him forth. At this time Little-Pestle was sixteen years old and wore his hair bound at the brow,[33] *although he was ten shaku tall.* Said Little-Pestle, "I wish to take with me some skilful bowmen," and being told there was in the Province of Three-Moors a skilful archer named

PRINCE-GIMI-YOUNGER

he sent, to bid that one to come to him,

PRINCE-MIYADO

of Mulberry-Castle. Accordingly Prince-Gimi-Younger came, bringing also

YOKOTACHI-OF-ISHIYURA

a country-lord of Tako and a country-lord of Chichika, of Omi Province, who went with Little-Pestle. Also his aunt, Princess-Mountain-Gate,[34] High Priestess of the temple at Isè, gave Little-Pestle her garment and skirt, and he hid a sword in his bosom and departed. *Passing the Province of Mimasaka, his comb dropped into a pool (which from this was named Comb-Pool).*[A]

When he came to the land of the Kuma-So he made inquiry into its condition and its point of entrance. Now near the dwelling of the two outlaw chiefs, who were named

ELDER-UPPER-RIVER-CURRENT-BRAVE
YOUNGER-UPPER-RIVER-CURRENT-BRAVE

was a roofed-pit [35] with a threefold girdle of warriors, and they were noisily preparing a feast. So Little-Pestle combed down his bound-up hair after the fashion of a girl's, and donned his aunt's garment and skirt, so that he appeared not other than a young girl,[36] and when the feast-day arrived he went inside the roofed-pit, mingling with the concubines. The two Kuma-So outlaws, rejoicing at the beauty of the pretended damsel, took her by the hand and set her between them, offering her the cup and making her drink for their amusement. So when it grew late and few of the people were left there, the Upper-River-Current-Braves were drunken, and Little-Pestle, plucking the sword from his bosom and catching the elder by the collar of his garment, thrust the blade through his breast. In fear the younger outlaw ran out, but Little-Pestle pursued him, and reaching him at the bottom of the steps of the roofed-pit, caught him by the skin of his back and thrust the sword through his buttock. Then the outlaw, bowing his head to the ground, said, "Do not move the sword; your servant has something to say." So Little-Pestle stayed his sword and gave him a moment's delay, holding him down prostrate. The outlaw then asked, "Who are you?" He answered, "I am the son of Prince-Great-Perfect-Ruling-Lord, the Sovereign, who rules the Land of the Great-Eight-Islands, and my name is Mountain-Gate-Boy.[37] Hearing that you two fellows were unsubmissive and disrespectful, the Sovereign sent me, commanding me to capture you." The Kuma-So outlaw said, "That verily must be true. There are none in the west as brave and strong as we two, and therefore none of the people have refused to be our followers. Yet truly in the Land of Great-Mountain-Gate is a man braver than us two. Therefore this contemptible robber, from his filthy mouth, offers you a name. Will you accept it?" Little-Pestle replied, "I will accept it." So the other said, "Henceforth, then, you shall be praised as Mountain-Gate-Brave." When he had finished speaking, Little-Pestle broke him up like a ripe muskmelon and slew him. So from that time Little-Pestle has been called by the name of Mountain-Gate-Brave.[38] He then sent Prince-Gimi-Younger with the others and they slew all the company, leaving no mouth.[39]

Now there was a great camphor tree, whose trunk and branches were high and its twigs dense, so that at sunrise its shade covered Mount Bullrush-River of Pestle-Island District and at sunset covered Mount Grass-Wide of Yafu District. When Mountain-Gate-Brave saw this camphor tree, he said, "This Land should be called Flourishing." (Therefore it was named Flourishing-District.)[40, A]

(Others say that it received its name in this wise: In the ancient time there was a violent Kami on the height of the mountain, who of all wayfarers slew half and spared half. So

GREAT-DESERT-RICEFIELD [41]

made divination and inquired of the Kami what to do. There were two Ground-Spider women, named Great-Mountain-Ricefield-Woman and Narrow-Mountain-Ricefield-Woman, who said, "If you take clay from Lower-Ricefield-Village and make shapes of people and horses of it and dedicate them to the Kami, he will be appeased." Accordingly Great-Desert-Ricefield made a festival which the Kami approved and he was appeased. Thereon Great-Desert-Ricefield said, "These women are wise indeed!" and he named the Land Wise-Princess District.) [42]

There is a stone statue there, on the upper side of the river, which is called Princess-World-Ricefield.[43]

Now there is a sea Kami that is a wani, and every year it comes up the stream, swimming to the side of the stone statue. Many sea fish follow it, and two or three days later they return to the sea. Those who avoid these fish get no harm, but those who catch and eat them die.▲

There were Ground-Spiders at Village-of-Small-Castle who built a fortress and did not obey the imperial command, so Mountain-Gate-Brave destroyed them. (Therefore the place was called Small-Castle-District.) He came at sunset to a port and anchored there, and next day, mooring his vessel, he viewed the wistaria. (For which reason the place was named Wistaria-Port.)

Thereon, having subdued and pacified all the Kami of the mountains and of the rivers, they returned by sea to Mountain-Gate. At the Passage-of-Hole [44] there was an evil Kami whom he slew, and also at Wave-Swift he slew the evil Kami of the Kashiba ford. After this he entered the Land of Sacred-Quarter, desirous of slaying the Sacred-Quarter bandit. When he arrived he at once cemented friendship with him, and having secretly made a sham sword of oak and girded it on, he went with him to bathe in the Fire River. Then, coming first from the water, he girded on the sword the Sacred-Quarter bandit had laid off, saying, "Let us trade swords." So the Sacred-Quarter bandit, coming after him from the water, girded on Mountain-Gate-Brave's sham sword, when Mountain-Gate-Brave reviled him, saying, "Ho! Let us join swords!" And he drew his sword, but the Sacred-Quarter bandit could not draw the sham sword and Mountain-Gate-Brave slew him.[45] Then Mountain-Gate-Brave returned to the capital and made report, saying, "Your servant has pacified the Kuma-So and tranquilized the western country, slaying the evil Kami who emitted baneful vapors to disturb wayfarers, and throwing open

---

[41] *Ancestor of the Governors of Saka-No Kori.*

land roads and water roads." So the Sovereign praised him and favored him exceedingly.

In this year the Sovereign sent his daughter, Princess-of-Iho,⁴⁶ to serve the spirit of Great-Sky-Shiner.⁴⁷

Mountain-Gate-Brave wedded Princess-Iwa-Tsuku,⁴⁸ his aunt, daughter of the Emperor Prince-Ikumè-Iri-Isachi, and begot

PRINCE-PERFECT-MIDDLE.

Also he took to wife

PRINCESS-YOUNGER-ORANGE

and there was born of the two

KING-YOUNG-BRAVE.

Also he took to wife

PRINCESS-FUTAJI

who was the daughter of

GREAT-TAMU-LORD ⁴⁹

by whom he begot

KING-RICE-GOOD-LORD.⁵⁰

Also he took to wife

PRINCESS-GREAT-MAISE-BRAVE

who was the younger sister of

PRINCE-BRAVE ⁵¹

Magnate of Maise, and there were born of the two

KING-BRAVE-COCOON ⁵²
PRINCE-TOÖKI-LORD.⁵³

Also he took to wife

PRINCESS-KUKUMA-MORI

---

⁴⁹ **Ancestor of the Rulers of the Land of Yasu in Chika-tsu-Omi.**
⁵⁰ **Ancestor of the Clan-Chiefs of Inugami (unidentified) and of the Brave-Clan.**
⁵² **Ancestor of the Clan-Chiefs of Aya (in Sanuki Province) and Isè, of the Lords of Towo (unidentified) and Miyagi (in Mikawa Province), and of the Head-Men of Masa (unidentified).**
⁵³ **Ancestor of the Clan-Chiefs of Wakè in Iyo.**

of Behind-the-Mountains, by whom he begot

KING-FOOT-MIRROR-LORD.[54]

By another wife, moreover, he begot

KING-LONG-LIFE-RICEFIELD-LORD.

Now there was rebellion in the eastern lands and the border was disturbed. *The cave-dwelling Ground-Spiders, Saheki of the mountain and Saheki of the moor, made themselves chiefs of tribes and ruled others, acting violently in the provinces, plundering and slaying. They dug holes in the ground, in which they dwelt; when they were pursued they ran into their holes and hid themselves, but when their pursuers departed, they came out on the moors to sport. They were by nature fierce and cruel and could not be tamed, their customs differing ever more widely from those of the people.* Then

BLACK-SLOPE [55]

made a stratagem, by which, watching for a time when they were frolicking outside their holes, he closed the inside of the latter with thorns, and made riders pursue them, whereon, thinking to run into their holes as usual, the thorns wounded them, so that they were destroyed. (For this reason that place was called Thorn.) [56]

(Others, however, say that he built a castle of thorn at the place, from which it was named.)

The high hill to the north of Thorn Village is called Mount Monkey-Slope-Time,[57] of which the aged tell that there were once a brother and sister named

PRINCE-NOGA [58]
PRINCESS-NUKA

and each night a stranger came to the latter's room and wooed her, departing by day. At length, since they were as man and wife, she conceived and in due time gave birth to a small snake. Until dark fell it spoke no word, but in the night it spoke to its mother. At that she and her brothers wondered, and deeming it a child of a Kami, put it in an empty vessel that they set upon an altar. However, the same night it swelled until it filled the vessel. They changed that vessel for another, which likewise it filled, swelling so greatly that though they changed the vessel three or four times in a night, none was sufficient for it.

---

[54] **Ancestor of the Lords of Kamakura, Wozu (in Omi Province), Iwashiro (unidentified) and Fukita (unidentified).**

Then the mother said to it, "By thus measuring with vessels I know you for a child of a Kami. As we cannot bring you up, you should not remain here, but should depart to the dwelling-place of your father." Then, weeping, it replied, "I would not disobey the bidding of my mother, but I do not like to go alone, so do you accompany me." The mother answered, "As you know, there is no one here save us two, my brother and myself, consequently there is no one to send with you." At that it was angered, and saying no word, tried, in ascending to the Sky, to shake its uncle to death. The mother, startled, took up a vessel and threw it, so that it struck the child, making it unable to ascend, so that it remained at the hill. The vessels in which the child was put still exist in One-of-Two-Hills [59]-Village, and its descendants built a shrine for the Kami and to this day celebrate its festival.

Black-Slope [60] chastised also the Izo tribes of Michi-no-Oku, coming back in triumph, but arriving at Mount Horn-Dead, he fell ill and died. (Wherefore Mount Horn-Dead was renamed Mount Black-Slope.) Now his coffin-wagon started from that place and proceeded to the Land of Sun-High-Looking,[61] the funeral cortege bearing red and blue flags that flapped as though they were flying clouds and sky-standing rainbows, making the fields and roads shine. (So the people of that time called it Country-of-Flag-Hanging,[62] but people of later ages called it Country-of-Shida.[63])[A]

The Sovereign said to the ministers, "Many violent Kami have arisen and the Emishi have rebelled and are carrying away the people. Who now shall be sent to put them down?" But they knew not whom to send. Thereon he summoned Mountain-Gate-Brave, saying, "Do you subdue and pacify the savage Kami and the unsubmissive folk of the twelve provinces of the east."

> (Some say that Great-Pestle was still alive and that when the Sovereign consulted with his ministers, Mountain-Gate-Brave spoke, saying, "It was I who pacified the west. This should be the task of Great-Pestle." But Great-Pestle, hearing, was stricken with fear and ran and hid in the grass. A messenger was sent to him and the Sovereign said, "We shall not compel you if you do not choose. Why do you fear before the enemy is met?" So he gave Great-Pestle the Land of Three-Moors and he went to rule it.)

Then Mountain-Gate-Brave, standing forth in warrior posture, said, "Only a few years ago I pacified the Kuma-So. Now the Emishi revolt in the east. Your servant, whatsoever the task, trusting in the Sky- and Earth-Kami, will subdue them." So the Sovereign gave him a spear of holly wood, eight hiro long, saying, "These savage people are turbulent and oppressive. Their villages have no head-men and they rob one another. Also there are evil Kami in the mountains and malignant Oni [64] who infest the roads. Of all, the Emishi are the strongest. Their men and women consort together without distinction even between parent and child, and brother is treacherous to brother. They live in caves in winter and in nests in summer. They wear skins and drink blood. They surmount mountains like flying birds and travel through the reeds like swift animals. They forget favors and avenge injuries, carrying arrows in their top-knots and swords in their clothing. Their bands overrun the border and rob the people of their harvest. When attacked they hide in the grass, and if pursued, take to the mountains. From olden times they have been uncivilized." Mountain-Gate-Brave took the spear and bowed twice, and the Sovereign joined to him, together with

PRINCE-GREAT-SUKI-FRIEND-EARS-BRAVE,[65]
BRAVE-SUN [66]

the Tribe-Master of the imperial guard, and giving him for steward

SEVEN-HAND-BREADTHS-SHINS [67]

sent him off.

Before he departed Mountain-Gate-Brave went into the temple of the Great Kami at Isè, and worshiping the Kami's courtyard, said he to his aunt, Princess-Mountain-Gate, "I have come to take leave of you. For surely it must be that the Sovereign intends my quick death. For after sending me to smite the evil people of the west, I am no sooner returned to the capital than, without giving me an army, he now sends me off anew to pacify the evil people of the twelve provinces of the east. Truly for this reason I think he intends that I shall quickly die." So when he departed lamenting and with tears, Princess-Mountain-Gate gave him the Sword-of-Sky's-Gathering-Clouds,[68] and a bag, saying, "If an emergency should arise, open the mouth of the bag."

Arriving in the Land of Owari, he entered the house of

PRINCESS-MIYASU [69]

who was the younger sister of

BRAVE-INA-TANÈ,[70]

minded at once to wed her. But thinking that he would do so on his

---

[65] **Ancestor of the Magnates of Kibi.**
[67] **Ancestor of the Governors of Kuma.**
[69] **Ancestress of the Rulers of Owari.**

return to the capital, when he had so covenanted with her, he went into the eastern Lands.

MOUNTAIN-GATE-BRAVE SLAYS THE RULER OF SAGAMI

When he reached the Land of Sagami, its ruler pretended obedience, and deceitfully said, "In the middle of this moor is a great lagoon and the Kami that dwells in its midst is a very violent one." So Mountain-Gate-Brave entered the moor to see the Kami.

> (Others say that he went first to the Land of Suruga,[71] where the outlaws of the place cunningly said, "On this moor are many huge deer. Their breath is like the mist of morning and their legs like trees close together. Do you go and hunt them," and that he, believing, entered the moor to hunt.)

The ruler of the Land then set fire to the moor-grass, so, perceiving that he had been tricked, Mountain-Gate-Grave opened the mouth of the bag that Princess-Mountain-Gate had given him, and behold, in it was a fire-striker.[72] So, having mowed away the grass with his sword, he took the fire-striker and struck fire, and kindling a counter-blaze, drove back the other fire and came forth again.[73]

> (By some, however, it is said that the sword moved of itself and mowed down the grass for him.)

Then, saying, "I was almost betrayed!" he slew all the chiefs of that Land and burned them with fire. The sword was after that called Herb-Queller.

> (It is related by some, however, that Mountain-Gate-Brave made a request, saying, "As the deeds of the Kami are greater than those of men, let it not be called Herb-Queller, but let it ever be known as Sword-of-Sky-Gathering-Clouds.")

The place where he burned the outlaw band is called Port-of-Burning.[74]

It is related also that in the Land of Suruga there was a Kami who visited his wife at Beach-of-Not-Come-See, in Hut-Plain District. This Kami was accustomed to cross Mount Rock-Tree, where resided a violent Kami who obstructed the way, so that the husband could not pass save with difficulty and when the violent Kami was absent. The female Kami came each night to the near side of Mount Rock-Tree, and when her husband failed to appear, she called his name, so that the place was called Groan-Slope-of-Wench.[75] The male Kami sang:

> *On Ah-My-Wife Road* || *Lies the Groan-Slope-of-Wench,*
> *Which I cannot pass.*
> *Thus I night on the mountain,* || *Where is no shelt'ring abode.*

On Ah-My-Wife Road || Lies the Groan-Slope-of-Wench,
If I could but pass!
Greatly I long to behold her || Though we two later may meet.

And the female Kami sang in reply:

Over Rock-Tree Mount, || Hasten to come, I pray you!
Here, beside Hut-Cape
Standing on Not-Come-See Beach, || Until you come I will wait.

(From the not-coming of the male Kami, Not-Come-See Beach received its name.) [A]

Mountain-Gate-Brave rested at the palace on the hill slope of Deer-Meet, and the kitchen being appointed at the beach, boats were lashed together to form a bridge to pass from the kitchen to the palace. The place of the kitchen was called Village-of-Great-Boiling Place.[76] Princess-Younger-Orange came from Mountain-Gate down to this place and met him here. (Therefore it was named Village-of-Meeting.)[77]

Now it was told him that on the mountain were such herds of deer that their horns were as thick as dead reeds and their breath like the mist of morning, that the sea-ears[78] were eight feet in length, and that rare products were in plenty. So he sent his consort, Princess-Younger-Orange, to the sea, while he himself went to the mountain to get game. But, though he chased and shot all the day long, he could take not even a single boar, while she speedily obtained many products of the sea. After the hunting and fishing were ended, a meal was offered to him, whereon he said, "Today I competed with the princess for game. I got no game in the field, but am now satisfied with these things of the sea. Name this place, therefore, Satisfied-Village." [79, B]

Afterward, gazing over the sea of Running-Water,[80] he said, "This is so small a sea that one might jump across it."

PRINCESS-YOUNGER-ORANGE STILLS THE WAVES

Then he took ship, but when he was in the middle of the sea the Kami of the ford raised the waves, and the sea was buffeted and the ship tossed about so that he could not cross. Then said Princess-Younger-Orange, his imperial consort: "The lifting of the waves and the blowing of the wind by which your vessel is likely to sink is the will of the Sea-Kami. I pray you, let me, your mean concubine, enter the sea in place of yourself, you who must finish the governing for which you have been sent, and take back report." So, when about to enter the sea, she spread eight thicknesses of sedge mats and eight thicknesses of skin mats and eight thicknesses of silk mats on the waves, and sat down on their top,[81] whereon the violent waves at once subsided and became like oil, and the ship was able to proceed to the shore. Then she sang:

> Where the true peak, || O'er the little moor rises,
> In Sagami—ah!
> Standing ringed by the fire-flame, || How were you there attended!

Seven days afterward her comb was washed up on the seashore,[82] and it was taken and placed in an august tomb made for it. (So the folk of that time called that sea Running-Water.)

At Tajima-Village Mountain-Gate-Brave slew one of the Saheki people who opposed his command, named

PRINCE-BIRD.

There were also people of the Kunisu [83] tribe, two of whom were named

PRINCE-OF-TREE
PRINCESS-OF-TREE

and the former was recalcitrant and would not pay respect to him, so he drew his sword and slew him. At that Princess-of-Tree, fearing and regretting the death of Prince-of-Tree, hoisted a white flag and received Mountain-Gate-Brave and worshiped him. So in compassion he forgave her. As for her, she brought her sisters and they devoted themselves to his service, avoiding neither wind nor rain, and served him day and night. And he was pleased at their kindness, which seemed to him beautiful. (Therefore the place was called Small-Field-of-Beautiful.) Also in his progress he had occasion to stop his sedan-chair [84] and washed his hands at a spring, and the sleeves of the garment he wore hung down and became wet. (Hence the place was called Soaking.) [85] From this arose the saying of the people of that Land: "The dark clouds hung over Mount Newly-Tilled [86] and the land was called the Land-of-Sleeve-Soaking." [87] Of Mount Newly-Tilled the very old say that it was built by the Kami He-Who-Invites and She-Who-Invites, as a rampart against the waves of the sea, which they forced to retire to the other side of Deer-Island, that was in the beginning an island.[88]

It is said likewise by those who hold that it was on this mountain that Great-Sky-Shiner in the beginning descended from the Sky, that she played on a koto, whereon the waves of the eastern sea rolled in to the mountain's foot, drawn by the koto music, the water that remained in a hollow of the ground being Kasumiga-Ura Lake. (The mountain, these say, was therefore named Mount Wave-Reaching, but it is now corruptly called Mount Newly-Tilled.) It is related, moreover, that of old time the ancestral Kami,[89] going round about to those places where the various Kami resided, came to Mount Fire-Wondrous [90] at sunset, and asked the Kami of the mountain to permit him to pass the night there. That Kami replied, "All of my household are strictly keeping the Festival of the New-Millet-Tasting,[91] so that today it cannot be permitted." The ancestral Kami resented this reply and cursed him, saying, "Since you will not permit your ancestral Kami to pass the night here, this mountain on which you reside shall, so long as you live, be visited repeatedly by snow, frost, and cold, so that people will not climb it, nor shall any offer you food!" Then he ascended Mount Newly-Tilled, of whose Kami he made the same request. That Kami replied, "Though this evening is the festival of the New-Tasting, how should I not obey your august will?" And he prepared food and drink and sedulously served the ancestral Kami, who was glad, and sang:

> Now how beautiful you are, my descendant!
> How lofty is your palace, O Kami!
> As long as continue the Sky, || The earth and the sun and the moon,
> The folk shall assemble and shall take joyance.
> Food and drink shall be abundant. || In all ages your posterity
> Shall flourish unending day by day. || Joy for a thousand autumns,
> For ten thousand years, shall not leave you.

Therefore Mount Fire-Wondrous has always had snow so that none can climb it, whereas Mount Newly-Tilled has never been without a gathering of people who sing and dance, eat and drink. Mount Newly-Tilled juts high above the clouds: its west peak is called Male-Kami and it is forbidden to climb it; its east peak is everywhere stony and steep for mounting and descending. On the way is a spring that never is dry either in summer or winter, and there come men and women, climbing from the provinces to the eastward at the time of spring flowers and autumn's red leaves, bringing drink and food, to sport there. They sing:

> On Mount Newly-Tilled || Asking whose child had told me
> To play. || It was the one I talked with.
> It was the one I played with before.

> At Nero, on Mount Newly-Tilled, || Making my house
> That shelters no wife. || The night time, while I slumber,
> Ah, may it pass away speedily!

So many songs there are that all cannot be mentioned. Wherefore people say, "If a daughter wins no treasure at the courting on Mount Newly-Tilled, then she cannot be called worthy."

Now in the ancient time there were in this land a damsel and a lad, who were named

LORD-NAKU-SAMU-RICEFIELD [92]

YOUNGER-LADY-OF-AJÈ-OF-UPPER-SEA.[93]

Both of them were fair to look upon and shone brightly in their native village, and each yearned after the other. After days and months they met at a song-hedge [94] and the lad sang:

> Hanging cotton cloths || On a young pine tree of Ajè,
> Lo, does it not seem
> Someone beckoneth to me? || Ah, little Ajè, mine isle!

Whereupon she sang this song in reply:

> Although you may start || When the tide is at flooding,
> Oh, my dearest one,
> Hidden by eighty islands, || Yet you did take note of me!

Both desired to converse, but feared to be observed by others, so they fled from the place of the merry-making and hid themselves beneath a pine tree, where they held each other's hands and drew knee to knee, expressing each to each their yearning, and satisfying their continued longing with pleasures ever refreshed. It was in a jewel-clear season of golden wind and clear moon, with the passing of crying cranes and the song of the breeze in the pine trees. The wild geese flew by to the eastern Lands. The mountain was quiet as an old well, the night peaceful, cloud and mist were fresh, and on the near hills golden leaves were scattered. They heard only the sound of blue waves dashing on the rocks, and that night they enjoyed unequaled happiness. In sweet converse they forgot how late was the night, till on a sudden cocks began to crow and dogs to bark, and the sun grew bright in the sky. Then the youthful pair knew not what to do, and so much were they ashamed to be seen by others that they were transformed into pine trees. The lad is called Nami-Pine and the damsel Kotsu-Pine. From ancient times the two pines have been so named, and up to the present the names have not been changed. (For this reason that place is called Younger-Lady-Pine-Forest.) [95]

By the people of the Land of Soaking, it is said that on Mount Ifukubè there was, in the ancient time, a Kami called

KAMI-OF-IFUKUBÈ

and that one day a brother and sister, toiling together in the ricefield, said to each other, "That one who is the last in planting the rice today shall receive evil of the Kami." The sister was the last in planting the rice, whereon thunder smote her to death. The elder brother lamented and in his resentment wished to revenge himself upon the Thunder-Kami, but did not know his place of abode. However there came flying a pheasant and perched on his shoulder, to whose tail he tied the end of a ball of thread. The pheasant flew to Mount Ifukubè, and the man, tracing the line of thread, found a cavern where a Thunder-Kami lay. He drew his sword and was about to cut the Kami down, when the latter, in fear, made his excuse, saying, "I will obey your words, nor will I permit your descendants to suffer from thunder during a hundred years!" So the man pardoned the Thunder-Kami and did not slay him. He was pleased, moreover, with the virtue of the pheasant, and took an oath that his descendants should be mindful of it for generations, lest, transgressing, one should suffer disease and life-long wretchedness. Now it cannot be told at present which mountain is Mount Ifukubè, but in High District, at the Village of Lower-River, there is a

PHEASANT-KAMI [96]

and three cho to the north is a mountain called Mount Ifuki. People of the village of Thread-Bell,[97] it is said, even now do not eat pheasant, and dislike even to have one brought there.

In this Land, also, there is a hill called Great-Rot Hill,[98] and the aged say that of old there was a giant who dwelt there. He was very tall and ate shellfish, and the shells accumulated till they were heaped up as high as a hill. His footprint is thirty paces long and twenty paces wide and the trace of his urination is twenty paces deep.[99] When he walked it was always bent over. He came from the southern sea to the northern sea, and then, going around from the east, he came to High-Land. There he said, "Other Lands are low, so that I always walked bent over, but since this Land is high, I walk erect. How high it is!" (From this it was named High-Land.[1]) His footprints here and there are transformed into marshes.

Now in Soaking-Province, Mountain-Gate-Brave went to the hill of Rough-Plain, where he partook of food. There, looking all about him, he turned to his attendants and said, "Stopping my sedan-chair and loitering, raising my eyes to gaze on the scene, I behold the crooked mountain ridges and beaches, with the clouds on the mountain peaks and mists on the mountain sides. The view is lovely and the province has a rare form. The name of this place should be Rare-Looking-Land." [2] Then, descending the hill, he proceeded to the Great-Benefit River, where he entered a vessel and went upstream, where his rudder broke. (Therefore the river was named Rudder-Without River.) [3] This river is on the border of the two Lands of Thorn-Castle and Rare-Looking. Landing from the river he shot a wild duck which he found flying there, and it fell, struck by the bowstring. (For this reason the place was called Wild-Duck-Field.) At Horn-Broken-Beach, likewise, he partook of food, but there was no water to drink, so the earth was dug with a stag's horn, which was thus broken. (Therefore the place was so named.)

> (Some say, however, that of old time there was a great serpent that desired to go to the eastern sea, so it dug up the beach to

make a passage, when its horn was broken and dropped off there, from which came the name.) ▲

After that Mountain-Gate-Brave crossed by sea in an indirect direction to Jewel-Beach. On his vessel was suspended a great mirror, and when he came to the Emishi border, the two Emishi leaders,

KAMI-OF-ISLAND
KAMI-OF-LAND

had camped at the harbor to give battle. But seeing Mountain-Gate-Brave's vessel, they were afraid, and knowing they could not gain the victory, threw away their bows and arrows, and making obeisance, said, "Your face is the face of a Kami. What is your name?" Mountain-Gate-Brave answered, "I am the child of a Kami of visible men." Then the Emishi, awestruck, girded up their garments, and entering the waves, brought the vessel to shore, and binding their hands behind them, waited their punishment. But he pardoned them, and added their leaders to his attendants. Then, having departed from there and subdued all the fierce Emishi and pacified all the savage Kami of the mountains and rivers, he proceeded southwest to the Land of Mid-Mountain-Place, where he dwelt in the Palace of Zigzag-Pass-Road. Here they built a fire and he took food, after which he sang:

> Nihiharu || And Newly-Tilled I have passed—
> How many sleep-nights ago?

None of his attendants could answer, but the old man who was the fire-lighter completed the song:

> Setting days in row, || Ah, of nights there are nine nights
> And of days there are ten days.

For this Mountain-Gate-Brave praised the old man and bestowed on him the rulership of an eastern Land. While he occupied the Palace of Zigzag-Pass-Road, he gave to Brave-Sun the Quiver-Clan. After this he entered the Land of Michi-no Oku.[4]

Now in this Land there were eight Ground-Spiders, called *Black-Eagle, Princess-Kami-Clothing, Miscanthus-Field-Haï, Ho-Ho-Ki-Haï,*[5] *Princess-Azanina, White-Boar, Kami-Stone-Eulalia,* and *Sashina.*[6] Each of these had a tribe that was encamped in a stone cavern in a commanding position, and none obeyed the rule of Mountain-Gate-Brave. The Land-Ruler,

PRINCE-IWAKI [7]

---

[7] **Ancestor of the Land-Rulers of Iwaki.**

had gone against them but had been defeated, and after that they plundered the people and would not cease, for which the Sovereign bade Mountain-Gate-Brave chastise them. They then joined their forces in defense and by guile prevailed upon some of the Emishi people of Tsugaru [6] *to join them. They shot the imperial troops at Iwaki with the bows and arrows with which they shot stags and boars, so that the troops could not advance. Then Mountain-Gate-Brave, taking his bow and arrows of keyaki wood, shot seven arrows and eight arrows. The seven arrows hummed like thunder, so that the Ezo folk fled, and with the eight he pierced eight of the Ground-Spiders, who straightway fell. Now the eight arrows took root and became keyaki trees. (Therefore the place was called Village-of-Eight-Kayaki.)* [8] *The descendants of Princess-Kami-Clothing and Kami-Stone-Eulalia, who were pardoned, live in this village. It is at this day called Ayato.*

> *(Others, however, say that Brave-Mountain-Gate at this place shot a turnip-shaped humming-arrow with many holes in it and thus slew the enemy, wherefore the place where the arrow fell was called-Arrow-Arrival.)* ▲

After that Mountain-Gate-Brave said, "Though the evil leaders of the Emishi have been subdued, in the Lands of Lime-Tree-Moor and Koshi there remain many who are uncivilized." So he proceeded northwestward to the Ashigara Pass.[9] There he remembered with sadness his wife Princess-Younger-Orange, and as he looked down to the southeast, he sighed three times, saying, "Ah, alas, my wife!" (So that Land east of the mountains is called by the name of Ah-my-wife).[10] From there he sent Prince-Brave-of-Maise around about to explore the Land of Koshi and to inquire concerning its people, and he himself entered the Province of Lime-Tree-Moor.[11] There the mountains were lofty and the valleys deep, with green ranges piled up ten thousand fold, difficult to climb for man or horse. But Mountain-Gate-Brave, daringly penetrating the mists, ascended Mount Great. On its top he partook of food, and while he ate, the Kami of the pass, in the form of a

WHITE-DEER

came and stood there. He waited its approach and struck it in the eye with a piece of wild garlic, so that it was struck dead. Presently he lost his way, but a

WHITE-DOG

appeared and guided him out into Three-Moors, where Prince-Brave-of-Maise, coming from Koshi, met him. Up to this time the Kami of the Lime-Tree-Moor Pass had exhaled a vapor, of which if any wayfarer breathed he sickened and was prostrated. After the White-Deer had been slain, however, people who crossed there chewed garlic and smeared their bodies and their cattle and horses with it, and were not affected.

Then, returning to the Land of Owari, Mountain-Gate-Brave abode in the house of Princess-Miyasu, to whom he was already affianced. There, presenting him with food, she lifted up a great liquor cup and offered it to him. Now her menses stained the edge of her veil, and he, seeing this, laughed, saying:

> As on Mount Fragrant || 'Neath the gourd-shaped firmament
> A stem striketh || Against the sharpened scythe—
> So as slender || And as wholly delicate
> Are thine arms, in which || I had been desirous
> To recline my head. || Therein I desired to sleep,
> But on the border || Of the veil which bedecks you
> Behold the moon [12] is rising!

And Princess-Miyasu replied to the verses, saying,

> O thou high-shining || August Sun-child!
> My puissant lord, || Tranquilly governing!
> While the years newly || Show their waxing and waning,
> So the new moons too || Show their waxing and waning.
> Be patient! Be patient! || While I, longing, await you,
> There on the border || Of the veil I am wearing,
> Behold, the moon is rising.*

Thereon they cohabited. *In the early night he rose and went to the privy, hanging his sword Herb-Queller on a mulberry tree. When he re-entered, he forgot it, and on returning for it, was astonished to find it shining with such a wondrous effulgence that he could not grasp it. Then said he to her, "This sword has a spirit which do you enshrine as an image of me." So a shrine was later built for it at the village of Hot-Field.*[13, A]

MOUNTAIN-GATE-BRAVE AND THE KAMI OF BLOWING

Afterward he made his imperial way to capture the Kami of Blowing.[14] *Now this Kami was named*

PRINCE-TATAMI

and was a son of

PRINCE-FROST-SWIFT.

He had two sisters,[15] *who were named*

PRINCESS-SUSASHI
PRINCESS-SHALLOW-WELL

and he quarrelled with Princess-Shallow-Well as to which one was the taller, whereon she increased her height in one night. At that he was angered, and drawing his sword, struck off her head and cast it into the bay. This head is Tsukubu Island.ᴬ

When Mountain-Gate-Brave came to Mount Blowing, he said, "As for the Kami of this mountain, I will take him merely with my empty hands." There met him then on the mountain side a white boar as big as an ox. So he raised his voice, saying, "This creature in the form of a white boar is truly a messenger from the Kami. However, after I have already slain Kami, a messenger is not worth pursuing. Though I do not slay it now, I will slay it on my return." And he went on

> (It is said by some that he met not a white boar, but a great serpent which lay in the road, over which he stepped.)
> (Others say that he slew it by winding his bare arms about it. Others, again, say that he met neither a boar nor a serpent, but that he was struck by a poisoned arrow.)

Now the creature in the form of a white boar was not a messenger from the Kami, but the very Kami himself, who, by reason of Mountain-Gate-Brave's words, appeared in order to mislead him; and he lifted up clouds and caused heavy ice-rain to fall, striking and disturbing him. Mist covered the hilltops and darkness was over the valleys, and there was no path, so that he was at a loss, knowing not where he was going. He forced his way on and out, however, through the mist, being like one who is drunken, and descended to the fresh-water spring of Jewel-Store-Clan,[16] of which he drank, and as he rested, his heart somewhat recovered itself. (So that spring is called Sit-Sober-Spring.) [17] At this time he became ill, and rising with difficulty, he returned to Owari. He did not go into the dwelling of Princess-Miyasu, but went on to Isè. On reaching Rudder-Moor, he said, "My heart was continuously feeling as though it was flying through the sky, and now my legs cannot walk. They have become rudder-shaped." (For this reason that place was called Rudder.) [18] Going a little further, he became very weary and leaned upon a staff to walk, (the place being called, for this reason, Leaning-on-Staff Place.) [19]

Thus he reached the single pine tree at Mount Declivity-Harbor.[20] While proceeding eastward he had stopped at this place to partake of food, and laying down a sword at the foot of a pine tree, had forgotten and left it there. Now this sword was found at this time, whereon he sang:

> O lone pine-tree, || Elder brother, directly
> Facing towards Owari || At Mount Declivity-Harbour! [20]
> If you, lone pine-tree, || Were but a living person,
> I would gird you with a sword, || I would clothe you in raiment,
> O lone pine-tree, elder brother!

Departing thence, he came to the Village of Three-Fold,[21] and said again, "My legs are like three-fold crooked things, and exceeding weary." (Thus that place received its name.) All this while illness was sore upon him, and when he came to Mounting-Moor [22] his suffering was intense. So he offered the Emishi whom he had made prisoners [23] to serve at the Shrine of the Kami. Also he sent Prince-Brave-of-Maise to report to the Sovereign, saying, "Your servant at your bidding penetrated the distant eastern wilds, and when I had put down the rebellious and pacified the savage Kami, I discarded my armour and weapons and was returning to report. But my preordained life is suddenly ending, as speedily as a four-horse carriage passes a rut in the road. I die alone on the empty moor. I regret not the losing of this body; I regret only that I may not come to you. Then he sang:

> At the couch-side || Where the maiden slept,
> That two-edged sword || Which I deposited!
> Ah, alas that sword!

When he had finished singing he died, and a courier was despatched with the news. He was thirty years old.

When the Sovereign heard, he could not sleep, and food was not sweet to his taste. Day and night he grieved and lamented, saying, "Oh, Our son Little-Pestle! [24] Though but a lad, when the Kuma-So rebelled he withstood the battle, and later assisted Us in the Government.

"When the east revolted We sent him to fight the savages. Each day he was in Our thought and day and night We longed for his coming! Oh, evil thing that has befallen Us! Who now shall aid Us in the rule?"

MOUNTAIN-GATE-BRAVE BECOMES A WHITE SWAN

The Sovereign bade his Ministers instruct the one hundred departments to bury him in Mount Mounting-Moor in the Land of Isè, and the imperial wives of Mountain-Gate-Brave and also his children, who dwelt in Mountain-Gate, all went down and built a tomb, and crawling here and there in the ricefields round about, wept and sang:

> We crawl about || Here amid the rice stubble,
> 'Midst the rice stubble || In the circling ricefields,
> Like five-leaved yam [25] vines.

Then Mountain-Gate-Brave, turning into a white swan [26] (or, as some say, a sandpiper eight hiro long), came from the mound, and soaring skyward, flew off toward the Land of Mountain-Gate,[27] while his imperial

---

[23] **Ancestors of the Saheki-Clans of Harima, Aki, Sanuki, Awa, and Iyo Provinces.**

consort and the children, though they tore their feet on the stubble of the bamboo grass, forgot the pain and pursued it with lamentations, singing:

> The plain's short bamboo grass || Encumbers our loins.
> We pass not through the sky; || Alas, we go afoot!

And when they waded through the salt sea, in pain as they went, they sang:

> As we pass through the sea, || Our loins encumbered,
> We waver in the sea || Like plants rooted
> In the great bed || Of a river.

And again, when the swan flew and alighted on the edge of the waves, they sang:

> The swan of the land-edge || Seeks not the land-edge, but goes
> Along the wave-edge.

Inasmuch as these four songs were sung at Mountain-Gate-Brave's burial, they are sung to the present day at the interment of a sovereign.

Now the Ministers opened the coffin and in it was no corpse, but only the empty raiment, so men were sent to follow the white swan. It first flew to the plain of Kotobiki in Mountain-Gate, and accordingly a mound was built there. Then it flew on and rested at Stone-Castle in the land of Kafuchi, and there also a mound was built. The three mounds are known as August-Tombs-of-the-White-Swan. At last the swan soared up to the sky again and flew away,[28] and nothing was buried of Mountain-Gate-Brave but his clothing and his ceremonial hat. To hand down the memory of his service, the Sovereign founded the Brave-Clan.

ROOT-BRANDISHER,[29]

Magnate of Kami-Gate, was appointed to this clan. Since that time the place where he and the Magnates of the Brave-Clan have resided, in Sacred-Quarter, is called Village-of-Brave-Clan. This place was originally called Village-of-Uya because the Kami

UYATSUBÈ [30]

descended from the Sky on the mountain there. The shrine of this Kami still exists there.[A]

During the whole time that Mountain-Gate-Brave went about pacifying countries, Seven-Hand-Lengths-Shins [31] always followed and respectfully served him as victualer. Of the children of Mountain-Gate-Brave, King-Long-Life-Ricefield-Lord begot

KING-PRINCE-KUMATA-LONG

to whom there were born

PRINCESS-QUITE-BLACK-OF-BOILED-RICE-MOOR
MOMO-SHIKI-IRO-BE.[32]

King-Young-Brave wedded Princess-Quite-Black-of-Boiled-Rice-Moor [33] and their grandchild was

PRINCESS-QUITE-BLACK [34]

whom the Sovereign, Prince-Great-Perfect-Ruling-Lord, took to wife.

At this time the Kami Brave-Awful-Possessing-Male said to

NARROW-MOUNTAIN [35]

Magnate of the Intercessors, "The vessels of the present shrine...." [36] *Narrow-Mountain answered, "I obey your great command with circumspection, nor would I presume to disregard it." The next morning the Great Kami said again, "Your vessel has been put upon the sea." So the owner of the vessel went there, but beheld it on a hill. Again the Kami said, "Your vessel is put upon a hill." Whereon the owner looked for it and found it on the sea. Two or three times this was repeated. Then he feared the will of the Kami and constructed three new vessels, each of them twenty shaku in length, and offered them to the Kami. Today on the tenth of the fourth month a festival is made, when sakè is sprinkled. The families of the Augur-Clan, men and women, drink sakè and sing and dance for days and nights. They sing:*

> *Now the sakè new, || The Kami's sakè supernal,*
> *Lift ye || Lift ye up!*
> *And lo the while I said it, || The drunkenness vanquished me!* [A]

On a day when the Sovereign feasted his Ministers, Prince-Young-Perfect [37] and Noble-of-Brave-Uchi [38] did not come, so he sent and asked the reason. They replied, "When there is festivity, the Ministers naturally amuse themselves and do not think of the government. As there may be miscreants to spy out a weak rampart, we keep guard at the august gate against surprise." This the Sovereign praised and showed them favor, and Noble-of-Brave-Uchi was made Great-Magnate. As for the Emishi whom Mountain-Gate-Brave had offered to serve at the shrine,

---

[35] *Ancestor of the Tribe-Masters of the Kashima Diviners.**

---

* The *Kashima-Daiguji-Keizu* says: "Prince Sayama (Narrow-Mountain) who is a son of the Magnate Sayama, descendant in the tenth generation of Sky-Beckoning-Ancestor-Lord, is an ancestor of the Nakatomi-no Kashima-no Muraji."

they created disturbance day and night and their deportment was disrespectful, so that Princess-Mountain-Gate would not keep them at the shrine and they were placed near Mount August-House. But they cut down the sacred trees and disturbed the villages and the people went in fear. So the Sovereign, saying, "These Emishi have beasts' hearts and must not dwell in the interior," gave them whatever places they chose in the remoter provinces.

At this time the empress, Princess-Elder-Lady-of-Wave-Hiding-of-Harima, died, *and a tomb in which to bury her body was built at Hiwoka. While they were crossing the Wave-Hiding River with the body, however, a great wind came from the lower river and blew the body into the water. Though they made search, they found only her comb-case and head-dress, and they buried these two articles in the tomb. (Therefore it was called Head-dress-Tomb.) The Sovereign's grief was great, and he took an oath that he would never eat anything that came from that river, so the trout from it were never offered to him.*

Afterward the Sovereign said, "When shall We cease to long for Our son, Mountain-Gate-Brave? I desire to visit the land he subdued." So he journeyed by carriage to Isè, from which he came to the provinces of the eastern sea.

Now at the village of Floating-Island in Kawaüchi District, in Hitachi Province, there was a kakuka bird [39] *the sound of whose singing charmed him. He therefore sent*

IKARI [40]

to take it with a net. The bird so delighted him that he gave Ikari the name of Bird-Bird.[41] *His descendants still dwell in that place. At the Palace-of-Tobari, of Floating-Island, there was no water, so he caused divination to be made and wells were dug in various places. These still exist in Male-Chestnut-Village.*[A]

Then, crossing over by sea to Foam-Harbor, he went out on the sea and gathered clams, when

IWAKA-MUTSUKARI [42]

twisted cords of reeds and, preparing a dish of the clams, bore it before the Sovereign, who praised him and gave him the Magnates-Imperial-Escort-Clan. After this the Sovereign returned from the eastern land to Isè.

Now while he was in Owari Province, there was heard from the west a sound of loud laughter, and wondering at it he sent there the Tribe-

---

[42] **Ancestor of the Magnates of Kashiwadè.**

Master of Ishitsuda, who beheld there beings whose faces were like the faces of oxen, and who were gathered together in groups, laughing loudly. The Tribe-Master of Ishitsuda, however, fearing them not at all, drew his sword and cut them down one by one. (Hence the place was called Village-of-Great-Cutting.) [43]

When the Sovereign went to the coast, he sang:

.Like to the target || Which the valiant man faces
Holding his arrows, || You, O shore of Target-Shape,
Shine forth in your brightness.

(Therefore this coast was named Target-Form.[44]) The place has now changed and has become a lake.[B]

PRINCE-SAJIMA

was made governor of the fifteen provinces of the east-mountain-road, but on the way he fell ill and died, so the eastern people, through sorrow, stole away his body and buried it in the Land of Upper-Grass-Moor.[45] Then the Sovereign bade Prince-Sajima's son,

PRINCE-AUGUST-HOUSE-LORD

to proceed there to rule that Land. Later the Emishi there rebelled and he gave them battle, so that their leaders made obeisance and submitted. Those who yielded he pardoned and the rest he slew, so that the land was tranquil. His descendants are now in the eastern land. In this reign also the Great-Victualer-Clan and the Ricefield-Clan were established, the Port of Aha in the east was fixed and the Mountain-Gate granaries founded. Also the Pool of Sakatè was made and bamboos were planted on its bank.

In this reign also a sakè spring gushed forth at Mount Sakè [46] (from which the place was so called). People drank of it and growing drunk quarreled and caused confusion, so that orders were given to bury and check it. Later, however, a certain man again unearthed it. Even now the place smells of sakè.[A]

The Sovereign lived one hundred six (or, as some say, one hundred and thirty-seven) years and died in the Palace of Taka-Anaho, at Shiga, in Close-Fresh-Sea, and his tomb is in the mound above the mountain-vicinity-road.

THE EMPEROR PRINCE-YOUNG-PERFECT
(ACCOMPLISH-DUTY [47])

Prince-Young-Perfect dwelt in the Palace of Taka-Anaho and ruled the empire. He had been born on the same day as Noble-of-Brave-Uchi and loving the latter exceedingly, made him Great-Magnate.[48]

This Sovereign established granaries in the villages, appointed the rulers of the great and small countries and the boundaries of the various Lands, and choosing able men of the provinces, appointed District-Chiefs of the great and small departments, so as to defend the interior, giving them shields and spears as tokens of office. Mountains and rivers were fixed as boundaries of provinces and districts, and lanes were drawn about villages to fix their limits, running with the sun and across the sun.[49] The sun-side of the mountains was called the white side and the shade-side was called the black side. Thus the empire was made tranquil.

In this reign

OTOYO

descendant in the tenth generation of *Sky-Shining-Earth-Shining-Sky's Fire-Ruddy-Comb-Jewel-Plenty-Swift-Sun* [50] *was appointed Land-Ruler of Owari.*[A] Now

RIVER-SHALLOW

a Tribe-Master in Spring-Clan [51] *District, Owari Province, tilled a ricefield that was called Bush-Clover-Ricefield, in which a wistaria grew in a single night. Wondering at this, he did not cut it down, and it grew to great size, being as large as a tree. (Hence the place was named Wistaria-Tree-Ricefield.)*[B]

The Sovereign's august years were ninety-five (or, as some say, one hundred and seven), and his tomb is at Row-of-Shields near Saki.[52]

THE EMPEROR PRINCE-PERFECT-MIDDLE [53]
(MIDDLE-SAD [54])

Prince-Perfect-Middle became Sovereign when he was forty-three years old, Prince-Young-Perfect having no son. He was ten shaku tall and of great comeliness. After he became Sovereign he said to his Magnates, "Since Our father's divine spirit, at his death, before We became a youth, turned to a white swan and went up to the Sky, we have longed for him daily. Therefore We desire white birds brought and kept in the pond by the mound, that We may look at them and be comforted." So the provinces were bidden to send white birds as tribute. The Province of Koshi sent four white birds and their bearers spent the night on the River Uji.

PRINCE-GAMA-MI-LORD

seeing them, asked, "Where are you carrying these white birds?" They replied, "We bear them as tribute to the Sovereign, who will keep them as pets because of his sorrow for his father." At which Prince-Gama-Mi-Lord, saying, "Truly these birds are now white, but roasted they will be black," seized them and took them away. So the men of Koshi reported this and the Sovereign, angry at the insult offered his father, sent soldiers and slew Prince-Gama-Mi-Lord. The latter [55] was his half-brother.

The Sovereign wedded Princess-of-Great-Middle,[56] and begot

KING-KAGOSAKA

KING-GREAT-BEAR.

Also he took to wife

PRINCESS-YOUNGER

who was the daughter of

GREAT-SAKÈ-MASTER [57]

and there was born to the two

HOMUYA-LORD

(who some say was born to him by Princess-Long-Life-Perfect. Also he wedded Princess-Long-Life-Perfect,[58] whom he made his Empress. In her youth she was intelligent and far-seeing, and her face was so lovely that her father marveled at it.

In the eighth year of his reign Koman-Wo, a descendant of King Kobu, descendant in the thirteenth generation of Shiko-Teï [59] *of Shin, visited Nippon.*[A]

The sovereign built the temporary Palace of Kehi at Blood-Strand [60] and dwelt there. Also he established the granaries of Foam-Way. Afterward he visited the provinces in the southward, and leaving behind him the Empress and court officers, he went on, in company with his highest Ministers and some hundreds of officers, to the Land of Tree. Later the Kuma-So folk rebelled and refused tribute, so he went against them, by sea, to the Ana Passage, and sending word to the Empress to meet him there, anchored in the harbor of Fertile-Shore, where he built the Fertile-Shore Palace, and dwelt there.

(*Others, however, say that the Empress proceeded with him, and that their vessels anchored at Wave-Hiding Beach, in the Land of Harima. At the time the sea was quite calm and there was neither wind nor waves, wherefore the Land was called Land-of-Wave-Hiding.*[A])

The Empress, desirous of coming to meet him, ordered all her retainers to prepare ships and left the harbor of Blood-Strand. She hung cotton

---

[57] **Ancestor of the Rulers of Kukumada.***

---

* Kukumuda (?).

cloths on sakaki trees of five hundred branches, and set these at bow and stern as gohei in honor of the sea Kami, and in person she played on a koto, also bidding Sky-Princess,[62] *her younger sister, who was in charge of the festival, to make divine music.*[63] (*This occurred at the place which is now called Kami-Music-Cape.*)[64] So she came to the Nuta Strait, and while she ate food on her vessel, many taï fish gathered there, and she poured sakè upon them till they became drunk and floated on the top of the water. So the fishermen caught many, saying, "These fish are the gift to us from our wise Sovereign." This was the origin of the habit the fish of that place have, by which in the sixth month they float belly up as if drunk.

Then the Empress came to Fertile-Shore Harbor, *where she stopped her ship at an island of the Land of Akawa. Resting on a rock* on the day of her arrival, she found in the sea a N'yoi[65] jewel, *which was as round as a hen's egg and, when she held it in her hand, shone brightly on every side. She took great joy in it, saying, "This is a white, true jewel, given by the sea Kami." (For this reason the island was named Jewel-Island.)*[B]

> (*Some say the jewel was shaped like a sword, and that it is the sword-jewel of Hiroda Shrine*[66] *in Settsu Province.*[67] *Others say that instead of a single jewel she found two jewels, and that these were the tide-flow-jewel and the tide-ebb-jewel, which Fire-Fade had brought from the sea realm, loaned to him by Great-Ocean-Possessor, by which he had subjugated his brother Fire-Glow.*)[A]

Later the Sovereign departed to Tsukushi. Now hearing in advance of his coming,

BEAR-WANI [68]

pulled up by the roots a sakaki tree of five hundred branches, set it on the prow of a vessel nine hiro long, and hanging on its top branch a white-copper mirror, on its middle branch a ten-hand-lengths sword and on its bottom branch yasaka gems, went to meet him in Saba Bay in Suwo, and presented to him a salt-fish pan. And he said to the Sovereign, "The Great Ferry, from the Ana Passage to the land opposite, is the eastern gate, and the Great Ferry of Nagoya is the western gate. The Islands of Motori and Abi are the august baskets. The Island of Shiba, cut in two, makes the august pans. And the Sea of Sakami is the salt-place." [69]

Now Bear-Wani piloted the Sovereign's vessel to the Bay of Oka, but the vessel could not enter, and stood still. So the Sovereign said, "It has

---

[68] **Ancestor of the District-Chiefs of Oka.**

been told Us that you have a true heart. Why does the vessel stay here?" Bear-Wani answered, "It is no fault of your servant. But at this entrance are two Kami,

GREAT-STOREHOUSE-MASTER
PRINCESS-TSUBURA

and it is their wish." Thereon the Sovereign offered prayers and sacrifice to these two, appointing his helmsman

PRINCE-IGA-OF-UDA

in Yamato Province as hafuri, after which the vessel proceeded. The Empress's vessel entered the Sea of Kuki, but the water ebbed and she could not proceed, and Bear-Wani, seeing that the vessel halted, was afraid. So he made a fish pool and a bird pool and put various sorts of fish and birds into them, and watching their play the Empress' anger lessened, and when the water flowed she anchored in the harbor of Oka. Hearing of the Sovereign's coming,

ITO-TE [70]

pulled up by the roots two sasaki trees of five hundred branches, set one on the prow of a vessel and the other on its stern, and hanging on their top branches yasaka gems, on their middle branches white copper mirrors, and on their bottom branches ten-hand-lengths swords, went to meet him at Hikejima, at the Ana Passage, and presented them. There he said to the Sovereign, "You govern with a wisdom as winding as the curves of these gems. Your gaze sees mountains, rivers, and the sea plain with a brightness like these mirrors of white copper. You tranquilize the empire with ten-hand-length swords."

On the Sovereign's asking his name, he said, "I am Ito-Te, a descendant of Sun-Spear,[71] who descended from the sky on Mount Oro [72] of Koma Province.[A]

So the Sovereign praised Ito-Te and gave him the name of Loyalty.[73] (Therefore people called his native place the Land of Iso. It is now called corruptly the land of Ito.) The village of Ito-Te is where he had his seat.[A] The Sovereign then came to the District of Naka, where he built the Palace of Evergreen-Oak-Sun and dwelt there.

THE PROMISE OF THE WESTERN LAND

After this he made plans for giving battle to the Kuma-So. When he was about to attack them, he played on his koto and the Great Magnate,

---

[70] **Ancestor of the District-Chiefs of Ito in Tsukushi.**

Noble-Brave-of-Uchi, being in the sacred enclosure, asked for the divine commands. Now at this time the Empress, Princess-Long-Life-Perfect, was possessed by a Kami, and charged and advised the Sovereign as follows: "Be not disturbed that the Kuma-So do not submit. Their land is one without courage, being like a stag's horn rather than a real Land, and, unworthy of meeting your army. But there is another better land to the westward, which has abundance of plenteous eye-dazzling treasures, a land opposite this, as lovely as a lovely woman, full of gold and silver and shining colors. It is called the Land of Silla, of the paper-mulberry quilts.[74] I will now bestow this land upon you. If you truly worship me, it will submit without your sword becoming bloodied, and afterward the Kuma-So also will submit.[75] In worshiping give me the vessel of the Sovereign and the flooded ricefield called Great-Field given him by the Governor of the Ana Passage,

HOMUTACHI.[76]

(*Some say that the Kami spoke first through the mouths of*

UCHI-SARU-TAKA [77]
KUNI-SARU-TAKA [77]
MATSU-YA-TANÈ,[77]

admonishing the Sovereign, saying: "If you desire to gain the treasure Land, I will presently give it to you"; and that thereon they said, "Bring a koto and give it to the Empress," which being done, she herself played accordingly, when the Kami spoke again through her mouth.)

Now the Sovereign doubted the words of the Kami, and going to the top of a high mountain, looked westward, but he saw no land, but only the wide sea. So he returned, saying, "If one ascends to a high place and gazes westward, no land may be seen. There is only the great sea. Can there be a land in the sky void? What Kami deceives Us with such false tales?" [78] The Sovereign, Our ancestors, have worshiped the Sky- and Earth-Kami, each one, without omitting any. Moreover, if Our vessel is offered them, in what vessel should We Ourselves set sail? The woman speaks ill-sounding words!" And saying, "Though these be Kami, they are lying Kami," he pushed away his koto and did not play upon it, but sat silent. At that the Kami became very angry and again spoke through the mouth of the Empress, saying, "I behold this land lying on the water like a reflection from the Sky. Why do you say there is no land and

---

[76] **Ancestor of the Governors of Anato.**
[77] **Ancestor of the District-Chiefs of Sawa.**

make a mockery of my words? Since you will not believe, this empire is truly a Land over which you should not rule. The child the Empress carries in her womb shall have it. Go then your one road!"

Then the Great-Magnate, Noble-of-Brave-Uchi, with dread spoke to the Sovereign, saying, "Continue augustly to play your koto." At which Prince-Perfect-Middle drew the koto to him and played, but feebly, and immediately its sound ceased and they made a light, and, lo, he was dead.

(Some say that the Sovereign did not die at this time, but remained unbelieving, and going out to give battle to the Kuma-So, was struck by one of the enemy's arrows and slain.)

Amazed and in fear, the Empress and Noble-Brave-of-Uchi made no mourning and kept the news from the people bidding

IGATSU

Tribe-Master of the Intercessors, the Clan-Chief of Great-Three-Threads, together with

IKUI [79]

Tribe-Master of the Warrior-Clan, and

TAKEMOTSU

Tribe-Master of the imperial guard, to keep watch inside the palace, and the body of the Sovereign was given to Noble-of-Brave-Uchi, who took it by sea to the Ana Passage and laid it for the time in the Palace of Fertile-Shore,[80] burying it without lights. The august years of the Sovereign were fifty-two.

THE REGENT PRINCESS-LONG-LIFE-PERFECT [81]
(DEITY-MERIT [82])

Sorrowing that the Sovereign would not obey the Kami's instructions and had thus died early, the Empress set the country's great offerings before the Kami and bade her officers purge offenses and right transgressions, and they sought out all sorts of crimes. *Now of the various faults and transgressions some are of the Sky;* to wit, the breaking down of the divisions of ricefields; the filling up of irrigation ditches; *the removing of water pipes;* sowing seed over sown seed; [83] *the planting of skewers,*[84] flaying alive, and backward-flaying.[85] *These are Sky-offenses.*[86] *Earth-offenses are the cutting of the living skin; the cutting of the dead skin;* [87] *leprosy;* [88] cohabitation in clear daylight; [89] calamities from creeping things, from the Sky-deities,[90] and from high-flying birds; killing animals by bewitchments; the evacuating of excrement and the voiding of urine; marriage between parents and children; marriage of a man to his mother-in-law or his stepdaughter; coupling with horses, with cattle, with fowls, and with dogs.⁹¹ Also they built a temple-of-abstinence in the Village of Woyamada.

Having thus made a great purification of the Land, Noble-of-Brave-Uchi again stood in the sacred enclosure and requested the Kami's commands, when the manner of the instruction and advice was exactly the same as on the former day. They declared, "This Land truly is a Land that should be ruled over by the child in the Empress' womb." Then said Noble-of-Brave-Uchi, "In awe, O great Kami! What is the child that is in the Empress' womb?" The Kami replied, "It is a male child." Then the Empress, wishing to discover what Kami had sent the curse and so that she might gain the Land of treasures, entered the temple and officiated in person. She bade Noble-of-Brave-Uchi play on a koto and Igatsu, Tribe-Master of the Intercessors, she appointed Master-of-the-Pure-Court. After that she placed a thousand pieces of cloth above the koto and prayed, saying, "I wish to know the names of the great Kami whose words earlier instructed the Sovereign." After seven days and nights the Kami replied, "It is the heart's wish of the Kami who dwells in the Shrine of split-bellied Fifty-Bells, in the District of Cross-Meet, in the Province of divine-winded Isè, Sacred-Jewel-of-the-Rooted-Sakaki-Princess-of-Sky-Distant-Opposite-Land." ⁹²

Then the Empress asked, "Are there other Kami present?" And a Kami replied, "I, the Kami who comes on the ears of the flag-like pampas-grass, dwelling in Foam-District in Adafushi in Oda." ⁹³ Again she asked, "Are there other Kami present?" And a Kami replied, "I, the Kami of the Thing-Sign in the Sky and in the Void, the Prince who enters the gem-casket, the sacred Eight-Fold-Thing-Sign-Master." ⁹⁴ Again she asked, "Are there others?" and answer was made, "We, the Kami who sank to the bottom of the water at the Little-Passage of Orange in the Land of Sun-Facing, who are born and dwell there like fresh-water weeds, Elder-Male-of-the-Bottom, Elder-Male-of-the-Middle, and Elder-Male-of-the-Surface." ⁹⁵

> (Some say that it was at this time that the august names of these Kami were first made known.)

Again she asked, "Are there others?" And it was answered, "It is not known whether there are others." Further the Kami said, "If you are truly minded to seek that Land, you must present sacred offerings to every one of the Sky- and Earth-Kami, and to the Kami of the mountains and of the rivers and of the sea, and set our spirits atop your vessel, and put into a gourd fir-tree ⁹⁶ ashes, and make a quantity of chopsticks and leaf platters, and scatter them all on the waves of the great sea. Thus you may cross over." So, having obtained the names of the divine Kami, the worship was done after their instructions, and afterward

LORD-OF-KAMO [97]

was sent to give battle to the Kuma-So, who soon made submission.

Now there was in the village of Notorita a man named White-Feather-Bear-Eagle,[98] of stubborn character, whose body had wings with which he could fly and soar on high, and who would not heed the imperial bidding, but robbed the people continually. Desirous of proceedings against him, the Empress removed from the Palace of Evergreen-Oak-Sun to the Palace of Small-Pine-Tree. At this time her hat was blown off by a sudden whirlwind (for which reason people called that place August-Hat). Then, going to the Sosoki Moor, she gave battle to White-Feather-Bear-Eagle and slew him, saying then to her attendants, "My mind is now at peace." (So that place was called Peaceful.) Proceeding to the District of Mountain-Gate,[99] she slew a Ground-Spider named Princess-of-Tabura, on which the latter's elder brother, Natsuha, who had raised an army to oppose her, fled. After this the Empress went to the District of Fir-Tree-Bay [1] in the Land of Hizen. *On the road she met a deer (for which reason that place was named Deer-Met-Station).*[A]

On the Little River in the Village of Jewel-Island,[2] she partook of food. It was then the first decade of the fourth month. There she pulled out threads from her raiment to make a line, and using a bent needle as a hook and grains of rice as bait, she stood on a sandy bar in the middle of the river, and threw in her hook, saying, "We are about to go to the west to take the Land of treasure. If We are to be successful, may a fish take Our hook." Then she lifted her rod and a trout was caught. At that she said, "Assuredly this is strange." (For this reason people named the place Strange-Land.[3] The present name, Fir-Tree-Bay, is a corruption of this.) The sandy bar is called Princess-of-Victory-Gate. It is on account of this event that to this day women, in the first decade of the fourth month, pull threads from their skirts and with grains of rice as bait, hook salmon-trout. If men fish there they can catch none.[4] So then, assured that the instruction of the Kami was right, the Empress sacrificed to the Sky- and Earth-Kami, and set apart and cultivated a sacred ricefield. To flood this with water from Middle River she dug a ditch as far as the Todoroki Hill.

Now there was a huge rock in the way, and summoning Noble-of-Brave-Uchi, she bade him pray to the Sky- and Earth-Kami, offering a

---

[97] **Ancestor of the Magnates of Kibi.**

sword and a mirror and beseeching them to let the ditch be completed. And the lightning and thunder broke the rock in two, so that the water ran through. (For this reason people called that ditch the ditch of Parted-Field.) *Also she went to Mount Mirror, in the Province of Buzen, and surveying the form of the land, she said, "May the Kami of Sky and of Earth assist me!" and she placed a mirror on the mountain. Afterward this mirror was turned to stone and remains there still. (For which reason the mountain received its name.)*[A] Then, returning to the Bay of Evergreen-Oak-Sun, the Empress let down her hair and gazing over the sea, she said, "I have been instructed by the Sky- and Earth-Kami, and trusting in the spirits of the imperial ancestors, shall cross the deep blue sea and personally punish the west. Therefore now I dip my head in the sea water, and if I am to succeed, may my hair part into two parts." So she went into the sea to bathe and her hair parted, and she bound it up in bunches,[5] saying to her Magnates, "Though a weak woman, I shall for awhile take the outward look of a man and use manly counsel."

While thus wearing man's attire she came to a village, where her elbow-pad dropped off (from which the place received the name of Elbow-Pad-Station. It has now become the two villages of Great-Elbow-Pad and Small-Elbow-Pad.[6, B]

It is also said by the people of Elbow-Pad-Beach,[7] *in Marsh-Corner District, Bingo Province, that in that place she prepared vessels and oars and stored provisions, and later, after her return, she made a festival there for the Kami of that port,*

SHIP-JEWEL.[8]

THE EMPRESS PREPARES THE EXPEDITION

Now she commanded that the various provinces collect vessels and practice with weapons, but she was unable to raise an army.

(Some say, otherwise, that the army was gathered, but ran away when she proceeded.)[A]

Then she said, "Truly this is the heart's wish of a Kami," *and she made divination that indicated the august Kami of Great-Three-Threads, and building the Shrine of Great-Three-Threads, she made offerings of a sword and spear, after which the troops were readily gathered.*[9]

At Mountain-Gate, in Nagato Province, was a great marsh in which was a camphor tree whose top reached the Sky and whose branches shaded a space two ri square. A village to the north of it saw no sunlight during the year (wherefore it was called True-Dark) [10] *and a village to the west of it saw no morning sun (wherefore it was called Morning-Shade). More than forty ships were built from the wood of this single tree.*[11] *Because* *the wood was thus used the name of Mountain-Gate was changed to Ship-Tree.*¹² Then the Empress called together many Kami at the pine field of Kami-Cape of Riverside District and besought their favor, when the Kami who dwelt at Mount Minumè, of Nose District, came and said, "I also will protect and aid you. At the mountain where I reside are cryptomeria trees. If you make proper choice of these to build vessels for your voyage, you shall be fortunate and happy." So the Empress commanded that vessels be built according to the Kami's instruction. Now these ships made deep sounds like the bellowing of cows, and they went of their own accord from Fort-Island to Minumè, but could be rowed no further. She made divination, by which it appeared that this was the heart's wish of a Kami, so she left the vessels there. (When she returned home she dedicated a shrine to that Kami at the seacoast where she had left the vessels, and named the place Minumè.) ᴬ

She then bade a fisherman named Womaro, of Ahe, to go into the western sea to see if there was land there, and he reported saying, "No land can be seen." Then she sent a fisherman named Nagusa,¹³ of Shika, to see, and he returned after some days and reported, "To the northwest there is a clouded mountain stretching across, which may be a Land." Now a Kami instructed her, saying, "There will be a gentle spirit who will go with you to guard your life and a rough spirit who will go in advance as guide to the vessels." And she worshiped this Kami,¹⁴ appointing

OTARIMA

the Lord ¹⁵ of Yosami, master of the worship.

At this time, *while she was reviewing the army,* the birth-time of the child with which she was pregnant approached. So, in order to restrain her august womb, she took a stone and twisted it in the girdle of her skirt, and prayed, saying, "May my delivery be in this Land on the day of my return from this adventure." The stone that she twisted in her skirt is now on the roadside at the village of Thread,¹⁶ in the Land of Tsukushi. *This was the origin of the practice of the people who, when they wish to postpone the birth of a child, carry a stone in the girdle.*¹⁷

> (By some it is said that she took two stones and put them in her girdle and prayed, saying, "I go to pacify the western land. If the child to be born is a Kami, it shall be born after I return here in triumph.") ᴮ
>
> These say that the two stones are two white stones that lie to the west of Ikofu-Moor of Thread-District, which the people of the time called Babe-Bearing-Stones,¹⁸ but which now, corruptly, are called Kafu-Stones. They are white and round and smooth as if polished. One is one shaku two sun long and one

shaku thick and its circumference is one shaku eight sun. Its weight is forty-one kin.[19] The other is one shaku one sun long and one shaku thick and its circumference is one shaku eight sun. Its weight is forty-nine kin.) [A]

In Harima Province, where she came to worship many Kami, the Kami

PRINCESS-OF-NIHO

a daughter of He-Who-Invites,[20] had possessed the governor

PRINCESS-STONE-SLOPE

saying through her mouth, "If you worship me, I will assure you good results. You shall subjugate the Land of Eight-Fathom-Hollywood-Spear-Bottom-Unreached, the Land of Maiden's-Eyebrows-Drawn, the Land of The-Shining-Jewel-Casket, the Land of Silla, of the Komomakura-Treasured-Mulberry-Cloth-Quilts, of the Red-Waves." [21] Thus she had spoken. So the Empress, marshaling her vessels, took red soil and with it painted Sky-jewel-spears that she stood at prow and stern, and with red soil she painted also the curtains [22] of the Imperial ships and the armor. Moreover, she stirred up the sea water so that it was murky.[B]

After the subjugation of Silla, when she had returned home, she pacified and offered worship to the Kami Princess-of-Niho, on Mount Wistaria-Sign [23] on Pipe-River, in Iyo Province. Now the Empress, desiring to obtain the two jewels of flood-tide and ebb-tide, instructed her younger sister, Sky-Princess,[24] saying, "Go swiftly to the sea palace and borrow and bring me the tide-jewels. By their power the subjugation of the enemy country will be certain. The child within my womb is a prince, who, if the Sea-Kami [25] lend them to me, shall wed his daughter.[26] Thus shall you say to him." Then she built a stage upon the sea at Kano-Island, on which an old man danced, while her attendants made music, hearing which the Kami

ISORO-OF-AZUMI

whose home was in the sea and who was a conductor to the palace of the sea Kami, loving the dance, came from the sea. He had shellfish attached to his face, which he covered with his sleeve. (So since that time a dancer of the dance called Seïno,[27] or Nara dance, covers his face with his sleeve.) Then, being asked, he conducted Sky-Princess to the palace of the sea Kami, who loaned the jewels, and these were delivered to the Empress the next morning.[A]

(Some say that Isoro-of-Azumi is the Great Kami of Deer-Island,[28] who resides in Soaking and in Shikuzen Provinces, and at Kasuga in Mountain-Gate Province.)

Setting sail, the Empress stopped at Stone-House in My-Shame, where a storm arose and all her people were made wet, when

GREAT-MIDDLE-CHILD

built a house of rough mats. (Accordingly he was called Head-Man-of-Rough-Mat-Weave, and since he lived there the river was named Middle-River and the village Village-of-Middle-River.) Stopping upon a certain hill, also, the Empress gave orders to her host, saying, "In this army let there be no complaint of anything!" (Therefore the place was named Hill-of-Special-Mentioning.) [29] Now her oarsmen asked, "When shall we come to yonder place?" (So that place was called When-Village.) [B]

She set sail from the Harbor of Wani, *stopping at the port of the Whirlpool River (so named because there was there a deep whirlpool), from which she came to Ito. There her vessel encountered a sudden contrary wind and could not proceed, though the vessels which accompanied it were able to do so. Thereon she called the people to drag her vessel. Among these was a woman, who, in trying to save her child that she carried on her back, fell into the bay (so the place was named Astonish-Port.)* [30] *She moored her ships northeast of Rescue-Village, and the stakes at the prow and stern of her vessel were transformed into rocks. They are twenty shaku in height, the circumference of each is more than one hundred shaku, and they are about ten cho distant from each other. No grass or trees grow on them. At this place one of the vessels of the Empress's army drifted on the waves before the wind, but a Ground-Spider, whose name was Utsuhiwomaro,*[31] *rescued it. (Accordingly the place was so named). She came at night to a certain island where she passed the night. She had two attendants,*

GREAT-BEACH
SMALL-BEACH

and the latter she bade search upon the island for fire, which he did and returned speedily. On Great-Beach's asking him whether there was a dwelling near by, he replied that the island was connected with Strike-Rise-Beach, and could almost be said to be the same. (So it was named Near-Island. It is now corruptly called Shika-Island.) [A]

THE CONQUEST OF THE WESTERN LAND

So she set sail, and in the crossing the wind Kami caused a strong, favoring breeze to rise and the sea Kami lifted the waves. *The fishes that dive in the depths of the sea and the high-flying birds crossed before the ship,* and the fishes of the sea-plain, great and small, rose to the surface and carried the august vessels on their backs, so that these, following the waves, arrived at the Land of Silla without the use of oar or steering-gear.

Now when the vessels were within one hundred sword-lengths of the shore, the Empress cast down the tide-ebb jewel and instantly the sea receded, so that all the vessels were stranded.[32] *Thereon the people of the Land, who had assembled to give battle, deeming them helpless, hastened to attack them, when the Empress cast down the tide-flow jewel and instantly the sea rose in a great wave and engulfed all their host.*[A]

The tide wave pushed the vessels up onto the Land of Silla, clear to the middle of the Land, on which the king, in fear and trembling, knew not what to do, and summoning his Ministers, said, "Since this state began, the sea has never been known to cover the land. Has our term of existence run out and is our Land to become a part of the sea?" He had scarcely spoken thus when the warlike vessels appeared, covering the sea, with shining banners and with drums and fifes that re-echoed from mountain and river, and believing that the Land was about to be destroyed, he was in such fear that his senses left him. At length, however, recovering, he said, "It has been told me that there is to the eastward a divine land named Nippon with a wise imperial sovereign. This army belongs to it. We cannot combat them with weapons." So he bound his hands behind him with a white cord, and taking a white flag, made submission, and sealing up his maps and records, made obeisance before the Empress' vessel, and made petition, saying, "From this time forward, obedient to the Sky-Sovereign's bidding, We will feed his horses [33] and will marshal vessels every year, nor ever let their bellies dry or their poles and oars dry, each spring and fall sending horse-combs and ships as tribute, and will respectfully serve him, without drawing back, while there is a Sky and an Earth. Also each year We will give male and female slaves, never deeming the sea distance too great." And he took an oath, over and over again, saying, "Not till the sun rises in the west instead of the east, and till the Arinarè River flows backward and its pebbles fly up and become stars, will We fail each spring and autumn to pay homage and send tribute. If We do, may We be punished by all the Sky- and Earth-Kami."

So the Empress loosed his cords and made him her forage provider. Then the Prince of Silla, Urosohorichi, came and knelt and took hold of the imperial vessel, and making obeisance, said, "From now on your servant will govern this inner Land for the child of the Kami who dwells in Nippon, and will not fail in tribute." Him, however, she made prisoner, and cutting off his kneecaps made him crawl on the rocks, after which she slew him and buried him in the sand.[34]

(Some say, however, that the Empress was advised to slay the king, but that she replied, "When I received the divine command and the promise that this Land of treasures would be given me, I ordered that the submissive should not be slain. Now that We have taken the Land and its people have made submission, it would be unlucky to slay them." So she slew neither the king nor the prince.)

Afterward she went into the Land, sealed up the storehouses of precious treasures and took the maps and records,[35] and planted the spear on which she leaned at the king's gateway as a token to later times, and this spear remains planted there to this day. Also the kings of the two countries of Koma [36] and Kudara,[37] hearing that Silla had made submission, sent spies to ascertain the imperial force, and despairing of victory, came and made obeisance, and with signs said, "From this time forever Our Lands shall be provinces of your western border and shall not fail in tribute." [38] So the Land of Silla was made feeder of the imperial horses and the Land of Kudara was made store-of-the-crossing. Governments were established for the three Lands, and the Empress made the rough august-spirits of the Great Kami of the Inlet of Pleasant-to-Dwell-In the guardian Kami of the Land, and gave them there a resting place.

(It is said by some, however, that these three Kami who had gone with the expedition, Elder-Male-of-the-Bottom, Elder-Male-of-the-Middle, and Elder-Male-of-the-Surface, instructed the Empress, saying, "Let our rough spirits be revered at the village of Mountain-Ricefield at the Ana Passage." Then Homutachi [39] and

NOBLE-OF-HAND-CRUMPLE [40]

said to her, "Surely you will set apart for these Kami the land they desire for a dwelling." So a shrine [41] was built in the village of Mountain-Ricefield and Homutachi was appointed master of their worship.)

Then the Empress, leaving a man as governor of Silla, crossed back to Nippon, and the king of Silla gave a prince named Mishikochi as a hostage, and filled eighty vessels with gold, silver, things of bright colors and figured stuffs and silks, and sent them after the imperial vessels. (This was the origin of the custom of the king of Silla's sending always eighty tribute vessels.)

---

[40] *Ancestor of the Tribe-Masters of Tsumori.*

Now after she had crossed to Chikuzen Province *in* the Land of Tsukushi, *thatching the roof of the bringing-forth-house with cormorant feathers, and standing a pagoda tree* [42] *upside down (which took root thus and still stands),* she gave birth at Kata to the child in her womb

GREAT-ELBOW-PAD-LORD.[43]

He was given this name because, when first born, he had on his arm a fleshy growth shaped like an elbow pad,[44] corresponding to the elbow pad worn by the Empress as masculine equipment. By this he was known, from the womb, for a ruler of countries. The place where he was born the people called Birth [45] (*or, as some say,* Birth-Moor,[46] *or* Birth-Palace.) From the womb the Kami of Sky and Earth granted to him the three Han.[47]

Now in Koyu District, in Sun-Facing Province, there is a mountain called Peak-of-Tono (or, as some say, Peak-of-Tsuno),[48] *whose Kami is called Great-Kami-Tono,*[49] *which Kami the Empress had invited to protect the prow of her vessel. After her return from Silla, she proceeded to Peak-of-Ushika,*[50] *where she shot an arrow, when a black substance appeared, issuing from the ground. This she dug up with the end of her bow, and found it to be a man and a woman, whom she employed as land-protecting Kami. Their descendants still exist, being called Head-Black, probably because their heads had at first appeared as a black substance when they were dug up. Their descendants multiplied, but died from a plague, till there were left only two. The ancient chronicle says, "They died from day to day till there remained, the story goes, but two mouths." This befell from the anger of the Great Kami (for the reason that they were made to labor at public works, though they were employed as land-protecting Kami), who sent the malignant plague from which they died. It is said that Great-Kami-Tono, if he be supplicated to cure ulcer, always effects a cure. After her return the Empress offered sacrifice to Great-Kami-Tono.*[A]

In Harima Province her vessel stopped at a certain place in which a hazel tree grew in one night some ten shaku high, (from which the place was called Hazel-Plain).[51] *Here the Empress' vessel listed (for which cause the place was called Inclined-Ricefield). This is the seat of the Kami*

LITTLE-PERFECT

for whom a festival is held. In this Land also the Kami

PRINCESS-ROAD-MASTER

settled. She gave birth to a child without an apparent father, so she planted rice in seven cho of ricefield, which grew and bore a crop in seven days and seven nights. From this rice she brewed sakè, and invited many Kami, when the child offered the sakè to Sky-Mara,[52] by which he was known to be its father. (Later the ricefield was deserted, so that the place was called Deserted-Ricefield-Village.)[A]

THE CONSPIRACY OF KING-KAGOSAKA AND KING-GREAT-BEAR

The Empress, with her Magnates and officers, journeyed to the Palace of Fertile-Shore at the Ana Passage, and taking the Sovereign's body, went by sea toward the capital. But King-Kagosaka and King-Great-Bear,[53] having learned of the death of the Sovereign, of the Empress's western expedition, and of the birth of the imperial child, conspired secretly, saying, "All the Magnates obey the Empress, and they will surely consult and make the infant the Sovereign. We are older than he, and shall we serve our younger brother?" So, on pretense of building a mound for the dead Sovereign, they went to Harima and built one at Akashi. To do this they made a line of boats across to the island of My-Shame and brought stones from there. Then they gave a weapon to every man and waited to seize the Empress. The two lords

KURAMI-LORD [54]

NOBLE-LEADING-ELDER [55]

joined King-Kagosaka and he bade them raise an army in the eastern Land. King-Kagosaka and King-Great-Bear went into the Moor of Toga [56] to search for a hunt-omen, saying, "If we are to succeed, we shall get good game." King-Kagosaka climbed an oak tree, when a huge and angry boar came forth, uprooted the oak tree, and straightway devoured him. At that the soldiers trembled, and King-Great-Bear said to Kurami-Lord, "This is an evil omen. Let us not await the enemy in this place." So he drew back his army and encamped at Pleasant-to-Dwell-In.

Now the Empress, learning of his purpose, bade Noble-Brave-of-Uchi take the imperial child in his bosom, and going across through the provinces of the southern sea, wait at the Harbor of Tree. Her own vessel went toward Wave-Swift. However, turning in the middle of the sea, it would not go forward, so she returned to the Harbor of H'yogo and made divination, when the Kami Great-Sky-Shiner instructed her, saying, "My rough spirit cannot come near the imperial dwelling. I must dwell in the Land of Hirota in August-Heart." So the Empress appointed

PRINCESS-HAYAMA

---

[54] **Ancestor of the Clan-Chiefs of Inugami.**
[55] **Ancestor of the Kishi-Clan of Naniwa.**

to worship her. Then the Kami Young-Sun-Female [57] instructed the Empress, saying, "I desire to dwell in the Land of Pleasant-to-Dwell-In in Ikuta." So

LEADING-ELDER-OF-UNA-GAMI

was appointed to worship her. Then the Kami Eight-Fold-Thing-Sign-Master instructed the Empress, saying, "Worship me in the Land of Nakata in August-Heart." And

PRINCESS-NAGA

younger sister of Princess-Hayama, was appointed to worship him. Also the three Kami, Elder-Male-of-the-Bottom, Elder-Male-of-the-Middle, and Elder-Male-of-the-Surface, instructed the Empress, saying, "Our tranquil spirits must dwell at Pleasant-to-Dwell-In,[58] in Nunakura in Ohotsu, that they may see the vessels going by." So these Kami were there enshrined. After this the Empress' vessel was able to cross the sea.

King-Great-Bear again drew back his army and camped, while the Empress went south to the Land of Tree and met the imperial child at Hitaka, and from there she removed to the Palace of Shinu. At that time the day became like the night and the darkness lasted many days, so that the people said, "It is the Eternal Night." The Empress asked

FERTILE-EARS [59]

the meaning of the omen, and an old man answered, "The name of this calamity that has been handed down is No-Sun. It arises from the fact that the two hafuri of the shrines of Shinu and of Amano have been buried together." So she made inquiry in the village, and it was told her that these two priests had been friends and that when the priest of Shinu became sick and died, the priest of Amano had wept and lamented, saying, "We have been friends since we were born. Why in death should we not have one grave?" And lying down by the corpse, he had died also, and the two had been buried together. The tomb was opened and this was found to be true, after which they were buried separately, when the sun again appeared and the night and day became distinguishable.

The Empress prepared a mourning vessel and setting the imperial child in it, spread a report that the child was really dead. Then Noble-of-Brave-Uchi filled the vessel with an army, and they set out, and when the army of King-Great-Bear lay in wait to attack the mourning vessel, thinking it empty, the army was landed from it and the battle began, Noble-Leading-Elder being King-Great-Bear's shogun and

---

[59] **Ancestor of the Governors of Ki.**

PRINCE-WAVE-SWIFT-BRAVE-FURU-BEAR [60]

being shogun on the side of the heir apparent.

(Some say, on the contrary, that Noble-of-Brave-Uchi and Prince-Wave-Swift-Brave-Furu-Bear, with an army of some tens of thousands of picked warriors, went by way of Behind-the-Mountains to Uji, where the two armies gave battle.)

In the forefront of the army of King-Great-Bear was

KORI-OF-BEAR [61]

who, to hearten his men, sang to them this song:

> Beyond the river || Lies the rough pine-clad plain.
> To that pine-clad plain || Let us now cross over,
> With our tsuki-bows || And supply of round arrows.
> Ah, my good comrades, || With my comrades together!
> My cousin also! || Cousins together!
> Come let us join in the battle || So transitory
> With the Noble of Uchi! || . . . .
> . . . .[62] || Come let us join in the battle!

King-Great-Bear's army was driven as far as Behind-the-Mountains, where it turned and made a stand, and both sides fought without retreating.

Prince-Wave-Swift-Brave-Furu-Bear, planning a stratagem, bade his men bind up their hair mallet-wise and hide extra bowstrings in their topknots and gird on sham wooden swords; then, circulating a report that the Empress was dead, he deceived King-Great-Bear, saying, "It is not I who long to rule the empire. We will guard the imperial infant and obey you. What is the need for further fighting? Let us all sever our bowstrings and throw away our weapons and agree, and you may take the Sky-rule and the government." So saying, he ordered his men to sever their bowstrings and to take off their swords and throw them into the river. But when their bows were unbent and they had laid aside their arms, Prince-Wave-Swift-Brave-Furu-Bear bade the three divisions of his army pluck from their topknots their prepared bowstrings and stretch

---

[60] **Ancestor of the Magnates of Wani.***
[61] **Ancestor of the Head-Men of Kadono-no Ki and of the Kishi † of Tako.**

* See p. 309, n. 2.
† Derived, no doubt, from the ancient Kishi-Clan (see p. 293, B). The name later would appear to have become a definite title or rank, whose precise meaning is uncertain. Motoöri thought it a Korean designation, which Chamberlain assumes to have been derived from the Chinese. Aston thought it identical with the Silla *Kilsa* (-grade).

them on again, and taking their real swords, they crossed the river and attacked their enemies. Then King-Great-Bear said to Kurami-Lord and Noble-Leading-Elder, "We have been fooled, and with no extra weapons we cannot give battle." So they retreated to Meeting-Hill [63] where Noble-of-Brave-Uchi's picked warriors, pursuing, came up with them and routed them. (Thus the place received its name.) From there they fled as far as Chestnut-Village [64] in Bending-Bamboo-Grass,[65] where they were cut to pieces, so that the blood ran into Chestnut-Village. For this reason the fruit of that village is not brought to the imperial palace.

There King-Great-Bear, with Noble-Leading-Elder, hard-pressed by the pursuit, and knowing not where to flee, boarded a vessel and floating on the sea, sang:

O my lord, come! || Sooner than the thrust
Of Furu-Bear's wounding hand, || Like unto wild ducks,[66]
Into the sea of Omi || Verily let us plunge!

Straightway they plunged into the sea at the ford of Seta and died. Thereon Noble-of-Brave-Uchi sang:

By the Omi sea || There at the ford of Seta,
Those birds a-diving!
Now my eyes see them no more, || Can it be that they still live?

They searched for the bodies, but could not find them, till after some days they were found on the bank of the river at Uji, when Noble-of-Brave-Uchi again sang:

By the Omi sea || There at the ford of Seta,
Those birds a-diving,
Passing Tanakami by, || There at Uji have been caught.

Later the body of the Sovereign, Prince-Perfect-Middle, was buried in the mound of Long-Inlet, near Wega in Kawachi, and the capital was established at Iharè, where the Empress dwelt in the Palace of Wakazakura.[67]

Now the king of Silla sent envoys with tribute, and they desired to bring about the escape of Prince-Mishikochi,[68] who had formerly been sent as hostage. So they caused him to petition the Empress, saying, "These have told me that the king, since I have not returned in so long, has seized my wife and family and made them slaves. I pray you grant me to return for a time to ascertain if this be true." The Empress granted this, sending with him

PRINCE-SOTSU-OF-MULBERRY-CASTLE.

When they reached Anchorage-Island,[69] the envoys gave Prince-Mishikochi another vessel in which to escape to Silla, after which they put a puppet of straw in his bed like a sick man, and said to Prince-Sotsu-of-Mulberry-Castle, "Prince-Mishikochi has suddenly become ill and is about to die." But the other sent men to care for him, and having thus laid bare the trick, put the envoys into a cage and burned them to death. The wife of the Silla prince Urushohorichi, whom the Empress had slain and buried in the sand of the seashore, wishing to know where the body of her husband had been buried, seduced the governor, who had been left there, saying, "If you will reveal the place to me, I will repay you and will be your wife." So he privately told her, whereon she and her people plotted together and slew him, and having taken up the body of Prince Urushohorichi, laid it in another place. Then they buried the body of the governor in the earth underneath it, with the coffin atop, saying, "Thus should punishment be meted out to the high and the low." Prince-Sotsu-of-Mulberry-Castle then proceeded from Anchorage-Island to the Harbor of Tatara and seized the Castle of Chhora, when the people of Silla were afraid, and took council and slew the wife of Prince Urushohorichi as apology, and Prince-Sotsu-of-Mulberry-Castle returned to Nippon, taking with him many captives.[70]

THE HEIR-APPARENT EXCHANGES NAMES WITH THE KAMI IZASA-LORD

When Noble-of-Brave-Uchi, taking with him the heir-apparent, for the purpose of purification passed through the Lands of Omi and Wakasa, he built a temporary palace at Horned-Stag [71] at the nearer end of the Province of Koshi for the child to dwell in. Then the great Kami

IZASA-LORD [72]

who dwelt in Kebi, appeared to Noble-of-Brave-Uchi at night in a dream, and said, "I desire to exchange my name for that of the child."

(For it is said by some [73] that, previous to this exchange, the name of the Kami of Kebi had been Great-Elbow-Pad-Lord, and that of the heir-apparent Izasa-Lord.)

The dreamer answered, "I give you reverence. The name shall be respectfully changed as you desire." Then the Kami charged him, saying, "Tomorrow morning let him go to the beach, and I will present my offering for the exchanged name." So when the heir-apparent went in the

---

[70] **Ancestors of the Han People * of the Villages of Kuhabara, Sabi, Oshinami, and Takamiya.**

---

* These are referred to as of Chinese descent, presumably on the theory that the portion of Korea from which they came had been settled by Chinese.

morning to the beach, the whole shore was lined with dolphins whose noses were broken, whereon the child caused it to be said to the Kami, "You give me fish for my august food." (For this reason the Kami is now called Food-Wondrous-Great.) The blood from the noses of the dolphins stank (for which reason the beach was called Bloody-Strand.[74] It is now called Horned-Stag.)

When the heir-apparent returned to the capital, his parent, the Empress, offered him a banquet in the great hall, and having distilled some sakè of the sort that one keeps in waiting for an absent friend, presented it to him, wishing him long life, and singing:

> This august sakè ‖ Is not my august sakè.
> The sakè-Kami, ‖ The Eternal-Land dweller,
> Firm as the rocks are, ‖ The august little Kami,[75]
> Benison high, ‖ Benison repeated,
> Benison rich, ‖ Benison redoubled,
> Sends as gift to thee, ‖ Augustly.
> Drink of it deeply, ‖ Sa! Sa![76]

Having thus sang, she offered him the liquor, when Noble-of-Brave-Uchi, replying for the child, sang:

> This august sakè! ‖ The man who did distil it,
> Did so setting up ‖ On the mortar his drum.
> Singing all the while ‖ He must have distilled it.
> Dancing the while ‖ He must have distilled it.
> This august sakè, ‖ Ah, this august sakè,
> Is ever sweeter! ‖ Sa! Sa!

(These are liquor-rejoicing songs.)

NOBLE-OF-SHIMA

after this was sent to the Land of Toku-Shu,[77] whose king said to him: "In the year before last three men of Kudara came to my Land, saying that their king, hearing there was a great country to the eastward, had sent them to beseech a passage to it. I answered that though I had heard of that country I did not know the way there, which was across wide seas and high waves, so that even in a huge vessel communication was difficult. They said then that they would return and make ready a vessel."

So Noble-of-Shima sent

NIHAYA

to inquire about the welfare of the king of Kudara. At this the latter was vastly pleased, giving Nihaya five rolls of different-dyed silk, a bow made of horn, arrows, and forty pieces of iron. Then he showed him the precious things in his treasury, saying, "In this Land is much treasure like this. I desired to send this as tribute to your Land, but did not know how to do so. I shall now send envoys to your Land." Nihaya came back and reported to Noble-of-Shima, who returned home, and later the king of Kudara sent three envoys with tribute and with them came an envoy from Silla. At this the Empress and the heir-apparent were delighted, saying, "People from the Lands desired by the dead Sovereign have now arrived. How pitiful that they cannot meet!" And all the Ministers wept.

However, when they examined the tribute, there were from Silla many precious things, but from Kudara things few and worthless. So they asked the envoys, "Why is Kudara's tribute less than Silla's?" They answered, "In coming here, we missed the way, and arriving at Sapi, the Silla people seized us and threw us into prison, and after three months were minded to slay us. But we looked up to the Sky and cursed them, and fearing the curse, they held back from slaying us, but took away our tribute, making it that of their own Land, and giving us in exchange the poor tribute of Silla, saying, 'Beware of speaking of this, or on your return you shall be slain!' So we were afraid and suffered it, and have come with difficulty to your Land."

The Empress and the heir-apparent accused the Silla envoys of this and prayed to the Sky-Kami, saying, "Who shall be sent to Kudara and who to Silla to inquire if this be true?" And the Sky-Kami instructed them, saying, "Noble-of-Brave-Uchi shall make a plan and

PRINCE-CHIKUMA-NAGA [78]

shall be sent." So the latter was sent to Silla. After this,

AREDA-LORD [79]

was raised to the rank of general, together with

KAGA-LORD

and raising troops, they crossed over to the Land of Toku-Shu. When they were about to go against Silla, however, they were advised that their army was too small, and they sent back to request reinforcements. So picked warriors were sent to Toku-Shu, who entered Silla and conquered it. They took several provinces, and proceeding to the west, slaughtered the savage people there and gave their land to Kudara. After that the king and the prince of Kudara came with more troops, four villages made submission, and the king and the prince, meeting Areda-Lord at the village of Tsurusugi, thanked and dismissed them with kind-

---

[78] **Ancestor of the Head-Men of Tsukimoto, of the Nukada-Clan.**
[79] **Ancestor of the Clan-Chiefs of Kozukè.**

ness. Prince-Chikuma-Naga, however, remained in the Land of Kudara, where he and the king of the Land made a sacred covenant on Mount Phi-ki. Later they ascended Mount Kos'ya, where the king took oath thus: "A seat of grass could be burned with fire; a seat of wood could be carried away by water. So, sitting on a rock, I swear a sacred compact which shall remain undissolved forever. From now on, for a thousand autumns and ten thousand years without end, this Land shall be called your province of the western border, and each spring and autumn we will render tribute." Then he took Prince-Chikuma-Naga to the capital, where he treated him with kindness, sending him home with an escort.

For three years after that the king of Kudara did not fail in his tribute. Silla, however, sent none, and at length Prince-Sotsu-of-Mulberry-Castle and Prince-Sachi [80] were sent to punish it. Now the Empress became angered with the latter [81] and he dared not return. His younger sister was one of the palace-ladies and she, to find out whether the Empress' anger had abated, said to her, "In a dream I saw Prince-Sachi." At this, however, the Empress, showing her wrath, said, "Would he dare to return, then?" and Prince-Sachi, hearing of this and believing that his pardon was impossible, died in a rock-cave.

The Empress died [82] in the Palace of Wakazakura at the august age of one hundred years. She was buried in the mound of Tatanami, in Saki.

THE EMPEROR GREAT-ELBOW-PAD-LORD [83]
(RESPONDING-DEITY [84])

Great-Elbow-Pad-Lord dwelt in the Palace of Brilliant at Karushima. He was intelligent, of clear understanding and of foresight.[85] He wedded three queens, daughters of King-True-Young-of-Elbow-Pad.[86] The name of the eldest was

PRINCESS-IRI-TAKAKI

by whom there were born to him

PRINCE-GREAT-MIDDLE-OF-NUKATA [87]
GREAT-MOUNTAIN-WARDEN [88]
TRUE-YOUNG-OF-IZA.[89]

The second whom he took to wife was

PRINCESS-MIDDLE.

---

[88] **Ancestor of the Clan-Chiefs of Hijikata, of Haïbara (in Totomi Province), and of Heki (unidentified).**
[89] **Ancestor of the Lords of Fukagawa.**

She was Empress, and by her he begot

GREAT-WREN [90]
NETORI.[91]

Great-Wren was so named because on the day he was born an owl flew into the bringing-forth house. Next day the Sovereign, summoning Noble-of-Brave-Uchi, inquired of him the meaning of the omen. He replied, "The omen is favorable. Yesterday, when the wife of your servant [92] brought forth a child, a wren flew into the bringing-forth-house, a strange thing indeed. Then said the Sovereign, "It is a Sky-sign that our children are born on the same day and both with a favorable omen. Let the name of each bird be used for the other child, as a sign for after generations." So the name of the wren was given to the heir-apparent and the name of the owl was given to the child of Noble-of-Brave-Uchi. Of these children, Netori wedded his younger half-sister,

LADY-OF-THREE-MOORS-OF-AYUCHI.[93]

(*Some say that the Sovereign wedded beside these,*

PRINCESS-GREAT-KAMI [94]

daughter of the Sea-Kami.)[95]

In the third year of his reign the Emishi came from the East bringing tribute, and were employed in road-making. Likewise

NOBLE-OF-GREAT-BEACH [96]

was sent to pacify the complaining fishermen and was made their overlord. (It was thus that the saying "boisterous fishermen" arose.) At this time the king of Kudara was not respectful to the imperial court, and

NOBLE-OF-TSUNO-OF-KI
NOBLE-OF-YASHIRO-OF-HATA
NOBLE-OF-STONE-RIVER

and Noble-of-Heguri's-Owl were sent to discipline him, and the people of Kudara slew the king as an act of penance. It was this Noble-of-Tsuno-of-Ki who first laid down boundaries for provinces and districts and set down in writing the things that each produced.

Now the Sovereign climbed the peak of Mount Great-Look [97] and gazed in every direction (*from which the mountain received its name*).

---

[90] **Ancestor of the Clan-Chiefs of Ohota.**
[96] **Ancestor of the Tribe-Masters of Azumi.**

The rock on which he stood is three shaku high, thirty shaku long, and twenty shaku wide. It has many impressions scattered over its face which are said to have been made by his foot-coverings and his staff. At Hill-of-Bell-Eat,[98] where he was injured, a hawk-bell fell off, and despite the great search made, it could not be found (for which cause the hill was thus named). A bell dropped upon another mountain, and however much it was searched for could not be restored, and finally search was made by digging the ground. (Therefore, the place was called Mount Bell-Dug.) When he made a hunt at Inner-River, many boars and deer appeared and were killed (so that the place came to be named Sega [99]). A village where he built a palace was named Great-Palace; later, when

MIDDLE-RICEFIELD [1]

governed the place, it was named Village-of-Great-House. Here a well was dug in the field, and a sakè-house was built. (Therefore it was named Sakè-Well.) When he made a hunt on the mountain, a deer stood before him and mewed "Hi! Hi!" (for which reason he called off the hunt and the place was named Mount Hiya). A dog of the Sovereign's gave chase on a mountain to a boar, which he shot. (So the place was named You-Shall-Shoot-Hill.) This dog was killed in the fight with the boar and was buried and a tomb was built over him on the western side of the hill. The place where the Sovereign proclaimed the Great Laws was named Great-Law.[2] Coming to a plain, he looked upon every side and asked, "Is it the sea or a river that is in sight?" His attendants answered that what he saw was fog, whereon he said, "I can see it completely, but there is no womè.[3] (Therefore the place was called Womè-Moor.) There his attendants dug a well, which was named August-Well-of-Bamboo-Grass.[4] Coming to Village-of-Immediately,[5]

CHILD-OF-AGA

of the Assistant-Chief-Clan, one of his attendants, with others, asked him concerning the place, to which he replied, "You have asked this immediately." (From this it received its name.) Coming to Great-Interior,[6] he said, "I thought this to be a narrow place, but entering, I find it large." (Therefore it was so named.) He washed his hands in a river, which was given the name Hand-Marsh-River. Then, his shadow falling on a mountain, the latter was named Mount Shadow. (It is also called Shadow-Hill.) [7] When he arrived at another place the sun set, and a mountain pine was used for a light (wherefore the place was called Hill-of-Pine-Peak). He ordered water to be drawn from a spring and it froze (whence the place was named Mount Freeze).[8] While upon a hunt, he shot at a running boar with a tsuki bow, and it was broken (whence the place was called Mount Tsuki-Break).⁹ From this mountain there was in sight a storehouse (for which cause the place was named Storehouse-Viewed-Village).¹⁰

> (Some, however, say differently that the head-man of the place, with others, stole a saddle from May-Night District and was carrying it home, admiring it, when its owner perceived it, and came to the village, whence it was named Saddle-Looking.) ¹¹

Pointing with his whip to a moor, the Sovereign said, "On that moor dwellings should be built and ricefields cultivated," (from which it was called Point-Out-Moor.¹² It is now known as Tashinu.) Coming from a mountain he met his attendants who were coming from the sea, (so the place was named Meeting-Moor).¹³ While he hunted on this moor, a boar raged at an arrow wound, (for which reason the place was called Anger-Moor.)¹⁴ His metal hunting arrow falling into a river, the latter was named Metal-Arrow River.¹⁵ When he stood on a hill in order to view the Land, the hill was consequently called August-Stand-Hill.¹⁶ Another hill on which he thus stood was named Grand-Stand-Hill.¹⁷ He mistook a dog for a boar and slashed open its eyes, whence the place was named Tearing-Eyes.¹⁸ When a road was made by the shore of the great river that formed the boundary of the Districts of Kami-Cape and Stag-ma, a whetstone was unearthed. (The place was consequently named Whetstone-Dug.¹⁹ It is still in existence.) Causing a well to be dug upon a hill, the water from it was extremely clear, and he said, "Since the water is clear, my heart is refreshed. (From that it was called Refreshment-Hill.²⁰ Another hill, on which a palace was built, was named Palace-Hill.)²¹, ᴀ

At this time the provinces were ordered to organize the Fisher-Clan, the Mountain-Clan, and the Game-Keeper-Clan, and the Isè-Clan was likewise established. The Land of Izu was then ordered to build a ship one hundred shaku in length. To the westward of the river Tsuki there was a tall tree, whose shadow, when the morning sun touched it, reached to the Island of My-Shame, and when the evening sun touched it, went beyond Mount High-Easy. This tree was felled and from it was fashioned a ship that, when it was finished, floated lightly and was of such swiftness, *passing seven waves with a single impulse of the oars,* that it was named Kurano.²² By means of this vessel, each morning and evening the water of My-Shame Island was drawn and augustly presented.²³

One day the ship was not used for this purpose, and the Sovereign sang:

> To Great Treasure-House, || Of Pleasant-to-Dwell-In flies
> The vessel Swift-Bird.
> Therefore rightly men name it. || But how is it Swift-Bird today?

After this its use was stopped.

On another day the Sovereign, crossing over into the Land of Omi, stood on the Moor of Uji,[24] *and gazing on Mulberry-Moor, sang:*

> On Chiba's || Thousand-leaved, vine-hung moor,
> One hundred thousand
> Home sites I distinguish, || And the plain, mountain-girdled.[B]

Now under the bridge of Uji dwells the female Kami

PRINCESS-BRIDGE.[25, A]

She is visited each evening by

KAMI-OF-RIKUYU [26]

who lives at a place at the north of the bridge of Uji (or, according to others, by the Kami of Pleasant-to-Dwell-In [27] *where in the early morning the waves roar loudly).*[A]

At the village of Kohata [28] a lovely damsel met the Sovereign at a fork of the road. He asked her, "Whose child are you?" She answered, "I am a daughter of

MAGNATE-OF-HIFURÈ-OF-WANI [29]

and the name by which I am called is

PRINCESS-TEMPLE-PRESIDER-EIGHT-RIVERS."

Immediately he said to her, "When I return tomorrow I will enter your house." So the princess told her father of this, and he replied, "Ah, it was the Sky-Sovereign. Pay respect, my child, and serve him respectfully." He decorated the house splendidly and waited, and the Sovereign came next day. Then, serving an august feast, he made his daughter present the great liquor cup, and the Sky-Sovereign, taking this, sang:

> Ah, behold this crab. || Whence, O crab, make you your way
> Through a hundred places, || Crab of far Tsunoga:
> Whither does it go || With its sidelong posturings?
> To Ichiji isle, || Or perhaps Mishima.
> Surely, like to it, || I pursued my hilly way
> By Sazanami, || Plunging like the wild duck
> And all breathlessly, || Never even making stop.
> But the maiden whom I met || On the road of Kohata,
> Had a back, ah me! || Formed like a little shield,
> And her small teeth || Like acorn rows!
> At Ichihiwi, || There at the Wani-Passage,
> Muddy the soil || Above, and red-black beneath.
> She selected || The middle soil, lying
> Like the middle one || Of three chestnuts in the burr,

---

[29] **Ancestor of the Magnates of Wani. (See also p. 241, n. 60.)**

> Drying it far || From the head-averting sun,
> To adorn her || Thickly painted eyebrows!
> The woman I encountered—
> The child I saw || And in this way desired—
> The child whom I saw || And in that way desired—
> Sits opposite. || While the feast is at its height,
> Ah, she sits by me now!

Thereon he lay with her. By her he begot

> YOUNG-LORD-OF-UJI
> YOUNG-LADY-OF-YATA [30]
> QUEEN-HEN-BIRD.

Also he took to wife

> LADY-OF-SMALL-KETTLE

younger sister of Princess-Temple-Presider-Eight-Rivers, and begot

> YOUNG-LADY-OF-UJI.

Also he took to wife Princess-Long-Life-True-Young-Middle, daughter of King-Prince-Kumata-Long,[31] and by her he begot

> KING-YOUNG-NUKÈ-FUTA-MATA.

Also he took to wife

> PRINCESS-ITOI [32]

who was the daughter of

> PERFECT-LORD-SHIMA [33]

and begot

> KING-FALCON-LORD.

Of these children, King-Young-Nukè-Futa-Mata wedded his mother's younger sister, Momo-Shiki-Iro-Be,[34] and begot

> GREAT-LORD [35]
> PRINCESS-GREAT-MIDDLE-OF-OSAKA [36]

---

[30] Ancestress (by proxy) of the Yata-Clan.
[33] Ancestor of the Tribe-Masters of the Ricefield-Clan (Ta-Be) of Sakuraï (in Kawachi Province).
[35] Ancestor of the Clan-Chiefs of Mikuni (in Echizen Province), of Hata (unidentified), of Okinaga (in Omi Province), of Sakabito in Sakata (in Settsu Province), of Yamaji (unidentified), of Meta in Tsukushi, and of Fusè (unidentified).
[36] Ancestress (by proxy) of the Osaka-Clan.*

---

* Not identical, presumably, with the Kami-Osaka-Be mentioned on p. 144. This Clan became the official executioners.

(Who, some say, was the child of the Sovereign Prince-Great-Perfect-Ruling-Lord,[37] by Princess-Quite-Black.)

PRINCESS-MIDDLE-OF-TAWI [38]
LADY-OF-KOTO-FUSHI-WISTARIA-PLAIN.

At this time there crossed over people from Koma, Kudara, Mimana, and Silla [39] and came to the court, and Noble-of-Brave-Uchi, taking these and setting them to labor on pools and embankments, made the Pool of Kudara. (This is also called the Pool-of-the-people-of-the-Han.)[40] The Pool of Sword,[41] the Pool of Karu, the Pool of Kakaki, and the Pool of Mumaya-Slope were also made.

Now in the western part of Kami-Island there was a stone Kami, whose shape was like a statue of Buddha,[42] and in its face were jewels of five colors. A man of Silla saw this wonder, and thinking the jewels in its face were ordinary ones, dug out the pupils of its eyes. At that the statue wept and the tears that streamed down upon its breast were also of five colors. In fierce anger it caused a great wind that broke the vessel of the Kara man and wrecked it on the south coast of High-Island, so that all on board lost their lives. The place where the corpses were buried was named Kara-Shore, and the island to which some things from the wreck drifted was named Kara-Cargo-Island. Even to this day people who pass the place are careful not to mention the fact that Kara men were concerned in the blinding of the statue.[A]

At this time Noble-of-Brave-Uchi was sent to Tsukushi to confer with the people, and Noble-of-Sweet-Uchi,[43] his younger brother, maligned him to the sovereign, alleging he had committed himself to the severance of Tsukushi from the realm, and intended to summon the people of the Han to serve him and seize the empire. So the Sovereign sent men to slay Noble-of-Brave-Uchi, who, learning of it, lamented, saying, "I have not two hearts toward the Sovereign, and shall I, being innocent, die?" Then one

MANÈ-KO [44]

who bore a great resemblance to him, grieved at this, came to him and said, "You are loyal and not of black heart, as all know. I beg you to go secretly to the court and yourself tell of your innocence. You can then die. People say I resemble you, and I will die in your place and prove that your heart is red." Speaking thus, he fell on his sword and slew himself. Then Noble-of-Brave-Uchi, sorrowing greatly, departed in secret,

---

[38] **Ancestress (by proxy) of the Kawa-Clan.**
[44] **Ancestor of the Governors of Iki.**

going around by way of the southern sea to Harbor-of-Tree, and, reaching the court with difficulty, protested his innocence. So the Sovereign examined him together with Noble-of-Sweet-Uchi. But they disputed so that he could not separate the true from the false, and he directed that the Kami of the Sky and the Earth should be appealed to by boiling water. Noble-of-Brave-Uchi, victor in this, took his sword, and throwing Noble-of-Sweet-Uchi down, would have slain him. The Sovereign, however, bade that he be let go and presented him to the ancestor of the governors of Iki.[45]

Now there were one hundred and eighty head-men of villages in Rice-field-Village in Harima Province, who fought one with another, and the Sovereign ordered that they be pursued and be put to death. The place to which they were pursued was called Stench-Bay, and the place where their blood streamed black was called Black-River.[A]

GREAT-WREN, THE HEIR APPARENT, AND PRINCESS-LONG-HAIR

Now it befell that some said to the Sovereign, "In the Land of H'yuga there is a beautiful damsel, daughter of

OX-MOROÏ

Clan-Chief of Many-Towns,[46] whose name is

PRINCESS-LONG-HAIR,"

and the Sovereign, pleased at this and thinking to make use of her, summoned her to the capital. So her father, who had been in the service of the court but was now old and unfit, offered her. Now the Sovereign, having journeyed to My-Shame Island to hunt, gazing westward, saw some tens of deer swimming toward him, which then entered Small-Deer [47] Harbor. It is for this reason that the place was so named, and it was perhaps at this time that people began to apply this word to sailors.

(Some say, however, that the swimmers entered the Harbor of Wave-Swift. He asked his attendants what these many sea-swimming deer were, and they gazed and wondered. So one was sent to examine and, reaching the place, perceived that all were men dressed in deer skins with the horns. When he inquired who they were, they answered, "Ox-Moroï offers his daughter, Princess-Long-Hair." At that the Sovereign was glad, and bade her follow his own vessel, and she was established in the village of Kuwazu.

According to others, Ox-Moroï came swimming alone in this guise and the Sovereign made him oarsman of the imperial vessel.)[B]

The heir apparent, Great-Wren, observed the damsel when she landed, and enthralled by her grace and beauty, felt a great love for her and straightway commanded Noble-of-Brave-Uchi to plead his cause before the Sovereign and bring about the granting of Princess-Long-Hair to himself. And when Noble-of-Brave-Uchi asked the august commands, and the Sovereign learned of Great-Wren's desire for Princess-Long-Hair, he was willing to unite them. Therefore, on a day when he held an abundantly bright feast in the after-palace, he for the first time summoned Princess-Long-Hair and gave her a seat, after which he summoned Great-Wren, and handing her the great august oak-leaf cup to give to him, pointing to him, he sang:

> Come then, my children! || Ah, as I go my way
> To pluck the garlic, || To pluck the garlic, fragrant
> The orange flow'rs! || The top branches withered
> By perching birds, || The low branches withered
> By plucking hands, || Yet, on its midmost branches,
> Like the mid-kernel || Of triple chestnut,
> This damsel-bud! || Ah, so flushing, if with you
> You should conduct her. || Ah, how joyful!

Then, Great-Wren, augustly given this song, by which he understood that he was to be given Princess-Long-Hair, much pleased, answered with this song:

> In the water hole, || In the Pool of Yosami,
> Driving the piling, || My innermost heart,
> (Unknowing where the caltrop || Sent out its rootlets
> To prick me—all unknowing || Where the mallow [48] twisted)
> More and more ridiculous,
> Now is truly repentant.

(Some have it, however, that this song also was sung by the Sovereign.) [49]

Then the Sovereign gave her to Great-Wren, and he, after having intercourse with her, cherishing her greatly, sang to her, alone:

> Ah, Kohata [50] maiden || From beyond the boundary!
> You hearing of her || As of a very Kami,
> We pillow, intertwining.

Also he sang this song:

> Ah, Kohata maiden || From beyond the boundary!
> With what affection, || Slumbering without dispute
> Here with me, do I behold her!

There were born to the two

GREAT-LORD-OF-HATABI [51]
YOUNG-LADY-OF-HATABI [52]

Now at this time King Shoko [53] of Kudara sent over two seamstresses named

MAKETSU [54]

and two tame horses, a stallion and a mare, for which feeding-houses were placed on the slope of Karu,[55] in charge of one

ACHI-KISHI [56]

who was made their fodder-master. (For this reason the place was named Stable-Slope.) Also he sent a cross-sword and a great mirror. Achi-Kishi, being able to read, was made tutor to Young-Lord-of-Uji, and the Sovereign inquired of him whether there were in the Land of Kudara any other men more learned than he. He replied, "There is one,

WAN-I [57]

who is my superior." So Areda-Lord [58] and

KAMU-NAGI-LORD

were sent to Kudara to fetch Wan-I, who came, bringing with him the Analects of Confucius [59] in ten rolls [60] and the One-Thousand-Character Essay,[61] and was taken as tutor by Young-Lord-of-Uji, who thus learned various writings, understanding every one. There came from Kara too a smith named Takuso, and from Go [62] came a weaver named Sai-So. Also there came from Kudara *in the fourteenth year of this reign*

YUTSUKI-LORD [63]

a descendant of Koman-Wo,[64] saying, "I purposed to come leading the people of one hundred and twenty neighborhoods, (or, as some say, of one hundred and twenty-seven) but the Silla people opposed them and made them all remain in the Land of Kara." Hearing this, the Sovereign despatched Prince-Sotsu-of-Mulberry-Castle to bring the people of Yutsuki-Lord. But during three years he did not return, so the Sovereign, saying, "It must be that he is restrained by the people of Silla," sent Noble-of-Heguri's-Owl [65] and

---

[51] **Ancestor (by proxy) of the Great-Kusaka-Clan.**
[52] **Ancestress (by proxy) of the Young-Kusaka-Clan.**
[54] **Ancestress of the Seamstresses of Kumè (in Yamato).**
[56] **Ancestor of the Head-Men of the Scribes of Achiki.**
[57] **Ancestor of the Head-Men of the Scribes of Kawachi Province.**
[63] **Ancestor of the Clan-Chiefs of Hada.**

NOBLE-OF-TADA

of Ikuba, to attack Silla and clear a path for him. These two therefore led picked troops to the Silla border, whereon the king of that Land, in fear, admitted his guilt. Then they brought back Prince-Sotu-of-Mulberry-Castle and the people of Yutsuki-Lord, *together with silver and gold, jewels and silk stuffs.*

Now when the Sovereign made his imperial way to the Palace of Good-Moor, the Kuzu,[66] seeing the august sword that Great-Wren bore in his girdle, sang:

> Sharp is the base, || Icy the point
> Of the sword of Great-Wren, || In Great-Wren's girdle—
> The August Sun-sprung child || Of Elbow-Pad-Lord.
> Ah, so frigid, || Frigid as the growth
> Underneath the stark tree-boles || In winter time!

Then they made a cross-mortar at Growing-Oak-Tree in Good-Moor, and mixing in it some august sakè, offered it to the Sovereign, and sang:

> At Growing-Oak-Tree || A cross-mortar we built,
> And within it— || That cross-mortar—we have mixed
> August sakè. || Pleasantly partake of it,
> Ah, honored one!

Singing thus, they laughed, and raising their eyes, made a drumming sound on their mouths. This was the ancient custom, and now, when the Kuzu people of the province offer its produce to the Sovereign, while they sing they laugh, and raising their eyes, make a drumming sound on their mouths. The song is sung to the present day when the Kuzu offer the Sovereign a feast.

At this time Great-Wren, purposing to hold an abundantly bright feast, proceeded to Princess-Island,[67] when a man informed him that a wild goose had had young there.

> (Some say otherwise that it produced its young on the Manuta Embankment, in Kawashi Province.)

A messenger, sent to see, reported it true,[68] whereon Great-Wren, sending for Noble-Brave-of-Uchi, inquired of him as to the producing of young by the wild goose, in this song:

> O Uchi's . . .[69] || court dignitary!
> You truly are || A person of long life.[70]
> When have you heard || In this Land of Mountain-Gate
> . . . . . . [69]
> That wild goose hatches || Out its young?

Whereto Noble-of-Uchi sang in reply:

> O thou high-shining || August Sun-child!
> It is natural || For you to inquire.
> It is but right || For you to inquire.
> Though truly I am || A person of long life,
> . . . . . .[69] || In this Land of Mountain-Gate
> That wild geese hatch || Their young ones ne'er heard I.

Then, taking the imperial koto, he sang:

> O august Sun-child! || The wild goose produced her young
> To show you at last should reign! [71]

(This is an incomplete song, and one of congratulation.)

Now the Sovereign journeyed to Wave-Swift and dwelt in the Palace of Great-High-Port. There he ascended a tall tower, when his concubine

PRINCESS-ELDER

who was with him, looking westward, wept loudly. He asked her, "Why do you weep thus?" and she replied, "Lately your slave has thought longingly of her father and mother, and now, while I looked toward the west, I wept unknowingly. I beseech you to allow me to go back for a time to see them." The Sovereign approved Princess-Elder's longing thought of her parents in heat and in cold, and said he, "You have not seen your father and mother for many years. That you should desire to go back to see them is right." And he gave her permission, and called eighty of the fisher people of Three-Beach in My-Shame to sail with her to Maise. So she departed from Great-Port. Watching her vessel from the tall tower, he sang:

> O My-Shame Island || With your double mountain peaks!
> Azuki Island || With your double mountain peaks!
> Ta-kata-sarè || Arachishi [72]
> Ah, with my wife of Maise || Face to face you have met!

Afterward he rode often in his carriage,[73] to hunt on My-Shame Island, and on a time he proceeded from there to Maise, and to the Island of Azuki. Later he removed to Hata and dwelt in the Palace of Reed-Forest, where

MITOMO-LORD [74]

came and entertained him, and his brother, children, and grandchildren assisted him. The Sovereign was pleased at the reverence that Mitomo-Lord showed him, and dividing the Land of Maize, bestowed it upon that one's children. To his eldest son he gave the District

INEHAYA-LORD [75]

---

[75] **Ancestor of the Magnates of Shimo-Tsu-Michi.**

of River-Island; to his middle son

PRINCE-OF-MIDDLE [76]

he gave the District of Upper-Road,[77] and to the third son

PRINCE-YOUNGER [78]

he gave the District of Three-Moors. Further, to his elder brother

URAKORI-LORD [79]

he gave the District of Sono, and to his younger brother

KAMO-LORD [80]

he gave the District of Hakukè. And to Princess-Elder herself he gave the District of the Weaver-Clan.[81] The descendants of Mitomo-Lord dwell still in the Land of Maise.

At another time, in Harima Province, two wild ducks nested and laid eggs, therefore the district was named Wild-Duck-District, and the place was named Wild-Duck-Village. This was divided into Upper-Wild-Duck-Village and Lower-Wild-Duck-Village.[82] When the Sovereign was at Well-of-Suck (which place is so named because if a woman tries to draw water from the well there, she is sucked into it). The wild ducks flew there and perched on a tree. He asked what birds they were and one of his attendants

TAJIMA

Clan-Chief of the Fire-Possessor-Clan,[83] replied that they were river ducks. Then the Sovereign gave an order to shoot them, and the pair were stricken with one arrow. (The place to which they flew, carrying the arrow, is called Wild-Duck-Slope, and the place where they fell, Wild-Duck-Valley. The place where a broth was made was named Boil-Slope.) Again, when he hunted on the moor, a horse ran away and on his inquiring whose it was, one of his attendants replied that it was the Sovereign's. Thereupon he exclaimed, "My horse!" (So the place was named My-Horse-Moor.)

The place where the bowmen stood in Stag-Ma[84] was called Bowman-Clan-Cape,[85] the place where a bow was broken was called Spindle-Tree-Hill and the place where the Sovereign stood was called August-Stand-Hill.[86] At this time a great doe came from My-Horse-Moor and, passing

---

[76] Ancestor of the Magnates of Kamu-Tsu-Michi and of Kaya.
[78] Ancestor of the Magnates of Mino.
[79] Ancestor of the Governors of Sono.
[80] Ancestor of the Magnates of Kasa.

by this hill, entered the sea and swam across to an island. Then the bowmen, gazing, said to one another, "The deer has already reached that island." (So it was called Ito [87] Island.) Also, in Upper-Wilderness-Moor [88] he ascended the hill of Dream-Cape, and gazing about him, saw something white. He inquired what it was, and one of his attendants replied that it was a Kami called

PRINCE-MANA.[89]

Accordingly the Sovereign ordered that it be investigated and it was found to be a waterfall that fell from a high place. Therefore the place was called Village-of-High-Shallow. Again when he made a circuit from Tajima Province, he brought no servants for the journey (for which cause the place was called Shadow-Mountain-Cape)[90] . . .[91] when the governor,

FRUITFUL-GREAT-LORD

was upbraided for his crime, the governor of Tajima Province

AKONÈ

pleaded for his freedom, offering to the imperial court salt-fields of twenty-thousand shiro [92] and other famous salt-fields, and made the people of Morning-Come, in Tajima Province, come to live there. (Thus the place was called Village-of-Morning-Fu.) The river there is called the Nagaünè River. Akonè wedded a woman of Aho-Village (which was so named because people of Aho-Village in Iyo settled there) and died and was buried there in a tomb. It is said, however, that his body was later removed. In this reign there was given to

CAPE-JEWEL [93]

a place that was for this reason named Fire-Possessor-Clan-Village.^A

At this time the king of Koma sent an envoy with tribute, but as he presented an address which angered Young-Lord-of-Uji, the latter tore it up and upbraided the bearer for its rudeness.

Now the Sovereign said to his Ministers, "The imperial vessel Kurano,[94] which was sent as tribute by the Land of Izu, has become decayed and can no longer be used. On account of its long service, let its name not be lost, but let it be perpetuated to later times." The Ministers, thus bidden, caused the ship's timbers to be used for fires to roast salt, five hundred baskets of which were thus produced and presented to the various prov-

---

[93] **Ancestor of the Fire-Possessor-Clan.***

---

* See p. 208.

inces. Strangely, some of the wood would not burn, and it was offered to the Sovereign, who had made of it a koto, whose resounding music could be heard for seven ri. Of this he sang:

> The Kurano || Was burned up for salt.
> Of the residue || There was framed a koto.
> When one plays it, || Then, lo, the brushing
> Of standing rocks || In the haven
> There at Yura— || The trees of summer
> Saya-saya [95]

(This is both an alternating and a tranquil song.)

In return for the salt, the provinces were made to build vessels, and five hundred being sent, these were brought together in Muko Harbor. Now the men who had brought tribute from Silla were housed there and, a fire breaking out and burning many of the vessels, they were held responsible. Hearing of this, the king of Silla was in great alarm and sent over cunning workmen.[96] Also there crossed to Nippon

MAGNATE-OF-ACHI [97]

together with his son whose name was

MAGNATE-OF-TSUGA

with the people of seventeen districts.

The people of Hada, Han, and Kudara who came to Nippon could be numbered by tens of thousands and some of these were worthy to be praised and rewarded. All of them have their ancestral shrines, though these are not included among those that receive government offerings.[A]

There came also one Nim-Pan,[98] who knew how to make sakè. This one, mixing some august sakè, offered it to the Sky-Sovereign, who, intoxicated by it, sang:

> By Susukori [99] || Compounded, the liquor
> August, has bestowed on me || Intoxication.
> Liquor soothing, || Augustly smiling liquor!

Thus singing, as he walked he struck with his staff a great rock in the middle of the Great-Slope road, when the rock ran away. (Thus arose the saying, "Hard rocks leave a drunkard's path.")

Now Magnate-of-Achi and Magnate-of-Tsuga, being sent to Go to secure seamstresses, crossed over to the Land of Koma, but arriving there, knew not the way and requested the King of the Land to furnish them guides. The King, therefore, sent with them two men named Go-Ha

---

[96] **Ancestors of the Wina-Clan.**
[97] **Ancestor of the Governors of the Han-Folk of Yamato.**

and Go-Shi. Thus they reached Go, whose ruler gave them four workwomen,

PRINCESS-ELDER [1]
PRINCESS-YOUNGER [1]
GO-WEAVER [2]
ANA-WEAVER.[3]

At this time also the king of Kudara sent his younger sister, Princess-Shi-Se-Tsu,[4] to be the Sovereign's concubine, and she brought with her seven serving-women.

The Sky-Sovereign, calling to him Great-Mountain-Warden and Great-Wren, asked of them, "Do you love your children?" They replied, "We love them greatly." Then he asked, "Which do you esteem the dearer, an elder or a younger child?" This question he asked because it was in his heart to give the rule of the empire to Young-Lord-of-Uji, and he desired to propitiate the minds of the two princes. Great-Mountain-Warden replied, "The elder is the dearer." At this the Sovereign was displeased. But Great-Wren, knowing the sentiment that made the Sovereign ask, and observing his countenance, replied, "The elder child, who has become a man, has passed through many colds and heats and causes no anxiety; but one knows not if the younger child will become a man, therefore he is the more pitiable and hence the dearer." At which the Sovereign, greatly pleased, said, "Great-Wren's words agree with my thought." And straightway the division was so decreed, that Great-Mountain-Warden should administer the government of the mountains, forests, and moors, the rivers and the sea; Great-Wren should assume and report on the realm's management; while Young-Lord-of-Uji should rule the succession of the Sky-Sun. Nor did Great-Wren rebel against the Sovereign's decree.

Now it came to pass that

GREAT-KAMI-OF-AUGUST-SHADE [5]

of Sacred-Quarter Province settled at Mount Kamiwo at Village-of-Hirakata, and ceased not to detain wayfarers, half of whom were slain and half spared. And

KOHOTÈ

who was a native of Broom,

FUKURO

---

[1] **Ancestress of the Seamstresses of Kurè and of Kaya.**
[3] **Ancestress of the Clan-Chiefs of Mitsukahi, in Tsukushi.**

who was a native of Rice-Leaves, and

TSUKIYA

a native of Sacred-Quarter, resenting this, reported it to the Sovereign. So

KURA

Tribe-Master of the Forehead-Ricefield-Clan, with others, was sent to make supplication, and these built a great mansion at Mansion-Ricefield and a sakè-house at Mount-Bamboo, and made a festival for the Kami. Then at a banquet they made merry and hung oak-leaves from Mount-Scrub-oak to their girdles and came down to Push-River, where they pushed one another.[6] (For this reason the river was thus named.) During this reign a bird house was built where all kinds of birds were gathered and fed in order that they might be made tame, to be offered to the court. (Therefore the place was named Village-of-Bird-House.[7] People later, however, called it Village-of-Tosu.)[A]

The Sovereign died at the age of one hundred and thirty years (or, as some say, one hundred and ten) in the Palace of Fruitful-Akira. (Some say at the Palace of Great-Sumi.) His grave is on the mound of Mofushi, at Wega, in Kawachi.

Now when Magnate-of-Achi and those with him arrived in Tsukushi from Go, the great Kami of Body-Form [8] demanded work women, therefore the former offered Ana-Weaver, and with the other three women came to the Land of Settsu. Reaching Muko, however, he found the Sovereign dead, so he offered them to Great-Wren.

THE EMPEROR GREAT-WREN
(BENEVOLENCE-VIRTUE)[9]

The Emperor Great-Wren was intelligent and comely and, as a man, was kind. After the death of the Sky-Sovereign he ceded the empire, in accordance with the command, to Young-Lord-of-Uji, who would not receive it, each wishing to give the rule to the other.

Prince-Great-Middle-of-Nukata,[10] desirous of taking in charge the official ricelands and storehouse of Mountain-Gate, said to

NOBLE-OF-OÜ [11]

who had them in charge, "These were at first Mountain-Warden lands, so I shall now control them." Noble-of-Oü reported this to Young-Lord--of-Uji, who directed him to take counsel with Great-Wren. The latter inquired of

---
[11] **Ancestor of the Magnates of Izumo.**

MARO [12]

who said, "I know nothing of this matter, but my younger brother

AKOKO

knows." Now Akoko had been sent to the Han Country and was not yet returned, so Great-Wren bade Maro go there himself, journeying day and night with speed, and bring Akoko. This Maro did, returning with him, when Akoko said, "It is stated by the aged that in the time of the Emperor Prince-Ikumè-Iri-Isachi, the official ricelands were given in charge to Prince-Great-Perfect-Ruling-Lord.[13] And it was decreed that they were to remain forever the lands of the Sovereign, and it is an error to call them Mountain-Warden lands." So Great-Wren sent Akoko to tell this to Prince-Great-Middle-of-Nukata, who, hearing, was nonplussed; but Great-Wren forgave him the error and forbore to punish him.

YOUNG-LORD-OF-UJI SLAYS GREAT-MOUNTAIN-WARDEN

Now Great-Mountain-Warden was resentful that he had been disregarded and not made the imperial heir, and disobedient to the Sovereign's command, and wishful nevertheless to obtain the empire, he planned to slay the prince his younger brother, and secretly raising an army, prepared to attack him. Great-Wren, hearing of this in advance, despatched a messenger to apprise Young-Lord-of-Uji so that he could protect himself, and he, startled, placed soldiers in hiding on the river's bank and spreading a curtain-fence and setting up a pavilion on the hilltop, placed there in view on a couch one of his men to pretend that he was the Emperor, the hundred officials coming and going reverently in the same manner as though they were in the Emperor's presence. Also, to prepare for the time when his elder brother should cross the river, he arranged and decorated a boat and oarsmen and having ground up roots of the japonica vine,[14] with the juice-slime he rubbed the grating inside the boat, so that whoever should tread on it would fall down. This done, he put on a hempen coat and trousers, and in the guise of a common fellow, mingled with the ferrymen and took stand in the boat, holding a scull.

His elder brother took with him some hundreds of soldiers, and starting by night arrived at Uji at daybreak, where, having hid his troops in ambush and donned armor beneath his clothes, not knowing of the ready soldiers, he came to the river bank. When he was about to enter the boat, seeing on the other side the grandly decorated place, and thinking the

---

[12] **Ancestor of the Governors of Yamato.**

Emperor, his younger brother, was seated on the couch—quite unknowing that he was standing in the boat holding the scull—he said to the oarsman: "It has been told me that on this mountain there is a large and vicious boar. I wish to capture it. Shall I be able to do so?" Then the fellow holding the scull replied, "You cannot." The other demanded, "Why not?" The boatman answered, "It is not to be captured, however often and in how many places it be chased. For this reason, I say you cannot."

Now when they had crossed to the middle of the river, Young-Lord-of-Uji caused the ferrymen to tilt the boat, so that Great-Mountain-Warden fell into the water and sank. Rising to the surface, floating down with the current, he sang:

> At the awful, stern, || Resistless [15] ford of Uji,
> Among the pole-men || He who is the swiftest one
> Let him come to assist me!

Then the soldiers in hiding on the bank of the river rose up together on both sides, and fixed their arrows as he floated down. And, unable to reach the bank, at last he sank and died at Rattling-Point. They searched the spot where he had gone down with hooks that rattled against the armor beneath his clothing, (for which reason the place was so called) and when they hooked up his bones, the younger brother, seeing, sang:

> You who now uplift, || Beside the stern and awful
> Resistless ford-reach of Uji, || Catalpa [16] bow, mayumi [17] tree!
> To sever you both || Had been in my inmost heart,
> To secure you both || Had been in my inmost heart,
> But ah, I thought || Principally of the lord—
> But, ah, I thought || At last of the young sister!
> On the former one || Pitifully I reflected,
> On the latter one || Sorrowfully I reflected,
> And left you both unsevered, || Catalpa bow, mayumi tree!

The bones of Great-Mountain-Warden were buried in Nara Hills.

GREAT-WREN AND YOUNG-LORD-OF-UJI MUTUALLY REFUSE THE RULE

Young-Lord-of-Uji dwelt in the Palace of Uji and having ceded the empire to Great-Wren, for a long while did not assume the rule, so that for three years there was no Sovereign. In this time there came fishermen with woven baskets of fresh fish which they offered at the palace for a feast. Each brother, however, proffered the gift to the other, Young-Lord-of-Uji saying, "I am not the Sovereign," sending them away with the command to present the gift at Wave-Swift, and Great-Wren sending them away with the command to present it at Uji. Many days elapsed during these mutual profferings, and the woven baskets stank. Then the fishermen went away and got other fresh fish, which they offered and which were declined as on the day before, and these also stank, and the fishermen wept from the fatigue of going backward and forward. (From this came the proverb "Lo, the fisherman weeps on account of his own plenty.")

Then Young-Lord-of-Uji, saying, "Clearly my elder brother will not yield; why shall I live longer to trouble the empire?" slew himself. Hearing of this, Great-Wren, astounded, hastened from Wave-Swift to the palace at Uji, and arriving three days after Young-Lord-of-Uji's death, wept, beating his breast and tearing his hair, not knowing what he did. Then, standing over the dead body, he called to him three times, saying, "Oh, my younger brother!" After a time, then, Young-Lord-of-Uji came to life and lifted himself and sat up. Great-Wren exclaimed, "Oh, grief and sorrow! Why did you slay yourself? If the dead are aware, what does the dead Sovereign think of me?" Young-Lord-of-Uji replied, "It is the divine will which none may gainsay. If I come where the Sovereign is, I will relate your wisdom and self-effacement. However, you yourself must be weary from the long and rapid journey which you made on learning of my death." Then he offered to Great-Wren his younger sister by the same mother, Young-Lady-of-Yata,[18] saying, "She is not fit to wed you, but may to some extent serve you in the side-apartments." [19] So saying, he lay down in his coffin and again died. And Great-Wren donned plain rough garments for the first mourning, and wept with pitiful lamentation. Young-Lord-of-Uji was buried on the height of Mount Uji.

Great-Wren dwelt in the Palace of High-Port at Wave-Swift and ruled the empire. There was no plaster on the palace or its buildings; its rafters and roof-poles, uprights and posts were plain and its thatch-roof was left unshorn, so that agriculture might not be hindered by his selfish indulgence. He wedded also his half-sister, Young-Lady-of-Uji, by whom he had no offspring. Also he wedded, as Empress,

PRINCESS-OF-ROCK [20]

daughter of Prince-Sotsu-of-Mulberry-Castle, by whom he begot

IZAHO-ELDER-BROTHER-LORD [21]
KING-MIDDLE-OF-PLEASANT-TO-DWELL-IN
NOBLE-OF-YOUNGER-CHILD-MALE-MORNING-WIFE

[20] **Ancestress (by proxy) of the Kazuraki-Clan.**
[21] **Ancestor (by proxy) of the Mibu (Nibu)-Clan.**

BEAUTIFUL-TEETH-LORD-OF-KNOT-GRASS.[22]

When this one was born his teeth were like a single bone, the upper and lower exactly alike, like strung jewels. Also there was a well called Beautiful-Well, whose water was used to wash the imperial hair, and into which a knot-grass blossom had fallen. These were the child's name. (*It was by reason of this that the Knot-Grass-Clan was founded in all the provinces, to be villages for the hot baths of the imperial princes.*)^

THE SOVEREIGN REMITS THE TAXES

Now the Sovereign said to his Ministers, "From a tall tower I looked abroad and beheld in all the Land no smoke arising, from which I assume that the people are in poverty and cook no rice." So he issued a decree that for three years taxes should be remitted and no labor be compulsory, but the people given leisure. From that time his imperial robes and footwear were not renewed save when they wore out, also the cooked food and drink were replaced only when they became sour.[23] The great palace buildings became ruined and were not restored, but rain everywhere leaked through the unrenewed thatch, and wind and starlight entered by the cracks and wet the exposed quilts. Yet repairs were not made, the rain being caught in boxes and the people removing to where were no leaks. So after three autumns of plenty, the people praised the Sovereign's virtues and the smoke of cooking rose plentifully. Then, seeing the people prosperous, he said to the Empress, "In Our prosperity, there is now no cause for complaint." [24] She replied, "What is prosperity?" Said he, "Surely when much smoke rises in the Land and the people grow rich." She answered, "When your palace goes to ruin unrestored, and its buildings are so worn that the quilts are exposed, is this what you call prosperity?" Yet, although petition was made by all the provinces that labor be again made compulsory in order to restore the palace, the Sovereign for a while longer delayed; and when labor was finally compelled the people worked willingly, without overseers, night and day, till the palace was quickly finished. So, in praise of that august reign, he is to this day called "the Sage Sovereign."

After that the Pool of Wani [25] and the Pool of Yosami were dug and the Yokono embankment built, the Wave-Swift Canal [26] was led to the western sea draining the moor to the north of the palace (for this cause that water was called Dug-Bay),[27] a bridge constructed at the ford of Wikahi (for which reason the place was called Little-Bridge) and the

---

[22] **Ancestor (by proxy) of the Tajihi *-Clan.**

* *Tajihi*, modern *itadori*. *Polygonum cuspidatum.*

port of the Inlet of Pleasant-to-Dwell-In was established. Also a road was built from the South Gate of the Capital to Tajihi Village, and canals were dug in Kuri-Bear District of Behind-the-Mountains, and in Konku, by which the waters of Stone-River were led to water the desert moors above and below Suzuka and Fertile-Shore,[28] for ricefields. Thus the people of these regions had plenty and the evil of fruitless seasons was unknown.

Now to the east of Dug-Bay there is a marsh three or four cho wide, which is called Eighty-Heads-Island. For it is said that once a woman who carried a babe on her back, while catching river-birds in a net, fell in and so perished. (A man made search for her head and found two human heads and seventy-eight heads of birds, eighty heads in all, so that the place was thus named.)[A]

At Dug-Bay, also, is the Log-Bridge-of-Dug-Bay, on which, if one has need to cross over, he should not look aside.[B]

STRONG-NECK AND CHILD-OF-CLOTHING

In this reign, lest the river to the northward overflow, the embankment of Mamuta was also built, and the people of Hada [29] were impressed to labor on it. Twice the portion that was built fell down and could not be raised, when the Sovereign had a dream in which a Kami advised him, saying, "In Musashi is one

STRONG-NECK

and in Kawachi dwells a certain man named

CHILD-OF-CLOTHING.[30]

If these two be offered to the Kami of the river, you shall succeed in stopping the openings. So, having sought out these two, he offered them to the Kami of the river, when Strong-Neck, lamenting, cast himself in and so died, and that embankment was finished. But Child-of-Clothing took two gourds and threw them into the river, where it would not be stopped up, and made a prayer, saying, "O Kami of the river, who sends the evil! I am now made an offering. If you still demand me, let these gourds sink, and not float on the surface, by which I shall know you are truly a Kami and will throw myself in with willingness. If, however, you do not make the gourds sink, then I shall know surely that you are not truly a Kami, and will not give my life uselessly." Then a wind came and tried to sink the gourds which, nevertheless, would not sink, but floated afar on the water. Thus that embankment was also finished, and Child-of-

---

[30] **Ancestor of the Tribe-Masters of Mamuta.**

Clothing did not die, but through his cunning kept his life. (For this reason people called the two places Chasm-of-Strong-Neck and Chasm-of-Child-of-Clothing.)

Later the Sovereign distributed the people of Hada among the various districts and bade them feed silkworms and weave silk, which he commanded should be presented to the court. Then he said, "I wear silk and floss offered by

HAN-MALE.[31]

These are smooth and soft, so that my skin is kept warm." (For this reason Han-Male was called Clan-Chief-of-Skin.) Now there was a certain Clan-Chief of Hada named

IROGU

of Ohoïta, who came to Ricefield-Moor,[32] a wide plain in Camphor District[33] in Bungo Province. Its soil was fertile and there was no better place for cultivation, and living there, he built a dwelling and planted many ricefields, becoming rich and happy. He left food on his fields to boast of his wealth, and lived in extravagant luxury. Once, having drunk sakè, he held a merry-making, at which time he took up his bow to shoot, and lacking a target, used a rice cake for this purpose, when the cake was transformed into a white bird and flew away southward. In that year all the people of the village died, his family gradually faded away, the ricefields were no more tilled and the place became a desolate moor. (From this the place was named Ricefield-Moor.) The white bird lived in the wood at the village of Minami-Bird-Clan[34] in Behind-the-Mountains Province (for this reason the place was called Bird-Clan). Since that time the ricefields have not been good.[A]

> (Others say that the bird settled on the peak of a mountain, at which rice-plants sprang up and bore a crop, so that the shrine there was named Rice-bearing Shrine.)[35]

One of Irogu's descendants, regretting that one's fault, uprooted a tree by the shrine and planting it beside his house, made a festival and prayed. Even now, if one plants a tree from this shrine and it takes root, he will be lucky, while if it withers he will be unlucky.[A]

At this time the Land of Koma sent as offerings shields and targets made of iron and for the entertainment of the envoys, the Ministers, and court-officials were bade to shoot at these. None could pierce them but

NOBLE-OF-SHIELD-MAN[36]

---

[36] **Ancestor of the Magnates of Ikuba.**

who did so, and the envoys, astonished at his bow-skill, rising, made obeisance to the Sovereign, who praised him and gave him the name of Noble-of-Toda-of-Target.[37] Also

MAGNATE-OF-NOBLE [38]

was given the name Magnate-of-Intelligent-Remainder. The imperial storehouse was built at Mamuta and the Miller-Clan [39] was created.

(According to some, it was at this time that the Kami Great-Mountain-Possessor,[40] coming from the Land of Kudara, settled at Three-Islands in the Land of Tsuno.[41])

THE JEALOUSY OF THE EMPRESS

Now the Empress, Princess-of-Rock, was very jealous, so that the concubines used by the Sovereign dared not even look into the Palace, and on occasion she stamped her feet with jealousy. So the Sovereign, pointing out

PRINCESS-KUGA-OF-KUWADA

one of his concubines, said to his attendants, "I greatly desire to make love to this damsel, but have not been able to have intercourse with her because of the Empress's jealousy for these many years. So her youth-time is wasted." Then he sang:

> Who will bring her up, || The daughter of the Magnate
> Who sweeps the under-water? [42]

Whereon there came before him alone one whose name was

HAYAMACHI [43]

who sang to him in reply this song:

> I will do so, || Harima's Hayamachi
> (Though I go in awe || As when great rocks tumble)
> Who sweeps the under-water!

So Princess-Kura-of-Kuwada was given to Hayamachi, who went the next night to her apartment. However, she would not yield to his desire, though he continually approached the curtain,[44] but said she, "Your slave will end her life without a husband. She cannot be your wife." The Sovereign nevertheless desired to bring about the wish of Hayamachi and sent her away with him, but she fell ill and died on the journey. Her grave exists to this day.

---

[38] **Ancestor of the Rulers of Ohasè.**
[43] **Ancestor of the Rulers of Harima (Province).**

At this time Silla did not send tribute, so Noble-of-Shield-Man and Magnate-of-Noble were sent there to ask the reason, at which Silla, in fear, offered as tribute eighty vessel-loads of silks and other things, altogether fourteen hundred and sixty articles.

Now the daughter of the Governor of the Fishers in Maise,

PRINCESS-BLACK,

was of great beauty, and the Sovereign, learning this, sent for her and cohabited with her. She, however, in fear of the jealousy of the Empress, fled away to her own Land. Watching from an upper story where her vessel departed by sea, he sang:

> On the horizon || Rows of little ships!
> My wife of Furozaya,[45] || Masazuko,[45] takes her leave
> To the country of her birth.

At the song the Empress was angered, and sent people to Great-Beach to send her ashore and drive her away on foot. The Sovereign, however, loving Princess-Black, told the Empress, to mislead her, that he desired to visit My-Shame Island, and going there, looking into the distance, he sang:

> When from the cape-end || Of Wave-Swift billow-beaten,
> I have departed, || Gazing o'er the far expanse,
> Isle of Millet, || Island of Self-Curdling,[46]
> You are in my sight, || With the Isle of Saketsu.

Then, proceeding, he came to the Land of Maise, where Princess-Black gave him an imperial residence at Mountain-Fields [47] and presented food to him. For this she gathered cabbage to make soup, when the Sovereign, coming where she gathered it, sang:

> The cabbage seedlings || At Yamagata growing—
> Maise-Land dweller— || Together with me plucking—
> Ah, delightful do I find it!

When the Sovereign departed on his return, Princess-Black sang:

> As the western wind || Blowing up toward Mountain-Gate
> Separates the clouds, || Although we be parted
> Ah, how can I e'er forget!

Also she sang to him this second song:

> Toward Mountain-Gate || Whose is the spouse that goes?
> And whose spouse is it || Coming creeping underneath
> Like to water that is hid?

At this time the Sovereign wished to make Young-Lady-of-Yata his concubine, but when he told the Empress, she would not permit it. At which he sang:

> According to rule || Established for the noble,
> As on occasion || One chooses extra bow-strings,
> I would make addition.

Thereon the Empress sang to him in reply:

> Robes—to speak of them— || Doubled are very good;
> But, my lord, to place || The nightly pallets a-row,
> Is it the part of wisdom?

On another occasion he sang to her a song which said:

> Widely shining || Promontory of Wave-Swift
> And shore beside it! || Surely that very child
> Should be put side by side with me!

To which she sang, in reply, these words:

> Like the insect's robes— || The fire-insect of summer,
> Whose robe is doubled! || With eight persons round about,
> How can it be agreeable?

Then the Sovereign again sang to her this song:

> On Mount Morning-Wife, || On the small slope of Hiika,
> When one weeps alone, || Even by a passer-by
> 'Tis sweet to be companioned.

But she would not consent, and kept silence. Loving Young-Lady-of-Yata, he then sent that one a song which said:

> The single || Stalk of the Yata sedge-grass,
> Without offspring || Will it stand all withering?
> Ah, sedge-plain pitiable! || I but use the word
> Sedge-plain, in lieu of my saying || "Pitiable, pure damsel!"

To which Young-Lady-of-Yata replied in this song:

> The single || Stalk of the Yata sedge-grass,
> Even though it stand lonely, || Yet my mighty lord
> Gives it his approval, || Even though it stand lonely.

KING-FALCON-LORD AND QUEEN-HEN-BIRD

Now the Sovereign requested leave to wed his younger half-sister, Queen-Hen-Bird, using as middleman his younger brother King-Falcon-Lord.[48] But Queen-Hen-Bird said to King-Falcon-Lord, "Because the Empress is so violent, the Sovereign has not taken Young-Lady-of-Yata, so I will not serve him, but I will become your wife. So they wedded one another, and for this reason King-Falcon-Lord made no report. Then the

Sovereign, going to the dwelling of Queen-Hen-Bird, stood on the sill of the palace, where she was weaving garments at her loom. And he sang:

> Ah, Queen-Hen-Bird, || Majestic Clan-Chieftainess!
> For whom is the loom || With which she now is weaving?

Whereon Queen-Hen-Bird sang in reply to him:

> For the high-going || Falcon-Lord she weaves it,
> An august covering.

Her women, too, made a song, which said:

> The long and hard [49] || Metal loom of the Sky,
> For Queen-Hen-Bird || A metal loom to weave,
> For her Falcon-Lord to use, || An august covering.

So the Sovereign, understanding that King-Falcon-Lord had wedded her in secret, was greatly angered. But because of what the Empress would say, and considering the rule which controls the relationship of the branch to the tree, he forebore to punish him, and returned to the palace. When her husband, King-Falcon-Lord, returned, Queen-Hen-Bird sang:

> Now does the lark || Soar up into the sky.
> O you high-going || Falcon-Lord, I pray you,
> Seize the wren in your clutches!

Then King-Falcon-Lord, reclining with Queen-Hen-Bird's knee for pillow, asked her, "Of the wren and falcon, which is the swifter?" She replied, "The falcon." Then he said, "That is to say I shall be first." The Sovereign heard of this saying, and again was angered. Also King-Falcon-Lord's attendants made a song, saying:

> Now let the falcon, || To the sky up-soaring,
> Darting upon it, || Seize the wren in the topmost
> Branches of the itsuki.[50]

Hearing of this song, the Sovereign was greatly enraged, and said, "I desired not to slay my relative because of private hatred, and forbore. Why should a private difference be made an imperial matter?" And, desirous of slaying King-Falcon-Lord and Queen-Hen-Bird, he raised an army. Falcon-Lord, however, fled away with her, purposing to place her in the Great Shrine of Isè, and the Sovereign sent one

WAFUNA

of the Honchi-Clan of Maise, and Child-of-Aga,[51] who was Governor of Saheki in Harima, bidding them overtake and slay them both. The Empress said, "Queen-Hen-Bird, in truth, should immediately be punished, but I hope her slain body will not be exposed." So the Sovereign commanded Wofuna and Child-of-Aga not to take the jewels on Queen-Hen-Bird's arms and legs.

King-Falcon-Lord and Queen-Hen-Bird, in their flight, ascended Mount Kurahashi,[52] when he sang:

> So like a ladder || Kurahashi Mountain is,
> That from its steepness || She cannot surmount the rocks.
> Therefore my hand she takes.

Also he sang to her this song:

> Though like a ladder || Is Kurahashi Mountain,
> With all its steepness || If my younger sister climb
> With me, it is not so steep.

Wofuna and Child-of-Aga pursued them to Uda, overtaking them at Mount Soni, where they hid in the bushes and, narrowing escaping, fled with speed over the mountain, when King-Falcon-Lord sang:

> Though like a ladder, || This precipitous mountain,
> When I surmount it || In company with my dear,
> Seems but a tranquil pallet.

But Wofuna and his company followed their flight rapidly and slew them at the moor of Komoshiro in Isè. They searched for Queen-Hen-Bird's jewels and took them from beneath her underclothing, and having burned the bodies on the bank of the Ihoki River, made report to the Sovereign. The Empress caused them to be asked if they had seen Queen-Hen-Bird's jewels, and they replied that they had not.

Now in the month of the First-Rice-Tasting ceremony, on the day of the feast, the princesses and ladies of both inner and outer corridors received sakè, and around the arms of two women were wound noticeable jewels. These women were the wife of

YOUNG-MOUNTAIN-WARDEN

who was Clan-Chief of the Mountains of Omi, and

PRINCESS-IWASAKI

of the Neck-Clan.[53] The Empress, Princess-of-Rock, took the great oak leaves of sakè and deigned to offer them to these women, when, seeing that the jewels were like Queen-Hen-Bird's, she bade an attendant ask how they came to have them. They replied that they belonged to the wife of Child-of-Aga. At that the Empress gave them no oak leaves of sakè, but had them sent away, and sent for Child-of-Aga, who, when questioned, said "On the day Queen-Hen-Bird was slain, I searched her and took the jewels." Then the Empress said, "On account of their unseemly actions those two were sent away. That was not strange. But you, slave! have stolen from the arm of the warm body of that princess the jewel she wore, and have given it to your own wife!" And he was straightway granted the penalty of death.

(*Some say, otherwise, that the chief general of the army, who stole the jewels, was*

BIG-SHIELD,

Tribe-Master of the Mountain-Clan, and that it was his own wife who wore them at the feast. Others, too, say that when they were about to put him to death, the condemned man offered all his private lands to the Sovereign, who accepted them, and remitted the penalty of death. These say that for this reason these lands were called Jewel-Price.)

THE RETIREMENT OF THE EMPRESS

Later the Empress journeyed to the Land of Tree to gather mustard and oak leaves for an abundantly bright feast, going as far as Cape Kumano, and the Sovereign, aware of her absence, wedded Young-Lady-of-Yata and installed her in the palace. The Empress was returning in her vessel, loaded with mustard and oak leaves, when a servant of Small-Island,[54] employed by the director of the water-caterers,[55] who was journeying to his own Land, met at the great passage of Wave-Swift the vessel of the Empress's mistress-of-the-Purse,[56] which had fallen to the rear, and said to her, "The Sovereign has consummated his marriage with Young-Lady-of-Yata, and disports with her day and night. Doubtless the Empress is ignorant of this, since she takes this imperial pleasure-trip."

When she heard this she straightway followed and caught up with the imperial vessel and reported all the servant had said. At that the Empress, reaching the Wave-Swift ford, and learning that the Sovereign had indeed become united to Young-Lady-of-Yata, was enraged, and cast into the sea all the mustard and oak leaves she had put on board. (For this reason the place is called Oak-Leaf-Ford, or, by some Cape-Three.) [57] Refusing to go ashore to enter the palace, she steered her vessel away and proceeded up the canal [58] against the current. The Sovereign, however, ignorant of her anger or refusal to go ashore, went to Great-Port to wait for her vessel. There he sang:

> O men of Wave-Swift, || The bell-vessel drag along!
> Wet to your middles, || That vessel drag you along!
> The ship great, august, drag you!

The Empress did not anchor there, but went on by way of the river to Behind-the-Mountains, where she sang:

> Behind-the-Mountains' || stream, where rows of saplings stand,
> As I follow it, || Follow up its current,
> There beside grows || A sashibu,
> A sashibu tree.[59] || There below stands
> A camellia. || Broad is its leafage and its branches
> Are five hundred. || Ah, like to it
> In bright blossom, || Like its wide foliage, too,
> In power, is my great lord!

After that she crossed Mount Level, and gazing at Mulberry-Castle, she sang:

> Behind-the-Mountains' || Stream, where rows of saplings stand,
> As I follow it, || Follow to my palace,
> Passing Level by, || Fertile of acres,
> Passing by || Mountain-girt Mountain-Gate,
> The land I fain would see— || Ah, 'tis Mulberry-Castle's
> Takamiya, || The countryside of my home!

Then she proceeded to Tsuzuki, where for a time she lived in the dwelling of a man of Kara,

MAGNATE-OF-NURI.

(Some say, otherwise, that she built a palace on the south side of Mount Tsuzuki, and lived in it.)

The Sovereign, hearing that she had reached Behind-the-Mountains, sent one of his retainers named

BIRD-MOUNTAIN

to conduct her back, singing to him this song:

> To Behind-the-Mountains || Follow her, O Bird-Mountain,
> Follow her, follow her! || My beloved wife, ah me!
> Will you follow her and meet her?

She would not return, however, and later he sent to her

PRINCE-KUCHI [60]

giving to him this song:

> At August-House, || Neighboring to Takaki,
> On the Owiko plain, || Owiko plain,
> Of my deepest heart, || Turning in upon itself,[61]
> Will you there remain || Without a thought?

---

[60] **Ancestor of the Magnates of Ikuba and of Wani. (See p. 216, n. 29.)**

He gave to him moreover this second song:

> Behind-the-Mountains, || With its saplings a-row—
> White as its radish || Cleft by women's hoe-lets
> Is your soft arm! || Since it has pillowed me,
> Can you offer such pretense, || Thus declaring, "Nay, I know not?"

When Prince Kuchi repeated to the Empress this august song, she remained silent and gave him no answer. So, although it was raining heavily, he prostrated himself in the downfall at the front entrance of her palace. At that she departed to the rear entrance and when he prostrated himself there, she returned to the front. He remained there day and night, wet by the rain and snow, and crawling back and forth on his knees, till the water reached his middle. He wore a robe that had been rubbed with blue-green,[62] with a red cord, and the water drenched the cord and its red tinged all the blue-green. His sister,

PRINCESS-KUCHI

who gave the Empress respectful service, seeing this, wept and sang:

> Behind-the-Mountains' || Palace hall of Tsuzuki,
> To my elder brother's || Repetitions I harken.
> What a tearful thing it is!

When the Empress asked her why she wept, she replied, "Your slave's elder brother has prostrated himself in the court-yard to beseech audience. Though wet with the rain, he still hopes for it. Therefore I weep." Said the Empress, "Bid him go back quickly. Never will I return."

So Prince-Kuchi and Princess-Kuchi conferred with Magnate-of-Nuri, and all three agreeing, sent report to the Sovereign, saying, "The Empress has made this journey by reason of certain insects that have been bred by Magnate-of-Nuri, which curiously change into three colors. At one time they are insects that crawl, at another they are . . . ,[63] and at another they are insects that fly. It is only to observe these that she has come here. She has no untoward intention." At which the Sovereign said, "If this is so, I too desire to go to observe, as I deem it curious." And he proceeded there from the imperial palace by river to Behind-the-Mountains. Seeing a mulberry twig floating down the river, he sang:

> Ah, you my Princess- || Of-Rock, creeper-covered,
> You will not harken || Ever so little
> To the mulberry's heart, || Nor may it attain;
> But by the river's borders || It seems to be tossing ever.
> Ah, that mulberry's heart!

When he came to the abode of Magnate-of-Nuri at Tsuzuki, the latter had already offered to the Empress the triple insects he had bred. So the

Sovereign, taking his stand at the entrance of the palace where she was dwelling, sang:

> Ah, Behind-the-Mountains ‖ With its saplings a-row!
> White as its radish ‖ Cleft by women's hoe-lets,
> Sweetly do you speak! ‖ Therefore journeyed I here
> Just to behold you, ‖ As gaze across at you
> The ever-increasing trees.

(These songs, by the Sovereign and the Empress, are both alternating and tranquil Songs.)[64] Then the Empress sent a messenger to say to the Sovereign that since he had taken Young-Lady-of-Yata for his concubine, she did not desire to live with him as wife. So she refused to see him and the Sovereign returned in his carriage to the imperial palace. He was incensed at her anger, but still loved her. Shortly after this she died and was buried on Mount Level, and Young-Lady-of-Yata was made Empress.

THE CRY OF THE DEER

Now the Sovereign, by reason of the heat, occupied with her a tall tower, and by night they could hear the cry of deer on the Moor of Toga, like plaintive music, so that both felt sympathy for them. But when there was no moon, the deer's cry was silent at which they wondered. Next morning one [65] of the Saheki-Clan of the District of Wina made an offering in a hamper. The Sovereign bade an attendant ask what it was, and he replied, "A male deer." On his asking where it came from, the man said, "From the Moor of Toga." Then the Sovereign, thinking the hamper was assuredly the deer which had cried, said to the Empress, "In our recent anxieties it has given us pleasure to listen to the cry of a deer. Reckoning days and nights, and the mountains or moor where this deer was taken, this is surely the deer that cried. This man knew nothing about our tender feelings, and took it without evil intent, but I cannot repress my anger. So let not the Saheki-Clan come near the palace." And he gave command that the man remove to Nuta in Aki.[66]

It is told that of old time there was a stag on the moor of Toga. The doe which was his legal wife lived on this moor, but his concubine doe lived at Field-Island in My-Shame Province, which the stag often visited, loving her exceedingly. At one time he came to his legal wife and passed a night, and in the morning he said to her, "Last night I dreamed that snow fell upon my back and moor-grass [67] *grew upon it. What does this dream portend?" The doe, displeased that her husband should go again to his concubine, said, deceivingly, "When a weed grows on the back it*

---

[65] **Ancestor of the Saheki-Clan of Nuta in Aki Province.**

is a sign that an arrow will be shot there, and the snow signifies the salt that is put upon a corpse. So if you cross to Field-Island in My-Shame, you will surely meet a boatman and be shot to death by him. You should never again go there." The stag, however, could not repress his yearning, and crossing to Field-Island, encountered a boatman on the sea, by whom he was shot to death. (Hence the moor was called Dream-Moor.) [68] Thus arose the saying, "Even a true stag standing on the Moor of Toga is only the interpretation of a dream,[69] or "Even the cry of the male deer is foretold in a dream." ᴀ

> (Others say that a man spent a night on the moor, when two deer, a male and a female, lay down near him. Just at dawn the male said to the female, "I dreamed that a white fog descended and covered me. Of what is it a sign?" The other replied, "When you leave this place, you will be shot by a huntsman and will die, and the white fog is the white salt with which your body will be strewn." While the man wondered at this, there came a huntsman who shot the male deer and killed it.)

Now at this time the grandson of the King of Kudara, Lord Sakè,[70] was disrespectful, and on being remonstrated with, the king, in fear, bound him in chains of iron and delivered him up.

> (Some say that it was at this time that Noble-of-Tsuno-of-Ki was sent to Kudara and that Lord Sakè was delivered up to Prince-Sotsu-of-Mulberry-Castle.) [71]

When he reached Nippon, Lord Sakè ran away and hid in the dwelling of

KAROSHI

Head-Man of Nishikori, in Stone-River, whom he hoodwinked by telling him that the Emperor had forgiven his offence, for which reason he had come to him to be cared for. In the end, though much later, the Sovereign pardoned him. After this

TSUCHIGURA

an Abiko of Yosami [72] caught a strange bird and offered it to the Sovereign saying, "I am used to catch birds in spread nets, but never have I caught one like this. Since it is strange, I augustly offer it." The Sovereign bade Lord Sakè be called, and showing him the bird, asked him what it was. He replied, "There are many such in Kudara, where people make them tame and obedient. They fly swiftly and pursue all other birds." So Lord Sakè took it and fed and speedily tamed it, and fastening to its foot a thong of skin and to its tail a little bell, he set it on his arm and offered it to the Sovereign. When he hunted on the Plain of Butcher-

Bird, many female pheasants rose, and when it was loosed, it quickly caught some tens of them. Thereon the Hawk-Feed-Clan was founded. (For that reason people called the place of the bird's rearing Hawk-Feed-Village.)

Now the Sovereign gave some chestnuts, whose after-parts were shaven, to

POND-CHILD

Tribe-Master of the Young-Mountain-Gate-Clan, who took them away and planted them in the village of Chestnut-Dwelling (for which the place was so called). Since that time all chestnuts from those trees have no after-parts.^A

It befell at this time that Silla failed to send tribute, and

TAKÈ-HASE

was sent to ask the reason. On the way he caught a white deer and returned to offer it to the Sovereign, after which he selected another starting-day. Later his younger brother

TAMICHI

was sent after him with the command, if Silla resisted, to raise an army and invade the country. At that Silla put her army against his and attacked the stronghold in which he had his forces. Then, capturing a man of Silla, Tamichi questioned him, and the man said, "On the right wing of the army is a valorous person named Hundred-Thrust, who is very active and brave and who always fights there. This being so, do you attack on the left and you shall be victorious." So, as Silla's left-wing was weak and the right strong, Tamichi attacked the left with picked horsemen [73] and the Silla army was vanquished. He pursued them and slew them by hundreds, and taking captive the people of four villages, returned with them to Nippon. Afterward he was sent against the rebellious Emishi, who conquered and slew him [74] at the Harbor of Ishimi.[75] One of his men brought his armlet to his wife and she, embracing it, strangled herself, and those who heard of it wept. Later, when the Emishi again rose and carried away the people, they broke open Tamichi's tomb, when a huge Serpent [76] rose up and issued from it. Its eyes shone and it bit the Emishi, who were poisoned by its venom, so that but one or two escaped death. From this arose the saying, "Tamichi, dead, was avenged. Can one say that the dead know naught?"

In this august reign, Noble-of-Brave-Uchi, who in earlier times had chastised the eastern barbarians, being now above three hundred and sixty years old, came to Mount Ubè, and at Kamè-Kanè, in Rice-Leaves Province, he left a pair of his sandals, after which time none knew where he went. There is a shrine,⁷⁷ dedicated to his spirit, at the foot of Mount Ubè, in Homi District, in Rice-Leaves Province.ᴬ

Now those who had guarded the August-Tombs-of-the-White-Swan ⁷⁸ were ordered to work on public structures, and when the Sovereign approached the place where they labored, one of them, who was named

MEKI

suddenly becoming a white deer, ran away. Seeing this, the Sovereign was awe-struck and said, "Since these august tombs have always held nothing,⁷⁹ I have purposed to remove their guards and to begin to use them for labor. Let them not, however, be removed." And he gave them to the Tribe-Masters of the Clay-Workers.⁸⁰

It befell at this time that the ruler of Totomi Province sent to the Sovereign the information that a huge tree, floating on the Great-Well River, ten measures ⁸¹ in size and with a two-forked end, had lodged at a turning in the river, and Akoko,⁸² Governor of Mountain-Gate, being sent, made it into a vessel, which he brought around by way of the southern sea to Wave-Swift Harbor and made it one of the imperial vessels.

Now Prince-Great-Middle-of-Nukata,⁸³ while hunting in Tsukè, saw from the mountain a hut on the moor and sent a messenger to observe it, who reported that it was a roofed-pit.⁸⁴ He asked

GREAT-MOUNTAIN-MASTER

Country-Lord of Tsukè, what kind of roofed-pit it was, and he replied that it was a roofed-pit for ice. On Prince-Great-Middle-of-Nukata asking how the ice was preserved and for what use, he answered, "A hole above ten shaku deep is dug and roofed with thatch. Reeds are strewn thickly in it and the ice laid on them. Thus it does not melt during the passing of the summer season. In the hot season it is used in water or sakè." ⁸⁵ Then Prince-Great-Middle-of-Nukata took away some of the ice and offered it to the Sovereign, who was must pleased with it. Always after that ice was preserved.

In Hida Province was one

SUKUNA

who had on a single body two faces which looked in opposite directions. The faces joined at the top and the neck had no back. Each face had two hands and two feet, and he had knees but no knee-hollows and no heels. He was vigorous and active, wearing swords on both sides and carrying bows and arrows in all four hands. Since he refused to obey the Sovereign but loved to rob the people, Prince-Wave-Swift-Brave-Furu-

Bear [86] was sent to slay him. After this the Sovereign proceeded to the plain of Ishitsu, in Kawachi, where he chose a place for a burial-mound. When the building of the mound began, a deer rose up and ran swiftly into the midst of those who were building it, and falling down there, died. As they looked to see the cause of its strange and sudden death, a butcher-bird flew from its ear, and when they looked, they saw that the skin was entirely eaten away. (For this reason the place was called Butcher-Bird's-Ear.) [87]

DISTRICT-WARDEN SLAYS THE WATER-SERPENTS

Now at a fork of the River-Island River, in the middle of the Province of Maise, was a huge water-serpent by which the people were afflicted. Many who passed that place died by its venom. So

DISTRICT-WARDEN [88]

who was violent of temper and very vigorous, took his stand by the pool at the fork of the river and threw into it three uncut gourds, crying, "O water-serpent, who always ejects venom to afflict people who are passing, you I will slay! If you can make these gourds sink, I will depart, but if you cannot, then I will cut you to pieces." At that the water-serpent became a deer and tried to sink the gourds, but they would not sink. So District-Warden drew his sword, and entering the pool, slew it, and finding a hole in the pool's bottom full of its kind, he slew them all, so that the river-water became blood. (Therefore the place was named District-Warden's-Pool.)

In this reign there were two persons

BLACK-HAIR-OF-GREAT-TREE
OYUKO-OF-RICE-LEAVES

who were extravagantly luxurious, so that they washed their hands and feet with refined sakè. The Sovereign deemed this too extravagant and sent

SAYA

Tribe-Master of Narrow-Well,[89] *to bring the pair. So Saya bound the members of their families, and on the way to the capital frequently immersed them in water to make them confess. Among these were two women who had jewels fastened to their hands and feet and, wondering, he inquired about them. They answered that their father was the Tribe-Master*

---

[88] **Ancestor of the Magnates of Kasa.**

AUGUST-CLOTHING-OF-WEAVING

and that their mother was

PRINCESS-ROUGH-SLOPE

a female Governor of Rice-Leaves Province, and that their names were

PRINCESS-UNA
PRINCESS-KUWA.

At this Saya was amazed, and saying, "These are daughters of Ministers!" sent them back. The place from which they were sent back is called Mount-See-Keep [90] and the place where they were immersed in water is called Mikatsuki Plain. During this reign the Clan-Chief of Asabè, who was a native of Fire, of Sun-Facing, brought some boars to the vessel [91] on which was Great-Sky-Shiner, the Great-Kami, and offered them, asking where they might be fed. So he was given a place in which to pasture them on Boar-Feeding-Moor, which thus received its name.[A]

The Sovereign died at the august age of eighty-three and was buried in the mound on the moor of Butcher-Bird's Ear.

THE EMPEROR IZAHO-ELDER-BROTHER-LORD (MIDDLE-TREADER [92])

THE REBELLION OF KING-MIDDLE-OF-PLEASANT-TO-DWELL-IN

It was the desire of the Sovereign, Izaho-Elder-Brother-Lord, to take as concubine

PRINCESS-BLACK [93]

who was the daughter of

NOBLE-OF-REED-PLAIN

child of Prince-Sotsu-of-Mulberry-Castle [94] (or, as some say, of Noble-of-Yashiro-of-Hata) so, having sent gifts for the bridal,[95] he despatched King-Middle-of-Pleasant-to-Dwell-In [96] to arrange a fortunate day. The latter, however, by using his brother's name, had intercourse with Princess-Black, but when he departed that night he forgot his wrist-bells and left them in her dwelling. So, on the next night, Izaho-Elder-Brother-Lord, ignorant that the other had lain with her, went there also and drawing the curtain of her room, seated himself upon her jewel-couch, when the bells sounded at its upper end. On his asking her, in surprise, what bells they were, she replied, "Whose but yours, which you brought last night?" From this he knew that King-Middle-of-Pleasant-to-Dwell-In had used his name and thus had lain with her, and he departed without replying.

King-Middle-of-Pleasant-to-Dwell-In, fearing calamity would result, planned to slay him, and raised an army in secret and surrounded the imperial palace. Three persons, however, Noble-of-Heguri's-Owl,

NOBLE-OF-GREAT-FRONT-LITTLE-FRONT

of the Army-Clan, and Magnate-of-Achi, informed the Sovereign, but he, having held an abundantly bright feast at the First-Rice-Tasting ceremony, was drunk and asleep, and could not rise. So they aided him, and Noble-of-Great-Front-Little-Front took him in his arms and put him on a horse so that he could flee, while King-Middle-of-Pleasant-to-Dwell-In, unaware of his flight, fired the palace, which burned unextinguished throughout the night. When the Sovereign reached the Moor of Knot-Grass, in Kawachi Province, he awoke sober and asked where he was, and Magnate-of-Achi replied, "King-Middle-of-Pleasant-to-Dwell-In set fire to the imperial palace, so we flee with you to Mountain-Gate." Thereon the Sovereign sang:

> On the Knot-Grass Moor || Had I known that I would sleep,
> Ah, I would have brought || Mats with me,
> To set up around— || Had I known that I would sleep!

Then, in great fear, he fled toward Mountain-Gate. When he came to Hanifu Slope, and looked at the Palace of Wave-Swift, where the fire glowed, he sang:

> As, standing, I gaze || From the Slope of Hanifu,
> All glowingly burns || The mass of houses beyond,
> There toward the dwelling of my wife!

When they came to the mouth of Mount-Great-Slope [97] (or, as some say, Mount-Asuka) they met a woman, of whom they asked if there were men on the mountain. She replied, "It is filled with men with weapons to oppose you. Go you across by way of Tagima." At which the Sovereign, reflecting that he had evaded misfortune through the words, sang:

> Ah me! At Great-Slope || I ask a damsel we meet
> As to the highway. || Says she, "Go not straight forward!"
> And speaks of Tagima.

Then he changed his course, and collecting an army in the district, led them across Mount Tatsuta, when some tens of men with weapons pursued them. Seeing these afar off, thinking from their swiftness that they might be enemies, they hid themselves, and when the others drew near, they sent a man to ask who they were and whither bound. The man replied that they were fishers of No-Island in My-Shame, whom

BEACH-CHILD [98]

Tribe-Master of Azumi, at the behest of King-Middle-of-Pleasant-to-Dwell-In, had sent in pursuit of the Sovereign. So they called out the army from hiding and surrounded and captured all of them.

Now Akoko, Governor of Mountain-Gate, who from old time had loved King-Middle-of-Pleasant-to-Dwell-In, had joined in his plan, raising secretly an army of some chosen hundreds at Kurusu, in Kakibami, and at his wish opposed the Sovereign. Ignorant that armed men fronted him, the former set out from the mountain, when he was stopped at some ri distance by a large company which forbade him to proceed. He sent a messenger to ask who they were, and they gave the name of Akoko. When they asked the messenger from whom he came, he answered, "From the Sovereign." So Akoko feared that there might be a great army there and said, "I heard that an accident had happened to the Sovereign and have gathered this army to assist him." The Sovereign however, knew his evil intent and would have slain him, when he, in fear, offered his younger sister

PRINCESS-OF-SUN

who begged for his pardon, which was granted. (Thus, people believe, arose the custom by which the Governors of Mountain-Gate send as tribute the Neck-Clan.) Afterward the Sovereign continued his journey and dwelt in the shrine of the Kami of Above-the-Rock. When he found he had gone, Beautiful-Teeth-Lord-of-Knot-Grass, his younger brother, followed and sent someone to see him. The Sovereign, nevertheless, being suspicious of his intentions, did not summon him but sent him word that inasmuch as he doubted whether his heart was not with King-Middle-of-Pleasant-to-Dwell-In, he would neither see nor speak with him. Then said Beautiful-Teeth-Lord-of-Knot-Grass, "Your slave's heart is not black, nor is it with him. I come here only because I grieve at your absence." At that the Sovereign sent to him, saying, "Because of the rebellious act of King-Middle-of-Pleasant-to-Dwell-In, I am here in fear and alone. I cannot but suspect you. Living, he will strive only to do me evil, and I desire, now or later, to be rid of this. If you speak the truth and your heart is not black, go down again to Wave-Swift and kill King-Middle-of-Pleasant-to-Dwell-In. Then I will see and speak with you." Beautiful-Teeth-Lord-of-Knot-Grass answered, "Your fear is over-great. Both the officials and the people despise that one's untoward actions and he is opposed even in his own family, to whom he is an outlaw. He is alone, with none to counsel him. While I was aware and was angered at his rebellious act, you had not given me orders, as you have now done. It will not be hard for me to slay him. But I fear that afterward you will still be suspicious of me. So I pray you to send with me one in whom you have confidence, that he may convince you of my good-faith." So the Sovereign sent with him Noble-of-Heguri's-Owl. Then Beautiful-Teeth-Lord-of-Knot-Grass grieved, thinking, "As both the Sovereign and King-Middle-of-Pleasant-to-Dwell-In are my elder brothers, I do not know which to obey and which to oppose. Slaying the evil and standing with the good, however, I shall be clear." So he journeyed to Wave-Swift, to spy upon King-Middle-of-Pleasant-to-Dwell-In, who was unguarded, believing the Sovereign fled and gone.

Now King-Middle-of-Pleasant-to-Dwell-In had for attendant a falcon-man [99] named

SOBAKIRI [1]

who was closely attached to him, and Beautiful-Teeth-Lord-of-Knot-Grass sent for the man in secret and flattered him, saying, "Do what I tell you, so that I may become the Sovereign, and what if I make you my chief-Minister, to rule the empire?" Sobakiri answered, "As you bid me." Liberally rewarding him, Beautiful-Teeth-Lord-of-Knot-Grass said, "Then kill him." He gave the other his robe and brocade trousers, and Sobakiri, fooled by his words, went alone and watched till King-Middle-of-Pleasant-to-Dwell-In went into the latrine, when he thrust him to death with a spear. So, taking Sobakiri with him, Beautiful-Teeth-Lord-of-Knot-Grass proceeded to Mountain-Gate, but when he came to the mouth of Mount Great-Slope, he reflected, "Sobakiri has already slain his lord and should be rewarded by me. Yet this is an unseemly thing. If I do not recompense him, men will call me liar. If I fulfil my word, I fear his intentions. Therefore, though I recompense his action, I shall kill his body." Then he told Sobakiri he would wait there that day to invest him with the title of chief-Minister and proceed on the morrow, and staying his progress in the mouth of the mountain, he had a temporary palace erected and hurriedly held an abundantly bright feast, investing the falcon-man with the title of chief-Minister and bidding the hundred officials prostrate themselves before him, at which the falcon-man was greatly pleased, believing that he had gained his object. Then, declaring that he would drink from the same sakè-cup with his chief-Minister, they drank together, a large cup that hid the face being filled with the offered sakè, he drinking first and afterward the falcon-man, the cup covering his face as he drank. On which Beautiful-Teeth-Lord-of-Knot-Grass took a sword that had been put beneath the matting and struck off the falcon-man's head.

(*By others it is said that the falcon-man was slain not by Beautiful-Teeth-Lord-of-Knot-Grass, but by Noble-of-Heguri's-Owl, who saying, "Sobakiri, though he has greatly aided us, has slain his own lord at the behest of another; being thus without feeling for his lord, he should not be allowed to live!" thereon slew him.*)

Straightway next day he went toward Mountain-Gate (for which reason the place was called Nearer-Asuka). When he came there, he determined to remain a day for purification and on the day following to go to worship at the shrine of the Kami (for which reason that place was called Further-Asuka.)

Now in the ancient time there was an old wolf [2] at Asuka which devoured many, so that the people feared him and named him

KAMI-OF-GREAT-MOUTH.[3]

(*Which is why the place was named Plain-of-Kami-of-Great-Mouth.*[4])[A]

Then, proceeding to the Shrine of the Kami of Above-the-Rock, Beautiful-Teeth-Lord-of-Knot-Grass reported, at midnight, that political affairs had been peacefully settled and that he had come to serve the Sovereign, who received him and treated him with great favor and gave him the grain storehouses of Ahasè Village. Afterward the Sovereign caused Beach-Child [5] to be brought before him and said, "You were with King-Middle-of-Pleasant-to-Dwell-In in his plan to seize the rule, and death is the fit punishment for this. Yet I will be merciful and instead of that will condemn you to be marked with ink." [6] So straightway he was marked with ink near the eye. (From this came the expression of that time, "The eye of Azumi.") Also the fishers who had served under him were pardoned and made to labor on the grain storehouses of Komoshiro, in Mountain-Gate. The Sovereign made Magnate-of-Achi keeper of the treasure-house and gave him food-lands.

The Sovereign wedded Princess-Black, by whom he begot

PRINCE-PUSH-TEETH-OF-NEAR-THE-MARKET

(whose august teeth were set unevenly like the petals of a lily)

PRINCE-AUGUST-HORSES
PRINCESS-IÏTOYO [7]

(who some have it was the daughter of Prince-Push-Teeth-of-Near-the-Market). Now the land was administered by Noble-of-Heguri's-Owl, and

NOBLE-OF-MANCHI-OF-SOGA

together with the Great Tribe-Master of Ikofutsu, of the Army Clan, and the Great Magnate of Tsubura. The Sovereign erected a palace at Assembling and there dug the Pool of Ichishi.

In it he set the two-forked boat [8] and entering it with Princess-Black, he made her a feast, each sitting apart from the other, when

ARESHI

Magnate of Kashihatè, offered imperial sakè. A cherry-blossom fell into the Sovereign's cup, and he, surprised, called the Tribe-Master of Nagamakè, of the Army-Clan, and saying, "It is not the season for these blossoms," bade him search out from where it had come. So the Tribe-Master made search and finding the blossoms on Mount-Muro-of-Young-Sacred, offered them to the Sovereign. He, much pleased by their novelty, named the palace, after them, Young-Cherry-of-Assembling. And he changed the title of the Tribe-Master of Nagamakè to Ruler-of-Young-Cherry-Clan and Areshi he made Magnate of this Clan. Moreover he founded the Assembling-Clan, and gave to the Clan-Chiefs of Princess-Ricefield the family name of Clan-Chief-of-Princess-Ricefield. Also the Canal of Above-the-Rock was made. It was at this time that provincial scribes were first appointed throughout the provinces who wrote down words and sent their records of the four directions.

Now the three Kami [9] whose seat is in Tsukushi, showing themselves in the imperial palace, said, "Because our people are stolen, we will bring shame upon you!" At that the Sovereign made supplication but without result. Later he made a hunt on My-Shame Island. The Horse-Tender-Clan served as bridle-holders, and as their faces had been recently marked with ink, the wounds were yet raw, so that the Kami He-Who-Invites, who has his seat there,[10] spoke through the mouth of a hafuri, saying, "The blood-smell is distasteful to me." Therefore by divination it was ascertained that it was the smell from the ink-marking of the Horse-Tender-Clan which offended the Kami, and from that time the ink-marking of this Clan was entirely done away with. After that there came a wind-blowing sound in the Great Void, crying, "You Prince who holds the Sword!" [11] Also it cried, "Your younger sister, Komotsu-of-Sanakita, of Hata the bird-thronged, is buried at Hasa." And immediately a swift messenger came who reported that the Sovereign's concubine was dead. So, deeply disturbed, he ordered his carriage and left My-Shame. When Princess-Black had been buried, he blamed himself for not having turned away the calamity of the Kami, thus bringing about her death, and made efforts to discover wherein wrong had been done. It was reported to him, then, that the Clan-Chief of the Carriage-Tenders, going to the Land of Tsukushi, had incorporated with them some of those appointed to serve the Kami. Since this seemed a wrong, the Sovereign sent for him and ascertaining the truth, said to him, "It is a crime that you, Clan-Chief of the Carriage-Tenders, have taken the Sovereign's people, and a crime also that without warrant you enrolled in the Carriage-Tender-Clan those appointed to serve the Sky- and Earth-Kami." He sentenced him, then, to expiate both evil and good, performing the ceremony at Nagasa Cape, and took from him the control of the Carriage-Tender-Clan of Tsukushi and gave this to the three Kami. In this reign a treasure-storehouse was etsablished and a Treasure-Storehouse-Clan formed.

Beside the sacred treasure-storehouse, there was built an inner treasure-storehouse where the imperial property was listed and kept, and the Kudara scholars, Magnate-of-Achi [12] and Wan-I [13] were ordered to set down what was put in and taken out. The inner treasure-storehouse had a chief who was in charge of gold, silver, jewels, valuable utensils, brocades, satins, sarsenet, rugs, pallets, and rare things sent as tribute from various barbarians.[A]

Now the Sovereign had taken two concubines

LADY-OF-FUTO-PRINCESS
LADY-OF-TAKATSURU

both of whom were daughters of

PRINCE-FUNASHI-LORD

and put them into the palace of the Empress. They made lament and on his asking the reason, they said, "Our elder brother,

PRINCE-WASHIZUMI [14]

who is so strong and swift that he can leap over a house of eight hiro, has departed. It is many days since we spoke with him, and we grieve." Since he delighted in great strength, the Sovereign summoned him but he did not come, and though many messengers were sent he would not, but remained in Pleasant-to-Dwell-In. After that the Sovereign ceased sending for him

Prince-Push-Teeth-of-Near-the-Market took to wife

PRINCESS-HAYÈ [15]

who was the daughter of

MAGNATE-OF-ARI

and there were born to the two

KING-BIG-BASKET [16]

(whose personal name was Large-Foot [17])

KING-LITTLE-BASKET.[18]

The Sovereign died in the Palace of Young-Cherry. His years were sixty-

---

[14] **Ancestor of the Rulers of Sanuki and the Lords of Ashikuhi in Awa.**

four (or, as others say, seventy, seventy-seven, eighty-five or eighty-seven) and his burial-place is at Butcher-Bird.

THE EMPEROR BEAUTIFUL-TEETH-LORD-OF-KNOT-GRASS (RESTORE-JUSTICE)[19]

Beautiful-Teeth-Lord-of-Knot-Grass dwelt in the Palace of Brushwood-Fence at Knot-Grass and ruled the empire. He was nine shaku, two and one half sun, tall. His teeth were one sun long and two lines [20] wide, and he was lovely to look at. He took to wife the two daughters of

KOGOTO.[21]

This Sovereign's years were sixty and his Burial-Mound is on Butcher-Bird Moor.

THE EMPEROR NOBLE-OF-YOUNGER-CHILD-MALE-MORNING-WIFE

(TRULY-RESPECTFUL)[22]

From babyhood's hair-style to youth's hair-style,[23] Noble-of-Younger-Child-Male-Morning-Wife was amiable and retiring, but when he grew up he could not readily move his limbs by reason of illness.

When the Sovereign Beautiful-Teeth-Lord-of-Knot-Grass died, his Ministers conferred, since there were then two sons of Great-Wren, namely Noble-of-Younger-Child-Male-Morning-Wife and Great-Lord-of-Hatabi.[24] The former, however, being the elder and by nature loving and dutiful, they selected an auspicious day and offered him on their knees the rule of the succession of the Sky's sons. He refused, saying that he unluckily was grievously ill and could not be cured sufficiently to walk. Without the knowledge of the Sovereign he had vainly mutilated himself,[25] so that, discovering it, the Sovereign had upbraided him as unfilial and declared that though he might attain to long life, he should not inherit the rule. "Therefore," he said, "and because, as you know, my two elder brothers who ruled hated me and considered me ridiculous, I will not rule the Sun's succession. For the empire is a thing that is great and of vast extent and only a wise man may be father and mother of the people. It may not be handed over to a ridiculous person. Choose another wise prince and let him imperially rule. I am unworthy and will not." Then all the Magnates, from the Empress down, besought him,

---

21 **Ancestor of the Magnates of Ohoyakè and of Wani.***

---

* See pp. 295 and 309. Apparently he was a descendant of Prince-Wave-Swift-Furu-Bear.

and the Ministers, prostrating themselves a second time, declared that the imperial office should not be long unfilled, nor the Sky intentions put aside through humbleness, and begged him, in spite of his bodily pain, to take the rule. As he continued to refuse, although the ministers insisted that he was worthy, his concubine, Princess-Great-Middle-of-Osaka,[26] sorrowful at their ill-success, said to him, "Since you have declined to take the rule, years with their months have gone by. So your Ministers and officials sorrow and are at a loss. I beseech you to yield and take the rule, even though you do not desire it." But he would not consent and remained silently sitting with his back toward her. Now when she came before him she was holding water to wash his hands. In fear, and not knowing how to withdraw, she waited there by him for two or three hours. As it was the twelfth month and there was a strong cold wind, the water from the basin ran over and froze to her arms. When she was ready to expire from the cold, Noble-of-Younger-Child-Male-Morning-Wife turned and to his amazement perceived her. Then, assisting her to rise, he said, "The matter of the rule is an important one and I could not take it without delay, so till now I have refused. But in truth my Ministers are right and I will not hold to it."

So Princess-Great-Middle-of-Osaka, greatly pleased, said to them, "He will listen to your desire. Offer him now the rule." And they straightway and with gladness prostrated themselves and did so, when he said, "This you do at the behest of the empire and I will no longer haughtily refuse." So he took the rule and Princess-Great-Middle-of-Osaka was made Empress and the Osaka-Clan [27] was founded for her.

Now once when she had been at her mother's dwelling, as she walked in the garden, the ruler of the Land of Tsukè passed in the road on horseback. Looking across the hedge, he jibed at her, saying, "You are a good gardener. Will you present me with an orchid?" So she gave him one, asking him why he desired it, when he replied, without dismounting, "To beat off the gnats on the mountain." Because of his disrespect she said, "I shall remember you, Head-Man!" So now, having gained the rank of Empress, she sent for the rider and reminding him of what he had done, would have put him to death, but he prostrated himself, beating his head against the ground, and said, "Justly should your slave suffer death ten thousand times. But I was then ignorant of your station." So she withdrew the death penalty but reduced his rank to that of Country-Lord.

By Princess-Great-Middle-of-Osaka the Sovereign begot

KING-KARU-OF-KINASHI [28]

---

[28] **Ancestor (by proxy) of the Karu-Clan.**

GREAT-LADY-OF-LONG-RICEFIELD [29]
KING-PRINCE-BLACK-OF-BORDER
ANAHO
GREAT-LADY-OF-KARU

(Some say, however, that she was not his child, but that this was another name of Lady-of-Robe-Passing, whom he later wedded.)

KING-PRINCE-WHITE-OF-EIGHT-MELONS
GREAT-HASÈ [30]

At the latter's birth a celestial light filled the palace.

Now an envoy was sent to Silla to fetch a learned physician, so the ruler of that Land sent tribute in one and eighty vessels and the great messenger who brought it,

KOMU-HA-CHIMU-KAMU-KI-MU,

having deep knowledge of medicine, treated the Sovereign and presently cured him of his disease. At which, greatly pleased, the Sovereign bountifully gifted him and sent him back.

THE SOVEREIGN RECTIFIES NAMES

At this time, regretting the falsities in the family-names and titles of the people who had them in the empire, the Sovereign issued this decree: "The Ministers, officials and rulers of the provinces claim either that their ancestors were emperors, or miraculously descended from the Sky. But it is many tens of thousands of years since the Three Powers of Nature [31] were formed, and families have increased and have invented ten thousand designations that cannot be proven. The people of the various families and names shall therefore bathe and practice abstinence and then, in presence of the Kami, dip their arms in boiling water." Accordingly hot-water jars for the trial were placed at Cape Sweet-Oak,[32] wonderful for eighty spoken evils,[33] and all the people were sent there, being informed that the truth-teller would be unharmed, but the liar would without doubt suffer. (This custom is called Kuka-Tachi.[34] Sometimes mud is made to boil in a jar and is stirred by the naked arm, and sometimes a red-hot axe is laid in the hand.) So all the people put on bands of bark [35] and thrust their arms into the jars of boiling water and the truth-tellers, as was expected, were unharmed, but the liars suffered. For this reason those who had lied feared to submit themselves and stole away in advance. Thus the Sovereign established the family-names and titles of eighty chiefs of companies, and after that family-names and titles took care of themselves, none altering them.

At this time the Karu- and the Kawa-Clans were founded. Now

NOBLE-OF-JEWEL-RICEFIELD

son of Prince-Sotsu-of-Mulberry-Castle [36] (or, as some say, his grandson) had been made director of the temporary burial of the Sovereign Beautiful-Teeth-Lord-of-Knot-Grass. It happened that there was an earthquake, and on the next night

ASO

Tribe-Master of Owari, was sent to examine the shrine. All came together save only Noble-of-Jewel-Ricefield, the high official, and this Aso reported to the Sovereign. Being sent again to Mulberry-Castle, he found Noble-of-Jewel-Ricefield carousing with men and women whom he had gathered. On Aso's telling him how the case stood, Noble-of-Jewel-Ricefield, fearing calamity, presented the other with a horse, after which he secretly lay in wait on the road and slew him. Then he fled and hid in the tomb of Noble-of-Brave-Uchi. When the Sovereign, learning this, sent for him, he was suspicious and came before him wearing under his robe armor whose edge showed beneath it. The Sovereign, in order to convince himself, commanded

OWARI-RICEFIELD

one of the Neck-Clan, to offer sakè to Noble-of-Jewel-Ricefield, and he, seeing the armor under the robe, so reported, whereon the Sovereign sent for armed men to kill Noble-of-Jewel-Ricefield, but he fled in secret and hid in his dwelling. The Sovereign, however, sent armed men who surrounded it, and seizing him, slew him.

Now a horse was offered to the Sovereign, when he said, "The forehead of this horse is like the border of a ricefield." Therefore he who offered the horse was given the name of

TRIBE-MASTER-OF-FOREHEAD-RICEFIELD.[37, A]

THE SOVEREIGN FALLS IN LOVE WITH LADY-OF-ROBE-PASSING

When he gave a feast at the new palace, the Sovereign played on the koto and the Empress danced. It was the custom then for the dancer at a feast, when the dancing ceased, to offer a damsel to the one of highest rank. When the Empress ceased dancing, however, she did not confer the customary favor, and when the Sovereign asked her why she had not, she was in fear. So she danced a second time and when she ceased, she

---

[37] *Ancestor of the Governors of Nuga (Nuka).*

made the offering. Thereon he asked, "What is the name of the damsel you offer?" Then perforce, she said, "It is

LADY-OF-ROBE-PASSING [38]

your slave's younger sister." (She was called Lady-of-Robe-Passing because the brightness of her body shone through her garments. Also her face excelled all in beauty.) The Sovereign already desired her, and for this cause forced the Empress to offer her, although the Empress, aware of this, did not wish to do so. He was pleased, and next day sent for Lady-of-Robe-Passing, where she dwelt with her mother, at Sakata in the Land of Omi. However, she would not come for fear of the Empress, though she was sent for more than seven times. The Sovereign, angered, sent a retainer of the Intercessor-Clan, named

MAGNATE-OF-IKATSU

saying, "Go and bring back with you this damsel who, though the Empress gave her to me, has not come, and I will abundantly reward you."

Thus commanded, he departed to Sakata where, having hidden food in his clothing, he went to the courtyard of Lady-of-Robe-Passing and prostrating himself, gave her the imperial summons. She replied, "I must regard the imperial command with awe, yet I will not offend the Empress. Even at cost of her life, your slave will not go." Magnate-of-Ikatsu answered, "Having been given the imperial word, I must take you back with me or failing, must be punished. Rather than go back and suffer the last penalty, I will die lying in your courtyard." So he lay there for seven days, refusing to eat and drink, while secretly eating food he had in his garments. Till Lady-of-Robe-Passing said, "Your slave has disobeyed the imperial command because of the Empress's jealousy: it would be a further crime for me to destroy you, you good servant!" and went with him.

When they came to Kasuga in Mountain-Gate, they took food at the Well of Ichihi, and she offered the Magnate sakè to calm his feeling. So he came to the capital, and putting her in the dwelling of Okoko, Governor of Mountain-Gate, made report, and the Sovereign, greatly pleased, abundantly favored him. The Empress, however, was angered, so that Lady-of-Robe-Passing dared not enter the palace, and a dwelling was especially built for her at Wistaria-Plain.[39] The Sovereign first visited this palace on the night the Empress brought forth Great-Hasè, and learning of it, she was incensed. Said she, "Many years ago I bound up my hair and became the Sovereign's consort in the inner-palace. It is brutal of him to go to Wistaria-Plain on this my night of labor, when I am between

---

[38] **Ancestor (by proxy) of the Fujiwara-Clan.**

living and dying." So saying, she set the bringing-forth-house on fire, and would have slain herself, but the Sovereign, greatly taken aback to learn of this, admitted his fault and pacified her.

At this time the Sovereign said to

MURUYA

Tribe-Master of the imperial guard, "I have recently taken to myself a lovely woman, the Empress's younger sister by the same mother's womb. I devoutly love her and wish her name transmitted to future ages. Can this be done?" Accordingly the Tribe-Master made a plan, which pleased the Sovereign, by which the rulers of the different provinces were commanded to form Wistaria-Clans for her benefit. The Sovereign, however, went again to Wistaria-Plain to see Lady-of-Robe-Passing in secret. And she, sitting alone, remembering him with love and knowing not that he was there, sang:

On this very night || Lo, my spouse will be coming,
'Tis the crablet's [40] rede,
She, the born of the spider! || Ah, 'ere it happened, I knew!

He, hearing with compassion, sang in answer this song:

Now my girdle, made || Of brocade, small of pattern,
I put by. Not oft
Have I given myself to slumber— || No, only one single night!

Next morning, seeing cherry-blossoms at a well, he sang:

If I other loved || As one loves the fragrant blossom
Of the cherry-tree,
Soon would I cease to cherish || The damsel I love so now!

When the Empress heard of this she was angry, so Lady-of-Robe-Passing said to the Sovereign, "Always would your slave be near the imperial palace and never cease, by night and day, to behold your effulgence. But my elder sister, the Empress, through me is vexed at us both. Therefore, I pray you, put me at a distance, far from the palace. This is my wish, that her jealous anger may cease." So the Sovereign erected a new palace in Chinu, in Kawachi, and let Lady-of-Robe-Passing dwell in it, and afterward he often hunted on the Hinè-Moor. But later, when the Empress declared her feeling was not one of jealousy, but of fear lest the Sovereign's frequent going there might cause anxiety to the people, he came to Chinu less frequently. On a time when he was there Lady-of-Robe-Passing sang:

Everlastingly || Would I my Lord were meeting—
Oft, as to the beach,
Out of the whale-hunted ocean || The seaweed drifts to the shore!

Then the Sovereign said, "No one else may know of this song, for if she heard it, the Empress would be sorely angered." (Therefore the weed of the seashore was named Telling-Not-Weed.[41])

Now when the Sovereign went hunting on My-Shame Island, deer, monkeys, and boars covered mountain and valley in masses like clouds of dust, leaping up like fire and fleeing like flies, but throughout the day none was taken. So they broke off the chase and again [42] made divination, whereon the Kami of the Island [43] declared that it was by his heart's wish that none had been taken, but that if there were offered to him a pearl which was on the sea-bottom at Akashi, much game would be taken. So the fishermen here and there were called together and commanded to search the sea-bottom, but the sea was so deep that they could not reach it. There was, however, one

OSASHI

of Naga-Zato,[44] in Awa Province, who was better than the rest,[45] and who bound a rope to his middle and went to the sea-bottom. Presently he returned, saying there was there a huge sea-ear [46] which shone. It appeared to all that the pearl which the Kami of the Island demanded was within this sea-ear, and Osashi again went for it and came up with it in his hands. However, he was without breath and died at the surface.[47] A measure-rope was let down and the sea-bottom was found to be sixty hiro. Then they cut open the sea-ear and in it was a true pearl as large as a peach, which was offered to the Kami of the Island, after which a hunt was made and much game taken. And, sorrowing for the death of Osashi the sea-plunger, they erected a tomb and buried him with honor. (This tomb stands to the present day.)[48]

The Sovereign died at the age of seventy-eight (or, as some say, eighty) years and was buried in the Mount of Long-Inlet, near Wega, in Kawachi (or, according to others, in the Plain of Nagano).

KING-KARU-OF-KINASHI AND GREAT-LADY-OF-KARU

Now King-Karu-of-Kinashi, who was to receive the rule, was comely and all who saw him loved him. Also Great-Lady-of-Karu, his sister by the same mother, was lovely. He held always in his mind the desire to cohabit with her, although fearing to do this wrong. But while he waited for the ceremony of accession, being well-nigh dead from the strength of his desire, and thinking that though wrong he could not withstand it and unwilling to die to no purpose, he cohabited with her in secret, which allayed his passion. Then he sang:

> Men delve ricefields || On the foot-dragging mountain,
> For that the mountain || Towers high, laying down

> Under-running pipes. || But today the young sister
> Whom I longed after || With under-longing, weeping
> With under-weeping— || Our bodies easily touch!

(This is a song whose after part is raised.)[49] Also he sang:

> The bamboo-grass || Sounds beneath stroke of the hail
> Its *táshi-dáshi*.[50] || To me, surely slumbering,
> What boots it that folk plot? || When entrancingly
> I shall have slept, let all things || Fall into disorder,
> Confused like cut kari[51] grass— || When I shall have soundly slept.

(This is a country song that is raised.)[49] Since he was heir-apparent penalty could not be meted to him, but by reason of this thing the one hundred officials and the folk of the empire turned against him and favored Anaho.

> (By some it is said that this occurred before the death of the Sovereign, who, when the soup which he was about to eat froze to ice, asked the meaning of it. On divination being made, the diviner said, "It is a sign of family confusion, such as incest by those nearly related." Thereon it was reported that King-Karu-of-Kinashi had had intercourse with Great-Lady-of-Karu, which, on examination, was found to be true.)

Then King-Karu-of-Kinashi, minded to attack Anaho, raised an army in secret, and Anaho did likewise and made ready to fight, both preparing a store of arrows. King-Karu-of-Kinashi put upon his arrows copper heads (for which reason they were called Karu-arrows) but Anaho's were like those used at present (therefore they have the name Anaho-arrows). But King-Karu-of-Kinashi, knowing that the Ministers would not side with him and that the people would not obey, fled in fear and concealed himself in the dwelling of two Magnates of the Army-Clan

NOBLE-GREAT-SAKI

NOBLE-SMALL-SAKI.

So Anaho, learning this, with his army surrounded the house. When he came to the gate heavy sleet was falling, and he sang:

> Your metal gate, || Great-Saki and Small-Saki,
> Will furnish shelter. || There let us take our stand
> Until the rain is over.

Then Noble-Great-Saki came out, raising his arms, beating his knees, dancing and waving his hands, singing:

> The folk of the palace— || The little bells have fallen
> From off their leggings, || So they are now in tumult.
> Ye rustics, also, be warned!

(This song is in palace-style.) Then he said, "O Child of the Sky-Sovereign! I beseech you, come not with arms to harm your elder brother, else will people laugh. Your slave will secure him and offer him to you as tribute." So Anaho withdrew his army and departed and Noble-Great-Saki secured King-Karu-of-Kinashi and brought him out and offered him. Then King-Karu-of-Kinashi made a song:

> O Sky-flying || Karu! If your damsel
> Cry violently, || Folk will be aware of it!
> As on Hasè Mountain || Do the doves.
> Cry, I pray you, quietly!

Also he made a second song which said:

> O Sky-flying || Karu! Let your damsel
> Come to me and sleep, || Passing then upon her way.
> O you maiden of Karu!

After this he was sent away to the Hot-Springs of Iyo.

(By some, however, it is held that he slew himself in the house of Noble-Great-Saki. Others say that it was impossible to punish the imperial heir, and that it was Great-Lady-of-Karu who was sent away to the Land of Iyo.)

When he was about to depart to his exile he made this song:

> The sky-flying || Birds, indeed, are messengers.
> When perhaps the voice || Of the crane you are hearing,
> Ask it then what my name is.

(These three songs are of a sky-flying style.) Also he made this song:

> Though I, a great lord, || To an island am banished,
> The return voyage || Of that vessel I shall make!
> O my pallet, have a care! || Say I my pallet?
> 'Tis but a way of speaking— || Wife of mine, have you a care!

(This is a country-song that is partly lowered.) Great-Lady-of-Karu, also, offered him this song:

> In the summer-grass || Of the shore of Ahinè
> Let not your feet tread || On the shells of oysters,
> But pass on when all is clear.

Later she was unable to hold her love in check, and followed him, singing

> My lord's departure || Is a thing of long ago,
> * * * * 52 || I will go to meet with you.
> Wait? No longer can I wait!

Then, when in her pursuit she came where he sadly waited, he made this song:

On the far-withdrawn || Mountain-side of Hasè, there
In its greater valleys || Setting on high your flags,
In its smaller valleys || Setting on high your flags,
This my great valley || Have you now discovered?
Well-away, my beloved wife! || Like a tsuki-bow,
Lying before me prostrate, || Like a cherry-bow,
Standing upright before me, || Now, afterward, I see you.
Wellaway, my beloved wife! [53]

Also he made this song for her:

On the far-withdrawn || River-bank of Hasè, there
In its upper stream || Driving sacred piling,
In its lower stream || Driving the true piling,
On that true piling || Hanging up a mirror,
On the true piling || Hanging the true jewels—
Like those true jewels || My dear younger sister.
Like to that mirror || My wife so beloved.
If they said || That you were thus engaged,[54]
Then would I go to my home—|| Then would I pine for mine own Land!

(These two songs are to be read.) Afterward the pair slew themselves together.

Now the King of Silla, in sorrow for the Sovereign's death, sent eighty vessels bearing tribute and eighty musicians of all grades, who, when they arrived at Port-Island and at Tsukushi, wailed exceedingly. They came to anchor in the harbor of Wave-Swift, and donning white robes, with the tribute-gifts and various musical instruments, they journeyed to the capital, wailing, singing and dancing, till they came to the temporary burial-place. Then when the burial ceremonies were finished they started to return home. The Silla men loved Mount Miminashi and Mount Unebi, close by the capital, and when they came to the hill of Katobiki they looked back, exclaiming, "Unemè haya! Mimi haya!" In their ignorance of the language they mispronounced the words, and the Horse-Tender-Clan of Mountain-Gate, who conducted them, when they heard, believed that they had had intercourse with the Neck-Clan,[55] and returned and made report to Great-Hasè, who straightway imprisoned and examined them. When they declared, however, that they had not wronged the Neck-Clan, but had spoken only from love of the two hills, they let them go. Nevertheless the Silla people were angry and sent fewer vessels and less tribute.

THE EMPEROR ANAHO
(PEACE-TRANQUILITY [56])

The Sovereign Anaho dwelt in the Palace of Anaho at Above-the-Rock and ruled the empire. His younger brother, Great-Hasè, desired to wed the daughters [57] of the Sovereign Beautiful-Teeth-Lord-of-Knot-Grass, but they answered, "You are a violent lord, prone to quick anger, who slays at evening whom you see in the morning and slays in the morning whom you see at evening. We, your slaves, have no great beauty nor are we wise, and if either our actions or our words should by ever so little displease your imperial desires, you would not take us. Therefore we cannot obey." So always they avoided him and would not listen. Then the Sovereign, desiring to give Young-Lady-of-Hatabi,[58] younger sister of Great-Lord-of-Hatabi, to Great-Hasè as a consort, sent

MAGNATE-OF-NE [59]

to Great-Lord-of-Hatabi's dwelling, to say for him, "I beg you to grant me, as wife to Great-Hasè, your younger sister, Great-Lady-of-Hatabi." Great-Lord-of-Hatabi answered, "I have been for some time ill of a disease which cannot be cured and am like a laden junk waiting its sailing. I dread not death, which is the common lot, but fear to die leaving my younger sister alone and uncared-for. Thinking her presence might be commanded, I have retained her, not suffering her to leave my house. If the Sovereign does not despise her homeliness but would permit her to be counted among the marsh-flowers, I shall offer her with gratitude and awe." Also, lest he seem to lack respect, he sent as a gift of ceremony from Great-Lady-of-Hatabi a jewel head-dress of oshi wood, saying, "This is of no value, but may show my heart."

Magnate-of-Ne, seeing its beauty, desired to steal the treasure for himself, and going to the Sovereign, slandered Great-Lord-of-Hatabi to him, alleging that he had refused to receive the imperial command, saying, "Shall my sister be made the mat under a man like him?" and had in anger seized the hilt of his cross-sword. The Sovereign credited this, and in great wrath raised an army and surrounded the dwelling of Great-Lord-of-Hatabi, and slew him.

Now there were a father with two sons, Kishi [60] of Wave-Swift, named

HIKAKA

who were servants of Great-Lord-of-Hatabi and lamented his innocent death. The father lifted the dead man's head and each of the two sons lifted one of his legs, and cried loudly, "Alas our Lord has innocently died! Now we three, who served him while he lived, will die also; thus shall we be loyal servants!" Thereon they cut their throats and died beside him, at which every man in the imperial army wept. Then the

---

[59] **Ancestor of the Magnates of Sakamoto.**

Sovereign took Great-Lord-of-Hatabi's chief wife, Great-Lady-of-Long-Ricefield [61] and brought her to the palace and made her his concubine and later his Empress, loving her greatly. Before this time Great-Lady-of-Long-Ricefield had given birth, by Great-Lord-of-Hatabi, to a son who was named

PRINCE MAYUWA [62]

who, for his mother's sake, was not punished, but was reared at the palace.

Now Great-Hasè made a journey, by way of the Straight-Cross Road of Kusaka, into Kawachi, and having ascended a mountain, as he was gazing from its top into the Land, he beheld a dwelling with a gable shaped like a dried bonito. He sent someone to ask whose it was, and was told that it was the dwelling of the Great District-Chief of Stone-Castle. Said he, then, "Does a slave build his dwelling after the pattern of the imperial palace?" And he sent men to burn the house, but the Great District-Chief, trembling with fear and with bowed head, said, "I am but a slave and like a slave am ignorant, and have built over-much. This gives me awe." And he offered as an entreaty-present a white dog, tied in a cloth and carrying a bell. He bade one of his relatives, a certain

LOIN-BELTED

to lead it on a leash and offer it, on which Great-Hasè bade them desist from the burning. Then, journeying to the dwelling of Young-Lady-of-Hatabi, Great-Hasè sent her the dog as a present, with a message, saying, "Today, on my way, I secured this strange thing, and make it one with which to pay my suit." She sent back to him the message, "For you to journey with your back to the sun is a fearful thing, so I will come at once and respectfully serve you." When he went back to the palace, he stood on the mountain's slope and sang:

'Twixt Mount Kusaka, || The nearer mountain height,
And the . . .[63] || Mountain height of Heguri,
The further mountain, || In the mountain-valley
Grows the fruitful stem || Of the broad-foliaged oak tree.
Beneath springs || The bamboo interweaving;
Above it springs || Bamboo all luxuriant.
Like to the bamboo || We sleep not thus twining,
Like luxuriant || Bamboo, we sleep not soundly.
But later twining, || O my wife so beloved,
We shall sleep!

He sent a messenger back to her with this song.

Great-Hasè made a pleasure-journey to Three-Threads River and on its bank there was a damsel of exceeding beauty washing clothes. He asked her whose child she was, and she replied, "My name is

BOAR-CHILD

of the Hiketa-Clan." He caused a message to be given her which said, "Do not take a husband. I will send for you." And he returned to the palace. Again he visited the Palace of Good-Moor and on the bank of the Good-Moor River was a lovely damsel. Her he wedded and returned. Later, going again to Good-Moor, he stopped where they had met, and setting there his great august couch, seated himself and playing his august koto, bade her dance. Then, in praise of her excellent dance, he sang:

> On the august couch || Now the hand of the Kami
> Plays on the koto.
> Ah, that the damsel's dancing || Might thus continue for aye! [64]

PRINCE-MAYUWA SLAYS THE SOVEREIGN

Now the Sovereign visited a palace on the mountain to take hot baths, where, going up into a tall tower to enjoy the view, he called for sakè and made a feast. While he was at ease and in enjoyment, he said to the Empress, "Have you something on your mind?" She answered, "Since I am so generously favored by you, what can be on my mind?" Said he, "I have always something on my mind. O Younger Sister,[65] you are my friend, but I fear Prince-Mayuwa, for he is the child of Great-Lord-of-Hatabi, whom I, heeding the slander of Magnate-of-Ne, put to death. And I fear, when he is become a man, learning of it, he may with an evil heart reward me."

Prince-Mayuwa, who was then a child only seven years old, was playing under the tower, and heard, and watching till the Sovereign, drunk, fell asleep at midday with the Empress's knees for a pillow, he took the great sword beside him and cut off his head. At which one of the high-retainers ran to Great-Hasè, saying, "The Sovereign has been slain by Prince-Mayuwa." Great-Hasè, who was then a lad, although endowed with great strength, shocked and angered, and suspicious of his elder brothers, armed himself and took his sword, and leading his troops, went to King-Prince-White-of-Eight-Melons,[66] and said sternly, "They have slain the Sovereign. What is to be done?" The other, seeing that he meant him harm, said nothing, but sat with unshaken heart, when Great-Hasè upbraided him, saying, "Not only the Sovereign, but your elder brother. What! Can your heart not be relied on, that you are unconcerned on hearing of the slaying of your elder brother?" Then he seized him by the collar and dragging him forth, slew him with his sword. He then went to his elder brother, King-Prince-Black-of-Border, and questioned him earnestly likewise, but that one also saw that the other meant him harm and sat with unshaken heart as King-Prince-White-of-Eight-Melons had done.

At this Great-Hasè's anger waxed even greater, and having in mind to kill also Prince-Mayuwa, he questioned him, when Prince-Mayuwa said, "Your slave has never sought the imperial rule, but has dealt vengeance upon the enemy of his father." King-Prince-Black-of-Border then, fearing that he was suspected, secretly sent word to Prince-Mayuwa and both fled together to the dwelling of

GREAT-MAGNATE-TSUBURA.

(Some say, however, that Prince-Mayuwa fled there alone, and that Great-Hasè, clutching King-Prince-Black-of-Border by the collar, dragged him forth to New-Tilled-Ricefield, where he had a pit dug, in which he buried him, standing, to the middle, when both his eyes burst out and he died.)

Great-Hasè then raised an army, and sending to the dwelling of Great-Magnate-Tsubura, demanded the pair. But he answered, "From of old I have heard of subjects in trouble taking refuge in imperial palaces, but never of princes hiding in the dwellings of subjects. King-Prince-Black-of-Border and Prince-Mayuwa, confident of your slave's heart, have entered his house and it is not in my heart to send them away, since I believe that while a mean slave, however he fight, may hardly be victorious, yet he should rather die than desert a prince who has trusted him." At that Great-Hasè summoned more troops and surrounded the dwelling, when Great-Magnate-Tsubura came into the courtyard and tied on his leggings. Then his wife, who had brought them, in grief, sang:

> Ah, the Magnate's child, || Having put on his trousers,
> Woven seven-fold, || Standing within the courtyard,
> Now adjusts his leggings!

Great-Magnate-Tsubura had also raised an army to beat them off and the arrows came like the falling of grasses. Then Great-Hasè, using his spear for a staff, peered in, saying, "The damsel I spoke with—is she perhaps in this dwelling?" So Great-Magnate-Tsubura, now fully dressed, hearing these imperial words, came to the gate of the stronghold, and, taking off the weapons he wore, knelt and prostrating himself eight times, said he, "It was said of old time that one cannot destroy the will of even a common man,[67] and thus it is with your slave.

PRINCESS-KARA

my daughter, to whom you have deigned to pay suit, awaits you. I humbly pray you imperially to receive her, with the five (or, as some say, seven)

Granaries of Mulberry-Castle, which I offer you besides, as quittance." (These Granaries are now the five Gardener [68]-Villages of Mulberry-Castle.) Great-Hasè, however, would not grant this, and Great-Magnate-Tsubura took his weapons and re-entered to fight. Then, when they had no more strength or arrows, he said to Prince-Mayuwa, "All our people are wounded and we have no more arrows. What now?" He replied, "Then nothing remains but to slay me." So Great-Magnate-Tsubura slew him with his sword and slew himself by cutting off his own head, after which Great-Hasè fired the dwelling and burned it, and all were consumed together.

(Some have it that King-Prince-Black-of-Border also died at this time in the fire.)

NOBLE-OF-NIYE

Tribe-Master of the Sakahi-Clan, holding Prince-Mayuwa's body in his arms, also was burned to death. His family gathered the burned remains but they could not separate the bones, so all were put into the same coffin and buried on the hill south of Tsukimoto in Han-of-New-Comer.[69] The Sovereign Anaho is buried in the Mound of Lying-See [70] at Sedge-Moor,[71] in Mountain-Gate Province.

This Mound of Lying-See is so called because a man once lay down upon it and neither rose up nor spoke a word during three years, from which he was believed to be dumb. He lifted his head only, and gazed toward the east. After three years, however, he rose up and danced, singing, "Now is the exact time! Now is the exact time!" People did not know what he meant nor his place of residence, and called him Venerable-Man-of-Lying-See.[A] The reference is no doubt to the man's having looked constantly toward the east.

THE EMPEROR GREAT-HASÈ
(MANLY-PLAN [72])

GREAT-HASÈ SLAYS PRINCE-PUSH-TEETH-OF-NEAR-THE-MARKET

Great-Hasè was angered because the Sovereign Anaho had desired to give the imperial rule to Prince-Push-Teeth-of-Near-the-Market,[73] so he sent a messenger to the latter to arrange deceitfully a hunt on the moor, and to say to him that

NOBLE-OF-KARA-BAG [74]

> [74] Ancestor of the Clan-Chiefs of Mount-Sasaki (in Omi Province).*

* See p. 418.

Clan-Chief of Mount-Sasaki, in Omi, reported that on the Kaya moor in Kutawata were many boar and deer, with horns like withered tree-branches, legs thick as reeds [75] and breath like morning mist. That now, in the beginning of winter, with the sky overcast and a cold wind, Great-Hasè would go with him to the moor, to take their pleasure in riding and bow-play. So Prince-Push-Teeth-of-Near-the-Market went with Great-Hasè to the hunt, and when they were come to the moor, each built a temporary palace to rest in.

Next morning, before dawn, Prince-Push-Teeth-of-Near-the-Market rode horseback, with a peaceful heart, to Great-Hasè's temporary palace, where he said to the latter's attendants, "Has he not yet awakened? Inform him at once that the night's dawning is over, and that he should come to the hunt." So saying, he spurred on. Then Great-Hasè put armor under his clothing, took his bow and arrows and mounted his horse. And while they waited he galloped up, and crying falsely, "There is a boar!" shot Prince-Push-Teeth-of-Near-the-Market dead.

Now

URUWA [76]

of the Saheki-Clan, who was one of the servitors of Prince-Push-Teeth-of-Near-the-Market, was so frightened that he did not know what he did. He took the body in his arms, trembling and crying aloud, and Great-Hasè slew him also. Then he cut up the body of Prince-Push-Teeth-of-Near-the Market, put it into a horse's food-box, and buried it, with that of Uruwa, in the same grave, without a mound.

> (By some it is said, however, that Great-Hasè made the hunt without evil intent, but that when he was about to ride forth, his servitors said to him, "Prince-Push-Teeth-of-Near-the-Market talks violently. Be on guard, therefore, and go armed." So, being thus made suspicious, he shot the other.)

The two sons of Prince-Push-Teeth-of-Near-the-Market, King-Big-Basket and King-Little-Basket,[77] learning that their father had been thus slain, fled in fear to hiding.

OMI

Tribe-Master of the Kusaka-Clan, an attendant, together with his son

PRINCE-ADA

secretly assisted them and they fled to Cut-Leaf-Well [78] in Behind-the-Mountains. There, when they partook of food, an old man whose face was marked with ink [79] came and seized it. Said they, "You are welcome to the food. Who are you?" He answered that he was a swine-herd of

Behind-the-Mountains. Then they fled across Dung-Trousers [80] River to the District of Yosa in the Land of Tamba. Omi changed his name to Tatoku, but nevertheless, *knowing his crime was serious, and* fearing he would be slain, he *cut his horse's tendons and freed him, burned his saddle and other articles, and* fled to a cavern in Mount-Shijimi in Harima Province, where he strangled (or, as some say, hanged) himself. King-Little-Basket, ignorant of his whereabouts, prevailed on his elder brother to go with him to the same province, *and they hid themselves and wandered now east, now west,* until in the District of Akashi, having changed their names to Lad-of-Tamba, they entered the dwelling of

HOSOME [81]

Ruler of the Oshinomi-Clan, head-man of the Shijimi Granaries. Prince-Ada went with them, remaining their faithful slave, and there, in concealment, they toiled as grooms and cattle-herders.

Afterward Prince-August-Horses,[82] being fond of Musa, which place was the property of the Clan-Chief of Three-Threads, went there to lighten his spirits. An army which was sent against him met him unawares and he fought them at Well-of-Iwa, in Three-Threads, but was taken. When he was put to death he called a curse on the well, by which its water might not after that be drunk by those of imperial rank, but only by the people. The Sovereign appointed officers to build a great pavilion at Morning-Storehouse [83] in Hasè, where he established his palace, and made Young-Lady-of-Hatabi his Empress.

MATORI

Magnate of Heguri he made Great-Magnate, and Muruya, Tribe-Master of the imperial-guard and

ME

Tribe-Master of the Warrior-Clan, he made Great-Tribe-Masters.[84] He wedded also Princess-Kara, daughter of Great-Magnate Tsubura, in Mulberry-Castle, by whom he begot

WHITE-HAIR-BRAVE-WIDE-LAND-GREAT-YOUNG-MOUNTAIN-GATE-PRINCE [85]

(whose hair was white from his birth.)

PRINCESS-YOUNG-PERFECT.[86]

(The latter attended to the worship of the Great Kami at Isè.

---

[85] Ancestor (by proxy) of the Shiraka Clan.

Now he gave one night to a damsel of the Neck-Clan, named

OGUNA-KIMI

who was a daughter of the Magnate of Wani in Kasuga,

FUKU-ME.

She became pregnant and gave birth to a daughter, named

PRINCESS-GREAT-LADY-OF-KASUGA [87]

But, being suspicious,[88] he would not rear her.

Once, when the child could walk, the Sovereign was in the main apartment with Me, Great-Tribe-Master of the Warrior-Clan, and she passed through the courtyard. Me, turning, said to the Ministers, "A lovely girl! There is an old saying, 'You resemble your mother.'" (This old saying now is not well known.) "Whose child do they say she is, who walks slowly through the courtyard?" The Sovereign asked, "Why do you inquire?" Me replied, "To your slave this girl seems greatly to resemble the Sovereign." The latter replied, "All who see her say the same. But it is unheard-of that she to whom I gave but one night should conceive and bear a daughter. For this reason my suspicions were aroused." Me replied, "But in that one night how often had you connection with her?" "Seven times," replied the Sovereign. Said Me, "If this woman was of pure body and spirit and you gave her one night, why have you so easily become suspicious and unwilling to believe in her chastity? Your slave has heard of women who easily become pregnant, conceiving even by an embrace of the arms. How much more reason, when you gave her a whole night! You should not have suspicions without good cause." So the Sovereign bade the Great-Tribe-Master make the girl an imperial princess and made her mother his concubine.

Now it befell that Princess-Iketsu of Kudara, whom the Sovereign had purposed to take to wife, had a liaison with

TATE-OF-STONE-RIVER [89]

at which the Sovereign was greatly angered, and bade the Great-Tribe-Master Muruya of the imperial-guard take some of the Army-Clan and stretch their limbs between trees. A wardrobe was set on fire beneath and they were burned to death. Later, on hearing of this, the King of Kudara, instead of sending women as tribute for the Neck-Clan, sent his younger brother

KOMU-KISHI [90]

---

[89] **Ancestor of the Head-Men of Momoahi in Ishikawa.**

to serve the Sovereign, sending with him one of his own concubines who was pregnant. She gave birth to the child in the Island of Kahara, in Tsukushi, and Komu-Kishi sent the child back to Kudara. He became King Mu-Nyŏng. Then Komu-Kishi proceeded to the Capital. He had five children afterward.

Journeying to the Palace of Good-Moor, the Sovereign proceeded to Munasè, where he bade his wardens prepare a hunt. Over high mountains and across broad wildernesses they took before dark seven or eight out of ten,[91] so large being the catch through all the hunting that birds and beasts were almost gone. Then, bidding his attendants desist, while they rested and walked about by the springs and fields, he counted the vehicles and horses. Said he to his Ministers, "The joy of the hunt is when the stewards cut the fresh meat. Let us do this ourselves." The Ministers, wondering, made no reply, at which he was angry and drew his sword and slew the steward

MUMAKAÏ-OF-OTSU.

When the imperial party reached the Palace of Good-Moor, all the people of the province were in fear and trembling, and the Empress-Dowager and the Empress, when they learned it, were filled with dread, and sent Princess-of-Sun [92] of the Neck-Clan of Mountain-Gate, to offer him sakè.

At the sight of her lovely face and elegance, he was pleased, and looked upon her kindly, saying, "What a joy to see you so pleasantly smiling!" Then he took her hand and led her into the after-palace, where he said to the Empress-Dowager, "Today, hunting, We took many birds and beasts. We desired to cut the fresh meat with the Ministers and to banquet on the moor, but when We proposed this, none replied, at which We were angered." She, knowing his thought, said soothingly, "The Ministers did not perceive that you deigned in connection with the hunting to form a Butcher-Clan and to ask their thought; their silence was just, for reply was difficult. However, there is time still to make the offering. To begin myself, my steward

NAGANO

cuts up meat well, so I beg to offer him to you." And the Sovereign, kneeling, accepted him, saying, "Good!" (Thus arose the country saying, "Nobles know each other's inner hearts.") The Empress-Dowager was pleased at the Sovereign's satisfaction, and desiring to offer more men, said, "I have also two kitchen-men,

MASAKIDA
HIGH-SKY

of the Mito-Clan of Uda.⁹³ Deign to permit me to offer these two, in addition, to form a Butcher-Clan." From that time on

NOBLE-OF-AKOKO

Ruler of Mountain-Gate Province, sent some of the Katori Lords of Soho to form the Butcher-Clan. The Magnates, the Tribe-Masters, the Rulers of the imperial-guard and the Land-Rulers as well, in succession, later offered some persons. Also the Scribe-Clan and the Retainer-Clan of River-Kami were formed, the Hasè-Clan retainers and the Kawasè-retainers were established, and the Shiraka-Clan was formed as the proxy of White-Hair-Brave-Wide-Land-Great-Young-Mountain-Gate-Prince.⁹⁴

The Sovereign's inclination led him to slay many unjustly, so that the people of the Land blamed him, calling him "The greatly wicked Sovereign." None loved him save

AWO

Village-Master of Musa, who was of the Scribe-Clan, and

HAKATOKO

who was a village-employer ⁹⁵ of Hinokuma.

Now at this time the Magnate of Abè

KUNIMI ⁹⁶

spread abroad a slander concerning the imperial princess Young-Perfect ⁹⁷ and the Tribe-Master of the Ihoki-Clan, who was bath-master,

BRAVE-PRINCE

stating that they had had secret intercourse by which she was pregnant. Brave-Prince's father

KIKOYU

hearing this and fearing evil for himself, made Brave-Prince accompany him to the River Ihoki, where, on pretence of causing cormorants to catch fish by diving in the water, he took him unawares and slew him. The Sovereign, when he learned this, sent an inquiry to the princess, who replied that she knew nothing about it. But straightway, taking with her a sacred mirror, she went to River Kami, of Fifty-Bells,⁹⁸ and choosing a time when none passed there, buried it and hanged herself. Wondering at her absence, the Sovereign sent men over by night to search everywhere. When they reached River Kami there appeared a rainbow, shaped like a serpent twelve or fifteen shaku long. Digging where the rainbow appeared, they found the sacred mirror and near by the princess' body. This they cut open for examination and found in her belly something like water in which was a stone. By this Kikoyu was able to prove that Brave-Prince was innocent and grieved that he had slain him, and for revenge slew Kunimi and fled for hiding to the Shrine of Above-the-Rock.

THE KAMI ONE-WORD-MASTER REVEALS HIMSELF TO THE SOVEREIGN

Once the Sovereign repaired to Mount Mulberry-Castle to hunt with bow and arrow, all the one hundred officials being clad in green-rubbed garments with red cords, that had been granted them. Presently there appeared people ascending the opposite slope of the mountain, in order exactly like the Sovereign's retinue, and also the style of clothing and the people themselves were similar and . . . .[99] When, behold, a tall man appeared who came and took his stand over Red-Valley,[1] in appearance and movement like the Sovereign, who sent to ask, "Since I alone am king in Mountain-Gate, who are you who proceeds in this manner?" The reply being that of a Sovereign, Great-Hasè was angered and fixed his arrow, and all his attendants did the same, whereon the other people fixed their arrows likewise. Then the Sovereign again made inquiry, saying, "Tell me your name! Let each one tell his name and then shoot an arrow." To this the reply was, "I being first asked, will first tell mine. I am the Kami who with one word puts aside evil and with one word puts aside good. I am the Great Kami of Mulberry-Castle

ONE-WORD-MASTER [2]

son of Brave-Swift-Impetuous-Male."

(Some say, however, that the Sovereign first told his name, whereon the Kami announced his own.)

At that the Sovereign trembled, knowing him a Kami, and asked, "Of what place are you, Lord?" The tall man replied, "I am a Kami of visible men." Then the Sovereign said, "I do the Great Kami reverence. I did not understand that your great Person would be present." And with these words he took off first his august sword and his bow and arrows and reverently offered them, together with the garments worn by the one hundred officers. One-Word-Master clapped his hands and accepted them, joining afterward in the hunting. When a deer was pursued each waited for the other to shoot. So they rode, their bits touching, in reverential conversation like that of spirits, till the sun set and the hunting ended. When the Sovereign returned from the mountain, the Kami accompanied him to its mouth, as far as Kumè-Water. Thus did the great Kami One-Word-Master announce himself, and all the people said, "What great virtues has the Sovereign!"

At another time the Sovereign repaired to Small-Moor of Upper-River for a hunt, and sitting on his august couch, bade his forest-wardens drive the wild game. As he waited to shoot, a horse-fly came flying swiftly and stung him on the elbow, but a dragon-fly came at once and stung the horse-fly and carried it off. Pleased at its action, the Sovereign bade his Ministers compose for him a poem in the dragon-fly's praise, but none dared, when he straightway composed this stanza: [3]

>   At August Good-Moor, || On the peak of Little-Cave,
>   That boars are lying || Who was it
>   In the Great Presence reported? || The mighty Sovereign
>   Who tranquilly governs, || Waited the wild-boar
>   On his august couch seated, || When in his fore-arm,
>   Clad in its sleeve of white, || A horse-fly, 'lighting,
>   Wickedly stings him. || But, behold, comes
>   A dragon-fly, who straightway || Stings the horse-fly.
>   That thus it should be famed, || The sky-filling
>   Land of Mountain-Gate was called || The Isle of the Dragon-Fly.

(Some say, however, that the last four lines of this poem were:

>   Even a creeping fly || Who guards the Great Lord,
>   Your form, Mountain-Gate, shall bear, || Land of the Dragon-Fly!)

(In honor of the Dragon-Fly, therefore, that place was called Dragon-Fly-Moor.)

Again the Sovereign visited the peak of Mount Mulberry-Castle to hunt, when there appeared a divine bird, of the size of a swallow, whose tail was so long that it touched the ground, which sang, "Be on your guard! Be on your guard!" And lo, there rushed from the trees a furious boar which they were hunting, and made for his attendants, who, in great fear, climbed trees.

(Some [4] say, to the contrary, that it was the Sovereign himself who climbed a tree.)

Then the Sovereign said to them, "When fierce beasts come upon men, they are to be stopped with bow-shots and sword-wounds." But the attendants, like women, though they were in the trees, paled and lost their five senses, so that the furious boar kept his course, roaring, and would have gored the Sovereign. But the latter straightway shot it with a humming-arrow so that it stopped, when with his foot he kicked it to death. So, the hunt being ended, he determined to slay the attendants, who, when led to execution, sang:

>   O our Great Sovereign, || Who so tranquilly rules
>   You did forthwith shoot || The roaring,
>   The wounded wild-boar, || While we, in dreadful terror,
>   In flight did climb || On Barren-Mound,
>   You, Alder-Limb— || O like an Elder Brother you! [5]

The Empress grieved for them and would have prevented it, but the Sovereign said, "Do you, the Empress, protect my attendants rather than your Sovereign?" She replied, "People say the Sovereign loves the hunting. This is not well."

At another time he repaired to Kasuga, where he wedded

PRINCESS-ODO

the daughter of the Magnate of Wani, who was named

SATSUKI.

On the way a damsel met him, who, at sight of the imperial cortège, ran away and hid on a hillock, whereon he sang:

> On the hillock, || See, the maiden is hiding!
> With spades of metal, || Had we but five hundred,
> Ah, then we might unearth her!

Again he proceeded to a small moor of Hasè, where, at sight of the hills and moors, he sang:

> The further withdrawn || Mountain-ranges of Hasè,
> They project themselves, || Mountains admirable:
> They hasten forward, || Ranges admirable.
> The further withdrawn || Mountain-ranges of Hasè—
> Ah, how abounding in beauty!

(Then he named the small moor Small-Moor-of-Road.)

THE LEAF IN THE AUGUST CUP

He there made an abundant, wine-bright feast under a tsuki tree of a hundred branches, when a female attendant from Three-Fold, in the Land of Isè, offered him a great drinking cup. Now a leaf fell from the tree and floated in the cup, and she, unknowingly, still offered it to him, who, seeing in it the floating leaf, struck her prostrate and aiming his sword at her neck was about to cut off her head, when she said, "Do not slay me. I have something to say to you." And she sang:

> At Makimuka, || The Palace of Hishiro,
> In the morning || Shining in the sun,
> In the evening || Lit by the setting-sun,
> Like the bamboo-root, || Plenteously rooted,
> Like the tree roots, || Spreading out its roots,
> Ah, eight-hundred-fold || Of earth is this palace builded.
> Its august gate || Of true-tree-splitting
> Hinoki wood anear, || Grows hundred-branched
> Tsuki, beside || The new-tasting house.[6]
> The topmost branch || Has the sky above it:
> The middle branches || They have the east above them:

> The lowest branch || Has the country above.
> Behold, a leaf || From the topmost branch-tip
> Falls and strikes || Against the middle branch,
> Down from whose tip || Falls a leaf, striking
> Against the lowest, || From whose tip falls
> A leaf in the oil— || In the fresh, jewelled goblet
> Which the Miyè damsel || Lifts on high to you.
> *Kowóro-kowóro* it goes. || Ah, this thing
> Very terrible is it! || O you high-shining
> August Sun-Child! || Let this song,
> To far tradition bear this event!

Through her offering this song, her crime was pardoned. Then the Empress made this song:

> At Mountain-Gate || In the high capital,
> The wide-timbered || Hillock of the city,
> By the new-tasting house, || Stands, broad-foliaged,
> A hundred-branched true camellia. || Like to its leaves,
> Spreading broad and burnished, || Like to its blossoms,
> Shining in brilliance, || Stands the Sovereign.
> To the august Sun-Child, || Rich august sakè
> Bring ye forth and offer! || Let this song
> To far tradition bear this event!

Whereon the Sovereign made this song in reply:

> Folk of the palace || (The mighty hundred-castled [7]),
> Like as the quail do || Putting upon them their scarfs,
> Like to the wagtails || Setting tail to tail,
> Like garden-sparrows || Gathering here together,
> May perhaps this day || Be truly soaked in sakè.
> Folk of the palace || Of the high-shining Sun!
> Let this song || To far tradition bear this event!

(These three songs are Sky-Word Songs.) At this abundant, wine-bright feast, the female attendant of Miyè was given praise and great gifts. Also on this day, Princess-Odo offered the Sovereign the great august sakè, when he sang:

> O . . . .[8] || Daughter of the Magnate,
> Holding the mighty flagon! || Hold the mighty flagon,
> Hold it with all firmness; || Hold firm its base,
> Hold it even more firmly, || Child holding the great flagon!

(This is a floating song.)[9] Then Princess-Odo sang:

> Our mighty Sovereign || Who tranquilly governs
> Stands at the door || In the morning, leaning—
> Stands at the door || In the evening, leaning
> Upon the arm-rest || Whose low rail would
> (Ah, elder brother!) || That I were!

(This is a tranquil song.)

The Sovereign desired the Empress and his concubines to plant mulberry-trees to assist the making of silk. So he ordered one

SUGARU

to gather silkworms [10] throughout the land. Sugaru, however, mistakenly gathered infants,[11] which he offered to the Sovereign, who, laughing heartily, gave them back, bidding Sugaru care for them himself. So the latter cared for them near the palace compound, and was given the title Tribe-Master of the Little-Child-Clan.[12] At this time the Land of Go [13] sent Envoys bearing tribute.

Now

PRINCE-COMPANION [14]

had a good maid-servant and a good horse of which he was fond, and when he was about to die, he said to his son, "After my death do you bury them like myself." So their tombs were made, the first for Prince-Companion, the second for the maid-servant, and the third for the horse: there were three in all. Later

OISHI

Governor of the province, dug a pool close by one of the tombs which he named Pool-of-Horse-Tomb.^A

THE KAMI OF MOUNT AUGUST-HOUSE

It befell that the Sovereign said to Sugaru, "I wish to see the form of the Kami of Mount August-House.[15] You are of greatest bodily strength. Go and seize him and bring him here." Sugaru replied, "That I will try." Then, climbing Mount August-House, he caught a huge serpent [16] and exhibited it to the Sovereign, who, because he had not restrained himself, when it caused thunder and flame came from its eyes, was in fear, and covered his eyes from it and ran into the palace. Later he commanded that it be loosed on the mountain and named it, anew, Thunder.[17]

Now an attendant of the Bow-Maker-Clan of Maise named

GREAT-VOID

went to his home for some pressing cause and was kept there for some months by

SAKITSUYA

Magnate of Lower-Maise, who would not let him return to the capital, so that the Clan-Chief of Mikè, who was a brave man, was sent to bring

---

14 **Ancestor of the Tribe-Masters of Owari.**

him. Thus summoned, Great-Void came, and reported that Sakitsuya had taken young damsels whom he called the Sovereign's men, and grown women whom he called his own men, and caused them to fight together; and when the young damsels won, he slew them with his sword. Again he took small cocks which he dubbed the Sovereign's cocks, which he plucked and whose wings he cut, and large cocks which he called his own cocks on which he hung bells and whose spurs he covered with metal, and made these fight together; and when the plucked cocks won, he slew them also with his sword. When he heard this the Sovereign sent thirty soldiers of the Army-Clan who slew Sakitsuya and seventy members of his household.

(Some, however, say that he who thus acted and was thus punished was the Magnate-of-Maise, the Land-Ruler,

YAMA.)

Now the Magnate of Upper-Maise whose name was

TASA

was at this time in attendance at the palace, and he had for wife

PRINCESS-YOUNG [18]

daughter of Noble-of-Jewel-Ricefield,[19] Magnate-of-Upper-Maise (or, as some say, of the Magnate of Kuboya, in Maise) by whom he had begotten

ELDER-CLAN-CHIEF
YOUNGER-CLAN-CHIEF.

He praised her excessively to his friends, saying, "My wife is incomparably the loveliest woman in the land. Is she not youthful and mild, with all attractions joyful and pleasant? Is not her face all perfect, without whitelead or extract of orchid? Never in the past was her equal, nor can she now be matched!" The Sovereign, hearing this indirectly, was secretly pleased, and desirous of making Princess-Young his own concubine, made Tasa Governor of Mimana,[20] and took her (or, as some hold, slew Tasa and wedded her). By her he begot

IWASHIRO [21]

(who some say was her son by Tasa)

YOUNG-MIYA-OF-HOSHI-RIVER.

After Tasa came to Mimana, he learned that the Sovereign had taken his wife, and went for assistance to Silla. At that time Silla was not subservient to the central Land, and the Sovereign bade Younger-Clan-Chief and

AKAWO

Governor of the Fishermen of Maise, to punish it. Two skilful workmen of the western [22] Han-folk, named Kwan-In and Chi-Ri, who were at hand, said to him, "The Han-Land has many more skilful than we your slaves are and they should be sent for to serve you." So the Sovereign bade the two go with Younger-Clan-Chief and the rest, through Kudara, and sent an order commanding the latter country to make offerings of skilful people. So Younger-Clan-Chief proceeded with a company of men to Kudara, but when he entered that Land, one of its Kami straightway met him on the road, in the form of an old crone, who, when he asked whether the Land [23] was near or distant, replied that he would arrive there within another day. Deeming it too distant, he returned, leaving it unpunished. He gathered on a great island the new skilful workmen offered as tribute by Kudara, and stayed there some months, alleging that he waited a favorable wind. Tasa, the Governor of Mimana, was pleased at his departure without having punished Silla, and sent privately to warn him, saying, "Your own head must be firmly fixed for you to punish others. I hear that the Sovereign has taken my wife and begotten children by her, and fearing evil, I wait to take a step. Since you are my son, cross into Kudara and let it not send word to Nippon; I will go to Mimana and take it and likewise will let it send no word." The wife of Younger-Clan-Chief, who was named

PRINCESS-KUSU

however, disapproving this treason, slew him by a ruse and buried him secretly in his room, she herself remaining at the great island with Akawo, in charge of the skilled workmen offered by Kudara.

> (Some say to the contrary, that Princess-Kusu did not slay him, but that Younger-Clan-Chief came back from Kudara, and offered a Han-Workman-Clan, a Tailor-Clan, and a Butcher-Clan.[24])

The Sovereign, when he learned of the disappearance of Younger-Clan-Chief, sent

KATASHIHA

the Kishi [25] of Hitaka, together with one named Ko-Au-Chon, who made report, and the workmen were finally placed in Village-of-Hirokitsu, in Ato, in Mountain-Gate Province. Since many of them fell sick and died, the Sovereign bade Muruya, Great-Tribe-Master of the imperial-guard, order

TSU-KAMI

Governor of the Han-folk of Mountain-Gate, to take of the new Han-folk Ko-Kwi and Kyon-Kwi (members respectively of the Potter-Clan and the Saddler-Clan), Insa-Raka and Chong-Ana (of the Painter-[26] Clan and the Brocade-Weaver-Clan) together with Myo-Ana, an interpreter, and to place them in Upper- and Lower-Momohara and Plain-of-Magami. At this time Awo and Hakatoko [27] were sent to the Land of Go.

During these eight years of the Sovereign's reign Silla was rebellious and spoke foolishly and sent no tribute, but fearing the central Land, made friends with Koma, which finally overran it. At that the king of Silla sent to the king of Mimana asking aid from the authorities of Nippon and the king of Mimana accordingly urged the Magnates of Kashiwadè [28] and of Maise

IGARUKA
ONASHI

together with the Kishi of Wave-Swift, who was named

AKAMEKO

to go to Silla's assistance, and these attacked and routed the Koma troops. At this time, also,

PERFUME-GIVER

Governor of Ofushi-Kawachi, and a woman of the Neck-Clan were sent to offer worship to the Kami of Body-Form, but when they came to the garden of the Kami and were ready for the ceremony, he lay with her. The Sovereign, learning this, despatched the Kishi of Hidaka in Wave-Swift to slay him, but he fled and could not be found. So he then sent

TOYOHO

Tribe-Master of the Bow-Makers, who, having searched the distant parts of the province, took him at Blue-Plain [29] in the District of Three-Islands, and slew him.

The Sovereign would himself have chastised Silla, but a Kami counseled him not to go, so he gave up the plan, and appointing as generals

NOBLE-OF-OYUMI-OF-TREE
NOBLE-OF-KARAKO-OF-SOGA

Tribe-Master of the Reciters, of the imperial guard, and

NOBLE-OF-OKAÏ,

bade them take imperial troops and do so. However, Noble-of-Oyumi-of-

Tree said to Muruya, "Your weak and foolish slave will respectfully obey the imperial command. But his wife is dead and he has none to cherish him. I pray you, lay the matter before the Sovereign." When this was done, the Sovereign sighed in sympathy and gave to him

GREAT-SEA

a woman of the Neck-Clan of Nearer-Maise, to cherish him. Thus encouragingly he sent him forward. So Noble-of-Oyumi-of-Tree and the others invaded Silla, slaying in the districts as they went, and conquered the land of Tok, at which the king of Silla fled. Then, joining Noble-of-Karako-of-Soga, and the rest, Noble-of-Oyumi-of-Tree attacked the remainder of the army,

MOUND-FRONT-OF-TREE

Tribe-Master of the Army Clan, being slain that night in valiant fight. Later both sides retreated.

Noble-of-Oyumi-of-Tree died of an illness and his son

NOBLE-OF-OÏHA-OF-TREE

proceeded to Silla and took from Noble-of-Okaï his cavalry, infantry and vessels, and assumed supreme command. For this reason the other hated him and reported falsely to Noble-of-Karako-of-Soga that Noble-of-Oïha-of-Tree had declared he would soon do the same in his case, begging him to beware. So that Noble-of-Karako-of-Soga abandoned his friendship for Noble-of-Oïha-of-Tree. The king of Kudara heard of this and sent to them, asking them to come to him so that they might together view the border of the land. Noble-of-Karako-of-Soga, therefore, with the others, rode bit to bit to the river, where Noble-of-Oïha-of-Tree let his horse drink, when the other shot at him from the rear, piercing the back of his saddle. Then Noble-of-Oïha-of-Tree, startled, turned and shot Noble-of-Karako-of-Soga, who fell in the middle of the river and died. Thus the three Magnates, being at first rivals, quarreled on the journey and went back without having reached the king of Silla's palace.

Now Great-Sea came to Nippon with the dead body of Noble-of-Oyumi-of-Tree and made complaint to Muruya, Great-Tribe-Master of the imperial-guard, saying, "Your slave knows no burial-place and I pray that a favorable one be chosen by divination." This being reported, the Sovereign commanded that officials be appointed to arrange the funeral, and Muruya despatched

OTORI

Tribe-Master of the Clay-Worker Clan, to erect a mound at the Village of Tamuwa, where the burial should be. Whereon Great-Sea, overflowing with joy, sent the Great-Tribe-Master six slaves [30] from Kara, named Muro, Temaro, Otomaro, Mikura, Wogura and Hari. Noble-of-Okaï attended the body, but himself remained in the Land of Tsuno, sending to Muruya, by the hand of the Tribe-Master

MOUNTAIN-GATE-CHILD

an eight-sided mirror, with this prayer: "Your slave cannot serve the imperial court in company with Noble-of-Oïha-of-Tree, therefore he begs that he be permitted to keep his residence in the Land of Tsuno." This the Sovereign granted. (Thus it was that the Magnates of Tsuno first came to reside in that Land.)

Now there was in the Province of Kawachi, in the District of Asukabè, one H'yakuson,[31] Scribe of Tanabè, whose daughter was given as wife to Kar'yu,[31] a scribe of the District of Furuchi. Hearing that she had borne a child, he paid her a ceremonial visit at Kar'yu's house, and returning by moonlight past the foot of the mound of Great-Elbow-Pad-Lord at Ichihiko Hill, met a man riding a red horse, that ran with extraordinary lightness and speed, like a soaring dragon,[32] or a wild-goose in flight. Seeing it, H'yakuson desired to have it, so he urged on his own spotted horse alongside the other. But being slow, it fell behind and was unable to overtake it. The other rider, however, knew his desire and stopped and traded horses with him. So they parted, and H'yakuson, rejoicing, went home, where he stabled the horse and unsaddled and fed him, after which he slept. In the morning there, instead of the red horse, was a horse of clay, and wondering, H'yakuson returned and found his spotted horse standing with the clay horses.[33] So he took it away, leaving instead the clay horse for which he had traded it.

Now it happened that Awo,[34] Village-Master of Musa, came to Tsukushi with two geese offered by the Land of Go, and these were bitten to death by a dog of the Clan-Chief of Minuma

(or, as some say, by a dog belonging to

NIMARO

District-Chief of Minè in Tsukushi)

who, overflowing with fear and grief, offered the Sovereign ten large wild-geese with bird-keepers. At his prayer, the Sovereign permitted these to offset his crime. These bird-keepers were made to settle in Karu-Village and Iharè-Village. Likewise, it being reported from the District of Kurimoto, in Great-Sea Province, that white cormorants lived on the Tana-

---

[30] **Ancestors of the Roaster-Clan of Kashimada Village, in Nearer Kibi.**

gami Beach, order was given to establish retainers at River-Stream. At this time there came from Kudara the man called

KWISIN [35]

who was said to be of the Land of Go.

A man of Uda had a dog which bit to death a bird that belonged to the Bird-Department, at which the Sovereign, greatly angered, branded him on the face and made him a member of the Bird-Keeper-Clan. There were some laborers from Lime-Tree-Moor Province and Musashi Province, who were at night in the offices of the palace, and these said one to another, "What! While we pile up the birds of our Land as high as a burial-mound, eating them morning and evening and yet having some over, the Sovereign brands a man on the face because of a single bird? A most unfair and cruel ruler!" Hearing of this the Sovereign bade them gather birds and heap them up, and when they were unable at once to do so, he made them also members of the Bird-Keeper-Clan.

There was also a carpenter named

MITA-OF-TSUKÈ [36]

whom the Sovereign bade begin a high building. Climbing upon this, he ran swiftly hither and thither, like one flying, till at the sight, a woman of the Neck-Clan of Isè, startled to see him run so swiftly on the top of a building of such height, fell prostrate on her face in the courtyard, spilling a platter of meat with which she was to serve the Sovereign. At this the Sovereign fancied that Mita-of-Tsukè had had connection with the woman, and being of a mind to slay him, bade the Army-Clan do so. But

SAKÈ-OF-HADA,[37]

who attended the Sovereign, laying his koto crosswise (in order by its music to convey a meaning to the Sovereign) played it, and sang:

> Now to the damsel || Of Isè
> Of the Isè moor, || Divine-winded,
> For five hundred years be weal!
> And until that time has ended
> On the mighty lord, || Let me wait,
> With my most faithful service.
> And let my life also || Be as extended, too.
> So now prays the carpenter. || This miserable carpenter!

And the Sovereign, understanding the koto's voice, pardoned the fault.

---

[35] **Ancestor of the Koto-Players of Iharè-No Kurè and of the Yakata-Maro of Sakatè.**

HADANÈ

great-grandson of King-Prince-Saö,[38] had a secret liaison with

KOSHIMAKO-OF-MOUNTAIN-CLAN

of the Neck-Clan, and learning it, the Sovereign delivered him to Me, Great-Tribe-Master of the Army-Clan, commanding that he try him. Then Hadanè gained pardon by paying eight horses and eight swords, whereon he made a song which said:

> Ah, Kashimako- || Of-Mountain-Clan! For her sake,
> Let it be asserted || That eight horses in no wise
> Are e'er to be regretted.

Me, hearing this, reported it to the Sovereign, who bade Hadanè spread his valuables on the ground at Orange-Base, in Near-the-Market, in Yega. And in the end he gave to Me the Village-of-Long-Moor in Yega.

Now in Miwikuma in Harima Province was a man of strength and courage named

OMARO-OF-AYASHI

who plundered the roads and stopped traffic at his pleasure, arresting merchants' vessels and robbing them, and who contrary to the Land's law would not pay his tax. So the Sovereign sent

OÖKI

Magnate of Wono, in Kasuga, with a hundred troops fearless of death, who, surrounding his house, set fire to it with torches. From the flames there ran out a white dog, of the size of a horse, which in a fury attacked Oöki. The latter's courage, however, did not falter, and he slew it with his sword, whereon it was transformed into Omaro-of-Ayashi. There was likewise a carpenter of the Wina-Clan, named

MANÈ

who smoothed wood with an axe, making his line straight by means of a stone. All day he did this, without a false blow turning his edge. The Sovereign, coming there, asked him in wonder whether he did not sometimes by a false blow strike the stone. He replied that he never did. Thereon the Sovereign assembled the Neck-Clan and made them disrobe and wrestle in plain sight, wearing only loin-cloths. At this Manè paused awhile to watch, when, continuing his smoothing of the wood, his hand slipped and he ruined the ax's edge. At which the Sovereign said in censure, "From what arises this person's disrespect, whereby he replied so carelessly and with such a haughty spirit?" And he gave him over to the Army-Clan to be slain on the moor. His companion, a carpenter also, grieved for him and sang:

> Ah, the much-grieved-for, || The Wina-Clan carpenter
> Who here stretched out his ink-cord! || When he is not here,
> Who is there to stretch it out? || Alas, that grieved-for ink-cord!

Hearing, the Sovereign felt regret and said, sighing, "How nearly had I slain the man!" and mercifully setting a messenger on a black Kahi [39] horse, bade him ride to stop the slaying and pardon the man. So they took off the ropes that bound him, when he also sang:

> Dark as the night is || Was the black horse of Kahi,
> Had they saddled him, || Wasted then had been my life;
> He would have arrived too late. || Ah, that black Kahi horse!

Great-Sky-Shiner said in an oracle (or, as some say, to the Sovereign in a dream [40]*) "My Food-Kami* [41] *is at Plain-of-True-Well, in Yosa District, in Tango Province. Summon her and let her prepare my repast in the morning." Accordingly the Food-Kami was moved from Plain-of-True-Well to Mountain-Ricefield-Plain, at the village of Swamp-Tree, in Cross-Meet District, Isè Province, and made to settle there. Later Great-Sky-Shiner declared in an oracle, "Do you make a festival for Female-of-Fruitful-Food before my own festival." For festival-makers, the Kami-Master* [42] *family, who are descendants of*

SKY-GATHERING-CLOUDS [43]

were appointed to serve the Kami. In accordance with an oracle, also, a food-palace was built to the northeast of the Shrine of Female-of-Fruitful-Food, where food is prepared, morning and evening, to offer to the Great Kami.▲

At this time Awo and Hakatoko, who had been sent on a mission to Go, returned with envoys from that land, bringing skilful workmen, whom it offered, such as weavers of Han and Go and two seamstresses named

PRINCESS-ANÈ [44]
PRINCESS-YOUNGER [44]

and anchored in the harbor of Pleasant-to-Dwell-In. For the Go envoys the Shihatsu road was continued, and it was called Go-Slope. To receive them the Sovereign sent the Magnates and Tribe-Masters, and the Go-people were settled on the Hinokuma Moor (which therefrom was called Go-Plain). Princess-Anè was offered to the Kami of Three-Threads, and

---

[44] **Ancestress of the Seamstress Clans of Asuka and of Isè.**

Princess-Younger was made a member of the Han-Seamstress-Clan. The Sovereign purposed to feast the Go envoys, and asked his Ministers, in the order, whom it would be best to seat with them. They replied that Magnate-of-Ne would be a fit one, so that he was bidden to eat with them. When at length they were regaled at Takanukuhara in Above-the-Rock, an attendant was sent secretly to observe their decorations, and he reported to the Sovereign that the Magnate's jewel head-dress was most distinguished and beautiful, and everyone added that he had previously worn it when he had gone to receive the envoys of Go.

So the Sovereign, desiring to see it, commanded that the Magnates and Tribe-Masters should appear at the hall in the costumes worn at the feast. At that the Empress, looking up into the sky, sobbed and wept bitterly. When the Sovereign asked why she wept, she left the couch and replied, "Your slave's elder brother, Great-Lord-of-Hatabi, offered this head-dress on your slave's behalf, when he offered her to you, by command of the Emperor Anaho. So that I suspect Magnate-of-Ne [45] and I was unaware that my grief made me weep tears." Surprised and angered, he charged Magnate-of-Ne fiercely, who answered, "Death for me is just —is just! Your slave has done wrongfully!" The Sovereign gave order then that Magnate-of-Ne, his children, and his descendants and relatives in the eightieth degree, should play no part as Ministers. He would have slain him but that he fled and hid himself at Hinè, where he built a Rice-Castle in which to defend himself. By the Sovereign's command the officials divided his descendants, half being made commoners of the Great-Kusaka-Clan, and given to the Empress, and half being made bag-bearers of the District-Chiefs of Chinu. Then search was made for a descendant of Hikaka,[46] Kishi of Wave-Swift, who was ennobled and made Kishi of the Great-Kusaka-Clan. The matter having been adjusted, Magnate-of-Ne's son

MAGNATE-OF-LITTLE-NE

on lying down one night, said to a certain person, "The Sovereign's castle is weak but my father's is strong." The Sovereign, when he heard this, sent one who found it was as the son had boasted, so he took Magnate-of-Ne and slew him. His descendants were made Magnates-of-Sakamoto. (This was their origin.) [47]

At this time the Hada family [48] was dispersed and Magnates and Tribe-Masters ruled them as they wished, preventing the rulers of Hada from governing them. Therefore Sakè-of-Hada was greatly angered, and took service under the Sovereign, who, loving and preferring him, gathered the Hada family and gave them to him. In return for this, Sakè-of-Hada, with one hundred and eighty skilled workmen of the Clans, offered as a tax a pile *as high as a hill* of fine silk, *thread, floss and cloth*,⁴⁹ sufficient to furnish the court, at which the Sovereign was glad and he was given the name of Uzumasa (or, as some say, Uzumori-Masa).⁵⁰ *The sword used in the Kami-festival had its hilt wrapped with silk offered by the Hada family. The common people do this even now.* The Sovereign ordered that mulberry-trees be planted in the proper districts and provinces, and sending the Hada family to other places, commanded them to bring taxes as tribute.

From this time the tribute from the various Lands became year by year more abundant, so that a great storehouse was built. Noble-of-Manchi-of-Soga was ordered to take in charge the three storehouses: the sacred-storehouse, the inner-storehouse, and the great-storehouse. The Hada family had charge of the incoming and outgoing of the stocks, and the families of the scribes of Mountain-Gate and of Kawachi registered and made account of them. Also the Sovereign assembled the Han-folk and appointed a ruler of the guard as their governor. (Some say the Magnate-of-Han-Folk was given this office.) *The Han families were given the family names of Inner-Storehouse and Great-Storehouse, and two families of Hada and Han became officers of the keys of the inner- and great-storehouses. (This was the origin of the Store-House-Folk-Clan.*⁵¹) ᴀ

Also, the Tribe-Masters of the Clay-Workers being ordered to offer new dishes for the Sovereigns' morning and evening repasts,

AKÈ ⁵²

offered him a Clan composed of his own vassals from Village-of-Kusasa in Settsu Province, Village-of-Uchi and Village-of-Lying-See in Behind-the-Mountains Province, Village-of-Fujikata in Isè Province, and from Tamba, Tajima, and Rice-Leaves, naming them the Clay-Worker-Clan of Food.⁵³

Now it befell at this time that two of the Army-Clan,

NOBLE-OF-USHIRO

and Me, its Tribe-Master, were despatched to attack

LORD-ASAHI

of Isè, who, learning that the imperial troops were coming, withstood them at Green-Mound in Iga. Boasting of his bow-skill, he called to them, saying, "Him who dare face me my arrow shall smite through his double armor." At which the imperial troops all feared, nor did Noble-

---

⁵² **Ancestor of the Tribe-Masters of the Clay-Workers.**

of-Ushiro dare go to meet him, both sides delaying for two days and a night. Then Me took his sword, and bade

GREAT-AXE-HAND

of the Army-Clan of Kiku, in Tsukushi, take his shield and raise a shout from the ranks, and the two went forward together. Lord-of-Asahi, seeing them at a distance, shot his arrow through Great-Axe-Hand's shield and double armor and pierced his body an inch deep, but he covered Me with his shield and the latter took Lord-of-Asahi and slew him. Noble-of-Ushiro, in shame at his failure, made no report to the Sovereign during seven days. When the Sovereign made inquiry of his Ministers, one

TAMUSHI-WAKE-OF-SANUKI

approached and said, "Noble-of-Ushiro has acted the coward. For two days and a night he could not take Lord-of-Asahi, till Me, Tribe-Master of the Army-Clan, with Great-Axe-Hand, took and slew him." At that the Sovereign was angered and took the Wina-Clan from Noble-of-Ushiro and gave it to Me. Also he formed the Anaho-Clan and made White-Hair-Brave-Wide-Land-Great-Young-Mountain-Gate the imperial heir.

At this time the Land of Koma attacked and utterly conquered the Land of Kudara, but the latter appealed to the Sovereign and he restored the country to its people. Later the pair,

MAGNATE-OF-ACHI-OF-TSUKUSHI,
MAGNATE-OF-UMAKAÏ,

with a company of vessels, went against Koma.

ISLAND-SHORE-OF-WATER-BAY-CHILD VISITS THE SEA REALM

There was in the District of Yosa in Tamba Province, a man named

ISLAND-SHORE-OF-WATER-BAY-CHILD [54]

in Village-of-Pipe-River, in Sun-Placing,[55] who was a child of

ISLAND-SHORE-OF-WATER-BAY.

He was handsome of feature and unequaled in taste. He went out alone in a boat to fish *with hook and line. Some say he was a crab-fisher. During three days and nights he caught nothing, but* at length he caught a turtle *of five colors.*[56] *Wondering, he put it in the boat.*

---

[54] **Ancestor of the Head-men of the Kusaka-Clan.**

(Some state otherwise that he did not keep it, but out of pity threw it again into the water, thus earning its gratitude.)

While he slept the turtle suddenly became transformed into a woman,[57] in form beautiful beyond description. He said to her, "This place is far from the homes of people, of whom there are few on the sea. How did you so suddenly come here?" Smiling, she replied, "I deemed you a man of parts alone on the sea, lacking anyone with whom to converse, so I came here by wind and cloud."

(Some say that he was fishing from the shore,[58] when he saw the woman in a boat, and that she besought his aid, saying that her friends had perished in a storm, whereon, promising to convey her to her own Land, he entered the boat and rowed seaward for two days, as she directed.)

He asked her again, "From where did you come?" She answered, "I am a habitant of the Plain-of-the-High-Sky, the Spirit-Land. I pray you, doubt not but converse with me in intimacy." From this Island-Shore-of-Water-Bay-Child [59] knew that she was a female Kami and was circumspect, fearing and doubting her. Then she said, "My will [60] lasts as long as sky and earth and ends with sun and moon. What of yours?" When he replied that he could say no more, she said, "You can come to that region by a turn of your oar. Obey me and shut your eyes." So presently they came to a broad island in the wide sea, which was covered with jewels. Its high gate and towers shone with a brilliance which his eyes had never beheld and his ears had never heard tell of. Together they walked to the gate of the great mansion, when she said, "Stand here a little while," and opened the gate and entered. At that seven children came out, saying, "This is the husband of

PRINCESS-TURTLE." [61]

Thereafter there came forth eight children, who said likewise. Thus he first learned her name. Then the maid came out and he asked her concerning the children. She replied, "The seven are the rising-stars and the eight are the setting-stars.[62] You must not think them anything else." Then, going in advance, she led him through the gate, where her parents received and greeted them. Seated, they conversed of the difference between mankind and the Land-of-Spirits, and the joy of man and Kami meeting. He was offered hundreds of kinds of fragrant delicacies. Her brothers and sisters, older and younger, offered and received cups of drink, and damsels of neighboring villages disported with ruddy faces, while spirit songs were interchanged and Kami dances were engaged in. Ten thousand times more pleasing than human feast was the joy of this. They did not note that the time drew to sunset, when at the fall of night, *all the Spirits vanished, leaving there only the damsel, who covered her eyebrows with her sleeves.*[63] Thereon the child of Island-Shore-of-Water-Bay felt affection for her and wedded her. *For three years, far from his aged parents, he lived his life in the Spirit capital, when he began to yearn for his home and for them. Often he sang sorrowful songs and day by day his sighs increased, till she said, "Your look is different from that of other times. I pray you, tell me your desire." He answered, "It is said by the old that the mortal longs for home, and when the fox is about to die, it turns its head to its hill. This saying I had deemed false, but now I find it true." She asked, "Do you desire to return home?" He replied, "To come to this far Spirit-Land, I parted from my near of kin. My yearning I cannot help. I speak without consideration, but I wish to return to my native place to see my parents for awhile."*

Then she wept and sighed, saying, "I deemed my desire would last ten thousand years, so long as metal and stones endure. Why do you, recollecting your native place, straightway forsake me?" Then, hand in hand, they walked conversing, and sleeve by sleeve they wept, till they came to where their ways diverged and where her parents and relatives, sorrowing to part with him, made their farewells. The princess informed him that she was indeed the turtle which he had taken in his boat, and she took a jewel-casket [64] *and gave it to him, saying, "If you do not forget me and desire to seek me, keep this casket carefully, but do not open it." Thus he parted from her and entered his boat, shutting his eyes as she bade him, and quickly he came to Pipe-River. He looked upon the village, but its people and objects were so altered that there was nothing of which he could be sure. So he asked a man of the village where was the dwelling of Island-Shore-of-Water-Bay-Child. The other answered, "Of what place are you, and why do you ask concerning a man of the olden time? I have heard a legend of one Island-Shore-of-Water-Bay-Child, who of old went alone on the blue sea and never returned. Three hundred years have gone by since then. How is it you have only now heard of it?"* [65] *So he wandered about his native place with a heart yearning to return to it, but not one of his relatives could he find in several tens of days, when, touching the jewel-casket, he thought of the female Kami, and he forgot his promise of a former day and opened it. But before he could look into it, something in the form of a blue orchid soared up to the blue sky with the winds and clouds. Then he knew that, having broken his oath, he could not go back and see her again. Thus he pondered, wandering here and there, choked with tears. Then, wiping his tears, he sang:*

> Lo, the mounting cloud || Seeks the country eternal,
> Set in the realm of sky.
> Ah, 'tis your life it carries,[66] || Island-Shore-Water-Bay-Child!

Then he and the female Kami exchanged parting songs, and afterward he went where no one knew.

(Some say, however, that when the cloud rose from the casket, he grew suddenly old, his body shrinking, his black hair becoming white, and his breath growing weaker, till he fell upon the ground and died.) [67, A]

THE OLD WOMAN BOAR-CHILD

Now Boar-Child [68] had awaited with reverence the Sovereign Great-Hasè's command during the passing of eighty years.[69] Then, thinking that waiting these many years her face and form had become thin and shriveled so that she could no longer hope for anything, but that if she did not demonstrate this faithful waiting she would not be able to withstand her loss, she prepared tables holding a hundred kinds of articles, and had them carried and offered as tribute, she herself coming with them. The Sovereign had entirely forgotten his former command, and asked her, "Who are you, old woman? Why do you come here?" She replied, "In a certain month and year the Sovereign laid command upon his slave, and for eighty years till this day she has been awaiting his word. I now am crippled and can hope for nothing, but have come to demonstrate my faith." Said he, much amazed, "That former incident I had entirely forgot, and in the waiting your youth-years have passed. How sad is this!" While it was in his heart to wed her, he could not bring himself to do so by reason of her old age. So he augustly sang to her:

At August-House || Stands the sacred oak tree.
Behold how awful
Does that oak tree appear! || O you maid of the oak plain!

Also he made for her this song:

At Hiketa, || The plain of the young chestnut,
Ah, if in her youth
I might have slept beside her! || Now, alas, she is old!

Then Boar-Child, weeping till the tears wet the red-rubbed sleeve she wore, sang in answer:

At August-House, || The jewel-wall is built,
And I left over!
Where shall she go, alas, || The Kami's temple-tender?

Also she sang this song:

At Kusaka Bay, || Grow the bay-side lotuses—
The lotus-blossoms.
She who is like them in bloom, || Ah, how much to be envied!

Thereon he dismissed her with rich gifts. (These four songs are tranquil songs.)

Now the Sovereign fell sick and lay upon his couch in anxiety of mind, putting the imperial heir in charge of great and small matters, of rewards, penalties and payments. He grew worse and bade farewell to all his officials and held their hands, weeping and lamenting. And he said to Muruya, the Great-Tribe-Master of the imperial-guard and to

TSUKA

Governor of the Han folk of Mountain-Gate, "Young-Miya-of-Hoshi-River has treason in his heart and is everywhere known to be of an evil and violent nature. If after my death he should attempt to wrong the imperial heir, you and your slaves are many." So saying, he died in the great hall, in the twenty-second year of his reign. His august years were a hundred and twenty-four, and he is buried in the mound of High-Eagle in Tajihi, in Kawachi. The falcon-men mourned beside it night and day and would not eat the food which was brought them, till after seven days, they died. A mound was raised north of the imperial mound and there they were fittingly interred.

THE EMPEROR WHITE-HAIR-BRAVE-WIDE-LAND-GREAT-YOUNG-MOUNTAIN-GATE-PRINCE (PURE-TRANQUILITY)[70]

At the time of the Sovereign Great-Hasè's death, the Magnate-of-Maise

OSHIRO

who commanded a force that had been sent against Silla, arriving at Maise, went to his own dwelling, when five hundred Emishi of his forces, hearing that the Sovereign had died, said to one another, "Since he who ruled the Land is dead, let us not miss the opportunity," and in a body overran the region adjoining. Then Oshiro left his dwelling and at Sawa-Port attacked them and shot at them. But they dodged or fell prostrate so that the arrows missed. Then he twanged his bare bow on the sea-beach and thus slew two bands who had dodged and fled. Having exhausted the arrows of his two quivers, he demanded more of a boatman, but the latter was afraid and took to flight. At this he stood his bow erect, and holding its tip, sang:

> On the road the Oshiro lad || Encountered them.
> Maybe in the sky || He will not be heard of.
> But in the land || He will be heard of!

Having thus sung, he slew many and pursued them to Port-Uragakè in the Land of Tamba, where they were all slain by men whom he sent.

Now Princess-Young went in secret to Young-Miya-of-Hoshi-River and said, "If you would take the rule, first seize the treasury." Her elder son, Iwashiro, hearing his mother's counsel to the younger, said, "The imperial heir, my brother, is younger than I, but do not betray him. Do not do this thing." But Young-Miya-of-Hoshi-River, disregarding him, and foolishly led by her counsel, seized the treasury and barred its entrance in anticipation of trouble, administering it as he chose and wasting the imperial property. At that Muruya said to Tsuka, "It is time to carry out the Sovereign Great-Hasè's dying command for the benefit of the imperial heir." So with their soldiers they laid siege to the treasury, and surrounding its approaches, fired it and burned Young-Miya-of-Hoshi-River to death, together with Princess-Young, Iwashiro the Elder-Clan-Chief, and

WARRIOR-OF-MOUND-FRONT-OF-TREE.[71]

Then trembling with fear, the District-Chief of Three-Moors in Kawachi,

ONÈ

burst his way out and escaped the fire, and clasping the feet of

PRINCE-AYA,

Kishi of the Kusaka Clan, besought that one to gain his life from Muruya, saying, "Though your slave faithfully served Young-Miya-of-Hoshi-River, he did not oppose the imperial heir, and begs that his life be granted him." So Prince-Aya made this plea, and he was not numbered with those executed. Then said Onè, through Prince-Aya, to Muruya, "In your great mercy to me, though my life was narrowly risked, it has been lengthened so that I shall see the day." And he straightway offered the Great-Tribe-Master ricefields of ten cho at Ohowido, in Warrior-Village, in Wave-Swift, and gave ricefields also to Prince-Aya. The Magnates of Upper-Maise, learning of the trouble at court, and wishing to assist Young-Miya-of-Hoshi-River, their brother by the same mother, came by sea with forty vessels of war, but hearing of the fatal burning, retired without disembarking. At that the Sovereign sent messengers to lay charges against the Magnates of Upper-Maise and took from them their Mountain-Clan.

The Sovereign erected his palace at Mikakurè, in Iharè, and ruled the Empire. He had no Empress and no children, and displeased at this, he sent Maruya into the provinces and formed as his proxy the White-Hair-Attendant-Clan, the White-Hair-Steward-Clan, and the White-Quiver-Bearer-Clan, desiring to leave nominal descendants. Also, in the search that was made for one who should rule the Sun's-succession after him, Princess-Iïtoyo,[72] younger sister of Prince-Push-Teeth-of-Near-the-Market, was found to be residing in the Palace of Tsunuzashi, at High-Castle in Oshinumi in Mulberry-Castle.

(Some say, however, that she was not found till later, after his death.)

THE SONS OF PRINCE-PUSH-TEETH-OF-NEAR-THE-MARKET DECLARE THEMSELVES

It befell at this time that the governor of Harima Province

LITTLE-SHIELD [73]

of the Warrior-Clan of Iyo, was sent to the District of Akashi to arrange the offerings for the New-Rice-Festival (or, as some say, was visiting the various districts to collect the land-tax) and he reached there when Hosomè was holding a celebration for a new roofed-pit,[74] which celebration had lasted all day and extended into the night. Then King-Little-Basket said to his elder brother, King-Big-Basket, "It is many years since we fled from disaster to this place. Is not tonight the time to tell our names and our high rank?" King-Big-Basket answered gloomily, "It would be our death. Could either of us escape safely from the danger?" Said King-Little-Basket, then, "We are the grandsons of the Sovereign Izaho-Elder-Brother-Lord, yet we labor for a man and fodder his horses and cattle. Better to tell our names and be slain." So then they two, overcome with feeling, clasped one another weeping, when King-Big-Basket said, "You alone, my younger brother, are of courage to make this declaration." But King-Little-Basket stoutly declined, declaring that he had neither the ability nor the courage, at which King-Big-Basket declared his ability and knowledge were greater than any other's, and so each retreated several times behind the other. In the end, however, it was decided that King-Little-Basket should do it.

So both left the house and seated themselves outside, as became very humble persons, and Hosomè bade them sit by the cooking-range and hold torches on either side. Late at night, in the midst of the merry-making, when all, one after the other, had danced, he said to Little-Shield, "Your slave sees how these young children,[75] the torch-holders, put others forward and themselves remain behind. Their respect indicates that they follow correct rule, and their self-abasement shows them courteous. They deserve to be called well-born." At this Little-Shield, playing on his koto, bade the torch-holders rise and dance, but for some time each drew back for the other and rose not, each saying to the other, "Do you dance first," so that the people there gathered and laughed at it.

---

[73] **Ancestor of the Tribe-Masters of the Mountain-Clan.**

Little-Shield pressed them, saying, "Why do you wait thus? Rise at once and dance."

So King-Big-Basket rose and danced, and when he ceased, King-Little-Basket rose after him and girding up his robe, in honor of the house, declaimed: "The kidney-bean [76]-roots of the house, newly-built, the erected pillars—are the peace of the august heart of the master of the house. The ridge-poles and the rafters—are the glade of the august heart of the master of the house. The rafters, put in place—are the good orderliness of the august heart of the master of the house. The thatch-frame,[77] put in place—is the equanimity of the august heart of the master of the house. The tied kidney-bean ropes—are the stability of the august life of the master of the house. The rushes used for thatch—are the excess of the august wealth of the master of the house. Sacred-Quarter has newly cultivated fields. How joyful to drink the sakè, made in a shallow vessel, from the ten-hand-length rice ears of these new fields! Oh, my lads, while you dance, upraising the antlers of a stag of this foot-beaten, secluded mountain—nor buying your sweet sakè from the market of Eka—strike softly together the palms of your hands! Oh, you immortal ones!" When he had finished this speech of honor, music was played and he sang:

By the sleeping-mats,[78] || The willow o'er the river
When water falls, || Its bent pole lifts aloft,
And its roots do perish not.[79]

Little-Shield said to him, "Excellent! Shall we not hear more?" So, in the end, King-Little-Basket danced a particular dance (this of old was called Stand-Out, it being danced with standing and sitting postures) and taking his position, said, "Of Mountain-Gate's rustling reed-plain, her shallow reed-plain, the younger serving-lad am I!" Deeming this extraordinary, Little-Shield asked him to speak more, when taking his position, he said, "The bole has been cut and the boughs have been stripped from the sacred cryptomeria of Furu, in Above-the-Rock. We are the august children of Push-Teeth-of-Near-the-Market, who in his palace ruled the myriad Lands, all that lie beneath the myriad skies."

(Some, however, say that he said: "On the mountain-side, as soon as they appeared, the sword of my warrior-companion, its hilt painted with red soil, its cord of cut red cloth, and his erected red flags, were hidden behind the bamboo!—yet of King-Push-Teeth-of-Near-the-Market, august child of the Sovereign Izaho-Elder-Brother-Lord who ruled the empire as one who cut and bent over its extremities and as one played an eight-stringed biwa, these beggars are descendants!")

(Others, also, quote his song in various other ways.)

At this, greatly startled, Little-Shield fell down from his couch and dismissed the people from the house, (*some say, however, that all present ran away from fear*) and nonplussed, repeatedly bowed before them. Then, setting the two Kami on his left and right knees, he took them on his breast, and recognizing them as his lords, wept and made lament. Afterward, summoning the people, whom he commanded to prostrate themselves before them, he took it upon himself to provide for them with great care. He taxed all the people of the district, and having thus (some say, from his private resources) within a few days erected a temporary palace of brushwood, lodged the two in it. *There were erected there the Palace of Small-Moor, and the Palace of Pool-Moor.* Then, proceeding on a swift horse to the capital, (or, as some say, sending a messenger there with the news) Little-Shield asked that one be sent to meet them. *Also, saying, "The mother of these children, Princess-Hayè,*[80] *neither eats by day nor sleeps by night. She is between life and death through yearning for them," he went to the place where she was and told her the news, so that she wept from joy and sorrow, and sent him for the princes so that she might see them.* Learning this, the Sovereign, amazed, made many exclamations, saying with feeling, "Wonderful and joyful it is! From abundant affection there are given me two Sky-children! I have no children and they shall succeed me." Princess-Iïtoya was also delighted to hear this. So, making a plan in the palace with the Great-Magnates and the Great-Tribe-Masters, the Sovereign sent Little-Shield, with emblems of authority and with attendants, to Akashi District to meet them. And he and those with him, bringing King-Little-Basket and King-Big-Basket, came to Settsu Province, where Magnates and Tribe-Rulers were sent with emblems of authority and with an imperial conveyance with a green cover, to meet them and bring them to the palace.

> (Some, however, say otherwise, that the two princes were not found till later, after the Sovereign's death.)

At this time the Princess-Iïtoya first cohabited with her husband in the Palace of Tsunuzashi, whereon she said to him, "Now that I have learned something of the habit of womankind, what is there wonderful in it? I desire never again to have connection with a man."

The Magnates and Tribe-Masters were given an imperial feast and were gifted with raw-silk, each carrying away as much as he could, and in going thus they taxed all their strength. Tribute was sent from the over-sea provinces, whose messengers were feasted and gifted variously. Also there was held throughout the empire a five-day sakè festival. The Sovereign released prisoners and the Emishi and falcon-men made obeisance together. He also held a shooting-contest in the bow-hall, the officials and messengers from over-sea taking part.

The Sovereign, being of great age,[81] died in the palace, and was buried in the mound on the Sakato plain, in Kawachi.

THE EMPEROR KING-LITTLE-BASKET (MANIFEST-ANCESTRY)[82]

Each of the princes, King-Little-Basket and King-Large-Basket, resigned the rule to the other, and for a long while it was not carried on. So Princess-Iitoya made a court [83] and ruled in the Palace of Tsunazashi in Oshinumi. A poet of that time sang thus of her:

In Mountain-Gate, || A thing so glad to behold
At Oshinumi—
This completed, high-castled || Palace of Tsunuzashi.

Dying, she was buried in the mound on the Hill of Haniguchi in Mulberry-Castle.

While they lived at the Palace of High-Moor, in Village-of-Shijimi, the two princes had sent Little-Shield to offer suit to

PRINCESS-ROOT

who was a daughter of the Governor

KOMA

who had given compliance. But while they yielded one to the other, the days passed, and Princess-Root died. Both princes grieved for her death and sent Little-Shield, bidding him build a tomb where the sun did not fail to shine by morning and evening, to bury her body and decorate the grave with jewels. (Therefore the place was named Jewel-Hill and the village there was named Jewel-Moor.)[A]

Now at a great gathering of officials, King-Large-Basket took the imperial seal and laid it on King-Little-Basket's seat and prostrated himself repeatedly before him, saying, "You it was who revealed our names when we dwelt in the dwelling of Hosomè, in Harima. Else we had not become lords of the empire. I resign the empire to you." King-Little-Basket said, "I may not take the rule, for I am the younger brother, and I know that the Sovereign had purposed to transmit it to you." However, when King-Large-Basket urgently resigned it, seeing that he was crossing his elder brother's desire, and being unable to refuse, King-Little-Basket consented. Nevertheless he would not sit in the imperial place. Till the Great-Magnates and the Great-Tribe-Masters appealed to him to take the inheritance, and accordingly he called together the Ministers and officials to the Yatsuri Palace in Nearer-Asuka and took the rule, to the joy of all of them there.

King-Little-Basket dwelt in the Palace of Nearer-Asuka (or, as some say, at Mikakuri) and ruled the empire. He had palaces also at Wono and Pond-Moor. The great-grandson of the Sovereign Noble-of-Younger-Child-Male-Morning-Wife [84] was

PRINCE-ROCK-CASTLE

who had for grandson

PRINCE-YOUTH-OF-MOUND

and Prince-Youth-of-Mound had as daughter

PRINCESS-SMALL-MOOR-OF-WAVE-SWIFT [85]

(who some [86] say was daughter to Prince-Rock-Castle) and her the Sovereign took to wife, but they begot no children.

OLD-WOMAN-KEEP-EYE

The Sovereign searched far and near for the august bones of his father,[87] but could not find them, so he called together aged persons and himself inquired of them in turn. There came from the land of Omi a poor and aged woman, a younger sister of

NOBLE-OF-MOUNTAIN-GATE-BAG [88]

who presented herself, saying, "I alone know well where the august bones were buried, and beg to point out the place. They may be known by his august teeth." [89] So the Sovereign and King-Large-Basket, taking the old woman with them, proceeded to the Kaya Moor in Kutawata, in Omi Province, where when people were impressed to dig the ground and make search, the bones were disinterred and it was found that she had spoken truly. Gazing on the grave they wept, for from old time till then there had been nothing so pitiful. The body of Uruwa [90] lay upon the august bones, which were so mingled that one could not be separated from the other. Then said the nurse of the imperial prince

ROCK-SLOPE [91]

"Uruwa's upper teeth had dropped out and thus they may be distinguished." So they were able to tell one skull from the other, but the bones of the four limbs could never be separated. For this reason a double-mound was built on the Kaya Moor, each part like the other, so

---

[88] **Ancestor of the Clan-Chiefs of Mount Sasaki.**

that they seemed a single one, and like ceremonies were performed for each. There the bones were buried. After his return, the Sovereign sent for the old woman, and praised her for having remembered the place, and gave her the name

OLD-WOMAN-KEEP-EYE

commanding that she should dwell near the palace and treating her with deep consideration and kindness, so that she needed nothing. Close by he had a dwelling built for her and sent for her every day. Also he said, "Old woman, you, being alone and decrepit, cannot easily walk. There shall be a rope drawn across to aid you in going and coming, at whose end there shall be tied a bell, so that no one need announce you. So, in coming, the bell will ring to inform me." Accordingly she rang the bell on coming, and he rang it when he desired to summon her. Hearing, far off, the bell's sound, he sang:

> By the sparse reed-plain || By the little valleys,
> A hundred passing—
> Hark! The bell is swinging. || I know Keep-Eye is coming!

Now at a feast, where King-Large-Basket was present, he took a melon to eat it, but lacked a knife, so the Sovereign bade his wife, Princess-Ono-of-Wave-Swift, take one and hand it to King-Large-Basket. She came to him and, standing, set it on the melon-tray. Also she poured some sakè, and, standing, offered him the drink. Therefore, having been wanting in respect, she feared she would be slain and so slew herself.

(Some say, however, that her disrespect to him had been long-continued, and that she did not slay herself till after the Sovereign's death, when King-Large-Basket inherited the rule.)

It fortuned that the Sovereign, as a reward of merit, asked Little-Shield what he desired. He, thanking him, replied that he always had desired the mountain service. So he was appointed to this, and the new title of Tribe-Master of the Mountain-Clan was granted to his family. The Magnate-of-Maise was joined with him in this and the Mountain-Clan were made their slaves. He was made to prosper exceedingly. Noble-of-Kara-Bag, Clan-Chief of Mount Sasaki, who had taken part in the murder of Prince-Push-Teeth-of-Near-the-Market, was to be slain, but he put his head on the ground and spoke such sorrowful words that the Sovereign could not bear to slay him, but made him one of the mound-guards, appointing him mountain-warden and taking his name from the list of population, gave him to the Tribe-Master of the Mountain-Clan. Noble-of-Mountain-Gate-Bag, because of the good service of his younger sister, Old-Woman-Keep-Eye, was granted the title the other's family had borne, of Clan-Chief of Mount Sasaki. Also the Sovereign made search for the old swineherd who had seized his food when first he had met ill-fortune and was in flight, and when he was found, he was beheaded in the bed of the Asuka River and the tendons of the knees of all his relatives were severed. (For this reason down to the present time his descendants always limp voluntarily whenever they come to Mountain-Gate. Since the place where this man dwelt was decided upon by divination, it was named Recognized.)

The Sovereign, deeply resentful of the slaying of his father by the Sovereign Great-Hasè, and desiring to avenge his spirit, said to King-Large-Basket, "Our father, innocent of wrong-doing, was slain by Great-Hasè with an arrow, and his bones were flung on the moor. I am minded to destroy that one's mound and break his bones and fling them away. Shall not this revenge be a filial thing?" But King-Large-Basket, weeping so that he could scarce reply, argued with him that it would not be well. When the Sovereign sent people to do it, said he, "Send no other than myself to destroy the mound. Your slave will go and will render report when I have destroyed it, according to your august heart." So the Sovereign bade him proceed there as he had said. (Some say, otherwise, however, that he withdrew his order for the work.) But King-Large-Basket, proceeding there in person, dug a little in the side of the mound, and returning, reported that he had dug it away and destroyed it. The Sovereign, wondering that he should have so soon returned, asked in what manner it had been destroyed. The other replied, "I dug a little in the side of the august mound." The Sovereign answered, "I desired to take revenge on my father's enemy, and expected it to be wholly destroyed. Why did you dig but a little?" The other replied, "For this reason. Your desire to avenge our father's spirit on his enemy is just; yet though he was our father's enemy, he was nevertheless our uncle and the Sovereign of this empire. So if now we regarded him solely as our father's enemy and wholly destroyed the mound, future generations would rightly curse us. Yet our father's wrong must not be left without vengeance. Therefore I dug a little in the side of the mound, a sufficient affront to show to after ages." At this the Sovereign said, "That too is most just. So shall it remain."

Now Old-Woman-Keep-Eye, who was very aged and infirm, besought permission to return home, saying, "I am old, weak and thin, and though I am aided by my rope, I cannot walk. I beseech you to permit me to return to the mulberry and oil-plant [92] trees, where I would pass my final days." So the Sovereign had compassion on her and gave her a thousand pieces [93] and sorrowing at their parting, over and over lamented that they should meet no more. He sang:

> Alas, now our Keep-Eye, || Our Keep-Eye of Afumi!
> After tomorrow
> We shall no longer see her. || She will be hid by mountains!

The empire was now tranquil, there was no levying of public labor, the grains ripened and the people prospered so that a measure of rice brought a silver piece, and horses and cattle were on the moors.

At this time

THING-SIGN

Magnate of Ahè, at the Sovereign's bidding, went on a mission to Mimana, where the Moon-Kami,[94] through a certain person's mouth, said to him, "My ancestor, High-Producer, with other Kami, admirably framed the Sky and the Earth. In his worship, dedicate to him both people and Land. I, the Moon-Kami, shall take pleasure in offerings made according to my wish." So Thing-Sign, returning to the capital, reported it to the Sovereign, who dedicated to the Kami the ricefields of Uta-Arasu and appointed in charge of his shrine

NOBLE-OF-OSHIMI.[95]

Also, the Sun-Kami,[96] through a certain person's mouth, said to Thing-Sign, "Dedicate to my ancestor, High-Wonder-Producer, the ricefields of Iharè." So Thing-Sign reported this to the Sovereign, who, according to her request, dedicated to the Kami fourteen cho of rice-land, and appointed in charge of his shrine the District-Governors of Shimo in Port-Island.[97]

The officers were summoned to a feast, at which time a three-stemmed plant grew in the palace courtyard. One of these was plucked and offered to the Sovereign, who thereon formed the Sakikusa [98] Clan and conferred upon the giver the title of Clan-Ruler.[A]

Now

PRINCE-NUSHI-MAN-PRINCE

descendant in the fourth generation of King-Young-Nukè-Futa-Mata,[99] learning while at his country-house at Miwo, in High-Island District, Omi Province, of the shining beauty of face of

PRINCESS-FURU

of High-Muka-Village in Mouth-of-Road-of-Koshi,[1] in the Land of Omi, descendant in the seventh generation of the Sovereign Prince-Ikumè-Iri-Isachi,[2] sent a messenger to Mawi-Slope in August-Land to ask for her. He wedded her and begot

---

[95] **Ancestor of the District-Chiefs of Yuki.**

LITTLE-HODO.³

While the latter was of child-age his father died, and Princess-Furu lamented, saying, "How can I bring him up thus distant from my birthplace? I will go back to my parents at High-Muka and respectfully bring him up there." At this time Noble-of-Oïha-of-Tree,⁴ relying upon Mimana, entered into relations with Koma. Purposing to govern the three Han on the western side, he set up a government and called himself a Kami. He cut off supplies from the provinces to the eastward so that its army suffered hunger, at which the king of Kudara, angered, sent troops against him. These he attacked, but his weapons being exhausted, he returned from Mimana.

The Sovereign died in the third year of his reign, and is buried in the mound on the Hill of Rock-Platter, at Side-Mound.⁵

THE EMPEROR BIG-BASKET
(BENEVOLENT-WISDOM)⁶

Big-Basket dwelt in the Palace of Hirotaka, in Above-the-Rock. He had palaces also at River-Village and at High-Moor in Shijimi.⁷ He had wedded Princess-Great-Lady-of-Kasuga,⁸ by whom he begot

PRINCESS-TASHIRAGA
PRINCESS-ORANGE ⁹
YOUNG-WREN-OF-LITTLE-HASÈ
PRINCE-MAWAKA

(who some say was a female child.) He took to wife also

HIYURI

and there was born to the two a daughter named

PRINCESS-MOUNTAIN-RICEFIELD-OF-KASUGA.¹⁰

In this reign the Above-the-Rock-Clan of attendants was formed. Also,

KASHIMA

Magnate of Ikuba, and the Clan-Chief of Honè were imprisoned for crime and died. Moreover all of the provinces and districts were searched for the Saheki-Clan, which had been scattered, and a descendant of Uruwa ¹¹ was made its ruler.

KISHI-OF-SUN-HEIGHT ¹²

was sent to Kara to bring skilful workmen. On his return he brought to the Sovereign from Koma the workmen

SURUKI [13]

TORUKI [14]

The Sovereign died in the eleventh year of his reign, in the chief bed-chamber, and was buried in the mound below Hanifu-Slope.

THE EMPEROR YOUNG-WREN-OF-LITTLE-HASÈ (BRAVELY-RAGING) [15]

When King-Big-Basket died, the Minister

MATORI

Magnate of Heguri, seized the government of the Land and attempted to rule the empire, building a palace under pretense that it was for the Sovereign's eldest son, Young-Wren-of-Little-Hasè, in which at length he dwelt himself.

MAGNATE-OF-TUNNY AND PRINCESS-KAGÈ

Now Young-Wren-of-Little-Hasè desired betrothal to

PRINCESS-KAGÈ

daughter of the Great-Tribe-Master of the Army Clan

ARAKAÏ

to whose dwelling he sent a middleman to arrange the marriage. She, however, had had secret intercourse with

MAGNATE-OF-TUNNY [16]

son of Matori. Yet, fearing to set herself against the proposal, she sent an answer saying that she desired to meet him on Tsubaki-ichi street.[17] So Young-Wren-of-Little-Hasè, purposing to go to the place of the meeting, sent an attendant to the dwelling of Matori to request, in his name, some imperial horses. But the Great Magnate derided him, saying, "Are not the imperial horses maintained for his use? He shall in truth be obeyed! Nevertheless a long time passed and they were not sent, for which reason Young-Wren-of-Little-Hasè was resentful, but covered it so that his face did not show it. At length he went to the place of the meeting

---

[13] **Ancestor of the Koma Tanners, of Nukada, in Yamabè District, Yamato Province.**
[16] **Ancestor of the Magnates of Heguri.***

---

* See p. 174. Presumably this man was in line of descent from Noble-of-Heguri's-Owl.

and joined in the Song-Hedge,[18] where he caught hold of the sleeve of Princess-Kagè and wandered about carelessly. Magnate-of-Tunny came to them there and thrusting him aside, put himself between them. At this Young-Wren-of-Little-Hasè released her sleeve and turning to regard Magnate-of-Tunny, sang:

> In the salt stream, || As I gaze on the breakers,
> By the tunny's fin,
> As he playfully passes || I see my wife is standing.

Whereon Magnate-of-Tunny sang to him in answer:

> The eight-fold screen [19] of bamboo, || Of the magnate's child,
> Say you, Prince, I yield thee?

At which Young-Wren-of-Little-Hasè sang the following song:

> Though the mighty sword || Which I carry suspended
> I may not draw forth,
> Yet I shall come unto it || Verily in the future.

Then Magnate-of-Tunny, in reply to him, sang:

> Though the mighty lord || His eight-fold screen enwoven
> May bind together,
> Still is it bound but loosely, || That screen that is thus enwove!

To which Young-Wren-of-Little-Hasè sang again:

> Child of the Magnate, || Thy eight-fold screen of branches—
> If, trembling neath,
> There come a shaking earth-quake— || Will be but a broken screen.

And he sang also to Princess-Kagè:

> To Koto-Kami,
> If Princess-Kagè should come,
> She would be a jewel,
> A jewel greatly desired,
> An awabi jewel of white.

And Magnate-of-Tunny sang in reply for Princess-Kagè:

> Now the mighty lord's || Girdle of figured weaving
> Has a hanging knot!
> Whosoever else there be, || Yearns she never for him! [20]

Then first Young-Wren-of-Little-Hasè understood that Magnate-of-Tunny had already made her his, and saw how father and son had held him in no esteem, and was unable to contain his fury. The same night he went to the dwelling of

KANAMURA

Tribe-Master of the imperial guard, the son of Muruya,[21] where he gathered soldiery and took counsel, saying, "All the court people go to the court in the morning and gather at noon at Magnate-of-Tunny's gate. Moreover now he is asleep and there will be no one at the gate. To snare him will be hard except it be done now." Whereon the Tribe-Master of the imperial guard ambushed Magnate-of-Tunny and slew him in his dwelling.

(Or, as some say, in the dwelling of Princess-Kagè, where he was passing that night. Others, again, say at Mount Level.)
(*By some,*[22] *too, it is said that this incident took place at the time when King-Little-Basket and King-Big-Basket were ceding each other the empire.*)
(Still others hold that it was King-Little-Basket who desired to wed, and that the damsel was one

BIG-FISH

daughter of a Head-man of Uda.)

Princess-Kagè, coming later to the place and seeing that he had been slain, was so startled that she knew not what she did, and shedding tears, in her grief she sang:

In Above-the-Rock || As I go by Furu,
And in Mat-Pillow || As I go by High-Bridge,
In Things-in-Plenty || As I pass Great-Storehouse,
And the spring-sun's || Kasuga as I pass,
The wife-confining || Small-Arrow as I pass,
Placing the boiled rice || Within my jewel-bowl,
In my jewel-jar || Placing fresh water, too,
I shall go drenched with weeping—
Princess-Kagè, piteous!

When he had been buried, when she was to return to her home, scarce able to speak for sorrow, she exclaimed, "Alas! This day I have lost a dear husband!" Then, weeping in grief, and beside herself, she sang:

Where the soil is blue, || In a ravine of Level,
Waits a lone boar || Hemmed in beside the water.
Here, all besprinkled, || Lies the young lord of Tunny.
Search him not out, O boar, I pray!

Now Kanamura said to Young-Wren-of-Little-Hasè, "The disobedient Matori must be slain. Let me go against him." So, the other agreeing, he led troops in person about the dwelling of the Great-Magnate and set it on fire and burned it. At which Matori, angry that his plan had been broken and thinking his life lost, his schemes brought to end, and his anticipations dispelled, set a spacious salt-curse, and at last was slain with his retainers. When he set the curse he forgot only one place, the sea-salt of Bloody-Strand,[23] on which he had not set it. (For this reason the Sovereign eats salt from Bloody-Strand and shuns eating any other sea-salt.) Then Kanamura, having put down the rebellion and given again the rule to Young-Wren-of-Little-Hasè, begged permission to give him the august name, and Young-Wren-of-Little-Hasè ordered his officials to make ready a sacred terrace at Row-of-Trees, in Hasè, where he assumed the rule and finally placed there the capital. On that same day he appointed Kanamura Great-Tribe-Master of the imperial guard.

At this time the king of Kudara sent

LORD-MANA

with tribute, but as tribute had not been sent during many years, the Sovereign held him and would not let him go. So the king of Kudara sent

LORD-SHIKA

with tribute and with another imperial letter, which said, "Since Lord-Mana, whom I previously sent with tribute, was not of the kindred of the Kudara kings, I send now Lord-Shika to attend the court." This one later had a son named

LORD-POPSA.[24]

The Sovereign wedded Princess-Mountain-Ricefield-of-Kasuga,[25] whom he made his Empress, and he ordered Muruya,[26] Great-Tribe-Master of the imperial guard, to levy workmen from Lime-Tree-Moor Province to build a castle in Village-of-Minomata, which was named Kinoüë. Also, having no posterity, he founded, as his august proxy, the Small-Hasè-Clan of attendants.

This Sovereign did great harm and did no good thing. He never failed personally to witness all manner of cruel punishments and all the people of the empire feared him. He cut open the belly of a pregnant woman to examine the womb. He caused men's nails to be pulled out and made them dig yams. He caused the hairs to be pulled from men's heads and made them climb to the tops of trees and shot them with bows, or felled the trees so that they were cast down and killed. In this he found pleasure. He caused men to lie prostrate in the waterways of embankments so that they were washed away, and thrust them through with three-pronged spears. In this also he found pleasure. He placed naked women on broad tables and causing horses to be brought, made these have commerce with them. Then when he had made examination, he slew those whose vaginas

---

[24] **Ancestor of the Clan-Chiefs of Yamato.**

were wet, and the others he made public slaves. In these things he found pleasure. Moreover he dug a pool and made a park which he filled with birds and beasts and in which he enjoyed hunting, dog-racing, and horse-training. He departed and returned at all times, nor was he mindful to escape storms and heavy rains; clad in his own warm raiment he took no thought of the people, who perished from the cold, and while he ate tid-bits, took no thought that the empire starved. He patronized many dwarfs and entertainers, and caused them to make boisterous music, arranging curious amusements and permitting vices without shame. By night and by day, with the palace women, he continued to drink sakè. He had brocade rugs and many robes of silk damask and of thin white silk.[27]

The Sovereign ruled the empire for eight years and died [28] at the age of fifty-seven in the Palace of Row-of-Trees. He is buried in the mound of Rock-Platter at Side-Mound.

THE EMPEROR PRINCE-LITTLE-HODO (SUCCEED-BODY)[29]

Now the Sovereign Young-Wren-of-Little-Hasè never had any child, either son or daughter, so there was none to succeed him and no prince to inherit the empire. So Kanamura, the Great-Tribe-Master, advised, saying, "There is now no successor to the rule, and to whom shall the empire adhere? From of old till the present this has brought calamity. Now there is in Kuwa-Ricefield-District, in Ricefield-Place Province

PRINCE-MOUNTAIN-GATE-PRINCE

descendant in the fifth generation of the Sovereign Prince-Perfect-Middle.[30] Let us, for a trial, arrange to have an armed force surround his carriage and sent to meet him, and make him our Sovereign." All the Great-Magnates and Great-Tribe-Masters agreed, and it was done as thus suggested. But Prince-Mountain-Gate-Prince, seeing from far off the soldiery sent to meet him, was frightened and his face changed, and he hid himself in a vale of the mountain so that none could discover his whereabouts. Thereon Kanamura again advised, saying, "There is

PRINCE-LITTLE-HODO,[31]

who is affectionate and dutiful, and is the proper one to inherit the Sky-succession. Let us respectfully offer it to him and thus carry on the prosperity of the rule." At this the Great-Tribe-Master Arakaï of the Warrior Clan, with the Great-Magnate

OBITO-OF-KOSÈ

and others, all said, "Considering carefully the lines of descent, there is none worthy but Prince-Little-Hodo." Then Magnates and Tribe-Masters were sent down to August-Land in the Land of Omi with insignia of authority and with an imperial sedan-chair,[32] and the troops forming his bodyguard came suddenly in impressive formation before him. But he remained quietly in his seat, self-controlled, with his attendants disposed according to rank beside him, as if he were already Sovereign. At that the messengers who bore the insignia of authority bowed down with a feeling of reverence, and gave him the rule, begging him to receive their loyalty and service. He, however, was still distrustful and for some time would not consent, till he learned that

ARAKO

Head-man of Mumakahi, of Kawachi, had secretly sent a messenger to let him know in detail the true purpose of the Great-Magnates and Great-Tribe-Masters in sending the guard. Then, at length, after waiting two days and three nights, he started. At the time he said in praise, "Good, O Head-man of Mumakahi! But for your messenger's information, I had likely been made a thing of ridicule for the empire." The common saying, "Set store by the spirit rather than regard the rank" had surely reference to such as Arako, whom Prince-Little-Hodo, when he became Sovereign, treated with special kindness.

When Prince-Little-Hodo thus reached the Palace of Kusuba,[33] the Great-Tribe-Master Kanamura knelt, and prostrating himself again and again, offered the Mirror, the Sword and the Jewels,[34] but Prince-Little-Hodo refused, saying, "It is no small thing to be father to the people and to rule the empire. I am unworthy and of poor ability and should not be considered fit. Therefore I beseech that, changing your plan, you choose one who is wise, since I am unworthy and fear to take it." The Great-Tribe-Master, however, prostrating himself, repeated his request, when Prince-Little-Hodo, facing the west three times refused, and facing the south twice. Then said the Great-Tribe-Master of the imperial guard and all the others, "In your slaves' humble wisdom, the great prince is well fitted to be the father of the people and to rule the empire. Considering the ancestral shrines and the shrines of the land and of the grains, your slaves' wisdom fears to be hasty. In the universal wish, we beg you graciously to deign to accept." Prince-Little-Hodo replied, "Since you Great-Magnates and Great-Tribe-Masters and all you high officers press it on me, though unworthy, I may not oppose it." Thereon he accepted the Jewels.[35] Kanamura was made Great-Tribe-Master, Obito-of-Kosè was made Great-Magnate and Great-Tribe-Master Arakaï of the Warrior-Clan was made Great-Tribe-Master, all being confirmed in the offices they held previously, and the Great-Magnate and the Great-Tribe-Masters each took up his duty and rank. The Emperor Prince-Little-Hodo transferred the Capital in the fifth year of his reign to Tsuzuki in Behind-the-Mountains, then to Otokuni, and last to Iharè, where he dwelt in the Palace of Tamaho. He wedded

YOUNG-LADY-OF-MEKO [36]

who was the daughter of

KUSAKA

Tribe-Master of Owari, and sister of the Chief

OFUSHI [37]

and there were born to them two sons

WIDE-LAND-GREAT-BRAVE-METAL-SUN [38]

BRAVE-LITTLE-WIDE-LAND-GREAT-SHIELD. [39]

He took to wife also

PRINCESS-YOUNG. [40]

Also he wedded Princess-Tashiraga,[41] whom he made Empress, and who governed the Interior,[42] and begot

SKY-LAND-GREAT-HARUKI-WIDE-COURT.[43]

He took to wife also

PRINCESS-MOUNTAIN-GATE

who was the daughter of

KATAÏ

Clan-Chief of Miwo, and there were born to the two

LADY-GREAT

(Who some say was a male child named Lord-Great)

PRINCE-MAROKO.[44]

He took to wife also

PRINCESS-WIDE

---

[37] **Ancestor of the Chiefs of Owari.**
[40] **Ancestress of the Clan-Chiefs of the Miwo.**
[44] **Ancestor of the Clan-Chiefs of Mikuni.**

who was the daughter of

PRINCE-NE

and there were born to the pair two sons

PRINCE-USAGI [45]
PRINCE-NAKA.[46]

It came to pass in this reign that a certain

YAHAZU-UJI-MATACHI

cleared the reed moors among the ravines in the western part of the district to cultivate new ricefields, and the deities of the ravines gathered and obstructed his labor. In anger he donned helmet and armor, and taking in hand a staff, thrust at the snake-deities and drove them away to the ravine-mouths, where he planted a border of piling, declaring that while it was granted to them to live beyond it, they were forbidden to enter men's ricefields. Also he covenanted with them that he and his descendants would make forever a festival in their honor, in return for which they should not resist or resent his presence. Then he built a shrine and instituted a festival. He thus cleared and made ten cho of ricefield, which his descendants inherited and these, to this present, celebrate the festival unfailingly.[A]

At this time Kudara sent as tribute a scholar of the Five Classics named Tan-Yang-ni; later it offered as tribute another scholar of the Five Classics named Ko-An-Mu-of-Han, for whom Tan-Yang-Ni was exchanged. Also

GREAT-MOUNTAIN

Magnate of Piled-Up-Rice-Ears, Governor of the Land of Tari,[47] was sent with fifty-four horses of the Land of Tsukushi, as a gift to Kudara, which, through him, made request that it be given four districts of the Land of Mimana, and Kanamura, the Great-Tribe-Master, laid the request before the Sovereign. So Arakaï, Great-Tribe-Master of the Warrior-Clan, was made imperial envoy. But when he was about to depart to the government-house at Wave-Swift, his wife protested to him, saying, "In the beginning the Great Kami of Pleasant-to-Dwell-In gave the Sovereign Great-Elbow-Pad-Lord, while in the womb, the over-sea Lands of gold and silver. Therefore the great Empress [48] Princess-Long-Life-Perfect and the Great-Magnate Noble-of-Brave-Uchi first founded granaries in each of these Lands and made them our protecting Lands over-

---

[45] **Ancestor of the Clan-Chiefs of the Sakè-Makers.**
[46] **Ancestor of the Clan-Chiefs of the Sakada.**

sea. This has come about with purpose, and if we now cut off and give them to others, we oppose our Land's interests. In after ages shall we be without blame?" The Great-Tribe-Master replied, "Your counsel is good, but I fear to disobey the Sky-bidding." But his wife protested the more, saying, "Pretend illness and take no message!" The Great-Tribe-Master yielded to this protest, so that another was made envoy to transmit the imperial will, and gifts were sent and the four districts were granted by decree to Mimana.

Wide-Land-Great-Brave-Metal-Sun, occupied with certain affairs, did not hear of this transfer of Land till too late. He was surprised and displeased and endeavored to have the decree altered to say, "The land of our granaries was founded in the time of the womb-enclosed Sovereign. Are we so readily to grant the desire of a foreign Land and give it away?" And he sent the Kishi of Sun-Eagle to give the strangers of Kudara a different reply. But they answered, "The Sovereign-father, in his imperial will, has given this for sufficient reason; is the prince-son to cross his declared wish and give another answer without authority? Truly this was not intended! But if so, is it worse to be beaten with the large end of a stick, than with the small end?" Thereon they departed. Afterward it was reported that the Great-Tribe-Master of the imperial guard and Great-Mountain, Magnate of Piled-up-Rice-Ears, had been bribed by Kudara.

Wide-Land-Great-Brave-Metal-Sun took to wife Princess-Mountain-Ricefield-of-Kasuga [49] and during an entire night of moonlight they talked sweetly together till dawn surprised them, when he sang, with words delicately expressing his sentiment:

> Seeking a wife || In the Great-Eight-Island-Realm,
> Vainly sought I, till learning || That in spring-weathered Kasuga
> Dwelt a lovely maid— || Learning that there
> Dwelt a pure maid— || The door of fir wood
> Of split maki || I pushed right open
> When I came here. || Grasping it by the lower end,
> I took hold of her hem— || Grasping it by the pillow-end,
> I took hold of her hem. || Then the arm enwound me
> Of my younger sister— || Then my own arm
> My younger sister enwound, || Like a lush creeper,
> Arm enclosed with arm || . . . . . . [50]
> Sweetly we slept together. || The courtyard bird
> Is the one that is crying. || The pheasant, moor-haunter,
> Is the one that is crying loudly. || Before I have told you
> All, alas! that I think,
> Dawn breaks, my love! [51]

Replying, she sang to him this song:

> Adown the stream || Of withdrawn Hasè
> Floats a bamboo || With joints close and long.
> Of the lower portion || I make me a biwa.
> Of the upper portion || I make me a flute.
> If, breathing into one, || Playing on the other,
> I climbed and stood || On August-House's top,
> Telling it there, || The fish that go
> Beneath the water-pond || Of creeper-covered Iharè
> Would come up to bewail it. || The small-patterned girdle
> Augustly worn || By my Great Lord
> Tranquilly governing || Hangs in a knot.
> There is no man anywhere || Who would not come to bewail it.

One morning she did not appear early, which was not as usual, and the prince wondered, so he entered the palace and found her lying on her couch in such tears and sobs that her feeling could not be controlled. In surprise the prince asked, "What causes you to sorrow this morning with tears and sobs?" She replied, "Your slave's sorrow is caused only by this: The sky-flying birds have such great love for their birdlings that they nest in the tree-tops so as to bring them up lovingly. Things that creep and crawl on the ground take such watchful care of their younglings that to protect them they make holes in the earth. Shall human-kind, then, lack foresight? The prince having to my sorrow no issue, your slave's name, too, dies out." Wide-Land-Great-Brave-Metal-Sun had pity for her sorrow and informed the Sovereign, who issued a decree, saying, "Your wife's words, O my son, are deeply reasonable. They must not be empty of the comfort of a reply. Let her be given the granary of Saö to carry on her name for ten thousand generations."

It came to pass that in order to protect Mimana from the inroads of Silla, the Sovereign bade

KENA

Magnate of Omi, leading an army of six thousand, to proceed there. At this time

ROCK-WELL

ruler of the Land of Tsukushi, prepared a secret uprising, by which some years time was lost, and while he watched for his opportunity, Silla bribed him to prevent the passing of the army of Kena. So he seized both Fire Province and Fertile Province, and forbade payment of the tax. Also he stopped the further sea-route and diverted the ships that each year brought tribute from the Lands of Koma, Kudara, Silla, and Mimana, while at home he barred the army of the Magnate Kena. Said he, harshly, "You are now an envoy who was once my comrade, when we stood shoulder to shoulder and elbow to elbow, eating the same food from the same platters. Do you so readily become an envoy so that I must come often and make obeisance before you?" So at last he repelled and refused to receive him, being arrogant and puffed-up, so that the Magnate Kena was stopped and held when his journey was but half accomplished. Then the Sovereign summoned Kanamura, Arakaï, and Obito-of-Kosè, saying, "Rock-Well of Tsukushi is in rebellion and has seized the uncultivated lands of the west. Who shall be made General?" Then the Great-Tribe-Master of the imperial guard and all the rest said, "As far as Arakaï is concerned, there is no one who walks at his right [52] in virtue, courage, and military knowledge!"

The Sovereign, agreeing to this, issued a decree, saying, "Great-Tribe-Master! Behold Rock-Well who is disobedient. Go and punish him." Whereon Arakaï, prostrating himself again and again, replied, "Rock-Well, the evil villain of the uncultivated lands of the west, counts rivers a barrier and comes not to court. Relying on steep mountains and fomenting discord, he puts the upright to naught, and his acts are undisciplined, prideful, and arrogant. From of old men have fought for the Sovereign, as well as to alleviate the wretchedness of the people, trusting to Sky-assistance, which your slave has always deemed necessary. Can he then fail dutifully to chastise these?" Then the Sovereign, charging him, with his own hand gave the battle-ax to the Great-Tribe-Master, saying, "East of the Ana-Passage We govern this Land. You shall govern it west of Tsukushi. Give rewards and penalties with authority and be not often at the trouble to refer to Us." Accordingly Arakaï took command, and fought Rock-Well in the District of Three-Wells, in Tsukushi, and in the end slew him and brought the border into subjection. Whereon

KUZU

Clan-Chief of Tsukushi, fearing that he would be slain with his father, offered the Sovereign the granary of Kasuya, which he begged might be accounted a ransom for his life.

Now the mound of Rock-Well was seventy shaku high, and sixty shaku in circumference. The ground of the tomb was six hundred shaku from north to south and four hundred from east to west. On its four sides are sixty stone men with stone shields, set opposite one another as if in a battle. At the northeast is a piece of ground called a Kitchen, in which is an erect stone man called the Trencher, and on the ground before him lies a naked man called the Thief. Beside these are four stone boars called Spoils. There are also three stone halls and two stone storage houses. The aged there say that this tomb was made for Rock-Well while he was still alive.[A]

(*Some say that when he was chastised by the imperial army Rock-Well fled alone to Buzen Province and died in a fold of a steep ridge of the southern mountains. To this place the army pursued but there lost trace of him, and in their anger they struck off the arms of the stone men and the heads of the stone horses.*[53])

After this Kena was sent on to Mimana to convey the Sovereign's commands. Later, however, an envoy from that Land complained of his conduct, and the Sovereign sent to recall him

MEZURAKO.

He returned as far as Port-Island,[54] when he fell ill and died. His funeral cortège went up the river into Omi, and his wife sang:

Up to Hira-Kata, || With the sound of the flute,
Goes young Kena || Of Omi—
With the sound of the flute.

On Mezurako's arrival in Mimana, Kenna's people who had remained there sent back this song:

The Land of Kara,[55] || Should it be called so
Now Mezurako has arrived? || Crossing afar
Iki, the opposite, || Mezurako has arrived.

Now in his youth Sky-Land-Great-Haruki-Wide-Court dreamed that a man came to him, saying, "If you show favor to one named

GREAT-TSUCHI-OF-HADA

when you are a man you shall without doubt rule the empire." When he woke he sent messengers to search in every place, and these brought from Fukusa-Village in Tree-District, in Behind-the-Mountains Province, a man with such a personal and family name. Then, filled with joy, exclaiming, "Never was there such a dream!" he said to him, "What has occurred to you?" Answering, the man said, "Only this. Your slave was returning from Isè, where he went to exchange goods, when he met on the mountain two wolves,[56] who, foul with blood, fought together. Your slave dismounted from his horse and washed his mouth and his hands, and besought them, saying, 'O Kami, august yet joying in violence! A huntsman, were he to come, would quickly take you captive.' Thus your slave made them cease fighting, cleansed their fur of blood, and at length released them, so that their lives were saved." At that Sky-Land-Great-Haruki-Wide-Court said, "Doubtless this is your recompense." And he caused him to take service near him and favored him more and more every day till he attained great riches.

The Sovereign died in the Palace of Tamaho in Iharè. His years were forty-three (or, as some say, eighty-two).⁵⁷ His august mound is on the plain of Awi in Three-Islands.⁵⁸

THE EMPEROR WIDE-LAND-GREAT-BRAVE-METAL-SUN (EASY-SPACE)⁵⁹

The Emperor Wide-Land-Great-Brave-Metal-Sun dwelt in the Palace of Metal-Bridge at Magari, in Mountain-Gate Province, and ruled the empire. The walls of his character were high so that it could not be looked into.⁶⁰ He was valiant and large-hearted and an able ruler. He continued Kanamura and Arakaï, the Great-Tribe-Masters, in office.

He had wedded Princess-Mountain-Ricefield-of-Kasuga, whom he made Empress. He wedded also

PRINCESS-SATÈ
PRINCESS-KAGARI

the two daughters of Obito-of-Kosè the Great-Magnate, taking to wife also

PRINCESS-YAKA

the daughter of the Great-Tribe-Master of the Warrior-Clan

ITAÏ.

It happened that the Sovereign gave command to

GREAT-MARO

the Magnate of Kashiwadè, to send a messenger to Ishimi for pearls. The Land-Rulers of Ishimi did not at once come to the capital and for some time failed to deliver these, so that Great-Maro was angered and seized and bound and questioned them. The Governor of Youth and other Land-Rulers, fearing, fled and hid in the inner part of the after-palace, and the Empress, not knowing that they had entered thus precipitately, fell down in agitation and in offended modesty. So the Governor of Youth and the rest were found guilty of intrusion, and being liable to a great penalty, respectfully besought the Empress, in atonement to accept the granary of Ishimi for her own. This was accepted and it was cut into districts which were added to the Province of Kazusa.

The Sovereign made a decree, saying, "Truly the Empress and the Emperor are one body, but as one is outside and the other inside, they are to be distinguished. Let there be set aside a portion of the granary-land from which to build a court-of-pepper,⁶¹ whose memory later generations may transmit." An imperial commission was therefore named to choose good rice-land. These, being charged, spoke to

AJIHARI [62]

Governor of Great-Kawachi, saying, "Offer now to the Sovereign the fruitful rice-land of Kiji." But he hoodwinked the commission, saying, "That rice-land is arid and difficult to water. Water put on it seeps through quickly, so that the harvest is too small for the great labor given it." The commission reported accordingly to the Sovereign, who said to Kanamura, "We have wedded four wives and as yet have had no offspring. Ten thousand years hence Our name will be extinct. What in your opinion should be done, O Our Uncle [63] of the imperial guard? Pondering this we are ceaselessly concerned." Said Kanamura, then, "Your slave is also concerned for this reason. The Sovereigns of this Land, ruling the empire, if they have offspring or if they have none ought to have what insures them a name. So I beseech you that for the Empress and your other consorts, granary-lands be set apart, so that to future generations they shall stand for the past." To this the Sovereign assented, and ordered such to be straightway set apart. Kanamura advised that the granary of Owari-Ricefield, with the Ricefield-Clans from every province, be given to Princess Satè, that the granary of Cherry-Tree-Well (some say, also, the granary of Mount Chinu) with the Ricefield Clans of every province, be given to Princess-Kagari, and that the granary of Wave-Swift, with spade-wielders of every district, be given to Princess-Yaka, for a sign to future generations and an example looking to the past. To this the Sovereign agreed.

The Sovereign proceeded to Three-Islands, with Kanamura in attendance. Through the latter he inquired of

IÏBO

the District-Chief, concerning good ricefields. Iïbo was extremely pleased and with loyal reverence offered as a gift Upper-Three-Moors, Upper-Kuwa-Plain and Lower-Kuwa-Plain, and also land in Takefu, altogether forty cho. Then the Great-Tribe-Master of the imperial guard, bidden by the Sovereign, said to Ajihari, "Of all the spread-out land, there is no portion but is in the imperial ownership. Beneath the wide sky there is no land which is not imperial land. But as for you, a mean and insignificant subject of the empire, you begrudged these imperial lands, and paid little heed to the message. Henceforth, you shall no longer be governor." At this Iïbo the District-Chief, his heart being filled with joy and dread, offered his son

TORIKI

to the Great-Tribe-Master as a slave, and Ajihari, in fear and remorse, made obeisance, and sweating, said to the Great-Tribe-Master, "The crime of this ignorant slave is worthy of death ten thousand times. I beseech you to permit me to offer in the spring and autumn five hundred spade-wielders from each district, to serve the Sovereign. My descendants will perpetually pray that their lives may depend upon this and will always remember this penalty as an example." In addition he offered the Great-Tribe-Master six cho of ricefield in Saï-Ricefield. (This, it appears, was the origin of the custom by which the Ricefield-Clan of the District of Kawachi are slaves of the granary of Takefu, in Three-Islands).

Now the Great-Tribe-Master of the Ihoki-Clan,

KIYOYU [64]

had a daughter, whose name was

PRINCESS-HATA

and she stole the necklace of the Great-Tribe-Master of the Warrior Clan,[65]

OKOSHI

and gave it to the Empress; but the affair at last was found out, and Kiyoyu gave her to be a slave of the Neck-Clan of the Kasuga-Clan, offering also the granary of the Ihoki-Clan of Koshibè in the Province of Aki, by which he atoned for her crime. Okoshi, in fear lest the affair involve him also, for his own safety offered the Ten-Market-Clan, the two villages of Kusaka and Toï, with the Hasè-Clan of Niye in the Province of Isè, and also the Isa-Mountain-Clan in the Land of Tsukushi.

It came to pass that the Land-Ruler of the Province of Musashi

OMI

Governor of Kasahara, quarrelled with his kinsman

OGI

as to who was rightly governor, the affair continuing for some years unsettled. Ogi was by nature obstreperous and rebellious, prideful and unmanageable, and secretly asking aid of

OKUMA

Land-Ruler of Kozukè, plotted with him Omi's death. Omi, learning this, fled to the capital and informed the court. So, when the affair was judged, Omi was made Land-Ruler and Ogi was put to death, after which Omi the Land-Ruler, in dread and joy, reverently offered the Sovereign the four granaries of Yokonu, Orange, Ohohi and Kurasu. After this, on account of the prosperity of the realm, the Sovereign decreed a great merry-making for five days, for the people's pleasure.

At this time the Retainer-Clan and the Bowman-Clan of Magari were formed. Also there were formed the granaries of Funami and of Kama in Tsukushi, of Tosa, Kuwabara, Kato, Ohonuka and Aka in Fruitful Province, of the Kasuga-Clan in the Province of Fire, of the Koshi-Clan and of Ushika in Harima, of Shizuki, Tanè, Kukutzu, Hawaka and Younger-River in the further Province of Maise, of Iyè and of the Itoshi-Clan in the Province of Millet, of Fusè and of the River-Clan in the Province of Tree, of Soshiki in the Province of Tamba, of Reed-Beach in the Province of Omi, of Mashiki and of Iruka in the Province of Owari, of Midono in the Province of Kozukè and of Wakanihe in the Province of Suruga. Also it was ordered that Dog-Keeper-Clans be formed in all provinces. The Sovereign appointed the Tribe-Master of the Ricefield-Clan,

CHERRY-TREE-WELL

to be Tribe-Master of the district Dog-Keepers and the Kishi of Wave-Swift to take in charge the income from the granaries. Likewise he bade the Great-Tribe-Masters, saying, "Cattle should be turned loose on Great-Sumi-Island and the fir plain of Princess-Island at Wave-Swift,[66] so that We may hope for a name transmitted to posterity.

The Sovereign died in the Palace of Metal-Bridge at Magari at seventy years. He was buried in the mound on the hill at Takaya-Village in Furuïchi in the Province of Kafuchi. In the mound were buried also the Empress and the Sovereign's younger sister, Lady-of-Kami-Cape.

THE EMPEROR BRAVE-LITTLE-WIDE-LAND-GREAT-SHIELD (SPREAD-CULTURE [67])

The assembled Ministers, on the death of the Sovereign, gave the Sword and the Mirror [68] to Brave-Little-Wide-Land-Great-Shield and caused him to assume the imperial rule. All of his qualities were evident, he was very intelligent and did not take the rule flippantly or boastfully, so that men of quality were true to him. He dwelt in the Palace of Ihori-Moor in Hinokuma and ruled the empire, making Kanamura of the imperial guard and Arakaï of the Warrior-Clan Great-Tribe-Masters as before. Also he made

NOBLE-OF-INAMÈ-OF-SOGA

Great-Magnate, and Great-Maro, Magnate of Abè, was made an official.

The Sovereign had wed Princess-Orange [69] whom he made Empress, and by whom he begot

KING-YOUNG-E-OF-KURA

(who, some say, was a female child named Princess-Young-Ya-of-Kura)

DIVINE-UË-HA [70]

(who, some say, was his daughter by Princess-Youth-of-Kafuchi). He took to wife also

PRINCESS-YOUTH-OF-KAFUCHI

and there were born to the two

PRINCE-FLAME-OF-FIRE [71]
PRINCE-YAKA-CLAN.

The Sovereign issued a decree saying, "Let the Clan-Chief of Asomo send from there more grain from the granary of the District of Mamuta in Kafuchi. Let the Great-Magnate of Soga and Noble-of-Inamè-of-Soga despatch the Tribe-Master of Owari to send grain of the granary of Nihinomi. Let the Magnate of Abè despatch the Magnate of Iga to send grain from the granary of the Province of Iga. Let there be built a granary at Mouth-of-Nanotsu. For since the Tsukushi, the Fire, and the Fruitful-Province granaries are separated and far off, the distance makes carriage difficult, so that it is hard to obtain supplies at need. Let the various districts each one make exchanges and build one together at Mouth-of-Nanotsu, that in special need there may be supplies and the lives of the people may be long continued. Go at once to the districts and tell them Our desire." Also the Sovereign bade Kanamura, Great-Tribe-Master of the imperial guard, to send his two sons

ROCK
PRINCE-SADÈ

to assist Mimana. Rock remained in Tsukushi, as head of its government, and prepared a campaign against Silla, Kudara, and Koma, but Prince-Sadè proceeded to Mimana.

It is related that on his way he came to the village of Bamboo-Moor, where he paid court to and wedded

PRINCESS-YOUNGER

who surpassed all in beauty. When he parted from her he gave her a mirror, and she sorrowed and wept. When she was crossing the Kuri River, the cord of the mirror was broken and it sank in the river. (Therefore the place was called Mirror-Crossing.) [A]

---

[70] **Ancestor of the Clan-Chiefs of Tajihi and of Ina.**
[71] **Ancestor of the Clan-Chiefs of Shihida.**

(*Some say that the wife was*

PRINCESS-SAYO-OF-PINE-TREE-BEACH

and that she ascended the hill named Mount Neck-Band-Wave [72] or Mount Mirror to gaze after his vessel, and taking off her neck-band waved it till it disappeared. From excess of grief at his leaving she was changed into a rock.[73])

(*Others say that after Prince-Sadè's departure, a man who closely resembled him came every night to his wife, Princess-Sayo-of-Pine-Tree-Beach, and slept with her, leaving at day-break. So, desiring to know who her visitor was in very truth, she fastened a hemp-thread to the hem of his robe and followed it, with her maid-servant, to the summit of a mountain, where was a pool, in which a creature lay sleeping whose body in the water was that of a man, but whose head that rested upon the bank was that of a serpent. Now he woke and saw her and instantly he became a man, who sang:*

> Since in Bamboo-Moor || Slept I with Princess-Younger
> But a single night,
> How can I gain her permission || Again to repair to her house?

The maid-servant, in affright, ran away and told the relatives of Princess-Sayo-of-Pine-Tree-Beach what she had seen, and these, gathering many of the people, straightway ascended the mountain, but neither the serpent nor Princess-Sayo-of-Pine-Tree-Beach was to be seen, and human bones were visible on the pool-bottom. They built a tomb south of the mountain in which the bones were interred, which exists to this day.)

Prince-Sadè took ship to go to Mimana, but it remained moveless, which

IWAKATSU

declared, "That the vessel does not proceed is by the heart's wish of a Sea-Deity who longs for

CLAN-CHIEFTAINESS-OF-NAKO

your mistress, who has been brought with you. If you leave her, you can proceed." Prince-Sadè and his mistress sorrowed, but he feared the imperial disgrace and loss of favor, so he compelled her to seat herself upon mats and to give herself to the waves.[74, A] Arriving in Mimana, Prince-Sadè assisted Kudara and brought about peace.

The Sovereign died in the Palace of Ihori-Moor at Hinokuma, at the age of seventy-three. He was buried in the mound at the top of the slope of Tsuki-Island, in Musa, in Mountain-Gate. The Empress and her young child, which probably died before reaching adult age, were buried with him in the same mound.

THE EMPEROR SKY-LAND-GREAT-HARUKI-WIDE-COURT (WISE-REVERENCE [75])

When the Sovereign Brave-Little-Wide-Land-Great-Shield died, Sky-Great-Haruki-Wide-Court [76] said to the ministers, "Being of few years and of little wisdom, I have not yet practiced the rule. The Empress is well-versed in government, and I beseech you that she be questioned and make decisions." The Empress however respectfully replied, "Your slave has received favor wider than sea and mountain, but the many operations of the government are far too difficult for a woman to be charged with. I pray you, O Ministers, to raise the imperial prince at once to the height, and let him rule the empire." So Sky-Land-Great-Haruki-Wide-Court became the Sovereign. Kanamura, the Great-Tribe-Master of the imperial guard, and Okoshi, Great-Tribe-Master of the Warrior-Clan, were made Great-Tribe-Masters and the Great-Magnate Noble-of-Inamè-of-Soga was made Great-Magnate, as formerly. Also he appointed Great-Tsuchi-of-Hada [77] Keeper-of-the-Purse.

The Sovereign dwelt in the Great Palace of Kanazashi at Shiki-Island, in the District of Shiki, in the Province of Mountain-Gate, and ruled the empire. He wedded Princess-Rock, whom he made Empress, and begot

PRINCE-OË-OF-JEWEL-KATSU-OF-YATA [78]
OSADA-NUNAKURA-BIG-JEWEL-SHIKI
KING-BROAD-HAT-SEW

(who, some say, was a daughter, named Princess-Broad-Hat-Sew, or Princess-Satakè).

At this time there came and dwelt in Mountain-Village in the District of Upper-Sofu, in the Province of Mountain-Gate, a man of Kudara named
KOCHIFU.[79]

Also the Emishi and the Hayato, with their people, came and gave allegiance, and Koma, Kudara, Silla, and Mimana sent envoys with tribute. The men of Hada,[80] Han, and others, who had come from the different nations on the border, were brought together and established in provinces and districts and written in the list of the people. The Hada men were altogether seven thousand and fifty-three families. The Keeper-of-the-Purse was appointed ruler of the Hada guard.

---

[79] **Ancestor of the Kochifu (Family) of Yamamura.**

The Sovereign proceeded to the shrine of the Hafuri at Wave-Shift with Kanamura the Great-Tribe-Master of the imperial guard,

INAMOCHI

Magnate of Kosè, and Okoshi the Great-Tribe-Master of the Warrior-Clan. He asked the Ministers how many soldiers would be needed to subjugate Silla, and Okoshi and others replied, "Few soldiers could not best Silla easily. When earlier Kudara's ambassadors asked that four districts of Mimana be given it, Kanamura straightway favored the request and it was granted, so that during many years Silla has been resentful. To subjugate it is no easy thing." At that Kanamura remained at home at Pleasant-to-Dwell-In, pretending illness, and did not come to court. When the Sovereign sent

MAGARIKO

Great-Toshi-of-Aöni, to ask him courteously, the Great-Tribe-Master offered the Sovereign his worthless thanks, saying, "It is only that the Ministers declare that I robbed Mimana, and through fear I came not to court." With that he gave the messenger a riding-horse and treated him as an honorable friend, so that the Great-Toshi-of-Aömi reported truly to the Sovereign, who, saying, "You, for long, have been true in all things. Pay no regard to the speech of the people," pronounced him innocent and favored him the more. The Sovereign took to wife likewise

PRINCESS-KITASHI

who was the daughter of Noble-of-Inamè-of-Soga, and begot

FERTILE-SUN-OF-ORANGE [81]
QUEEN-ROCK-KUMO [82]

(who served the Great Kami at Isè but was found to have had a liaison with King-Umaki [83] and was therefore dismissed)

PRINCESS-FRUITFUL-AUGUST-FOOD-COOK-HOUSE.[84]

He took to wife also

PRINCESS-LITTLE-E [85]

the aunt (or, as others say, the sister) of Princess-Kitashi, and begot

KING-UMAKI [86]
PRINCESS-ANAHO-CLAN-OF-HASHI-MAN [87]
PRINCE-HASETSUKA-CLAN-ANAHO-CLAN [88]
YOUNG-SAZAKI-OF-HASÈ-CLAN.[89]

In this reign it was reported from the Province of Koshi that at Mina-Clan-Cape, Mishi-Hasè [90] men came in a boat to the north of Sado-Island and remained there, eating fish which they took in spring and summer. The Island people said they were not human but Oni, and feared to go near them.

The people of Umu-Village, to the east of the Island, gathered acorns which they made ready to cook for food. They covered them with ashes to roast them, when the hulls became two men, which rested more than a shaku above the fire. Presently they fought, when the village-folk, in amazement, took them and set them in a courtyard, whereon they flew up and fought again in the same manner. A man made divination by which he declared, "Surely the Oni bewitch us!" And indeed, soon after, they were robbed by them. After that the Mishi-Hasè men departed to Segawa Bay.

The Kami of this bay is so fearful a Kami that no one dares approach it. Half of all the thirsty who drink that water perish and piles of their bones are on the rocks of the slopes. The people call this Kami

BEAR-OF-MISHI-HASÈ.

Now it befell at this time that

HASUI

Magnate of Kashiwadè, returning from Kudara, reported, "Your slave sent on this errand proceeded with his whole family to the Kudara coast, where at sunset we spent the night, when one of my children on a sudden could not be found nor could it be discovered where he had gone. In the night much snow fell so we were unable to search for him till day, when we came to a row of tiger's tracks leading away. So your slave took his sword and donned his armor and searched, and at a rock-wall drew the sword, saying, 'I reverently took up the cords and ribands of silk, toiling over land and sea, the wind my hair-comb, the rain my bath, the grass for my mat and briers for my cushion, and came to this place, by reason of my love for my child and my desire as his father that he should take over my dignity. You, awful Kami, have for one of your qualities love of children. By night my child has vanished, and following his trail I have searched for him up to this spot. I will avenge him without regard for my own life. This is why I am here.' Then the tiger came upon me, opening his devouring mouth. But swiftly with my left hand I caught the tongue of the tiger and with my right hand thrust it to death and flayed it and came back with the skin."

The District of Imaki, in the Province of Mountain-Gate, reported that

MIYA-KAWARA

Governor of Tami, a man of Hinokuma-Village, looking at the view from the upper story, saw a good horse of the breed of the mares that bear the food from the fisheries of the Land of Tree for the imperial table, a horse which at the sight of a shadow neighed loudly and leaped high over the back of its dam. He went out and bought it and had it for some years. When grown it moved like a frightened wild goose or a flying dragon, being different from the others and better, obeying command and being of regular gait. It leaped a ravine eighteen jo [91] wide on the Hill of Ohochi.

KUDARA SENDS THE BUDDHA TO NIPPON

Now the king of Kudara [92] sent as gift to the Sovereign a statue of Shaka [93] the Buddha [94] in gold and copper, some flags and umbrellas and some rolls of the sutras, with a personal communication, setting forth the meritoriousness of sending abroad this religion, which said: "This teaching is the best of all teachings, though difficult to convey and to learn. Even the Duke of Chow [95] and Confucius did not fully comprehend it. It can confer merit and infinite and endless reward, and by it one reaches full comprehension of the highest enlightenment. This wondrous learning has riches like those of a man who has all his soul desires and can gain his every wish by spending them. It fulfills all prayers without exception, and from far Tenjiku [96] it has spread to the Three Han where, when it is disclosed, all receive it reverently. So your slave, Myöng, king of Kudara, has dutifully sent his servant Nuri-Sachhi to carry it to the Sovereign Land and to spread it widely in the home provinces, so as to carry out Buddha's written word 'My law shall spread eastward.' " Thereon the Sovereign, hearing all, sprang up in delight and said to the envoys, "As we never before were able to hear so wondrous a learning, we personally cannot make a decision." He asked his Ministers separately, saying, "The Buddha offered by the border country on the west has a face of stern authority such as we never before beheld. Should it be given worship?" Noble-of-Inamè said, "The border countries on the west, every one, give it worship. Is only Mountain-Gate of the dragon-fly to refuse?" However, Okoshi, Great-Tribe-Master of the Warrior-Clan, and

KAMAKO

Tribe-Master of the Intercessor-Clan, together, said to the Sovereign, "The rulers of the empire always took care to worship the one hundred and eighty Sky-Kami and Earth-Kami and the Kami of the Land and of the grains in spring, summer, autumn and winter. If we were now to replace their worship by that of foreign Kami, we fear that our Land's

Kami would be angered." So the Sovereign bade that the Buddha be given to Noble-of-Inamè, who had expressed desire to have it, and that he give it worship, as a trial. And the Great-Magnate received it joyfully on his knees and made it a shrine at his dwelling in Owari-Ricefield, where he retired from the world, with all due observances, and to this end he purified his dwelling at Muku-Plain and made it a Buddhist temple.

Later, however, a plague came upon the Land, by which the people died before their time and it became worse as it continued. There was no healing for it. Okoshi and Kamako spoke to the Sovereign together, saying, "The people die thus from the plague because the previous advice of your slaves was not approved, but retracing your path before it is too late will in truth bring happiness. It is better to dispense with this at once and eagerly seek happiness hereafter." To this counsel the Sovereign listened, and the officials took the statue of Buddha and cast it into the Wave-Swift Canal,[97] and fired the Buddhist temple and burned it wholly. But the sky being cloudless and without wind, the fire from it destroyed the great hall.[98] And presently from the Province of Kawachi it was reported thus: "A voice echoing thunderously comes from the sea off Chinu, in Izumi District, and there is a refulgence which glows like a shining sun." At that the Sovereign's heart was amazed and he sent the Governor of the Miso-Clan to the sea to inquire into this thing. That one went there accordingly, and lo, he found floating on the surface a camphor wood log which shone brightly. He took this and offered it to the Sovereign and an artificer was bidden to make of it two statues of Buddha. (These are the shining camphor wood statues in the present Buddhist temple of Good-Moor.)

At that time the Magnate of Uchi was sent on an errand to Kudara, taking as gifts two fine horses, two boats, fifty bows and fifty sets of arrows, with an imperial order saying, "Let scholars of medicine, of geomancy and of the calendar, take turns in coming to court and returning home. It is the year and month in which these ranks shall be replaced, so they shall be sent back with the envoy to be replaced, with rolls of geomancy, calendars and medicines for our imperial use." The Sovereign proceeded to the Palace of Magari in Kusunoki, and bade Noble-of-Inamè, Great-Magnate of Soga, to appoint

GREAT-SHIN-MI [99]

[99] **Ancestor of the Tribe-Masters of Funa.***

* *Funa* (*funè*), ship.

to keep record of the ship-tax. So he was appointed Chief-of-Ships and the name Scribe-of-Ships was given him. Also Noble-of-Inamè, Great-Magnate of Soga, and

IWAYUMI

Magnate of Piled-up-Rice-Ears, were sent to the five districts of Maise to found the granary of White-Well, Noble-of-Inamè was sent with others to Small-Island District in Nearer-Maise to found a granary, and

MIZU-KO

Governor of Mountain-Ricefield in Mulberry-Castle, was appointed its Governor-of-Ricefields.[1] Noble-of-Inamè, Great-Magnate of Soga, was sent with others to High-Market District in Mountain-Gate to found the granary of Great-Musa of the Kara people and the granary of Little-Musa of the Koma people. The granary of Ama in the Land of Tree was founded in that Land. The Kara men of different places were made the Ricefield-Clan of the granary of Great-Musa and the Koma men were made the Ricefield-Clan of the granary of Little-Musa. (It was because of the making of the Kara and Koma men Ricefield-Clans that these were called granaries.) [2]

Now it befell that a certain man circulated a libel upon

UTA-GOOD

Magnate of Mumakahi, alleging, "That one's wife came upon me at Sanuki with an odd saddle-cushion, and when I regarded it, behold, it was the saddle of the Empress." He was given up to the officers of inquiry, who closely questioned him. Then Uta-Good swore an oath saying, "If this be true and no false accusation, may Sky-calamity fall on me!" In the end he fell down and died from the torture. Soon afterward sudden evils befell in the imperial palace, so the officers of inquiry took his two sons,

MORISHI
NASEHI

and repeating an incantation, saying, "It is not by our hand that they are thus treated," were about to cast them into the fire, when the mother of Morishi made supplication, saying, "Great misfortune will befall you if my son is cast into the fire; let him, I pray, be given to the Hafuri as a slave to serve the Kami." So, as the mother prayed, permission was granted to give him to the service of the Kami.

At this time Silla sent envoys[3] with tribute, who remained, not return-

---

[3] Ancestors of the Silla Folk of Uno-Mura in Sarara District, Kawachi Province.

ing to their Land, but being compelled to become subjects of the Sovereign. Also an army, under the command of

NOBLE-OF-OMARO-OF-TREE

its general-in-chief, and the Magnate of the River-Clan

NIYÈ

was sent against Silla to make inquiry into its attack on Mimana. It arrived there at length, and

TONI

Head-man of the Komo-Tsumè-Clan, was despatched to Kudara to arrange a plan of campaign. On the way to his wife's dwelling, where he stayed, he lost a letter and a bow and arrows, by which Silla learned his full plan and gathered a great force, but was beaten and became subject. The victorious Noble-of-Omaro-of-Tree led his army to the Kudara camp, where the troops all rendered him affection and earnest service. Niyè, advancing alone, in continuous fighting captured the entire enemy force, so that the Silla troops lifted the white banner, and throwing down their weapons, submitted themselves, but Niyè, who was without knowledge of soldiering, raised his white banner in return, meaning only that they should advance. At which the Silla leader, exclaiming that Niyè desired to surrender, led up his troops and they attacked in haste with all their weapons unsheathed and put the advance guard to flight, very many being wounded.

TAHIKO

Land-Ruler of Mountain-Gate, believing no aid could come, left his men and fled. The Silla leader, holding a curved spear, pursued him to the moat of the castle, and lifting the spear aimed a blow, but Tahiko, who rode a fast horse, leaped the moat of the Castle, barely saving his life. The other, standing on the edge of the moat, cried. . . .[4] Thereon the Magnate of the River-Clan retreated with his troops and made a hurried camp on the moor, but the troops despised him and would not obey him, and the Silla leader came himself into the camp, making prisoners of Niyè and all his troops, with his wife

PRINCESS-MUMASHI

the daughter of the Magnate of Sakamoto, who was with him. At that time father and child and husband and wife had no compassion for one another, and when the leader asked Niyè, "Which do you love best, your life or your wife's life?" he replied, "Is the love of a man worth my ruin? Nothing is more loved by me than life." And in the end he gave her for a concubine, and the Silla leader had public connection with her. When later she returned, the Magnate of the River-Clan would have come near and spoken with her, but so great was her mortification that she would not live with him, saying, "How shall I live with a former Lord who sold his slave's body without cause?" And she steadfastly refused to speak with him.

IKINA

Kishi of Mitsugi, was taken prisoner at the same time, but he, being of stout soul, refused absolutely to submit, whereon the Silla leader, drawing his sword, made him, under threat of death, take off his trousers and turn his posterior toward Nippon and bade him shout aloud obscenities to its generals. But he shouted obscenities to the Sillan king and continued to shout these however much they tortured him, till they slew him. His son

OJIKO

taking his father in his arms, died in like manner. Ikina's mind, set upon holding to his own words, was thus unshakable, and therefore all the generals grieved for him. Also his wife

PLANTAIN [5]

was taken prisoner at the same time, and sorrowing for her they sang:

> See how Plantain, there || Taking stand by the castle
> Of the Kara Land, || Waving afar her head-dress,
> Turning toward Mountain-Gate.

And one, replying to it, made this song:

> Plantain I behold || Standing there by the castle,
> Of the Kara Land, || Waving afar her head-dress,
> Turning to face Wave-Swift.

The Sovereign sent Prince-Sadè,[6] Tribe-Master of the imperial guard, as chief general, at the head of a force of some tens of thousands of troops, to attack Koma, and he, proceeding on the plan of Kudara, put it to flight. The king escaped by scaling a wall. Prince Sadè, after this victory, took possession of the palace, fetching away all its treasures, gifts, hangings from the king's own room woven in seven thicknesses, and a building of iron [7] that was on the roof of a storyed building in the west of Koma. The hangings of seven thicknesses were given as a gift to the Sovereign, and to Noble-of-Inamè of Soga, the Great-Magnate, were sent two suits of armor, two swords with golden decorations, three chased copper bells, many-colored banners and a lovely woman named Yomè, with Atako, her attendant. The two women the Great-Magnate in the end took for concubines, giving them quarters in the Palace of Magari of Karu. After this Silla sent envoys [8] with tribute, but these did not go back to their own Land and were compelled to become subjects. Likewise

TU-MU-RYA-PHYE [9]

and other Koma men came to Tsukushi and settled in Behind-the-Mountains Province. At this time there befell floods and famine in districts and provinces so that sometimes men ate each other, so that grain to aid these was sent from near districts.

Now the Sovereign commanded as follows: "The founding of Ricefield-Clans is an ancient custom, yet during ten years past many have shirked their labor, their names being omitted from the lists. Let

ITSU

be sent to make new lists of the Ricefield-Clan of White-Well." He accordingly did so and, as commanded, made these lists permanent in order to establish Ricefield families, and the Sovereign, approving the manner in which he had done this, made him Head-man of White-Well and also Governor-of-Ricefields under Mizu-Ko.

When the Sovereign proceeded to the Palace of Shibagaki in Hasè, one

MOSHIRO

of Koshi, Magnate of Yenu, coming to the capital, said to him, "Koma envoys, ill-treated by wind and wave, lost their way and did not find the port, drifting on the tide till they made shore. The district ruler hid this fact, which I now disclose to you." Thereon the Sovereign commanded, saying, "Koma men, for the first time since I began to reign many years ago, have gone astray and come to the Koshi shore. They have met with shipwreck to their hurt and have been cast into the sea, but have escaped with their lives. The officers charged with such matters shall build a hall in Sagaraka District in Behind-the-Mountains Province, and shall make it clean and cordially assist in their entertainment." He returned then from the Palace of Shibagaki in Hasè, and Arako,[10] Governor of the Family of the Han-folk of the east, and

WAVE-SWIFT

Governor of Mulberry-Castle, were sent to meet the Koma Envoys and

---

[8] Ancestors of the Silla Folk of Hani-ïho in Mishima (Three-Island) District, Settsu Province.
[9] Ancestor of the Present Koma Folk of Unè-Hara, Nara (Level), and Yamamura.

to conduct them, while

LITTLE-KATA-CLAN

Magnate of Kashiwadè was despatched to Koshi to entertain them. Their chief, well aware that the Magnate had been sent by the Sovereign, said to

OX-OF-MICHI

ruler of Koshi district, "So, as I suspected, you yourself are not the Sovereign, for you have made obeisance to the ground to the Magnate of Kashiwadè, fully proving your vassalage, after you fooled me and took the tribute for yourself. Return it therefore speedily, and waste no words in excuse." The Magnate, hearing of this, sent to demand the tribute, and it was all given back, and he returned to the capital to make report.

When the Koma envoys came to Omi,

SARU

Magnate of Kosè was sent from Wave-Swift port, together with

AKABATO-OF-KISHI,

to drag a boat to Mount Sasanami, where they decorated it and went to meet them at Mount North in Omi, fetching them finally to the official hall at Komahi in Behind-the-Mountains. So

LITTLE-MARO

Governor of Uhe-of-Saka of the Han-folk of the east, and

GREAT-OSHI

Head-man of Nishikori, were despatched to conduct them, and the Koma envoys were entertained again in the official hall of Sagaraka.

Now the Sovereign lay on his bed ill and in anxiety, and the imperial prince was summoned by a swift mounted messenger. The Sovereign, taking his hand, said to him, "We are desperately ill and the future is your charge. Attack Silla and make Mimana a dependency." He died in the inner room, being of great age.[11] He was buried in a temporary tomb at Furuichi in Kawachi and later was buried in the mound of Sakahi at Hinokuma. Silla sent envoys to condole and to lament.

THE EMPEROR OSADA-NUNAKURA-BIG-JEWEL-SHIKI (CLEVERNESS [12])

The Sovereign Osada-Nunakura-Big-Jewel-Shiki dwelt in the Palace of Great-Well in Kudara [13] (some say in the Palace of Osada) and ruled the empire during fourteen years. He was not a Buddhist, but loved letters. He confirmed in his office

MORIYA-OF-YUGÈ

as Great-Tribe-Master of the Warrior-Clan, and appointed as Great-Magnate the son of Noble-of-Inamè of Soga,[14]

NOBLE-OF-MUMAKO-OF-SOGA.[15]

(The people of that time also gave him the name Great-Magnate-of-Island because in the courtyard of his dwelling on the bank of the Asuka River a small pool had been made, in whose midst was a little island.) He was versed in military operations and was eloquent. Also he paid reverence to the Three-Precious-Things.[16]

The Sovereign asked the imperial princes and the Great-Magnate where the Koma envoys then were, and the Great-Magnate replied, "In the official hall at Sagaraka." Hearing this the Sovereign was greatly angered and answered hotly, "I am most regretful! Their names, as envoys, had been announced to the Sovereign, my sire, when he died." He despatched Ministers to the official hall at Sagaraka to examine and list the tribute they had brought and to send them to the capital. He also submitted to the Great-Magnate the Koma letter, and calling together all the scribes, bade them read and expound it, but for three days they could not do so. Great-Shin-Mi,[17] however, was able to read and expound it, at which the Sovereign and the Great-Magnate both said in praise, "Good, O industrious Shin-Mi! But for your love of learning who could have expounded it? Henceforth do you wait near Us in the palace." Later the Sovereign declared to the scribes of the east and the west, "Why has your especial art failed? Of all you many, none is Shin-Mi's peer." The Koma letter was on crows' feathers, in characters black like them, so that none could read them; but Shin-Mi held the feathers in boiling-rice steam and pressed them on silk, by which the characters were set on the silk, so that the court was amazed.

The Koma chief-envoy said to the vice-envoys, "In the time of the late Sovereign, because you did not take my word, you let others fool you and without permission divided up our Land's tribute and gave it, thoughtlessly, to persons not in authority. You were blameworthy, and if our king learns of it, he will surely put you to death." So the vice-envoys said to one another, "When we return to our Land evil will come to us if the chief-envoy tells of our dereliction. Better kill him in secret so as to prevent his speaking." That night, however, the plan became known to the chief-envoy, who dressed himself and took a station alone in the inner court of the official hall, not knowing what to do. While he was there a ruffian came and struck him on the head with a mace and fled; then another came face to face with him and struck him on the head and hand and fled. The chief-envoy silently stood still, wiping the blood from his face. Then another ruffian, running up, stabbed him in the abdomen with a sword and fled. The chief-envoy fell down in fear and prayed for mercy, but another ruffian came and killed him and fled. Next morning Little-Maro, Governor of Uhe-of-Saka, of the Han-folk of the East, one of those who had in charge the official entertainment, made inquiry, and the vice-envoys, concocting a lie, said that the chief-envoy, disobediently to the Sovereign's command, had refused to receive a wife which had been given him, for which great insolence they, though slaves, had slain him in the Sovereign's name. He was given ceremonial burial by the officers.

On their departure the envoys anchored on the coast of the sea of Koshi, and their ship being wrecked, many of them were drowned. The court wondered that they should so many times lose their way and were allowed to leave without being entertained, but the Sovereign despatched Wave-Swift, Governor of the Ama-Clan of Maise, to accompany them back. He met them at the coast, and putting on board their vessel two of his sailors

IWAHI

the Head-man of Great-Island, and the Head-man of Saöka who was named

MASA

and putting two of the Koma men on his own vessel, to guard against treachery by this exchange, they set sail. However, after going some ri, Wave-Swift, in fear of the waves, threw the two Koma men into the sea. He then returned, and reported that many whale had gathered and had hindered and swallowed the ships, oars and steering-gear, so that he and his men feared they would be swallowed by these fish and could not make the voyage. The Sovereign, knowing this a lie, forbade him to go back to his own province, but used him in one of the official departments.

The next year the Koma Envoys again cast anchor on the coast of the sea of Koshi, and going to the capital, said to the Sovereign, "Last year your slaves left for their Land with the envoy who accompanied them, and when they reached their Land, Iwahi, Head-man of Great-Island and those with him were entertained with all fitting ceremony as envoys and the Koma king gave them especial welcome and respect. But the vessel of the envoy who accompanied us has not arrived, so he has sent us envoys again, with Iwahi and his men, to ask respectfully why those envoys have not come." Thereon the Sovereign weighed Wave-Swift's crime, and said to him, "You have committed two crimes, first deceiving the court, and second causing the drowning of envoys of a Land which is our neighbor. Because of these grave crimes you shall not be freed." So he was judged and punished.

Now the Great-Magnate, Noble-of-Mumako-of-Soga, was despatched to the Province of Maise to increase the White-Well granary and its Ricefield-Clan, and having listed the Ricefield-Clan and given the list to Itsu, Scribe of White-Well, he returned to the capital and made report. Also the Sovereign gave to

OX [18]

younger Brother of Great-Shin-Mi, Scribe of Ships, the name Scribe-of-Ports.

The Sovereign wedded Princess-Fruitful-August-Food-Cook-House, by whom he begot

PRINCESS-KAÏ-TAKO-OF-UJI [19]

who wedded Shotoku, the heir-to-the-throne. Also he took to wife one of the Neck-Clan,

LADY-OF-LITTLE-BEAR-CHILD [20]

and there was born to them

QUEEN-TAKARA. [21]

He took to wife also

PRINCESS-WIDE

who was the daughter of

KING-MADÈ-OF-LONG-LIFE [22]

of Long-Life, whom he made Empress, and there were born to the two

KING-PRINCE-MAN-OF-OSAKA [23]
PRINCESS-SHITSU-KAÏ-OF-UJI [24]

(who some say was a male child named Prince-Uji).

Also he took to wife

LADY-OF-OMINA-CHILD [25]

daughter of the Magnate of Kasuga, the Clan-Chief

NAKATSU [26]

and there were born to the two

PRINCE-WAVE-SWIFT
PRINCE-KASUGA.

Of these children, King-Prince-Man-of-Osaka wedded his half-sister, Queen-Takara, and begot

LONG-LIFE-PERFECT-SUN-WIDE-NUKA.[27]

The diviners chose by divination a spot for the dwellings of the imperial princes

PRINCE-AMA-CLAN
PRINCE-ITOÏ,[28]

and a palace was built at Wosa-Ricefield, called Palace-of-Saki-Jewel. On the death of the Empress, Princess-Wide, Princess-Fruitful-August-Food-Cook-House was made Empress, and there were founded a Sun-Worship-Clan and a personal Clan.[29]

PRINCE-GREAT-WAKÈ

and the Kishi of Oguro were despatched to administer the Land of Kudara, and by these envoys, when they came back, the king of that Land offered to the Sovereign some religious rolls, and an Abstainer, a Practicer of Meditation, a Nun, a Reciter of the Mantra, a Maker of Buddhist Statues, and a Designer of Buddhist Temples, all six of these. Thus there was built at Wave-Swift the Buddhist temple of Prince-Great-Wakè. Later Silla sent a statue of Buddha. At this time Princess-Shitsu-Kaï-of-Uji [30] served the Shrine at Isè, but was found to have had illicit relations with

PRINCE-CLAN-OF-IKÈ [31]

the imperial prince, and the appointment was withdrawn.

Now the Emishi by thousands rebelled on the border, so their chiefmen Ayakasu and others [32] were summoned, and the Sovereign addressed them, saying, "In the reign of the Sovereign Prince-Great-Perfect-Ruling-Lord [33] you Emishi who deserved death were slain and those who deserved pardon were pardoned. Accordingly, We shall slay your leaders." Then they felt great fear and dread, and going into the middle current of the Hasè River, faced Mount-August-House and washed their mouths and swore, "From now on we Emishi, our children and our children's children, will serve the Sky-gate with true hearts, and if we prove false to this oath, let all the Sky- and the Earth-Kami, and the spirits of the Sovereigns, destroy our people."

The Magnate of Kafuka, who had come from Kudara, had a stone statue of Miroku,[34] and the Tribe-Master of Saheki had a statue of

Buddha, and Noble-of-Mumako-of-Soga, asking for the two Buddhist statues, sent

SHIBA-TATTO [35]

SUKURI-OF-KURA-CLAN

together with the Governor of Clan-of-Ikè, who was named

HIDA,

everywhere to find people who were believers. As a result he found in the Province of Harima one Hye-Phyön,[36] of Koma, who had been a Buddhist priest but was then a layman, whom the Great-Magnate caused to teach him, and to confer religious orders upon

SHIMA

daughter of Shiba-Tatto, under the name Zen-Shin-the-Nun. He conferred religious orders also upon her two pupils

TOYOMÈ

who was the daughter of

YAHO-OF-HAN-MAN

under the name Senzo-the-Nun, and

ISHIMÈ

who was the daughter of

NISHIKORI-TSUBU

under the name Keïzen-the-Nun. And Noble-of-Mumako-of-Soga, according to Buddhist law, gave respect to these three nuns, giving them to the Governor of Hida and to Shiba-Tatto, whom he commanded to feed and clothe them. Also he built a Buddhist temple to the eastward of his house and enshrined there the stone statue of Miroku, and made the three nuns meet together for religious worship. Shiba-Tatto, finding a Buddhist relic [37] in the food-of-worship, gave it to Noble-of-Mumako-of-Soga who, to test it, laid it on a piece of iron, and lifting high an iron hammer, beat it, when the pieces of iron and the hammer flew to pieces without the relic's being crushed. Then he cast it into the water, but it floated or sank as he willed, so that Noble-of-Mumako-of-Soga, Hida and Shiba-Tatto believed in Buddha and devoutly worshiped him. He built also another Buddhist temple at his house at Stone-River, from which place Buddhism began, and building a Pagoda on the north side of the hill of Great-Moor, he held a meeting for worship and placed Shiba-Tatto's relic atop its pillar. Also, Noble-of-Mumako-of-Soga, being sick, consulted a diviner, who declared it a punishment sent by the heart's wish of the Buddha-Kami that had been worshiped in the time of his father.[38] So Noble-of-Mumako-of-Soga sent a youth of his family to report the divination to the Sovereign who bade that the Kami of his father be given worship, and Noble-of-Mumako-of-Soga gave worship to the stone statue and besought long life.

Presently a plague spread through the Land and many people died, so Moriya-of-Yugè, Great-Tribe-Master of the Warrior-Clan, with the officer of the Intercessors,

KATSUMI

(or, as some say, the Tribe-Master of the Intercessors

IWARÈ,

together with the Clan-Chief of Great Three-Threads

SAKAË)

made a plot to destroy Buddhism, wishing to burn the Buddhist temple and the pagoda and to fling away the Buddhist statues. But Noble-of-Mumako-of-Soga set himself against the plot and would not consent. So the others said to the Sovereign, "Because you were unwilling to follow your slaves' advice, the plague has spread, from the time of the Sovereign your father to your own time, till the people face destruction. Is this not the direct result of the founding of the Buddhist religious worship by Noble-of-Mumako-of-Soga?" The Sovereign answered, "True. Buddhism shall be made to cease." So Moriya-of-Yugè went to the Buddhist temple, where he took his seat on a couch and caused the pagoda to be cut down and burned with fire, burning also the statue of Buddha and the Buddhist temple, and what the fire left of the statue of Buddha he threw into the Wave-Swift Canal. It was a windy and rainy day but cloudless, and wearing a rain-coat, he berated Noble-of-Mumako-of-Soga and his religious disciples so that they were ashamed and repentant. Also he despatched

AUGUST-HOUSE [39]

Ruler of Saheki, to bring Shima and the others who had been caused to be made nuns by Noble-of-Mumako-of-Soga, and he, fearing to disobey the command, summoned these nuns with sorrowful tears and gave them to August-House, and when officers had taken from them their three robes, they were imprisoned and beaten at the Ichi-of-Tsubaki road-house.

But the Sovereign and the Great-Tribe-Master were all at once stricken with ulcers. Throughout the Land were many who were thus stricken and died, and those stricken said it was as though their bodies were burned, beaten and broken, and died sorrowing. And the aged and the young whispered to one another, "Is this the penalty for burning the statue of Buddha?" Then Noble-of-Mumako-of-Soga said to the Sovereign, "Your slave is not yet recovered from illness and cannot possibly be aided except by the efficacy of the Three-Precious-Things." [40] So the Sovereign bade him worship Buddha himself but to refrain from teaching it to others, and the three nuns were restored to him. These he took with joy, and grieving because of their special suffering, made obeisance before them, and building another Buddhist temple for them, put them into it and supported them. But the illness of the Sovereign increased, till he died in the great chamber.

A temporary burial-palace was built at Hirosè, and wearing his sword, Noble-of-Mumako-of-Soga made a funeral address, when Moriya-of-Yugè laughed, saying, "A sparrow stricken by the huntsman's arrow!" Then Moriya-of-Yugè made his funeral address, and because his arms and legs shook, Noble-of-Mumako-of-Soga, the Great-Magnate, laughed, saying, "A bell should be fastened to him!" Thus, beginning in a small incident, these two Ministers hated one another. Sakaë sent falcon-men [41] to guard the courtyard of the temporary tomb, at which Prince-Hasetsuka-Clan-Anaho-Clan,[42] who desired to seize the reign, was angered and exclaimed, "Do you serve the court of a dead Sovereign and not the person of the living one?"

The burial mound of the Sovereign is at Shinaga, in Kafuchi. The Empress, his mother, was buried in the same mound.

THE EMPEROR FERTILE-SUN-OF-ORANGE
(EMPLOY-REFULGENCE [43])

The Sovereign Fertile-Sun-of-Orange made Iharè his capital, the palace being named Namitsuki-of-Clan-of-Ikè (some say Palace of Clan-of-Ikè) and ruled the empire for three years. He believed in Buddha's law and had respect for the Kami-Way.[44] He confirmed in office both Noble-of-Mumako-of-Soga as Great-Magnate and Moriya-of-Yugè as Great-Tribe-Master of the Warrior-Clan, as before.

He wedded Princess-Anaho-Clan-of-Hashi-Man, his half-sister, whom he made Empress, and begot

PRINCE-EAR-QUICK-WISE-VIRTUE.[45]

who was called Prince-Stable-Door, because the Empress, on the day her pregnancy came to end, made a circuit of the secluded district, examining the various departments, and had just reached the stable-door in the horse-section, when he was painlessly brought forth; and he was called also after the upper-palace because the Sovereign, who loved him, made him occupy its southern portion. There was born to the two also

PRINCE-ARMY.

Also he took to wife

CHILD-OF-IÏ-ME [46]

who was the daughter of

KURA-MAN-WIDE-OF-TAGIMA

and there were born to the two a son and a daughter

PRINCE-TAËMA [47]

PRINCESS-NUKADÈ-PRINCESS.[48]

Princess-Nukadè-Princess was charged with the worship of Great-Sky-Shiner at the Shrine of Isè.

Now Prince Hasetsuka-Clan-Anaho-Clan would have broken into the temporary burial place in order to seduce the Empress, Princess-Fruitful-August-Food-Cook-House, but the Minister who was her favorite, Sakaë, Clan-Chief of Three-Threads, summoned the imperial guard, who made fast the gates of the palace against him and denied him entrance. Prince-Hasetsuka-Clan-Anaho-Clan asked them who was there, when they replied that Sakaë, Clan-Chief of Three-Threads, was there. He cried to them seven times to open the gates, but they continually denied him entrance, whereon he declared to the Great-Tribe-Master, "Sakaë persists in his affronts. It was an affront for him to say in his mortuary address, 'Your court shall not remain empty, but shall remain like the clear face of a mirror, while your slave dutifully serves you in maintaining peace.' Now many youths of the Sovereign's family and the two chief Ministers are here, so whose place is it to speak thus, boasting of dutiful service? Also I desired to see the interior of the temporary burial place but was denied entrance, and though I personally cried seven times to open the gates, there was no obedience. I pray you to let me slay him." The Great-Magnates answered, "As you have declared, do." So Prince-Hasetsuka-Clan-Anaho-Clan, whose secret plan was to seize the empire, stating that he purposed to slay the Clan-Chief Sakaë, with Moriya-of-Yugè took soldiery and invested Clan-of-Ikè in Iharè. Sakaë, when he learned this, hid himself on Mount August-House, and that midnight he left the mountain secretly and hid himself in the after-palace. His relatives, however,

SHIRATSU-TSUMI
MOUNT-YOKO,

---

[47] **Ancestor of the Clan-Chiefs of Taëma.**

disclosed his whereabouts, and Prince-Hasetsuka-Clan-Anaho-Clan at once sent to Moriya, bidding him go and slay Sakaë with his two children; and the Great-Tribe-Master departed, leading armed soldiery. Noble-of-Mumako-of-Soga, hearing of this plot from others, went to the prince, and reaching his gate as he was leaving to join the Great-Tribe-Master, opposed this, saying that a ruler should not in person approach a criminal. The prince, however, would not hear him, but went, whereon Noble-of-Mumako-of-Soga at once followed after him to Iharè, where he vehemently withstood him, so that the prince paused and waited, seated on a couch, for a long time till the Great-Tribe-Master, coming with the soldiery, reported that he had slain Sakaë and the rest.

(By some, however, it is said that Prince-Hasetsuka-Clan-Anaho-Clan went himself and slew them with arrows.)

At this Noble-of-Mumako-of-Soga grieved greatly, saying that disturbance must soon come in the realm, but the Great-Tribe-Master, hearing, replied, "You, being a Minister of little influence, have not knowledge." Now Sakaë, Clan-Chief of Three-Threads, had been favored by the Sovereign Osada-Nunakura-Big-Jewel-Shiki, and had had in his charge all affairs both inside and outside,[49] so that the Empress, Princess-Fruitful-August-Food-Cook-House, and Noble-of-Mumako-of-Soga both hated Prince-Hasetsuka-Clan-Anaho-Clan.

Now on the day when the Sovereign performed the ceremony of New-Rice-Tasting on the bank of the river at Iharè, he fell ill, and returned to the palace attended by all the Ministers. He said to them, "We desire to give faith to the Three-Precious-Things. Take council as to it." So all the Ministers entered the court for conference, when Moriya and Katsumi, Tribe-Master of the Intercessors, opposed the Sovereign's word, saying, "Shall we pay worship to foreign Kami and turn away from the Kami of our Land? Surely we know nothing of these." But Noble-of-Mumako-of-Soga said, "Shall any one counsel against our aiding to carry out the Sovereign's bidding?" At which the prince, the Sovereign's younger brother,[50] brought inside the palace a priest of the Land of Toya. Moriya watched in great anger, till

KEKUSO,

scribe of the Great-Saka-Clan, came in haste, and in secret told the Great-Tribe-Master that all the Ministers were in conspiracy against him and intended to ambush him, and hearing, Moriya fled to Ato where he had a country residence, and gathered troops. Katsumi gathered soldiery at his dwelling and took them to aid him, and afterward he made images of King-Prince-Man-of-Osaka,[51] of the Heir-to-the-Throne, and of Prince-

Brave-Ricefield, and hated [52] them. Finding he could not succeed, however he soon went to the palace of King-Prince-Man-of-Osaka at Mimata. But

ICHIHI

Head-man of Tomi, a retainer of that one, watched Katsumi's departure from the place and slew him with his sword. At that Moriya sent word from his house at Ato to the Great-Magnate Noble-of-Mumako-of-Soga by

WO-SAKA

Ruler of the Warrior-Clan of Great Ichi of Yasaka, and to

ANI

Ruler of the Painter-Clan,[53] that he was absenting himself because of news that the Ministers has conspired against him, and Noble-of-Mumako-of-Soga sent the Tribe-Master of Yajima-of-Hashi to

HIRAFU

Tribe-Master of the imperial guard, to tell him what the Great-Tribe-Master had said. So Hirafu, grasping a bow and arrows and a skin shield, went and stayed at the house of the Great-Magnate at Tsukikuma, guarding that one night and day without leaving.

Now the Sovereign's ulcers grew continually worse till near the last, when

TASUNA [54]

of the Saddle-Makers-Clan, came and said to him, "For the sake of the Sovereign your slave will retire from the world to worship and will make a statue of Buddha sixteen shaku tall and a Buddhist temple." This profoundly touched the Sovereign. This statue is the wooden Buddha which stands, with Bosatsu,[55] in the Temple of Sakata, at Minabuchi. The Sovereign died in the great chamber. He was buried in the mound by the bank of Lake Iharè, and was later moved to the Middle Tomb of Shinaga.

THE EMPEROR YOUNG-SAZAKI-OF-HASÈ-CLAN [56]
(VENERABLE-UPLIFTED [57])

After the death of the Sovereign the troops of the Great-Tribe-Master of the Warrior-Clan three times caused trouble. From the beginning it was Moriya's desire, disregarding the rest of the princes, to make Prince-Hasetsuka-Clan-Anaho-Clan the Sovereign, and he planned a hunt which he hoped would be the means of giving him, rather than the others, the rule. To this end he secretly sent him word that he desired to hunt with him in My-Shame. The conspiracy, however, became known, and Noble-of-Mumako-of-Soga and the rest of the Ministers, acting under instruction of Princess-Fruitful-August-Food-Cook-House, commanded

NIFUTÈ

Tribe-Master of Saheki, to go immediately, together with

ROCK-VILLAGE

Tribe-Master of Hashi, and the Magnate of Ikuba

MAKUI

all strongly armed, and slay Prince-Hasetsuka-Clan-Anaho-Clan and Prince-Yaka-Clan. So that midnight Nifutè and those with him surrounded Prince-Hasetsuka-Clan-Anaho-Clan's palace and the guard, climbing to the upper story, smote him on the shoulder so that he fell from the upper story and fled into an adjoining building where the guard, fetching a light, slew him. Prince-Yaka-Clan also, who supported him, was slain.

Now Zen-Shin-the-Nun and the rest said to the Great-Magnate, "Those whe retire from the world act according to self-government, and we beseech you to grant us permission to go to Kudara to learn the laws of self-government." So, as envoys came at this time bringing tribute from Kudara to the court, the Great-Magnate bade them take the nuns with them when they were ready to cross to that Land, and to let them learn the law of self-government, and when this had been done, to send them back. The envoys replied that there would be time to send them after they themselves had returned to the border of their Land and informed its king.

THE CONSPIRACY AGAINST THE GREAT-TRIBE-MASTER, MORIYA-OF-YUGÈ

Noble-of-Mumako-of-Soga, the Great-Magnate, began to conspire with the princes and the Ministers to slay Moriya, so Young-Sazaki-of-Hasè-Clan, Prince-Brave-Ricefield, Prince-Ear-Quick-Wise-Virtue, Prince-Wave-Swift,[58] Prince-Kasuga,[58] Noble-of-Mumako-of-Soga,

NOBLE-OF-LITTLE-MARO [59]

the Magnate of Tree, Hirafu the Magnate of Kosè, and

KATAFU

the Magnate of Kashiwadè, together with

ONARA

Magnate of Mulberry-Castle, all led troops against the Great-Tribe-Master.

KURAFU

a Tribe-Master of the imperial guard, together with

HITO

the Magnate of Abè,

ITÈ

the Magnate of Heguri, the Magnate of Omi, and

NUKADÈ

Magnate of Sakamoto, all led troops from the District of Shiki up to the house at Shibu-River. The Great-Tribe-Master himself, leading the youths of his family and a force of slaves, made a rice-castle and fought. He climbed into the fork of an enoki tree [60] and sped his arrows like rain, and his troops were valiant, so that from the full house they spread over the plain, while the troops of the princes and the Ministers were cowardly and retreated three times in fear. So Prince-Ear-Quick-Wise-Virtue, whose hair was tied on his forehead (for of old time youths of fifteen or sixteen were accustomed to tie the hair thus till they were seventeen or eighteen, when it was divided into bunches, as at present) [61] following behind the soldiery, reflected, "We shall be defeated and if we do not pay worship will fail." Then he cut down a nuridè tree,[62] and quickly making images of the Four-Heavenly-Kings,[63] put them on his top-knot and swore, "If we defeat the enemy I will surely revere these Four-Heavenly-Kings who guard the world, by building in their honor a Buddhist temple and a pagoda." Also the Great-Magnate, Noble-of-Mumako-of-Soga, swore, "If you, Heavenly Kings and Great King-Spirit, as I beseech you, do help and guard us and give us victory, I will build in your honor a Buddhist temple and a pagoda, and everywhere I will spread a knowledge of the Three-Precious-Things." And having thus sworn, they encouraged all the armed troops to press home the attack. Thereon Ichihi, Head-man of Tomi, shot the Great-Tribe-Master, who fell from the tree-fork, and slew him and his child, so that his troops retreated. Then, all coming together, each one dressed himself in black [64] and separated to hunt on the moor of Megari, in Hirosè.

Certain of Moriya's children and relatives fled from the battle and hid themselves on the Plain of Reed-Plain, changing their personal names and surnames, while others fled none knew where. It was said by the people of that time that the wife of Noble-of-Mumako-of-Soga being the younger-sister of Moriya, the Great-Magnate had unwisely slain him at his wife's behest.[65]

After the disturbances had ceased in the realm, a Buddhist temple [66] to the Four-Heavenly-Kings was built in Settsu Province. Half of the slaves of the Great-Tribe-Master were made the slaves of the great Buddhist temple, and his house was given to it [67] and ten thousand shiro [68] of ricefield were given to Ichihi.

Now there was a retainer of Moriya, of the Bird-Catch-Clan, named

YOROZU

who with a hundred guarded the house at Wave-Swift. Hearing of the ruin of the Great-Tribe-Master, he fled at night on a galloping horse toward Arimaka-Village in Chinu District, passing his wife's dwelling, and finally hid himself on a hill. The court held conference and it was advised that as Yorozu was recalcitrant his relatives should at once be slain. Then Yorozu, with his clothing torn and dirtied, and with woe in his look, came out by himself, with his bow in his hand and his sword in his girdle. The officers despatched some hundreds of the guard to surround him, but in fear he hid in a bamboo-forest, and tying cords to the bamboo, pulled them, which made the bamboo shake so that people were uncertain where he was inside. Thus he fooled the guard, who pointed to the shaking bamboo and ran in, crying that Yorozu was there, whereon he shot his arrows, never missing, and the guard in fear dared not go near. Then he unstrung his bow and ran off to the hills with it under his arm, the guard following and shooting arrows at him from both river banks, without hitting him. One of the guard, however, swift of foot, outstripped him, and lying on the river bank, shot at him and hit him on the knee. At this Yorozu drew out the arrow and stringing his bow shot his own, after which he prostrated himself on the ground, crying, "Yorozu would have given his strength serving the Sovereign as a shield, but the matter was not looked into, and he has been set upon, so that he is now desperate. Come, someone, and speak, for I wish to know whether I am to be slain or imprisoned." The guard came running up and shot at him, but he warded off the swift arrows and slew thirty more. Then he took his sword and cut his bow into three pieces, and wheeling the sword threw it into the middle of the river, and thrust his extra dagger into his throat and died.

The Governor of Kawachi made report of his death to the court and a stamped order [69] was issued, directing that his body be cut into eight pieces for exposure in the eight provinces. The governor, obeying the stamped-order, would have cut him to pieces, but thunder sounded and much rain fell, and a white dog of Yorozu's, gazing up and down, went howling to the body and took the head in its mouth and laid it on an old burial mound, and lying down by it, starved there. The Governor of

Kawachi, wondering at the dog's act, reported it to the court, which, unable to hear it for compassion, issued a stamped-order saying, "Seldom has such a thing as this dog's act been known in the world, and it should be cited for later ages. Yorozu's relatives shall make a tomb and bury the bodies." So Yorozu's relatives came and made a tomb in Arimaka-Village and there buried Yorozu and the dog.

Now report was made that in the Province of Kawachi, on the bed of the Ega River, were some hundreds of corpses, so rotted that their names could be told only by the colors of their clothing, which were taken up for burial. There was a dog belonging to

INU [70]

Tribe-Master of the Tana-Clan of Cherry-Tree-Well, who clung to a corpse by his teeth and lay by it to guard it, not leaving until it was taken up for burial.

The Sovereign ascended the throne by the counsel of Princess-Fruitful-August-Food-Cook-House and of the Ministers. He confirmed in their rank Noble-of-Mumako-of-Soga as Great-Magnate and the Ministers and officers. He dwelt in the Palace of Shibabaki at Kurahashi and ruled the empire for four years. He wedded

OTÈ-CHILD [71]

who was the daughter of

NUKADE [72]

Tribe-Master of the imperial guard, and there were born to the two

PRINCE-HACHIKO
PRINCESS-NISHIKIDÈ.

He took to wife also the daughter of Noble-of-Mumako-of-Soga,

LADY-OF-UPPER-RIVER. [73]

Now the Land of Kudara sent envoys, with Buddhist priests and gifts of Buddhist relics, and officers also with tribute and a Buddhist priest, abstainers, carpenters for Buddhist temples, a man skilled in making braziers and platters, men skilled in pottery and a painter. Noble-of-Mumako-of-Soga asked the Kudara priest concerning the acquiring of self-government, and putting Zen-Shin-the-Nun [74] and her colleagues in charge of the Kudara envoys, sent them to study. Then destroying the house of

KONOHA [75]

---

[75] **Ancestor of the Rulers of Kinunuhi of Asuka.**

he started the building of the Buddhist temple of Hokoji, in Asuka, in accordance with the oath he had taken. The place was called Plain-of-Magami-of-Asuka, and also Toma-Ricefield-of-Asuka. Later its worship hall and roofed corridor were built.

KAMAFU

Magnate of Omi, was despatched to the eastern-mountain-circuit to examine the Emishi border, the Magnate of Shishibito,

KARI,

to the eastern-sea-circuit to examine the border of the eastern-sea-provinces, and the Magnate-of-Abè to the Hokuriku-circuit to examine the border of Koshi Province and other places. Zen-Shin-the-Nun and the nuns with her returned from their study in Kudara and resided in the Buddhist temple of Cherry-Tree-Well. Also people went and brought logs from the hills to build Buddhist temples, and

ZEN-TOKU

daughter of Prince-Sadè, Tribe-Master of the imperial guard, and his Koma wives (a Princess of Silla and a Princess of Kudara) became nuns, the two latter under the names

ZEM-M'YO
M'YO-KWO.

Also Tasuna [76] retired from the world, with certain Han-men, under the name of Priest-Tokusaï.

At this time a wild-boar was offered to the Sovereign who said, pointing to it, "When shall the ones we hate have their throats cut like this wild-boar's?" A large over-supply of weapons was made ready also. Otè-Child, angry that the Sovereign no longer favored her, sent a messenger to Noble-of-Mumako-of-Soga to tell him of this saying, and he, in fear of the Sovereign's hatred, summoned his people and plotted with them to slay him. Then, telling the Ministers falsely that he was offering the taxes of the eastern provinces, he despatched

KOMA

Governor of the Han-folk of Mountain-Gate, and son of

ROCK-WELL

Governor of the Han-folk of Mountain-Gate, who slew the Sovereign.[77]

This Koma had illicit relations with Lady-of-Upper-River, daughter of Noble-of-Mumako-of-Soga, and took her secretly to wife, and Noble-of-

Mumako-of-Soga thought she had died. But discovering Koma's act, as she had been the imperial consort, the Great-Magnate slew him.

The Sovereign was buried in the mound on Kurahashi Hill.

THE EMPRESS PRINCESS-FRUITFUL-AUGUST-FOOD-COOK-HOUSE
(ANTIQUITY-REASON [78])

The Empress Princess-Fruitful-August-Food-Cook-House was lovely of face and of correct deportment. After the slaying of the Sovereign by the Great-Magnate Noble-of-Mumako-of-Soga, there being no heir to the succession, the Ministers prayed her to take the rule, but she refused till the officers had formally requested this three times, when she agreed and they gave to her the imperial seal. She dwelt first in the Palace of Fruitful-Shore, and later removed to the Palace of Owari-Ricefield, ruling the sky-under for thirty-seven years. At this time Buddhist relics were placed in the foundation-stone of the building of the Buddhist temple of Hokoji and the pillar of the pagoda was erected.

Prince-Ear-Quick-Wise-Virtue was declared the imperial heir, and was given the management of governmental affairs small and large. He could speak at his birth, and when of adult age had wisdom that could consider the representations of ten men at one time and give correct decision. He had foreknowledge of the future. Besides this he studied the inner-wisdom from the priest

EJI [79]

of Koma, and the outer-classics from the scholar

HAK-KA [80]

till he knew both studies fully. He built his palace in Ikaruga, and the building of the Buddhist temple of the Four-Kings [81] was begun at Tomb-Rui in Wave-Swift. The Empress bade the heir to the throne and the Great-Magnate enhance the progress of the Three-Precious-Things, and the Magnates and Tribe-Masters all competed in the building of Buddhist shrines on behalf of their lords and their parents, calling these Buddhist temples.[82] Also a log of aloes wood a hiro in circumference came ashore at My-Shame Island and the folk of that island, not knowing what aloes wood was, burned it in a cooking-range with other wood and a perfume went afar with the smoke, so in wonder they offered it to the Empress. It was at this time that the Koma Priest Eji came to Nippon and became the tutor of the heir. Also the Kudara priest

HYE-CHHONG

came, and these two taught the worship of Buddha widely and together were the chief support of the Three-Precious-Things. When the Buddhist temple of Hokoji was completed, the Magnate

ZEN-TOKU [83]

son of the Great-Magnate, was made its director and the priests Eji and Hye-Chhong lived in it.

IWAGANÈ

Kishi of Wave-Swift, having been despatched to Silla, returned with a pair of magpies which he offered to the Empress. They were kept in Wave-Swift forest, where they nested on a tree-branch and hatched young. Also Silla sent a peacock and the Land of Koshi offered the Empress a white deer. Later Kudara sent as tribute a camel, a pair of sheep [84] and a white pheasant.

At this time there was an earthquake which ruined all houses, and it was accordingly commanded that in all districts sacrifice should be made to the Kami of Earthquake.[85] The Empress then dwelt in the temporary Palace of Miminashi, and there being severe rain, the river swallowed and submerged the courtyard.

Now Prince-Army [86] was made general to invade Silla, and was given the different Clans which served the Kami, with the Land-Rulers, the Rulers of the Guard, and troops numbering twenty-five-thousand. So, coming to Tsukushi, he made his camp in Island-District and got together vessels to carry his army and supplies. However, he fell sick and could not go on with the enterprise. At this time the Kudara Priest

KANROKU [87]

came, offering as tribute books concerning the calculation of the calendar, astronomy, geography and geomancy, with the method of rendering things invisible, and incantations; and three or four persons were chosen to study under his direction.

O-CHIN [88]

learned the calculation of the calendar;

TAKATOSHI

Village-Master of Atomo learned astronomy and the method of rendering things invisible;

HI-NAMI-TATSU

---

[88] **Ancestor of the Scribes of Yako.**

Magnate of Behind-the-Mountains learned magic; and all these became so proficient in these studies as to be thoroughly master of them.

Prince-Army died in Tsukushi and a messenger was sent on horseback to inform the Empress. When she heard it she was greatly shocked, and sending at once for the heir to the throne and Noble-of-Mumako-of-Soga the Great-Magnate, said, "Prince-Army, chief general for the punishment of Silla, is dead. When about to undertake this great plan, he has been unable to carry it through. How much to be mourned is he!" He was temporarily buried at Saba in Suwo Province,

WITÈ [89]

Tribe-Master of Hashi being despatched there in charge of the burial. (For this reason his descendants were called Tribe-Masters of Saba.) Later Prince-Army was buried on the crest of Mount Hanifu in Kawachi. Prince Taëma, elder brother of Prince-Army, was then made general to punish Silla, and sailing from Wave-Swift, came to Harima. However, his wife

PRINCESS-TONERI

who went with him, died at Akashi and was buried on the crest of Higasa Hill, whereon he went back and did not carry through the punitive expedition.

The heir to the rule said to all the officers, "I have a statue of the revered Buddha. Who will take it and give it reverent worship?" At this

RIVER-KATSU

Ruler of Hada came forward, saying, "Thy slave will give it worship." Accordingly he took the statue of Buddha and built the Buddhist temple of Hachi-Oka [90] for it. Also the Heir received permission of the Empress to make large shields and quivers and painted banners.[91] After this he personally for the first time drew up laws,[92] in seventeen sections, concerning the following:

> Harmony in men's relations
> Reverence for the Three-Precious-Things
> Obedience to the Sovereign's commands
> Propriety of behavior in Officials
> Just judgment of complaints
> Appreciation of the evil and good in men, and sycophancy
> Distribution and distinction of duties
> Zeal in carrying on affairs of state

---

[89] **Ancestor of the Tribe-Masters of Saba.**

The keeping of good-faith
Repression of anger
Just punishments and rewards
Levying of improper taxes by Land-Rulers
Officials' attention to their duties
Envy in officials
Private feeling and public spirit
Forced labor of the people
The need of the counsel of many in Sky-Affairs.[93]

Changes, too, were made in the court-ceremony, it being commanded that one who enters the gate of the palace shall kneel on both knees, both hands flat on the ground, and shall rise and walk only after passing the threshold. At this time also the yellow-writing [94] painters and the Behind-the-Mountains painters were first organized. Also the Empress bade the heir to the throne, the Great-Magnate, the princes and the Ministers, all alike, to swear to make statues of Buddha, of copper and of tapestry, each one sixteen shaku tall, and she appointed

TORI-OF-SADDLE-MAKE

to plan their construction. Hearing that she was making the statues of Buddha, the Koma king sent three-hundred r'yo [95] of red metal. On the day the two statues were completed the copper statue was shrined in the Golden Hall of the Buddhist Temple of Gangoji. Being taller than the door of the Golden Hall, it could not be taken in, and the workmen, after conferring, would have broken the door to take it in, but Tori-of-Saddle-Make skilfully managed it without doing so. On this day a meeting for religious worship was held, attended by innumerable folk. At this time began the holding of festivals at all Buddhist temples on the eighth day of the fourth moon and the fifteenth day of the seventh moon. After this the Empress said to Tori-of-Saddle-Make, "For this your service We give you the rank of Daïnin and twenty cho of irrigated land in Sakata District in Omi Province." With the income from this land Tori-of-Saddle-Make built for the Empress the Buddhist Temple of Diamond, which is now called the Nunnery of Sakata in Minabuchi. On the Empress requesting the heir to discuss the Sho-Man-G'yo,[96] he finished expounding it in three days. Also, in the Palace of Okamoto, he discussed the Hokke-K'yo,[97] and the Empress, much pleased, gave him a hundred cho of irrigated land in Harima Province, which were added to his Palace of Ikaruga. The heir and the Great-Magnate, together with all officers, worshiped the Sky- and Earth-Kami. A Mibu Clan [98] was formed, and also the Pools of Brave-Uchi, of Wistaria-Plain, of Katawoka and of Sedge-Plain [99] were made in Mountain-Gate Province and the Pools of

Takari and of Yosami [1] in Kawachi Province, while granaries were built in all Provinces.

IMO-CHILD

Magnate of Little-Moor was sent to the Land of Thang,[2] together with

FUKURI-OF-SADDLE-MAKE

as interpreter, returning accompanied by an envoy of Thang named P'ei-Shih-Ch'ing, with a party of twelve, to Tsukushi, where

LITTLE-NARI

Kishi of Wave-Swift was sent to bring them, while a new official residence was built for them above the Koma official resident at Wave-Swift. The guests anchored in the Port of Wave-Swift, when thirty decorated vessels were despatched to Yeguchi to meet them.

TORI-MARO

Tribe-Master of Miyatoko of the Intercessors, Nukadè Governor of Great-Kawachi, and

O-HEI

Scribe of Ships were made official entertainers. Imo-Child reported to the Empress, "On my departure the sovereign of Thang gave me a letter, but in passing through the Land of Kudara, its people searched me and took it from me." The Ministers, for this, adjudged that he should be banished, saying, "An envoy, though he lose his life, should not lose his message. How lacking is one who loses the letter of the Great Land!" But the Empress pardoned him and remitted the penalty, saying, "If we punish it, the Great Land's guest will learn of it, which we do not wish." When the guests of Thang reached the Capital seventy-five caparisoned horses were despatched, to meet them, to the Road of Ichi-of-Tsubaki, and there Hirafu, Tribe-Master of the Nukada-Clan, gave them the imperial greeting. Then they were called to court, being introduced by

TORI

Magnate of Abè, and the Tribe-Master of Yosami

IDAKU

of the Warrior-Clan. The gifts from the Land of Thang were set in the courtyard. The chief envoy, holding his letter in his hand, twice prostrated himself and then rose. The letter said, "The Emperor sends greeting to the Crowned-Head [3] of Wa. Your envoy, Imo-Child, came with his companions and communicated with us. We rule the sky-under, having with reverence received the High Command. We wish to include all life within the scope of our civilization, and far and near our affection and guardianship extend. We know that you, dwelling apart over-sea, bless with peace and placid methods all subjects within your borders. In greatest loyalty you have sent us tribute from a distance, and we received the sign of good-faith with joy. In spite of the warmer weather,[4] We are in usual health. Now we send P'ei-Shih-Ch'ing, Entertainment Officer of the Foreign-Envoy-Ceremony-Bureau, and those with him, to speak thus, sending also articles which are listed elsewhere." Tori advanced and took the letter, which Kurafu,[5] coming forward to him, took and laid on a table before the great-gate and reported to the Empress. After the ceremony they withdrew.

The Thang guests were entertained at court and at Great-Koöri in Wave-Swift until P'ei-Shih-Ch'ing departed, when Imo-Child as chief-envoy, Little-Nari as vice-envoy, and Fukuri-of-Saddle-Make as interpreter, were sent to escort them. The Sovereign said to the Thang Sovereign: "The Eastern Sovereign respectfully to the Western Sovereign.[6] Your envoy, P'ei-Shih-Ch'ing, and those with him, came to relieve Our long anxiety. Autumn's last month is cold.[4] How are you? Well, We hope. We are in usual health. We send to you Ima-Child, Little-Nari and others. With respect, but informally sent." Also there were despatched to the Land of Thang, to study,

FUKU-IN

Governor of the Han-folk of Mountain-Gate,

EM'YO

an interpreter of Level, Kuro-Maro a Han-man of Takamuku, and Great-Land a Han-man of Imaki, with student-priests, namely the Han-men Nichi-Bun of Imaki, Sho-An of Minabuchi, E-On of Shiga, and Kosaï of Imaki. At this time many Silla folk came and settled in Nippon.

Now the Dazaï[7] of Tsukushi reported to the Empress that Kudara Buddhist priests named Dokin and Emi,[8] conducting ten other priests and seventy-five laymen, were anchored in the Port of Ashigita in Higo Province, so

TOKO-MARO

Kishi of Wave-Swift, and the Scribe of Ships

TATSU

were despatched to ask why they came. They replied, "The Kudara king bade us go on a mission to the Land of Wu, but there is internal war there and we were not permitted to enter, and were returning to our own Land when we were smitten with a sudden tempest at sea, till happily we anchored on the shore of this empire, to our great joy." So Toko-Maro and those with him returned and informed the Empress, and he and Tatsu were sent back at once to go with the Kudara men to their own Land. Coming to Port-Island, however, the ten priests desired to abide there and a dwelling was given them in the Buddhist temple of Gangoji. At this time Imo-Child returned from the Land of Chang, but Fukuri the interpreter remained there. Also the Koma king sent as tribute two Buddhist priests, the former of whom knew the Five-Classics and also knew how to prepare painter's colors, paper and ink. Also he made mills. (This seems to be the first making of mills.) Moreover an envoy from Silla and an envoy from Mimana came to Tsukushi and messengers were despatched to bring them to the capital. On their arrival Hirafu, Tribe-Master of the Nukada Clan, was put in charge of the decorated horses despatched to meet the guests of Silla, and

GREAT-COMPANY

Magnate of Kashiwadè, was put in charge of the decorated horses despatched to meet the guests of Mimana. These were lodged in the official residence at River-Clan in Ato. When they came to court, River-Katsu and

USAGI

Tribe-Master of Hashi were appointed to present Silla, and

SHIWO-FUTA

Tribe-Master of Hashi-Man, and the Magnate of Omi

GREAT-CHILD

to present Mimana. These conducted them in at the southern gate and they took a position in the middle of the court. Then Kurafu, Tribe-Master of the imperial guard,

FRUITFUL-SHORE-OF-SOGA

Magnate of Emishi, Nukadè Magnate of Sakamoto, and

TORI-CHILD [9]

all rose and went forward and made obeisance in the court, whereon the guests of the two Lands did the same over and over. The four officers then rose and advanced and informed the Great-Magnate, who rose and heard them standing. Afterward gifts were given the guests appropriate to their ranks. Later they were entertained at court,

NIYÈ [10]

Governor of the Han-folk of Kawachi being Silla's companion at the feast, and

KUSO

Head-man of Nishikori, Mimana's. After the reception ceremonies the guests departed.

Now the Empress went to gather plants for medicine on the Plain-of-Uda, all coming together at cock-crow at the Pool of Wistaria-Plain and starting at dawn.

HOSOME

Magnate of Awata was appointed to lead, and Hirafu followed. A feast with sakè was given to all the superior officers, at which the Great-Magnate sang in honor of the Empress:

> When I cast my eyes || On the High-Sky, forth stands
> From its eight-fold fence || Augustly concealing her,
> The mighty Sovereign || Who tranquilly governs
> For myriad ages. || Thus may it be forever—
> Thousands of ages. || Thus may it be forever!
> We would be her slaves, || Rendering reverence deep.
> We would be her slaves, || Giving her low obeisance.
> So has my song its ending.

At which the Empress deigned to sing in answer:

> Excellent Soga! || Truly the sons of Soga,
> If they were horses, || Would be horses of H'yuga.
> If they were sword-blades, || They would be blades of Wu.
> Well the Great Sovereign || Has chose that sons of Soga
> Be here to do her service!

When the body of Princess-Kitashi, the former Empress, was taken away and buried in the great mound of Hinokuma, mortuary addresses were made on the Karo road. First Tori, Magnate of Omi,[11] spoke officially in praise of the Empress and offered to the spirit of the dead sacred dishes and robes and fifteen thousand things of like sort. Second the imperial princes gave mortuary addresses in order of rank. Third Tori, Tribe-Master of Miyatoko, of the Intercessors, delivered a complimentary address for the Great-Magnate. Fourth the Great-Magnate, leading the Magnates of the eight descents,[12] commanded

MARISÈ

Magnate of the Boundary-Clan, to read addresses of praise written by the noble families and holders of titles. The people of the time said that Marisè and Great-Maro spoke their addresses well, but that the Magnate Tori spoke his poorly.

At this time there came from Kudara a man with face and body spotted with white all over, which may have been caused by white ringworm, and the people, feeling repulsion at his strange look, would have put him upon an island of the sea. But said he, "Do you who feel repulsion at my spotted body raise no more horses and oxen that are white-spotted in this Land? Now I have the small ability of making shapes of hills and mountains. Let me remain and be employed to the Land's profit. Would it not be waste to put me on an island of the sea?" So they did not send him away, but caused him to draw the shapes of Mount Sumi [13] and the Bridge of Wu at the southern court. The people of the time called him

TAKUMI-OF-MICHIKO.[14]

Also there came to Nippon a Kudara man named

MIMACHI.

As he stated that he knew the Wu style of music and of the dance, he was given a residence at Cherry-Tree-Well, and the young assembled to learn these from him, and

DESHI

Head-man of Manu and a Han-man of Imaki named Seïbun, learning the dance from him, transmitted it. At this time, moreover, the Pools of Upper-Waki, Unebi and Wani [15] were made and a great road was constructed from Wave-Swift to the capital.

Now the heir to the rule journeyed to Katawoka and a starving man lay by the road. He asked that one his name, and when he made no reply the heir to the rule gave him food and drink, and taking off his own robe, clothed him and bade him lie in peace. Then he sang:

> O Wanderer || That lies by the wayside,
> Empty of rice, || On the Katawoka Hill,
> The sunshine-laved! || Have you no parents?
> Have you no lord || Like to the fruitful bamboo?
> Ah, welaway! || O Wanderer here lying,
> Empty of rice!

Later the heir sent a messenger to see the starving man, who reported that he was dead, at which he sorrowed much. He commanded that he be buried there, and a mound was made and sealed up. Many days later he summoned his own attendants, saying, "The starving man who formerly lay by the road was not a common man, but surely was righteous," and sent a messenger to inspect the mound, who reported that the pile of soil had not been altered, but that when he opened it and examined the tomb, there was no body in it and only the folded robe was on the coffin. So the heir sent the messenger back again to bring the robe, and he wore it again as formerly. The people of the time were much amazed at this, saying, "It is true that one wise man recognizes another," and they revered him the more. At this time the Great-Magnate fell sick, and to benefit him men and women to the number of a thousand took up a religious life.

MITASUKI

Kimi of Inukami and the Ruler of the Yata Clan were despatched to the Land of Thang. When they returned an envoy from Kudara came with the latter to the court and a feast was given him. Also thirty of the people of Yaku Island [16] came to Nippon and resided in Inoï, never leaving it till they died. Moreover Silla sent as tribute a statue of Buddha, and Koma sent envoys with products of that Land as tribute, together with gifts of two captives, flutes, cross-bows and slings—ten things—with a camel raised in that Land.

At this time the Magnate of the River-Clan was despatched to Aki Province to build ships, and going into the mountains looked for trees for these. Finding a tree that was good he put a mark on it and would have felled it, when one came to him saying that it was a Thunder-Tree [17] and should not be felled. The Magnate of the River-Clan, saying that not even the Thunder-Kami should oppose the Sovereign's commands, made many offerings and sent laborers to fell the tree. Then immediately much rain fell, the thunder pealed and the lightning flashed, at which the Magnate of the River-Clan, drawing his sword, said, "O Thunder-Kami! Me you should harm, but not the laborers!" He waited, gazing upward, but while the Kami caused the thunder to peal more than ten times, he was unable to harm the Magnate. Then he took the shape of a small fish which was caught among the tree's limbs, and the Magnate of the River-Clan took it and burned it up, and thus the ships were made.

Also report was made that in the Gamo River in Omi Province was a creature formed like a man. Moreover when a fisherman of Settsu Province set a net at Dug-Bay,[18] there came into it something shaped like a child, not a fish nor a man, whose name was not known.[19] At this time two of the people of Yaku were cast up on Izu Island. The top of the mound of Hinokuma was covered with small stones, and outside of its edge the soil made a hill, on which each family [20] was ordered to set up a great pillar.[21] The pillar set up by

UË-OF-SAKA [22]

Governor of the Han-folk of Mountain-Gate, greatly overtopped the rest, so that the people of that day called him the Governor-of-Great-

Pillar. At that time something red came in the Sky, more than a jo long, shaped like the tail of a bird.[23] The heir, with the Great-Magnate, set down a History of the Sovereigns, a History of the Land, and the first Annals of the Magnates, Tribe-Masters, Rulers of the Guard, and Land-Rulers, of the one hundred and eighty Clans and of the citizens.[24]

The heir, Prince-Ear-Quick-Wise-Virtue, died on a midnight in the Palace of Ikaruga, at which all the princes and Magnates and the people of the realm, like aged persons who lose a loved child, had no relish in their mouths for salt and vinegar, and like youths who lose a loved parent, sorrowed till the sound went everywhere, while the peasant left the plow and the pounding-woman the pestle, saying, all of them, "Sun and moon have lost radiance and sky and earth have fallen into ruin. From now on who is there to trust?" The prince was buried in the mound of Shinaga.[25] The Koma Buddhist priest Eji, learning the prince had died, sorrowing much, invited the priests to a repast in his honor, when he expounded the sacred writings, and made a prayer, saying, "In this Land of Nippon the imperial Prince-Ear-Quick-Wise-Virtue was a wise man, truly given a wise man's virtues by Heaven. He was born in this Land, and understanding completely the Three-Worlds,[26] he carried forward the great projects of former wise men. He worshiped the Three-Precious-Things and aided folk who were afflicted. Truly the heir had great wisdom and now he is dead. I am a foreigner, but in spirit was in close sympathy with him. Why should I survive without him? I have decided to die next year, the second month and the fifth day, in order to meet him and with him go through the soul-transmigration of all life." Eji in fact died on the specified day, so that all the people of that time said to each other, "Prince-Ear-Quick-Wise-Virtue was not alone in being a wise man; Eji was one also."

Silla and Mimana each sent an envoy, who came together to court, bringing as tribute a golden statue of Buddha, a golden pagoda, with relics and flags for baptism, one large and twelve small. The statue was put in the Hada Buddhist temple at Kadona, and the relics, the pagoda and the flags were put in the Buddhist temple of the Three-Heavenly-Kings. With the envoys came also two Buddhist priests, with Em'yo and Fuku-In,[27] the physicians, who had studied the knowledge of the Land of Thang, and Em'yo and the others said to the Empress, "Let all those who have been living in Thang to study be summoned, as they have finished. Also let communication with the Land of Thang be kept up, as it is a land to extol, with an established system of law."

Now the Empress, hearing that a Buddhist priest had struck his father's father with an ax, summoned the Great-Magnate, saying, "A man who has taken up the religious life should give his attention to the Three-

Precious-Things. Is he so easily and without remorse to commit crime? We learn that a priest has struck his grandfather. Gather together all priests and nuns of the different Buddhist temples and make inquiry, punishing severely such as are found guilty." But when the priests and nuns were brought together for inquiry and all the guilty were about to be punished, the Buddhist priest of Kudara, Kanroku,[28] represented as follows: "Buddhist law came from a country in the west of Han, and after three hundred years was transmitted to Kudara. Scarcely a hundred years later our king, learning of the wisdom of the Sovereign of Nippon, sent to him as tribute a statue of Buddha and Buddhist Sutras. That is not yet a hundred years ago, so that the priests and nuns have not yet learned Buddha's law and easily do wrong. Therefore they fear, not knowing the proper conduct. I, lowly one, beseech that all the priests and nuns except the criminal ones be pardoned and punishment remitted. This would be a most meritorious act." The Empress gave assent, and it was commanded as follows: "Can laymen be called to account when priests, too, disobey the law? From now on, therefore, officers are appointed to have jurisdiction over priests and nuns." The priest Kanroku, and

TOKU-SEKI

of the Kura-Clan, were appointed to this duty. Also the Koma king sent as tribute the Buddhist priest

HYE-KWAN

who was made one of these officers, and the Tribe-Master of Azumi was made Chief-of-Laws.[29] Moreover examination was made of Buddhist temples, priests and nuns, and the details of the building of the Buddhist temples were carefully recorded and of the entering into religious life of priests and nuns, with the dates of their entrance. There were then forty-six Buddhist temples, eight hundred and sixteen priests and five hundred and sixty-nine nuns, thirteen hundred and eighty-five all told.

Now the Great-Magnate sent two Ministers, the Tribe-Master of Azumi and

MARO

Magnate of Abè, to the Empress to say, "I originally lived in Mulberry-Castle District, from which I took my name. I beseech therefore that this district may be established as mine and be made my fief." So the Empress commanded, saying, "We are descended from the house of Soga, and the Great-Magnate is Our maternal uncle, so that We confirm the Great-Magnate's words, if spoken at night before night becomes morning and if spoken by day before day becomes night. No word of his have We disregarded. But if We now, in this reign, were so unwise as to give away this district, Sovereigns to come would say, "Because a foolish woman ruled the empire this district was unwisely lost." Beside Our being called unwise, the Great-Magnate would be considered a traitor. Thus we should have an evil reputation in after ages." So she refused it.

The Great-Magnate died and was buried in a tomb at Peach-Moor.

After this there were prolonged rain in the empire and a great famine, so that aged folk devoured the roots of plants and died by the roads, while nursing babies died with their mothers. Also very many thieves and bandits appeared whom it was not possible to suppress. In Michinoku Province a Mujina [30] took the form of a man and sang. Moreover very many flies assembled in a mass ten jo [31] thick and flew across the Lime-Tree-Moor Pass with a thunderous noise. There was also a total eclipse of the sun.

At this time the Empress fell sick abed with a severe malady, so that she clearly was near her end. So she summoned Prince-Tamura, saying, "The assumption of the Sky-rule and the control of the great foundation and the many details of the realm by which the people are fed, is a thing not easily explained, and it requires deep and unremitting consideration. So do you be circumspect and make no hasty pronouncement." Also, at the same time she summoned

GREAT-E-OF-TAMASHIRO

saying, "You are of youthful spirit. Put now your secret wish into words, but carefully wait till the general desire is clear, and then act." She died at the age of seventy-five and was buried in a temporary tomb in the southern court. Her august tomb was in the mound of Great-Moor and later it was removed to the great tomb at Shinaga.

> With the close of this reign Japan was officially to recognize the art of writing, and though three centuries were to elapse before its first history, the *Kojiki*, was to be written, the epitaph of its legend had been spelled. Japan's mythical period had ended, and the myth-narrative of its people may appropriately close with the *Kojiki's* final record, in which the race's ancient traditions were crystallized. The written character henceforth was to record more or less authentic history. And it is not unfitting that the curtain fell upon the introduction into the archipelago of Buddhism, which was henceforth to leave such an ineffaceable mark upon Japanese thought and literature: sacred legendary material of later appearance for the most part attaches to Buddhist propaganda, bears all the earmaks of priestly invention, and like the new importation has roots which are not of Japan's soil.

KAMI LIST
(DEITIES AND PERSONAGES)

A

Achi-Kishi	221
Again-Forging-Old-Woman	24
Ajihari	318
Akabato-of-Kishi	331
Akameko	282
Akano-Jewel	9
Akawo	281
Akè	289
Akoko	229
Akonè	225
Anaho	257
Ana-Weaver	227
Ani	342
Apparent-Country-Jewel (*see* Great-Land-Master)	
Arakaï	305
Arako	310
Areda-Lord	211
Areshi	253
Asahi	39
Ashi-Nadaka	51
Aso	258
Attach-Name-Pass-Light-Prince-Eight-Island-of-Refreshment (*see* Eight-Island-Rule-Master)	
August-Brilliant-Ugly-Female	118
August-Clothing-of-Weaving	248
August-Earth-Ancestor (*see* Great-Earth)	
August-House	338
August-Luck-Spirit-August-Wondrous-Spirit (*see* Great-Land-Master)	
August-Moor (*see* Fruitful-Shape-Moor)	
August-Spirit-of-Snap (*see* Thrust-Snap)	
August-Spirit-Plunged-in-Mountain-Stream-Water	134
August-Tranquil-Waver	134
August-Year	39
August-Year (*see* Great-Year)	
Augustly-Distant	52
Awful-Lady	4
Awful-Snap (*see* Thrust-Snap)	
Awful-Swift-Sun	13
Awo	274
Azuki-Island	9

B

Beach-Child	249
Bear-Hand-of-Clothes-Sewing	103
Bear-of-Mishi-Hasè	325
Bear-Wani	192
Beautiful-Teeth-Lord-of-Knot-Grass	232
Beautiful-Ugly-Female	118
Beautiful-Ugly-Male	118
Big-Fish	307
Big-Shield	240
Bird-Bird (*see* Ikari)	
Bird-Ears	50
Bird-Mountain	241
Bird-Rock-Camphor-Tree-Boat	7
Bird-Sounding-Sea	50
Black-Falcon (*see* Shiki-Younger)	
Black-Hair-of-Great-Tree	247

Black-Slope	172	Brave-Yotsuka	104
Black-Thunder	15	Breast-Bone (*see* Noble-of-Nomi)	
Blade-Possessor	86		
Blue (or Green)-Awful (*see* Perfect-Face)		Bubble-Calm	10
		Bubble-Flowering-August-Spirit (*see* Prince-Monkey-Ricefield)	
Blue (or Green)-Awful-Lady (*see* Awful-Lady)			
		Bubble-Wave	10
Boar-Child	267	Buretsu (*see* Young-Wren-of-Little-Hasè)	
Boar-Hand-of-Clothes-Sewing	103		
Body-of-Eighty-Evils	18		
Body-of-Great-Evils	18	**C**	
Body-of-Swift-Autumn (*see* Prince-Swift-Autumn)		Cape-Jewel	225
		Cherry-Tree-Well	320
Body-of-Swift-Autumn (*see* Princess-Swift-Autumn)		Chi-Nushi-of-Ricefield-Place	129
		Child-of-Aga	214
Bottom-Earth-Stander (*see* Eternal-Earth-Stander)		Child-of-Clothing	233
		Child of Iï-Me	340
Bottom-Master-Treasure-August-Treasure	134	Child-of-Offering-Holder	97
		Child-of-Rock-Push-Divide	97
Bottom-Touching-August-Spirit (*see* Prince-Monkey-Ricefield)		Clan-Chief-of-Skin (*see* Han-Male)	
Brave-August-Name-Firm	62	Clan-Chieftainess-of-Nako	322
Brave-Awful-Possessing-Male	13	Clay-Mountain-Lady (*see* Princess-Clay-Easy)	
Brave-Awful-Possessor	125		
Brave-Chinu-Ears (*see* Ears-of-Suwe)		Cleaving-Thunder	15
		Cock-Pheasant	58
Brave-Deer-Island	128	Complete-Advancer-of-Great-Maise	117
Brave-Horn-Body	69		
Brave-Ina-Tanè	174	Crumbling-Prince	53
Brave-Kura-Oki	89	Crying-Weeping-Female	12
Brave-Lagoon-River-Lord	119		
Brave-Leaf-Elder	25	**D**	
Brave-Little-Wide-Land-Great-Shield	311	Dark-Mountain-Body	13
Brave-Male-Kumi	128	Dark-Mountain-Possessor	13
Brave-Morogi	157	Dark-Okami	13
Brave-Mina-Kata	47	Dark-Water	13
Brave-of-Three-Rooms	159	Deer's-Blood-Island	9
Brave-Prince	274	Dense-Mountain-Possessor	14
Brave-Snap (*see* Brave-Awful-Possessing-Male)		Deshi	356
		District-Warden	247
Brave-Rock-Spreader (*see* Brave-Stone)		Ditch-Stake-of-Three-Islands	111
		Divine-Eight-Wells-Ears	113
Brave-Stone	53	Divine-Lagoon-River-Ears	113
Brave-Sun	174	Divine-Life-Wonder-Producer	38
Brave-Sun-Direction-Lord (*see* Small-Island)		Divine-Producer	3
		Divine-Producer-Ancestor (*see* Divine-Producer)	
Brave-Swift-Impetuous-Male	19		
Brave-Uchi-Nokori	26	Divine-Rectifying-Body	18

KAMI-LIST

Divine-Uë-Ha 321
Door-Conceal-Kami (*see* Sky-Hand-Strength-Male)
Double-Name-Island 8
Dread-Sky-Star (*see* Kagasè-Male)

E

Ears-of-Suwe 126
Earth-Dark-Door 10
Earth-Hill-Pass-Elder 10
Earth-Mist 10
Earth-Pillar (*see* Lady-Long-Wind)
Earth-Soil 4
Earth-Stander (*see* Earth-Soil)
Earth-Thunder 15
Earth-Water-Divider 10
Earth-Water-Drawing-Gourd-Possessor 10
Eightfold-Great-Kami-of-Sacred-Stone 141
Eight-Fold-Thing-Sign-Master 49
Eight-Footed-Crow 96
Eight-Forked-Serpent-of-Koshi 34
Eight-Island-Possessor 50
Eight-Island-Rule-Master 36
Eji 348
Elder-Clan-Chief 280
Elder-Male-of-the-Bottom (*see* Male-Bottom-Possessor)
Elder-Male-of-the-Middle (*see* Male-Middle-Possessor)
Elder-Male-of-the-Surface (*see* Male-Surface-Possessor)
Elder-Sister-Haë 115
Elder-Upper-River-Current-Brave 168
Em'yo 353
Entrance-Limit 39
Eternal-Earth-Stander 4
Eternal-Sky-Stander 4

F

Feather-Shining-Jewel (*see* Wondrous-Shining-Jewel)
Female-Kami-of-Summer (*see* High-Summer-Sun)
Female-of-Fruitful-Food 111
Female-of-Izu 18
Fertile-Ears 206
Fertile-Sun-of-Orange 324
Field-Possessor 41
Fifty-Brave 33
Fire-Climax 80
Fire-Fade 80
Fire-Father (*see* Fire-Shining-Swift-Male)
Fire-Glow 79
Fire-Producer (*see* Fire-Shining-Swift-Male)
Fire-Shining-Elder (*see* Fire-Shining-Swift-Male)
Fire-Shining-Swift-Male 11
Fire-Thunder 15
Five-River-Currents 89
Float-Pass-Moor-Fruitful-Buy (*see* Fruitful-Shape-Moor)
Flower-Waves 118
Foam-Calm 9
Foam-Wave 10
Food-Wondrous-Great (*see* Izasa-Lord)
Foot-Stroke-Elder 34
Foot-Stroke-Hand-Stroke (*see* Foot-Stroke-Elder)
Four-Kami 77
Fresh-Water 117
Fruitful-Earth-Master (*see* Fruitful-Shape-Moor)
Fruitful-Earth-Moor (*see* Fruitful-Shape-Moor)
Fruitful-Great-Lord 225
Fruitful-Jewel (*see* Jewel-Ancestor)
Fruitful-Mouth-Moor (*see* Fruitful-Shape-Moor)
Fruitful-Perfume-Joint-Moor (*see* Fruitful-Shape-Moor)
Fruitful-Rock-True-Gate (*see* Sky-Hand-Strength-Male)
Fruitful-Shape-Moor 4
Fruitful-Shore-of-Soga 354
Fruitful-Snap (*see* Brave-Awful-Possessing-Male)
Fruitful-Three-Hairs-Moor (*see* Young-Three-Hairs-Moor)

Fuku-In	353	Great-Iri-Ki	123
Fuku-Me	272	Great-Island	8
Fukuri-of-Saddle-Make	352	Great-Jewel	26
Fukuro	227	Great-Kami-of-August-Shade	227

G

Germ-Integrator	4	Great-Kami-of-Carry-Across (*see* Great-Mountain-Possessor)	
Go-Weaver	227		
Good-Sword-of-Han-Man	103	Great-Kami-of-Hoe-Mountain (*see* Great-Mountain-Integrator)	
Governor-of-Great-Pillar (*see* Uë-of-Saka)			
Grand-Ears	37	Great-Kami-of-Rock (*see* Great-Land-Master)	
Great-Army-Master (*see* Sky-Round-Eye)		Great-Kami-of-Sakè (*see* Great-Land-Master)	
Great-August-Kami-of-Kamo (*see* Prince-High-Lord-of-Aji-Spades)		Great-Kami-of-Soda	43
		Great-Kami-of-the-Land-of-Night (*see* She-Who-Inviteth)	
Great-Ax-Hand	290		
Great-Beach	201	Great-Kami-Tono (*see* Great-Land-Master)	
Great-Child	354		
Great-Company	354	Great-Lady-of-Karu	257
Great-Country-Jewel (*see* Great-Land-Master)		Great-Lady-of-Long-Ricefield	257
		Great-Land-Jewel	104
Great-Desert-Ricefield	170	Great-Land-Maker (*see* Great-Land-Master)	
Great-Divine-Fruit	16		
Great-Door-After (*see* Great-Place-Elder)		Great-Land-Master	37
		Great-Law-King (*see* Prince-Ear-Quick-Wise-Virtue)	
Great-Door-Before (*see* Great-Place-Elder-Lady)			
		Great-Lord	217
Great-Door-Place (*see* Great-Place-Elder)		Great-Lord-of-Hatabi	221
		Great-Magnate-of-Island (*see* Noble-of-Mumako-of-Soga)	
Great-Door-Sun-Lord	9		
Great-E (*see* Fertile-Sun-of-Orange)		Great-Magnate-Tsubura	268
		Great-Male-of-Great-Thing	9
Great-E-of-Tamashiro	360	Great-Maro	317
Great-Earth	39	Great-Master-of-Things-of-Three-Threads (*see* Great-Land-Master)	
Great-Elbow-Pad-Lord	204		
Great-Elder-of-Come-not-Place	17		
Great-Eyes	117	Great-Middle-Child	201
Great-Female-Noon-Possessor (*see* Great-Sky-Shiner)		Great-Middle-Ishiji	154
		Great-Mountain	312
Great-Hasè	257	Great-Mountain-Gate-Fertile-Dragon-Fly-Island	8
Great-Hasè-Young-Brave (*see* Great-Hasè)			
		Great-Mountain-Integrator	39
Great-Hawk-of-Mountain-Neighborhood	145	Great-Mountain-Master	246
		Great-Mountain-Possessor	10
Great-House-Prince	44	Great-Mountain-Top-Master (*see* Great-Mountain-Integrator)	
Great-House-Ricefield-Child	167		

Great-Mountain-Warden	212	**H**	
Great-Mount-Sa	38		
Great-Name-Possessor (*see* Great-Land-Master)		Hadanè	286
		Hakatoko	274
Great-Ocean-Possessor	9	Hak-Ka	348
Great-Oshi	332	Han-Male	234
Great-Palace-Female	28	Hand-Placing-Soil-Carrier	25
Great-Pattern-Body	19	Hand-Stroke-Elder	34
Great-Pestle	154	Harima-Great-Tribe-Master	141
Great-Place-Elder	4	Hasui	325
Great-Place-Elder-Lady	4	Hayamachi	235
Great-Rectifying-Body	18	He-Who-Invites	4
Great-Refulgent-Mountain-Dwelling-Magnate	39	Head-Man-of-Telling	154
		Herb-Queller	36
Great-Ricefield	149	Hi-Nami-Tatsu	349
Great-Ruler-of-Invisible-Things (*see* Great-Land-Master)		Hida	337
		High-Male (*see* Brave-Awful-Possessing-Male)	
Great-Sakè-Master	191		
Great-Sasu-Land-Kami	37	High-Producer	3
Great-Sea	283	High-Sky	273
Great-Shin-Mi	327	High-Summer-Sun	39
Great-Sky-Creator-of-the-Beneath (*see* Great-Land-Master)		Hikaka	265
		Hinamori-Elder	163
		Hinamori-Younger	163
Great-Sky-Shiner	19	Hino	92
Great-Snap-Kami (*see* Brave-Awful-Possessing-Male)		Hirafu	342
		Hiroko (*see* Child-of-Iï-Me)	
Great-Stone	50	Hisa-Females (*see* Ugly-Females-of-the-Land-of-Night)	
Great-Storehouse-Master	193		
Great-Tamaru-Lord (*see* Great-Island)		Hito	344
		Hiyuri	304
Great-Tamu-Lord	171	Hohoro	75
Great-Thing-Master (*see* Great-Land-Master)		Homuda-Lord (*see* Great-Elbow-Pad-Lord)	
Great-Thing-Master-Wondrous-Dread-Spirit-of-Mountain-Gate (*see* Great-Land-Master)		Homutachi	194
		Homuya-Lord	191
		Hosomè	271
		Hosomè	355
Great-Thunder	14	Hot-Spring-Mountain-Master-of-Refreshment-Three-Names-Saro-Prince-Mountain-Bamboo-Grass (*see* Eight-Island-Rule-Master)	
Great-Tribe-Master-of-Tochinè	144		
Great-Tsuchi-of-Hada	316		
Great-Void	279		
Great-Water-Master	37		
Great-Wealthy-Ground (*see* Great-Place-Elder)		Hot-Spring-Mountain-Master-of-Refreshment-Three-Names-Saro-Prince-Eight-Island-Moor (*see* Eight-Island-Rule-Master)	
Great-Wealthy-Place (*see* Great-Place-Elder-Lady)			
Great-Wren	213		
Great-Year	38	Hundred-Complete	66

Hye-Chhong		Iwaki (see Iwashiro)	
Hye-Kwan	348	Iwarè	338
	359	Iwashiro	280
I		Iwayumi	328
Ichi-Fukaya	161	Izaho-Elder-Brother-Lord	231
Ichi-Kaya	161	Izasa-Lord	209
Ichihi	342		
Ichikawa	144	**J**	
Idaku	352	Jewel-Ancestor	24
Igaruka	282	Jewel-House (see Jewel-Ancestor)	
Igatsu	195		
Iïbo	318	Jewel-of-Storehouse-Rice	9
Iï-Iri-Ne	133	Jewel-Pile-Wondrous-Producer	107
Ikari	188		
Ikatomi	109	**K**	
Iki-Island	8	Kaga-Lord	211
Ikina	330	Kagasè-Male	64
Ikobaya-Lord	144	Kamafu	347
Ikochini	50	Kamako	326
Ikui	127	Kami-Buto (see Brave-Swift-Impetuous-Male)	
Ikui	195		
Imo-Child	352	Kami-of-Great-Mouth	252
Inamochi	324	Kami-of-Eight-Thousand-Spears (see Great-Land-Master)	
Inehaya-Lord	223		
Inmost-Mountain-Possessor	13		
Intermediate-Shore-Direction	18	Kami-of-Ifukubè	179
Inu	346	Kami-of-Island	181
Irogu	234	Kami-of-Kara (see Fifty-Brave)	
Iroë (see Young-Lady-of-Meko)		Kami-of-Land	181
		Kami-of-Merit (see Fifty-Brave)	
Ishimè	337		
Island-Child-of-Three-Rivers-Pipe-River (see Island-Shore-of-Water-Bay-Child)		Kami-of-One-Eye (see Sky-Mara)	
		Kami-of-Rikuyu	216
Island-Maise-Child (see Small-Island)		Kami-of-Storehouse-Rice (see Jewel-of-Storehouse-Rice)	
Island-of-Koshi	8	Kamo-Lord	224
Island-Shore-of-Water-Bay	290	Kamu-Nagi-Lord	221
Island-Shore-of-Water-Bay-Child	290	Kanamura	306
		Kanroku	349
Isoro-of-Azumi	200	Kara-Land-That-Big-Arrive (see Fifty-Brave)	
Itaï	317		
Itè	344	Kari	343
Ito-Te	193	Karibata-Tobè	151
Itsu	331	Karoshi	244
Iwaganè	349	Kaseko	140
Iwahi	334	Kashima	304
Iwaka-Mutsukari	188	Katafu	343
Iwakatsu	322	Kataï	311

KAMI-LIST

Katashiha	281	King-Noble-of-Shibumi	121
Katsumi	338	King-Ochi-Lord	151
Kayanarumi	63	King-of-Great-Kusaka (*see* Great-Lord-of-Hatabi)	
Keïzen-the-Nun (*see* Ishimè)			
Kekuso	341	King-Prince-Black-of-Border	257
Kena	314	King-Prince-Cave	121
Kenso (*see* King-Little-Basket)		King-Prince-Elder-of-Great-Kuro	157
Kihisa-Possessor	147		
Kikoyu	274	King-Prince-Imasu	121
Kimi-of-Little-Elder-Sister (*see* Princess-Little-E)		King-Prince-Kumata-Long	186
		King-Prince-Long-Life	122
King-Anaho-Clan-of-Kusa-Clan (*see* Prince-Hasetsuka-Clan-Anaho-Clan)		King-Prince-Man-of-Osaka	335
		King-Prince-Saho	121
		King-Prince-Severe-Perfect	151
King-Big-Basket	254	King-Prince-White-of-Eight-Melons	257
King-Brave-Cocoon	171		
King-Brave-Fruitful-Hazura-Lord	121	King-Prince-Yatsuri-Iri (*see* King-Divine-Great-Lord)	
King-Broad-Hat-Sew	323	King-Prince-Younger-of-Great-Kuro	157
King-Dawn-Rise	122		
King-Divine-Great-Lord	122	King-Rice-Good-Lord	171
King-Divine-Wondrous	155	King-Tatatsu-Road-Master-Prince-of-Tamba	121
King-Falcon-Lord	217		
King-Foot-Mirror-Lord	172	King-True-Young-of-Elbow-Pad	155
King-Fruitful-Land-Lord	162	King-True-Young-of-Great-Tsuzuki-of-Behind-the-Mountains	122
King-Great-Bear	191		
King-Great-Elder-Brother	156		
King-Great-Hodo (*see* Great-Lord)		King-True-Young-of-New-Rice-Ears	122
King-Great-Mata	121	King-Umaki	324
King-Great-Winding-Ascent	122	King-Unakami	122
King-Itoshi-Lord	151	King Wiha (*see* Divine-Uë-Ha)	
King-Iwa-Tsuku-Lord	151	King-Wondrous-Tsunu-Lord	154
King-Kagosaka	191	King-Yata (*see* Prince-Oë-of-Jewel-Katsu-of-Yata)	
King-Karu-of-Kinashi	256		
King-Law-Master (*see* Prince-Ear-Quick-Wise-Virtue)		King-Young-Brave	171
		King-Young-E-of-Kura	320
King-Little-Basket	254	King-Young-Nukè-Futa-Mata	217
King-Little-Maro (*see* King-Prince-Man-of-Osaka)		Kishi-of-Sun-Height	304
		Kisu-Ears	90
King-Little-Saho	121	Kiyoyu	319
King-Long-Life-Ricefield-Lord	172	Kochifu	323
King-Lord-August-Gate	122	Kogoto	255
King-Madè-of-Long-Life	335	Kogoto-Jewel	26
King-Ma-Yowa (*see* Prince Mayuwa)		Kohotè	227
		Koma	347
King-Middle-of-Pleasant-to-Dwell-In	231	Koma	299
		Komotsu-of-Sanakita (*see* Princess-Black)	
King-Noble-of-Long-Life	122		

Komu-Ha-Chimu-Kamu-Ki-Mu	257	Lady-Yasaka-Furu-Ama (see Princess-Great-of-Ama)	
Komu-Kishi	272		
Konoha	346	Land-Great-Wealth	51
Kori-of-Bear	207	Land-of-Fire-Brave-Male-Pure (see Brave-Male-Kumi)	
Koshimako-of-Mountain-Clan	286		
Kotè-Child (see Otè-Child)		Land-of-Night-Gate-Block	16
Kuehaya	143	Leading-Elder-of-Una-Gami	206
Kuni-Saru-Taka	194	Leaf-Tree-Earth-Moor (see Fruitful-Shape-Moor)	
Kunimi	274		
Kura	228	Leech	7
Kura-Man-Wide-of-Tagima	340	Life-Integrator	4
Kurafu	344	Life-Island	107
Kuraji-Elder	102	Life-Wondrous-Producer	107
Kuraji-Younger	102	Little-Hodo	304
Kurami-Lord	205	Little-Kata-Clan	332
Kurando (see Magnate-of-Achi)		Little-Left	163
		Little-Maro	332
Kusaka	311	Little-Nari	352
Kuso	355	Little-Perfect	204
Kuwa-Male	93	Little-Pestle	154
Kuzu	315	Little-Shield	296
Kwisin	285	Living-Hikana-Saku	19
K'yotan-Shoraï	41	Loin-Belted	266
		Long-Life	153
L		Long-Life-Perfect-Sun-Wide-Nuka	336
Lady-Beautiful-Teeth	156		
Lady-Great	311	Long-Road-Space	17
Lady-Long-Wind	9	Long-White-Leaf	25
Lady-Mud-Earth	4	Long-Wind-Chief (see Prince-Long-Wind)	
Lady-of-Aömi (see Princess-Itoyo)			
		Loosen-Put	17
Lady-of-Futo-Princess	254	Lord-Asahi	289
Lady-of-Koto-Fushi-of-Wistaria-Plain	218	Lord-Great-Mountain-Gate-of-White-Hair (see White-Hair-Brave-Wide-Land-Great-Young-Mountain-Gate-Prince)	
Lady-of-Little-Bear-Child	335		
Lady-of-Mountain-Ricefield-of-Kasuga (see Princess-Mountain-Ricefield-of-Kasuga)			
		Lord-Mana	308
Lady-of-Omina-Child	335	Lord-Mud-Earth	4
Lady-of-Robe-Passing	259	Lord-Naka-Samu-Ricefield	178
Lady-of-Small-Kettle	217	Lord-of-Great-Tata	125
Lady-of-Sugashiroko (see Princess-Nukadè-Princess)		Lord-of-Kamo	197
		Lord-Popsa	308
Lady-of-Takatsuru	254	Lord-Shika	308
Lady-of-Taku-Hata (see Princess-Young-Perfect)		Lord-Sky-Rock-Soil (see Sky-Feather-Feather)	
Lady-of-Three-Moors-of-Ayuchi	213	Lord-Stem-Tree-Young-House-Rope	39
Lady-of-Upper-River	346	Lovely-August-Feather-Waver	134

M

Loyalty (see Ito-Te)	
Luck-Jewel	5
Magariko	324
Magnate-of-Achi	226
Magnate of Achi-of-Tsukushi	290
Magnate-of-Ari	254
Magnate-of-Hifurè-of-Wani	216
Magnate-of-Ikatsu	259
Magnate-of-Intelligent-Remainder (see Magnate-of-Noble)	
Magnate-of-Little-Ne	288
Magnate-of-Ne	265
Magnate-of-Noble	235
Magnate-of-Nuri	241
Magnate-of-Sun	108
Magnate-of-Tsuga	226
Magnate-of-Tunny	305
Magnate-of-Umakaï	290
Maiden-Sacred-Stone	141
Maketsu	221
Makui	343
Male-Bottom-Possessor	18
Male-Middle-Possessor	18
Male-Surface-Possessor	18
Manè	286
Manè-Ko	218
Many-Handed-Boat-of-Bear-Moor (see Bird-Rock-Camphor-Tree-Boat)	
Mariko (see Divine-Uë-Ha)	
Marisè	355
Maro	229
Maro	359
Masa	334
Masakida	273
Master-of-Mikuma-of-Great-Boiled-Rice	32
Matori	271
Matori	304
Matsu-Ya-Tanè	194
Me	271
Meki	246
Menoko (see Young-Lady-of-Meko)	
Mezurako	316
Mi-Wistaria-Weir	159
Mid-Sky-Master	3
Middle-Mountain-Possessor	14
Middle-Ricefield	214
Miho-Susu-Mi	47
Mikagè	121
Mikasa-of-Kugamimi	129
Mimachi	356
Miro-Na-Mi	51
Mishiru-Male	110
Mita-of-Tsukè	285
Mita-of-Winabè (see Mita-of-Tsukè)	
Mitasuki	357
Mitomo-Lord	223
Miya-Kawara	326
Miyoya (see Princess-Jewel-Good)	
Mizu-Ko	328
Moji-Ku-Moor-Su-Moor-of-Fuwa	36
Momo-Shiki-Iro-Be	187
Monkey-Great-Sea	165
Moon-Bow (see Moon-Darkness-Possessor)	
Moon-Darkness-Possessor	19
Moor-Elder (see Princess-Reed-Moor)	
Moor-Thunder	15
Morishi	328
Moriya-of-Yugè	333
Morning-Katsumi	164
Moshiro	331
Mound-Front-of-Tree	283
Mount-Yoko	340
Mountain-Descent-Possessor	13
Mountain-Gate-Boy (see Little-Pestle)	
Mountain-Gate-Brave (see Little-Pestle)	
Mountain-Gate-Child	284
Mountain-Gate-Possessor	14
Mountain-Plain-Possessor	14
Mountain-Spur-Possessor	14
Mountain-Thunder	15
Mulberry-Castle-One-Thing-Master (see Eight-Fold-Thing-Sign-Master)	
Muruya	260
Mumakaï-of-Otsu	273

My-Shame-Island	7	Noble-of-Okaï	282
M'yo-Kwo	347	Noble-of-Okara-of-Kosè	120
		Noble-of-Omaro-of-Tree	329
N		Noble-of-Oshimi	303
Nagano	273	Noble-of-Oü	228
Nagaöchi	141	Noble-of-Oyumi-of-Tree	282
Nagöchi-of-Ichishi	125	Noble-of-Reed-Plain	248
Naka-Chiko (see Uruwa)		Noble-of-Shield-Man	234
Nakatsu	335	Noble-of-Shima	210
Naked-Hare-of-Rice-Leaves	42	Noble-of-Soga-of-Stone-River	120
Nameless-Female	58	Noble-of-Stone-River	213
Narrow-Mountain	187	Noble-of-Sweet-Uchi	119
Nasehi	328	Noble-of-Tada	222
Nashitomi	110	Noble-of-Toda-of-Target (see	
Netori	213	Noble-of-Shield-Man)	
Natsubana	157	Noble-of-Tsuno-of-Ki	213
Nifutè	343	Noble-of-Tsunu-of-Tree	120
Nihaya	210	Noble-of-Ushiro	289
Nimaro	284	Noble-of-Yashiro-of-Hata	213
Nishikori-Tsubu	337	Noble-of-Young-Child	120
Niyè	329	Noble-of-Younger-Child-Male-	
Niyè	354	Morning-Wife	231
Noble-Great-Saki	262	Noble-Small-Saki	262
Noble-Leading-Elder	205	Nukadè	344
Noble-of-Akako	274	Nukadè	346
Noble-of-Brave-Rice-Seed	155	Nunoshi-Wealth-Bird-Grow-	
Noble-of-Brave-Uchi	119	ing-Ears	51
Noble-of-Great-Beach	213		
Noble-of-Great-Front-Little-		**O**	
Front	249	O-Awful (see Awful-Lady)	
Noble-of-Great-Mina-Kuchi	125	Obito-of-Kosè	309
Noble-of-Great-Moor-of-		Ocean-Bottom-Possessor	18
Three-Threads	158	Ocean-Middle-Possessor	18
Noble-of-Hand-Crumple	203	Ocean-Surface-Possessor	18
Noble-of-Hata-Shrine	120	O-Chin	349
Noble-of-Heguri's-Owl	120	Ofushi	311
Noble-of-Inamè-of-Soga	320	Ogi	319
Noble-of-Jewel-Ricefield	258	Oguna-Kimi	272
Noble-of-Kara-Bag	269	O-Heï	352
Noble-of-Karako-of-Soga	282	Oïshi	279
Noble-of-Little-Maro	343	Ojiko	330
Noble-of-Manchi-of-Soga	252	Okami	51
Noble-of-Mountain-Gate-Bag	300	Oki-Island	8
Noble-of-Mumako-of-Soga	333	Okoshi	319
Noble-of-Nagaöchi (see Naga-		Okuma	319
öchi)		Old-Man-of-Salt-Sea (see Salt-	
Noble-of-Niyè	269	Possessor)	
Noble-of-Nomi	143	Old-Woman-Keep-Eye	301
Noble-of-Oïha-of-Tree	283	Old-Woman-Shiritsuki	155

Omaro-of-Ayashi	286	Port-Swift-Jewel	25
Omi	270	Possessor-of-Tahiri and	
Omi	319	Kishima	51
Onara	343	Priest-Tokusaï (see Tasuna)	
Onashi	282	Prince-Ada	270
Onè	295	Prince-Aga	50
One-Thing-Master (see Eight-Fold-Thing-Sign-Master)		Prince-Ama-Clan	336
		Prince-Army	340
One-Thousand-Jewel	25	Prince-Assembling-of-Divine-Mountain-Gate (see Young-Three-Hairs-Moor)	
One-Word-Master	275		
Oöki	286		
Open-Mouth	17	Prince-August-Horses	252
Open-Mouth-Master	17	Prince-August-House-Lord	189
Oru-Ke (see August-House)		Prince-Awful-Master	51
Osada-Nunakura-Big-Jewel-Shiki	323	Prince-Aya	295
		Prince-Bear	163
Osashi	261	Prince-Bird	177
Oshiro	294	Prince-Brave	171
Oshizaka-Oïnè-of-Prince-Man (see King-Prince-Man-of-Osaka)		Prince-Brave-Clay-Easy	119
		Prince-Brave-Cocoon	171
		Prince-Brave-Land-Kori-Lord	156
Otarima	199	Prince-Brave-Red-Brow	68
Otè-Child	346	Prince-Brave-Tube-Grass	69
Otori	283	Prince-Blue-Cloth-Sa-Grass	38
Otoshi-of-Little-Muna-Kimi (see Lady-of-Omina-Child)		Prince-Chikuma-Naga	211
		Prince-Child-of-Sky-Tsuka (see Prince-Hasetsuka-Clan-Anaho-Clan)	
Otoshi-of-Unako (see Lady-of-Little-Kuma-Child)			
Otoyo	190	Prince-Clan-of-Ikè	336
Owari-Ricefield	258	Prince-Clay-Easy	11
Ox	335	Prince-Companion	279
Ox-Moroï	219	Prince-Divine-Comb	156
Ox-of-Michi	332	Prince-Ear-Quick-Wise-Virtue	339
Oyuko-of-Rice-Leaves	247	Prince-Eight-Wells	113
		Prince-Elder-Brother-of-Tokonè	115
P		Prince-Fierce-of-Long-Inlet-of-Mulberry-Castle	120
Perfect-Distant-Mountain-Cape	52	Prince-Fire-Possessing-Lord	138
Perfect-Face	4	Prince-Fire-Shining (see Fire-Shining-Swift-Male)	
Perfect-Lord-Shima	217		
Perfume-Giver	282	Prince-Flame-of-Fire	321
Pheasant-Kami	180	Prince-Frost-Swift	183
Plant-Slope	166	Prince-Fruitful-Ears-of-Stable-Door-of-Upper-Palace (see Prince-Ear-Quick-Wise-Virtue)	
Plantain	330		
Pleasant-Reed-Sprout-Prince-Elder	4		
Pond-Child	245	Prince-Fruitful-Jewel (see Great-Ocean-Possessor)	
Port-Island	8		

Prince-Fruitful-Ki-Iri	123	Prince-Iwaki	181
Prince-Funashi-Lord	254	Prince-Jewel-Good	69
Prince-Gama-Mi-Lord	190	Prince-Kasuga	336
Prince-Gimi-Younger	168	Prince-Kuchi	241
Prince-Great	118	Prince-Kunichi-Lord	156
Prince-Great-Ears-Young-Mountain-Gate-Lord	118	Prince-Kuë (see Crumbling-Prince)	
Prince-Great-House	9	Prince-Land-of-Okè	121
Prince-Great-House (see Fifty-Brave)		Prince-Land-Pacifier	130
Prince-Great-Middle-of-Nukata	212	Prince-Land-Ruler-Great-Mountain-Gate-Lord	117
Prince-Great-Mountain-Gate-Suki-Friend	115	Prince-Little-Hodo	309
		Prince-Life-Lord	31
Prince-Great-Perfect-Ruling-Lord	143	Prince-Little-Maro (see Prince-Taëma)	
Prince-Great-Rice	119	Prince-Little-Renowned	54
Prince-Great-Suki-Friend-Ears-Brave	174	Prince-Long-Marrow	66
		Prince-Long-Wind	9
Prince-Great-Toma (see Great-Place-Elder)		Prince-Lord-Shinè-of-Mima	116
Prince-Great-Vale	11	Prince-Madè (see King-Madè-of-Long-Life)	
Prince-Great-Wakè	336	Prince-Mana	225
Prince-Hachiko	346	Prince-Maroko	311
Prince-Hasè Clan (see Young-Sazaki-of-Hasè-Clan)		Prince-Mayuwa	266
		Prince-Mawaka	304
Prince-Hasetsuka-Clan-Anaho-Clan	324	Prince-Measure-Knowing	25
		Prince-Metal-Mountain	11
Prince-High-as-Sky's-Sun-Great-Rice-Ears-Lord-Ears (see Fire-Fade)		Prince-Miyado	168
		Prince-Monkey-Ricefield	71
		Prince-Mountain-Gate	123
Prince-High-as-Sky's-Sun-Wave-Marge-Brave-Cormorant-Thatch-Making-to-Meet-Incompletely	88	Prince-Mountain-Gate	155
		Prince-Mountain-Gate-Prince	309
		Prince-Mountain-Gate-Sun-Facing-Brave-Sun-Facing (see Yatsu-Nada)	
Prince-High-Lord-of-Aji-Spades	48	Prince-Mountain-Gate-Old-Stone-Castle-Tomi-Fruitful-Asakura-Dawn-Rise (see King-Dawn-Rise)	
Prince-Hinokuma-High-Ricefield (see Brave-Little-Wide-Land-Great-Shield)			
		Prince-Mountain-Gift (see Fire-Fade)	
Prince-Ibaraki (see King-Umaki)			
Prince-Iga-of-Uda	193	Prince-Mulberry-Castle	68
Prince-Ikumè-Iri-Isachi	123	Prince-Naka	312
Prince-Ini-Stone-Castle-Iri	143	Prince-Ne	312
Prince-Iniyè-Mima-Kiri	120	Prince-Noga	172
Prince-Iri-of-Ihoki	155	Prince-Nushi-Man-Prince	303
Prince-Iri-of-Inasè	156	Prince-Oë-of-Jewel-Katsu-of-Yata	323
Prince-Isaseri	130		
Prince-Itoï	336	Prince-of-Abeshi	148

Prince-of-Great-Maise (see
   Prince-Valorous-Advancer-
   Prince)
Prince-of-Great-Middle   144
Prince-of-Inside   39
Prince-of-Isè   103
Prince-of-Middle   224
Prince-of-Oak-Root   93
Prince-of-Rock-Ricefield   52
Prince-of-Shiki   115
Prince-of-Shiki-Tamadè-Ears   115
Prince-of-Taki   50
Prince-of-Tree   177
Prince-of-Usa   92
Prince-of-Wherefore   164
Prince-Oïnè-of-Magari (see
   Wide-Land-Great-Brave-
   Metal-Sun)
Prince-Perfect-Great-Mountain-
   Gate-Country-Great-Man   116
Prince-Perfect-Jewel   50
Prince-Perfect-Middle   171
Prince-Pure   142
Prince-Push-Teeth-of-Near-
   the-Market   252
Prince-Rice-Chariot   119
Prince-Rock-Castle   300
Prince-Rock-Earth   9
Prince-Rudder   116
Prince-Sachi   153
Prince-Sadè   321
Prince-Sajima   189
Prince-Samema   117
Prince-Sanuki   52
Prince-Sashi-Kata-Lord   117
Prince-Sea-Gift (see Fire-Glow)
Prince-Sky-Five-Hundred   74
Prince-Sky-Great-Man   68
Prince-Sky-Great-Perfect   116
Prince-Sky-Jewel-Wondrous   74
Prince-Sky-Little-Renowned   75
Prince-Sky-Lord   31
Prince-Sky-Plenty-Earth-Plenty-
   High-as-Sky's-Sun-Fire-
   Ruddy-Plenty   66
Prince-Sky-Yasaka   74
Prince-Sky-Young   57
Prince-Sotsu-of-Mulberry-Castle   208
Prince-Sotsu-of-Sun-Facing   156
Prince-Stable-Door (see Prince-
   Ear-Quick-Wise-Virtue)
Prince-Swift-Autumn   9
Prince-Taëma   340
Prince-Tatami   183
Prince-Tide-Possessor   38
Prince-Toöki-Lord   171
Prince-Uzu   119
Prince-Usagi   312
Prince-Valorous-Advancer-
   Prince   117
Prince-Vast-Great-Truth   118
Prince-Vast-Jewel-Great-
   Mountain-Gate-Lord   117
Prince-Washizumi   254
Prince-Wave-Swift   336
Prince-Wave-Swift-Brave-
   Furu-Bear   207
Prince-Yaka-Clan   321
Prince-Yasaka-Iri   123
Prince-Yoso-of-Oki (see Prince-
   Mulberry-Castle)
Prince-Young   114
Prince-Young   167
Prince-Young-Ki-Ni-Iri   144
Prince-Young-Mountain-Gate
   (see Prince-Mountain-Gate)
Prince-Young-Perfect   155
Prince-Younger   224
Prince-Youth-of-Mound   300
Princess-Aga   50
Princess-Ahira   90
Princess-Ahira-Good   68
Princess-Akami (see Princess-
   Mountain-Ricefield-of-
   Kasuga)
Princess-Akami-of-Mountain-
   Ricefield (see Princess-Moun-
   tain-Ricefield-of-Kasuga)
Princess-Akuto   115
Princess-Anaho-Clan-of-Hashi-
   Man   324
Princess-Anè   287
Princess-Ata   130
Princess-August-Food (see
   Jewel-of-Storehouse-Rice)
Princess-August-Sword-of-
   Mimuku   162
Princess-Autumn   39

Princess-Avoiding-of-Mulberry-Castle	68
Princess-Awaka	37
Princess-Awo-Numa-Oshi	51
Princess-Awa-of Iitoyo-of-Oshinumi (*see* Princess-Iitoyo)	
Princess-Ayato (*see* Princess-Jewel-Ornamented-With-Clusters-of-August-Jewels)	
Princess-Beautiful	117
Princess-Black	236
Princess-Black	248
Princess-Blooming-Tree-Blossom	78
Princess-Bridge	216
Princess-Bridge-of-Uji (*see* Princess-Bridge)	
Princess-Brilliant	140
Princess-Clam	43
Princess-Clay-Easy	11
Princess-Clay-Easy	118
Princess-Comb-Ricefield	34
Princess-Cockle	43
Princess-Divine-Great-Ichi	38
Princess-Divine-House-Shield	49
Princess-Divine-Nashi	157
Princess-Dog	38
Princess-Eagle	121
Princess-Eight-Rivers (*see* Ashi-Nadaka)	
Princess-Eighty-Bells-Good (*see* Princess-River-Fork)	
Princess-Elder	156
Princess-Elder	223
Princess-Elder	227
Princess-Elder-Lady-of-Wave-Hiding-of-Harima	153
Princess-Falling-Tree-Blossom	36
Princess-Fish-Hawk (*see* Princess-Three-Cook-House)	
Princess-Flourishing-Good-of-Long-Life	121
Princess-Forward	44
Princess-Fragrant	67
Princess-Fruitful-August-Food-Cook-House	324
Princess-Fruitful-Food	11
Princess-Fruitful-Jewel	81
Princess-Fruitful-Stone-Castle-Iri	123
Princess-Futaji	171
Princess-Furu	303
Princess-Good (*see* Princess-Lovely-Island)	
Princess-Great	116
Princess-Great-Food (*see* Jewel-of-Storehouse-Rice)	
Princess-Great-Furnace (*see* Princess-of-Inside)	
Princess-Great-Kami	91
Princess-Great-Kami	213
Princess-Great-Lady-of-Kasuga	272
Princess-Great-Lady-of-Mountain-Ricefield (*see* Princess-Mountain-Ricefield-of-Kasuga)	
Princess-Great-Maise-Brave	171
Princess-Great-Middle-of-Osaka	217
Princess-Great-Moor-Clapper-Bell (*see* Azuki-Island)	
Princess-Great-of-Ama	123
Princess-Great-Sun	68
Princess-Great-Toma (*see* Great-Place-Elder-Lady)	
Princess-Great-Vale	11
Princess-Hasetsuka-Clan-Anaho-Clan (*see* Princess-Anaho-Clan-of-Hashi-Man)	
Princess-Hata	319
Princess-Hayama	205
Princess-Hayè	254
Princess-Hibasu	122
Princess-Hibasu	143
Princess-High (*see* Princess-Under-Shining)	
Princess-High-Brow-of-Mulberry-Castle	122
Princess-Hikami	52
Princess-Hinaga	147
Princess-Hisura	154
Princess-Hoï (*see* Princess-Akuto)	
Princess-Horn-House	68
Princess-Hoso (*see* Princess-Beautiful)	
Princess-Iho-Nono (*see* Princess-of-Iho)	

KAMI-LIST

Princess-Iitoyo 252
Princess-Ikakoya 69
Princess-Imè (*see* Queen-Rock-Kumo)
Princess-Inamè (see Queen-Rock-Kumo)
Princess-Iri-of-Azami 122
Princess-Iri-of-Futaji (*see* Princess-Iwa-Tsuku)
Princess-Iri-of-Nubata 122
Princess-Iri-Takaki 212
Princess-Iseri 110
Princess-Ishiki-Island 39
Princess-Island 9
Princess-Ito (*see* Princess-Itoï)
Princess-Itoï 217
Princess-Iwasaki 239
Princess-Iwa-Tsuku 151
Princess-Izumi (*see* Princess-Vast-True-Young)
Princess-Izumi 163
Princess-Jewel (*see* Sky-Princess)
Princess-Jewel-Comb 111
Princess-Jewel-Good 69
Princess-Jewel-Good 88
Princess-Jewel-of-Uji (*see* Princess-Bridge)
Princess-Jewel-Ornamented-With-Clusters-of-August-Jewels 47
Princess-Kagari 317
Princess-Kagè (*see* Princess-Under-Mountain-Flow)
Princess-Kagè 305
Princess-Kago (*see* Princess-Ikakoya)
Princess-Kaï-Tako-of-Uji 335
Princess-Kami-Cloth 76
Princess-Kanarachi 68
Princess-Kara 268
Princess-Kasuga (*see* Princess-Mountain-Ricefield-of-Kasuga)
Princess-Ke (*see* Princess-Young)
Princess-Kitashi 324
Princess-Kuchi 242
Princess-Kuga-of-Kuwada 235
Princess-Kukuma-Mori 171

Princess-Kusu 281
Princess-Kuwa 248
Princess-Lagoon-River 45
Princess-Life-Jewel-Good 126
Princess-Life-Spirit-Luck-Spirit 51
Princess-Listen 17
Princess-Little-E 324
Princess-Long-Hair 219
Princess-Long-Life-Perfect 122
Princess-Long-Life-True-Young-Middle 217
Princess-Long-Marrow (*see* Princess-Three-Cook-House)
Princess-Lovely-Island 30
Princess-Luck-Spirit 51
Princess-May-Night (*see* Princess-of-Jewel)
Princess-Metal-Mountain 11
Princess-Middle 212
Princess-Middle-of-Orange (*see* Princess-Orange)
Princess-Middle-of-Tawi 218
Princess-Mika-Yori 92
Princess-Mima-Ki 123
Princess-Miyasu 174
Princess-Mountain-Gate 144
Princess-Mountain-Gate 311
Princess-Mountain-Gate-To-To-Hi-Momoso 118
Princess-Mountain-Gate-To-To-Kami-Asachi-Harama-Guhashi 125
Princess-Mountain-Ricefield-of-Kasuga 304
Princess-Mumashi 329
Princess-Myriad-Looms-Fruitful-Dragon-Fly-Island 65
Princess-Naga 206
Princess-Nagaï (*see* Young-Lady-of-Hatabi)
Princess-Nakashi (*see* Great-Lady-of-Long-Ricefield)
Princess-Naseri 110
Princess-Nishikidè 346
Princess-Noga 172
Princess-Nuka 172
Princess-Nuka-Ricefield-Clan (*see* Princess-Fruitful-August-Food-Cook-House)

Princess-Nukadè-Princess (see Queen-Takara)
Princess-Nunaki-Iri 123
Princess-Nuna-So (see Princess-Akuto)
Princess-Nutsu 81
Princess-Odo 277
Princess-of-Aga 77
Princess-of-Deer-Reed (see Princess-Blooming-Tree-Blossom)
Princess-of-Divine-Ata (see Princess-Blooming-Tree-Blossom)
Princess-of-Great-House 34
Princess-of-Great-Middle 144
Princess-of-Great-Middle 156
Princess-of-Haya 160
Princess-of-He (see Princess-Torrent)
Princess-of-Iho 156
Princess-of-Inside 39
Princess-of-Isè 103
Princess-of-Jewel 52
Princess-of-Maise 153
Princess-of-Miho 49
Princess-of-Niho 200
Princess-of-Okè 120
Princess-of-Okè 122
Princess-of-Old-Port 161
Princess-of-Quick-Arrive 159
Princess-of-River (see Princess-Akuto)
Princess-of-Rock 231
Princess-of-Rock-Ricefield 52
Princess-of-Sun 250
Princess-of-Tree 177
Princess-of-Tsuma 34
Princess-of-Usa 92
Princess-of-Wherefore 164
Princess-of-Yamè 165
Princess-Oki-of-Owari 68
Princess-Orange (see Young-Lady-of-Hatabi)
Princess-Orange 304
Princess-Oshinomi-Be (see Princess-Iïtoyo)
Princess-Over-Shining 49
Princess-Perfect-Jewel 50
Princess-Perfect-of-Hina 51
Princess-Perfectly-Ornamented 69
Princess-Vagina-Tatara-Fleeing 111
Princess-Pure-of-the-Land-of-Great-Mountain-Gate (see Elder-Sister-Haë)
Princess-Quite-Black 187
Princess-Quite-Black-of-Boiled-Rice-Moor 187
Princess-Reed-Moor 10
Princess-Refulgent 38
Princess-Rice-Sun (see Princess-Vast-True-Young)
Princess-River-Fork 114
Princess-Road-Master 204
Princess-Rock-Long 78
Princess-Rock-Nest 8
Princess-Root 299
Princess-Rough-Slope 248
Princess-Sacred-Stone-of-Mulberry-Castle (see Princess-Horn-House)
Princess-Sahaji (see Princess-Saho)
Princess-Saho 121
Princess-Satè 317
Princess-Sayo-of-Pine-Tree-Beach 322
Princess-Sea-Horizon-Island (see Princess-Tagiri)
Princess-Seya-Tatara (see Princess-Jewel-Comb)
Princess-Shallow-Well 183
Princess-Shitsu-Kaï-of Uji (see Princess-Kaï-Tako-of-Uji)
Princess-Sky-August-Servant 74
Princess-Sky-Awful 146
Princess-Sky-Governing-Fresh-Karu 39
Princess-Sky-Hand-Good (see Port-Island)
Princess-Sky-Hand-Loom 25
Princess-Sky-Mikaji 50
Princess-Sky-Mikatsu (see Princess-Sky-Mikaji)
Princess-Small-Moor-of-Wave-Swift 300
Princess-Stone-Slope 200
Princess-Sun-Oki (see Princess-Perfectly-Ornamented)

Princess-Sun-River	36	Princess-Yakami-in-Rice-Leaves	41
Princess-Susashi	183	Princess-Yasaka-Iri	155
Princess-Swift-Autumn	9	Princess-Yoto (*see* Sky-Princess)	
Princess-Tagori	30		
Princess-Tagiri (*see* Princess-Tagori)		Princess-Young	280
		Princess-Young	311
Princess-Takachima-of-Mulberry-Castle	119	Princess-Young-Eight-Moors	47
		Princess-Young-Forward (*see* Princess-Forward)	
Princess-Takahashi (*see* Princess-Great-Lady-of-Kasuga)		Princess-Young-of-Sasu-Land	37
		Princess-Young-Perfect	271
Princess-Tamura (*see* Queen-Takara)		Princess-Younger (*see* Princess-Iri-of-Nubata)	
Princess Tashiraga	304	Princess-Younger	155
Princess-Tatara-Fifty-Bells-Princess (*see* Princess-Vagina-Tatara-Fleeing)		Princess-Younger	156
		Princess-Younger	191
		Princess-Younger	227
Princess-Tatara-Startled-Good-Princess (*see* Princess-Vagina-Tatara-Fleeing)		Princess-Younger (*see* Lady-of-Robe-Passing)	
		Princess-Younger	287
Princess-Temple-Presider-Eight-Rivers	216	Princess-Younger	321
		Princess-Younger-Orange	171
Princess-Three-Cook-House	66	Princess-Younger-Princess-True-Young (*see* Momo-Shiki-Iro-Be)	
Princess-Toneri	350		
Princess-Torrent	30		
Princess-Toto-Mountain-Gate (*see* Princess-Mountain-Gate-To-To-Hi-Momoso)		Princess-Youth (*see* Princess-Young)	
		Princess-Youth-of-Kafuchi	321
Princess-Trout-Eyed-Beautiful-Eyes-of-Far-Harbor	123	**Q**	
Princess-True-Hair-Touch-Comb-Ricefield (*see* Princess-Comb-Ricefield)		Queen-Hen-Bird	217
		Queen-of-Wave-Swift (*see* Princess-Ono-of-Wave-Swift)	
Princess-Tsubura	193		
Princess-Turtle	291		
Princess-Una	248	Queen-Rock-Kumo	324
Princess-Under-Mountain-Glow	119	Queen-Takara	335
Princess-Under-Shining	48		
Princess-Vagina-Tatara-Fleeing	111	**R**	
Princess-Vast-True-Young	116		
Princess-Water-Hanomè	11	Red-Possessor	19
Princess-Water-Sasara	104	Refulgent-Mountain-Dwelling-Magnate	39
Princess-Wealth-House (*see* Princess-Three-Cook-House)		Refulgent-Ugly-Male	126
		Resistance-Calmer (*see* Sky-August-Bird)	
Princess-Weaving (*see* Young-Sun-Female)		Rice-Boiled-Rice	89
Princess-Wide	311		
Princess-Wide	335	Rice-Ear-Youth (*see* My-Shame-Island)	
Princess-Yaka	317		

Ricefield-Palace-Mistress-Eight-Ears-of-Refreshment (*see* Hand-Stroke-Elder)		Sea-Body (*see* Great-Ocean-Possessor)	
		Sea-Horizon-Distant	18
River-Katsu	350	Senzo-the-Nun (*see* Toyomè)	
River-Shallow	190	Seven-Hand-Breadths-Shins	174
River-Weed	12	Shake-Jewel	5
Road-Keepers-of-the-Land-of-Night	17	She-Who-Invites	4
		Shiba-Tatto	337
Road-Reaching-Great-Kami (*see* She-Who-Invites)		Shijumi (*see* Hosomè)	
		Shiki-Elder	101
Road-Spread-Out	18	Shiki-Mountain-Master	51
Road-Turn-Back (*see* Land-of-Night-Gate-Block)		Shiki-Younger	102
		Shikotoi (*see* Kunimi)	
Rock	321	Shima	337
Rock-Possessor	19	Ship-Jewel	198
Rock-Slope	300	Shiratsu-Tsumi	340
Rock-Splitter	12	Shiwo-Futa	354
Rock-Village	343	Shore-Distant	18
Rock-Well	314	Shunned-Awful-Lady (*see* Awful-Lady)	
Rock-Well	347		
Root-Brandisher	186	Sit-Place	107
Root-Splitter	12	Sky-Akaüra	75
Rudder-Ears	90	Sky-Assembling-Town-Lady	37
Rustic-Illuminator-Nukata-Bichi	50	Sky-August-Bird	32
		Sky-August-Shade	74
S		Sky-August-Year (*see* Great-Year)	
Sacred-Jewel-of-the-Rooted-Sakaki-Princess-of-Sky-Distant-Opposite-Land (*see* Great-Sky-Shiner)		Sky-Awful-Master	51
		Sky-Beckoning-Ancestor-Lord	26
		Sky-Bird-Boat (*see* Bird-Rock-Camphor-Tree-Boat)	
Sacred-Male-Pillar	13	Sky-Blowing-Male	9
Sacred-Quarter-Brave-Child (*see* Prince-of-Isè)		Sky-Change-Sun-Sky-Mist-Land-Change-Moon-Land-Mist (*see* Mid-Sky-Master)	
Sacred-Quarter-Root-Brandisher	133		
Sado-Island	8	Sky-Cloud-Man	21
Sakaë	338	Sky-Country-Jewel	58
Sakè-of-Hada	285	Sky-Dark-Door	10
Sakitsuya	279	Sky-Deer	60
Salt-Possessor	77	Sky-Divine-Stander	3
Saru	332	Sky-Door-Eye	68
Sashihirè (*see* Sobakiri)		Sky-Eagle-Stander	5
Sato-Tomo (*see* Beach-Child)		Sky-Eight-Descend	4
Satoï (*see* Ajihari)		Sky-Eight-Hundred-Days	5
Satsuki	277	Sky-Eighty-Myriad-Jewel	5
Saya	247	Sky-Elder-Brother	74
Scribe-of-Ports (*see* Ox)		Sky-Feather-Feather	26
Scribe-of-Ships (*see* Great-Shin-Mi)		Sky-Feather-Field	75

KAMI-LIST

Sky-Fertile-Dragon-Fly-Prince-Lord (see Great-Mountain-Gate-Fertile-Dragon-Fly-Island)
Sky-Frightening-Female 26
Sky-Gate 24
Sky-Gathering-Clouds 67
Sky-Gathering-Clouds 287
Sky-Gourd 11
Sky-Great-Heart-Youth (see Three-Children-Island)
Sky-Great-Male (see Deer-Blood-Island)
Sky-Great-Male 68
Sky-Great-Sun 31
Sky-Hand-Strength-Male 26
Sky-Hard-River 5
Sky-Hibara-Great-Long-Wind-Wealth 52
Sky-Hill-Pass-Elder 10
Sky-Ikishiniho 74
Sky-Isafu-Jewel 74
Sky-Jewel-Owner (see Sky-Feather-Feather)
Sky-Kami-Jewel 74
Sky-Kunono 74
Sky-Land 124
Sky-Land-Great-Haruki-Wide-Court 311
Sky-Leaf-Elder (see Brave-Leaf-Elder)
Sky-Life-Jewel 74
Sky-Lower-Spring 75
Sky-Mara 24
Sky-Mara 75
Sky-Mara 114
Sky-Maüra 75
Sky-Maüra 76
Sky-Meet 5
Sky-Milk-Swift-Sun 74
Sky-Mirror 10
Sky-Mist 10
Sky-Moon-Spirit 75
Sky-Mount-Fragrant 66
Sky-One-Eye (see Sky-Mara)
Sky-One-Pillar (see Iki-Island)
Sky-One-Root (see Princess-Island)
Sky-Pillar (see Prince-Long-Wind)

Sky-Place-True-Seeing 74
Sky-Point-Blade-Extended 14
Sky-Princess 122
Sky-Push-Man 109
Sky-Red-Mara 76
Sky-Red-Star 75
Sky-Red-Star 76
Sky-Rice-Bran-Door 74
Sky-Road 74
Sky-Road-Sun 66
Sky-Rock-Door-Opener (see Sky-Hand-Strength-Male)
Sky-Round-Eye 71
Sky-Seed 92
Sky-Shiner-Great-Noon-Female (see Great-Sky-Shiner)
Sky-Shining-Earth-Shining-Sky's-Fire-Ruddy-Comb-Jewel-Plenty-Swift-Sun 66
Sky-Shining-Jewel (see Jewel-Ancestor)
Sky-Soso 75
Sky-Southwest-Wind-Wondrous-Southwest-Wind 112
Sky-Spying-Female 58
Sky-Sun-Eagle 25
Sky-Sun-Lord 102
Sky-Sun-Spear 139
Sky-Sun-Spirit 74
Sky-Taneko 108
Sky-Ten-Thousand 10
Sky-Thing-Five-Hundred 75
Sky-Three-Descend 5
Sky-Tomi 106
Sky-Tree-Falling 74
Sky-Two-Houses (see Two-Children-Island)
Sky-Upper-Spring 75
Sky-Wani 93
Sky-Water-Divider 10
Sky-Water-Drawing-Gourd-Possessor 10
Sky-Winter-Clothing 37
Sky-Yukawa-Tana (see Great-Hawk-of-Mountain-Neighborhood)
Small-Beach 201
Small-Island 8
Small-Person-Jewel 153

KAMI-LIST

Snap-Master	13	Takuzu-Well	158
Sobakiri	251	Tamichi	245
Somin-Shoraï	41	Tamushi-Wakè-of-Sanuki	290
Soödo (see Crumbling-Prince)		Tasa	280
Soöri	38	Tashiraga (see Princess-Hayè)	
Spirit-of-Great-Land	38	Tasuna	342
Stem-Year	39	Tatè	132
Storehouse-Rice-Possessor (see Jewel-of-Storehouse-Rice)		Tatè-of-Stone-River	272
		Tatsu	353
Storehouse-Shelf-Kami	20	Ten-Thousand-Jewel	5
Strong-Neck	233	Thing-Excel-Land-Excel-Long-Narrow (see Salt-Possessor)	
Sufficient-Wondrous-Producer	107		
Sugaru	279	Thing-Sign	303
Sukuna	246	Thought-Includer	24
Sukuri-of-Kura-Clan	337	Three-Children-Island	8
Sumè-Irodo (see Prince-Hasetsuka-Clan-Anaho-Clan)		Three-Hairs-Moor	89
		Thrust-Snap	96
Sumi-Zaka-of-Uda	56	Thrust-Stand-Funo-Place (see Great-Elder-of-Come-Not-Place)	
Sumoto (see Prince Hasetsuka-Clan-Anaho-Clan)			
Sun-Governing	38	Thunder (see Great-Land-Master)	
Sun-Maë	24		
Sun-Minister	96	Toko-Maro	353
Sun-Place-True-Seeing	74	Toku-Seki	359
Sun's-Swift-Sun	13	Toni	329
Suruki	305	Tori	352
Sweet-True-Hand	67	Tori-Child	354
Swift-Awful-Brave-Land-Ruler-of-Sahaya	51	Tori-Maro	352
		Tori-of-Saddle-Make	351
Swift-Banishment-Kami (see Brave-Swift-Impetuous-Male)		Toriki	318
		Toruki	305
		Toyoho	282
Swift-Father	59	Toyomè	337
Swift-Jewel-Male	17	Tree-Elder	10
Swift-Mountain-Dwelling	39	Tree-Fork-Kami	45
Swift-Passing-Lord (see Swift-Father)		Tribe-Master-of-Forehead-Ricefield	258
		Trouble-Master	17
T		True-Kind-Lovely-August-Mirror	134
Tachi-Swift (see Swift-Father)			
Tahiko	329	True-Pass-Mountain-Possessor	13
Tajima	224	True-Young-of-Iza	212
Tajima-Mori	142	Truly-Conquerer-I-Conquer-Swift-Sun-Sky-Great-Great-Ears	
Tajima-Sun-Height	142		
Takè-Hasè	245		30
Takatoshi	349	Tsuka	294
Takè-Moro-Sumi	133	Tsu-Kami	282
Takemotsu	195	Tsuchigura	244
Takumi-of-Michiko	356	Tsukiya	228

Tsuku-Hi-Mi	25	Wave-Edge-Sea-Horizon-Prince	18
Tsunè	109	Wave-Edge-Shore-Prince	18
Tsuruginè	68	Wave-Swift	331
Tu-Mu-Rya-Phye	331	Weaving-Lady (*see* Princess-Sky-Hand-Loom)	
Two-Children-Island	9		
		Well-Shine	97

U

Uchi-Saru-Taka	194	White-Deer	182
Uë-of-Saka	357	White-Dog	182
Ugly-Females-of-the-Land-of-Night	15	White-Hair-Brave-Wide-Land-Great-Young-Mountain-Gate-Prince	271
Ugly-Male-of-the-Reed-Plain (*see* Great-Land-Master)		White-Stone	135
		White-Sun	38
Ugly-Maro (*see* Takumi-of-Michiko)		Wide-Land-Great-Brave-Metal-Sun	311
Ujimè-of-Hada (*see* Princess-Jewel-Good)		Witè	350
		Wo-Saka	342
Ukashi-Elder-Brother	97	Wondrous-Eight-Fold-Jewel	64
Ukashi-Younger-Brother	97	Wondrous-Jewel (*see* Prince-of-Isè)	
Ukatsu-Kunu	133		
Unade	157	Wondrous-of-Bear-Moor	31
Under-High-Storehouse	95	Wondrous-Rock-True-Gate (*see* Sky-Hand-Strength-Male)	
(Unnamed)	115		
Unu (*see* Great-Stone)		Wondrous-Shining-Jewel	31
Urakori-Lord	224	Wondrous-Sun-Kata-Sky-Kata (*see* Princess-Life-Jewel-Good)	
Uruwa	270		
Usagi	354		
Ushi-of-Worship (*see* Worship-Master)		Wondrous-Well-of-Oki	46
		Worship-Master	61
Uta-Good	328		
Uyatsubè	186	**Y**	
Uzumasa (*see* Sakè-of-Hada)		Yahazu-Uji-Matachi	312
Uzumori-Masa (*see* Sakè-of-Hada)		Yaho-of-Han-Man	337
		Yama	280
		Ya-Nushi-Oshiho-Brave-Boar-Heart	119

W

Wa-chi-tsu-mi	115	Yard-Fire-High-Kami	39
Wafuna	238	Yard-Fire-Kami	39
Waiting-to-See-Holly-Flowers	51	Yatsu-Nada	137
Waki-Thunder-of-Kamo	70	Yes-or-No-Shins	62
Wan-i	221	Yokotachi-of-Ishiyura	168
Wanasa-Okina	110	Yorozu	345
Wanasa-Oöma	110	Young-Brave-Prince-of-Maise	129
Warrior-of-Mound-Front-of-Tree	295	Young-Child-of-Kumè (*see* King-Little-Basket)	
Warriors-of-the-Land-of-Night	16	Young-Child-of-Shima (*see* King-Big-Basket)	
Water-Spoiled-Deep-Pool-Blossom	37	Young-Country-Jewel (*see* Princess-Under-Shining)	
Water-Sprinkler	39		

Young-Day-Female	52	Young-Wren-of-Little-Hasè	304
Young-Kusaka-Be (see Young-Lady-of-Hatabi)		Young-Year	39
		Younger-Clan-Chief	280
Young-Lady-of-Hatabi	221	Younger-Lady-of-Aje-of-Upper-Sea	178
Young-Lady-of-Meko	311		
Young-Lady-of-Uji	217	Younger-Sister-Haë	115
Young-Lady-of-Yata	217	Younger-Upper-River-Current-Brave	168
Young-Lord-of-Uji	217		
Young-Miya-of-Hoshi-River	280	Youth-Mist-of-Spring-Mountain	141
Young-Mountain-Integrator	39		
Young-Mountain-Warden	239	Youth-Nakatsu-of-Kasuga (see Nakatsu)	
Young-Prince-Brave-Prince-of-Maise	117	Youth-of-Wind-Great-Male	9
Young-Producer	11	Youth-Under-Ice-of-Autumn-Mountain	141
Young-Rice-Transplanting-Female	39	Yutsuki-Lord	221
Young-Sazaki-of-Hasè-Clan	324		
Young-Snap-Master	50	**Z**	
Young-Sun-Female	23		
Young-Three-Hairs-Moor	89	Zem-M'yo	347
Young-Thunder	15	Zen-Shin-the-Nun (see Shima)	
Young-Thunder (see Great-Mountain-Integrator)		Zen-Toku	347
		Zen-Toku	349

ANALYSIS OF THE NARRATIVE

I. MYTH-PARALLELS

The reader who follows the myth-story will at first deem his bark afloat in strange waters. It creates on the Occidental mind a profound impression of weirdness, of uncouthness and of unfamiliarity.

One searches it in vain for certain myth-ideas well distributed throughout the rest of the world—such, for example, as an early fire-worship, of which relics are so frequent in the systems of eastern Asia. Its list contains only a single proper deity of fire (Fire-Shining-Swift-Male) and his worship is negligible, being confined to little-known Shrines of low rank.[1] And nowhere in the legends is there any indication that the Sun-Goddess is a later development from a more primitive fire deity. The deity of the hearth (Princess-of-the-Inside) and the deity Kami-of-the-Yard-Fire, by some Japanese scholars identified with her, are mere lesser divinities of household economy. Moreover the few scattered superstitions and housewife observances of Japan which at first glance seem to possess some such connection (as, for example, the planting of the sunrise-grass [*hinodè*] on country roofs to insure the dwellings from conflagrations) [2] without exception classify themselves with sun- rather than with fire-ceremonial.

There is the meagerest suggestion of mating by capture,[3] whose traces are so readily distinguished among the Mongol peoples of the mainland without exception.[4] The rape of the daughter of Brave-Swift-Impetuous-Male by Great-Land-Master is the nearest approach to bride-capture, and this is not a true instance, since the pair were wedded, presumably with consent, before their flight. The strait observances, too, which among so many peoples surround the nuptial approach, are wholly lacking. There is no suggestion of preliminary stealth in a man's first visit to his affianced, no prohibition for a wife to see her husband naked, no period of "reserve" or silence upon either side after the wedding ceremony—omissions the more remarkable for the reason that these ceremonials obtain to this day on the near Korean mainland. There is no trace of the worship of the double-sex hermaphrodite, or of the *couvade*, that strange custom by which the male symbolically partakes of the female labor in child-bearing.[5]

There is no rainbow myth—except as one may identify with the prismatic arc the "Floating-Sky-Bridge," which in origin is probably the vessel in which the *pseudo* Sky-folk came to the islands.

And the Narrative is oddly deficient, too, in star-myth. Only one star-episode is mentioned (that of the submission of the rebel Kami, Kagasè-Male [Dread-Sky-Star]) and but one other probable star-divinity is cited, in the retinue of the Sky-ancestor. Perhaps the reason for this, however, is a very simple one. The excessive humidity over the greater part of the archipelago, added to during much of the year by the mist from the flooded ricefields, makes a starry night rare indeed. The Japanese has never had the incentive of the Arab and the Greek to speculation upon the nightly firmament. Only in the northernmost island do even the brighter planets shine with any brilliancy—and among the Ainu, who have persisted in those latitudes, there is a more copious star-lore than in all the rest of Japan.

For all these curious omissions, however, the legends are full of old landmarks. Here and there one discerns a world-wide superstition-fragment. He-Who-Invites, when he parted with She-Who-Invites at the Level-Pass-of-the-Land-of-Night, "spat out spittle." Great-Ocean-Possessor, the ruler of the sea realm, giving Fire-Fade the lost fishhook of his brother Fire-Glow, which has been found in the mouth of the *taï*-fish, advises him, "*spit thrice* and fling it to him with your hand behind your back." Spitting has been a custom among many savage peoples at the sight of what is impure or tabu; as a charm against evil luck it is still well-nigh universal. In the southern part of the United States a child makes a mark with his foot and spits on it.

The sea deity counsels Fire-Fade: "When he (Fire-Glow) goes a-fishing, take your stand on the sea-beach and do that which raises the wind. Now that which raises the wind is whistling. When you do this I will overwhelm and harass him with the hurrying waves." This superstition is common to modern sailor-men the world over.

Preparatory to luring the Sun-Goddess from her cave, the Sky deities seek a portent in scapulimancy, "divination by the shoulder-bone," that is, by observing the cracks caused by heat in the shoulder-bone of a stag —the "speal-bone" divination known to the early English. It was practiced by the Arabs, by the Mongols in the time of Genghis Khan,[6] and is still made use of by the Lapps and the Tatars of the Khirghiz. Confucius mentions its early use in China. To this day the method is employed by the Japanese, except that tortoise-shell takes the place of the deer's bone.

It is told of Mountain-Gate-Brave that during his campaign against the recalcitrant peoples of the east, a certain pass exhaled a deadly vapor, but "folk who crossed there chewed garlic and smeared with it themselves and their cattle and horses, and were not affected." Belief in the peculiar efficacy of the garlic plant is world-wide. The modern Chinese use it to keep away evil spirits, and wherever the vampire superstition is known it is employed, from Servia to Scotland.[7]

In the reign of Yomeï-*Tenno*, when the newly imported religion, Buddhism, had split the court into two factions, Katsumi, Tribe-Master of the Intercessors, "*made images of King-Prince-Man-of-Osaka, the Heir to the Rule, and of Prince-Brave-Ricefield, and hated them.*" Here is a Japanese variety of the sorcery of the waxen image, perhaps as ancient a kind of witchcraft as is known to the modern world, and one common, in some form or other, to all races.[8] These puppets, made of straw or clay, are to this day employed in China and are more rarely met with in Japan.

In the earliest legend with which the recital opens, one recognizes the primal myth of what later science was to recognize as the true process of cosmic creation, the development from a primordial darkness and chaos, whose grosser parts precipitate to form the earth, and whose more ethereal portion becomes the firmament. This is the Kronos legend, in its thousand forms, the father of all mythologies, upon which so many peoples have constructed their cosmogonies. The theogony based upon this is thus similar to many other systems, including the Polynesian, wherein Rangi and Papa represent the Heaven and the Earth, but suggesting most nearly the elaborate Pantheon of the Greeks and Latins, the High-Sky-Plain corresponding to Uranus, and the Earth to Gaea, Mid-Sky-Master to Hyperion, and finally the creative pair, He-Who-Invites and She-Who-Invites, to Jupiter and Juno.[9] The derivation of the land from elements of the watery waste is familiar to Babylonian, Egyptian and Hebrew legend. Relics of this fundamental myth are to be met with in cosmogonic fragments and songs on every continent.[10]

He-Who-Invites and She-Who-Invites are the Japanese equivalents of the Babylonian Adam and Eve whose myth was later re-echoed in those of Deucalion and Pyrrha, of Cadmus and Hermione. The "Central Pillar" of their earthly dwelling is Indra's World-House-Pillar, the Indian Mt. Meru, the Scandinavian Branstock. The retirement of the Sun-Goddess to her cave and her placation and return re-tell what is one of the world's oldest stories, a version of which exists among every people whose history has known the variation of winter and summer.[11] The rebellion and expulsion of Brave-Swift-Impetuous-Male (the Loki of the

Japanese epos) is the Japanese version of the fall of Lucifer, echoing the familiar dualism of Set and Osiris, of Ormuzd and Ahriman.

The creation of light and the vegetable world before that of the sun, and the subjugation of the rebellious princes of the Sky, recall the story of the Hebrew Genesis. The abandonment of the first-born infant deity Leech in the reed-boat is a variant of the story of the Indian Karma, son of the sun deity; of that of the Egyptian Horus, reincarnation of Osiris; of the Accadian myth of Sargon and his bullrush ark and of that of the hidden Attis, identical in origin with the Mosaic legend.

The creation of other deities from the blood and portions of the body of Fire-Shining-Swift-Male has its parallels in the god-myths of almost all nations, from the Chaldeans and the Egyptians to the American Indians. When Kronos mutilates his father Uranus (Heaven) with the iron sickle to end his embraces of his mother Gaea (Earth), the blood produces the Melian Nymphs, the Gigantes, and (according to some legends) Silenus, and when Perseus cuts off the head of Medusa the blood produces the winged steed Pegasus.

The visit of He-Who-Invites to his wife in the nether-world parallels the Babylonian myth of Ishtar and Du'uzu (Greek forms of which appear in the legends of Orpheus and Eurydice, and of Protesilaus and Laodamia), as certain of its features correspond with the rape of Persephone by Pluto and the journey of Hermod to the Halls of Hela (Death) to ask the return of Balder to the upper-world. In the same way the Hawaiian Hiku follows his wife Kawelu to Hades to regain her.

The fatal eating of the food of Hades is Indian,[12] Hebrew,[13] Greek and Scandinavian, and is found in folklores as wide apart as those of Samoa, New Zealand, the Tonga Islands,[14] Finland, Picardy and the Isle of Man. Persephone eats the seven pomegranate seeds and so is bound to the under-world, just as She-Who-Invites eats of the furnace of Hades and may not return with her mate. So the Hawaiian Hitu pursues Paré and is counselled not to eat of the spirit food if he would return. So, too, Thomas the Rhymer is warned not to partake of the pottage of fairyland, Ogier the Dane eats the fatal apple,[15] and the water and grass of the middle-earth are poison to Kan Pudai.

The lustration of He-Who-Invites on his return suggests that of Juno after her descent to Hades, and of Alcestis after her rescue from Thanatos, a myth that was old before the Greek race was born. His flight, with the pursuit, is among the oldest known myths of the world. One of its episodes appears in the Egyptian tale of "The Two Brothers"—whose earliest manuscript form is of the time of Rameses II, fourteen hundred years before the Christian era—where Ra causes a river of crocodiles to flow between the fugitive Bitou and his vengeful brother Anapou.

Its poetical version is seen in the tale of Atalanta and the golden apples.

The distribution of the rule among the three children of the earlier creator—like the division of the world, after the rebellion against Saturn, among Zeus, Poseidon and Pluto—is familiar to the student. The creation of grains and domestic animals from fragments of the slain deity of food has its parallels in Iranian as in Indian story: from the body of the bull created by Ormuzd sprang all herbage, the vine from its blood and wheat from its spinal-marrow. The quarrel of the Sun-Goddess and the Impetuous-Male-Deity has a legion of prototypes. The Mongol version is found even among the Eskimo, who hold the moon and sun to have been brother and sister: when he attempted to ravish her, she fled to the sky. There are a dozen versions among the Slavonic peoples.

The Eight-Forked-Serpent of Koshi is Python whom Apollo slew with his arrows, and the combat of Brave-Swift-Impetuous-Male with the monster classifies itself with the legend of Hercules and Hydra, of Cadmus and the dragon, of the Egyptian Hathor-Sekhet who was made drunk from blood-red beer poured from jars so that she would cease from slaying mankind, of Siegfried and Fafnir, of the Scot Martin and the serpent which had devoured nine maidens, of the Lambton Worm—not to speak of Christian St. George and innumerable others—as a variant of the Perseus and Andromeda story which has impressed itself in so many forms upon the myth-fabrics of the world.

The persecution of the youthful deity Great-Land-Master by his eighty brothers and his rise to pre-eminence is the tale whose Hebraic variant is that of Joseph and his Brethren. His elopement with the daughter of Brave-Swift-Impetuous-Male is a version of one of the oldest and most widely distributed folk-tales—the myth of Jason and Medea,[16] daughter of Aeëtes. It appears in Celtic as in Greek mythology, in Russian, Italian and Magyar folklore, in tales of Scotland and Madagascar; and plainly recognizable incidents of it are common to the Finns, the Samoans, the Algonquins and the Samoyeds, and to Eskimo, Zulu and Bushman.

In his theft of Brave-Swift-Impetuous-Male's life-preserving sword, his bow and arrows, and his Sky-speaking lute, one recognizes the prototype of our own Jack-and-the-Beanstalk—a tale familiar to all Slavonic peoples [17]—while the burial of Prince-Sky-Young, at which the various birds officiate, is Cock-Robin in more dignified dress. And harking still further back, the contest of Fire-Fade and Fire-Glow and the whelming of the latter by the jewel of flood-tide constitute a version of the ubiquitous "flood-story."

The divine cross-sword which falls from the Sky for the aid of Jimmu, the first earthly emperor—like the sun-god Elagabalus of Syro-Phoenicia, the Palladium of Troy and the sacred shield of the Romans—together with the supernatural crow which appeared to guide him in his campaign, recall features common to the story-fabrics of all peoples.

The tale of the bird-maiden who is captured by a mortal through the stealing of her feather-robe is found in well-nigh every folklore of the world. It is Arabic,[18] Teutonic, Slavonic,[19] Norse, Welsh, Eskimo, Borneoese, South African and Red Indian, and is found even in the Shetland Islands, where the part of the feather-robe is played by a seal's-skin.[20]

Perhaps the most lovely of all the myths of the Narrative is the legend, ascribed to the reign of the Emperor Yuriaku, of Urashima [21]—the fisher-boy who, angling in his boat, takes a sea-turtle of five colors, which becomes transformed into a maiden "beautiful beyond description," who conducts him to her realm in the empyrean (strangely confused with the sea), where her folk welcome and entertain him with pleasures unknown on earth. It is the familiar tale of the long ecstasy, the final nostalgia and the return with the casket which may not be opened to find that centuries have passed as years, the disregarded injunction and the closing catastrophe. "He knew that, having broken his oath, he could not go back and see her again." . . . "When the cloud rose from the casket he grew suddenly old, his body shrinking, his black hair becoming white, and his breath growing weaker, till he fell upon the ground and died." This legend, in its myriad forms, appears in Egyptian, Greek, Teutonic, Slavonic, Celtic, Norse, and a dozen other tongues [22]—Atlantis, Avalon, the Hesperides, Ogygia, Cocaigne. Diodorus Siculus cites the older Latin tradition.

II. PRIMEVAL CULTS

Woven in the Narrative are a hundred episodes and allusions that link unmistakably with one or other of the great world-cults to which we must assign an origin more ancient than the present-day races of whose folklores they form a rapidly disappearing feature—the adoration of the Sun and of the Sword, the Phallus-Cult, Serpent-Worship, Tree-Worship, Living-Entombment, Human Sacrifice, and suggestions of an ancient Matriarchy.

1. THE CULT OF THE SUN

Sun-Worship, universal among barbaric peoples (particularly widespread among the Tatar tribes of the near mainland) is the pivot of this ancient lore. The Sun-Goddess was the prime deity of the early Japanese, as she is the great, over-shadowing divinity of Shinto today. And the most detailed and venerated of these earlier legends is the universal story of the return of the sun to a world desolated by cold and darkness—the Japanese version of the solar-myth with which all sun-worshiping peoples have begun their deity-stories—the re-welcoming of spring after the winter solstice, the victory of day over night, of summer over winter.[23]

The early pre-archipelagoan Sun-Cult had to do with the actual fiery planet, as distinct from its later personification in deity. The older myth-tales show the inevitable confusion that attends the process of this conceptual development. Presumably, for example, both Sky and Earth were lighted by the luminary previously to the birth of Great-Sky-Shiner; with her appearance, however, she begins to usurp the light-giving function. It is said that "she was of a shining and a beautiful nature, made to shine upon the Sky and the Earth" and that "the resplendent lustre of Great-Sky-Shiner shone throughout all the six directions." And in conclusion, when the persecutions of her brother, the Impetuous-Male-Deity, drive her to retire into the Sky-Rock-Cave, the sunlight vanishes from both worlds: "*so that* the whole Plain-of-the-High-Sky was darkened and all the Central-Land-of-Reed-Plains unilluminated, and *from this* unchanging night befell and the alternation of day and night was unknown. The Kami had no place to set their hands or feet, and all their affairs were carried on by means of lights." When, puzzled by the apparent gaiety, she peeps from the cavern, she says, "Methought that *since I have withdrawn and shut myself in the Rock-Cave*, the Plain-of-the-High-Sky and the Central-Land-of-Reed-Plains would be in continued darkness." On her emergence "her radiance filled the Sky-Under, and both the Plain-of-the-High-Sky and the Central-Land-of-Reed-Plains again became light, so that all could see each other's faces distinctly." It is apparent that by the time this myth had attained its final form, what had once been the sexless globe of fire had, as with the Persians and Mexicans and no doubt with all other systems, taken on person and sex as the prime member of the Japanese Pantheon.[24]

In the contest between the Sun-Goddess and the Impetuous-Male-Deity in the production of offspring, the lesser deities created from the crunching of her hair- and arm-jewels were undoubtedly solar deities also. Plenty-Swift-Sun, whom the Narrative names elder brother of the imperial grandchild, and whose descendant the latter, on his Sky-descent, is to find ensconced in Mountain-Gate (Yamato), may be assumed to have been the Sun-deity of the earlier folk of that region, incorporated by the later conquerors into their own Pantheon. The names of numbers of deities appearing in the Narrative surrounding the divine descent assign them to a similar place. Such are Sky-Road-Sun, White-Sun, Sun's-Swift-Sun, Awful-Swift-Sun, Princess-Great-Sun, and (in the imperial ancestor's own entourage) Sky-Sun-Spirit, Sky-Milk-Swift-Sun and Sky-Round-Eye.

The three sons of the celestial heir, Fire-Glow, Fire-Climax and Fire-Fade, are to be likewise classified. The first syllable in each name, translated "Fire," may as correctly be rendered "Sun." It seems more than probable that the myth-story of their birth in the blazing "bringing-forth-house" was invented to explain names they already possessed, and that the three represented the rising, noon-tide and setting sun.

As a symbol of the early Sun-worship there appears throughout the Narrative the sacred Mirror—from its light-reflecting property a Sun symbol for all races which acknowledged the cult, including even the Peru of the Conquistadores. To tempt the Sun-Goddess from her seclusion in the Sky-Rock-Cave, the assembled deities make a Sky-mirror *"in shape like the sun,"* and it is this mirror which she later sends to earth with the celestial ancestor—to remain forever the chiefest of the Three Sacred Treasures of the dynasty and symbol of the power imperial—*as an image of herself*. In the earliest times, it appears certain, the mirror was itself a true deity, worshiped under the name of Sky-Mirror, as such a deity is named by one legend the child of Eternal-Earth-Stander, one of the primal deities and great-grandfather of He-Who-Invites.

And as time goes on, the distinction between the Sun-Goddess *in persona* and the Sun-mirror (which in origin was the image of the orb itself) fades out, and the sacred Mirror is spoken of as "Great-Sky-Shiner," without qualification. When it is transferred to Isè it is said "The Kami Great-Sky-Shiner was put in charge of Princess-Mountain-Gate, who searched for a spot where she might dwell."

The mirror is continually used, not only as a badge of Sun-allegiance, but as an emblem of Sun-sovereignty. When Mountain-Gate-Brave goes against the Emishi, "on his vessel was suspended a great mirror," and it is this emblem of deity which strikes the barbarians with awe. It is used also in appeal to the deities. In Yuriaku's reign an imperial princess employs it to demonstrate her innocence under accusation. And the Empress-Regent Jingu, preparing her descent upon the coast of Korea, "went to Mount Mirror in the Province of Buzen, and surveying the form of the land, she said, 'May the Kami of Sky and Earth assist me!' and placed a mirror on the mountain."

Indication that the ancient Sun-Worship is not yet dead in the archipelago is to be seen in the attitude of the peasants toward the great luminary today. They call it O-Tento-Sama (Honorable-Sky-Path-Personage) and Nichi-Rin-Sama (Day-Wheel-Personage) and give it what seems to approach actual worship—a spirit reflected in a lesser degree in the modern crowd which gathers to watch the sun rise on the first day of the New Year. In country sections prayers are still offered it, with ceremonial hand-clapping, as to a deity.

The Mirror remains the chief symbol of Shinto [25] and there is no shrine in the empire without it, though modern shintoists are prone to assign to it a spiritual significance which is not justified by its origin.

2. THE CULT OF THE SWORD

Next to that of the Sun, the Sword-Cult is pre-eminent in this myth-epos. It obtained among the Sun-folk well into recorded history—if indeed it is not a living cult today. Perhaps more anciently the Sun-folk worshiped the naked blade, as Herodotus, writing in the fifth century B.C., says the Sythians did. But the sword-worship of the Narrative more nearly resembles that which the Greeks bestowed on the sword of Agamemnon in the time of Pausanias.

The great storied blades are all greater or lesser deities. The sword with which He-Who-Invites kills his son is the Kami Sky-Point-Blade-

Extended, and it is the Impetuous-Male-Deity's sword which the Sun-Goddess uses in her contest with him in offspring-bearing. While he sends it to the Sky to Great-Sky-Shiner, it comes to Earth again with her descendant, the celestial ancestor of the earthly Emperors, one of the Three Treasures with which he is invested preparatory to his divine descent. The Land-Master, visiting the Impetuous-Male-Deity in the nether-world, steals his host's sword—and on his return to the upper-world, it is with this that he vanquishes his eighty Kami brethren and makes himself Lord of Izumo.

When the descent of the Sky-deity to the earth-rule is preparing, the Kami sent down to spy out the land are the sword with which He-Who-Invites cut his son to pieces, and his own son by a portion of the blood of the slain fire-deity that spattered the knob of his sword-guard. When Jimmu, the first earthly emperor, is resisted by the savage Kami of the mountains, a celestial blade is sent down to him from the Sky. Most of these blades of the early Narrative are true Kami. Their great head is the sword Herb-Queller, which was found by the Impetuous-Male-Deity in the tail of the eight-forked serpent which he slew, and which is the second member of the sacred triad of the divine regalia, the first being the Mirror and the third the Necklace. It has never ceased to receive the imperial worship. It is the symbol of the dynastic power, so considered by the Sky-Deities themselves: "There came a wind-blowing sound in the Great Void, 'You Prince who holds the Sword! (i.e., the Emperor).'"

And the Sword, as distinct from the Sword-Kami, has a sacred character per se, as is evidenced throughout the Narrative from the frequency with which blades are listed among sacred possessions or are presented as holy objects to shrines. Prince-Ini-Stone-Castle-Iri, son of the Emperor Suinin, has a thousand cross-swords made which he presents to the temple of the Kami of Isonokami. They are called the Naked-Companions, and the Sovereign, at the Kami's request, puts them in charge of the great ancestor of the Head-men of the imperial guard. In the same reign the imperial Department of Worship decrees, after divination, that cross-swords be placed in the shrines of "all the Sky- and Earth-Kami." An instance is the so-called "Sword-Jewel" of Hirota Shrine in Settsu Province, which is sword-shaped and which, one legend says, was found by the Empress Jingu just before she entered upon her campaign for the subjugation of Korea. It is named in various shrine lists as an object of worship, and one authority says it was anciently preserved in a shrine reared especially for it.

With the beginning of real history the character of deity begins to vanish from the storied swords, but some of them, whose divine origin is not now claimed, still occupy a unique position in ceremonial that is semi-sacred. Such is the sword known as Tsubokiri (the origin and meaning of the word are not now known) with which the Emperor invests the prince imperial in the ceremony attending what was, previously to the Restoration and the new constitution, his "Nomination" as such. The first record of its ceremonial use is in the reign of Uda-*Tenno* [26] (888-897) and its earliest description is that of the *Enk'yu-G'yoki* (Record of the Era of Enk'yu [1069-1074]). Nothing is known of its previous history save that it had been a possession of Fujiwara-no Nagayoshi. Since Daïgo's time it is believed to have been used in the nomination of every heir imperial except that of the insane Atsuakira (Go-Ichijo-no In) in 1017. In the burning of the palace in the eleventh century its fittings were destroyed but the blade was uninjured; once, too, during the wars of the early thirteenth century, it was lost and a substitute was made for it, but it was later found.

Throughout the middle ages there was scarcely a noble family which had not its sacred blade (or blades) to which actual worship, or a veneration that is difficult to distinguish from worship, was given. The "Kojima-Maru," made in the seventh century by Amakuni of Yamato, the father of Japanese sword-smithery, was a sacred inheritance of the Taira. In that Clan it was an ancient custom to transmit the two swords "Ko-garasu-Maru" (Little-Crow-Blade) and "Nukè-Maru" (Spring-Out-Blade) to the eldest son, and it was the refusal of Tadamori to do this in his turn (says the legend) that gave birth to the family hatred which finally drove his fifth son, Yorimori, into the arms of the Minamoto Clan, acquiescent in the ruin of the Taira Clan in the sea-battle of Dan-no Ura. The most prized heirloom of the Hatakeyama was the sword "Sodè-Seba" (Narrow-Sleeve). The boasted inheritance of the governors of Omi was the supernatural blade "U-no Maru" (Cormorant-Blade) forged by Yoshiïyè, son of Munechika, for the temple of Sumiyoshi at Naniwa (Osaka). It was his own sacred sword which Nitta Yoshisada, when he was besieging Kamakura in 1333, cast into the waves, as an offering to the divinities of the sea, with a prayer for victory.

Many of the famous blades cherished religiously by noble families were believed to possess miraculous powers. The "Nukè-Maru" earned this, its modern name, by leaping unaided from its scabbard to kill a serpent which was about to attack the sleeping Tadamori. One of the great shrine-swords invoked with special rites is the famed "Amakuni-no Hoken" at the Narita-Shingo-Shinsho-Ji (Narita-Divinely-Protected-Recent-Victory-Shrine), said to have been forged by Amakuni in the seventh century for Mommu-*Tenno*, which was presented in 940 by the Emperor Shujaku to Fudo the deity of Narita, in gratitude for the defeat of Taïra Masakado. This relic, which is never shown to foreigners, is believed to cure insanity and to relieve fox-possession with a touch.

The shrine-swords are commonly considered to lie under the divine protection. There is one sword in the Homuda Hachimangu Shrine on which is engraved the warning that he who steals it will incur the vengeance of the Sky.

The ancient sword-worship was instinct in the veneration given these vanishing symbols, and it has persisted down to modern times in the peculiar attitude of the warrior toward his blade—a feeling expressed by Iyeyasu, the founder of the last shogunate dynasty, when he wrote (in his famous "Legacy," drawn up for the guidance of his successors), "The girded sword is the living soul of the samurai."

As the sacred blades were to the Kami of his race, so even the ordinary sword was to the individual Japanese warrior. It partook of the sacredness that attached to them as he himself partook of the divine Kami nature. The swordsmith of old Japan was no mere smith, but in general a man of gentle blood and of proud and austere life—the one exception to the rule which esteemed a manual trade a degradation. For a period before he began work upon a blade he abstained from meat, *sakè* and sexual intercourse. He began his work with solemn purification and with prayer and sacrifice to the deities. His forge, across whose threshold no woman's foot might pass, was a shrine decorated with sacred pictures and holy emblems, and his anvil was consecrated as an altar. He labored in fresh ceremonial clothing. The processes of tempering and polishing were performed in secrecy and according to religious formulae, and the blessing of deity was besought for the finished product.

The weapon thus produced was more than mere metal of offense and defense. To the wearer such a blade possessed something akin to a soul. It was surrounded with a punctilious etiquette—never touched with the bare hand but with a silken napkin, lifted reverently to the forehead when girded on or laid down, and its rack set in the sacred alcove of the room, the place of honor. Its wearer took oath upon it and (in the ceremony called *kincho*) vowed eternal friendship by touching its hilt. Laid beside the head it protected the sleeper and set by the pillow of the sick it hastened recovery. A self-respecting Japanese of today cannot be brought to handle a sword as though it were a curio, and to sell a really fine one to a foreigner would be to him an offense unpardonable—which accounts for the very limited number of worthy blades in European collections.[27]

That the sword, to modern Japan, has by no means lost its sacred character is seen in the presentation to the Great Meïji Shrine of three swords forged by authorized sword-smiths of the era (Teiïchi Tsukiyama of Osaka, Masaji Moriyoka of Shizuoka and Masahiro Hayama of Totomi) offered to the spirit of the Emperor Meïji, there worshiped.

3. THE CULT OF THE PHALLUS

Presumably Phallus-Worship, the oldest form of fetichism, had a cult even more ancient than that of the sun and sword. Its traces are worldwide. In the Narrative it appears in the earliest story of all—that of the thrusting down, by the primal creative pair, of the jewel-spear (symbol of the male-stalk) to create the first land. It is made the central pillar of the first matrimonial dwelling. Later the symbolic spear is used to tempt the Sun-Goddess from the cavern into which she has withdrawn. It appears as a sacred emblem even as late as the reign of the Regent Jingu. "So the Empress, marshaling her vessels, took red soil and with it painted Sky jewel-spears which she stood at prow and stern."

The staff, which appears in the myth of the descent of He-Who-Invites to the nether-world to see his dead wife, is the same symbol, and was so understood by the old commentators.[28] When pursued by his outraged spouse, "He also threw down his staff, which became the Kami Great-Elder-of-Come-Not-Place, saying, 'Come no further!'" This was the chief male deity of the early phallic pantheon. Its chief female deity was the peach, to whom he gave the name Great-Divine-Fruit. This association is not fortuitous: the peach from its shape is the symbol of the female organ (vulva). It retains its phallic significance in modern China (where the peach-tree (*t'ao*) remains an emblem of marriage, as well as of longevity) as do the apricot in India and the pomegranate in Greece—and was a concomitant of the ancient phallic worship. If other evidence were needed of this peach deity's place in this cult, it is to be found in her identification by the earlier commentators with the Kami known as Princess-Great-Road-Fork.

One is more than justified, too, in concluding Brave-Swift-Impetuous-Male himself to have been, in origin, one of the older phallic divinities; for there is good evidence that the great *Goriyoë* festival held now in his honor at K'yoto was anciently a festival of the pestilential Preventive-Deities (Sahe-no-Kami)—admittedly phallic—the halbert that figures in the fête being the relic of the conventionalized phallus.

In the first conclave of the Sky-Deities called to concert a plan to tempt Great-Sky-Shiner from her retirement, appears the smith-Kami, Sky-Mara (*mara: membrum virile*), whose name bespeaks his high place in this ancient cult. As shipmaster and helmsman he later accompanies the Sky-ancestor to Earth. The word *mara* appears in the names of later deities also,[29] whose phallic status had been lost long before the age of the earliest writings, such, for example, as another of the shipmasters, Red-Mara, who appears in the list of the entourage of the celestial ancestor in his divine descent.

It is a female deity who plays the principal part in inducing the Sun-Goddess to quit her Sky-cave—Sky-Frightening-Female, whose licentious posturings link her unmistakably to the phallic cult. As she sang, "she pulled out the nipples of her breasts and pushed down her skirt-string to her mons-veneris so that the Plain-of-the-High-Sky shook and all the eight hundred myriad Kami laughed together." Her popular name is Otafuku (Big-Breasts) and she is given especial honor during one of Tok'yo's greatest *matsuri*, the so-called *Tori-no Machi* of the eleventh month. On the days of this festival the rear gate of the *Yoshiwara* (brothel section) is thrown open. Still stronger evidence that her place is in the phallic list is her connection with the Kami who later becomes the guide for the celestial ancestor in his descent from the Sky to assume the earthly rule, and who remains a phallic deity to this day. Later, after the Sky-ancestor had chosen a site and built his first palace, "he gave Sky-Frightening-Female as consort to the Kami Prince-Monkey-Ricefield, who served as her guide, and the Clan-Chieftainesses of Saru (Monkey), though they are women, bear the name of the male Kami. He is invariably pictured carrying a long staff and as deity of the road is besought by travelers today. He is the popular deity of the brothel, which sometimes maintains a small shrine in his honor, to whom the proprietor prays for prosperous business, associating his worship with small conventionalized stone *phalloi* before which stands the tiny, ever-burning lamp. The larger shrines dedicated to his worship are seldom without their larger symbols of this cult.

Scattered through the early myths are deity names which lend themselves to phallic interpretation—such for example as Sacred-Male-Pillar—and about one of the major Kami clusters a group of unmistakable phallic stories. This is Great-Land-Master, descendant of the Impetuous-Male-Deity, whom the latter, when he finally departs to his rule of the netherland, leaves in control of the Earth, a tenure finally brought to a close by the descent of the Sky-ancestor.

There can be little doubt that the Land-Master was in the beginning a phallic deity. His youthful incineration by his embrace of the red-hot stone boar, his bringing to life by the milky tricheration, his second death in the tree-cleft, point back to a symbolism that belongs only to the obscenities of a savage epoch. The epithet "Eight-Thousand-Speared" (*Yachi-hoko*) applied to him, is also significant, and one of the legends of his cycle preserves a relic of phallic ritual. His first wife, Princess-Forward, daughter (in the nether-world) of Brave-Swift-Impetuous-Male, appears to belong, with him, in the same category. The principal episodes in which he appears after his earthly abdication are unmistakable phallic stories.

In the later legends Princess-Bridge (Uji-Himè) who is worshiped locally as a goddess-of-lust and supplicated by women for marriage, with her companion deities, Kami-of-Rikuyu prayed to for divorce, and Agata, patron of geïsha and healer of venereal diseases, belong to the same series.

Phallic traces are, of course, commonly to be seen in the study of the Ainu. Aston thinks the *inaö* (or *nusa*), the whittled-stick which is connected with their worship, is itself to be so explained. If this surmise is correct and the *inaö* was, in fact, the progenitor of the Shinto *goheï* (the peculiar ornament of cut-paper, foil or sheet-metal, alleged to take the place of the ancient offerings of cloth, and supposed not only to ward off evil but to be the actual medium of communication between the deity and the priesthood) we have, as he has remarked, a significant instance of phallic survival in the most spiritual aspect of modern Shinto.

The visitor in modern Japan may see the relics of its once extensive phallic cult in a number of famous shrines, notably the Daïseki (Ra-no seki)-Jinja: Great-Stone (Penis-Stone)-Shrine, at Kandè, near Kobè, whose object of worship is four feet high, and according to local legend was anciently of gold. Another shrine scarcely less celebrated is at the village of Uji-Yamada, Isè, near the *Naïku* shrine of the Sun-Goddess. In each of these the emblem has a companion *vulva*. The observant traveler cannot stray far from the beaten track in Japan, too, without coming upon some rustic rite which is significant of this early worship.[30] Onogoro, the "Island of the Congealed Drop," the first land created by the primal creative pair of the Narrative, has always been celebrated for the number of stones of phallus and vulva shape found there. Aston records that he found the road from Utsunomiya to Nikko lined with the stone symbols, and many country neighborhoods still show a multitude of *phalloi* scattered along the highway [31] or piled under the porches of old temples. Some of the emblems, in altered form, appear in modern ceremonials—as, for example, the cornucopia-banners used in the New Year festival—and the recognizable symbols were in popular use up to 1872, when the imperial government prohibited their exposure and sale.

It is still common for the barren and impotent to offer small *phalloi* or *vulvae* at shrines (as, for example, at the shrine of the Goddess of Fuji at Isè, from which women borrow *phalloi* to insure easy delivery) and the emblems, for various purposes, are often worshiped in secret.[32] In the countryside, also, it is not unusual to find reverence paid to certain natural objects in the same way, well-known instances being the In-yo-no

Taki (Female-Male waterfall) in the Nachi Valley, so called from the fancied resemblance of a projecting rock to a phallus, and the rock known as the "woman-stone" at the Temple of Hachiman, in Kamakura. Hirata Atsutanè cites three famous instances of natural formation which I have not seen—a phallus twenty feet in height, with its companion *vulva*, in Inushima, Bizen Province, and two sets of four *phalloi*, the largest of which is two hundred feet in height, at Reïgan-Ji (-Temple) in Chikugo Province.[33] Up to 1880 ascension of the sacred mountain Nantaï (Male-shape) at Nikko was denied to female pilgrims.

There are various survivals of phallic symbols in modern Japanese art, such, for example, as the wild-goose, emblematic of matrimony and the male-principle, and the mushroom, emblem of sexual vigor and longevity.

4. THE CULT OF THE SERPENT

It is not surprising to find distinct traces in these legends of a cult whose relics are to be seen in every country which has a savage or semi-savage history.[34] There is, indeed, more than a suspicion that some of the lesser deities of the early portion of the Narrative were serpent-deities. Such a one is Princess-Water-Hanomè, born from the urine of the dying She-Who-Invites, some more modern Japanese commentators rendering the name "Female-Water-Snake." Aside from these, however, the earliest and most significant fragment is to be seen in the detail of the legend of Brave-Swift-Impetuous-Male's slaying of the Eight-Forked-Serpent-of-Koshi, in whose tail was found the wondrous Sword Herb-Queller.

The legend-series of Great-Land-Master which relates his visit to the Impetuous-Male-Deity in the nether-world, represents the latter as compelling his unwelcome guest to sleep in the "snake-house."

> His host's wife, however, Princess-Forward, gave him a "snake-scarf," saying, "When the snakes make to bite you, wave this scarf thrice to drive them off."

This seems to indicate that when this myth was born, people held in memory a time when serpents were preserved alive in numbers in captivity, and it is difficult to conceive of any use to which these can have been put (in the absence of any record of the snake having been used for food)[35] unless one assumes their employment—like the prototypes of the tame snakes kept in the Greek Temples alluded to by Aristophanes in his *Plutus*—in worship or ceremonial.

The assumption of serpent-form by deity points unmistakably to the cult, and of this the myth-fabric shows many examples. One very ancient vulgar legend represents Great-Sky-Shiner herself as floating on the sea in the guise of a huge golden serpent. In the Narrative Great-Land-Master takes the snake-form—which indicates the aboriginal character of the portion of the epos in which he especially figures. At the insistence of his wife, who has seen him only by night, that he show her his face, he appears as a small serpent in her toilet-box.[36] To the Emperor Yuriaku he appears as a huge serpent from whose eyes come thunder and flame. In a later legend of the middle ages he shows himself in serpent-form to Matsudaïra Naōmasa (1601-1666), grandson of Iyeyasu. When *Däim'yo* of Izumo he demanded that the inner sanctuary of the Great Shrine at Kizuki be exposed that he might see the sacred body of the deity. Both of the *kozuko* (high-priests) protested, but he insisted and the sanctuary was opened. In it he beheld a great *awabi* ("sea-ear": *Haliotis tuberculata*) which, while he gazed, became a serpent fifty feet long. It is related that he fled in terror and after that gave the deity all reverence.

The serpent figures still in shrine ceremonial in the Land-Master's legendary habitat. What is known as the "Kami-ceremony" is today one of the local Izumo mysteries. This commemorates the completion of the Great Kami's palace after his subjugation by the ambassadors from the Sky, when the latter "built a Sky-dwelling for his worship." The Narrative relates that, "all the Kami assembled to assist in the raising and building" of this palace. It is in celebration of this rite that to this day all the Kami leave their various residences to assemble in Izumo Province in the tenth month. During the period of the annual festival which celebrates this event, a small white snake, whose head is marked with the crest (*mon*) of the Great Shrine, comes swimming to the shore. It is caught in a peculiar manner by an aged man selected for the purpose, and given to the chief priest, who deposits it, with certain rites, in the inner sanctuary.[37]

Another major deity which in later myth takes serpent-form is Benzaï-Ten (Benten), the modern Japanese goddess of conjugal love, learning and eloquence, and popularly (though mistakenly) thought to be a divinity of music, possibly because she is often represented holding a *biwa* (lute). She is considered to be another form or manifestation of the Kami Jewel-of-Storehouse-Rice, who was procreated by the first deity-pair, He-Who-Invites and She-Who-Invites, when they were hungry. This deity of food (as an illustration of the tenacity with which the symbol will cling after the disappearance of the associated legend) has for emblem a bale of rice *guarded by a serpent*. Benzai-Ten is always associated with water, her shrines being invariably set on islands or on the shores of lakes or ponds, and is pictured commonly with, or mounted upon, a serpent. "She is to be found," says the *Bukk'yo-Iroha-Jiten* of Miyura

Kensukè, "on rugged mountains or in holes in thick forests. . . . In her coronet is a white serpent with the face of an aged man and white eyebrows. . . . This is Benten's real form and nature." [38] A snake is represented on her amulets. The day sacred to her is the day of the snake and she is especially invoked in the hour of the snake (9 A.M. to 11 A.M.). At her principal shrines—Enoshima, Chikubushima in Lake Biwa, and Miyajima—the serpent is sacred and in each a number of white snakes are maintained which are treated with reverence as messengers of the deity. Her prime shrine is that of the Island of Enoshima, near Kamakura, where she first manifested herself (Kimmeï-*Tenno's* reign) on a snakeday. There she was besought, during twenty-one days, by Hojo Tokimasa (1138-1215), for the prosperity of his house, and revealed herself to him as a serpent two hundred feet in length. On the spot where she plunged into the sea he picked up three huge scales, which he arranged in a design still used as the Hojo family crest. There is an old picture [39] by Kosè Kanaōka, the founder in the ninth century of the Kosè-R'yu, the oldest school of painting in the archipelago, which shows her with a body scaled below the waist.

In many legends, a serpent-deity assumes human form for the prosecution of his amours, and some of the legends, quoted above, bear phallic earmarks, which goes to show what has long been recognized by students, the close connection one with the other of these two primeval cults.

The serpent being a menace to primeval man, the early Serpent-Cult was principally propitiatory. The serpent-Kami were maleficent deities, whose influence must be nullified by incantation or who themselves must be destroyed or placated by worship or sacrifice. When Keïko-*Tenno* despatches his fiery son, Mountain-Gate-Brave, to subdue the recalcitrant *Kuma-so* folk, Prince-Tatami, the deity of Mount Ibuki, stretches himself across the warrior's path in the form of a great serpent. Eventually the deity smites him with an illness which causes his death.

The texts are sprinkled with legends of lesser unnamed and venomous serpent-Kami such as the huge water-snake at the fork of the river in the Province of Maise (Kibi) which slew so many of the people with its venom, and was in turn slain by the fierce District-Warden, ancestor of the rulers of Omi. A snake-deity, also, no doubt, is the Kami of the river who continually throws down the embankment of Mamuta and for whose placation Nintoku-*Tenno* is directed, in a dream, to sacrifice two men. In all these legends it is significant that the texts employ the honorific character belonging to the true Kami.

In rare cases the malevolent Kami, overcome, are turned into guardians of sacred objects—like the famous "snake-willows" of the Avenue of the Dead on Mount Koya, which were once reptiles, but for molesting pilgrims were turned into trees by the great Kobo-Daïshi and now have the power to resume their scaly form only to punish sacrilege.

When, too, the spirits of the great dead deign to show themselves to the living, it is sometimes in serpent-form. The spirit of the imperial princess Taku-Hata, who hangs herself when accused of unchastity, appears to the searchers for her body as a rainbow, *shaped like a serpent.* And the spirit of Tamichi the warrior, slain in Nintoku's reign by the rebellious Emishi, wreaks revenge in serpent-form upon the violators of his tomb.

There is a well-defined cycle of legends of the Province of Mimasaka (till the eighth century a portion of Bizen) which indicate that one of its two most ancient deities—"Kaya" by name—was a serpent, to which a virgin girl was sacrificed each year. Echizen Province, also, had two great serpent-deities, the "Rainy-Night-Kami" and the "Great-Worm-Kami," both of whom the Emperor Kammu elevated in rank at the end of the eighth century.[40] A serpent-deity was worshiped in Akumi District of Dewa Province, and there are indications that the principal snake-deity of Suwa was revered widely throughout the archipelago.

So much for the Narrative's serpent-legends. These were fragments of the epos of the land, with which the Sun-Folk—for whom Serpent-Worship as a distinct cult had disappeared before their archipelagoan history began—came into contact with their advent.[41] But the snake-superstition was deeply implanted, and the records of later eras teem with allusions to the practices of the decaying cult. In the centuries following the reduction of the Narrative to written form, the serpent's sacred character was generally recognized. In the tenth and eleventh centuries *bonzè* (Buddhist priests) were sent by imperial command to recite *keitan* (*sutras*) over the bodies of dead snakes found in temples. And in the seventeenth century Nakayama Chugi writes in his *Daïgo-Zuihitsu,* "It is said that in the middle provinces (the sixteen forming the great section of central Japan called the Chugoku) and in the southern provinces (K'yushu) there are folk who have snake-Kami which they make possess and torture others." Kaïbara Atsunobu, in his *Yamato-Honzo* (1708) locates this plague "In Aki and the surrounding provinces," where, he says, "there are snake-Kami called *Sho-Kuchinawa* (Small-Viper); in the same locality other snake-Kami called *Tob'yo* are used. Those who do this have in their dwellings many *Sho-Kuchinawa* which possess others and bring misfortune." The *Toruyuko-Zuihitsu* of Oguri Huyakuman (1724-1778) calls these deities *Suikatura* and says they are to be found everywhere. "The way of worshiping these Kami," he writes, "is thus: A hole is dug in a secret spot and in this they put many snakes and worship them. . . . The snakes are made to possess those for whom their owners feel hatred, and straightway these are seized by a fever of madness. Folk say that when one is thought to be possessed by a *Suikatsura*, if those who live with him send gifts of value to the owner of the snake-Kami, the sick one quickly recovers."

In Tosa Province, in the same century, a snake-deity (*hebi-gami*) was worshiped by certain families upon whom it was currently believed to bestow wealth,[42] and there still stands at the foot of Mount Koda a Shrine dedicated to the Hakuja-no M'yojin (Clear-Deity of the White-*Ja* [-Supernatural serpent]). According to legend the inhabitants of an entire village (Manako-mura, Hidaka District, Kii Province) worshiped as their ancestral deity a serpent from which they claimed to be descended. They all intermarried with one another, since folk of other villages would not consort with them. Stories declare that there never failed to be one woman of the village who did not marry, and whose body was scaled like that of a snake.[43]

But when all has been said, the ancient Serpent-Worship of Japan, like the Phallus-Worship, has left fewer traces, both in the myth Narrative and in modern folklore and observance, than have either of the great living cults of the Sun and the Sword. As with the cult of the phallus, these traces will persist longest in the far and untraveled interior, where there are still to be found men who keep snakes in cages and offer them supplication as "honorable-lords-serpents."

In the Japan of the new Western sophistication the one-time general veneration is echoed, perhaps, only in the popular feeling which protects the snake, particularly in temples or their enclosures. There is no province of the archipelago in which it is not counted unlucky to kill one,[44] be it harmless or venomous, and tales of catastrophe following harm done to the species are legion. Conversely, its protection brings prosperity, and from this follows the association of the snake, in the Japanese mind, with good luck. This is worked out in a thousand ways—for example, one pronunciation of the character for snake (*mi*) also means fruit: therefore the year of the serpent in the Japanese cycle is traditionally a lucky and fruitful year.

5. TREE-WORSHIP

Tree-Worship, like that of the sun, the sword, the phallus and the serpent, belongs to the dim epochs before the dawn of human history.[45] It appears early in the Narrative.

Among the offspring of He-Who-Invites and She-Who-Invites are "Tree-Elder, a tree-Kami who was the ancestor of the trees," and "Princess-Reed-Moor, the ancestress of the plants." And a little later appear the deities Long-White-Leaf (probably the deity of hemp, since the Narrative names him ancestor of the hemp-spinners of Isè Province) and Brave-Leaf-Elder. The worship paid to these deities decayed at such an early period, however, that no record other than their names has persisted, but there can be no doubt that at some early epoch they had their separate cults.

In the Narrative certain trees have become veritable Yggdrasils, such as the great camphor tree whose shade at sunrise "covered Mount Bullrush-River of Pestle-Island District and at sunset covered Mount Grass-Wide of Yafu District," from which Mountain-Gate-Brave named the Land of Saka; or the tree at Yamato in Nagato Province "whose top reached the sky and whose branches shaded a space of two ri quare"; or the prostrate tree of the land of K'yushu, "which was eight thousand seven hundred and thirty *shaku* long, and the one hundred officers walked back and forth upon it." A song sung of this tree calls it "sacred," and the Emperor Keiko-*Tenno*, seeing it, said, "This tree is a divine tree and this Land shall be called the Land-of-August-Tree." There is also the interesting tradition (referred to in a footnote under the reign of Koreï-*Tenno*) of the prodigious tree at the concussion of whose fall Fuji Mountain sprang into being.[46]

But the worship accorded individual tree-growths passed with them, and if the legends indicate that the ancient Japanese gave reverence to any particular species (as, for example, the Slavonians offered sacrifices to the birch in the season sacred to Lado, divinity of the springtime), it is to be distinguished only in the sacredness attached to the *sakaki* tree (*Cleyera japonica*).

It is as a symbol of worship rather than an object of worship itself that the tree appears throughout the Narrative. This is seen in the primal myth of the return of the Sun-Goddess from her cavern, when the assembled deities employ the *sakaki* trees and the *suzuki*-grass in the ritual.[47] In the later Narrative the tree-symbol is thus presented, with prayer, to deity. It is this usage which obtained among the early Romans, who took it from the Greeks.[48] The Empress-Regent Jingu, going by ship to meet her imperial spouse Chuaï, "hung cotton cloths on sakaki trees and set these at bow and stern *as goheï in honor of the sea Kami.*" In this is a suggestion that the tree so used had a very peculiar religious significance, since the *goheï* is held by modern Shinto authorities to have been the very medium of communication between man and deity.

By a natural further step, the decorated tree was offered to the divine lineage of the Sun. Thus the mirrors presented in token of allegiance to Keïko-*Tenno* and to Chuaï-*Tenno* by the Land-Ruler Princess-Divine-

Nashi, by Bear-Wani, and by the chieftain Ito-te, were suspended on *sakaki* trees carried or set up on their vessels.

A belief in the sentient life of the tree is inseparable from its worship. In the earliest cycle of the land there is an echo of this where we are told that some trees and plants could speak until, with the savage Kami, they were called to account by Great-Land-Master and "put to silence." Later the scion of the Sun-Goddess discerns among the evil deities certain "tree-stems and herbs" that have power of speech, and in the pacification preceding the descent of the divine ancestor "they put to death all the rebellious and malignant Kami and the tribes of herbs, trees and rocks." Presumably the willow was the retreat anciently of some special deity which cannot now be identified; in some localities still the sufferer from toothache thrusts a needle into a willow tree, whose resident spirit, to save itself pain, cures the ailment.

In Japanese folklore of today, however, the ancient deities of the trees have lost their divine character and have become mere elementals, spirits beneficent or maleficent as the case may be. The tree-spirit is commonly called Ki-no O-Bakè (Tree's-Honorable-Transformation) and the echo (*ko-dama*) is its voice. It is generally of the female sex and often leaves its leafy residence in the form of a woman. There is a series of legends in which it takes on human guise, marries man and bears him human babes.

Japanese thought today is saturated with ideas that have come to it from this ancient cult. The *sakaki* tree is still sacred to Shinto ceremonial and it is probable that the *hinoki* tree (*Thuya obtusa*) also had anciently a sacred character, since no other wood may be used in the construction of the Daïjingu, the Great Shrine at Isè, which is rebuilt every twenty years. The later folklore shows traces of tree-burial, tree-marriage, tree-haunting, and the use of trees in medicine, divination, and witchcraft.

Modernly certain individual trees are besought for specific blessings. A cryptomeria near Matsuo, Osugimura, Tamba Province, is prayed to for relief from the rice insect. There is a shrine called Koshiyo at Teradamura in Ugo Province whose unknown deity is invoked by mariners or boatmen in danger of shipwreck. It seems probable that the deity of this shrine was originally a tree deity, since it is the local belief that when prayer is thus offered it, a flame-colored camboge tree appears over the shrine, towering high into the sky, as a beacon for the distressed craft.

A few deities are invariably associated with particular tree species, though the reason for this is no longer known. There is, for example, Kojin, the deity of the hearth or kitchen, who is believed to have residence in the *enoki* tree (*Celtis sinensis, Willdenowiana*), as in Danish legend the elf Hyldemoer (Elder-mother) inhabits the elder. To the *enoki* tree very old dolls are modernly presented, a custom whose origin and significance are now forgotten. In the popular belief it is a goblin-tree whose resident spirit is sometimes baleful; there is one such standing on the outskirts of Tok'yo, which is known as the *En-kiri-Enoki* (Karma-Cutting-*Enoki*) to which jealous lovers offer petition.

6. LIVING-ENTOMBMENT AND HUMAN-SACRIFICE

The practice of Living-Entombment has been so widespread among primitive peoples [49] that it would be strange indeed if these legends contained no allusion to it. The form of the rite of which the Narrative makes record is not connected with the marriage relation, nor is it to be classed with cognate practices growing from motives such as developed the burial of living wives with their dead husbands among the old Slavonians, or the Indian *suttee*. It more nearly resembled the living entombment of the ancient Sythians at the dolmans of their chieftains.

That the practice, which is known as "dead-following" (*junshi*), prevailed in the archipelago down to the Christian era is shown in the legend of the burial of Prince-Mountain-Gate, in the reign of Suinin-Tenno, when all his attendants were buried alive upright about the mound.[50] We may disregard the very patent gloss of the Narrative which alleges, with the convenient "some say," that this occasion was the first in which this practice had been followed. It is far more reasonable to suppose that it was, as the *Nihongi* text says, "an ancient custom" not mentioned in connection with previous imperial burials for the reason that it was an habitual feature, and mentioned at this time only because the Emperor then decreed that it should cease.

Soon after the burial of Prince-Mountain-Gate, Suinin's second Empress dies and the interment is prepared. The Emperor asks advice of his ministers and one proposes the substitution for living persons of clay puppets. The plan delights the Emperor, who issues a decree that these "set-up things" shall henceforth take the place of living men at burials.[51]

While the custom of image-burying at imperial funerals lasted till the beginning of the eighth century, the Narrative contains but one more record—in the following reign (Keïko's)—of the use of these manikins which are offered to a deity in lieu of human lives. There is nevertheless some ground for belief that the custom of "dead-following" obtained in some sections of the archipelago for several centuries after this in connection with the burial of men below imperial rank. Chinese accounts speak of the existence of the custom in A.D. 247, in the time of Jingu. There is, too, a hint of its survival in the Narrative, in the account in

Yur'yaku's reign of a noble who had his maid-servant and his horse buried with him.

There is perhaps no Asiatic people of whose early history Living-Sacrifice for the propitiation of deity has not been a feature, particularly in the form in which it was known to the old Japanese—the hito-bashira (person-pillar), the burying of living persons, as with the ancient Bulgarians, to ensure the stability of castle, bridgehead or dyke.[52] The Narrative furnishes a typical instance in the record, in Nintoku-*Tenno's* reign, of the building of the Mamuta Embankment, which I have cited in connection with the cult of the serpent. After the embankment has twice fallen, the Emperor, counselled by a deity in a dream, offers two men of Musashi to the Kami of the recalcitrant river. One saves his life by a cunning artifice, but the other is sacrificed and the embankment is finished.

The practice lasted well through the middle ages. Kiyomori, the most renowned of the Taira, legend says, finding the dykes with which he was constructing the harbor of H'yogo in the twelfth century were continually washed away, planned to seize thirty strangers and sacrifice them. A page in his retinue offered himself as a substitute, the deity was thus placated and the harbor work finished.[53] The artificial island Tsukijima, near Kobè, still remains to tell of this labor.

If legend is to be believed, Kato Kiyomasa, the relentless foe of Christianity, when he built his castle at Kumamoto, at the close of the sixteenth century, buried alive the architect and a number of his chief workmen in a pit within its moats. Nor was this done solely to conceal the secrets of its construction, but rather that their spirits might jealously protect their handiwork.

A decade later Horiwo Yoshiharu, made *Daïm'yo* of Matsuë, Izumo, by the grateful Iyeyasu whose cause he had espoused, building his bridge there, found its foundations sinking in spite of the vast quantities of stone which were thrown into the quicksand. He thereon seized the first man who crossed wearing a *hakama machi-nashi* (trousers without a stiff girdle) and buried him alive in the bed of the river. His resentful spirit was placated by the erection of a shrine. Legend says also that a dancing girl was buried alive under the foundation of his castle and that it was found necessary to put a ban upon dancing on the hill on which it was built as it caused the ground to shudder so that the castle quivered.

As recently as 1925, in making repairs necessitated by the great earthquake two years previously, eight human skeletons were found buried in an upright position beneath the cornerstones of the double bridge at the main entrance of the imperial palace grounds at Tok'yo. Whether these "man-pillars" date from Ota Sukenaga's (Dokan's) first castle built in 1456, or to the later building of Tokugawa Iyeyasu, at the close of the sixteenth century, is a matter of surmise.

7. MATRIARCHY

There is grave doubt that matriarchy, in the broad sense of gynocracy (the domestic supremacy or political rulership of women) ever existed in any land or in any period of any race's development. Matriarchy in the technical sense, however (that is of "mother-right" [*mutterrecht*], or the rights and customs which pertain to true uterine descent), which signifies descent reckoned only in the female line, with the assignment of all children to the mother's rather than to the father's Clan, has been found among many primitive races. It is of this that traces are to be distinguished in these legends. The most casual reading of the Narrative, indeed, suggests that from whatever state of more or less savage society it had descended, the system of the pre-legendary Sun-Folk was a matriarchal one, although the earlier myths show this in an enfeebled and disappearing stage. The true patriarchy had not yet arrived.

The earliest of all the myth-stories, which deals with the making of the first land and the first natural birth, embodying the dispute between the primal creative pair, in what appears to be a relic of an ancient marriage ceremony, as to who should of right speak first, echoes the sex-conflict in the decay of the old matriarchal system. The struggle is to be seen later in the cycle of legends dealing with landholdings or inheritance-rights of the earthly dynasty before the divine descent. The Land-Master's "younger sister" (the phrase throughout the Narrative is synonymous with wife) "strove with him in securing land, and yielding to her, he departed to another place." His son quarrels with his wife over the water supply, but she outwits him and gains her way. There is also the curious statement of the Narrative that "the Clan-Chieftainesses of Saru (Monkey) like the Clan-Chiefs, bear the name of the male-Kami, . . . though the Clan-Chieftainesses of Saru are women." The myth-explanation of this custom is, of course, an insufficient one.

When He-Who-Invites purifies himself, after his visit to the netherworld, the first of the three great Kami to be born from his lustration is a female deity, who, as the Sun-Goddess, is to become the great head of the Sun hierarchy. She is born from his left eye—the left being to the Japanese the side of honor. From her first appearance, though the general direction of Sky-affairs is seen to be in the hands of the earlier male deities (as is the rule of the matriarchy), it is she who holds the real title. A female deity makes the sacred mirror with which the Sky-Kami tempt her from the rock-cave, and a female deity is appointed to attend her. It is the Sun-Goddess who has the naming of the earthly Sovereign and her choice falls first upon her own son and next upon her grandson.

On the Earth, when his eighty revengeful brothers torture and kill Great-Land-Master, it is his mother who twice comes to his rescue. It is the Sky-Spying-Female whose evil counsel leads Prince-Sky-Young, the recreant envoy to the Earth from the Sky-assemblage, to kill the Pheasant-Messenger sent to remind him of his duty, thus bringing death upon himself.

Many female tribal chiefs and leaders appear in the Narrative of the early earthly rule. When Jimmu-*Tenno*, first of the earthly Emperors, ascends a mountain to view the whole Land, he discerns "an army of women." The female Kami, whom he first wins to his cause, is no doubt a local chieftainess with whom he finds peace easier than war. The Narrative, while recording his seduction of the two Shiki chiefs, tells us that it is Princess-of-Shiki (presumably their mother) against whom his campaign is directed. When Sujin-*Tenno* wars against the rebels in the Land of Koshi, it is a local princess who conspires with her husband and uses black magic to defeat him. When Keïko-*Tenno* proceeds against the recalcitrant Kuma-so folk in K'yushu (Tsukushi) he finds at Suwa that "the ruler of the Land, Princess-Divine-Nashi, ruled many folk." . . . "Now at the village of Mayami there was a chieftainess named Princess-of-Haya." . . . "At Hinamori Princess-Izumi, Clan-Chieftainess of Murokata, desired to offer the Sovereign a banquet, wherefore her tribe were gathered together."

Throughout the early myths of the Deity-Age the spousal choice is the woman's. When the youthful Land-Master, whom his eighty brethren have made the "bag-carrier" in their journey to wed Princess-Yakami-in-Rice-Leaves, teaches the naked hare-deity how to regain his lost fur, the princess declares to the eighty, "I will not listen to you. I intend to wed Great-Land-Master." The wife whom he later finds in the nether-world rules her own choice no less than has Princess-Yakami-in-Rice-Leaves: "He . . . came to the august seat of Brave-Swift-Impetuous-Male, when the latter's daughter, Princess-Forward, . . . issuing forth, saw him and they regarded each other and were wed." Later he weds Princess-Tagiri, though "when first he paid court to her she would not listen."

While this female independence in the spousal-choice is not characteristic of a primitive pure matriarchy, it springs from the woman's exalted status in her own place—the family (i.e., her mother's) home—and is to be regarded as a relic of the disappearing matriarchal system, in which the husband is always the intruder, who enters for a shorter or longer period the household (and Clan) of the wife.

The stay of the wife at the parental dwelling long after the quasi-marriage is the telltale feature of these early espousals. When the Land-Master flees to the nether-world to escape the malignancy of his brothers, his wife does not accompany him, and on his return declines to leave her home with him. Princess-Forward, his second wife, whom he has stolen from her father, his host of Hades, goes with him no further than Izumo, which has been her father's earthly habitat. When the assembled Sky-Deities send their ambassador to the Earth, his celestial wife and children as a matter of course remain behind, while he, "wedding Princess-Under-Shining, and many daughters of Kami of the Land, . . . during eight years brought no report." We hear of his celestial family only incidentally, when they are sent to accompany the messenger ordered to bring the corpse of the recreant prince to the Sky.

Fire-Fade, he of the lost fishhook, when he journeys to the sea-realm, weds the sea Kami's daughter, and remains an inmate of her house for three years. When he elects to return to the Land, there is no obligation upon his wife to accompany him. The matter is not even broached. Nor is it taken for granted that he will revisit the place: what decides her to visit her husband's Land is her pregnancy and the consideration that "the child of a Sky-Kami should not be brought forth in the sea-plain." And on her arrival her babe is hardly born before, at her husband's first act of disobedience (which she takes as an affront to her dignity), she abandons the child and returns forever to her own realm in the sea.

As the matriarchal system faded and the patriarchy established itself —as the true marriage came more and more to be signalized by the removal of the wife to her husband's home—there arose naturally the ancient custom of cohabitation following the betrothal and before the marriage. This is the marriage "for a single night" continually referred to in the Narrative. In the wooing of Princess-Lagoon-River by the Land-Master, on the day of his arrival at her house she sings him her nuptial song and on the second night they assume the marital relation. The divine ancestor weds his first earthly consort "for one night." *Jimmu-Tenno* sees "seven lovely maidens playing on the Takasaji Moor, Princess-Vagina-Tatara-Fleeing among them. . . . He made his imperial way thither and slept there one sojourn." Later she becomes his Empress. *Anko-Tenno* weds a maiden, whom he sees dancing on the bank of a river, for one night, but eighty years pass before he remembers her existence. The custom was still alive in Yur'yaku's time: "Now he gave one night to Oguna-Kimi, . . . who became pregnant and bore a girl, whom, being suspicious, he would not rear." When the child has grown, however, her resemblance to him convinces him and she is declared an imperial princess.

The matriarchal wife, even when taken from her Clan and an inmate of her husband's home, is slow in yielding up her independence. When Princess-Blooming-Tree-Blossom, whom the celestial grandchild, as has been said, has wedded "for one night," gives birth to three sons, he presumes to sneer at her pretentions: "How can I, Sky-Kami though I be, cause one to become pregnant in the course of one night? The children cannot be mine. They must be the children of a Kami of the Land." At this affront to her dignity she builds "a doorless hall," enters it with her children and after plastering up the entrance with earth, sets it afire, vowing, "If these . . . are not the offspring of the Sky-grandchild, let them surely perish." When all issue forth unharmed by the flames, the accuser realizes the enormity of his deed and attempts to make amends, but she will not speak to him and his parting song bemoans her unforgiveness: "Yet for me, alas! never henceforth is thy bed!" There is small suggestion here of the husband's conjugal rights.

The later Narrative tells of the jealousy of Nintoku-*Tenno's* Empress. His concubines "dared not even look into the palace." He wishes to marry his younger half-sister and sends his own younger brother as middle-man, but on account of the Empress' violent temper she refuses. When during the Empress' absence on a journey, the Emperor dares to bring his half-sister, whom he loves, into the palace, the Empress flees and takes refuge in the distant house of a Korean noble, where she remains till she dies.

Ink'yo-*Tenno's* Empress is as intolerant. When he proposes to bring Lady-of-Robe-Passing to the palace, "she dares not come for fear, though she is sent for seven times over." He has her brought by force, and a dwelling is especially built for her. He visits her there when the Empress is in labor, at which the latter sets the bringing-forth-house on fire and tries to kill herself.

Under the matriarchal system the husband never becomes a member of the wife's Clan in the sense in which the children do. It follows that the tie between uterine brother and sister is stronger than that between husband and wife. This Clan-tie still holds when most of the matriarchal earmarks have vanished. The later Narrative furnishes some striking instances of this principle still at work. It is told of Suinin-*Tenno* that his wife's elder brother, plotting to overthrow the Emperor, proposed to her that she stab him while he slept. When she demurred he demanded which was the dearer to her, her husband or himself, her brother. She admitted that he, her brother, was the dearer. But while the Emperor slept, as she bent above him, girdle-sword in hand, her tears fell on his face and woke him and she confessed the pact, after which she fled to her brother to perish with him when his castle is fired. At Yur'yaku's death his consort advises her younger son to seize the rule. As a preliminary he takes possession of the treasury but is surrounded and both of them are slain. Yur'yaku had stolen her from the Magnate of Upper Maise (Kibi) Province, to whom she had borne sons, and these latter, "Wishful to assist *their brother by the same mother*, came by sea with forty vessels of war," to turn back only when they find they have come too late.

There can be no question that something approaching real matriarchal conditions obtained down almost to historic times in isolated sections of the archipelago. Recent legend says that they prevailed in Hida, which is so isolated by lofty mountain ranges that it is known as the "Island Province" and which in feudal times acknowledged the rule of no *Daïm'yo*. Of Onna-Takè (Woman-Hill) a settlement near Takato, whose name was derived from the fact that its wives were the heads of its households, it is recorded, "If a man from any other place weds a woman from this place he straightway droops and dies." Only a few years ago the Reverend Walter Weston, sometime British Chaplain at Yokohama, found a hamlet in the southern Japanese Alps wherein the heads of all the households were women.

But these few traces are fast vanishing. If the ancient matriarchate has bequeathed any lasting legacy to modern Japan, it is distinguishable only in the far wider liberty and equality possessed by females of the lower than by females of the higher classes in whom Chinese culture has had its unrestricted way, and in certain persisting social formulae, the most noticeable, perhaps, being the vesting of heirship in the daughter in case of absence of male issue.

III. WESTERN ELEMENTS

In any speculation as to the sources from which the archipelago derived its mass of myth, it is natural to suppose that the great bulk came from the west, since, in the ages preceding written records, the effect upon its people—even assuming that they did not themselves originally come from the west—of that part of the continent that lay nearest their most ancient seat, Izumo, would have been preponderant. It is not surprising, therefore, to find the bond between the Sun-empire and the kingdoms of Silla,[54] Okara (or Kara,[55] later called Mimana) and Kudara, which occupied the lower Korean [56] plain, an intimate one even in the Deity-Age (Jindaï).

In some telltale instances the Japanese legend has unmistakable Korean earmarks for the student of the language—as, for example, in the account of the murder of the Food deity, Jewel-of-Storehouse-Rice, by Moon-Darkness-Possessor (or, as some variants say, by Brave-Swift-Impetuous-Male), and the creation of articles useful to man from portions of her body. From her nose it is said the bean was created. Now between the Japanese words for nose (hana) and bean (mamè) there is no similarity or root connection; in the Korean, however, the likeness is striking. The Korean words for all of the articles created show similarities to the Korean words for the portions of the body from which they are born. Thus: The bean (khong) was created from her nose (kho); the horse (mar) from her head (mori); the silk-worm (nui) from her eye -[brow] (nun); rice (pio) from her belly (pai); wheat (pori) from her genitals (pochi).[57] The philological consideration alone seems to show this legend to be (in its Japanese form, at least) beyond reasonable doubt, Korean.

The Land-Master cycle of the Narrative contains many names that are unmistakably Korean, and there is more than a suspicion that a number of the earlier Kami (notably some that seem to classify as deities of fire, though, as has been said, there is scarcely a trace in the Narrative of fire-worship) were of Korean importation.

The deity Great-Mountain-Possessor, whose alternative name was Great-Kami-of-Carry-Across, came, according to one legend, from Kudara. The name itself would seem to enshrine his importation. And it is most significant that what is probably the oldest variant of the legend which chronicles the expulsion from the Sky of the Impetuous-Male-Deity (who takes to wife Great-Mountain-Possessor's granddaughter) recites that he also came to the archipelago via the mainland. According to some legends not given in the Narrative, his son Fifty-Brave became Silla's king, and one of his alternative names is "Kami-of-Kara." Under this appellation, or that of Idatè (That-Big-Arrive) he was anciently worshiped at the imperial palace,[58] and obscurer deities such as the Kami Sagiri,[59] were worshiped at numerous shrines. The sword with which Brave-Swift-Impetuous-Male slays the Eight-Forked-Serpent also is called "Serpent's-Kara-Blade." His own popular name, the Ox-Headed King (Gozu-Tenno) is retained in the name of a Korean mountain, G'yuto (Gozu)-Zan, at which it is believed he was anciently enshrined, and in the archipelago he is still worshiped as Shiragi (Silla)-M'yojin, under which appellation he is the guardian of Miï Temple, in Omi Province. The Narrative pictures him, after his arrival in Izumo, where his first three descendants have "scattered well the seeds of trees," finding the new land too small for his needs, severing portions of the mainland and sewing them to Izumo to make it sufficiently large for his progeny, after which he departs to his exile in the nether-world.

One might look in vain for a legend more significant of the mainland's influence upon Izumo. It is visible from the Island of Tsushima, and must have been known to every age.[60] While the legend that recites the Empress-Regent Jingu's expedition against Korea represents that land as hitherto unknown, it is frequently mentioned in earlier portions of the Narrative, and there is little doubt that it was visited by a brother of Jimmu-*Tenno*, whom some scholars identify, with apparent reason, with Hyukkusa, founder of Silla's first dynasty (Pak: 57-4 B.C.).

If one supplements the Narrative by even a casual examination of contemporary records, he finds many more indications of intimate and constant exchange. The Emperor Suinin, in 29 B.C., according to one account, sent an expedition to help Mimana against Silla, already beginning that vigorous career which was to continue for almost a thousand years. According to the annals of the later Han dynasty (25-220), the folk of thirty-two provinces of the archipelago maintained, in the first century B.C., a postal service with the Chinese authorities in the peninsula.

Even in this early period the influx to Japan from the several nations of this nearest portion of the Asian continent must have been considerable. It had left its impress upon such proper names as Umashi-*Kara*-Hisa long before Japan's first recorded relations with the mainland began. The word *kori* (as in Kuma-no Kori) is also, perhaps, referable to Kara. It has been suggested, too, that the Japanese *Kishi* and *Aso* (*Asomi*) may be derived from the Korean grade-titles *Kilsa* and *Ason*. A like suspicion hangs about many terms. Aston thinks the word *kuma* (bear), which so frequently appears in Japanese place-names, is the Korean Koma [61] (*kom*: bear), which was the Japanese name for the kingdom of Kokuryö (Koryö) and was also the ancient name of one of the capitals of Kudara (Pèkché); and he supposes the folk of Korean Koma to have had their Japanese seat at Kumamoto. When, on the rebellion of the *Kuma-So* folk, the deity counsels the expedition against the westward land, the Emperor Chuaï is promised, "If you truly worship me, it (Korea) will submit without your sword becoming bloodied, and afterward the *Kuma-So* also will submit." Only the hypothesis that there was a tie between the Kuma people and Korea will offer an explanation of this implied connection.[62] The Korean Koma folk bestowed their nomenclature upon Japan as the German Saxons did upon English soil. Later the peninsula was to have a cultural effect upon the islands comparable only to the effect of Norman France upon Saxon England.

When, after Chuaï's death, the Empress-Regent (Jingu) inquires the name of the deity who advises her campaign, the Kami answers that it is the desire of the Sun-Goddess. The reply uses the term "Opposite-Land" (*Mu-Katsu*) which lends itself to no other interpretation than Korea, and compels the conclusion that the Sun-Goddess here designates herself as a deity of the mainland.

With the so-called epoch of the San-Kan (so termed from the three states that formed the southern part of the Korean peninsula) following the expedition of Jingu, Japan's relation to Korea is to become that of suzerain. After her conquest, she leaves there her Minister, who put into effect what history claims was to all intents a Japanese administration.[63] Such as it was it was to last two centuries, before the more powerful states of Korea intervened, and during that time the Sun-nation profited greatly as one by one the features of the foreign culture crept across the waters.

The Narrative records the arrival of oversea agriculturists, silk clothiers (*kinu-nui*), potters, carpenters and architects. From Odin's reign on even the imperial palace (*Mi-araka* or *Mi-ya*) is built in Korean style. Scholars arrive with books. Whole villages come *en masse* to settle in villages of their own in the hospitable land. Those of one village dig the great Naniwa canal to preserve the capital from inundation. When in the sixth century Japan's suzerain hold on Korea breaks, more than five thousand families of various occupations and grades have settled in the archipelago.

Following the earlier wave of immigration come groups of Korea's literati, with astronomers (*reki-hakasè*) and calendar-makers, and in the reign of Bidatsu-*Tenno,* the thirtieth Sovereign, these are followed by Buddhist priests (*bonzè*) bringing copies of the *sutras,* temple furniture and a statue of Buddha, to inaugurate the long and bitter struggles which are finally to culminate in the closure of the empire against the outer world.

So far the Narrative carries us. Soon history is to record the definite abandonment by the Sun-Folk of the Korean peninsula and the return to the archipelago of the remnant of their army. That the infusion of Korean blood at this time was great may be inferred alone from the numbers of Koreans of various grades, from the meanest guild of laborers to collateral branches of the royal house, many of them possessing names already known to letters and art, who thus removed, bag and baggage, to Japan. For many centuries the record of this influx persisted in the country names of various provinces.

Such an association, reaching back to the Deity-Age and resulting in such wholesale immigration must have been profound upon the Japanese as a people. And as the infusion significantly modified the strain, so just as directly the thought, manners, customs and legends of the western mainland must have welded with those of the islands. One cannot find a people adopting in a large degree foreign religion, architecture and ethics, foreign fine and useful arts,[64] a foreign calendar and foreign measures,[65] without anticipating the discovery in the adopter's oral and written literature of a great share of borrowed mythic material inseparable from the new culture and scholarship.

Much such material doubtless reached the archipelago from China, some at first-hand but more via Korea. Taoist and Confucian fragments in the mass are legion. The phallic legend of the peaches with which He-Who-Invites smites the fifteen hundred pursuing warriors of the Nether-Distant-Land, is Taoist; in Chinese myth the peach (a phallic symbol) has magical properties, drives off demons of disease and even confers the gift of immortality.[66]

The story of the creation of the Sun-Goddess and the Moon-Deity from the left and right eyes of He-Who-Invites is a broken portion of the Taoist myth of P'an Ku,[67] the Chinese Kronos. This deity "came into being in the Great Waste; his beginning is unknown. In dying he gave birth to the existing material universe. His breath was transmuted into the wind and clouds, his voice into thunder, his veins into the rivers, *his left eye into the sun, and his right into the moon.*" [68] The deity Brave-Swift-Impetuous-Male, the "Ox-Headed King," too, shows a significant resemblance to Shen-nung,[69] the Heavenly Husbandman, one of China's mythical rulers. The latter was conceived through a celestial dragon, was "horned like an ox,'" cut down trees to make tools for the cultivation of the land, invented the art of medicine, and taught the people commerce.[70]

The deity of the kitchen-range (Kama-no Kami) who was "reverenced of all the people," can be traced to China, and the same is true of a sufficient number of lesser deities to lend probability to the statement of the Narrative that the Chinese folk who came to the archipelago in Ojin's reign, who with the Korean immigrants, "could be numbered by tens of thousands," maintained, all of them, *their own ancestral shrines*.

Others assign a Chinese origin, likewise, to the archipelago's many-syllabled appellation, "Luxuriant-Reed-Plains-Land-of-Fresh-Rice-Ears-of-a-Thousand-Autumns-of-Long-Five-Hundred-Autumns," to the names of the personal entourage of the Sun-Goddess, the Sky-river, the curved jewels, etc. The posthumous names, of course, of every Emperor of the mythical story, from Jimmu to Buretsu, are quasi-Chinese in form.

The practice of "dead-following" came also from the Middle-Kingdom. The living-burial of the household of a dead chieftain is recorded as late as the third century B.C. From China came also the substitution of clay images for living men at imperial interments, where it was known in the seventh century B.C.[71]

Chinese also is the *metier* of the "falcon-men" (*hayato*), whose origin the Narrative ascribes to the vanquishment of Fire-Glow by Fire-Fade by means of the jewels of flood- and ebb-tide. In the ancient Middle-Kingdom like officers were appointed to protect the imperial palace by hooting at baleful spirits (*shen*). The concept of the tailed-men encountered by Jimmu-*Tenno* also is Chinese, as is the notion of proceeding with the sun and not against it. The legend of Tajima-Mori's, "weak water," the portion of the sea where the water is of such a consistency that the lightest junk will sink in it, is borrowed from Chinese legend, which locates it to the north of Fuyu, off Manchuria.

The Narrative records the slow but sure infiltration of Chinese culture, as the centuries pass, by way of the Korean land-bridge. It is a Chinese imperial prince of the Shin (Tsin) Dynasty who becomes the father of Japanese sericulture. He brings the folk of one hundred and twenty districts, which are organized into a guild that a hundred and seventy-five years later numbers nearly twenty thousand persons. Another (the great-grandson of the Emperor Ling Ti of the after-Han dynasty) in the third century brings the inhabitants of seventy more districts to form a guild for the designing of figured fabrics. The later story is sown with references to Chinese personages of note who came, with their culture and customs, to the archipelago.

Many fragments of the Japanese myth-mass are unmistakably Indian. In his flight from the nether-world, He-Who-Invites throws his comb behind him, and the teeth become bamboo shoots which deter the pursuing Ugly-Females-of-the-Land-of-Night. Similarly, the deity Salt-Possessor, when he is assisting the journey of Fire-Fade to the sea realm, throws a comb on the ground, where it becomes a five-hundred-fold clump of bamboo. This artifice is a stock property of Indian, as of Persian myth. The piebald colt which Brave-Swift-Impetuous-Male flays and flings through the roof of the Sun-Goddess' weaving-hall with disastrous consequences, is probably identical with the celestial spotted cow (or deer) of Indian story. It is to be noted that the turbulent deity does not fling down the spotted hide, which is symbolic of the starry sky.

What is probably the most ancient example of Indian influence in the myths is that of the deity Buto-no Kami, whom popular Japanese thought, since the early centuries, has identified with Brave-Swift-Impetuous-Male, brother of the Sun-Goddess. A single legend of him is given in the Narrative. It recites the appeal of Buto to two brothers, Somin-Shoraï the poor and K'yotan-Shoraï the rich:

The Kami visits the pair, asking a night's shelter. The rich one refuses it, but the poor one gives him shelter and food. Years later Buto returns, asks what family the charitable brother has, and bids him tie belts of reeds about their waists. In the night he kills the uncharitable brother's family, announces himself as Brave-Swift-Impetuous-Male, and bids the other's family to counsel their descendants to wear bracelets of reeds when the plague appears, promising they will not be stricken.

There can be no doubt that this kami is the Indian Gava-Griva (Ox-Head). The *Gion-Engi* says: "There is a kingdom to the north of India, named K'yuso. Its king is named Gozu-*Tenno* (Ox-Head-Heaven-King) and also Buto-Tenjin. He married Shakatsura, a daughter of the dragon king." This deity is named in the *sutra* known to the Japanese as the *Himitsu-Shinten-N'yoï-Zawo-Darani-K'yo*, in the following lines: "At this time Buddha explained the hymn again: Buto-Tenjinwo is by nature a free perceiver and his past was endless. It is very long since he became a Buddha . . . and his name alone can expel all evil diseases." This makes it clear that it is from his Indian prototype that Brave-Swift-Impetuous-Male derives his quality as a protector against plagues.

Other Indian deities crept into the Sun-list surreptitiously by the vehicle of Buddhism, after its triumph in 587, gaining a vague place by association with some picturesque festival which won to vulgar esteem. The popular name of the phallic Prince-Monkey-Ricefield, Koshin, is an example of this. The all-night feast called *koshin-machi* (*-matsuri*) was originally a festival in honor of the two deities Taïshakuten and Shomenkongo. Both of these are Indian, the former being the Vedic Indra (Buddhistic Sakradevendra) and the latter another form of Vajrasattva.

Some authorities believe the torii gate [72] and the custom by which each Emperor erected a new habitation were in origin Indian. Certain German critics (see D. Seckel's *Der Urstrung des Torii*, Tok'yo, 1942) deny this. I have myself seen, however, in Indian ruins near the Tibetan border far older than any in the Japanese archipelago, what I believe may well have been the torii's progenitor. And the custom of the new habitation is world-wide and must be classed as universal. In the sub-Arctic Eskimo-Tukudh tribes in the northern Yukon Territory and in Alaska north of the Porcupine, with one of which I lived for a time a half century ago, every new Chief burned his tribal lodge and built a new one before his authority was acknowledged even by his own tribe.

To India may be referred various customs and observances of which one may read between the lines of the Narrative: the custom of *ink'yo* (retirement from active life), the so-called "true-name," and certain phases of the ancestor-worship, which, grafted upon the earlier natureworship and fetishism, has produced the Shinto of today. And one must admit the debt owed to India by Japan's art and architecture. From it, for example, came the influences which inspired a large part of the interior decoration of the Hor'yu Temple,[73] the oldest religious structure in the archipelago, and Indian motives are discernible in the art of the Nara period (A.D. 710-784) and in the work of several of the early painters, notably Kanaöka, the first great secular painter of Japan.

Here and there in the Narrative stands out a myth-fragment that is more familiarly Greek or Roman. She-Who-Invites gifts the earth with the sky's fire [74] at cost of her life, as did Prometheus; like the maidenly entourage of the Sun-Goddess, Minerva and the Graces wove the robes of the Greek deities; the assemblage of the deities to concert a plan to entice Great-Sky-Shiner from her rock-cavern recalls the efforts of the Greek divinities to bring Hephaistos back to the celestial sky. The smith-deity summoned to make the mirror with which she is at length tempted forth, like the Greek Cyclops, has but one eye; the aid given by wind, wave and fish to the Empress-Regent Jingu's fleet is reminiscent of the Aeneid of Virgil. Greek and Roman, too, is the tree with decorated branches, which the deities display to placate the Sun-Goddess, and which the

Land-Ruler, Princess-Divine-Nashi, bears as a sign of allegiance to the Emperor Keïko. The legend (cited in the discussion of the Phallus-Cult) in which the Great-Land-Master reveals himself to an Empress in the form of a serpent in her toilet-box, as a result of which she kills herself, is paralleled in the story of the daughters of Cecrops, the half-dragon, half-human founder of Athens, in whose hands was placed the box that held Erichthonius, son of Vulcan and Atthis, and who committed suicide by throwing themselves down from the Acropolis.

Other fragments are to be found in the Narrative which identify themselves more especially with the folklores of the still further west. To this group belong the use of the numeral *seven* (neither the Ainu six nor the Sun-Folk's eight) seen particularly in the older fragments; the episode of the well, the overhanging tree and the sea deity's daughter [75] (in the tale of Fire-Fade's visit to the sea realm); and, of the larger stories, the phallic tale of Princess-Life-Jewel-Good, to whom each night comes the youth whose identity is established by surreptitiously fastening to his clothing the end of a hemp thread which, in the morning is found to lead through the hole of the door-hook to the shrine of the deity of Mount Miwa. It is safe to say that there is not a branch of the folklore family of western Europe that does not contain a variant of this last-mentioned root-theme.

The concept of the pillar uniting Sky and Earth is Semitic. It is said of He-Who-Invites, after Great-Sky-Shiner had been born as a result of his ablution, "Now at this time the Sky and the Earth were still not far separated and were connected by the Sky-Pillar, by which he sent her up." In the Talmud a like pillar unites the two Paradises: "There is an upper Paradise and a lower Paradise, and between them is fixed a pillar, by which they are joined together, and which is called 'The Strength of the Hill of Sion.'"

The exchange of names between the Kami Izasa-Tara and the prince imperial, later the Emperor Ojin, likewise has a Semitic root.

In Korea the journey of western myth to the eastward met the sea. There in what Hulbert calls "the back-attic of Korean folklore" was assembled a miscellaneous lot from which Japan could draw *ad libitum*. As Egypt and Arabia poured their myths into the melting-pot of Greece, so Greece passed her stories to India, and India to China, and in Korea the lore of the vast Middle-Kingdom, with all its accretions, merged with the hoary myths of Tartary and Tibet. Small wonder that the myth-mass of the neighboring archipelago shows interwoven fragments common to them all.

IV. SOUTHERN ELEMENTS

The second grand division of the myth-mass of the archipelago is southern —the flotsam and jetsam from the southern seas.[76] The swift, warm, dark *kuro-shiwo* (black-current) which is the Pacific's Gulf-Stream, flowing up past Luzon and Formosa to lave the lowermost island, must, during the ages, have borne many a strayed raft or lost boatload from the Malay archipelago or the isles of Polynesia to mingle with the blood and lore of aboriginal Japan.

The impact from the south would naturally have been greatest upon K'yushu (Tsukushi), on which island the myth places the descent from the Sky of the divine ancestor, and here according to the Narrative— on the southern tip of this, the most southerly of the larger islands of the archipelago—the advent of the Sun-warriors found ensconced a stubborn and tenacious people.

These latter were, at bottom, the *So*—believed to have been a shoot of the *Sow*[77] tribe of Danii (Borneo), who had landed on the Satsuma coast some centuries earlier. They had amalgamated with another stock (probably referable to the Korean mainland) called the *Kuma*, and had thus developed the tribe known to the Sun-Folk as the *Kuma-So*, apparently a co-related people like the Anglo-Saxons. One of the four faces of K'yushu Island (which was brought forth by He-Who-Invites and She-Who-Invites, the original creative pair) was named for these people. They had a tribal organization, living in villages under the governorship of Head-men, and appear to have been the most contumacious of all the tribes to be brought into the common fold (they were in intermittent armed rebellion during all the Yamato campaigns), a fighting spirit perhaps due in no small measure to their admixture of Malay blood.

The task of the Sun-Folk here was to absorb or to annihilate. This was no easy process, for the *Kuma-So* resisted stoutly. There are many indications that their chiefs married into the Sun-line. The great bulk of the vanquished, however, were made serfs. Save by assuming it to have been made up of these *Kuma-So*, there is no way to account for that strange body of retainers known as *hayato* (*haïto*) or "falcon-men" (already spoken of in connection with the legend of Fire-Fade and Fire-Glow) on which the imperial court made such various use in the early centuries. They were not *Emishi*, certainly, yet they would appear to have been treated with the same reserve as were those ancestors of the Ainu. Their leaders formed a kind of bodyguard for the sovereign's person and palace. At the death of the Emperor Yur'yaku (A.D. 479), "the falcon-men mourned beside it (the *tumulus*) night and day and would not eat the food which was brought them, till, after seven days, they died."

They would appear to have revolted on occasion, the earliest record of such a rising, in Osumi Province, being in Keïko's reign (A.D. 71-130). At times they suffered massacre. The record of some of these human battues is perpetuated in the festival known as Hoshoë, celebrated by Hachiman shrines throughout the empire on August 15. In the modern Hoshoë festival offerings are still paid to their resentful spirits. An echo of these early risings may be distinguished in a curious group of myth-stories reciting a war against a demon giant named Hayato, against whose castle at Kamiï, in Osumi, Mountain-Gate-Brave strove for years in vain, gaining final victory by the aid of a giant, Yagoro, and the favor of the Sky-deities.[78]

The effect on the myth-mass of the southern coast-epos was a very material one. The first myth of the K'yushu series, that of the contest of Fire-Fade the hunter and Fire-Glow the fisherman, is unmistakably a local and incorporated story. The Sun-Folk were neither hunters nor fishers but agriculturists—the true type of fighting-farmer. It was the aboriginal *Emishi* who "got his luck upon the mountains, and caught rough-haired beasts and soft-haired beasts"; it was the south-sea intruder who "got his luck on the sea and caught broad-finned fish and narrow-finned fish." Hence the assumption that this famous contest enshrined the pre-historic struggle between the *Kuma* tribe of the *Emishi* and the then foreign *So*-folk of the coast. The legend was no doubt ancient before the incoming tide of Sun-warriors turned against the amalgamated *Kuma-So*, then strongly entrenched on the southern shore.

The legend of Fire-Fade's journey to the palace of the sea deity, his marriage to the sea princess and the latter's consequent prohibition disregarded with such fatal consequences, the assemblage of the fishes, and the jewels of ebb-tide and flood-tide is clearly southern. Some legends definitely place R'yugu, the sea king's sanctuary, in the Lu-Chu[79] Islands. The detail of the lost fishhook and its recovery, which the aboriginal story had incorporated, is widely spread throughout Indonesia, occurring in

Halmahera, Celebes and Sumatra. In the variant of the Kei Islands, in the extreme southeast of the Indonesian area, the borrowed hook is restored to the younger brother by a fish from another fish's throat, as in the Japanese version.[80] In the Minahassa legend the hero dives into the sea and finds a village where the hook is found in a girl's throat, and he comes home fish-back where, by prayers, he brings rain down upon his evil friend. In taking over the tale, with all its south-sea earmarks, the newcomers in the archipelago (whose myth contains no such cycle) had only to identify its demigod with their own ruling line, while the story was perpetuated with the vanquished folk (in their new status of serfdom) playing the part, in mimes and dances, of the descendants of the worsted Fire-Glow. An odd hint of the south-sea origin of this legend of the sea realm is to be seen at Kagoshima. The authorities of the Great Shrine there (originally dedicated to the worship of Fire-Fade) sell during festival time a rough wooden box said to be a copy of a toilet-case given this deity by his wife of the sea realm, and this box is painted in red and yellow in a conventional design which is certainly not Japanese, and which bears a striking resemblance to well-known South Sea patterns.

The myths are punctuated throughout with smaller fragments that point as unmistakably to the southern seas. The notion that the first land was due to a divine angler in the watery waste is found in Tahiti, Tonga, New Britain (Melanesia), New Zealand, and the southern New Hebrides. The conception of the first islands as offspring of the celestial mating, also, is Maori. Many things mentioned in the Narrative, such as tattooing, religious dances and hand-clapping, together with various customs and practices unmentioned but characteristically Japanese—the use of the mask, the bamboo hat, certain styles of hair-dressing, the part in war played by the severed head of an enemy, the open aspect of the dwellings, tooth-blacking—these are all Malay or Polynesian in their origin. Ghost-masks, very similar to those seen today in Japan, are still employed in the dances of Borneo and Sarawak. The Hawaiian masks, indeed, affect the movable pieces (jaw, ear and eyelid) just as do ancient Shinto masks, and in the Philippines we find even the huge noses.

The Narrative's "bringing-forth house" is the Polynesian "house of retreat," and the superstition that cormorants' feathers bring relief to women in childbirth belongs to the south sea category. In later Japanese folklore a cowry shell takes the place of the feather, on account of its shape, that of the female organ (*vulva*), and becomes an amulet to increase fertility.

One of the most noticeable myths, that of the Earthquake-Fish [81]—the nearest approach to an earthquake deity to be found in the whole myth-fabric—is of the south, and its lack of earthquake divinities and legends suggests very strongly that the Sun-Folk came originally from a land not subject to such disturbances. On the other hand, with the indigenous Ainu the myth has retained its primal and dignified place. The earth-shaker is the world-backbone-trout (*moshiri-ikkewe-chep*) which existed in the pre-creation morass, the creating deities having made this fish the foundation of the world. The ebb and flow of the tide is caused by its alternately sucking in and expelling the sea water from its mouth. When it shakes itself it creates earthquake and tidal-waves, and to insure the safety of the world two deities stand, one on either side, to hold it down.

In the larger myth-fragments, too, there are many references that seem unexplainable save as they pre-suppose, in the people to whom they belonged before the advent of the Sun-warriors, a knowledge of southern lands. There is the appearance of the *wani*: It is a vengeful *wani* which the Hare-Deity, succored by the youthful Land-Master, blames for the loss of its fur. The story is one with The Tale of the Ape, the Heron, and the Crocodile, in the Dutch East Indies. According to one legend it is riding *wani*-back that Fire-Fade journeys to the sea realm and at the end of his three years' stay he returns in like fashion, seated on a *wani's* head. He presents this *wani* with his sword and it receives a Kami-name.

When his sea-bride, having come to join him on the land, is about to be delivered of her babe, she tells him, "When an outlander is about to give birth to offspring, she assumes the shape *common to her native land*. Look not upon me, I pray you, while I am in travail." He, however, peeps into the parturition-house, "When she turned into a *wani* of eight hiro, crawling and writhing about on her belly," so that he flees in terror.

All the *wani* of the Narrative, similarly, are sea- or water-creatures; and it is significant that the principal legends which introduce the *wani* are localized in K'yushu, the southernmost island, which justifies its reference to the south seas, and its classification, in general, with the water-fairies of medieval Europe—such, for example, as the Melusina [82] of French legend—which folklorists unite in tracing, through Persia and India, to a further southern source. In his translation of the *Kojiki*, Chamberlain, following the more modern commentators, translates the word "crocodile," and considers its introduction an indication of the well-known appetence of the myth-maker for furbishing his legend with foreign wonders. This, however, is a begging of the question. For how did the Japanese myth-maker learn of this particular marvel? If the knowledge of the *wani* could get to him overseas, so could the legend.

Suggestive of the south, too, is the region of Tok'yo-no Kuni [83] repeatedly mentioned. To it sails the adventurous Tajima-Mori, in quest of the "fruit of perpetual scent," the orange. The legend of the fisher-lad Urashima, who went out alone in his boat, met the turtle-maiden, and visited the realm of the undying, belongs to the "universal" category, but the detail of the Japanese version—the turtle, the "broad island in the wide sea which was covered with jewels"—came to the archipelago via the south seas. The legend, too, of the midget deity Prince-Little-Renowned—glorified modernly as the father of medicine, master of charms and incantations and the inventor of *sakè*—who comes to assist Great-Land-Master in his conquest of the savage wilderness, on internal evidence should be assigned to this cycle. The Lilliputian character of this deity (there is nothing similar in the whole field of Japanese mythology) marks the legend as southern in origin. His inability at first to make himself known in the language of the Sun-Folk and his later acknowledgment as son by one of the original trinity, point to foreign origin and absorption by the Sun-Folk, just as his approach by sea, coupled with his final departure to the unidentified southland across the waters, set him apart from the legend-cycle of Great-Land-Master.

Only one of these legends which point to the south seas enters the myth of the Sun-Folk before their Izumo epoch is over [84] and they have transferred their center of conquest to Southern K'yushu. This indicates that the race found the rest there.

V. LOCAL ELEMENTS

Underneath this interwoven mass of foreign myth are to be discerned fragmentary incorporations from a native, more savage lore, which belonged much more nearly than the rest to the soil itself.

These presumably reached the archipelago also from the western mainland, in some far-distant era. There are geological indications of ancient connection,[85] and the strait to the north of Karafuto (Saghalien) is but five miles wide at its narrowest point, Norato. For months during the winter this is frozen over, and so shallow is the channel that in summer junks can pass through only at high tide, and a high wind has been known to leave the bottom practically dry. At all times communication between the Asian continent and the northernmost island of the Japanese group must have been continuous. There is, indeed, good ground for believing the earliest race of which more than the merest mention has been preserved in the legends—the "Ground-Spiders"[86] (*Tsuchi-Gumo*), so called from their custom of living in underground habitations—to have been a collateral line of some of the tribes of lower Kamtchatka and Saghalien. History describes as of much the same character and habit the ancient Yih-Lou folk of Primorsk, who some ethnologists are disposed to believe were the immediate ancestors of the Manchu.

The Ainu [87] (the present-day descendants of the ancient *Emishi* of these myths) have preserved many legends of these Ground-Spiders. They called them under-dwelling-folk (*koropok-un-guru*), picturing them as dwarfs (*kobito*), of whom "ten could lie under one burdock leaf," [88] the Ezo burdock being a shrub whose leaves, according to Batchelor, rarely attain a measurement of more than four feet across. They called them, also, mud-bakers (*toi-chi-kuru*) and mud-hut-folk (*toi-chi-sekuru*). Tradition pictures them as beardless, possessors of light skiffs which they carried at need on their shoulders, and as making small dolls—all strongly suggestive of the Eskimo and of certain Mongol tribes of the mainland.

In only one place in the Narrative, however, are they pictured as undersized, where one tribe is encountered with "short bodies and long arms and legs, like pygmies, and the troops wove nets of mulberry fiber which they threw over them and so slew them." In character they were like the "Gubbings" of old Devonshire—"deceiving folk," the record calls them, "who lived in holes in the ground," hence their name, and were not amenable to discipline.

In the Narrative they are known by outlandish names, such as "Competent-Nose," "Smite-Monkey," "Hang-Ear" and "Great-White," and the names of their chiefs are never written with the honorific character. During the early history of the Sun-Folk they were dispersed in small bands over Yamato and Harima, and were occasionally met with in H'yuga and Higo in K'yushu. They appear to have had little cohesion, however, and in but a few places are their villages mentioned. They are trouble-breeders and incorrigible resisters of all authority. The Narrative records that they "made themselves chiefs of tribes and prevailed upon some of the *Emishi* folk of Tsugaru to join them." [89] From the standpoint of the Sun-warriors they are mere outlaws, a despicable folk of filthy habit who are to be exterminated without mercy as defiant to the imperial authority. It is probable that all save their last dwindling remnants had disappeared from the archipelago long before the dawn of its recorded history,[90] bequeathing whatever of their myth epos might survive to the folk by whom they were overruled.

The latter autochthones—the ancestors of the present-day Ainu—were the so-called *Ebisu* (barbarians) or *Emishi* (*Emishu*) whom the Sun-invaders absorbed or forced east and north—"the hairy people beyond the mountains" of the Chinese chroniclers of the T'ang Dynasty. When the Sun-folk arrived they found the archipelago in great measure held by these people, whom the legends represent as of a far lower level of culture than the newcomers. Correspondences between their myths and those of Izumo point back to a rudimentary common myth-possession, and from this it may be inferred that they too (although long before the continental settlers of Izumo), had come from the western mainland.[91] As to their origin there has been much dispute. Motoöri thought they were a northern race seeking a warmer habitat when they were met half-way by the Sun-warriors pressing from the south. This hypothesis, however, will not hold in the light of more modern research. But whatever their source, the myth-mass they possessed (some of it doubtless bequeathed them by their predecessors, the Ground-Spiders, and some of it brought with them from their further habitat), at the time of the incursion of the Sun-Folk had a source comparatively so remote that it may be classed as aboriginal.

From a study of local nomenclatures, which disclose Ainu place-names in every one of the sixty-eight provinces, Chamberlain concludes, with Professor Milne, that the *Emishi* overran the entire archipelago. He traces their place-names to K'yushu, the southernmost province of Osumi, and even to Iki and Tsushima Islands, far south of the mainland. Nor is this survival seen alone in place-names, but as well in a group of words of universal and daily use—such, for example, as the modern Japanese *nobori* (an ascent), whose relation to the Ainu *nupuri* (mountain) seems apparent, the word *rakko* (seal) or the word *kami* (anciently *kamu*), whose identity with the Ainu *kamui* would seem as clear. There is some reason to think, also, that Fuji is a corruption of Fuchi (*Huchi*), the Ainu Goddess of Fire. All of these can scarcely be accounted for on a theory that they represent Ainu borrowings from the Japanese.

And that the *Emishi* were not only widespread but numerous may be inferred from the resistance they offered to the newcomers. For centuries they harried their conquerors as the Picts and Caledonians of Britain harried the Romans. Mountain-Gate-Brave smites them in Izumo and in the central portion of the Great Island in A.D. 110, but those of Shinano and of the north remain unsubdued. In the same century, under Prince-August-House-Lord's rulership of the fifteen eastern-mountain-provinces (Tosando), they rebel, and again in Kazusa in 367 against the Japanese General Tamichi, whom they kill. There is a serious insurrection in 581.

The Sun-Folk knew the *Emishi* as of three great divisions: the *Tsugaru* (the northern, most distant ones), the *Ara* (rough) and the *Nigi* (docile). The last were submissive, and so were painlessly absorbed, the second either were exterminated or fled to join the *Tsugaru* in the northern fastnesses. Their settlements were to linger to the twelfth century, and their reputation for savagery clung through the middle ages. According to some Japanese authorities there were still a few remaining on the main island [92] even at the end of the eighteenth century.

The racial divergence at that time must have been marked, if one may judge by the significant differences that persist in the Ainu of today. The latter is a meat-eater, rather than an agriculturist. His features are more European than Asiatic, his eyes brown as often as black, and his hair frequently reddish. His robe is folded over from right to left, which is tabu to the Japanese, and used only in dressing a corpse. He turns his toes out, not in. His language is at base Aryan, is without honorifics, possesses true pronouns, prepositions, a passive voice, traces of number and case and reflexive verbs, while the Japanese is far more largely agglutinative. He has another sacred number (six instead of the Japanese eight) and a different method of notation. He holds the earth to be round, while the Japanese counted it flat. He strives not to remember, but to forget the dead. Ainu women consider exposure of the breasts immodest and are said to kiss their children, whereas the kiss was not known to the Japanese; in Ainu families the heirship is with the youngest rather than the eldest son.

Moreover, the manners and habit of the *Emishi* set them apart from their more fastidious conquerors. A clear hint of this appears in the ritualistic portion of the legends, in the distinction drawn between Sky-Offenses and Earth-Offenses. The former are transgressions such as a race of fighting agriculturists would know—disturbance of boundaries, tampering with water-supply and irregularities in the sowing of seed and the dressing of meat. The derelictions of the lower stock, however, are bestial ones—mutilation, vivisection, snake-bite, injury from lightning, animal-magic, filthiness, incest and crimes unmentionable.

But with all this, the *Emishi* were not regarded with the peculiar detestation accorded the Ground-Spider, and intimate contact through many centuries of the Sun-Folk with these neolithic aborigines at length had its way. Many *Emishi* customs would seem to have been adopted by the Sun-Folk, who even learned to "tie their hair mallet-wise and ink (tattoo) their bodies." While the unregenerate retired to the north, the milder married into the dominant race, and the history of expulsion was linked to a parallel history of absorption. The Kami Plenty-Swift-Sun, elder brother of the Sky-ancestor, whom he precedes to the earth, weds a sister of an *Emishi* chief. Many of the land-chiefs whom the imperial ancestor finds in possession when he descends (numbers of whom are speedily incorporated) are *Emishi*; they retain in many cases their local power and mingle their blood, from the beginning, with the Sun-strain. The first unmistakable record of the *Emishi* in the Narrative—the legend of Ukashi-Elder-Brother and Ukashi-Younger-Brother, of whom Jimmu demanded allegiance—is, in fact, a record of absorption. The former, who threw in his lot with the invaders, is named as ancestor of the Uda water-caterers (a Clan whose function it was to furnish the ice and water used on the imperial table). Other local chiefs are listed as the ancestors of the rulers of the Land of Yamato, the cormorant-fishers of Ata and of the Head-men and the Kuzu-folk [93] of Yoshino. The latter persist for centuries, growing less and less distinct and uncouth and more and more Japanese as the welding progresses. There is a clear echo of race-absorption, too, in the Narrative's statement that the *Emishi* whom Mountain-Gate-Brave had captured and offered as servitors at the Great Shrine are the ancestors of the Saheki Clan of Harima, Aki, Sanuki, Awa and Iyo Provinces. The later record (seventh century) is to note one incorporation *en masse*, when seven thousand families [94] that had been taken captive were given to the submissive *Emishi* of Koshi [95] to found a district.

Griffis concedes the mass of Japanese people today to be "substantially of Ainu stock"; he accounts for the difference between the unreconstructed Ainu of today and the typical Japanese, mainly by infusion of foreign blood, adoption of Chinese civilization and the hot bath, and the substitution of an agricultural for a hunter's mode of life.[96] The truth, it seems probable, lies somewhere between these two extravagances.

Indeed, one can hardly observe the wide physical differences between the typical northern peasant and the typical member of the ruling aristocracy of southern Japan today without the conviction that the former represents large borrowing by the conqueror from the coarser strain of the land, and the latter a proportionally large inoculation from the more cultured strains of early immigration, the one reflecting the Ainu lowstature and shorter arm, the bushy true-black hair, straighter eye-angle, thick nose and larger hand and foot, and the other the narrower eye set at a slightly oblique angle, nose more approaching the aquiline, small wrist, shapely hand and foot, finer texture of hair, and taller yet less muscular frame.

But, even were the racial effect of this impact less than is to be presumed, the effect of the myth epos of this savage *Emishi* people (whose richness and extent may be gauged from the folklore of the Ainu, their dwindling descendants today) can be clearly distinguished in the legends. There has been heretofore a disinclination to acknowledge this considerable debt, on the assumption that wherein Ainu myth shows resemblance to the Japanese it is to be considered an imitation of the latter.[97]

A priori this is rather an indication of a contrary process, or at least of a common possession of rudimentary legends which hark back to the same origin; that some Ainu myths seem to be cruder variants of those of Izumo would no more suggest that they are debased versions of the latter than that both had a common parent. And a very clear indication that the latter is the case is seen in the fact that, while there is scarcely one of the so-called "universal" myths which has not its variant in Ainu as well as in Japanese lore, some of them are the more fully developed in the former.

An example is the story of the sending from the Sky of the Cock-Pheasant, to investigate the defection of Prince-Sky-Young, the first ambassador to the Earth. In the Japanese myth it is merely stated that the bird, attracted by the fields of millet and pulse, remains there. In the Ainu legend, he lingers, but at length returns, when the creator, angered at his delay, strikes him back to earth, saying, "No longer are you desired in the Sky!"—an incidental explanation of the modern barnyard cock's inability to fly.[98]

Many larger elements the mythology of the Sun-Folk gained by accretion as they over-rolled, now pacifying and absorbing, now extirpating or expelling, the stubborn and untutored *Emishi*. Some major deities of the latter they took over bodily. We can be confident that the Kami Sky's-Sun-Spear, whom the Narrative names merely as the chief actor in a fading phallic myth, was at some primeval epoch a powerful native prince of whom the Great-Land-Master once went in awe and whom the Sun-warriors at length subjugated.

The triumphal progress of the first earthly emperor (Jimmu-*Tenno*) is punctuated by the discovery and adoption into the Sun-Pantheon also of numbers of lesser deities of the land—the same process by which, in the pre-Homeric age in Greece, soil-born tribal Pelasgian deities swelled the ranks of the Olympians. Such was Sky-Spying-Female, who joined Prince-Sky-Young, the first ambassador sent from the Sky, and the Sky-ancestor's guide in his descent to the Earth. Kagasé-Male (the only star-deity mentioned in the myths) also was no doubt a recalcitrant Kami of the Land who later submitted. Such were the Kami accosted in the Quick-Sucking-Channel, who came riding on the back of a tortoise, the Kami found on the lower reach of the Yoshino River catching fish in a weir, the tailed Kami who issued from the well, and the Kami, also tailed, who came forth "pushing the cliffs apart." These were deities of the Land, the last two, perhaps, bequeathed to the native Pantheon originally by the Ground-Spiders who, in one later legend, are themselves represented as tailed.

Ainu worship today shows correspondencies with Shinto that suggest a far greater debt on the part of the latter than is usually presupposed. There is, for example, the distinction between the "rough"- and the "gentle"-, or "blessing"-spirits of the Kami. Japanese teaching is that these Kami are not to be considered separate personalities, but rather one of the dual manifestations which are so often predicated of Shinto deities. The distinction drawn is somewhat like that made by some Christian theologians between the first two persons of the Trinity, the "rough" spirit being the deity in his character as punisher of the wicked and the "gentle" spirit the same deity in his character as pardoner of the penitent. The Ainu in the worship of their *Kamui* [99] (deities), have precisely this distinction [1] in their *Shi-Acha* (Rough-Uncle) and *Mo-Acha* (Peace-Uncle)—a distinction too subtle to allow us to suppose that they could have borrowed it from the Japanese.

There is also the use of the *goheï*, the folded strips of cut paper, foil or metal, hung in shrines and borne in festivals. The relationship of these to the whittled stick (*inäo*) of the Ainu is beyond question; if the *goheï* be, in fact, descended from an *Emishi* prototype, we have, as Aston has pointed out, a survival of the primitive worship "in the most spiritual aspect of modern Shinto."

It is inconceivable that the adoption of the heroes or demigods of the aborigines themselves into the Sun-Deity list, and the wholesale assimilation of the land stock as the result of centuries of association and interbreeding, should not have involved a large incorporation of native myth, and examination of the legends shows that this occurred.

Smaller *Emishi* fragments are easily discerned here and there in the Narrative. The building and pounding of the land by Brave-Swift-Impetuous-Male, assisted by the other Kami, and the spade work of Great-Land-Master, is Ainu. In its legend the sixty mattocks used were thrown away and, rotting, became ghosts and demons. A rock on the seashore, near Moruran, in Ezo, called *Mukara-So* (Ax-rock) is believed to be an implement used by one of the deities. The water that laved the decaying tools brought forth elves and mer-women, and sinking to Hades became Kunnepet, the Black-River, whence issue the demons which, entering a human being, cause epilepsy.

The wagtail, in the primal myth of the first pair, is Ainu. In that tongue it is still called the "bird of sensual desire" (*ochiu-chiri*). According to Batchelor, young men of Ezo keep the bones and skins of these birds as love-amulets and worship them to secure the objects of their affections.[2] In the Ainu story the wagtail plays even a larger part, since it was sent by the Great Deity to assist in making the Earth out of the primordial morass, and smoothed the rough clods upturned by his mattock—in memory of which to this day it is seen beating the earth with its tail. Ainu also is the use of the body-sword in the ancient marriage ceremony—as witness the song of the dying Mountain-Gate-Brave:

> At the couch-side || Where the maiden slept,
> That two-edged sabre || Which I deposited!

Today, in Ezo, the sending of the body-sword to the woman is the universal sign that the man is ready to take her to wife.

There is reason to believe that the primitive phallus-worship, already treated of, was Emishi. The huge phallus and *vulva* worshiped at Kandè Shrine are named, respectively, Okko-San and Mekko-San, which are the ancient names for the two adjoining hills upon which these relics originally stood, and two companion hills in Ezo [3] still bear the Ainu names Oakkan and Meakkan, bestowed upon them, presumably, for similar reasons.

It seems evident, too, that almost all the traces of serpent-worship which remain in the legends are aboriginal. By a number of these legends the Land of Koshi which was the home of the Eight-Forked-Serpent slain by Brave-Swift-Impetuous-Male, is identified with Ezo, the abode of the *Emishi*. Legends that were foreign to them, and so bizarre, the Sun-Folk would not unnaturally have attributed to Ezo. Among the Ainu today the legend persists of the great serpent of Rishiri, which was so huge that it could coil its length six times about the island of that name. It devoured the people till the deities took council and slew it with their divine blades. The legend closes with the characteristic Ainu detail that the fragments became wasps and gadflies. What is here trivial and inconsequential has gained size and dignity in the later Sun-variant; the detail is now used to trick out the western Perseus and Andromeda legend; the snake-fragments become no less than Thunder-Deities, and the mystic six of the aboriginal has become the sacred eight of the Japanese.

It is not too wide a conclusion, perhaps, to assume that the entire Great-Land-Master cycle is, in origin, *Emishi*. Up to the Sky-descent it presents a barbarous, untutored myth-series, appropriate to a land whose deities are "uproarious," a savage pot-pourri of filth and license. Of the conquest of the Land by his ancestor, Brave-Swift-Impetuous-Male, after the latter's slaughter of the Eight-Forked-Serpent (in itself an *Emishi* variant of a "universal" myth) the Narrative contains not a single episode—a fact inexplicable on the hypothesis that that conquest belonged originally to the Sun-epos.

To approach the question of the aboriginal element in the Sun-legends from another side: Japanese folklore, as we know it today, is strangely deficient in the apologue, or beast fable, whose finished form antedated the most ancient *faibleau*. Its animal stories show always the beast *in its relation to man*. For the beast-dialogue proper, in which man's craft and logic are saddled upon his humbler neighbor, we find in well-nigh every case a foreign root, and as often as not an Ainu one. And this is significant in the light of the fact that Ainu folklore is peculiarly rich in the true beast fable. For it is precisely those myths which contain traces of the apologue that, from other features, seem least at home in the Japanese mythology.

The fragments of beast fable interwoven with the fibre of the earliest legends of the Deity-Age, leaving out of account the beast episodes for which a southern and over-sea origin has been assigned (the flaying of the White-Hare by the vengeful *wani*, the recalcitrancy of the *bêche-de-mer*, the council of the fishes to obtain Fire-Fade's lost fish-hook and the selection of the *wani* which escorts him to and from the realm of the sea deity) are:

The prophecy of the White-Hare to Great-Land-Master.
The bringing to life of Great-Land-Master by Princess-Cockle and Princess-Clam.
The giving of aid to Great-Land-Master by the Speaking-Rat.
The sending of the celestial Pheasant to recall Sky-Young-Prince to his duty, and the part played by it, together with the wild goose, the heron, the kingfisher, the fish-hawk, the crow, the sparrow, the pheasant and the wren, in his funeral ceremonies.

These beast fragments are non-essential portions of the story, indeed they are peculiarly extraneous in the context. The White-Hare prophesies that Great-Land-Master will prosper in his wooing but in no way assists that enterprise; the intercession of Princess-Cockle and Princess-Clam are not necessary to bring Great-Land-Master to life—his mother is able to resuscitate him without assistance after he has been tortured to death by his brethren in the split tree trunk; the part played by the Speaking-Rat, when he is entrapped in the blazing moor, is an unessential one; there was no reason why the rat should have spoken at all, since it was not itself in possession of the information which the Scarecrow Deity furnished; the bird-episodes are quite immaterial to the Narrative.

This is by no means to imply that myth-fragments need to be interdependent. In fact, most mythologies are masses of narrative inconsistencies. But in these cases the fragments possess not only the quality of irrelevancy, which is a prime badge of incorporation, but one of primeval childishness, which inevitably links them to a further background—like the mouse attached to the earlier worship of Apollo Smintheus, and the rat that was sacred to the totem-age of Egypt.[4] Even at the early date at which the legends were committed to written form, there was, in fact, a belief that these fragments were not true parts of the whole, justifying Tachibana Moribè's nineteenth century characterization[5] of them as "puerile expressions" (*wosano-goto*) since from the *Nihongi*, the next to the earliest of the great Shinto scriptures, the legends of the White-Hare and of the Speaking-Frog and Rat are omitted altogether—exactly as Pindar omits, as "foolish and unworthy," some of the animal episodes given by the earlier Hesiod.[6]

All but the last-named of these beast fragments belong to the same sub-cycle of legends dealing with the career of the deity Great-Land-Master—a group evidently drawn, virtually *in toto*, from the older *Emishi*-epos.

Finally, while the western myth-fragments appear among the very first in the legends corresponding to the earliest epoch of the Sun-folk in the archipelago (that of Izumo), and the southern elements enter the story later, after their K'yushu epoch begins, these fragments which appear to be aboriginal cling to every part, just as throughout all their career the Sun-Folk came into contact with the savage, unruly people to whom these belonged.

As might be expected, it is in the ancient *Fudoki* portions of the Narrative, which were not incorporated in the later court compilations the *Kojiki* and *Nihongi*, that such fragments are generally to be recognized. They adhere to every cycle. The sewing of the lands by Brave-Swift-Impetuous-Male; the contentions of Prince- and Princess-of-Rock-Ricefield, children of Great-Land-Master; the courtship of Prince-Sanuki; the cycles of the turbulent Sky-Sun-Spear and Prince-of-Isè; the coming of the white-bird woman; the giant of Hitachi whose footprints were thirty paces long; the laughing monsters with cows' faces, slain by the fearless Tribe-Master of Ishitsuda, and the black folk dug from the ground by the Empress Jingu's bow-tip; the insolently wealthy Irogu whom the Kami punished for using rice cakes as targets; the sea *Wani*, which each year visited the stone Princess-World-Ricefield, the Thunder-Kami who flew as a pheasant; the ancient festivals of Mount Tsukuba and Mount Hitachi, and the formulae of incantation against rice insects—all these were myths deeply imbedded in particular localities; and they contribute not a little to give to the resultant mass that primeval combination of weirdness and artlessness, that peculiar quality of the naive and inconsequential, which would probably have disappeared in the process of thorough Nipponization which its final reduction to written form effectually prevented.

VI. THE RATIONALE OF THE NARRATIVE

From this brief inquiry into these legends it will not be difficult to make certain generalizations as to the Sun-Folk themselves and their early archipelagoan history.

First of all, there are a vast number of myth-fragments scattered throughout the stories which are palpably of Western origin, and the largest fragments, and those showing the most unmistakable resemblances, center in the Province of Izumo, on the southwest shore of the Great Island (Hondo)—almost the nearest point to the Korean coast. From this fact, coupled with the long and intimate connection, antedating even the Deity Age, between the archipelago and the mainland, it can be concluded that Izumo was held, at the time of the conquest of the Sun-Folk, by a stock descended from related tribes that had crossed the narrow stretch of estranging sea, and developed there a prehistoric and well-developed cosmogony based on the continental myths they brought with them.[7]

Second, linked to the southernmost Island of K'yushu is a group of myths that had their origin in the south seas, indicating an early settlement of a southern race who had brought with them the legends of their homeland and developed others of their own on the new soil. The most vigorous southern tribe, the *So* (primarily of Malay stock) later combined with the *Kuma* people from Korea. We see the legend of this welding of western *Kuma* and southern *So* in the myth of Fire-Fade the hunter and Fire-Glow the fisherman, and in the conquest of the latter and his consequent subserviency we hear the echo of that early struggle between the upland and coast peoples which resulted in the mixed stock of *Kuma-So*, a folk that had so strongly entrenched itself before the arrival of the Sun-warriors that the latter were several centuries in bringing about its subjection.

Third, we find throughout the greater part of the archipelago the myth-relics of an aboriginal people (that had absorbed or exterminated other peoples before them), a savage and untutored stock, whose legends have interwoven with the myth-fabric.

Consideration of these contrasts, which are so apparent even in the larger and more coherent episodes of the myth-mass, force the conviction that here is no homogeneous lore of a single stock, but one variously compounded of elements so dissimilar as to suggest an artificial welding that has been but partially successful. And this will suggest what has assuredly been the case, the struggle of old, perishing, local legend with two distinct bodies of more vigorous foreign myth, the gradual absorption of the older by the newcomer either by modification or wholesale appropriation, and the final binding together with a *callida junctura* into a single whole whose progress toward homogeneity was forever checked by its crystallization in written form.

Whence the Sun-Folk came [8]—this, the great crux of the ethnologist, is a question which has, primarily, no part in this discussion. Folklore furnishes no key to the riddle. The presumption is, however, that they came at the close of the bronze- or the beginning of the iron-age, from the western mainland [9] to Izumo, as numberless waves of emigration had preceded them, in a vessel which later story picturesquely designates as the "Floating-Sky-Bridge," bringing with them myth-materials which blended naturally with what they found. The Narrative shows a telltale confusion between Earth and Sky which points the conclusion that the episodes were invested with a Sky-character at a later period than their occurrence. For example, when He-Who-Invites slays his son, Fire-Shining-Swift-Male, the blood bespatters the rocks of both Earth and Sky, from which Kami are produced in both places. The rock-cave, into which the Sun-Goddess retires when insulted by her brother Brave-Swift-Impetuous-Male, is in the Sky, yet Sky-Hand-Strength-Male, when he leads her forth placated, rests his feet on the Earth, since there is the mark of his footprint on Togakushi-Mountain. The rock-door also, which he hurls away, comes to rest on Mount Tsukuba. Similar examples might be multiplied. In later episodes there is attempt at distinction—as when the mortuary of Prince-Sky-Young falls to Earth and becomes an earthly mountain. The distinction is more clearly drawn as the Narrative proceeds, the whole showing the usual steps in the familiar process by which deification is finally conferred upon historical personages and the earthly events with which history connects them are given a divine character and locale.

The invaders in the archipelago were rice-eaters, as were the great bulk of the peoples of the mainland. The staple of the aborigines had been millet, which accounts for the many recurrences of the word *awa* (millet) in place-names.[10] That tremendous, honorific-burdened "Fruitful-Reed-Plain-Land-of-Fresh-Rice-Ears-of-Thousand-Autumns-of-Long-Five-Hundred-Autumns looked forward to what the under-country was to become when the imperial grandson and his Kami-following should have sown there the rice-ears brought from the festival grounds of the High-Sky. It is the millet-fields and the bean-patches which seduce the pheasant, the *avant-courier* of the legend, and the Sky-ancestor, when he lands on Mount Takachiho, scatters the sacred Sky-grains (rice) to dispel the earthly darkness.

It cannot be well doubted that the Sun-folk came first to Izumo, though the legend of the celestial descent is localized in K'yushu. When their leader views the land from this vantage ground, he declares the place to be "over against the Land of Kara, coming straight across to this august cape." K'yushu is *not* directly opposite Korea, while Izumo *is*, and the discrepancy explains itself readily as an early uncertainty as to the real spot of the descent. This same uncertainty persisted in the name of the western and higher peak of the mount of the legendary landing (Nishi Kirishima)—"Opposite-Kara-Land-Peak" (Kara-Kuni-mi Dakè).

The blood-relationship of the Sun-Folk, too, with the Izumo ruling race is clearly insisted on; Great-Land-Master, whom they find in possession, is a son of Brave-Swift-Impetuous-Male, one of their prime deities. They claim the realm on the ground of superior descent and heirdom—a specious dictum that has been put forward a hundred times in real history. The myth seems to indicate that the primary claim to the Izumo territory was set up, indeed, by a younger collateral line. This acquires additional meaning from an identification of the celestial Takama-ga hara, the "Plain-of-the-High-Sky," (whose rivers, trees, mountains, caves, wells and ricefields endow it with a strangely earthly character) whence came the creative pair He-Who-Invites and She-Who-Invites, as Izumo itself. It is significant that the Sun-Goddess is said to have received as her portion of the land "the former abode of her parents," and while Japanese commentators are prone to pronounce this Izumi and its neighboring provinces on the eastern side of the Great Island, the opinion is vitiated by the fact that she proceeds against the progeny of Brave-Swift-Impetuous-Male, the Earth-deity who had overrun Izumo, to recover for her own heir *the region she conceives herself to have been deprived of.*

In the Narrative the claim to Izumo, though disallowed, is steadfastly maintained. Various chiefs are sent to spy out the land, who are corrupted by the local rulers and remain. The first, Sky-Great-Sun (who by one legend is a son of Brave-Swift-Impetuous-Male, and hence half-brother, at least, to Great-Land-Master, the Izumo ruler), ingratiates himself with the latter, as does his son, who follows him. The third, Prince-Sky-Young, marries the ruler's daughter and thinks to usurp the rule himself. A messenger (the Cock-Pheasant) sent after him finds the flesh-pots of Izumo too tempting to return. A second messenger (Nameless-Female) is killed by the recreant Prince-Sky-Young. A more ambitious embassy, led by the deities Brave-Awful-Possessing-Male and Bird Rock-Camphor-Tree-Boat, is more successful. One son of Great-Land-Master they win over, another they coerce, and the ruler at length abdicates in favor of the choice of the Sun-Folk. This is effected, however, by compromise, Great-Land-Master, as the price of his abdication, specifying that he be made high-priest, that a temple-palace be erected for him, and his worship fittingly incorporated. This episode would account naturally for a grafting of the salient features of the Izumo epos upon the cosmogony of the Sun-warriors.[11] We may infer that Sky-Great-Sun was able to make his peace with the successful claimant (indeed one variant of the legend represents him as true to the Sun-cause and as hypocritical in his apparent ingratiation) since the myth, in another place, names him [12] ancestor of the rulers of the Land of Izumo—which seems to indicate that the Sun-warriors, when they passed on to their more southerly conquest in K'yushu, left him seated firmly as suzerain.

The question of Izumo having been thus peacefully disposed of, the newcomers are ready for the second chapter of their archipelagoan history, which the myth enshrines in the descent upon far-distant K'yushu, the southernmost of the islands, where credible history at length overtakes them. Here they come into contact with the *Kuma-So*, who had brought the myths of the south sea to gain lodgment on the soil, and here the celestial chronology proper comes to end with the birth of the first earthly Emperor, Jimmu. Here, some thousand years after their appearance in the seventh century B.C., we find them accounting for their own origin by a preliminary Deity-Age of indefinite duration and comprehensively elastic geography, and for the divinity of their great ancestress through the descent of Sky-Plenty-Earth-Plenty-High-as-Sky's-Sun-Fire-Ruddy-Plenty, the descendant of the Sun-Goddess, from the Sky upon H'yuga. And here we find them exhibiting a passionate love of the great luminary and a horror of the outer savagery and of the dark which argues an ancestry of a considerable mental culture, in whose progress the slow gradation up from barbarity had been long overlaid.

The absorption of K'yushu well finished, the Sun-warriors turn their attention to the eastward—or, more properly, to the northeastward—whence rumors of the rich land of Yamato (Mountain-Gate) have reached them. From the legend, they were not the first who had left Izumo for new fields of eastern conquest. Plenty-Swift-Sun—a paternal uncle of Sky-Great-Sun, the first scout sent into Izumo (whom we have supposed to have been invested with the rule of Izumo)—had anticipated them in Yamato, having presumably gone overland. Jimmu has heard of him from the deity Salt-Possessor. Later, when Jimmu comes to grips with the line of Plenty-Swift-Sun, the latter's son gains consideration by proving his descent from the same ancestry, exhibiting as evidence weapons such as Jimmu himself carries. To Yamato Jimmu leads his victorious troops, by way of the Inland Sea—a journey that, even in the legends, takes some sixteen years to accomplish—and there embarks on an era of conquest, embodied in the legend-group which concerns itself with the establishment of the empire in central Japan and is the repository of the Sun-Folk's own later myth.

The Sun-warriors had meanwhile been all along absorbing the aboriginal myth of the Land itself (*Emishi*), softening its cruder barbarities, eliminating its filth and obscenities, dignifying it, using its larger episodes to clothe some of their own legends, and incorporating their own theogony and racial adventures, so that in time the various cycle-groups came to be woven into a more or less coherent pageant by a thread of *soi-disant* history.

So that the lesson of the legends is that the race whose ancient lore they embody is a heterogeneous one. They speak of three streams, aboriginal, Mongol and south sea or Malay, mingling to form a nation to whose stock each strain has contributed its own salient characteristics. Beyond this the most ardent folklorist cannot venture far without other materials, and speculation that leads further afield must be taken with much reserve.

NOTES

NOTES

THE MYTH NARRATIVE

PAGES 3 - 17

¹ The *In* and *Yo* (Chinese *Yin* and *Yang*). The tenet is *Wo konomu mono-wa hiyasu; in yo niki-no hataraki nitè ban-butsu naru.* (All things are produced by the action of the female and male principles.)
² Ancient tradition has it, "disappeared": i.e., either died or became true spirits. Those who adopt the latter view will find in it an early indication of that lack of distinction between nature-deities and deified souls which has always marked the national beliefs.
³ Alternative name: Sky-Change-Sun-Sky-Mist-Land-Change-Moon-Land-Mist (in the *Kujiki* only). According to the *Shojiroku*, this deity is claimed as Ancestor by several noble families.
⁴ Alternative name: Divine-Producer-Ancestor.
⁶ Alternative name: Bottom-Earth-Stander.
⁷ Alternative name: Earth-Stander.
⁸ Alternative names: Fruitful-Earth-Moor; Fruitful-Earth-Master; Fruitful-Perfume-Joint-Moor; Float-Pass-Moor-Fruitful-Buy; Fruitful-Mouth-Moor; Leaf-Tree-Earth-Moor; August-Moor.
⁹ Alternative names: Prince-Great-Toma; Great-Door-Place; Great-Door-After; Great-Wealthy-Ground; Great-Place (probably the Earth).
¹⁰ Alternative names: Princess-Great-Toma; Great-Door-Before; Great-Wealthy-Place. Later Shintoists generally regard the above four mated pairs as representing, not separate Kami, but processes of development through which He-Who-Invites and She-Who-Invites passed in their progress to perfection.
¹¹ Alternative name: Blue (or Green)-Awful. In Japanese one word (*awo*) does duty for both colors.
¹² Alternative names: Shunned-Awful-Lady; Blue (or Green)-Awful-Lady; O-Awful.
¹³ He is enshrined at Taga-village in Awaji (see p. 22, n. 30), at Kawaüchi, Ishikawa District, in Kaga Province and at numbers of other shrines, generally in company with She-Who-Invites, and occasionally with Prince-Monkey-Ricefield (see p. 71).
¹⁴ Alternative names: Great-Kami-of-the-Land-of-Night: Road-Reaching-Great-Kami (see p. 71). The shrine known as Oba-no O-miya or Kamoshi-

Jinja, at Oba, near Yaëgaki, Izumo Province, and the Taga Shrine at Taga, Inukami District, Omi Province, are dedicated to her. Her spirit, also, is the Kumano Gongen of Kii and the Kamosubi M'yojin of Izumo. At the Hakusan-Himè-Shrine, at Kawaüchi, she is enshrined in company with He-Who-Invites and Princess-Listen (see p. 17). The Kamoshi-Jinja is said to have among its treasures a grain of rice an inch long, believed to have been preserved from the Deity-Era, and a stone caldron in which the first *Kozuko* (High-Priest) descended from the Sky. There are many minor shrines at which she is worshiped.

[15] See p. 10.

[16] In archaic Japanese the two terms are interchangeable. A gloss in the *Nihongi* says, "In olden time a woman called her brother 'elder brother' and a man called his sister 'younger sister,' whatever their ages."

[17] Eternal-Earth-Stander and Fruitful-Shape-Moor.

[A] This Kami and the four preceding are mentioned only in the *Kujiki*.

[18] The phallus, male pillar (*nu-boko*), root of coition, the Chinese "jewel stalk" (penis). The first suggestion of the ancient phallic worship. Some see in the spear a symbol of the earth-axis.

[19] What this was is disputed. Hirata identifies it with the Kami Bird-Rock-Camphor-Tree-Boat (see p. 7). Motoöri says it was a real bridge, and points to certain elevations in Harima and Tango provinces as being its overthrown "landing-places" or abutments. Brinkley supposes it to have been the vessel which brought the Sun Folk's ancestors to the new land. This obvious explanation, however, seems insufficient, for on Great-Land-Master's abdication of the Earth-Rule, it is promised him *"that you may take pleasure on the sea,* I will make you *a floating-bridge* and a Sky-Bird-Boat." In the later poetical development of the myth there is little doubt—Aston to the contrary —that it became identified with the rainbow.

[B] The lost *Tango-Fudoki,* quoted in the *Shaku-Nihongi-Jutsugi,* vol. I.

[20] Yasohashi.

[C] The *Harima-Fudoki.*

[21] Onogoro. One of the tiny pendants at the northwestern extremity of the Island of Awaji, which bridges the Inland Sea, between the Great Island and Shikoku. There is doubt which one deserves the honor. On Awaji itself is a great *tumulus* which popular legend declares was once an island. It is named Onogoro and on it is a shrine dedicated to He-Who-Invites and She-Who-Invites.

[22] The Japanese "fathom," defined as the stretch of the arms, about five feet, English measure.

[23] The twirling of the spear to set the Earth revolving and the flying-off of clods to make stars and comets (ideas fathered by Sato Nobuhiro and his school) are of course modern inventions and have no part in the old myth form.

[24] There is a Wagtail Island (Sekireï-Shima) near the Island of Onogoro, which testifies to the age of the story. Onogoro has also a Wagtail-Rock (Sekireï-Ishi) which is visited by women in labor. The bird is sacred to these two deities. There is an old saying that not even Crumbling-Prince, the Scarecrow-Deity (see p. 53), can frighten it.

[25] This circumambulation Aston surmises to be a relic of an ancient marriage ceremony.

²⁶ It was anciently the custom for a newly married pair, on the third night after the first cohabitation, to offer a kind of small cakes to these two Kami.

²⁷ Hirugo. Hirata, whose identifications are sometimes fearfully and wonderfully made, identifies this Kami with Prince-Little-Renowned (see p. 54). In later times he has been identified with the Izumo deity Ebisu, one of the seven Deities-of-Happiness (*Shichi-Fuku-Jin*) who, as the first angler and patron of fishermen, is represented with a rod and line under one arm and a *taï* fish under the other, and (since fish and rice are the main articles of the Japanese diet) is worshiped as the deity of daily food. By merchants in some sections he is supplicated also as a deity of wealth, in association with Daikoku-Ten (another of the *Shichi-Fuku-Jin*).

Ebisu is also known as Ebisu Saburo, though scholars are loath to accept this identification with the deity of Iki. The *Shinsha-Keïmo* warns against giving the Leech-Deity this name, "as the vulgar do." An author translated by the Italian Puini (*I sette Genii della Felicità, notizia sopra una parte del culto dei Giapponesi; Traduzione dal Giapponese di Carlo Puini*. Firenze, 1872) supposes that the word *Iki* may be taken here in lieu of its homophone *ikki* (revolt) and hence that the name *Ara* (rough)-Ebisu, given this deity, may be an alternative for Ikki-no Kami (Kami of the Rebels). It seems tolerably certain, however, that Hirugo, if not the progenitor of the *Emisu* folk, was one of the earlier deities to whom they gave worship.

One authority (cited in the *Nihon-H'yakwa-Jiten*) identifies Ebisu with Fire-Fade (Hiko-Hohodemi), on the assumption that the word is a corruption of *emisu* (smile) and the syllables *hohodemi* are for *hohoëmi* (smiling). In the later Narrative, in the discussion of its sources, I have suggested that the Fire-Fade and Fire-Glow legend was a native one, taken over from the aboriginal *epos* by the Sun-Folk, the myth itself embodying the mastery gained by the inlanders over the coast or fishing-people of K'yushu. If this be so, the identification of the former's deity (Ebisu) with the sun-deity who usurped the niche in the Pantheon occupied by the victor, is not an improbable one. To find proof of this, however, in mere syllabic corruption is an unnecessary strain.

Others identify Ebisu with the Kami Thing-Sign-Master, since the legend later pictures the latter as fond of fishing, and Ebisu is the patron of the industry. One legend identifies him with Prince-of-Oak-Root (see p. 93).

There are two shrines dedicated to Ebisu in the enclosure of the Hirota Shrine in Settsu Province, the Ebisu-Miya or Nishi-no Miya-Ebisu (West-Ebisu-Palace) and the Minami-no Miya (South-Palace). The second is locally known as the Oki-no Ebisu Shrine. He had anciently shrines also in Satsuma and Aki provinces and there is every indication that his worship was widespread. The *Azuma-Kagami* (a chronicle of the Kamakura Government covering the period 1180-1266) says, under date of 1253, "At the shrine beside the west gate Saburo Daim'yojin was invited to settle for the first time." From this it may be inferred that the deity had by this date become one of general acceptance in the Sun Pantheon.

Aston thinks Hirugo (Hiruko) was merely a masculine form of Hirumè (Sun-Female).

²⁸ See p. 19.

²⁹ Alternative names: Sky-Bird-Boat; Many-Handed-Boat-of-Bear-Moor (*Kumano-no Morota Bunè* [*Funè*]. *Morota*: Many-Handed (-oared?).

Mr. Shinji Nishimura of Tok'yo, well known for his work in the Anthropological Society and the Society of Naval Architecture, and editor of the *Gakuseï*, has published a monograph (Waseda University Press) on the subject. There seems no doubt, from the age of this legend, that this many-oared vessel was an importation from the mainland. Mr. Nishimura connects it, indeed not without reason, with the Amur barge, of which the triangular Korean boat is the descendant, the Ainu skiff belonging rather to the northern type than to the western.

The name Kumano (Kuma-nari) is considered by the older commentators to be a corruption of Komori-nu (Retirement-Moor). The legend is given (p. 12) which fixes the burial of She-Who-Invites in this Kumano. The village, a very ancient one, contains three of the oldest shrines in the archipelago (Hongu, Shingu and Nachi) whose generic designation is Kumano-Jinja (Kumano-no San-Zan). The Hongu, founded 81 B.C., is dedicated primarily to the Great Deity of Kumano, and a local legend, whose immense antiquity is unquestioned, points to the place as that to which the folk of Izumo migrated from their native land. Nothing is known of this Great Deity, unless it be considered Wondrous-of-Bear-Moor (see p. 31) whom, by the way, Hirata is disposed to identify with his elder brother, Sky-Great-Sun, which would suggest an early Sun-Deity.

ᴬ The *Nihon-H'yakwa-Jiten* (see p. 7, n. ᴀ). Of the West Palace (Ebisu-Miya) the *Nippon-Ki* says: "His (Hirugo's) skiff reached the shore of the bay of Nuko-no Kori, in Settsu Province, where accordingly the people erected a shrine in his honor, and many prodigies were performed there."

³⁰ Awa-jima. A tiny island near Awaji.

³¹ Alternative name: Rice-Ear-Youth. Awaji-no Shima, written with the characters signifying, by one reading, "Foam-Way Island," and by some so translated. Motoöri thinks it so called because it is on the way to Awa Province. Here it is considered to be a corruption of Agahaji (*aga*: my; *haji*: shame).

³² In Japanese a single word does duty for both placenta and elder-brother. The *Kujiki* alone, in this place, employs the character which means the latter.

³³ Alternative name: Sky-Fertile-Dragon-Fly-Prince-Lord.

³⁴ It is singular that this island is given this place in the order in every text but that of the oldest—the *Kojiki*—which puts it last of the "Great Eight Islands."

³⁵ Modern Shikoku.

³⁶ Alternative name: Sky-Great-Heart-Youth.

³⁷ K'yushu. The name was anciently applied to the whole island. The texts of the legends throughout use the ancient form. For various derivations of the name, see p. 92.

³⁸ Alternative name: Sky-One-Pillar. Iida Takesato derives Iki from *yuki* (snow), and Motoöri from either *ikohi* (rest) or *yuki* (the sacred ricefield fixed by divination in the year preceding a coronation, whose crop is used in the first post-coronation Taïshosaï [Great Festival of First Rice-Tasting]). In ancient times the *yuki* was chosen also at other than coronation occasions. There is, however, no early myth record of the fixing of the sacred ricefield on Iki-Island. Other texts confuse it with Oki-Island (see p. 8).

³⁹ Alternative name: Princess-Sky-Hand-Good.

⁴⁰ It has been stated that Foam-Island, the first created, "is not reckoned amongst their offspring," but apparently it is counted in the total.
⁴¹ Koshi in earliest times signified the northern or barbarous country, Ezo, the land of the Ainu (Emishi). Later it designated the northwestern Provinces of Etchu, Echigo, and Echizen. It is not properly an island.
⁴² Alternative name: Great-Tamaru-Lord.
⁴³ Alternative names: Island-Maise-Child; Brave-Sun-Direction-Lord. Ko-jima (*Ko*: child, small). The *Kujiki* gives it as Kibi-no Ko-jima (Child-of-Maise, or Small-Maise Island).
⁴⁴ Alternative name: Princess-Great-Moor-Clapper-Bell. Unless regarded as here, phonetically, the characters signify the small bean (*Phaseolus radiatus*).
⁴⁵ Alternative name: Sky-One-Root.
⁴⁶ Alternative name: Sky-Great-Male.
⁴⁷ Alternative name: Sky-Two-Houses.
⁴⁸ Alternative names: Long-Wind-Chief; *Sky-Pillar*. Motoöri renders this word as *breath*.
⁴⁹ Alternative name: *Earth-Pillar*. Hirata Atsutanè, in his form of prayer to be used in adoring the residence of the Emperor, mentions these two deities: "From a distance I reverently worship with awe before Amè-no Mi-Hashira (Sky-Pillar) and Kuni-no Mi-Hashira (Earth-Pillar), etc." It is difficult to guess why special stress should be laid on these in this connection. A deity of the site of the imperial palace also was given worship (see p. 107, n. 61).
⁵⁰ The *Kujiki* and one of the *Norito** make this deity a double one. The *Nihon-Shoki-Tsushaku* says, "These two names signify one male deity. It is found in the *Norito* that this wind-deity is male, but his divided forms are a male and a female, Prince and Princess, as in the case of Prince-of-Swift-Autumn (see *supra*), whose divided forms are two deities, a male and a female, who ruled river and sea respectively and also gave birth to offspring."

Hirata supposes this wind-Kami acted as messenger between the Sky and the Earth (see, however, p. 59).

His principal shrine is at Tatsuta, in Yamato Province, and his worship is closely related to that of Uga-no Kami at Hirosè, the similar festivals of the two deities being identified in the popular mind. They are invoked together to expel calamities of wind and water and to bring abundant harvest. The Tatsuta and Hirosè festivals were inaugurated in 676, in the reign of the Emperor Temmu.

The Kaza-Miya (one of the four detached shrines of the *Gegu* [exterior shrine] at Isè) is also dedicated to him. Originally a subordinate shrine, its rank was raised in 1293, the deity being considered responsible for the tornado which destroyed the invading fleet of Kublai Khan off the coast of Chikuzen in 1281.
⁵¹ Alternative names: Princess-August-Food; Kami-of-Storehouse-Rice; Storehouse-Rice-Possessor; Princess-Great-Food. This deity is Uka (Uga)-no Kami, popularly known as Inari-M'yojin, deity of rice. It is extremely unlikely that she was ever associated with Double-Name-Island (Awa) (see p. 8).

Her best-known shrine is one at Fushimi, near K'yoto, founded in 711 and dedicated (according to the *Engi-Shiki*) to the trio Brave-Swift-Impetuous-

---

* Liturgies.

Male, his wife Princess-Divine-Great-Ichi, and Jewel-of-Storehouse-Rice, who, according to one legend, was their daughter. The name of this shrine is Inari (Rice-Bearing), hence the rice-deity's popular name, Inari-M'yojin. The K'yoto Inari is the patron, in particular, of sword-makers and *femmes de joie* (*joro*), and is crowded with worshipers each month on a Day of the Horse. It has Festivals on April 9 and the second Day of the Horse in the same month.

Since the sixteenth century the fox has been popularly associated with this deity. There have been many attempts to explain this. Some authorities would trace the connection to an etymological confusion due to the similarity, in their written form, of the words *mi-kitsunè* (Three-Foxes) and *miketsu* (August-food-provider). The real fact is, doubtless, that fox-worship—which is very ancient in the archipelago—had its seat on Mount Inari. The ancient fox-deity was a male, which would account for the modern confusion in the sex of this Kami by which Inari (which name came to be applied to the latter) is often represented nowadays as an old man with a white beard, riding fox-back. Gradually the newer Sun-deity forced the older land-deity into the background until his devotees, the foxes, came to be regarded as the mere messengers of the female deity of rice. The *Engi-Shiki* says, "In the fourth year of Wado (711) these (i.e., the three Sun-deities to whom the Inari Shrine at Fushimi is dedicated) began to settle at level places of the three peaks of Inari-Mountain." The fox-worship was localized at the place long before this time.

Anciently Jewel-of-Storehouse-Rice was the patron deity of silk culture (see p. 21, n. 25).

The *Benten K'yo* (*Benzāi-Ten-Keïten* [-Sutra]) identifies her with Benzaï-Ten (Benten), one of the *Shichi-Fuku-Jin* (Seven-Deities-of-Happiness).

[52] The one version of her subsequent murder, which makes Brave-Swift-Impetuous-Male her murderer (see p. 21) would seem to oppose this paternity. It is thus given, however, by the *Kojiki* and the *Engi-Shiki*.

[53] See p. 38.

[A] The *Jin-Sho-Sho*.

[54] This name appears in only one variant. It seems likely that it is a copyist's error, and that this deity is identical with Jewel-of-Storehouse-Rice.

[55] I identify him with Prince-Long-Wind.

[56] Alternative names: Sea-Body; Prince-Fruitful-Jewel. A sea-deity (see p. 82).

[57] Alternative name: Body-of-Swift-Autumn.

[58] This is presumably the early deity of the divine Mirror (see p. 24).

[59] Alternative name: Great-Kami-of-Carry-Across. A mountain-deity, generally considered a male, but which the *Nihongi* makes a female. There is a shrine dedicated to the worship of this deity at Yamada, Isè, near the *Nāigu* (inner shrine) of the Sun-Goddess (see p. 235).

[60] See p. 10.

[61] Alternative name: Moor-Elder. A moor deity.

[62] A mist deity.

[63] Alternative names: Prince-Fire-Shining; Fire-Shining-Elder; Fire-Producer; Fire-Father. Deity of Fire and of Summer Heat. His worship, which has almost disappeared, is still maintained at Nagusa in Kiï Province, and (under the name of Fire-Producer) on the summit of Atago-San, a mountain near K'yoto. There are occasional hill shrines dedicated to him. He is besought for protec-

tion against conflagrations. The deity popularly known as Atago is regarded as his avatar.
64 A deity of metals.
65 Alternative name: Clay-Mountain-Lady.
66 I am disposed to identify this deity with Jewel-of-Storehouse-Rice.
▲ The *Jinsho.*
67 The Clay-Deity, the Water-Deity, the Gourd-Deity and the River-Weed-Deity are associated in one of the *Norito* (liturgies) as protectors against fire. The inclusion of the Clay-Deity is an obvious reference to the fact that clay vessels were used, like the gourd, to hold water. The river-weed *kuwaï* (*sagittaria sagittata*) is modernly molded on the face of the wide tile used for roof-edging, as an amulet against conflagrations, and formerly ornamented the fronts of helmets, symbolic of power and victory.
▲ *Norito* of the *Hi-Shizumè-no Matsuri* (Fire-Calming-Service).
68 This Kumano (Bear-Moor), is in Kishu (Kiï), though popular belief fixes her tomb at a place called Hana-no Iwaya (Flower-Cave), near Kinomoto, in Kumano Province. The latter spot is marked by a sacred straw-rope (shimè-nawa) stretched from the top of a cliff to a pine-tree at its base, the rope being renewed twice a year, in February and October, with a *fête de fleurs* (see p. 7, n. 29).
69 Hoki (*haha-ki*). Motoöri's supposition.
70 Kagu.
71 Ama (amè)-no Kawa, also called Tenga or Ginja (Silver) River. The *via lactea*, the Milky Way. To the Ainu it is the "River-of-the-Kamui (-Kami)" in which the deities fish.
72 Alternative names: Brave-Snap; Fruitful-Snap; *Great-Snap-Kami*; High-Male. Enshrined by Jimmu-*Tenno*, according to legend, in 659 B.C., at Kashima, in Hitachi Province (see p. 90).
73 Izu-no Wo-Bashira (*wo-bashira*: male-pillar) (see p. 5, n. 18). Evidently one of the older phallic deities. I count this an alternative name of the Kami Sky-Mara (see p. 24).
74 See p. 28. This male Kami is given, in this earlier place, by the *Kujiki*. It seems most probable that he is to be identified with the Kami Sky-Shining-Earth-Shining-Sky's-Fire-Ruddy-Comb-Jewel-Plenty-Swift-Sun (see p. 66).
75 Deities of darkness.
76 From a method of reasoning which would, by the way, argue this translation of his name (Futsu-Nushi) a wrong one, Aston believes this deity to have been a fire god of Korean origin. He is worshiped particularly in the shrines of Katori and Kashima, in Hitachi Province. He has always been held in special reverence by the imperial family, from the legend of his later success in pacifying the under-realm preliminary to the descent from the Sky of the imperial ancestor (see p. 60 *et seq.*).
77 According to popular belief, this deity is buried at the foot of the cliffs near the town of Kinomoto, in Kumano Province, at a place known as Oji-no Iwaya (Prince-Cave). A celebration is held there every July, with a huge bonfire.
78 See Note 85.
79 I believe this *Kami* is to be identified with Inmost-Mountain-Possessor.
80 Alternative name: Majestic-Point-Blade-Extended.

⁸¹ He is believed to have descended through a passage on the boundary of Izumi and Iwami provinces.

According to Ainu legend, there was an entrance to the underworld at the mouth of the river Sarubutsu, in a cave that is now engulfed by the waves.
⁸² This expression for the nether world is Chinese.
⁸³ Or, "as I reverence your coming." An extreme honorific.
⁸⁴ I.e., Family.
⁸⁵ These Kami are referred to as one, under the name of Ikazuchi (Naru Ikazuchi). Aston believes this collective deity to be identical with Brave-Awful-Possessing-Male (Takè-Mika-Zuchi), but there seems to be little warrant for this, other than a similarity of particles. There are numerous shrines to this collective Kami.
⁸⁶ There is no justification, in the oldest texts, for translating, as does Motoöri, "had been born in her" (*Kojiki-Den*). The character used means "were present in their form." For example, *Takamagahara-ni Nareru Kami*: "the Kami who was existing, in his form, at Takamagahara."
⁸⁷ Alternative name: Hisa-Females. The *Wamyosho* says these are the same as the *Gogo-me*, used as bogies to frighten children with. Hirata Atsutanè identifies them with the eight Thunder-Kami.
^A *Norito* of the *Hi-shizumè-no Matsuri* (Fire-Calming-Service).
⁸⁸ He threw down his *kuro-mi-katsura* (*kuro*: black; *mi*: honorific; *ka* [*kami*]: hair; *tsura*: joining), which turned into *ebi-katsura* (wild grapes). In the Japanese the pun is obvious.
⁸⁹ These, with the Ugly-Females-of-the-Land-of-Night, the Thunder-deities, and those deities produced from the contaminated clothing and bodily impurities washed away by He-Who-Invites in his lustration (see p. 17) are called pestilence-Kami (*Yakushin*) and represent disease, against which they are invoked. Hence they are known as preventive deities (*Sahe-no-Kami*). They are all in origin phallic deities, like the peach. No shrines are dedicated to them, but a festival in their honor is held on the first full moon of the year. In modern phrase the character *sahe* (prevention) is written *sai* (good luck). In Isè the name is now written with the same characters as Dosojin (see p. 17, n. 95).
⁹⁰ From its shape the peach in myth is representative of the female organ (vulva). The apricot in India and the pomegranate in Greece are modernly so used. It was a concomitant of the ancient phallus worship, as may be seen from its identification with Princess-Eight-Road-Fork (see n. 91, *infra*), who is grouped with Great-Elder-of-Come-Not-Place, deity of roads. The latter was produced from the staff of He-Who-Invites, which itself was a phallic emblem, like the Jewel-Spear used in the creation of the first land (see p. 3). In the ceremony of demon-ousting (*oni-yarahi*), which takes place on the last day of the year throughout modern Japan, rods of peach wood are used.
⁹¹ By some identified with a Princess-Eight-Road-Fork (Yachimata-Himè), named in one of the *Norito* as one of the three Kami-of-Prevention which were produced from He-Who-Invites' flung-down garments or from his lustration (see p. 17) and given various names. The three thus grouped are Prince-Eight-Road-Fork, Princess-Eight-Road-Fork, and Great-Elder-of-Come-Not-Place (see p. 17).
⁹² Alternative name: Road-Turn-Back.

⁹³ *Ifuya* (*Yuya*), i.e., *Yufu-Yami* (Evening-Darkness). Moribè in the *Izu-no-Chi-Waki*.
⁹⁴ Izumo.
ᴬ The *Kujiki*.
⁹⁵ One ancient commentator observes, in relation to this passage, "This is the reason why people now spit when they see something that is impure."
⁹⁶ Alternative name: Thrust-Stand-Funo-Place. The Deity of Roads, Kunato (Kunado). This deity drives away pestilence and evil spirits from the roads and is worshiped by wayfarers (see p. 63). He is identical with the popular deity Dosojin, who is often wrongly confounded with Prince-Monkey-Ricefield (see p. 71). He is worshiped at the shrine called Izumo Wi-no Kami Yashiro (shrine of the Izumo well-Kami) or Izumo-ji-no Yashiro (shrine of the Izumo road), at Kizuki-Machi, Izumo Province. The festival of Dosojin is celebrated by boys. On January 14 decorated bamboo is burned, together with writings made on the first two days of the year, and rice cakes are cooked on the fire thus made.
⁹⁷ Kukuri-Himè (kikurè: listen). Iïda Takesato's rendition. According to the *Jinshosho*, she is the present Hakusan-Himè, worshiped in the middle shrine at Kawaüchi Village, Ishikawa District, Kaga Province, the other two shrines being dedicated respectively to He-Who-Invites and She-Who-Invites. The *Engi-Shiki* lists her also there.
⁹⁸ This descent is given in the *Jinja-Benran* of Sakaüchi Naoyori (1685).
⁹⁹ Naruto Kaik'yo (-no seto). A strait between Awa (in Shikoku Province) and Awaji Island.

PAGES 17 - 33

¹ Haya-sufu-na. In the Bungo Channel.
² Tachibana.
³ H'yuga (ancient Himuka).
⁴ Omitted in the *Nihongi* text.
⁵ Alternative name: Elder-Male-of-the-Bottom.
⁶ Alternative name: Elder-Male-of-the-Middle.
⁷ Alternative name: Elder-Male-of-the-Surface.
⁸ Hirata (followed by Kurida) identifies the trio with Great-Ocean-Possessor (see pp. 19 and 82). Their chief shrine is at Sumiyoshi, near Sakaï.
⁹ According to the *Kojiki*.
¹⁰ Suminoë (Sumiyoshi). This, the popular rendition, is a play upon words.
¹¹ It seems clear that these three deities are to be identified with three of those named above, but the dissimilarity of characters and particles makes this difficult.
¹² Alternative names: Great-Female-Noon-Possessor; Sky-Shiner-Great-Noon-Female; Sacred-Jewel-of-the-Rooted-Sakaki-Princess-of-Sky-Distant-Opposite-Land. Amaterasu, the Sun-Goddess, the Chief Deity of the Japanese people, known as Shimmeï, or more popularly, as Tenshoko (Tensho) -Daïjin. Her holy of holies is in the Great Shrine at Isè. There is a popular shrine dedicated to her near Shiba Park, Tok'yo; its festival (the *Shimmeï-Matsuri*) is held

September 11-21. She is worshiped also at the Hongu Shrine (founded 81 B.C.) in Kumano, Kiï Province.

In the eighth century G'yogi-Bosatsu (670-749), the Korean *Bonzè* who first preached in Japan the doctrine of *R'yobu-Shinto* (which, holding the ancient Shinto deities to be temporary manifestations [*gongen*] of Buddhist divinities, was responsible for the rapid progress of the new religion) asked permission to erect the colossal statue of the Buddha at Nara. He was referred for authority to the Great Shrine at Isè and watched before its altar through seven nights, when the Sun-Goddess appeared to him, declaring that she was herself a manifestation of Amida Buddha, the highest of all the Buddhas.

[13] Alternative name: Moon-Bow. The Moon-Deity. Identified by later Shinto writers with Brave-Swift-Impetuous-Male (see Note 15, *infra.*). Aston thinks the latter was originally the moon god of the pre-Japanese Izumo folk, and that Moon-Darkness-Possessor was the moon god of the conquering race. He is worshiped at Isè, Kadono, etc., at the former place being represented as a man of heroic size on horseback, wearing a purple robe and carrying a golden sword. In ancient times live horses were offered to him annually. In 772 a noted tempest was ascribed to his displeasure by the Isè priesthood, and in 853 an oracle from him is believed to have saved the nation from a great epidemic of smallpox. He is still supplicated when this disease is prevalent.

It is a singular fact that in modern times the Japanese poet refers to the moon as feminine.

▲ The *Jinjako*.

[14] Isè-ni Itsukimatsuru O-Kami.

[15] Mabuchi's rendition. Alternative names: Swift-Banishment-Kami; Kami-Buto (see p. 57). This deity is identified by commentators of Hirata's school with Moon-Darkness-Possessor, and by others with Emma-O, the Judge of the Buddhist Hells. He is worshiped as Gozu-*Tenwo* (Indian, Gava-Griva, the Ox-Headed) who also belongs to the Buddhist infernal pantheon. Shinto shrines where he is worshiped are called Yasaka and Buddhist temples dedicated to him are called Gion, the latter name being referable to an oracle of Yozeï-*Tenno's* reign (877-884) in which the deity declared, "I am a protecting Kami of Gion-Shoja (a temple in which the Buddha preached) in India." His ancient shrine, the Yasaka-Jinja, in K'yoto, was the most popular of the capital. This, later called Gion-no Yashiro, under the *R'yobu-Shinto* (the amalgamation of Shinto and Buddhism) was called Gion-Ji. It is also known as Kanshin-in. The Restoration made this again pure Shinto.

The *Shinto-M'yomoku* makes this deity a trinity under the collective appellation of Sampo-Kwojin (Three-Treasure-Rough-Deity), whose members are called Susa-no Wo, Kami-Susa-no-Wo, and Haya-Susa-no-Wo (Impetuous-Male, Kami-Impetuous-Male, and Swift-Impetuous-Male) in which manifestation, and as Gozu Tenwo, he is besought against plague. Among his ten forms Amano Nobukagè gives that of a plague deity and the *Tenkeïseï-Himitsu* declares that "Gozu-Tenwo strikes demons of disease and expels the calamity of plague."

While he is generally identified with Kami-Buto, the identification is not universally conceded. The *Gozu-Tenwo-Ben* of Nobukagè says: "The government order of *Shoheï* Era (1346-1369) calls Buto a Sky-Kami. Sorcerers believe him to be Susano-wo (Brave-Swift-Impetuous-Male), while scholars and diviners think him a Sky-deity or Taïzanfu Kun." But it seems clear that Buto and Gozu-Tenwo, in his aspect as Plague-Protector, are identical.

O'Neil (*Night of the Gods*) and Dr. Buckley believe Brave-Swift-Impetuous-Male to have personified the rain or thundercloud (whirlwind). Aston is disposed to dissent, by reason of the fact that he is invoked as protector from shipwreck and tempest. But worship is as often as not offered for placation.

He is named (wrongly) ancestor of the Rulers of the Land of Izumo, by Florenz, Murray, Brinkley, and Hearn. These Land-Rulers claimed descent from Sky-Great-Sun (see p. 31).

16 Notably that of the *Kujiki.*
17 North, south, east, west, zenith and nadir.
18 Takama-ga-Hara. Certain commentators consider this to have been Izumi, with the Go-Kinaï (Go-Ki) region: i.e., the five Provinces of Yamato, Yamashiro, Kawachi, Settsu and Izumi. It might more plausibly be identified with Izumo, if on the earth at all. Aston very pertinently asks, "What would those Japanese euhemerists, who think Takama-ga-Hara to be the name of a country, make of a passage like 'reared aloft roof-timbers to the Plain-of-High-Heaven'?" (See p. 111.)
19 Called also "Sky-Uniting-Pillar." Much dispute exists as to its nature and origin. The diagrams of early commentators picture it as a kind of umbilical cord uniting the two bodies, which was later severed.
A Katsura-no Sato. The *Yamashiro-Meïshoshi* quotes, to this effect, a lost fragment of the *Yamashiro-Fudoki.*
20 The Ainu have their own explanation of this separation. "Formerly it was the female luminary that came out at night. But she was so greatly shocked at the immoralities which she saw going on out of doors in the grass, that she exchanged with the male luminary, who, being a man, did not care so much" (Chamberlain, *Ainu Folk-Lore*, vol. XX).
21 *Yoru-no-wosu-Kuni.*
22 *Una-bara.* Some Japanese commentators profess to identify this with Korea, and some incline to think it the R'yuk'yu (Lu Chu) Archipelago. A variant of this myth names it as the portion of Brave-Swift-Impetuous-Male, and another gives him the land of *Amè-ga-shita*, which some believe to have indicated the western San-yo and San-in, or the sixteen provinces that make up the southwestern portion of the Great Island (Hondo).
23 Identified with Yes-or-No-Shins (see p. 62) by the *Izumo-Mondo* and with Sky-August-Bird (see p. 32). The syllables as written are *kuma* (bear) but commentators are agreed that this is an error for *kumo* (cloud).
24 *Panicum italicum.*
25 This food-Kami was anciently the patron deity of sericulture, her worship being perhaps justified in the legend according to which the silkworm was produced from her eyebrows. It is worthy of note, however, that one prefecture (Ibaraki) worships a Chinese deity as patroness of the silk trade. Its shrine, known as Kokagè (Silkworm-Shadow), is dedicated, according to legend, to Princess Konjiki, daughter of King Rinyi of China. Hated by her stepmother, she was exposed to lions and hawks, and buried alive, all of which she survived. Her stepmother at length sent her to sea in a skiff made of mulberry wood, in which she reached the harbor of Toyora-no-Ura in Hitachi

Province, Ibaraki Prefecture. There she died, and from her body was produced the silkworm.

Weston, from the inclusion of the silkworm in the legend of Jewel-of-Storehouse-Rice, postulates a recent origin of the tradition, as in point of fact the silkworm was not introduced into Japan until the third century. But incorporation is common enough in all cosmogonic myth.

[26] *Phaseolus radiatus.*

[27] *Soja clycine.*

[28] It is interesting to note that while the *Kojiki* text gives this reference, it does not give the legend of his natural birth.

[29] *Ne-no kata-tsu Kuni.* Identical with *Yomo-tsu Kuni*, the Land-of-Night. Modern commentators frequently call it Izumo and some confound it with Korea itself. Brinkley holds that *ne*, in archaic Japanese, signified mountain.

[30] His most ancient shrine is probably that on Awaji (My-Shame) Island. The *Engi-Shiki-Jimmeï-Cho-Tochu* says: "Izanagi (He-Who-Invites) in Tsuna District, Awaji Province, is also called Taga." References in the *Daïdo-Ruishu-Sho* and the *Awaji-Jobanso* show that the shrine existed there from very ancient times. The oldest portion of the present structure dates from about 1280.

[A] Omi. Ancient Afumi (*Awa-umi*). This derivation is given in the *Sasanami-Iri-Ayobiki*, a manuscript in the possession of the Asawi family, quoted from the lost *Omi-Fudoki*.

[31] Anciently this ceremony—the festival when the new rice is offered to the imperial ancestors—was threefold, consisting of the *Kannamè-saï (-matsuri)*, the *Onamè-saï (-matsuri)*, and the *Niinamè-saï (-matsuri)* (see p. 178). Nowadays the first is celebrated on October 17, and the last on November 23. They are also known as *Shinjo-saï*.

[B] The *Kogo-Shui.*

[32] "Backward flaying," whatever that was, was accounted a crime in ancient times and was legislated against (see p. 195, n. 85).

[33] Alternative name: Princess-Weaving (Ori-Himè). Motoöri counts this Kami also a Sun-deity. It seems probable that this is true and that she represented Aurora, the sunrise. A temple called Karasu Gozen-no Yashiro (Crow-Temple) at Isè is dedicated to her. The crows give her service. The *Ohotashi* (Geographical Dictionary) says the Tamatsushima Shrine, in Kaïso District, Kii Province, is dedicated to her. The common people mistakenly count this shrine, however, sacred to Lady-of-Robe-Passing (see p. 259).

[34] One version, apparently very ancient and little known, credits him with violating her.

[35] Explained by many modern works, notably the *Kokushi-Riyaku* (History), as an account of the first eclipse of the sun.

[36] *Ama-no-ya-se-kawa.* Motoöri reads *Amè-no-yasu-no-kawa* (Sky-Tranquil-River), the Milky Way.

[37] In the ceremonies at Isè these birds are represented by posturers called Bird-Cry (*Tonako*).

[38] Tokoyo-no Kuni. The *Hitachi-Fudoki* locates this in Hitachi. Aston thinks it the mainland of Asia. Greater probability, however, attaches to the view that it is located in the far southern seas, or Fokien.

[39] *Toriï*: fowl. The so-called "sacred-gate," of wood, stone, or metal, seen nowadays in great numbers before Shinto shrines, Buddhist temples, monu-

ments, or other objects (natural or otherwise) that are accounted sacred. It was originally Shinto but was adopted by Japanese Buddhism in the eighth century, when the two systems were married. The Restoration of *Meïji*, with its revival of "pure Shinto," pronounced the divorce, but the *torii* clung.

[40] Alternative names: Kami-of-One-Eye; Sky-One-Eye. (Ama-tsu-mara. *Mara: membrum virile*). The name, with his connection with the spear (a mark of the cult) indicates this deity's place to have been in the ancient phallus worship. Hirata denies this on the ground that *mara* appears in the names of other deities, but the argument seems more plausible that these others, in origin, were phallic deities also. And Hirata admits that the earlier "jewel-spear" was a phallic emblem.

[41] Motoöri renders it "Stone-Coagulating-Old-Woman." Hirata thinks this Kami a male.

[42] This mirror is the prime symbol of the imperial power and the chief object of worship at the Great Shrine at Isè. According to Aston, it is about eight hands in diameter. It would be interesting to know his authority, as no eye is believed to have seen it since the mythical age. If legend is to be depended upon, it would seem clear that the sacred symbol is round, not octagonal, as it is sometimes represented. It would naturally be sun-shaped. The *Yamato-Himè-no Mikoto Seïki* says, "The *Mafutso-Kagami*, which is an image of Great-Kami-Sky-Shiner and is enshrined at the shrine of Wataraï, in Isè Province, is a *round* mirror" (see, however, p. 73, n. 62).

[43] Alternative names: Jewel-House; *Sky-Shining-Jewel; Fruitful-Jewel.*

Worshiped at the Tama-no Oya Shrine (Suwo Ichi-no Miya) at Osaki, in Saba District, Suwo Province, where he is believed to have resided after his descent with the sky-ancestor, and where one legend says he died. Among the treasures of this shrine is a sword said to have been offered by Keïko-*Tenno*, who visited it when he made his expedition against the Kuma-So of Tsukushi (Kyushu). A place near by, in the ricefields, called Palace-Castle (Miyagi) is supposed to be the site of his temporary palace. Later, according to legend, the Empress Jingu visited the shrine and made an offering of earthenware vessels. Nowadays, at the September festival, a three-legged kettle and some shallow earthenware pans are made by the priests, in which rice is boiled and offered to the deity.

This shrine anciently perpetuated a curious ceremony, whose origin and meaning are now unknown, called Hook-and-Line-Fishing-Kami-Affair (*Tsuri-tare-no Kami-goto*), in which the priests offer to the deity fish caught by themselves from three boats furnished by the villagers of Tajima-ura. This has now been discontinued.

The present structure was built in the Era of *kanen* (1748-1752).

[45] *Shiro*: white; *ha*: feather, leaf. It is abbreviated to *shira*.

[46] This deity is mentioned only in the *Kujiki*.

[47] I identify him with Sky-Eagle-Stander (see p. 5). Curiously enough, the Narrative does not name him as ancestor of the Paper-Mulberry Cloth Clan (*Yu-be*).

[48] *Yu.*

[49] Alternative name: *Sky-Leaf-Elder.* He is said to be enshrined (with Mountain-Gate-Brave) in the Chotori Shrine in R'yusenji-Machi, Shitaya-Ku, Tok'yo.

⁵⁰ Alternative name: Weaving-Lady. This is the weaving-maiden once mentioned later in the Narrative in a song, as the "Weaving-Maiden in the Sky" (see pp. 60 and 140, n. 59). Later a Chinese legend, connected with the star *a Lyrae, (Vega)* with its appropriate festival *Tanabata* was linked to her, and the character for weaver, used for this star, is employed in writing her name. But there seems no reason for assuming, with Aston, that the weaving-maiden herself was taken from the Middle-Kingdom.

The *Engi-Shiki* mentions a shrine dedicated to her in Yamada District, Owari Province.

ᴬ Shokujo-no Kami. The *Hizen-Fudoki* and the *Kogo-Shui*.

⁵¹ Ta-oki-ho-ohi.

⁵² Hiko-Sa-Shiri (-Chi).

⁵³ See p. 10.

⁵⁴ *Cleyera japonica*. The sacred tree of Shinto.

⁵⁵ See p. 10.

⁵⁶ The rendition is a most problematical one. There are almost as many Japanese opinions as there are Japanese authorities, and Chamberlain and Aston differ as widely, as do Hirata and Motoöri. The descent is as given in the genealogies of the Fujiwara and Arakida families.

This deity is worshiped at the Kashima shrines at Kashima in Hitachi Province, at the Kasuga Temple (Kasuga Daim'yojin) at Nara, at Honjo in Settsu Province, and other places (see p. 90, n. 65).

⁵⁷ Nakatomi (Naka-tsu-Omi), Ministers-of-the-Middle, i.e., intercessors or mediators. From the ancestral Kami of the Nakatomi descended Kamatari, the famous minister of Tenji-*Tenno*, who broke the despotic yoke of the Soga line and made possible the great political reforms of the Taïra period. He was given the name of Fujiwara, and his house held the reins of power for nearly four hundred years. Many noble families (including those of Kujo, Konoë and Ichijo) trace to him.

* This deity is mentioned only in the *Kujiki*.

⁵⁹ It is probably from this use of the deer's bone by this deity that the animal has become in a sense sacred to his shrine at Kasuga (Nara).

⁶⁰ Aston and some other authorities believe these blue and white offerings to have been the prototypes of the *goheï* (folded, irregular strips of cut paper, foil, or sheet metal) which are hung in every shrine and play a prominent part in festivals. These are believed to be efficacious in warding off evil, and to the popular mind represent the spirit of the deity itself.

Later Brave-Swift-Impetuous-Male makes like white and blue offerings from his spittle and nasal mucus (see p. 28).

⁶¹ Alternative names: Door-Conceal-Kami; Sky-Rock-Door-Opener; Wondrous-Rock-True-Gate; Fruitful-Rock-True-Gate. Popularly this Kami is often referred to under the alternative name Togakushi (*to*: door; *gakushi*: conceal). There is a shrine erected to him on a mountain of the same name (Togakushi-San) in Shinano Province. He is invoked also at Isè, and (according to the *Wakan-Sansaï-Zuë*) at Shitsu Shrine in Hitachi Province. He is today the Patron-Deity of wrestlers.

ᴬ The *Kogo-Shui*.

⁶² Alternative names: Lord-Sky-Rock-Soil; Sky-Jewel-Owner. This descendant is listed in the lost *Tosa-Fudoki*.

⁶³ Amè-no Uzu-me. Supplicated for honors, posterity, longevity, and protection from evil. Her popular name, Otafuku (Otafuku-men) means "Big Breasts." At the November festival (*Tori-no Machi*) held during the days of the Cock, at the shrines known as O-Tori Jinja, in Tok'yo, her picture is carried about on bamboo rakes. The fête dates from the K'yoho Era (1716-1735).

It is difficult to account for her connection with this festival. According to legend a great eagle appeared at Ajiki, Shimosa Province, east of Edo Bay, to which the people erected a shrine that was later brought to Shitaya District, Edo (modern Tok'yo) and the festival was instituted in its honor. Thus the name *Tori-no Machi* (*Machi* [*Matsuri*]-of-the-Bird). The rakes are testimony of the popular confusion of the word "bird" with that meaning "catch" or "gain." The teeth of the rakes used in the fête are said to be made from the wooden boxes in which coffins are carried to the cemetery.

⁶⁴ *Masaki. Euonymus japonicus.*

⁶⁵ Represented by the courtyard fire (*nihabi*) used in the Shinto ceremonial. This is said to have been the origin of the Japanese custom of lighting a fire when a bride departs from the house of her parents.

⁶⁶ This chronicles the invention of the *koto*, a zither-like instrument six feet long, which when played is set flat upon the floor.

⁶⁷ The first recorded dance. This incident was perpetuated by the *sarumè* (monkey-women) of the ancient Shinto ceremonial, who were attached to the imperial court and performed *saru-maï* (monkey-dances) before the shrines, from which originated the later pantomimic dances called *kagura* (*Kami-kura*), or *Kami-Isami*. The *no* dances, which arose in the fourteenth century, are believed to be an outgrowth of these. Both *kagura* and *no* are features of Shinto festivals today.

⁶⁸ The first record of an utterance under divine inspiration. This is confusing, since she was herself a Kami. Inspiration is common in Shinto, and has given forth many oracles. It is nowadays a possession of the *miko*, female shrine dancers who practice auto-hypnotization (see p. 164, n. 13).

⁶⁹   *Hito, futa, miyo* || *Itsu, muyu, nono,*
          Ya, kokono, tari (to) || *Momo, chi, yorozu.*

ᴬ The authority for this feature of the legend is the *Kogo-Shui*, but the legend deserves a primary place in the Narrative. Hirata assigns it to this episode, and to this day the syllables are sung by priestesses in the *kagura* at Kizuki, in Izumo. Hirata argues that the application of the syllables to the numerals came later, but of course it is far more probable that any song-meaning is a comparatively modern production of forced and artificial translation. He would have us believe the meaning is:

      Lo, ye gods, the rift see || Whence the Kami's splendor
      Shineth for your pleasure. || My charms so excelling!

Aston translates:

          "Majesty appears; hurrah!
          Our hearts are quite satisfied.
          Behold my bosom and thighs!"

⁷⁰ The *Kujiki* (see p. 27, n. 70).

⁷¹ Where this word is employed in the Narrative it is to be understood as

meaning more properly "chanted." The so-called "songs" of the later text are almost without exception of irregular meter, and classify themselves with the rhythmic extempore vocalizations which are characteristically Japanese today.

72 Popular legend ascribes this act to Sky-Hand-Strength-Male, who it is said clapped his hands and stamped his feet before putting forth his strength. Wrestlers, since he is their patron-deity, on entering the ring commemorate his deed in this manner.

73 The *no* which commemorates this myth is invariably performed at night.

74 Making the cave *tabu*. This straw-rope (*shimè-nawa*) is in everyday use in modern Japan to repel evil influences. It is employed in festivals, in the New Year ceremonial, before shrines, during the rite of sword-making, in fire-walking, etc. It is made of rice-straw, twisted backward, i.e., left-wise (because the left is the pure and fortunate side), the lower ends of the straws being left to project here and there in tufts, in the sequence 3, 5, 7. It is often decorated with *goheï* (see p. 26, n. 60). (For its connection with a later legend see p. 41, A.)

It has been plausibly surmised that the *shimè-nawa* has its origin in the custom which has prevailed in many savage tribes of Asia of stretching about their encampments ropes to which are tied fragments of skins or rags, to frighten away night-prowling beasts.

75 Tsukuba. This mountain can be seen from Tok'yo.

76 Togakushi-San, in Shinano Province (eight thousand feet).

A The *Kogo-Shui*.

77 See p. 26, n. 60.

78 Polite form. He was in fact born later.

79 The first invention, says popular legend, of the *hakama*, the wide-girdled trouser worn by both sexes in Japan.

80 Part of the armor worn by a Japanese warrior, designed to protect the arm from the recoil of the bow-string. It was as a rule made of deer-skin and painted in colors, on which was etched a design in India ink. It was worn on the left elbow.

81 This seems to bear out the legend of her digging the three True-Pool-Wells.

82 Alternative names: *Princess-Sea-Horizon-Island: Princess-Tagiri*.

83 Alternative name: *Princess-Good*. Ichiki (Itsuku)-Shima. The modern Miyajima, the Sacred Island in the Inland Sea.

84 Alternative name: *Princess-of-He*. This name (according to the *Munakata-Shaki*) was given her in the lost *Saïkaïdo-Fudoki*.

86 Schwartz (see *Transactions of the Asiatic Society of Japan*, vol. XLI, pt. IV, ap. B, n. 11) prefers Heavenly-Fire-Sun, and Chamberlain translates Heavenly-Great-Wondrous.

88 A ninth is mentioned in the *Kujiki*—Sun's Swift-Sun (see p. 13).

89 *Hachi-o-Ji*.

90 See p. 1.

91 Alternative name: *Feather-Shining-Jewel*. I think there is little doubt that this Kami is to be considered identical with Jewel-Ancestor (see p. 24).

A The *Kujiki*.

92 It is called Kitsuki-no Kami-no Miya.

93 Alternative name: *Resistance-Calmer*. Motoöri, Chamberlain, and others

render this name Brave-Rustic-Illuminator. He is identified with Sky-Cloud-Man (see p. 21), Yes-Or-No-Shins (see p. 62) and Bird-Rock-Camphor-Tree-Boat (see p. 7). He is especially worshiped in the modern village of Takuwa, Ihishi District, Izumo Province. There is a rock beside the Takuwa River which is said to be the stone onto which this Kami descended from the sky.

Kurita identifies this deity with the Sky-Young-Bird (Ama-no Hina Tori) of the *Engi-Shiki-Jinmeïcho*.

The *Izumo-Fudoki* gives him the name Resistance-Calmer. This would seem to be a local appellation of Izumo Province. It is Kurita's rendition, which is assisted, no doubt, by his identification of this deity with Bird-Rock-Camphor-Tree-Boat, who calmed the resistance of Great-Land-Master (see p. 60, *et seq.*).

94 *Wakiko*.
95 *Wakako*.
96 Akito. The *Munakata-Shaki* (quoted in the *Kojiki-Den*).
97 Tsunè Hoshino and Sugè Masatomo agree that this is identical with the Uzankoku (Utsur'yo To) of the *Sangokushiki* (King Chisho of Shiragi: thirteenth year). The modern Takeshima.
A The *Harima-Fudoki*. Rotten straw is used as manure on Japanese paddy-fields. This is known as *tsumikoë* (heaped-manure).
98 Munakata. In the *Engi-Shiki-Jinmeïcho* this shrine is mentioned with annotation, "Three Deities, M'yojin. Great."
B The lost *Saïkaïdo-Fudoki* quoted in the *Kojiki-Den*.
C The *Shaku-Nihongi*, vol. VII (see p. 33). These are not the jewel-necklace given to Great-Sky-Shiner by He-Who-Invites (see p. 20) which she later sends down from the Sky with the Sky-Ancestor (see p. 73).
99 Alternative names: Kami-of-Kara; Kami-of-Merit; Prince-Great House; Kara-Land-That-Big-Arrive. Kara: Okara or Kan (Korean, Imna; Japanese, Mimana). Kara was one of the ancient kingdoms of Korea and at one period gave its name to the entire peninsula. It is only modernly that the word has been used to designate China. This Kami is not identical with the Kami Prince-Great-House previously mentioned (see p. 2). That-Big-Arrive: Idatè. The *Jinmeïcho* says the shrine called Kamu-Kara-Kuni-i-da-te-Jinja is dedicated to Fifty-Brave.

PAGES 33 - 47

1 See p. 33. This descent is given by the *Kujiki*. If Princess-Dog was of the Sun-descent, as the genealogy indicates, and not a Kami of the *Emishi*, the name is a strange one.
2 Unidentified. This is said to have been a place-name, as well as the title of an ancient song, of Shiragi (Silla).
3 *Tori-Kami*.
4 Hi (Hiï). Supposed to have received its name from the first syllable of the name of the Kami Fire-Shining-Swift-Male (see p. 11).
5 Izu-mo. The *Izumo-Fudoki* derives this name from the incident related in Brave-Swift-Impetuous-Male's nuptial song (see p. 36), considering it a corruption of *idè-kumo* (arise, clouds!). Chamberlain would render it Promontory-Bay.

⁶ *Podocarpi.*

⁷ Near Nagano is a tree called Deity-Age-Cherry-Tree (*Jindaï-Zakura*) which legend says was planted by this deity. It is thirty-five feet in circumference and its limbs cover a space of ninety feet. It stands in the grounds of Suwa Shrine at Izumi-daïra.

⁸ See p. 10.

⁹ Alternative names: Foot-Stroke-Hand-Stroke; Master-of-Rice-Temple-Eight-Eared-Kami-of-Refreshment.

¹⁰ Alternative name: Ricefield-Palace-Mistress-Eight-Ears-of-Refreshment.

¹¹ Alternative name: Princess-True-Hair-Touch-Comb-Ricefield. Brinkley translates "Lady Wonderful."

¹² The *Gempeï-Seïsui-ki* (1255?) says this deity was the second son of a dragon-king, who had been expelled from his ancestral palace. This was probably invented with reference to the loss of the sword at the Dan-no Ura sea-fight in 1185 (see p. 71, n. 62), suggesting its return to its original owner. By some later legends the infant ex-emperor, Antoku, lost with the sword in that battle, is regarded as an avatar of the dragon deity.

If one may judge by the "Official Guide to Eastern Asia" (1914) prepared by the Imperial Japanese Government Railways, the view is permitted in Japan that the serpent symbolized a chief of a band of outlaws. That painstaking compilation says, "In a campaign against Yamada-no Orochi, *a rebel chief*, he (Brave-Swift-Impetuous-Male) obtained as a war-trophy a sword known as Murakumo-no Tsurugi, etc." (vol. II, p. lvii). If literalism is to be thrown away, it seems as plausible to consider the monstrous reptilian a voracious river with a many-mouthed delta.

¹³ *Physalis alkekengi.*

¹⁴ *Hi-no-ki.* The *Thuya obtusa.*

¹⁵ As between brother and sister, whatever the real order of birth, the male is given a courtesy-precedence.

ᴬ This is mentioned in the *Azuma-Kagami.*

¹⁶ Archaic *ki.* Modern *sakè.* Sometimes rendered "rice-beer" and Rein calls it "rice-brandy," though the process of *sakè*-making is neither simple brewing nor distillation.

¹⁷ Tradition places this incident on a mountain, back of the Great Shrine of Great-Land-Master at Kizuki (Izumo Province), anciently called Serpent's-Mountain (Ja-no Yama), but now known as Eight-Cloud Mountain (Yakumo-Yama) (see p. 36, n. 25). The slaying of the serpent appears on Japan's paper currency.

Inada-Himè, the Lady of the Eight-Fold-Hedge, is worshiped at Izumo as the Goddess of Love, to whose shrine lovers flock with their petitions from all corners of the Land.

¹⁸ See p. 174, n. 68.

¹⁹ *Kusanagi.* Alternative names: Sword-of-Sky's-Gathering-Clouds; Fly-Cutter; Serpent's-Kara-Blade; Serpent's-Rough-True.

²⁰ Atsusa. Present-day Atsuta, near Nagoya, in Owari Province. This Shrine (see p. 183, n. 13) is dedicated primarily to Mountain-Gate-Brave (Yamato-Dakè), i.e., Little-Pestle (see p. 154) but also to the Sun-Goddess (Great-Sky-Shiner), Brave-Swift-Impetuous-Male, Princess-Miyasu (wife of Mountain-Gate-Brave) and her brother Brave-Ina-Tanè (see p. 174). It was founded

A.D. 86, but the present buildings date only from 1893. Seven subsidiary shrines are grouped about the Great Shrine; of these the most important is the "Eight-Sword-Shrine" (Yatsurugi-Jinja) founded in A.D. 708. The sword "Herb-Queller" is kept in the main shrine, which numbers among its treasures 1,509 objects.

This, next to the Great Shrine in Isè, is the most venerated in all Japan. Portions of its towers, gates, and walls were built by Minamoto Yoritomo, Oda Nobunaga, Toyotomi Hideyoshi, Tokugawa Iyeyasu, Asano Nagamasa, and various others, and many Emperors have especially favored it. A camphor tree in the compound was planted by the late Emperor Yoshihito.

[21] Isonokami (see p. 96, n. 3). Curiously this sword is not specifically called a Kami.

[22] Kibi.

[23] Suga. Some versions give Susa.

[24] The first poem of the typical Japanese tanka form—five syllabic groups, numbering 5, 7, 5, 7, 7 syllables.

[25] The first line of this song (*Yakumo tatsu*) is said to have given the name to Eight-Cloud Mountain (Yakumo Yama) at Kizuki where, according to legend, this incident occurred (see p. 35, n. 17). It is said, also, to have taken place at the village of Sakusa-in-Iü near Matsuë Izumo, on the site of the shrine called Yaëgaki-Jinja. Hence this shrine, as well as that at Kizuki, claims to be the "Shrine of Love and Marriage." It is dedicated to Brave-Swift-Impetuous-Male, Princess-Comb-Ricefield, and their son. The lovesick are carried to it.

[26] The cloud-screen symbolizes the marital relation, the Japanese phrase for the act of cohabitation being "to be in cloud and rain."

[27] This song has been a bone of contention for the commentators. Aston thinks it of far less antiquity than the rest of the legend, declaring that it cannot be older than the sixth or the seventh century. There is, however, no internal evidence of this, and when one takes into account the greater facility with which verse is remembered and the relative longevity of its forms as compared with those of prose, there seems reason for considering the verse-portion to be among the oldest portions of the myth.

[28] Alternative names: Hot-Spring-Mountain-Master-of-Refreshment-Three-Name-Saro-Prince-Mountain-Bamboo-Grass; Attach-Name-Pass-Light-Prince-Eight-Island of Refreshment; Hot-Spring-Mountain-Master-of-Refreshment-Three-Name-Saro-Prince-Eight-Island-Moor.

[29] Motoöri, Hirata and Aston consider the characters phonetic and render this name Heavenly-Brandishing-Prince-Lord.

[30] This, however, is in contradiction with the main story, according to which Prince-Sky-Plenty-Earth-Plenty-High-as-Sky's-Sun-Fire-Ruddy-Plenty was invested with the jewels on his descent from the Sky (see p. 73, n. 61).

[31] Alternative names: Great-Name-Possessor; Great-Thing-Master; Ugly-Male-of-the-Reed-Plain; Spirit-of-the-Living-Land; Kami-of-Eight-Thousand-Spears; Great-Master-of-Things-of-Three-Threads; Great-Country-Jewel; Apparent-Country-Jewel; *Great-Kami-of-Sakè; Great-Sky-Creator-of-the-Beneath; Great-Land-Maker; Great-Ruler-of-Invisible-Things; Great-Kami-of-Rock*; August-Luck-Spirit-August-Wondrous-Spirit (see p. 56, n. 51); *Great-Thing-Master-Wondrous-Dread-Spirit-of-Mountain-Gate*; Thunder (see p. 280).

"Eight-thousand-spears" (*yachihoko*) is a "pillow word" (*makura-kotoba*) (see Introduction, p. XXXI), having probably a phallic signification explained by his numerous amours. For Three-Threads (*Miwa*), see p. 125. Great-Country-Jewel was his particular designation in Yamato, where (by that curious separation of attributes or personification of separate persons in Kami-essence, which is a feature of Shinto) it seems at times almost to designate a separate deity from Great-Land-Master, as in one case where two separate Masters-of-Worship are appointed for the Kami under these two designations. Great-Sky-Creator-of-the Beneath is preferred by the *Kujiki*. The *Kojiki* gives five alternative names and the *Nihongi* seven.

There has been much speculation as to the name Great-Kami-of-Rock, which appears in the *Harima-Fudoki*. That authority states that "in ancient time Princess-Sea-Horizon-Island (an alternative name of Princess-Tagori), the Great Kami of Body-Form (*Munakata*), conceived a child by Great-Kami-of-Rock and settled in Kurota-no Sato, in Harima. The *Kojiki* makes Princess-Tagori the wife of Great-Land-Master (see p. 48). Iida and Kurida agree in identifying the two Kami as one.

This is the Great Deity of Izumo Shinto. His chief shrine is the Izumo-Taïsha, Izumo-no O-Yashiro, or Kizuki-no O-Yashiro, the Great Shrine at the village of Kizuki, in Izumo Province. Its buildings cover an area of nineteen acres. This is the oldest Shinto seat in Japan (see p. 63, n. 3). At Kizuki the Great Deity, once each year, rides on a bronze horse through the town. Popular belief is that any human being he meets is turned into a dog; the people, therefore, upon that day, do not venture out till the equestrian feat is well over.

Outside of Izumo the Land-Master is worshiped especially, in conjunction with Prince-Little-Renowned (see p. 54), at Kanda, Tok'yo. There the pair are believed to protect the worshiper from smallpox. His *nigi-tama* (gentle-spirit) is worshiped at the Shrine of Miwa, in Yamato Province. He was anciently worshiped on Mt. Hiyeï (Hiyeï-Zan) at a shrine known as Hiyoshi-Jinja or Sanno, Hiyeï and Sanno being presumed to be his local appellations. The priests of the Enr'yaku Shrine, which superseded this, formerly carried the image of the deity with them to the capital when they presented imperial petitions.

Hirata identifies this deity with Daikoku-Sama ("Big-Bag"), one of the Seven Deities of Happiness (*Shichi-fuku-jin*), as also does the *Kokoku-Kaïb'-yaku-Yuraïki* (1856) of Shiro G'yosho; the *Wakan-Sanzaï-Zuë*, however, says this belief arose by a confusion of the deity's alternative name, Daïkoku-Shu (the Chinese pronunciation of the characters). This seems likely. Hayashi Razan, the Confucianist, contemporary of Iyeyasu, identified him with Brave-Swift-Impetuous-Male (see p. 19).

By Great Land, modern Shintoists insist, is meant the entire Earth.

The Land-Master is especially worshiped by the modern *Taïsha K'yokwaï* (Great-Shrine-Sect) whose headquarters are at Kizuki. It was founded in 1873 by Baron Sengè Takatomi (Sompuku), eightieth High-Priest of the Great Shrine of Izumo, who inherited this office from his Kami ancestor, Sky-Great-Sun. The *Izumo-Mondo*, the Sect's Credo and Catechism, contains the following:

"By the august permission of Male-Who-Invites, Great-Sky-Shiner assumed control of affairs above the Sky and Brave-Swift-Impetuous-Male of the great Earth. But for a certain reason the latter descended into the Land-of-Roots, where his divine mother dwelt, wherefore the great government of the great Earth descended to his divine son, Great-Land-Master. As this Kami is the ruler of the hidden world, he has in charge the rulership of spirits. The place to which spirits go after death differs according to their virtues and demerits. Some rise to the Sky. Some descend into the Earth. Others must follow the path to the Land-of-Roots, etc. But as all these must dwell in some portion of the hidden world, it behooves us to put trust in Great-Land-Master, the hidden world's ruler."

32 She is cited, at least under this name, only in the *Harima-Fudoki*.
33 According to the *Engi-Shiki*, this Kami is worshiped at Matsu-no Wo, with Great-Mountain-Integrator. Various identifications which suggest themselves are unsatisfactory.
34 Unochi (*ushiyo-mochi*)-Hiko. The father in this place is called Suganè, but the identification seems sufficiently certain (see p. 36, n. 23).
35 Ushigo-no Sato.
A The *Izumo-Fudoki*. It alone makes mention of this last named deity.
36 Alternative names: August-Year; Sky-August-Year.
37 Alternative name: Princess-Great-Furnace. Kami of the Kitchen.
38 Alternative names: Great-Mountain-Top-Master; Great-Kami-of-Hoë-Mountain; Young-Thunder. The second of these names is employed in his worship at the Kuwayama-no Jinja (shrine of Hoë-Mountain) in Tamba Province, which is dedicated to him. The third is a local one in that Province. He is not to be confused with the earlier deity of like name (see p. 15). He is worshiped, according to the *Engi-Shiki*, at Matsuno Wo, where he divides honors with Princess-Ishiki-Island (see p. 38).
39 Hirata identifies this deity with the Kami of the kitchen, above-mentioned.
40 Alternative name: August-Earth-Ancestor.
41 In their composite character. There was anciently a shrine at Kojin-Kawara (Kojin-River-Bed) in K'yoto, called a shrine of Kojin, but believed to enshrine this (or these) Kami. The *Yoshu-Fushi* records that on the last day of every month a *miko* (priestess, or seeress) performed before it a dance which included the ringing of bells in front of a kitchen-range. This was called Kitchen-Range-Evil-Expulsion (*Kamado Harai*). A similar service was performed there also by men wearing carved lion-heads.

The Kojin who has usurped the place of this double deity properly belongs to China, where legend says he was a beggar of Kiangsi. He became cook for a schoolmaster and thus was able to feed a poor pupil who, becoming in later years a high official, decreed worship to his spirit as deity of the kitchen. In Japan he has three faces (whence his popular name Sambo-Kojin) and four arms, and is a terror to the evil-doer. The *enoki* tree is sacred to him. He is not to be confused with Koshin (see p. 71, n. 51).

42 Chika-tsu-Afumi (-Omi).
43 Matsu-no Wo.
44 Kazu-nu. *Kazu* (*Kozu*): the paper mulberry (*Pueraria*).
45 I am of opinion that this is an error which crept into the myth through the use of his local name "Young-Thunder," causing a confusion between this

deity and the later one of like name (Waki-Ikazuchi), whose father Ho-no-Ika-Zuchi (Fire-Thunder) transformed himself into an arrow (see p. 69).
ᴬ The *Kujiki.*
⁴⁶ Previously murdered, according to one legend, by Moon-Darkness-Possessor (or Brave-Swift-Impetuous-Male) (see p. 20).
⁴⁷ Alternative name: Female-Kami-of-Summer.
⁴⁸ Literally, *"Kuni Ko!"*: Country, (be) drawn! The meaning of the expression is much disputed among the older commentators.
⁴⁹ Kizuki.
⁵⁰ The *Jimmeï-Cho* says, "This mountain is now called Sanbeï-San."
⁵¹ Iwami: *Iwa* (rock) *-umi* (sea). The *Wamyosho* derives this name from a rocky range several hundred feet high at Hamada village, borough of Iwami, Naka District.
⁵² Nagahama. Local legend makes the long promontory of Yomi-ga-hama a portion of the rope.
⁵³ Sono.
ᴬ This is without doubt a very ancient tradition, but I have been unable to trace it to any great antiquity in written form. The *Tsurezurè-Gusa* of Yoshida Kenko (1283-1350), in a comment, says, "We can find no document regarding this." References to it, however, are legion. The same author is authority for the statement that in the Namboku-cho Era (1336-1392) one legend placed this gathering of deities at the Great Shrine (Daïjingu) of Isè. But he is the only one to record this, and the legend is now practically unknown. And if this were the true variant, the Great Shrine should have festivals in the tenth month, yet it has none.

During this month, except in Izumo Province, shrine observances are for the most part avoided. Except for one *matsuri* at Sumiyoshi, one at Hirawoka (Kawachi), the Eight Services at Matsu-no Wo and the Kompira Festival in Sanuki Province, I know of none, and the few historical instances of imperial visits to shrines in this month are, generally, unlucky ones.

The *Shirinsäiyosho* of the Priest Yua of Fujisawa (written in the Tenji Era, 1362-1368) says: "When all the Kami come to the shores of the province (Izumo), myriad boats made of bamboo leaves, like those made by children, float on the waves. All the deities gather at Kamiari (Kami-Present) Shrine—they do not go to the Great Shrine. Kamiari Shrine is at Furo-Zan (Not-Grow-Old-Mountain) and its deity is Great-Kami-Sada (-Saruda). This deity is he who conveys their message." According to a document of this shrine, which is in Akita District, it is dedicated to She-Who-Invites.
⁵⁴ See p. 91.
⁵⁵ *Kamina-tsuki.* There are many conflicting derivations of the word. Following are the more usual:
(a) A corruption of *Kami-namè-tsuki* (*Kannamè-tsuki*). (Kami-eat-moon. The *Kannamè* festival falls in this month.)
(b) A contraction from *Kami* (*Kaminari*)-*na* (*nashi*)-*tsuki* (Thunder-without moon. This month has no electric storms.) Derivation of Lord Mito *Chunagon* Mitsukuni *et al.*
(c) From *Kami-na* (*nashi*)-*tsuki.* (Kami-without moon. According to the Urabè Family, the Kami She-Who-Invites died in this month. According to the *Shirin-Säiyasho,* it was the Kami Brave-Swift-Impetuous-Male.)

NOTES: PAGE 40

(d) From *Kami-na* (*nashi*)-*tsuki*. (Kami-without moon. The month has no major shrine festival.)
(e) From *Kami-na* (*nashi*)-*tsuki*. (Kami-without moon. In this month Great-Land-Master ascended to the Sky, leading eight hundred deities.) The Kunimiyatsuko families of Izumo.
(f) From *Kami-na* (*nashi*)-*tsuki*. (Positive-without moon. October is a month in which the negative principle is uppermost. The word *kami* signifies the positive, as the word *oni* (demon) signifies the negative.)
(g) From *Kami-na* (*nashi*)-*tsuki*. (Spirit-without moon. In the tenth month the babe leaves the womb.)
(h) From *Kazu-minè-tsuki*. (Number-all moon. Since ten ends the series of the simple numbers.) The *Wakun-no Shiyori*, the *Shino-no Hashu*, etc.
(i) From *Kami* (*hami*)-*na* (*nashi*)-*tsuki*. (Leaves-without moon. The month of falling leaves.) The *Seïgen-Mondo*.
(j) From *Kami-nari-tsuki*. (Brew-Complete moon. The new *sakè* is brewed in this month.) The *Oho-Oho-Hitsugo*.

⁵⁶ From October 11 to 17 the Kami-Present Festival (*Kamiari Matsuri*) is held. Its great day was anciently the fifteenth (old style). It is celebrated before the two so-called Ju-ku-Sha (Nineteen Shrines) which derive their name from the fact that they have nineteen doors. The visiting Kami are believed to occupy these two shrines during their stay in Izumo. Leech (Hirugo), the first-born of all the deities, identified with Ebisu, is the only one of the Kami who does not attend this assemblage. He, being deaf, cannot hear the summons.

During the period of this *matsuri* (to quote the *Izumo-Ohoyashiroshi*) "the . . . Kunimiyatsuko and superior officers purify themselves and remain at the shrines. During this time feasts, songs and dances are suspended and musical instruments are unhung. The shrines are left unswept. House building and repairing are postponed, the pounding of rice is set aside, and all affairs are carried on with circumspection."

It is popularly believed that during this period of seven days a white snake, about a foot in length, whose head is marked by a brocade-like design which is the crest of the Great Shrine, comes swimming to the shore. It is caught by an aged man who spreads sea-weed on his hands and brings it in this manner to the shrine, whose chief priest puts it in a round box which he deposits in the inner sanctuary. This, which is known as the *Kami-goto* (Kami-ceremony), remains one of the local mysteries. The snake is known as the "dragon-snake" and is believed to come as a messenger from the dragon deity of the sea.

There are many popular stories dealing with this divine assemblage. A typical one (given in the *Izumo-Mondo*) relates that in the Kambun Era (1661-1673) a fleet of one hundred and fifty ships were storm-bound in the tenth month at Fukura. One of them was from Kizuki, and her crew, praying to the Daïm'yojin of the place, were informed that the deity wished to take passage with them to attend the council. They put out and reached home safely, those who attempted to follow being driven back baffled.

The origin of this gathering of the Kami is explained otherwise by various popular legends. The *Tsurezurè-Gusa-Sanko* says they meet as an act of filial piety, in memory of She-Who-Invites, Izumo being the seat of her son, Brave-

Swift-Impetuous-Male. The *Heïkizan-Nichiroku* says it is in respect for the Kami Brave-Awful-Possessing-Male, who descended to Izumo for the conquest of Great-Land-Master. The *Wakan-Sanzaï-Zuë* cites a legend (without authority) to the effect that "Fukusa-no Wo-no Mikoto (probably Brave-Swift-Impetuous-Male) is a Kami of great virtue and can be approached only in the tenth month." The *Gohin-Tsuko* says the Kami go to Izumo in October in accordance with a compact made by Great-Sky-Shiner with the refractory Brave-Swift-Impetuous-Male, by which the latter received the Provinces of Izumo and Iwami and in return "became her son" during one month in each year.

It is the popular belief that the Kami gather to consult Great-Land-Master as to temporal problems. The *Izumo-Mondo* says they come "to report to him, their ruler, the conditions of the invisible administration of the places and lands for which they are responsible, and in particular they treat of the souls under their tutelage (*ujiko-no tamashïi*)."

The peasantry today believe that human romances and marriages are discussed and arranged at this conclave. Thus the *Shin-on-Ki* (Annals of Divine Benevolence), published 1881, records that one Isoshichi, of Mibushi Village, in Iwami Province, in order to gain as husband for his daughter a lad affianced to another, spent a night at the shrine and overheard the council of the Kami when they agreed to his plan. It fell out as he wished, and in gratitude he performed the Thousand-Visits (*Sendo-Maïri*) and had a *kagura* performed at the great *matsuri* of the third month.

57 A Korean name. There was a Mount Shaki in Mimana.
58 Sado-no Kuni. Later named Autumn-Deer Country, after Prince Akika (Autumn-Deer).
59 Tashimi. Corrupted, according to the *Eïfuku*, from Tayui. Kurami is now Shimanè-gori.
60 In this place the Districts of Sanin and Hokuriku are meant.
61 This is Cape Miho in Izumo, not the well-known Miho in Suruga. For a legendary derivation of the name, see p. 47.
62 Yomi (Yumi).
63 The meaning is, set up in a leaning position: leaned.
64 A mere exclamation of relaxation. It has no meaning.
A The *Izumo-Fudoki*.
65 I.e., Brave-Swift-Impetuous-Male (see p. 19, n. 15).
66 Enokuma.
67 I am of opinion that this episode originally belonged to the legend of Brave-Swift-Impetuous-Male's first expulsion from the Sky, when he vainly begged shelter from the Earth-deities (see p. 29).
68 His wife.
A The lost *Bingo-Fudoki*, quoted in the *Shaku-Nihongi*. The legend which the myth mass has incorporated is Indian. The Indian story relates that the Ox-Headed King (Buto) had passed through three cycles of existence and was ruler of the stars. He descended to India to get a wife, and failing there, was directed by a bird to the under-sea dragon-palace. After traveling ten thousand leagues, at sunset, he asked shelter of Kotan, King of southern India, who closed his gate upon him. After his return from his marriage with the

sea-ruler's daughter, he made war on Kotan, slaughtering him and his people, and hewing his body into five pieces.

A variant of the Japanese form of the legend says that Buto bade Somin-Shoraï hang a straw-rope (*shimè-nawa*) across his house-door to insure it against the pestilence. The incident is located at the village of Futami, on the coast of Isè Province, where there is a small temple called Somin-Shoraï-no Yashiro. Jutting from the sea close by are two high rocks called M'yoto-Seki (Married-Rocks), which from time immemorial have been joined together by a cable of tufted straw-rope. These, which embalm the legend, are familiar to tourists and collectors of photographs. Buto (Brave-Swift-Impetuous-Male), according to local tradition, installed the whole company of the Kami in a niche in the seaward side of the larger of these two rocks. The plague-warding *shimè-nawa* used as one of the household decorations for the New Year, suspended across the house-door, is referred by some to this legend, although it had been in existence before (see p. 28, n. 74). These count the pine saplings used in the door decorations, from which the rope is hung, as representing K'yotan-Shoraï's gate.

Those who adopt the Indian detail of the story say that the five fragments of K'yotan-Shoraï's body were offered as a sacrifice at the Five-Festivals (*Go-Sekku*), which is now represented by the food eaten on these occasions: the rice-cakes that are a feature of the *Hina-Zekku* (Doll Festival) standing for the flesh and bones; the rice- and bean-cakes steamed in bamboo-leaves eaten at the *Tango-no Sekku* (Boy Day) the hair; the vermicelli served in the *Tanabata* festival the arteries; and the *sakè* drunk at the Feast-of-the-Chrysanthemum the blood from the liver. This legend, however, is comparatively little known and is not approved by cultured people.

Anesaki thinks Shoraï (which is usually understood to mean "Future") is a corruption of a Korean title.

ᴀ The *Izumo-Fudoki*. This deity is mentioned in no other writing. A note calls him "Possessor of the region of Hata (Field)" and in that neighborhood is one Hata-mura and six Hata-no Sato (see Introduction, p. xxxiii, note *).

69 The horizon. (*Fudoki* and *Engi-Shiki: Toshigoë Matsuri*).

70 Kumanu (Kumano).

71 Rice-leaves: *ina-ba*.

72 There has been much dispute as to the nature of this creature. (See p. 88, n. 50.)

ᴀ The italicized portions here are from the *Inaba-ki*, quoted in the *Chiribukuro*, and the *Chirisoë-Aïnosho*.

73 *Typha japonica*.

74 Alternative name: Hare-Kami. There is a shrine (Hakuto-Jingu) dedicated to this deity near Hogi, Tottori Prefecture (see also p. 62).

75 *Kisa-gahi*, modern *aka-gahi* (*arca inflata*). Motoöri attempts to assign the name to the word *kisagè* (*triturate*), and that of Princess-Clam (*-umugi*) to *omo*: mother, or nurse—a fair example of the frequent methods of the older commentators!

76 Kaka-no Kamusaki (*Kakayaku*: to sparkle).

ᴀ The *Izumo-Fudoki*.

77 The word used in the text is *hohoki*, the modern *uguisu* (*Cettria cantans*).

78 Identified by some with the Kami Fifty-Brave (see p. 33).

⁷⁹ Ki.

⁸⁰ Alternative name: *Princess-Young-Forward.* Suseri-Himè (*Sasu-rahi*: to advance). Motoöri's rendition. The root here is probably the same cited by Mabuchi as employed in the name of Brave-Swift-Impetuous-Male (see p. 22). She is believed to be identical with the Sasura-Himè of certain of the *Norito*, whose habitat is the Land-of-Eternal-Night (Yomi) and who "banishes" the pollutions of which the people are relieved by the ceremony of purification. Brave-Swift-Impetuous-Male was made the deity of the Japanese Hades and his alternative name of "Swift-Banishment-Kami" would seem to strengthen this identification. Hirata, however, regards Sasura-Himè as his "side-spirit," or spiritual double.

Lovers nowadays carry on the person as a charm (known as a "Relation-Binding-Amulet") the names of Great-Land-Master and Princess-Forward, written on a paper which is sealed within a wrapper of red brocade.

⁸¹ *Hachi.* Any of the *vespidae*.

⁸² An arrow with a hollow head which turned on the shaft with a humming sound as it flew. It is generally believed to have been a Chinese invention. Parker claims that it was a device of the Huns.

⁸³ Great-Land-Master has been identified with the deity Daïkoku-Sama (see p. 37, n. 31). This deity is always associated with a rat, which fact may perhaps point back to this legend. If I am not mistaken it was Lafcadio Hearn who first suggested this.

⁸⁴ These expressions *hora-hora* (*hora*: cavern) and *subu-subu* are two of the naive onomatopes in which Japanese abounds.

⁸⁵ *Muku. Aphananthe aspera.*

⁸⁶ Presumably the sword Herb-Queller (see p. 36).

⁸⁷ *Uka* (*Ukagaü*: to inquire) (see p. 45, n. 87). The mountain had lost this name before the ninth century.

⁸⁸ This is by some construed "to make the land," having reference to a continuance of the actual creation by the earlier-born deities. The later use of the words thus translated (*kuni tsukuri*), however, as a mere family name signifying Land-Ruler, seems to forbid this.

ᴬ The *Izumo-Fudoki*.

⁸⁹ The first record of feminine jealousy—frequently to appear later.

⁹⁰ Alternative name: August-Wells-Kami.

⁹¹ Shima-mura. In Harima.

⁹² Uë-to. The *Wamyosho* says "a *uë* was a kind of bamboo basket used to trap fish."

ᴮ The *Harima-Fudoki*.

⁹³ "A bird larger than a pigeon and having a loud and mournful cry" (the *Wakun-Shiwori*). "Like a pheasant, with markings on its head, white wings, and yellow feet, whose flesh is a certain cure for the hiccough" (The *Sankaï-k'yo* [Chinese]). Mabuchi and Dickins think it an owl. Other old books say that its color is reddish-yellow, that it has black stripes on the wings, that it flies by night and remains hidden in the daytime, and that it has a cry like that of an infant.

During the Middle Ages it took on monstrous shape, with the head of a monkey, the body of a tiger, wings of swords, and the tail of a serpent. Such was the prodigy slain by Gensanmi Yorimasa in later legend. The *nuë* of

the Kami-legends, however, is a very harmless bird.
⁹⁴ For a similar song exchange, see p. 313.
⁹⁵ Unnamed in the previous genealogies.
ᴬ The *Izumo-Fudoki*. I am inclined to think the name of this deity a scribe's error for Miho-tsu-Himè (Princess-of-Miho), whom one popular legend makes the wife of Eight-Fold-Thing-Sign-Master. The later legend which makes Princess-of-Miho wife to Great-Land-Master would, however, contradict this.
⁹⁶ See p. 1.
⁹⁷ Alternative name: Princess Ayato. I identify her, on the evidence of like parentage and habitat, with the Princess Ayato of the *Izumo-Fudoki*, although some commentators identify her with Princess-of-Miho. The *Shinr'yo* refers to a Princess-Aya-Kado in Uga-no Sato, who is probably this same person.
⁹⁸ Koï-Yama.
⁹⁹ See p. 45, n. 87.

PAGES 47 - 62

¹ Asayama.
ᴬ The above-italicized portions are from the *Izumo-Fudoki*.
² Literally, according to Motoöri's reading, "fins."
³ As, for example, the wild goose, with whose organized flight the gazer on the autumn sky in Japan is familiar.
⁴ Literally, necks.
⁵ See p. 30.
ᴬ The *Izumo-Fudoki*. In this her name is given as Princess-Ashi, whom I identify with Princess-Tagori on the authority of the *Ashihan-Jinjasho-Jocho*.
⁶ Alternative name: Great-August-Kami-of-Kamo. This Kami has a "resting place" (as one of Great-Land-Master's five "Guest-Kami") at a shrine at Kizuki, Izumo Province.

According to the *Genr'yaku-Sojo-Ki* (records presented to the Emperor in 1184-1185), the *Izumo-no-Oho-Yashiro Shoën-Ki* (Short Account of the Great Shrine of Izumo), etc., this deity is identical with Great-Mountain-Integrator (see p. 39). The name as here given, A-ji-Suki (Shiki)-Taka-Hi-Ko-ne no Kami, has many variations. The *Nihongi* gives Aji-Suki-Taka-Hiko-ne no Kami and A-ji-Su-Ki-ta-ka-hi-ko-ne, the *Izumo-Fudoki* A-ji-su-ki-taka-hi-ko no Mikoto, etc.

⁷ Alternative names: Princess-High; Young-Country-Jewel. The *Jinja-Keïmo* places her shrine (Himekoso-no Jinja) in Higashinari District, in Settsu; the *Chijin-Hongo* says it is the Kumokushi Jinja in Katsurakami District, in Yamato. The *Engi-Shiki* calls it the Ohokurahimè Jinja, and Iïda Takesato is quoted as stating that it is at Kowaï Village, in Kosè, where it is known as Ukuisu Miya. According to other authorities she is enshrined at the Mishima-e Jinja, at Mishima, in Settsu Province, although this is dedicated primarily to Eight-Fold-Thing-Sign-Master.
⁸ Ofuyama.
⁹ Kihè-no Woka.
ᴮ The *Harima-Fudoki*.
¹⁰ Takashi.

¹¹ Literally, to *swing*, as in a cradle.
¹² Sakakami.
¹³ Mitsu.
ᴬ The *Izumo-Fudoki*.
¹⁴ Alternative names: One-Thing-Master; Mulberry-Castle-One-Thing-Master. This deity, I am of opinion, is to be identified with Prince-High-Lord-of-Aji-Spades (see p. 48). Some commentators identify him with Great-Mountain-Integrator (see p. 39).

He is worshiped especially at Futara-Yama (Nikko), at Mount Katsuragi (Yamato) and at the Miho-Shrine known as Seki-no M'yojin, at Miho-no Seki (Miyonoseki) (see p. 53, n. 37). This shrine is dedicated also to Princess-of-Miho who, in this locality, is claimed to have been wife to Eight-Fold-Thing-Sign-Master. They are jointly worshiped as protectors of travelers by sea. Popularly he is identified with the Izumo deity Ebisu (see p. 7, n. 27) patron of fishermen and market-places.

He frequently figures in later folklore. The *Genk'yo-Shakusho* cites one legend which represents him as refusing to obey the orders of the anchorite En-no Shokaku (En-no G'yoja), who had his retreat on Katsuragi Mountain, whereupon the hermit binds him and leaves him in durance at the bottom of a ravine.

¹⁵ Later given as wife to Great-Land-Master (see p. 65). Worshiped at Miho Shrine, at Matsuë, with Eight-Fold-Thing-Sign-Master. People visiting this shrine eat no eggs, believing that the deity's curse will follow a violation of this prohibition, and no farmer in the district raises poultry. The shrine, nowadays very popular, is dedicated to the imperial ancestors. Its chief *matsuri* is on April 7. On this date the image of the deity is placed in a boat surrounded by a high wall of evergreens, with a huge *gohei* rising in the middle. The boat sails out on the lake, and as it approaches the coast a free fight ensues to secure the *gohei*, hundreds of people taking part, many of whom fall into the water in the struggle, although few are drowned. The shrine does a large business in the sale of charms, the most usual of which is a *tamagushi* (a strip of white paper attached to a branch of *sakaki*). This, placed before the family altar, is believed to protect a house against fire and water.

ᴬ This is a very old legend in Izumo. The oldest printed form in which I have found it given in full, however, is the *Izumo-Jinja-Junpäiki* (Narrative of a pilgrimage to the shrines of Izumo), 1833. There is a popular song which states that the deity is prone to anger and is a raiser of storms, so that, in order that he may not be awakened from sleep, cocks are *tabu* there.

Hearn relates that the steamer which plies daily between Matsuë and Miyonoseki (Miho-no seki: Cape Miho) on one occasion met foul weather. The crew insisting that the ship carried something displeasing to Eight-Fold-Thing-Sign-Master, search was made and the brass figure of a cock was found on a passenger's pipe. This was thrown overboard and the storm lifted.

Japanese eat no eggs on the day they visit Miyonoseki. The people of near-by Yasugi, however, who worship the Sign-Master, eat both eggs and chickens, arguing that the best service that can be rendered the deity is the destruction of his enemies, which is reminiscent of the American argument of the prohibition era, of "putting down the demon rum."

¹⁶ These are given in the *Harima-Fudoki* (Aga-no Sato).

¹⁷ Alternative name: *Unu*. *Unu* popularly means "You." But here it is written with characters which signify "Cloud-Thick."
¹⁸ This deity is mentioned only in the *Izumo-Fudoki*. Kurida says there was anciently a shrine dedicated to his worship, but it is now unknown.
¹⁹ The *Fudoki* explains this as an abbreviation of Mita-mochi (August-Rice-field-Possessor).
²⁰ Alternative name: Princess-Sky-Mikatsu. The *Owari-Fudoki* gives it thus.
ᴬ The *Izumo-Fudoki*.
²¹ Alternative name: Princess-Eight-Rivers.
²² *Olca aquifolia*.
²³ See p. 10, n. 62.
²⁴ Alternative name: *Princess-May-Night*.
²⁵ Sayo.
²⁶ Koshibè-mura. Its more ancient name was Mikoshiro-mura. Legend says it was renamed from the fact that folk from Tajima Province passed across it.
²⁷ Izumi-mura.
²⁸ The only known manuscript (the *Harima-Fudoki*), which gives this incident, is worm-eaten at this point and the reading of the character is not certain.
²⁹ Kuwahara-mura.
³⁰ Minashi-kawa.
³¹ Alternative name: *Brave-Rock-Spreader*.
³² *Tsutaki*: wretched, cowardice.
³³ In ancient times the headdress, or hair-ornament (like the beads) appears to have been used in this way as a symbol of authority.
ᴬ The *Harima-Fudoki*.
³⁴ See p. 31.
³⁵ Izumo-no Kami-be.
³⁶ See p. 39.
ᴮ The *Izumo-Fudoki*. Some details are included from records of the Kuwayama-no Jinja (Shrine of Hoë-Mountain) in Tamba Province.
³⁷ On the eastern extremity of Shimamè promontory, Tottori Prefecture, Izumo Province.
³⁸ Native commentators identify the plant named with the *chichi-gusa*. Chamberlain supposes the *Ampelopsis serianaefolia*.
³⁹ The *Kojiki* gives goose. One account in the *Nihongi* says wren. Motoöri prefers to assume a copyist's error and reads silk-worm-moth.
⁴⁰ Alternative names: *Soödo;* Prince-Kuë. *Soödo* (sohotsu: to become wet?) is an obsolete word for scare-crow. This deity is presumed by Tominobu to be the *inventor* of the scarecrow. Motoöri says there is a shrine dedicated to his worship in Noto District, Noto Province.
⁴¹ Yamada.
⁴² *Tenka*. The Chinese gave this designation to their empire, and the Japanese adopted the phrase to designate Japan.
⁴³ Sukuna-bikona. This deity in modern times has become one of the most popular of Japan. He is glorified (see Hirata's *Shizu-no Ihaya*) as the father of medicine, the master of charms and incantations, and the inventor of the art of *sakè*-brewing. Hence in some districts he is worshiped as the god of *sakè* (Kushi-no Kami). Hirata identifies him with the deity Leech (see p. 7) who, in turn, is identified with the deity Ebisu. An attempt has been made

to classify him as an incarnation of Yakushi, the Indian deity of healing. He is worshiped especially (in conjunction with Great-Land-Master) at Kanda, Tok'yo (see p. 37, n. 31).

⁴⁴ It seems possible that this phrase in the ancient text is the basis of the later legend that this Kami was born from the hand of Divine-Producer.

⁴⁵ Shisawa. I render according to the *Harima-Kotohagimè*. The *Wamyosho* regards the word as from *shika-aü* Deer-Meet).

⁴⁶ Yata-Mura.

⁴⁷ Haniyoka.

⁴⁸ Hajika-mura.

ᴀ The *Harima-Fudoki*. A local legend relates that the pair attempted to build in a single night the Cave-Temple of Ishi-no Hoden, but failed, and it remains incomplete.

ʙ The *Iyo-Fudoki*. This spring is that of Dogo, in Iyo Province, a mile from Matsuyama, north of Izumo-Oka (-Hill) and south of the Sagi valley. The *Shaku-Nihongi* states that, "not only was this hot-spring a mysterious thing in the Age of the Kami, but it is a surpassing remedy for the folk when they are sick. Five Sovereigns among others visited it, the Sovereign Keiko and his Empress once, the Sovereign Chiuaï and his Empress once, Shotoku-Taïshi once, the Sovereign Yomeï and his Empress once, the Empress Kok'yaku and the Sovereigns Tenchi and Temmu once." The Emperor Meïji visited it while crown prince. It is also called Sagi-no Yu (Egret's Spring) from a legend of an egret which cured its wounded foot by dipping it in the water.

ᴀ The *Izu-Fudoki*, cited in the *Jinko-Shimboki*. This account specifically excepts from the list the hot spring of Hashiru, which it states was first used in the reign of Gemmeï's Empress (A.D. 715-723).

ʙ The *Engi-Shiki*, Norito No. 10. The Great Purification (*Oho-harahi*).

⁴⁹ See p. 12, n. 68.

⁵⁰ Tokoyo-no Kuni. There is much dispute as to this locality. The "Official Guide to Eastern Asia" (published by the Imperial Japanese Government Railways), says (vol. II, p. 289) "Sukuna-Hiko (i.e., Prince-Little-Renowned), also a member of the imperial family, who had returned from a visit to Tokoyo-no Kuni (*Southern China*)." The same volume, in another reference, says it is "believed to be Korea." This confusion, after all, only echoes the squabbles of the early (and later) commentators.

⁵¹ This is considered not a separate Kami but one of Great-Land-Master's dual manifestations. For a distinction between the "rough" Spirit and the "gentle" or "blessing" Spirit, see p. 203. Many of the deities were thus regarded as a spiritual duality. Hirata defines the rough-spirit as the deity in his character as punisher of the wicked, and the gentle-spirit as the deity in his character as pardoner of the penitent. An incident illustrating this distinction is recorded in the *Izumo-Fudoki*, under a reign later than is covered by the Narrative (Temmu's):

"A daughter of Imaro, Magnate of Katari, was playing at Cape Calm (Yasuki), when a wani did evilly by her. Then her father buried the daughter thus slain at the cape and lamented loudly, shouting to the Sky, leaping from the ground. Standing and sitting he mourned, nor did he leave the place where his daughter was buried. After several days, in his indignation he chose sharp-headed arrows, and sitting in an auspicious place, he prayed: 'Oh you fifteen million Kami of the Sky, and you fifteen million Kami of the Earth, you Kami of three hundred and ninety-nine shrines whose seats are in this Land, and you Kami also of the sea! I beseech your mild-spirits to be tranquil but your harsh-spirits to assemble for that which I, Imaro, request of you. If your spirits do indeed exist, I beseech you to help me in my sorrow, and thus shall I know what Kami are Kami in truth.' Presently more than one hundred wani gathered around another and conducted it beneath the place where Imaro was, where they waited, neither advancing nor withdrawing. Thereon Imaro took a spear and thrust it through the wani's middle, halfway its length, and killed it, after which the one hundred withdrew. Cutting it open he found in it a leg of his daughter, and he hewed the body in pieces and spitted them on skewers by the roadside."

Ordinarily this spiritual distinction is too subtle for the popular comprehension, and except in special cases is disregarded. In the case of Great-Land-Master, above, August-Luck-Spirit-August-Wondrous-Spirit, his own "gentle" double, is unrecognized by him (see p. 126, n. 96). For another name of his "gentle" spirit, see p. 63.

52 Mimoro (Mimuro).
53 See p. 69.
54 See p. 37.
55 The *shitoto* is Temmink's Japanese bunting. The method of augury by use of the kettle-ring is now unknown. According to some commentators the characters here used signify merely "men-festival-makers" and "women-festival-makers."
56 *Karasu-afugi (yakan) Pardathus chinensis*. The leaf of this grass is fan-shaped. At the ceremony of rice-planting at Isè Shrine, a fan made of ground-cypress, decorated with a red ball, is used to fan the rice-plants to ensure their safety from insects.
57 These directions, presumably, indicate operations to be performed against the insects themselves, though the language is ambiguous.
58 *Phalloi*.
59 *Coix lacryma*.
60 This singular remnant of old ritual is preserved in the *Kogo-Shui*. Korea even today employs similar charms; in the eighteenth century King Yung-jong, following the prescribed formula, went into the blighted fields, caught a rice-worm and bit it, saying, "Through thee my folk starve! Get thee gone!" the priests, meanwhile, performing sacrifice to the deities.
61 This is a very curious fragment, suggesting, as it does, fore-knowledge of the imperial grandson's descent.
62 The leaving of beads or jewels was a ruler's notice of ownership.
63 Mori.
A The *Izumo-Fudoki*.
64 In the preceding Narrative, however, Great-Land-Master is said to have reduced these Kami to submission (see p. 57).
65 See p. 5, n. 19.
66 Up to the close of the second world war it was suicidal for a Japanese scholar to suggest that the Kami thus sent from the sky to the earth were spies and envoys despatched from the earlier base of the Sun Folk to Izumo, the earliest of whom were debauched by the local rulers.

⁶⁷ Born from Great-Sky-Shiner's Jewels (see p. 37).
⁶⁸ The first record of a measure of time.
ᴀ The *Engi-Shiki, Norito* No. 27. Festival of New-Food-Offering.
⁶⁹ Ama-no Sagu-Me (Ama-Saku-Me). She is today known as Ama-no Sako (Shaku or Japu) and in popular belief is a perverse spirit which delights in misleading mortals. It is an old folk-belief that the crow builds its nest in the tree-top in a year which is to be one of great storms and in the lower branches in one which is to bring great floods, being advised to this unlucky procedure by Ama-no Shaku, and old women tell children that if they go out at night contrary to the permission of their parents, they will be carried off by the same maleficent being. In some sections the weird evening note of the buff-backed heron (*ama-sagi*) is believed to be its cry. Villagers in some sections give the name Ama-no Shaku to the mountain echo. The name is borne also by a species of water-insect which is found in pools, whose characteristic habit is to swim on the surface belly-up.
⁷⁰ Takatsu.
ʙ The lost *Settsu-Fudoki*, cited in the *Manyo-Daïsho-Ki* and the *Shoku-Karin-R'yosaïshu* (vol. I). I suspect here an ancient connection of this legend with the Kami Bird-Rock-Camphor-Tree-Boat, which some identify with Sky-August-Bird. The latter, it is to be noted, was a son of Sky-Great-Sun. At least the similarity of name is very odd.
⁷¹ See p. 48.
⁷² *Cercidiphyllum japonicum*. The word is believed by some commentators to have meant the cassia.
⁷³ This latter saying is no longer known.
⁷⁴ Alternative names: Swift-Passing-Lord; Tachi-Swift. *Haya-chi*, the whirlwind, Kami of gales. I identify with him the Kami Tachi-Swift, mentioned only in the *Hitachi-Fudoki*, in connection with the legend of Matsusawa (Pine-Swamp) (see p. 67). If we account Swift-Father the whirlwind, this identification seems certain. The close similarity in names, the tree-fork abode, the visitation of disease through blown ordure and the final removal to the windy mountain-top are badges of identification. In some texts of the *Fudoki* the name Tachi-Swift is given as Tachi-Swift-Sun (-*bi*) but the *Kaga* text omits the extra character.
⁷⁵ There seems little doubt that this legend and that of the death and burial of Plenty-Swift-Sun (see p. 66) were in origin identical, if, indeed, the two Kami are not themselves to be identified one with the other.
⁷⁶ They bore food on their heads.
⁷⁷ The broom was to sweep the road before the cavalcade. The description of an Emperor's funeral in an early century of our era shows that in the old Shinto rite broom-bearers led the procession, and a record of the obsequies of a prince imperial in the seventh century shows the custom then prevailed. In the eighteenth century the brooms were sometimes replaced by bundles of reeds.

In China the broom-bearing is symbolic of purification and appears in the ceremonial procession for the expulsion of pestilence.
⁷⁸ The fiber was used, it is believed, to enwrap the corpse in the coffin.
⁷⁹ The kite and crow are added on the authority of Hirata, whose commentary quotes "certain ancient writings," but does not give their names.

⁸⁰ The rice was to regale the guests.
⁸¹ This merry-making by friends was to tempt the dead to return to life. It was a very ancient Japanese custom, supposed by some to have originated in the ceremonies invented to lure the Sun-Goddess from her cave (see p. 27) and obtained into historic times. At the death of the Emperor Ink'yo (reigned 412-453) the king of Silla sent eighty "musicians," who wailed and sang and danced until the day of the provisional interment.
⁸² The suggestion of day and night in the Sky, as on Earth, is a curious feature of the Narrative.
⁸³ Neither mountain nor river can now be identified.
⁸⁴ Minu (Mino).
⁸⁵ See p. 25, n. 50.
⁸⁶ This was the sword with which He-Who-Invites cut off the head of his son, Fire-Shining-Swift-Male (see p. 12).
⁸⁷ This Kami was the boat in which He-Who-Invites and She-Who-Invites set adrift their child Leech (see p. 7).
⁸⁸ Brave-Awful-Possessing-Male's great-nephew (see p. 13).
⁸⁹ Alternative name: Ushi-of-Worship.
⁹⁰ Azuma.
⁹¹ Inasa (*ina-se*: yes or no?) or Itasa. Unidentified.
ᴬ The *Izumo-Fudoki*.
⁹² See p. 49.
⁹³ See p. 40, n. 61.
⁹⁴ His Shrine is at Kizuki-machi, Izumo Province, where he shares honors and worship with the Hare-Kami (see p. 42). He is identified with Sky-Cloud-Man (see p. 21), and with Sky-August-Bird (see p. 32).
⁹⁵ Hirata contends that he drowned himself, and in this is followed by Chamberlain and Brinkley. But the legend of his island residence makes this untenable. It would seem that these commentators were unaware also of the twin festivals of the people of Miho-no Seki (see p. 62, n. 96). He capsized his boat to indicate that he abdicated his fishing-rights, made his farewell, and disappeared in the "fence of green branches," the island habitation he had chosen.

The *Manyoshu-Kogi* (ancient meaning of the *Manyoshu*) in a comment on Lay No. 5 of Bk. I, pt. 1, "On the Three Mountains," by Nakano Ohoë, says that two of the three quarreled as rivals for possession of the third, and the *Kami* Aho, hearing of it, left Izumo with the purpose of reconciling them. On the way he heard that the struggle was ended, and instead of pursuing his journey, *turned his boat bottom-upward* and remained at Inami-no Hara in Harima.

The incident referred to by the Lay is told in the *Harima-Fudoki*. "Abo-no Kami of Izumo Province heard that the three deities of Kagu-Yama, Miminashi, and Unebi, of Yamato Province, were fighting, and set out to admonish them. But when he came to this place (Kami-Oka) he heard that they had finished their quarrel. So he *turned his boat bottom upward* and sat upon it. For this reason the place was named Kami-Oka. The shape of the hill is like that of an overturned boat."

Some Shinto authorities claim that in this gesture of farewell originated the custom of hand-clapping in worship. Shinto worshipers clap four times;

Buddhists strike the palms together only three times—once for each of the Three powers, heaven, earth, and man. Commonly, however, Buddhists rub the palms together soundlessly when praying.

⁹⁶ The former of these festivals is celebrated on April 7, and is called *Aofushi-gaki* (a rude sort of dwelling) day; the other, known as *Morota-bunè* (Morota-boat) day, is celebrated December 3-6. In the latter a sacred boat is employed. The hand-clapping (*Kashiwadè*) which forms a part of the ceremony is said to represent the conversation between Eight-Fold-Thing-Sign-Master and Yes-or-No-Shins.

⁹⁸ Tsubutè-Iwa. This great stone is still pointed out in the water near the Inasa beach. It is now called Chihiki-no Iwa.

⁹⁹ Shina-no (-nu).

^A This legendary derivation is given by Dr. Yoshida Togo on the authority of an ancient manuscript preserved at Futamata Shrine, Tsunu District. *Suwa!* is an exclamation of sudden surprise (English, "There now!").

PAGES 62 - 75

¹ See p. 17, n. 96. Often confounded with Prince-Monkey-Ricefield (see p. 71).
² See p. 55, n. 51.
^A The *Engi-Shiki*, Norito No. 27. Greater Festival of New Food Offering.
³ The great Shinto shrine (see p. 63, n. 3). The Holy of Holies itself is within the edifice called the "Eight-Legged-Gate."

The shrine is believed to have been, originally, three hundred and twenty feet in height, which was later reduced to one hundred and sixty. It is now eighty feet high and thirty-six feet square. The history of its various reërections may be traced in the shrine-maps of the *Kwaneï, Kwambun* and *Meïji* Eras. The present structure dates from 1744.

A legend relates that in 1110 one hundred huge timbers were thrown up by the sea on the beach at Kizuki and a piece of timber one hundred and fifty feet long and fifteen feet thick on the beach near Jogu in Inaba Province. The people tried to cut the great timber into pieces, but found a monster serpent coiled about it and desisted, and those who had attempted to cut it were stricken with illness. Worship being made, the deity of Ubè Shrine delivered an oracle which declared, "When the Great Shrine of Izumo is rebuilt the deities of all Provinces are put in charge of the work by turns. I am this time in charge. The great timber is for myself and my shrine is to be built from it." For this reason the Izumo shrine erected at that time was called Yoriki-no Zoëi (Re-Built of Thrown-Out-Wood).

The best account of the Great Shrine is the *Izumo-Ohokami* of Baron Sengè Takatomi (Sompuku) (1913).

⁴ See p. 32.
⁵ Tatenui.
^A Curiously the *Izumo-Fudoki* is authority for both of these legends.
⁶ According to Motoöri, meaning the long road leading to the Land-of-Night, the Nether-Distant-Land, the Japanese Hades.
⁷ See p. 9.

⁸ If he (Kushi-Ya-Tama-No Kami) is to be identified, as I believe he should be, with the Kami Amè-No-Kushitama-No Mikoto of the *Kujiki*. He is worshiped at the Minato-no Yashiro (Harbor-Shrine) at Izumo.
⁹ Ancient *komo* (Holocholo macrantha), see p. 64, n. 9.
¹⁰ The Izumo priesthood claim still to possess this fire-drill, given to their ancestor (Sky-Great-Sun) by the deity Rare-Offerings (Kushi-Mikenu-no Mikoto) at the order of Great-Sky-Shiner and Brave-Swift-Impetuous-Male, at the Shrine of Kumano.
¹¹ One suspects this old myth is the basis for the legendary connection of a white-deer with the deity at Kashima Shrine (see p. 90, n. 65).
¹² Alternative name: *Dread-Sky-Star* (*Kagayasu*: to shine?). This Kami is one of the only two star-deities mentioned in the entire myth-Narrative. The nightly firmament seems to have attracted little attention from the sun-folk, a testimony, perhaps, to their horror of the dark and worship of the Sun-deity. The only nightly object that impressed itself upon their imagination was the moon. The Chinese system of star divination was not introduced until 675, and then from Korea.
¹³ See p. 25, n. 49.
¹⁴ The *Kunimiyatsuko* families of Izumo.
ᴬ The *Hitachi-Fudoki*.
¹⁵ See p. 49, n. 14.
¹⁶ See p. 24.
¹⁷ The shorter form given in most texts is Amè-no Ho-Akari-no Mikoto. Aston supposes this Kami to have been the sun-deity of the earlier Yamato people (see p. 13, n. 74).
¹⁸ Alternative names: *Princess-Long-Marrow; Princess-Wealth-House; Princess-Fish-Hawk*.
ᴬ The *Kujiki*.
¹⁹ Kata-woka.
²⁰ Commentators say this is the present Mount Kirishima.
ᴮ The *Hitachi-Fudoki*.
²⁴ Alternative name: Princess-Sacred-Stone-of-Mulberry-Castle.
²⁵ Alternative name: Prince-Yoso-of-Oki.
²⁷ Alternative name: *Princess-Sun-Oki*.
²⁸ See p. 116.
²⁹ Takachiho. This is believed by modern scholars to have been, not the modern Takaschiho-Yama, but Kirishima-Yama (see p. 89, n. 54). Ancient arrow-heads, however, have been found on the modern Takachiho.
³⁰ The characters used here mean the *Cercidiphyllum japonicum*.
³¹ Alternative name: *Princess-Kago*. The *Tochu-Engi-Shiki* says her shrine is the Kaminu-Jinja in Hikami District, Tamba Province.
³² Taniha (Tamba).
³³ Alternative names: *Ujimè-of-Hada; Miyoya*. The latter name is employed by the *Kujikongen*.
ᴬ The main features of the above are from the lost *Yamashiro-Fudoki*, quoted in the *Shaku-Nihongi*. Some smaller details are added from the *Jinjako* and the *Kujikongen*. The story is re-echoed in a later one which concerns Great-Land-Master (see p. 111). It is probable that in origin the two legends are identical.

35 According to the *Yucho-Sho* and the *Seïshiroku*. There is an apparent contradiction here in the ancestry, since earlier (see p. 56) we find the same claim made for the Kami August-Luck-Spirit-August-Wondrous-Spirit. I believe this to be correctly explained in a statement in the *Shiki-Den* of Kamo Chomeï, to the effect that the Lower Kamo Shrine (Shimo-Kamo) was originally the Taka-Kamo Shrine at Katsuragi-gori, Yamato Province, and was moved to its present place in 676. That shrine, however, was dedicated to the Kami Eight-Fold-Thing-Sign-Master (son of Great-Land Master) and to Princess-Tagori (who was, by one legend, his mother). This would tend to explain one point of difficulty: the statement of the legend that Prince-High-Lord-of-Aji-Spades (son of Great Land-Master) is known as Great-August-Kami-of-Kamo (see p. 48) and the legendary records which claim both August-Luck-Spirit-August-Wondrous-Spirit, who is regarded as a manifestation or "spiritual double" of Great-Land-Master (see p. 56) and the deity of the present story, Prince-Jewel-Good, as ancestors of the hereditary chiefs of Kamo. If we identify Prince-High-Lord-of-Aji-Spades, however, with Eight-Fold-Thing-Sign-Master (as I have suggested on p. 49, n. 14) and assume his shrine (Taka-Kamo) to have been merged into that at Kamo, it is easy to explain both his appellation Great-August-Kami-of-Kamo and the apparent contradiction as to the ancestry of the Kamo chiefs.

36 *Kamo*. This is a pun, as the character used originally in writing the place-name is not the same which is used for "wild duck." No doubt the wild duck feather is a more recent addition to the legend, given it by the identity of the syllables. At present the character "wild duck" is used in writing the name of the lower shrine (Kamo-no Mioya), though anciently it was used of both, without distinction. The upper shrine is that of the child, and the lower that of the mother. The head priests of both have the same title (*Kamo-no-Agata-no Nushi*).

37 The Thunder-Deity who, in the nether world, sat on the breast of She-Who-Invites (see p. 14). Various Japanese commentators do not admit this identification, but arguments *contra* are weak. The *Shinsho-Sho* identifies this deity with Great-Land-Master, on the strength, no doubt, of that Kami's similar liaison (in the guise of a red arrow) recited in a later legend (see p. 111).

38 By analogy drawn from the use of the same characters in the *Kojiki* and the *Nihongi*, it should be thus written. The *Engi-Shiki*, however, gives both W*aki* and W*aka*.

A The story of the red arrow is given in the preface to the *Hojo-ki* of Kamo Chomeï (twelfth century).

39 The *Nihon-Soshi*. In the multitude of subsidiary shrines it is not possible to identify this so-called "middle shrine" at present. There were anciently many shrines in the group, as may be seen from a record in the *Kokushi-Daïjiten*: "Kami-Kamo Shrine has tens of adjoining shrines such as Ohota, Shirahigè, Niï-miya, Yama-wo, Fuji-wo, Shiro-Taïfu, Fukutoku-sha, Waka-miya, Nara-sha, Hanishi-wo, Kawa-wo, Kata-woka, Su-Wo, Sugino-wo, Sawada, Kajita, and others. Shimo-Kamo has Hiraki, Kawaäï, Kokarasu, Miwi, Kuga, and others."

40 Presumably the child's grandparents, Brave-Horn-Body and Princess-Ikakoya.

⁴¹ Here the myth shows a later incorporation. The Japanese of this early era had no horses.
⁴² The *Kamo-K'yuki*. The festival referred to (*Kamo-no Matsuri*), celebrated at K'yoto in the fourth month on a day of the Cock, is also called *Aöi-Matsuri* (Hollyhock Festival). It is said by some authorities to have originated during the reign of Kimmeï-*Tenno* (540-571) in a plague which the deity sent upon the people, who chose a lucky day in April and offered it worship, running horses and wearing the heads of wild boars; certainly it was already a great festival in the time of Mombu and Gemm'yo (697-748). It is still a major rite of Shinto, and is attended by the high dignitaries of the imperial court, wearing collars of hollyhock leaves, while the townspeople wear head-dresses of the same. Uda-*Tenno* inaugurated a second festival, known as *Kamo-Rinji-no Matsuri*, in the eleventh month.
⁴³ Ono (Wo-nu).
⁴⁴ There were originally two separate Kamo shrines, the Kami Kamo (upper Kamo) and the Shimo Kamo (lower Kamo), both at the village of Kamo, a little to the north of K'yoto.

The Kami Kamo, which is said to have been founded in 677, is dedicated to Waki-Thunder. The *Engi-Shiki* states that it is dedicated also to Brave-Horn-Body. The enclosure covers a space of 28,000 tsubo. The ancient structure was rebuilt by the Tokugawa government in 1628.

The Shimo Kamo is dedicated to the Princess-Jewel-Good of this myth. One old legend affirms that it is dedicated to Jimmu-*Tenno*, but this doubtless is an error, growing from the enshrinement there of his *image* (see p. 113, n. 90).

Ruishu Kokushi says it was anciently known as Tadasu-Ancestral-Forest (Tadasu-Miyoya-no Mori), after Brave-Horn-Body, who settled at Tadasu.

The two shrines were joined (according to the *Shoku-Nihongi*, in 785) under the title Kamo-Jinja (Kamo-Daïjin) and ten years later, when Kwammu-*Tenno* took formal possession of his new capital of Heïan-k'yo (K'yoto), in a special festival he constituted the two deities protectors of the city. Before the juncture, Kami Kamo had been worshiped especially, but later Shimo Kamo would appear to have become the more prominent, since in 810 an imperial princess was appointed to serve it (as *Saï-in*) as at the Great Shrine of Isè, a custom that continued, under succeeding Emperors, till the opening of the thirteenth century. Isè, Hachiman, and Kamo shrines are called "The Three Shrines."

The *Engi-Shiki* styles these deities "The Great Kami." Kami Kamo was given the rank of *Kampeï-Taïsha* (Government-Ceremony-Grand-Shrine) in 1871.
ᴬ The *Engi-Shiki*.
⁴⁵ Matsu-no Wo. A detached shrine of Kamo. This is given on the authority of the *Kujikongen*. There appears here to be record of a very ancient confusion between the deity of Kamo and the Kami Great-Mountain-Integrator (see p. 39) of whom the earlier legend states that he "is also the Kami dwelling at Pine-Tree-Declivity, who was changed into an arrow." Motoöri, in his Commentary on the *Kojiki* (sec. XXIX) cites the Yamashiro legend of Princess-Jewel-Good as applied to this deity. I can find no trace of such a connection beyond the association with him of the arrow and the bare statement that

the red-arrow is worshiped at Matsu-no Wo. Ban Nobutomo (see his *Semi-Ogawa*) attempts to prove that the arrow was originally worshiped at the Otokuni Shrine and was later removed to Matsuno Wo as the spirit (*tama*) of Great-Mountain-Integrator, who there divides honors (according to the *Engi-Shiki*) with the Kami Princess-Ishiki-Island (see p. 38) the daughter of Brave-Swift-Impetuous-Male. In the *Engi* of Kamo Shrine, the arrow is known as *Ninuri-no Ya*.

46 The Mii Shrine of Tadekura-no Sato. This town has now vanished.

A The lost *Yamashiro-Fudoki*.

47 See p. 31.

48 Alternative name: *Great-Army-Master*. There is strong probability that the Kami Sky-Great-Sun and Sky's-Round-Eye were, in origin, identical. The commentators have spent much toil on this abstruse point. The most significant evidence pro is perhaps to be found in a poem of Ohotomo-no Yakamochi (in the *Manyoshu*) which names Ohokumè-mushi (an alternative name of Sky-Round-Eye) as ancestor of the Oho-tomo (see p. 31, n. 86). The *Jimmu-Tennoki* substantiates this view.

The question naturally arises whether this deity is not identical with the "Prince-Eight-Road-Fork" of the *Norito*, one of the three *Kami*-of-Prevention (see p. 16, n. 89).

49 The *Kogo-Shui* says "seven *da*" (one *da*: eight inches).

50 Her popular name, Otafuku (Big-Breasts) is in allusion to this episode (see p. 27, n. 71).

51 Alternative names: Bottom-Touching-August-Spirit; Bubble-Flowering-August-Spirit (see p. 77).

Saruta-Hiko, a deity of the road, in the popular worship often confounded with the deity Dosojin, Great-Elder-of-Come-Not-Place (see p. 17). He is represented as of huge stature with an enormous nose, carrying a long staff and sometimes with many arms. Like the other deity of the highway with whom he is confounded, he is of phallic origin. He is the popular deity of the brothel, which is apt to contain a small shrine in his honor and whose proprietor prays to him for prosperous business. He is also appealed to by one starting on a journey and in certain forms of divination. Images dedicated to him are frequently to be seen at crossroads, where offerings are sometimes made of straw miniature horses, in supplication that the real animals they represent may be kept from sickness and accident. The monkey is his attendant.

He is sometimes known as Koshin. This title springs from a connection in the popular mind between his name, Prince-Monkey-Ricefield (Saru-ta-Hiko) and the Day of the Monkey. The year of the sexagenary cycle, employed by the Old Calendar, in which the two terms of the Ka-no E or Elder-Brother-Metal (*Ko*) and the *Saru* or Monkey (*Shin*) coincide, is called a Koshin year. This is often represented by the ubiquitous monkey-trinity of the *Saru-biki-zaru*, one member of whom covers his eyes, one his ears, and one his mouth, popularly held to exemplify the Buddhist rule-of-conduct, "I see, hear, and speak no evil," but implying the higher truth that the ultimate wisdom cannot be seen, heard, or told. They are designated Mizaru (Non-Seeing Monkey), Kikazaru (Non-Hearing Monkey) and Iwazaru (Non-Speaking Monkey)—a play on words, as *zaru* means either "monkey" or "not." Since

Koshin is a deity of the road, the trio are to be seen over the entrance of the *Umaya* (Stable) at Nikko, which houses the sacred white horse kept for the use of the Kami. The group is one of good omen, however, and nowadays is to be found even on shrine tablets and gravestones. Most travelers are familiar with the carvings at Nikko and some will have seen the painting of "The Three Exemplary Monkeys" by the great Mori Sosen.

The festival of the *Koshin-Machi* (*Matsuri*) was first observed at the imperial palace in 939. It is celebrated on a *Ka-no E Saru day*, and modernly is an all-night feast. Papinot (*Dictionaire: Histoire et Geographie de Japon*) says of it, "Fervent believers spend the whole night *in worshiping a star* which is also called Koshin." This is without foundation.

Prince-Monkey-Ricefield's most famous shrine, at Kasashima near Sendaï, legend says was founded by Mountain-Gate-Brave in the third century B.C. He is worshiped also, jointly with He-Who-Invites and She-Who-Invites, at the shrine of Makibori Village, in Iwadè, and there is a small shrine dedicated to him on Kasuga Hill, at Nara. Enoshima has a small shrine, now deserted, where an image of Koshin is put on view once in every sixty-one years.

As this deity was the guide of the bright Kami in their journey from Sky to Earth, one sect of Shinto (the *Deguchi*) has constituted him guide of the *moral* way from Earth to Heaven, and worships him as the deity of morality and right living.

[52] There is held yearly at Atago Temple (Tok'yo) the *Miko-no Tsukaï*, commonly called *Tengu*, a *matsuri* commemorative of the guiding of the Sky-ancestor by the big-nosed *Kami*. The *Tengu* is a semi-supernatural which, in Japanese popular belief, partakes of the nature of both man and bird. Modern folklore contains a hundred varieties, ranging from the harmless forest creature to the maleficent demon. It is pictured with a bird's bill or an exaggerated nose, the last feature explaining its connection, in the popular fancy, with this Kami, Prince-Monkey-Ricefield. An ancient manuscript commentary on one of the texts observes, "The beings called Tengu were emanations from the excessive ardor of the Kami Brave-Swift-Impetuous-Male" (see p. 19).

[53] Takachiho. The eastern of the two peaks called Kirishima-Yama, on the boundary between H'yuga and Osumi provinces, Island of K'yushu, now bears this name.

[54] Isuzu. The name of the site of the inner shrine at Isè. The *Jimmeï-Hisho* gives the derivation as I-se (Fifty-Shallows). The *Isè-Fudoki* says, "On this day eight men and eight women (i.e., the sacred number who took part in the festival ceremony) gathered here and made merry *in a confused manner* (*isusuki*). Therefore it was named Isuzu."

[55] See p. 24.

[56] See p. 31.

[57] What this was is a subject of much dispute. It was clearly an appurtenance of worship (see p. 141, n. 62).

[58] A *sakaki* tree upon which was hung a mirror. A note in the *Kogo-Shui* says the *torii* is here meant.

[59] This reference is made clear in the Ritual for the Praying-for-Harvest: "The offerings which the Clan of Abstainers, *hanging thick sashes to their weak*

shoulders, have reverently prepared and lifting, bring." (Satow's translation.) The straps were to support the tray which held the offerings.

⁶⁰ See p. 36.

⁶¹ This is the necklace named Storehouse-Shelf-Kami, given her by He-Who-Invites (see p. 4). These ancient jewels (*magatama*), specimens of which have been found in burial mounds, were of stone and comma-shaped. It has been plausibly suggested that they derive their peculiar shape from the custom, obtaining among many savage peoples, of wearing necklaces of the curved claws of animals. The necklace is also called *shinshi*.

⁶² Two of these Three-Sacred-Treasures (*San-shu-no Shinki* or *Mikusa-no Kan-dakara*) the Mirror and the Necklace, with a substitute Sword, are popularly believed still to be preserved, symbols of the imperial power. The Mirror is held to represent knowledge, the Necklace mercy, and the Sword courage.

The Mirror (*Yada-no Kagami*) was kept in the palace where the Emperor lived till the sixth year of Sujin-*Tenno* (92 B.C.) when it was enshrined at Kasanui-mura, Yamato Province (see p. 124, n. 83), the Emperor's virgin daughter being appointed high-priestess of the shrine. Eighty-seven years later, in the twenty-fifth year of Suinin-*Tenno* (5 B.C.), the *Nihongi* relates, "Great-Sky-Shiner—the Mirror, upon which the Emperor was to look as upon herself—" was taken from Princess-Fruitful-Stone-Castle-Iri (Toyo-suki [shiki]-iri-Himè) and given in charge of Princess-Mountain-Gate (Yamato-Himè) who, by imperial order, fixed a new site for its worship at Isè (see p. 148, n. 9). It is preserved there in the inner shrine (Naïgu). According to Murray's *Japan*, it is kept "in a box of chamaecyparis wood, which rests on a low stand covered with a piece of white silk. It is wrapped in a bag of brocade which is never opened or renewed, but when it begins to fall to pieces from age, another bag is put on, so that the actual covering consists of many layers. Over the whole is placed a sort of wooden cage, with ornaments said to be of pure gold, over which again is thrown a cloth of coarse silk falling to the floor on all sides." It has also been stated that the Mirror is wrapped in many layers of white silk, and that each Emperor, during the ceremonies incident to his accession to the throne, adds another silk wrapping (see p. 24, n. 42).

The Mirror of the palace (a duplicate) has had many vicissitudes. In 930 in a thunderstorm, fire broke out in the palace, so that the Emperor (Go-Daïgo-*Tenno*) fled to another refuge. The Mirror, however, says the legend, removed itself, depositing itself in a tree, where a lady of the court later found it. In 960 a fire again consumed the palace, with the shrine (*Kashikodokoro*) in which it is kept. It was found next day, however, bright and unstained in the ashes. The Emperor (Murakami-*Tenno*) recorded in his diary that "None witnessed this miracle but was struck with awe and reverence." In 1005 a fire originated in the *Kashikodokoro* itself, which was wholly consumed without injury to the relic. A court official of the time has recorded that when it was being removed to a cabinet, a light issued from it that dazzled all present. A more severe conflagration in 1040 is said not to have left it unscathed. The original Mirror was in the possession of the seven-year-old ex-Emperor Antoku in the sea fight of Dan-no Ura, in the great struggle between the Taïra and Minamoto clans, in 1185. When the conquering Minamoto took the imperial ship, they attempted to remove it from its locked coffer, but were struck down by its power, senseless and bleeding from the nose.

The Necklace (*Yasakani-no Magatama*) was lost in the same battle. Some authorities hold that it floated and was restored to its place. Better authority says it was not recovered. Satow states that "its place is taken by a stone of three or four inches in diameter, kept in the charge of a special officer who always accompanies the Mikado." I am ignorant of the sources of his information. Its duplicate is preserved in the imperial palace at Tok'yo, with those of the Mirror and Sword which were made in 92 B.C., when the originals were enshrined at Kasanuhi, in Yamato. The copy of the Sword is kept in a room called the "Room of the Sword," adjoining the imperial bedchamber, and that of the Necklace in a room called the "Room of the Jewels."

The Sword (*Murakumo-no Tsurugi*), like the Mirror, had a troublous history. The *Kogo-Shui* cites a legend according to which it was once stolen by a foreign thief who would have fled with it, but found himself unable to leave the shrine enclosure, by which its miracle-working power was demonstrated. It was also lost in the Dan-no Ura sea-fight. Some say it was recovered by a diver. According to another legend, a Buddhist priest of Isè, having supplicated the Great Deity for one thousand days, saw a bright object floating on the sea, which proved to be a sword two feet six inches long. A boy of thirteen, claiming to be inspired, stated this to be the lost sword of the divine regalia. It was not, however, officially recognized by the authorities. Ariga says that in the sixth year of *Bunji* (1190) the sacred sword "Hinogoza" was chosen in its stead, and that twenty years later a revelation of the Great Deity at Isè named one of the blades in its treasury as a perpetual substitute. This is now preserved in the Eight-Sword-Shrine (Yatsurugi-Jinsha) of the Great Shrine (Daïjingu) at Atsuta, in Owari Province (see pp. 36, n. 20, and 173, n. 68). According to others the sword lost at Dan-no Ura was not the sacred emblem, but one called Hiru-no Omashi-no Mitsurugi, made in the reign of Ichijo-*Tenno* (987-1011) by the famous Sukenari and Tomonari, father and son, of Bizen Province. Others say that the blade thus named was a copy made later in the reign of Go-Toba-*Tenno* (1184-1194) by whom it was made one of the Three Great Treasures.

Thus far the records, and it seems doubtful whether anyone now living knows more. Mr. Ukita Goji, one-time counsellor of the Japanese Embassy in London, stated (see *Trans. and Proc. of the Japan Society*, London, vol. VI)—though the sources of his detailed information he did not divulge—that the Mirror is of copper, sixty-four (eight x eight) inches in circumference, about two feet in diameter, and many-sided (see, however, p. 24, n. 42). He exhibited before the Japan Society a miniature model, loand by H.E. Baron Hayashi, the then ambassador. A duplicate of the Mirror, he stated, was hung in the center of the Great Shrine at Isè, where worshipers were permitted to see it. I have found no Japanese who was able to verify this.

The Sword, he stated, was of tempered steel, straight, two-edged, and two feet one inch in length, showing on one side the sun, the six stars of Nanto, the stars of *Su-Jaka* (Red-Sparrow), and the stars of *Seï-R'yu* (Blue-Dragon) and on the other side the moon, the seven stars of *Hoku-to* (Northern Dipper), a portion of Ursa Major, the stars of *Gem-bu* (Black-Tortoise), and the stars of *B'yakko* (White Tiger). If this information is trustworthy, it is interesting to note, as regards the Sword's origin, that these constellations are all in the ancient Chinese zodiac and that before Jimmu-*Tenno* two-edged swords were unknown in the archipelago.

The Necklace, according to the same authority, consists of three crescent-shaped stones, one red, one white, and one blue, of very hard agate, of a variety never found in Japan. He showed also some models in wax, made by himself.

The acquisition of the Three Sacred Treasures is the prime act of the assumption of imperial rule: "Upon the demise of the Emperor, the imperial heir shall ascend the throne and shall acquire the divine treasures of the imperial ancestor."—Article X of the Imperial Court Law (promulgated twenty-second year of *Meiji*, i.e., 1889).

63 There seems no adequate explanation of this, since Great-Land-Master had been given the rule of the nether-world. Motoöri evades the difficulty unsuccessfully by suggesting that the Kami commanded by him were not living deities, but their spirits.

64 See p. 26. The deity is called in this place by his alternative name, Sky-Rock-Door-Opener.

65 See p. 25.

66 The first suggestion of the later shogunate.

67 This word is a "pillow word" coupled with the place name of Isuzu. It has no particular signification.

68 Watarahi (Wataraï).

69 See p. 27, No. 68.

73 Earlier in the Narrative the Kami Again-Forging-Old-Woman is cited as ancestress. It is assumed by some commentators that Sky-Rice-Bran-Door was a son, and by others a father, of this Kami, but I have been unable to find any recorded legends upon which these opinions could be based.

74 This deity is not to be identified with the Kami of like name listed on p. 1.

75 Mikagè (August-Shade). The word was used anciently to denote a ceremonial chaplet. If this deity is not identical with Prince-Sky-Lord (see p. 31) he is presumably his descendant. Sky-Place-True-Seeing also presumably has the same ancestry. On the same evidence Prince-Sky-Jewel-Wondrous is probably a descendant of Sky-Great-Sun.

88 The similarity of name with that of the Kami who had appeared from overseas to assist Great-Land-Master in his making of the land (see p. 54) will be noted. They can be scarcely identical, however. The former is not named in the legends as having left descendants and there is no episode which attaches his activities in especial to Totori.

92 Aston suggests that this Kami was originally a local moon deity.

98 It seems probable that this is not the Sky-smith (see p. 24) but one of his descendants of like name. I identify him with Sky-Soso (see p. 75).

99 The list gives two deities of this name, but they cannot be identical, as different descendants are ascribed to them.

PAGES 76 - 95

1 The Broad-Hat-Sewers claim several ancestors (see p. 75). Similarity of names suggests that some of these Kami are in origin identical.

A The *Kujiki*.

⁴ The lost *H'yuga-Fudoki* specifies this peak (Futa Kami-no Minè). Quoted by the *Shaku-Nihongi*.
⁵ See Analysis of the Narrative: P. 424.
⁶ *Tsuchi-gumo* (ground-spider). The name is believed to have been given by the early Japanese to a tribe of the aboriginal (pre-Ainu) pit-dwellers, the remains of whose semi-underground dwellings are dotted over several provinces. These cave-dwelling savages doubtless overran parts of the country; they were, however, quite distinct from the Ainu (*Emishi*) of the early legends. Some commentators, notably the author of the *Yorimitsu-Ason-Kunko-Zuë* (Pictured Record of the Mighty Deeds of the Noble Yorimitsu), consider the word *Tsuchi-gumo* to have been confused with *tsuchi-gomori* (earth-burrower). Both Dickins and Chamberlain take this view also. The explanation, however, seems superfluous. It would have been quite natural for the early Japanese to call these burrowing savages literally "Ground-Spiders." Later writers use the word loosely as a mere nickname for bandit or bog-trotter. The Emperor Jimmu is later credited with the invention of the name (see p. 106).
⁷ Today uncooked rice is scattered on the waves by junk-men to insure safety at sea, and in a house before child-birth to drive off evil spirits.
ᴬ The lost *H'yuga-Fudoki*.
⁸ Kamu-Hata-Himè. The *Wamyosho* says *kamuta* (kamu-hata?) is "like a brocade, but thin." I am inclined to identify her with Princess-Sky-Hand-Loom (see p. 25). The *Hitachi-Fudoki* cites a shrine known as Nagahata-be-no Yashiro at Ohota-no Sato.
ᴮ The *Hitachi-Fudoki*.
⁹ Some versions give it Nagasa. According to Hirata, the modern Nagasaki.
¹⁰ Alternative names: Thing-Excel-Land-Excel-Long-Narrow; Great-Ocean-Possessor; Old-Man-of-Salt-Sea. The deity of the salt-manufacturers.
¹¹ To be sure, K'yushu (Tsukushi) was *not* directly opposite.
¹² Presumably as his consort.
¹³ The *Jimmeï-Hisho* says, "Of old time the great ancestor fixed upon Swift-Wind-Isè Province and there threw down from the Sky a Sky-Upside-Down-Sword, an Upside-Down-Spear, and a metal bell."
¹⁴ This Kami by some is identified with Great-Sky-Shiner.
¹⁵ Tengashino.
ᴬ The *Sokoku-Fudoki*.
¹⁶ Ancient *hirabu*. *Arca subcrenata*.
¹⁷ Ko. Genus *Pentracta*.
¹⁸ Alternative names: Princess-of-Deer-Reed; Princess-of-Divine-Ata. Ata is in Satsuma Province. She is called, modernly, Sengen or Asama.

According to the sect of Fuji-worshipers founded by Shishi-no Han, this Kami is the especial protector of Mount Fuji. She is popularly called Fuji-Himè and is pictured wearing a large sun-hat and with a branch of flowering wistaria (*fuji*) in her hand. She is reputed to be the creator of flowers, and in ancient times was believed to hover over the mountain summit in a shining cloud, surrounded by hosts of invisible attendants who hurled down all attempting its ascent who were not pure of heart. The Nitta family of Izu Province cherishes a legend that one of its members (Nitta Tadetsunè Shiro, a retainer of Yoritomo) in the twelfth century pursued a boar too far up the mountain and was thrown down by the angry goddess and dashed to pieces. Up to about forty years ago no Nitta ever ascended the peak. Shinto shrines, called Sengen-Jinsha, dedicated to her worship, are found at several places on the mountain, that at Omiya-guchi being the head shrine of the group. There are shrines to this deity in other parts of the country also—notably one at Shizuoka, Suruga Province. This latter, which was earlier dedicated to a deity whose name is not certainly known, is nowadays celebrated for the relics it contains of Yamada Nagamasa, famous for his adventures in Siam in the seventeenth century, who was a great devotee of the Sengen shrines. Fuji mountain itself is popularly worshiped under the name Sengen.

There is a shrine at Yamada, in Isè, near the Naïgu Shrine of the Sun-Goddess, dedicated to the worship of this deity.

[19] See p. 10. By some lesser authorities the name (Princess-Blooming-Tree-Blossom) is given as that of a daughter of Prince-Sky-Plenty-Earth-Plenty-High-as-Sky's-Sun-Fire-Ruddy-Plenty, and not as an alternative name of his wife.

[20] There is a shrine dedicated to her worship on Mount Oyama, in Sagami Province.

[21] In a voluminous note in his commentary on the *Kojiki*, Motoöri says of the "Weaving-Maiden," "All work is aided by singing or beating time, and thus women, when they weave, used the sound made by swinging jewels." The Nineteenth Lay of the *Mayoshu* contains the expression *naru-hata* (-loom) *wotomè* in which the *naru-hata* seems to signify "sounding loom." In the Narrative, also, in Nintoku's reign, the song of the women of Queen-Hen-Bird (Medori) (see p. 228) uses the phrase *Hisa-kata-no Ametanabata* (Long, hard Sky-loom) on which the *Shiki* comments, "In ancient times the loom was worked in time to the jingling of metal chains."

[22] The ancient custom of cohabitation following the betrothal and before marriage. When the Emperor Jimmu chose Princess-Tatara-Startled-Good as Empress, he first visited her at her residence at Saïgawa, Shikami-no Kori, and remained with her one night (see p. 113).

[23] Local legend fixes the place of this birth at Kaseda Village, in Kawa-no Be District, Satsuma Province.

[24] Alternative name: Prince-Sea-Gift. Worshiped anciently at Kawashima Shrine, which, according to the *Engi-Shiki-Jemmeïcho*, was in Hakuri District, Owari Province; the *Shinsen-Minoshi*, however, places it in Mino (Minu) Province. The *Noyoshi-R'yaku* quotes from the *Rikoden* as follows: "K'yusho-Daïmyojinsha was formerly at Kawashima Village, but the shrine was carried away by a flood and stranded here (at Tokuta Village, in Hakuri District). The folk of Kawashima Village asked the folk of Tokuta Village to return it, but they did not, giving them, however, the Hachiman Shrine of Tokuta. So now there is at Kawashima Village a Hachiman shrine which is called the Tokuta Hachiman." This is apparently the Kawashima Shrine referred to in the *Engi-Shiki*, whose deity, however, the *Engi-Shiki-Jemmeïcho* says, is not known. Kurida is authority for the statement that the Kawashima folk worshiped Fire-Glow, and that during the reign of Shomu-*Tenno* (749-758), the deity having performed a miracle, they petitioned the Emperor, as a result of which he was entered upon the government list and worship decreed him.

ᴬ The *Harima-Fudoki*.
²⁵ Alternative names: Prince-Mountain-Gift; Prince-High-As-Sky's-Sun-Great-Rice-Ears-Lord-Ears. These three, Fire-Glow, Fire-Climax and Fire-Fade, Aston supposes, may have originally been names for the rising-, noonday-, and setting-sun. It is well to state that a maze of conflicting variants entangles these three Kami. Scarcely two accounts give their names the same, and many texts give but the first and third.

Fire-Fade's Great Shrine (Kampeï-Taïsha-Kagoshima-Jingu) is at Nishi-Kokubun-Village, in Kagoshima. It is believed to have existed since the time of Jimmu-*Tenno*. During the reign of Kimmeï (540-571) the spirits of the Emperors Chuaï and Ojin and of the Empress Jingu were also enshrined there. The shrine was later known as Osumi-Main-Hachiman-Shrine (since it is the principal shrine of Osumi Province) and the worship of Fire-Fade became forgotten. The ancient name was revived, by imperial decree, in 1874, and in 1895 the shrine was raised to the highest rank.

In ancient times, at Ohoyama village, near Kagoshima, there was celebrated a fishing-festival (*Sunadori-Matsuri*) called by the vulgar *Okiyè-Matsuri* (Ocean-Catching-Festival) which is believed to represent Fire-Fade's return from the sea-palace. During the spring festival of the shrine wooden fish and toilet-caskets (which latter are decorated in designs which suggest a south sea origin) are still sold. The caskets are supposed to be duplicates of one given Fire-Fade by his sea wife on his departure from the sea realm.

According to the *Nihon-Shoki-Tsusho*, Fire-Fade is enshrined also in the N'yoï Shrine, to the south of Sakaï, in Izumi Province. The *Shimiyoshi-K'yuki* says, "He entered the palace of the sea-deity and obtained the two jewels of ebb and flow, after which (since he so *willed*) he was called the Sea-Deity N'yoï-M'yojin (Will-Clear-Deity), but popularly he is called Neü-no Kami or Neï-no Kami by error."

²⁶ See p. 66.
²⁷ Ancient local custom prescribed cutting, with a knife sometimes of bamboo, sometimes of copper. Sometimes the cord was bitten through, like the tails of several breeds of dog in some Occidental countries.
²⁸ The lost *H'yuga-Fudoki* located this place in Ata District, Satsuma Province.
ᴬ The *Chiri-Bukuro*, vol. VI.
²⁹ Near Mukoda, twenty miles north of Kagoshima.
³⁰ The modern Mt. Hashiriyu.
ᴬ The lost *Izu-Fudoki*, quoted in the *Kamakura-Jikki*, vol. III.
³¹ Funa-Oka and Nami-Oka.
³² Mikashiho and Norisè.
ᴮ The *Harima-Fudoki*.
³³ See p. 77.
³⁴ See p. 9. According to later legends the sea-deity's palace was in the Luchu (R'yukyu) Islands.
³⁵ See p. 42, note 72.
³⁶ Presumably skins of the seal.
³⁷ Ancient *tahi*. A species of perch. (*Serranus marginalis*).
³⁸ Kuchimè: "Mouth-Female." This is an old name for the mullet (*nayoshi, bora*).
³⁹ A luck charm whose efficacy is well known to the children of many countries.

⁴⁰ Interesting in its bearing upon one of the world's oldest marine superstitions.
⁴¹ The parturition house has been known to various semi-savage peoples. Childbirth, like menstruation, and to a greater degree, rendered the woman unclean and a special hut was constructed to avoid contamination to the common dwelling. Satow found this practice still obtaining on the Island of Hachi-jo as recently as 1878. Like birth, defloration was anciently considered to carry with it pollution, and a small hut was built in which the bridal pair passed the first night together. According to the author of the *Kogi-Manyoshu*, the custom still prevailed in Tosa in the early part of the last century.
⁴² A legend of the Great Shrine of Kagoshima relates that she gave him a toilet-casket, and the shrine authorities nowadays sell a rough wooden box said to be made after the pattern of the original. One of these in my possession is painted in red and yellow, in a conventional design very similar to south sea patterns.
⁴³ See p. 86.
⁴⁴ The episode of Fire-Glow and Fire-Fade I consider less a memory of the invention of hook-and-line fishing, as Dickins supposes (which would hark back beyond the age of the oldest repeated legend of the world), than an echo of an ancient conquest of a coast of fisher people by a hardier huntsman tribe of the uplands.
⁴⁵ This was performed with certain arbitrary movements of the feet.
⁴⁶ By the *Hayato* (*Hayabito*) (see p. 79, n. *) in the court dances called *kagura* (see p. 27, n. 67). These "falcon men," or "dog men," had particular places in certain ceremonials. They wore red wigs and barked and howled, loudly or in low register, according to an elaborate ritual. They also perpetuated the legend by means of a mime (*Hayato-maï*) in which the drowning struggles and the submersion of their ancestor were depicted. At the date of the writing of the *Nihongi* (A.D. 720) this was still danced before the court. The mime, however, has no part per se in the mystery of the return of the Sun-Goddess, as various writers have assumed. The fact that the two are so closely linked is an indication only of the very early date of the welding of the local and indigenous lore of the land and the vigorous legends of the newcomers. The *Hayato* were formed into an imperial guard probably before the end of the sixth century.
⁴⁷ In Japanese a single word does duty for both fish-hook and needle.
⁴⁸ See p. 68.
⁴⁹ Kanimori (*Kani*: crab).
ᴬ The *Kogo-Shui*.
⁵⁰ See p. 42. This episode stamps it a sea-creature as the Hare-Kami called it, but it could not well be Satow's "sea-shark," as for Princess-Fruitful-Jewel, in her human shape, to turn for the process of parturition into a fish, presupposes that a fish can live on dry land. The one variant, supplied by the *Nihongi*, which states that she turned into a dragon, is palpably a version that has been colored by Chinese influence. Some Japanese scholars even try to make the *wani* a *ship*—according to which ships can speak and sea-going ones measure less than six feet in length! There is a painting by Sensaï Eïtaku which shows Fire-Fade returning from the sea-realm on the back of an unmistakable crocodile, and that would seem to be the best guess. The more modern commentators are a unit for the saurian.

⁵¹ A small shrine (Udo-Jingu) is dedicated to him in a cavern called Udo-no Iwaya on the sea-beach near the little port of Aburatsu, H'yuga, which legend has fixed as the place of his birth. This was the chief shrine of the governmental Bureau of Ceremonies. Old geographical dictionaries mention a village of Udo (Cormorant-Door) in Naka District, seven and a half miles north of Aburatsu. Popular legend states that Hayabi-minè, a peak behind the cavern, is the deity's grave mound. There are ruins of ancient mausolea in the same neighborhood.

⁵² Not to be confounded with the Kami, earlier mentioned, of the same name (see p. 88).

⁵³ Agè-uta.

⁵⁴ One legend says the site of this palace is at Kaseda Village, in Kawanobè District, Satsuma Province.

"Of the palace on Takachiho," says Mr. J. Morris (A *Pilgrimage to Isè: Transactions and Proceedings of the Japan Society* [London], vol. VII, pt. II, 1905-1906), "there is today not a vestige to be found, but it is said that traces are to be discerned of the rocks having been leveled as though for its foundations. At one spot, moreover, there is to be seen a pile of stones, arranged altar fashion, on which rests, or rested not many years ago, an ancient sword, three feet six inches long, thick and broad in the blade, with a massive cylindrical handle, made altogether of bronze, to which vast interest must ever attach, for it is palpably a relic of antiquity, be its true history what it may."

Mr. Morris, however, is in error as to the sword. That relic belongs to the summit of the eastern, lesser peak (Higashi) of Kirishima, also called Taka-Chiho-Dakè and locally O-Takè, which modern scholars hold to have been the real place of the divine descent. Ancient records call it a "sky spear," of bronze, about four and one-half feet long, which was fixed in the ground hilt upward. It was possibly this sword which was shown to Rein, in 1875.

⁵⁵ The first mention of the duration of a life.

⁵⁶ Mabuchi's translation.

⁵⁷ Motoöri (followed by Aston) translates this name August-Food-Master, and the next, Young-August-Food-Master.

⁵⁸ Alternative names: Fruitful-Three-Hairs-Moor; Prince-Assembling-of-Divine-Mountain-Gate (see p. 108). This is the Emperor known canonically as Jimmu-*Tenno*. The period before his accession is called the Deity Age (*Jin-dai* or *Kami-yo*) and was made up of five or seven generations. The *Kojiki* gives seven; all but one version of the *Nihongi* gives five, two at Izumo and three at H'yuga.

⁶⁰ Various popular legends state that he lived from six hundred to nine hundred years.

⁶¹ With this emperor what may be called the human history of the empire begins. The official chronology fixes his birth at 711 B.C. and his accession at 660.

⁶² Jimmu. This was his posthumous name, bestowed upon him many centuries after his death.

There has been much dispute as to the time of the importation of this custom, which is Chinese. Motoöri, in his *Kojikiden*, quotes the *Shiki* of the *Shaku-Nihongi* as testimony to the fact that by an imperial order of the Emperor Kwammu (782-805) certain posthumous names, including that of

Jimmu-*Tenno*, were offered by Afumi-no (Mahito) Mifunè. The *Kwaïfuso*, however, which dates to 751, contains the names of Temmu and Jingu, and a memorial of Hanishi-no Sukunè Michinaga, dated 781, contains that of Suinin. The *Kwaïfuso*, also, was prepared by the same Afumi-no Mifunè. Takesato Iïda's assertion, therefore, that the use of posthumous names antedated the Era of Enr'yaku (782-805) seems to be substantiated. He assigns the beginning of their use to the year 751. Moreover, the phrase "the posthumous name of an Emperor" occurs in the statutes, which were published in 701 and revised seventeen years later, and there are several records of the bestowal of posthumous names upon subjects (notably upon Fujiwara-Fuhito [died, 720]) earlier than Kwammu-*Tenno*.

Though the custom was Chinese, it was not till the time of the Emperor Konin that the names bestowed were in the true Chinese style.

[63] In H'yuga Province.

[64] February 11 (the alleged date of Jimmu's accession) is observed as a national holiday under the name *Kigensetsu*. The Constitution of 1889 was promulgated on this date. April 3 is also sacred to him. He could not have visited Hitachi Province in the first year of his reign as he had not then begun his Yamato campaigns.

[65] Kashima. Hence the name, as popularly applied to the principal deity of the place. The shrine (at Nakamura, Kajima District, Hitachi Province) has, annually, 133 festivals, the most important of which is the *Mi-Kusa*, July 10, Old Calendar. This festival is believed to have been established by the Emperor Ojin, in honor of the victory of his mother, the Empress-Regent, Jingu, over Korea, in which victory the deity assisted. On a hill behind the shrine, known as Mikasa-Yama, the helmet of Brave-Awful-Possessing-Male is said to be buried. The shrine is enclosed in a double deity-fence, and has a temple, a *kagura* (dancing) temple and a tower gate. In ancient times it was rebuilt every twenty-one years, but the custom was abolished in 812. The present building dates to the early part of the seventeenth century.

There is a Kashima shrine also on the Kasuga hill at Nara, said to have been established by the deity while visiting there, the journey having been made on the back of a white deer. In point of fact, it was founded in 710 by Fujiwara Fuhito, of whose family the deity was the protector, on account of the distance from Kashima. This shrine is called Kasuga-Jinja. Hence the name Kasuga-Daïm'yojin as applied to this deity.

A third well-known Kashima shrine is in the village of Honjo, in Settsu Province. The *Settsu Gundan* says that at the beginning of the Era of Kwaneï (1624-1643) a plague prevailed throughout the empire and countless numbers died. An oracle of Kashima-Daïm'yojin bade that his *mikoshi* (carrying-shrine) be borne through all the provinces. The oracle was obeyed and the plague ceased wherever it appeared. The people manifested their joy by leaping and dancing, whence originated the "kashima dancing." When one of the *mikoshi* reached Honjo-Village it became immovable and an oracle declared that the deity desired a shrine to be built on the spot. From this legend arose the custom which still prevails, by which members of the families of those who serve the Kashima shrine go about foretelling the approach of epidemics. This is known as *koroburè* (thing-announcing).

⁶⁶ Hitachi (*hitashi:* soaking). For the legendary origin of the name, see p. 177, n. 85.
⁶⁷ Who had subdued Brave-August-Name-Firm, son of Great-Land-Master.
⁶⁸ See p. 13.
⁶⁹ See p. 26.
⁷⁰ It is at Wakamatsu-mura, Kajima-gun, Ibaraki-ken.
ᴬ This legend is widely distributed in Hitachi Province. It is cited in the *Nihon-Densetsu-Shu* of Dr. Takagi Toshiyo.
⁷¹ *Namazu.* This is the legendary *Jishin-Uwo* (Earthquake-Fish). It is popularly believed to have a body like that of an eel, with flattened head and long feelers on the sides of its mouth, to be 700 miles long and to hold Japan on its back, its head being beneath K'yoto and its tail beneath Awomori, in the north. In some sections its head is believed to be beneath the northern part of the main island of the archipelago (where earthquakes seldomest occur) and its tail beneath the Province of Shinano, midway between K'yoto and Tok'yo. In seashore regions it is believed to be a submarine creature one *ri* (nearly two and one-half miles English) in length, which causes earthquake by striking the ocean-bottom and tidal-waves by arching its back. In some sections local legend substitutes an Earthquake-Beetle (*Jinshin-Mushi*) with a dragon's head, ten spider-legs and a scaly body, which lives deep in the earth.

The *Jinshin-Uwo* is the nearest approach to an earthquake deity that is to be found in Japanese myth. There is a later statement in the Narrative (Empress Suiko's reign, see p. 349) that, following a severe quake which destroyed many houses, orders were given to all districts to sacrifice to the "Kami-of-Earthquake," but the latter is not named and Isè Sadatakè (see his *Afuhizukuri*, 1779) says this deity is unknown.

⁷² This sword is the famous "Rivet-Rock" (Kanamè-ishi [*Kanamè*, fan-nail, literally, "crab's-eye": *ishi*, rock]) about 100 yards south of the shrine. Its rounded knob projects about three feet above the ground. It is mica-granite, similar to a formation found throughout central Japan, and is probably the mark of a prehistoric tomb. It no doubt penetrates to a great depth below the surface, since it is said that Mitsukuni, grandson of Tokugawa Iyeyasu and second *Daïm'yo* of Mito (Mito-no Komon: *Giku*) dug for six days without reaching its root. It is enclosed in a deity-fence and is approached by a *torii*.

According to the *Junikagetsu Na-no Kaï* (Explanation of the Names of the Twelve Months) the modern term is a corruption of *Kami-Namè-Ishi* (Kami-Eat-Stone), the rock being merely the ancient altar upon which the peasants of the locality offered the new rice to the deity of Kashima.

⁷³ In ancient times this was the soldiers' shrine—seeming to argue a general currency for the alternative legend (see p. 61) by which Snap-Master was the Kami originally chosen to pacify the land. The present building was erected in 1700.

The deity of Katori is often pictured holding a gourd, for what reason is not clear. Hence arises the saying, "A gourd against a *namazu* (catfish)," expressive of useless effort.

The main festival of the shrine is on April 14. On this date, in a year of the horse, the deity-car is taken by boat to Kashima, where a joint festival is held. This is an indication of the close historical relation between the two shrines. They are styled the Nidaïsha (Two-Great-Shrines) of Eastern Japan, and a visit to them and to the Ikisu Shrine constitutes the so-called *Sansha-meguri* (three-shrine-pilgrimage).

[74] This name has been the cause of much dispute. Dr. Kurida Hiroshi, compiler of the *Kofudoki-Ichibun-Kosho*, the *H'yochu-Kofudoki* and the *Santeï-Kofudoki-Ichibun*, holds that Katori Shrine was originally dedicated only to Snap-Master and Brave-Awful-Possessing-Male, but that the Fujiwara family (which worshiped Sky-Beckoning-Ancestor-Lord and Princess-Great-Kami as its ancestors and patron deities at Kashima) enshrined also at the latter place Snap-Master and Brave-Awful-Possessing-Male, and that through this Katori came also to worship the two former. Amano Nobukagè, in the *Shiyojiri*, identifies Princess-Great-Kami with Great-Sky-Shiner. According to others she is the deity of the silkworm. Some also claim that she is a deification of the Empress Jingu. Authorities of the middle-ages, also, state that she stands for the three female deities born of the Sun-Goddess in her contest with Brave-Swift-Impetuous-Male (see p. 30). Dr. Kurida's guess is perhaps the best— that she was wife to Sky-Beckoning-Ancestor-Lord. In addition to the Great Shrine at Kashima she is worshiped at Usa Shrine, in Buzen Province, at the Hachiman Shrine at Otokoyama near K'yoto and at the Sumiyoshi shrine in Settsu Province.

Princess-Great-Kami is mentioned in the *Buntoku*, the *Jitsuroku* and the *Engi-Shiki*.

[75] See p. 204.

[76] See p. 200.

[77] Looseness of number is a characteristic feature of Japanese myth. A deity group belonging to a single locality is often considered as but a single person as well as an essence. The *Shin-Kokinshu*, in reference to the shrine of Kamo, says, "He-Who-Invites is only one deity, but his spirit can be invited at Udo and various other places. Kamo-no Taketsu numi-no Mikoto, Tamayori-Himè and Wakiïkazuchi are different deities, but when we speak of 'Kamo-Daïjin,' these three deities become one deity in idea."

[A] This legend is localized in Miyagi Prefecture. The two trees, which are locally called "Tarobo" and "Jirobo," are at the village of Hiraïso, Shizukawa-machi, Motoyoshi-gun. They are about thirty feet in circumference and for centuries have been a landmark for fishermen.

[78] It need scarcely be stated that the chronology of the Deity-Age does not bear the light of critical inquiry. The dates of the *Kojiki* do not agree with those of the *Nihongi* and the latter often contradicts itself. The official Japanese chronology follows sometimes one and sometimes the other and at times rejects both. Motoöri noted a discrepancy of two cycles (one hundred and twenty years) between the Japanese records and responsible Korean annals. The modern rationalistic view concedes ten cycles (six hundred years) to have been interpolated in the first thousand years, and assigns Jimmu-*Tenno's* probable date to the period 61-1 B.C.

[79] See p. 77.

[80] For the longer form of his name, see p. 66.

[81] Kura-Shitakura-Tsukushi-no Kuni.

[A] The *Tsukushi-Fudoki*.

[82] Hito-no Inochi Tsukushi. The *Settsu-Fudoki*.

[83] Tsukuji. The *Shaku-Nihongi*, vol. V.

⁸⁴ The *Tsukushi-no Kuni-no Shiki* gives a simpler derivation: "The shape of the province is like the body of an owl (*tsuku*); therefore the province was named Tsuku."
⁸⁵ Unidentified.
⁸⁷ Enshrined, according to some authorities, in the Ohotori Shrine, at Ohotori-mura, Sempoku District, Izumi. According to others this shrine is dedicated to Little-Pestle (Mountain-Gate-Brave) (see p. 154). Presumably Sky-Seed is enshrined also in the Ohotori Shrine at Meguro, Izumi Province, as it is of the same character as that at Ohotori-mura.
  Beginning as a hereditary title of religious significance, Nakatomi became finally a mere extra family name. In this case probably Sky-Seed counted his descent from the Kami Sky-Beckoning-Ancestor-Lord (see p. 26).
⁸⁸ In Chikuzen Province.
⁸⁹ A province on the upper shore of the Inland Sea.
⁹⁰ Kibi. Anciently it included the provinces of Bingo, Bizen, and Bitchu.
⁹¹ See p. 17, n. 1.
⁹² See p. 25.
ᴬ The *Kujiki*. Presumably he was a son of Brave-Kura-Oki.
⁹³ *Shihi. Quercus cuspidata.*
⁹⁴ Alternative name: Prince-of-Pole. Worshiped at the Awoümi Shrine, in Kambara District, Echigo. Awoümi (Blue-Sea) is mentioned in the *Wamyosho* as a village in this district.
ᴮ The *Settsu-Fudoki*, quoted in the *Jinjakako*, vol. VI. Dickins supposes this legend to preserve the memory of a tarn or pool which was subject to overflow with consequent destructive freshets till the water was led off.
⁹⁵ Naniha (Nani-haya). Naniwa.
⁹⁶ *Tomi* (*tobi: Milvus melanotes*) (see p. 66).
ᴬ This legend is quoted in the *Wakan-Sanzäi-Zuë*, with the prefatory remark, "It is related that. . . ."
⁹⁷ Taketsu (Tadetsu), (Tadè: Polygonum).
⁹⁸ Wo.
⁹⁹ See p. 86.

PAGES   95 - 115

¹ See p. 60.
² Alternative names: Awful-Snap; August-Spirit-of-Snap.
³ Isonokami, in Yamato Province (see p. 36, n. 19). This sword was at first kept at the imperial palace, but was enshrined at Isonokami-Jingu in the first century, in the reign of Sujin-*Tenno*.
⁴ *Yata-garasu*. An effort dating from the ancient *Shiki* (commentary on the *Nihongi*) has been made to identify this Kami with the three-clawed bird (*yang-wu*) of Chinese myth which inhabits the sun. Aston discusses the question in an exhaustive paper on the Sun-Flag of Japan (*Hi-no Maru*) (*Transactions of the Asiatic Society of Japan*, vol. 22, p. 27). The fact that the Crow was sent by the Sun-Goddess is scarcely conclusive, however, and later a normal golden fish-hawk serves as well (see p. 104).
  A fanciful view sees in the eight feet a metaphoric reference to the compass, *yata* signifying the eight segments of the circle.

⁵ See p. 69.
ᴬ The *Seishiroku*, the *Kamo-no Agata-Nushi-no Fu*, etc. Few Japanese commentators are sufficiently rationalistic to accept the supposition that "Eight-Footed-Crow" was merely a surname given by Jimmu to this Kami, previously met with, who served as his guide through Yamato to Yoshino. It is quite in line, however, with the phrase *Yatsu-mimi-no Oji* ("Prince having-eight-ears") applied to Shotoku Taishi, because he could listen to eight persons at one time and reply appropriately to each. Those who insist on the feathered octoped should find it hard to explain the ancestry claimed. Kamo Mabuchi (1697-1769) the scholar, pupil of Kada and master of the great Motoöri, claimed descent from the Crow.

A Shrine in honor of this Kami is mentioned in the *Engi-Shiki*. It is at Uda, in Yamato.
⁶ Alternative name: Road-Minister.
ᴬ The *Kogo-Shui*.
⁷ Yoshino (Yoshi-nu). In Yamato Province.
¹¹ These brothers, with scarcely a doubt, were *Emishi* (see p. 101, n. 28). The modern Ainu word for Elder is *Ekashi*. They were presumably the District Elders.
¹² See p. 71.
¹³ *Phontinia glabra*.
¹⁴ Here probably a larger variety of the *Cleyera japonica* that cannot now be identified.
¹⁵ I.e., tones and gestures indicated the difference in size between woodcock and whale and the portions given to elder and younger wife.
¹⁶ This was the counterpart of the Mount Fragrant (*Kagu*) in the Sky (see p. 12, n. 70).
ᴬ The lost *Iyo-Fudoki*. (Quoted in the *Jindaiki-Koketsu*, vol. III, and the *Shaku-Nihongi*.)
ᴮ The *Senkaku-Manyoshu*.
¹⁷ Yama-to. The Province of the ancient capitals. It very early gave its name to the whole archipelago. The phrase Nihon (Sun-Root), the Niphon of the older map-makers and the modern Nippon, did not come in till the seventh century. Aston places its first use in an elegy on the death of Shotoku-Taishi, by a Korean Buddhist priest in 620. Fifty years later Korea officially employed it, and China also adopted the practice.
¹⁸ The meaning of this phrase is very problematical.
¹⁹ *Maki. Podocarpus macrophylla*.
²⁰ There being, presumably, no women of rank present.
²¹ These are not to be considered Kami.
²² *Turbinidae*.
²³ *Muro*.
²⁴ Not the modern Osaka.
²⁵ See p. 76, n. 6, p. 100, n. 21, and p. 106, n. 49.
²⁶ Mouth:Eater:Man.
²⁷ The line is *Imada-ni mo ako yo*, which Iida Takesato says is for *Ima naritomo ako yo*. He explains it as meaning, "Now is our indignation appeased and we may be at ease."
²⁸ This is the first specific mention in the legends of this people (variously

called *Ebisu, Emisu,* or *Emishi*), who were the ancestors of the present-day Ainu. They are to be distinguished from the Ground-Spiders. The old commentators derive the word from *ebi* (prawn) and suppose the name to have been given them because their hairy faces resembled the crustacean. Modern scholarship, however, is doubtful.

29 Alternative name: Black-Falcon.
30 In order to pass the fiery barrier.
31 According to the *Isè-Fudoki,* a descendant in the twelfth generation of the Kami Mid-Sky-Master (see p. 3).
32 Alternative names: Sacred-Quarter-Brave-Child; Wondrous-Jewel.
33 Here called by his alternative title, Great-Kami-of-Rock.
34 Anashi-no Yashiro.
A The lost *Isè-Fudoki,* quoted in the *Nihon-Shoki-Shikembun.*
35 The *Shojiroku* says this Kami was a descendant of Kami-Tama (Prince Jinreï) of Kudara.
36 Nashi-Mimi.
A The lost *Isè-Fudoki.*
37 The *Gencho-Sankeï-Monogatari* (1480) says, "The mountain in front of the *geku* (outer-shrine) is called Takakura, Takasa-Yama, Higashi-yama or *Karisa*-no Minè." There is a cavern near by which tradition says was used by Prince-of-Isè.
38 Wataraï (*watariäi nu:* cross).
39 The *Rottlera japonica* (or *Catalpa kaempferi*). Some think the cherry tree.
40 The character thus rendered means "small designs" (delineation).
41 Tsuchi-Hashi (Tsugihashi).
B The episode is related in the *Richo-Kanchu* (*Yamato-Himè-no Mikoto-Seïki*).
42 See pp. 66 and 93, n. 96. He was known as Prince-of-Tomi. While the word *tomi* is popularly referred to *tobi* (fish-hawk) in order to fit the accompanying legend of the golden fish-hawk which flew from the Sky to turn the tide of battle for Jimmu-*Tenno,* it is more probably the Ainu word for war, and Tomibiko an Ainu-Japanese combination signifying War-Prince.
43 *Tobi* (see p. 93, n. 96). In this legend is to be found the origin of the present-day Japanese order of the Golden-Kite. This decoration is given for military services.
44 Tobi-Mura. Corrupted now to Tomi-mura.
45 Chamberlain states that the genealogy of this deity is unknown. The *Kujiki,* however, makes it clear that he is to be identified with Sky-Shining-Earth-Shining-Sky's-Fire-Ruddy-Comb-Jewel-Plenty-Swift-Sun (see p. 66).
46 See p. 66.
47 So the *Kojiki* version, but the weight of legend is on the other side.
48 This sword is not designated as a Kami. It is not to be confounded, therefore, with the blade Thrust-Snap, worshiped at Isonokami (see p. 96, n. 3) or with the Kami Brave-Awful-Possessing-Male, two of whose alternative names are Brave-Snap and Fruitful-Snap (see p. 13).
A The *Kujiki.*
49 See pp. 76, n. 6 and 101, n. 25.
A The lost *Settsu-Fudoki,* cited by the *Nihon-Yakuki,* vol. IX.
50 The use of this word in this connection is difficult to explain, unless it is

a mere coincidence of sound. *Hafuri* (*Hofuri*) was a lesser grade of Shinto priest. The term could scarcely be applied to the Ground-Spiders unless we are to conceive of them as possessing a kind of priesthood of their own. Even so, it seems unlikely that the Sun-folk would have applied the term to them.

51 *Kazu.* The paper mulberry. Chamberlain derives the name from *kuzu* (*Pueraria, dolichos*).

52 Kazuraki. In Yamato Province.

53 Kashiwabara (Kashibara), in Yamato. Most historians count this as the first capital of the empire.

54 *Mihogi-tama.*

55 *Ara-taë.* A rough weave carrying blue stripes. The *Kogo-Shui-Shochu* derives the word from *ara* (rough)-*hadaë* (surface).

56 The grand festival that follows a coronation.

57 Fusa-no Kuni, *fusa* being the ancient name for hemp. Hence the present Province of Kazusa (Upper-Hemp) and Shimosa (Lower-Hemp).

58 Notably the *Jinno-Jitsuroku.*

59 See p. 28.

60 See p. 2, n. 51.

61 Wigazuri.

62 I.e., by the Sun-folk. Satow has elaborated this theory of sky and earth offenses. He concludes that as for long the two races did not intermingle and "as they (the Sun-folk) came from beyond the sea, where sea and sky touch, they acquired a celestial character," which attached to their derelictions. Florenz, on the other hand, holds that the sky-sins came to mean those which affected the community as such and were thus "apt to bring down upon them the wrath of the gods," while earth-sins were "trespasses against the welfare of individuals." These theories seem, however, an evasion of the obvious, since the later Narrative gives lists of both classes (see p. 195).

63 For this Cremony of Purification.

64 See p. 77.

▲ The *Kogo-Shui.*

65 Apparently these were charms or incantations.

66 See p. 7.

67 This reference alone bespeaks for this legend an origin far later than the rest of this cycle.

▲ Quoted in the *Wakan-Sanzai-Zuë.*

68 See p. 26. The *Shojiroku* gives this ancestry.

69 This legend's exact place in the Narrative is not certain. But a comparison of the genealogies of the Fujiwara and Arakida families seems to show the descent as given, from Sky-Beckoning-Ancestor-Lord, who accompanied the divine ancestor from the Sky. Jimmu-*Tenno* was the sixth generation from the Sun-Goddess. The *Seïshiroku,* however, claims Ikatomi to have been the eleventh generation.

I consider him identical with Iga-tsu-Omi (Magnate-of-Iga) mentioned in fragments of the lost *Iga-Fudoki,* who was probably a descendant of Princess-of-Aga, daughter of Prince-Monkey-Ricefield. According to the previous Narrative, she governed the Province of Aga (Iga), a small portion of the ancient Province of Isè (see p. 77).

Joly says he was "a fisherman named Hakurio": I do not know upon what authority.

^A What is perhaps the original *Fudoki* form of this legend appears in the *Teïwo-Hennen-Ki* (723 A.D.). The *Kofudoki-Ichibun-Kosho* so credits it, under the heading "Omi Province; Small Bay of Ikako (Ikako-no Woë) introducing it with the phrase "The *Kuroden* (old legend) says." Its antiquity in the archipelago cannot be doubted.

The *Tango-Fudoki* places the episode at the borough of Hiji, Tamba District, Tango Province. Other variants locate it in Yamato Province, on the mountain called Ama-no Kagu Yama. The *Tango-Fudoki* gives a number of versions.

^B This version is the subject of a thousand poems and literary references to it are legion. In modern variants the maiden of the feather-robe is often confused with the Buddhist angelic being called the *Tennin*, which is female and, in Chinese tradition, wears a robe of the five heavenly colors. One of the most pleasant of the *No*, The *Ha-Goromo* (Feather-Robe), is founded on the story. It is attributed to Seämi, but it is no doubt much older, being of the most primitive type, scarcely more than a pantomime, with words largely irrelevant. It has been attractively translated by Chamberlain. There is often served in Japan a kind of sweet cake called *hagoromo*, generally placed on trays which, in allusion to the legend, are painted with pine trees.

One tradition says that in the reign of Temmu-*Tenno*, fortieth sovereign, a number of these sky-maidens descended and danced before him at Yoshino, "fluttering their celestial sleeves five times," and that this was the origin of the court dance known as *Gosetchi*. (This dance is still performed. I saw it at K'yoto, at the "Coronation" of the late emperor, by five girls of ancient noble families selected for their beauty. These were afterward besieged with proffers of marriage.) In modern times, however, the legend attaches itself to Cape Miho, in Suruga Province. A half mile from the Miho Shrine (at Miho-no Matsubara, on the Bay of Suruga) on the sandy beach, grows what is known as the *Hagoromo-no matsu* (Feather-Robe-Pine) on which the bird-maiden is said to have hung her robe. This tree, which is of fantastic shape, one hundred feet in height and more than ten feet in circumference, is said to have been planted some two centuries ago, to take the place of the decayed and fallen original. A remnant of the robe of feathers is currently believed to be preserved in the shrine.

In the R'yuk'yu (Lu Chu) Islands version of the legend, a poor peasant sees a light coming from his well and a woman bathing in it, with her clothing "as ruddy as the sunset" hanging on a near-by pine tree. In displeasure at her fouling the water, he takes her robe. When she upbraids him, seeing her beauty he begs her to marry him. She consents and bears him a daughter and a son. When the girl is nine years old, on a day when her husband is away, she dons her ruddy dress and flies to a tree branch, where she bids the lad, "obey your father and forget me," and takes flight. The king endows the peasant with land, gives the lad schooling, and has the girl brought up in the palace.

Bronislaw Pilsudski, in his "Materials for the Study of the Ainu Language and Folklore," gives an interesting Ainu version.

[70] Manawi.

⁷¹ Hiji-Yama. Dr. Yoshida says the present shrine of Hi-numa-manawi is at Tojotomè, Gokason, and that the name of Hishi (Yama) is a corruption of Hiji. The *Jingi-Shir'yo* says it is now called Fuji-Koso Daim'yojin (Wistaria-Shrine Great-Deity) and is dedicated to Female-of-Fruitful-Food.

⁷² Hijikata.

⁷³ Hinuma. The *Yamato-Himè-Seïki* says it was so named after the well dried up. The *Engi-Shiki* refers to the deity Female-of-Fruitful-Food as "the Kami who settles at Hinuma Manawi-no Hara."

⁷⁴ Arashiyo-mura.

⁷⁵ Nakiki-no mura.

⁷⁶ *Planeca japonica.*

⁷⁷ Nagu-no mura.

⁷⁸ I am of opinion that she is to be identified with Jewel-of-Storehouse-Rice (see p. 9).

She is popularly known as Toyukè-Daïjin, and is deity of food and clothing, having in her charge all the fruits of the earth. She is a patron-deity of farmers. She was at first enshrined at Manaï (Tamba Province) but was removed to the outer shrine (*Gegu*) of Yamada, Isè, in the year 478, in the reign of Yur'yaku-*Tenno*, in accordance with a revelation of the Sun-Goddess to the Emperor (see p. 287).

An eruption of a volcano in Dewa, in the ninth century, was declared to be due to the anger of this Kami at the pollution by dead bodies of the mountain streams. She was prayed to anciently by agriculturists, and modernly is worshiped by all classes and besought for every imaginable favor.

ᴬ This version is given in the *Gengen-Shu*, the *Kojiki-Urogaki-Sho*, the *Manyoshu-Chukaï*, and the *Ruishu-Jingihongen*.

⁷⁹ Mishima. In Settsu Province.

⁸⁰ Miwa.

⁸¹ Alternative name: Princess-Seya-Tatara.

⁸² Alternative names: Princess-Tatara-Startled-Good-Princess; Princess-Tatara-Fifty-Bells-Princess.

⁸³ I.e., tattooed (?). This is Chamberlain's hazard at a most abstruse problem in translation.

⁸⁴ These two lines, which the best commentators read

Amè tsutsu
Chidori mashitoto

are hopelessly unintelligible—except to Motoöri and Moribè, whose renditions are very far apart.

⁸⁵ See p. 78, n. 22.

⁸⁶ According to another account this song was in two portions, the first by him and the second by her, and they were sung on the morning after they had first slept together, when they "made their toilet with the dewdrops from the red lilies (*saëgusa*)." The incident is the legendary origin of the *utagaï* (song-hedge) (see p. 179, n. 95).

⁸⁹ Alternative name: Brave-Lagoon-River-Ears.

⁹⁰ The *Zokusetsu* states that his image was later enshrined at Shimo-Kamo in Yamashiro Province (see p. 70, n. 44).

⁹¹ Suizeï.

⁹² See p. 90.

⁹³ According to the *Nihongi,* he was over a hundred years old.
⁹⁴ Probably a descendant of, but not identical with, the Kami of the same name who, one legend says, descended with the Sky-Grandchild (see p. 75, n. 98).
⁹⁵ Katawoka.
⁹⁶ Alternative name: Princess-Eighty-Bells-Good.
⁹⁷ Tsukida, in Yamato Province.
⁹⁸ Annei.
⁹⁹ Katashiho (Katashiha). In Kawachi Province.

PAGES 115 - 127

¹ Alternative names: Princess-Nuna-So; Princess-of-River; Princess-Hoï.
³ This word occurs only in the *Kojiki.* It is practically synonymous with prince.
⁵ Alternative name: Princess-Pure-of-the-Land-of-Great-Mountain-Gate.
⁶ Itoku.
⁷ In Yamato Province.
⁸ Alternative names: Princess-Rice Sun; Princess-Izumi.
¹⁰ Manago (Masago) in Yamato Province.
¹¹ Kosho.
¹² See p. 69. According to the previous genealogy, she was his niece.
¹⁴ In Yamato Province.
¹⁵ Koän.
¹⁶ Motoöri's translation.
¹⁷ In Yamato Province.
¹⁸ Koreï.
¹⁹ Kuroda. In Yamato Province.
²⁰ Alternative name: Princess-Hoso.
²⁴ Alternative name: Prince-of-Great-Maise.
²⁶ See p. 115, note 3.
ᴬ The *Harima-Fudoki.*
ᴮ Lake Biwa (lute). This legend is very ancient, and one of the most widely distributed of the archipelago, although the earliest known references to Fuji-San are in the eighth century *Manyoshu.* The date 285 B.C. is given by the *Wakan-Sanzaï-Zuë* (1714), which calls the story "absurd." The legend states that the mountain appeared in a Monkey hour of a Monkey day of a Monkey month of a Monkey year. Anciently women were permitted to ascend it only in a so-called *Koshin* year (the fifty-seventh year of the sexagenary cycle, when *Ko* of the Stem Circle combines with *Shin* (Monkey) of the Sign Circle: *Ka-no E Saru*). The Monkey, also, is the attendant of the Kami Koshin (Prince-Monkey-Ricefield). Since the earth that formed the mountain came from Omi Province, its people, before ascending it, fasted and mortified the flesh during only seven days instead of the usual one hundred. Similarly legend says that Lake Ikada in K'yushu was formed by an eruption of Mt. Kaïbun-takè, and Lake Suwa by an eruption of Mt. Asama.

There is another ancient tradition to the effect that Fuji Mountain sprang up at the concussion caused by the fall of a giant tree, whose bole was many *ri* in diameter, whose top reached the sky, and whose branches covered all

Japan. This tree is said to have been called *Fusao-Buko*. Since the Chinese pronunciation of the characters with which "Fusao" is written is "Fusang," some writers claim that the Middle Kingdom's "Fusang" was an appellation of Japan—"the land of the *Fusao-Buko*." This, of course, is not to be taken seriously.

Chamberlain sees in the story "an echo of some early eruption, which resulted in the formation, not indeed of Lake Biwa, but of one of the numerous small lakes at the foot of the mountain."

[27] In Yamato Province.
[28] Kogen.
[29] This apparent contradiction leads most translators to render these names "Beautiful-Frightening-Female (Male)," but the character is the same as that used with the "Ugly-Females-of-the-Land-of-Night," etc., where the meaning is obvious.
[32] Alternative name: *Princess-Toto-Mountain-Gate*.
[34] Alternative name: Princess-Kagè.
[36] This Japanese Methuselah reappears in the Narrative for many generations. Some accounts represent him as attaining to the age of three hundred and sixty years. He is worshiped at the Ubi-Jinja (-Shrine) at Kokubu-Mura, Inaba Province, and at Sumiyoshi (Suminoë), Settsu Province. There is also a shrine (Takè-Uchi-Jinja) dedicated to him on the edge of Matsuë, Izumo.
[37] The Emperor Keïko.
[38] The name as given in this variant (the *Nihongi*) is Princess-Glow, but the two are no doubt identical.
[45] Nintoku (see p. 228).
[46] See p. 213.
[50] *Tsurugi*. In Yamato Province (see p. 218, n. 41).
[51] Kaïkwa. The word properly indicates the culture that produces civilization.
[58] Alternative name: Princess-Sahaji.
[60] Local legend relates that this deity descended upon Mount Mikami, Omi Province, in the reign of Koreï-*Tenno*. There is a shrine dedicated to him in Mikami-Village, at the mountain's foot.
[61] Chika-tsu-Omi.
[63] Alternative name: King-Prince-Yatsuri-Iri.
[64] This was his mother's name. Its use here is probably a scribe's error.
[65] Alternative name: Prince-Mountain-Gate-Old-Stone-Castle-Tomi-Tomi-Fruitful-Asakura-Dawn-Rise.
[67] Alternative name: Princess-Younger.
[69] Later to become the Empress Jingu.
[70] Alternative names: Princess-Jewel; Princess-Yoto.
[73] In Yamato Province.
[74] Sujin.
[75] Shiki. In Yamato Province.
[77] High Priestess of the Great Shrine (see p. 124).
[78] Alternative name: Lady-Yasaka-Furu-Ama.
[80] In this place the Kami is called by his alternative name of Great-Country-Jewel.
[81] Kami-of-One-Eye. An alternative name of the Kami Sky-Mara (see p. 24), who forged the original Mirror.

⁸² There are two ceremonies attending the installation. The one indicated here is the *real* ceremony. The official "Coronation" comes sometimes many months later.
ᴬ The *Kogo-Shui*.
⁸³ Kasanui.
⁸⁴ See p. 123. According to the *Shinto-M'yomoku-Ruïju-Sho*, the female thus selected (by the tortoise-shell divination) does not menstruate and attains to great age.
⁸⁵ The words are:

Miya bito-no || Oho yosu gara-ni
Isa tohoshi.
Yuki-no yoroshi mo || Oho yosu gara-ni.

corrupted to

Miyabito-no || Oho yoso goromo
Hiza tohoshi.
Yuki-no yoroshi mo || Ohoyoso goromo.

ᴮ The *Kogo-Shui*.
⁸⁶ See page 118.
⁸⁹ This is Great-Land-Master under another of his designations (see p. 37, n. 31).
⁹⁰ In Izumi Province.
⁹¹ Not the Kami Brave-Awful-Possessing-Male (see p. 13).
⁹² Alternative name: Wondrous-Sun-Kata-Sky-Kata.
⁹³ Alternative name: Brave-Chinu-Ears.
⁹⁴ Great-Land-Master's alternative name is "Great-Master-of-Things-of-Three-Threads" (see p. 37, n. 31).
⁹⁵ For a similar amour of Great-Land-Master's, see p. 111.
⁹⁶ See p. 56, n. 51, and p. 126, n. 96. Pointing to an early lack of understanding, in the popular mind, of the distinction between the deity and his spiritual "double."
⁹⁷ Mimuro.
⁹⁸ Motoöri's rendition.
⁹⁹ In Yamato Province.

PAGES 127 - 147

¹ Oho-Zaka. On the border between Yamato and Kawachi Provinces.
² Kashima (see p. 90, n. 65).
³ An alternative name of Great-Land-Master.
⁴ The original contains an untranslatable pun on the brewer's name (Ikui) and the word *ikuhisa* ("how long ago").
⁵ Asakina. It is difficult to identify this mountain. The *Higo-Kembun-Zakki* says, "At Fukuwara-Mura, Masuki District, there is a mountain called Asaki. On it is a cavern whose walls are of stone, and which is covered with a huge rock thirty or forty *shaku* long. The cavern is not an artificial one, and is like a stone castle, capable of holding some tens of persons. At present the locality is deserted. The natives call it '*Oni's* (demon's) cavern.' There is no other place called Asaki in the country."
⁶ Alternative name: *Land-of-Fire-Brave-Male-Pure*.
⁷ Later it was divided into the two provinces of Hizen and Higo.

ᴬ The lost *Higo-Fudoki* and *Hizen-Fudoki*.
⁹ Aba. Probably the present Ukishima (Floating-Island) in Shida District. The latter has an Aba-M'yojin shrine which is dedicated to Great-Land-Master. Aba-no Sato (Village-of-Easily) also has a shrine to this deity, whose spirit is called by the vulgar Ohosuji-M'yojin.
¹⁰ No doubt these are *Emishi* names, as the characters used are evidently phonetic.
¹¹ Presumably down a river.
¹² Hats?
¹³ Songs of Mount Kishima.
ᴬ The *Hitachi-Fudoki*.
¹⁴ Probably a descendant of Young-Prince-Brave-Prince-of-Maise, of four generations earlier (see p. 117).
¹⁵ Taniha (Tamba). Taniwa.
¹⁶ Yamashiro.
¹⁷ There are two versions of this song in the *Nihongi* and a third in the *Kojiki*. They have been combined in this.
¹⁸ See p. 119.
¹⁹ The first instance of Black-Magic. For a later one see p. 142.
²¹ Nara (*Narasu*: to make level).
²² Idomi.
²³ Izumi. A corruption of Idomi.
²⁴ The first arrow shot in a battle was dedicated with special prayers.
²⁵ Kuso-bakama. Corrupted to Kusuba.
²⁶ Kawara.
²⁷ Lit. "finger-work."
ᴬ The *Kogo-Shui*.
²⁸ See p. 33 *et. seq.*
²⁹ See p. 76.
³⁰ *Kuji (Kujira)*.
³¹ Evidently the Kami's descendant, as she had resided at Three-Moors (see p. 76, n. B).
³² Presumably because of the bird's color.
ᴬ The *Hitachi-Fudoki*.
³³ See p. 118.
³⁴ See p. 63, n. 3.
³⁷ The *Kokuzo-Honki* calls him Uji-Oya (Clan-Ancestor).
³⁸ Mo.
³⁹ See p. 170.
⁴⁰ Sonaka-Shichi (Korean: *Cheulchi*). A note in the commentaries says that Arashito (Korean: Arasateung) was the name of the Kara king. Aston thinks it the name of some Korean rank or office. Some texts give Arishito.
⁴¹ See p. 140, n. 58.
⁴² Tsunoga (*tsuno-nuka*). Corrupted now to Tsuruga. In Echizen Province.
⁴³ Anato (modern Choshu).
⁴⁴ See p. 92.
⁴⁵ Suïnin.
⁴⁶ See p. 135. In this place he is called simply "Prince-Saho."
⁴⁷ Alternative name: Prince-Mountain-Gate-Sun-Facing-Brave-Sun-Facing.

⁴⁸ *Ina-ki* (rice-castle). The word later came to be applied to the imperial granaries.
⁴⁹ Only four are mentioned in the genealogies.
⁵⁰ See p. 121.
⁵¹ Kara. (See p. 33).
⁵² A kingdom of Korea adjoining Great Kara.
⁵³ This is a singular statement as to which Japanese commentators are silent. There had been exchange, to be sure, with the mainland before this time— an embassy had come from Mimana in the preceding reign—but the claim of this Kami to descent from the Sun-deities is no doubt an addition that the legend acquired after being transplanted to Japanese soil.
⁵⁴ Uzu-kawa.
⁵⁵ Called here by his alternative name, Ugly-Male-of-the-Reed-Plain (see p. 37, n. 31). This Kami, however, had long since abdicated and retired (see p. 63). This confusion would seem to indicate that the coming of Sky-Sun-Spear belonged in fact to a far earlier epoch.
ᴬ A lost portion of the *Harima-Fudoki*, quoted in the *Shaku-Nihongi*.
⁵⁶ Ubaï-tani.
⁵⁷ The modern Kozu.
⁵⁸ See p. 135. No doubt these two legends are in origin identical.
ᴬ The lost *Settsu-Fudoki*, quoted in the *Senkaku-Manyoshu*, vol. II.
⁵⁹ Presumably Kaseko erected a Himegoso shrine at Tamura, and a second shrine to the Weaving-Maiden (Princess-Sky-Hand-Loom) (see p. 32). There would seem to be an attempt here to identify these two Kami, but there is no further record of such an identity. It is, however, curious that an ox is connected with both versions of the legend of this Kami's arrival in the archipelago, and that the lover of the Weaving-Maiden of Chinese myth (to whom Princess-Sky-Hand-Loom was finally linked) was an ox-herd (see p. 25, n. 50).
ᴮ The *Hizen-Fudoki*.
⁶¹ Alternative name: Noble-of-Nagaōchi. Presumably to be identified with Nagaōchi-of-Ichishi (see p. 182).
⁶² See p. 72, n. 57. In this place the expression has been variously rendered as "shrine," "offering," and even "bear's claws."
⁶³ Izushi (Izu-ishi).
⁶⁴ I.e., fill a jar as tall as himself.
⁶⁵ Black-magic (see p. 142).
⁶⁷ The Empress Jingu.
⁶⁸ In Yamato Province.
⁶⁹ Alternative name: Breast-Bone (*Kanesumè*).
⁷⁰ He is called in this place Noble-of-Nagaōchi, but the identity seems clear, as he is named here also as ancestor of the Governors of Yamato (see p. 141, n. 61).
⁷¹ The word thus rendered is used to describe all personal meetings without weapons. The ancient trial of prowess corresponded to the Greek παγκρατιον or the modern French *savate*. It had no similarity to modern Japanese wrestling.
⁷² See p. 138.
⁷³ This daughter is not mentioned in the genealogy previously given.
⁷⁴ Sagariki (Sugari-ki).

⁷⁵ Ochi-kuni. Unidentified.
⁷⁷ High Priestess of the Great Shrine of Isè (see pp. 147 and 168).
⁷⁸ I suspect some confusion between the genealogies here and those given previously of Suïnin-*Tenno*.
⁸⁰ Supposed to be the sea of Blood-Lagoon mentioned on p. 94.
⁸¹ Sayama. In Kawachi Province.
⁸² Tosori. In Izumi Province.
⁸⁴ The list gives only nine, unless the River-Head Clan is to be considered the tenth.
⁸⁵ This princess is not named in the preceding genealogy.
⁸⁶ Oho-Muraji. Here the word *muraji* has lost its original signification and become merely a portion of the proper name.
⁸⁷ See p. 138.
⁸⁸ Alternative name: Sky-Yukawa-Tana.
⁸⁹ Wanami (unidentified).
⁹⁰ The whole incident is suspiciously reminiscent of the tale told of Prince-High-Lord-of-Aji-Spades (see p. 48).
⁹¹ Tottori (Tori-tori). Later this was to become a surname (see p. 145, n. 91).
⁹² In ancient times the same word did duty for both "temple" and "palace," the emperor's residence being the chief place of worship of the deities.
⁹³ Tagu.
⁹⁴ Tachi (Takè)-waka. His name is not given.
⁹⁵ Hanaka.
ᴬ The lost *Fudoki* of Owari Province, quoted by the *Shaku-Nihongi*, vol. X.
⁹⁶ See p. 122, n. 65.
⁹⁷ Amakashi (see p. 257).
⁹⁹ Ajimasa.

PAGES 147 - 161

¹ See p. 123.
² See p. 144, n. 1.
³ Robes used in the ceremonial worship.
⁴ Oümi.
⁵ Isè is on the upper part of the Isuzu River, in Wataraï District, Isè Province.
ᴬ The *Jimmeï-Hisho*.
⁶ See p. 102.
⁷ Kurida supposes him to have been a native deity of Iga Province.
ᴮ The lost *Isè-Fudoki*, quoted in the *Nihon-Shoki-Shikembun*.
⁸ Totomi (Totsu-Afumi). Ancient accounts state that there was a fresh-water lake there, but that in the Era of Meïyo (1492-1501) an earthquake demolished the neck of land between it and the sea.
ᴬ This record of her wanderings is given in the *Daïjingu-Shozatsuji-Ki* (1093).
⁹ According to the Narrative, the shrine was founded a few years before the beginning of the Christian era, and has been in existence, therefore, over nineteen centuries. In ancient times it was called Wataraï-no Miya, Iso-no Miya, Uji-Miya, or Sakukushiro Isuzu-no Miya. It is now called Isè-Daïjingu or simply Daïjingu. It consists of two portions, the Toyoükè Daïjingu or Gegu (outer shrine) and the Kwo Daïjingu, or Naïgu (inner shrine), which latter

the imperial court calls Sob'yo (Ancestral Hall). The two together are called Nisho-Daïjingu (Two-Place-Great-Shrine).

It is dedicated to Great-Sky-Shiner, but the deities Sky-Beckoning-Ancestor-Lord and Great-Jewel are also worshipped there, the *tama* or spirit of the first residing in a bow, and that of the second in a sword. Offerings cannot be made to the shrine at will, even that of a crown-prince requiring a special imperial sanction, and it is considered as too sacred to possess a rank. No one may enter its compound bearing a weapon, nor is a Buddhist priest admitted.

The structure is of plain wood, roofed with rice-straw thatch, in striking contrast to the ornate temples of Buddhism, every detail of the original being faithfully copied (it is wholly rebuilt every twenty years) so as to preserve the simplicity of architecture of the early era. During the periodic reconstruction of the building a sacred structure called *Kuroki-goten* is erected in the compound of the outer shrine as a temporary abode (the Shinto Holy-of-Holies) of the sacred Mirror. The sanctuary containing the latter is then removed from the inner shrine and placed in a small portable shrine of wood covered with white silk brocade, which is then transferred with solemn ceremonies to the *Kuroki-goten*. This takes place at night, the cortege being lighted by two torches borne by ritualists, and the relic being guarded by Shinto priests and a guard of honor composed of imperial troops, a representative of the Emperor, distinguished nobles and officials. A subsequent ceremony consoles the spirit of the deity. The year in which this periodic removal occurs is known as *shikinen*, and the official day of the ceremonial removal is September 15.

Its main festivals are on February 12 (*Tashigoi*), April 14 and September 14 (*Kamumiso*), June 17 (*Tsukinamè*), and September 17 (*Kamunamè*). Lesser festivals are held on January 1 and 15, March 3, and May 5.

Every Japanese cherishes a desire to visit Isè Shrine at least once in his lifetime. There are in every section of the country associations called *Daïdaï-Ko*, that collect funds to defray the expenses of the journey for their members, the order of whose going is determined by lot.

[10] See p. 274, n. 93.

[11] Tsukuba. The peak gives its name to one of the two Districts of the ancient Province of Hitachi, the other being Nihibari (modern Nihiharu). The *Hitachi-Fudoki* relates that its former name was Kino-Kuni, but that in the reign of Sujin-*Tenno* a governor was appointed whose name was Tsukuba-no Mikoto, and that he changed the name of the district in order to immortalize his own. Another legend (see p. 177) gives the origin of the name as *tsuku* (reach)-*ha* [Chinese] (waves).

[A] The *Nihon-Densetsu-Shu* of Dr. Toshiyo Takagi.

[13] Who after guiding the Sky-ancestor in his descent, had settled in Isè (see p. 77). This ancestry is given in the *Kogo-Shui-Tosetsu*.

[14] See p. 38. He is called here by his alternative name, Sky-August-Year.

[15] Referred to here by his alternative name, Great-Country-Jewel.

[16] See p. 124, n. 84.

[17] See p. 141.

[18] See p. 143.

[19] Tatenu. The clay articles he invented were called *tatemono* (set-up things). They are modernly called *tsuchi-ning'yo*. There are some excellent specimens

in the Imperial Museum at Tok'yo. This custom of image burial died out at the beginning of the eighth century.

²⁰ Hakaya.

ᴬ The *Harima-Fudoki*.

²¹ A very curious word to employ here, since this was in the reign of the Emperor Suïnin, more than half a millennium (by the *Kojiki* itself) before the first tentative knock of Korean Buddhism upon the door of the Sun-empire. Presumably this was a later name which had displaced the original one long before the *Kojiki* was written.

²² The last portion of the song is missing from the text. Indeed, the whole reading is problematical.

ᴬ The *Hitachi-Fudoki*.

²³ Shiratori-no Sato.

²⁸ Alternative name: Princess-Iri-of-Futaji.

²⁹ Aston says "a kind of badger," Hepburn "something like a badger." I cannot satisfactorily identify it.

³⁰ See p. 142.

³¹ Sugawara, in Yamato Province.

³² See p. 142.

³³ *Tachibana*.

³⁴ A portion of the northern sea where the water was believed to be of such a consistency that ships sank in it. The legend of the "weak water" belonged to the Chinese, by whom it was said to be found north of Fuyu (off Manchuria).

³⁵ Keiko.

³⁶ In Yamato Province.

³⁷ See p. 129.

³⁸ *Mafutsu* (*ma-futu*)-*kagami*. This is Motoöri's supposition.

³⁹ See p. 153.

ᴬ The *Harima-Fudoki*. If the alternative legend is the true one, Keïko-*Tenno* could not have been the hero of this adventure, as Seïmu (Prince-Young-Perfect) was his son. However, the later Narrative states that Keïko-*Tenno* made her his Empress and that she died before Seïmu's rule began. Besides, there is the record of the sending of Young-Brave-Prince-of-Maise to the western province in the reign of Sujin, who was of the second generation before Keïko.

⁴¹ This is the only reference in the Narrative to a go-between in the marital affairs of the Emperors themselves.

⁴² *Niyebito*. One who hunts wild fowl or catches fish for the imperial table.

⁴³ *Oto-katsura* (*oto*: younger; *katsura*: headdress). Probably a headdress of a youthful style is meant.

⁴⁴ *Kashiwadè* (*kashiwa*: oak leaves; *de*: hand). In ancient times food was served on leaves, and the term *kashiwa* was employed indiscriminately, no matter what variety of leaf was used. *Kashiwadè* meant those who were concerned with the preparation and service of food. Motoöri renders it "cook."

⁴⁵ Mutsugi-mura.

⁴⁶ Niyeta-mura. *Niyè* means birds or fish offered to the deities or to the imperial court. *Niyeta* means the fields that produce them.

⁴⁷ Tatemura (*tatè: tachi*).

^A^ The *Harima-Fudoki.*
^50^ Alternative names: Mountain-Gate-Boy; Mountain-Gate-Brave.
^51^ There appears to be record here of some household observance that is now unknown. The mortar, in which the daily rice was pounded would naturally have been an object of importance and the center of housewives' superstitions. Some authorities suppose "the Great" and "the Little" to indicate the upper and lower stones of the handmill, but this implement, according to the Narrative record itself, was not introduced until the seventh century.
^52^ Alternative name: Prince-Young-Mountain-Gate. He bore the same name as one of his great-uncles (see p. 123).
^55^ See p. 123.
^56^ See p. 187, n. 34. She was, according to the genealogies, his great-great-granddaughter. Some authorities believe a confusion to have arisen in the genealogy through a copyist's error in writing the name of Mountain-Gate-Brave (Yamato-Takè) for that of Young-Prince-Brave-Prince-of-Maise, son of the Emperor Prince-Vast-Jewel-Great-Mountain-Gate-Lord (see p. 117). The genealogy, however, is given twice in the *Kojiki* in different connections.
^57^ Not to be confused with the princess of like name mentioned earlier (see p. 144).
^58^ Alternative name: *Princess-Iho-Nono.*
^64^ It seems probable that this Princess-Younger is the same whom the earlier genealogy (see p. 122, n. 67) lists under her alternative name Princess-Iris-of-Nubata, as the daughter of King-Divine-Great-Lord's elder brother, King-Tatatsu-Road-Master-Prince-of-Tamba.
^67^ The correlative tribes of Kuma and So occupied the southern portion of the Island of K'yushu, i.e., H'yuga, Satsuma, and Osumi Provinces.
^68^ The *Gunk'yoko* derives this name from *Sawa* (many). Dr. Yoshida Togo derives it from *saba* (mackerel) and cites the *Engi-Shiki* and the *Shin- Sarugakki* as naming this fish among the chief products of this province.
^69^ See p. 62, n. A. Not to be confounded with Suwo, in Shinano Province.
^73^ Kamikawa.
^74^ Mikè.
^75^ These names are written with honorifics, but their bearers were not counted Kami.
^76^ Nakatomi (naka-tsu-omi)-mura. The modern Nakatono.
^77^ Toyo-Kuni. Later this province was divided into Toyokuni-no Michi-no Kuchi (Buzen) and Toyokuni-no Michi-no Shiri (Bungo).
^A^ The *Bungo-Fudoki.*
^78^ The characters used mean Long-Tail. There is a hamlet called Nagawo in Buzen which Dr. Kurida supposes marks the place of this palace.
^79^ Miyako. The *Bungo-Fudoki* calls it Miyako-Nu (*nu:* moor).
^80^ The characters with which this name is written in the *Fudoki* mean High-Come-Port-Settle, but they are no doubt used phonetically.
^A^ The *Hizen-Fudoki.*
^81^ Yutari-mura.
^82^ Miyofu-Wi.
^83^ Ohokida.
^84^ Kunimi-Mura.
^85^ Anamisu-Nu.

▲ The *Bungo-Fudoki*.
86 Kashiro.
87 Hayaku.
88 Mi-Fuji-Yama. There is doubt about the rendition of these characters. The *mifuji* was an ancient instrument used in catching fish.
89 Sonai-Tama-no Kuni. Later corrupted to Sonoki-no Kori.
▲ The *Bungo-Fudoki*.
90 Awo (see p. 4, n. 11).
91 Negino (Neginu).
92 See p. 128.
93 Dickins (*Japanese Texts*) cites a work of the fifteenth century as saying, "There is a stone kept at the shrine of Saï-no Kami (Sahe-no Kami) by lifting up which people practice divination. If they succeed, good luck will attend them."
94 Fumi-Nu (the *Bungo-Fudoki*).
95 Haya-tsu-Himè-no Kuni.
96 Hotsumè-to.
97 Hi-muka (H'yuga).
98 Hisazu (corrupted to Hita).
▲ The *Bungo-Fudoki*.
99 The numeral here is used as a complimentary adjective.

PAGES 162 - 180

2 Koyu.
3 The line arrangement here is Motoöri's.
5 Mizushima.
6 This mysterious light seen by the Emperor was the famed *shiranuhi* (unknown fire), one of the so-called seven wonders of K'yushu (Tsukushi). It appears in various localities, but that of Ariakè Bay, on the west coast, is best known. Shimabara Peninsula people say it comes on August 1, and the famous *Shiranui-Kenbutsu-Ki* of Nankeï Tachibana assigns it to the last nights of July. Sumoto, Kamiyo, and other villages report its appearance also on December 31, old calendar (February 3 in the new), and it is seen off Kohama on July 14 and December 13. The *R'yuto* (Dragon-Fire) visible on January 6 from Misen in Itsukushima is similar. It is at its best on calm nights and at high tide, appearing generally at midnight and fading at dawn.

Testimony differs as to the color and appearance of this extraordinary radiance; some say it is red like a torch or yellowish red like a smoking lamp; others that it is red at first, changing later to white; and still others that it advances in waves from north to south. Some of the older legends describe it as a greenish tint. Mr. Goto Ichiro, chief of the Nagasaki Meteorological Observatory, was of opinion that it is red on misty nights and white in clear weather.

Nankeï Tachibana, above referred to, describes the phenomenon as follows: "At ten o'clock a point of red fire became visible, which soon divided into three parts. Then other like fires appeared, till thousands of them covered the sea, over the space of four or five *ri*. Some were bright and others dim, some faded out and others grew brighter. Some were high and others low. They were a fine sight and we were amazed at it. The color of the light was as red as lanterns seen from a distance." The report of a party of observation, a few years ago, whose station was at Inasayama Shrine in Saga Prefecture, reads: "At 3:25 on the morning of the 13th . . . a wonderful fire as large as a *sakè*-barrel appeared suddenly on the sea off the coast between Ohomuda and Kurosaki. It disappeared in a few seconds, but appeared again, drawing a long line of fire to the south, after which it leaped across a space of thirty *ken*. Four minutes later it divided into two parts and leaped to the left, multiplying itself gradually into thirty or forty, which now appeared and now vanished. The fires covered about one square mile. The color of the fire was yellowish-red. . . . They disappeared suddenly at five o'clock."

The *shiranui* has naturally called for much scientific investigation. Many private expeditions have been formed for its study, and in 1916 four prefectures (Nagasaki, Fukuoka, Saga, and Kumamoto) cooperated in an enterprise to establish the true cause of the phenomenon. These attempts have borne little fruit, and the most noted Japanese experimenters hold very different hypotheses. The opinion of Professor Matsushita of the Imperial University of K'yoto that the light is caused by phosphorescent bacteria seems to be borne out by a series of test-tube cultures that he made with sea water from the localities affected. Professor Kichisaburo Endo, however (see the *Shin-Nihon*, 1916) combats this theory. It is the belief of the fisher folk that the fires are kindled by dragon deities, and they will not venture out in their boats while the glow can be seen.

At least one province still retains an ancient custom in which the *Shiranui* is imitated in a special *matsuri*. On the day of this festival, lanterns are hung on the ships in harbor and set along the beach, and in the early evening there is a feast with music and singing. At nine o'clock the bells of the village temples are rung and a great quantity of board-floats are set adrift on the water, each bearing a lighted candle, after which all the craft of the place, great and small, sail to and fro amongst them.

▲ The lost *Higo-Fudoki*.

7 Tamana. This is the Tamakina (Jewel-Pestle-Name) of the *Nihongi*. The *Wamyosho* calls it *Tama-ina*.

8 Nibeïwo (*Nibesani*): the local word for many.

▲ The lost *Higo-Fudoki*, cited in the *Shaku-Nihongi*, vol. XVI.

9 Aso (*nanzo*, *nazo*).

10 Possibly to be identified with Princess-of-Old-Port (see p. 161).

11 Kashi-shima (Kashima).

12 Ki (Kinè)-Shima. Suzuki Shigetanè disputes this rendition, deriving the name from *ki* (*tree*)-shima (island), assigning its origin to the legend according to which the Kami Fifty-Courageous planted trees throughout K'yushu (see p. 34). The characters employed in the *Fudoki* texts, however, are against him.

13 Miko. There are two classes of *miko*, the *miko-han* and the *tataki-miko* or *kuchiyosè*. The former is attached to a shrine, and takes part in its processionals, ceremonials, and dances.

The characters with which the word *kuchiyosè* is written indicate a deity so remote that by ordinary means man cannot communicate with him. In common parlance, however, it means a woman who possesses the power to receive and communicate the message of the dead or of the absent (*iyahiko*) (the western "medium"). Usually the *kuchiyosè* adds fortune-telling to the list of her accomplishments and has no fixed residence. She is looked down upon by the shrine *miko*. While sometimes these traveling *miko* worship recognized Shinto deities or even *Bodhisattva*, as a rule they carry with them their own secret deities, concealed in a box wrapped in cloth or in a bamboo tube encased in gold brocade. A specimen of one of the latter may be seen in the Imperial Museum at Ueno, Tok'yo. It is called *mamoribukuro* (amulet). In Aïzu and Shirakawa the *Kuchiyosè-miko* are known as *waka*.

There were anciently *miko* attached to the imperial court, and in distinction the *miko* of the various provinces came to be known as *agata* (land, country)-*miko*. In Luchu the *miko* generally were called *yuta*.

At some of the principal shrines (as, for example, the Kasuga Shrine at Nara) the young girls, who wear skirts of white and scarlet and dance with small bells in their hands, are called *miko*, but not properly so.

ᴬ The *Hizen-Fudoki*, quoted in the *Senkaku-Manyo-Sho*, vol. III.

14 Yama-ka. Local legend says it was named from the fact that it had a hot spring in which a mountain deer was once observed bathing.

15 The Land of Fire (Hi-no Kuni) was divided into Hi-no Kuni-no Michi-no Kuchi (Hizen: Fire-Front) and Hi-no Kuni-no Michi-no Shiri (Higo: Fire-Rear), Provinces.

ᴮ The lost *Chikuzen-Fudoki*, quoted in the *Shaku-Nihongi*, vol. X.

16 Ikuha (*ukuha*).

17 Chiku (*Tsuku*)-go:rear. The character is the same here as in Tsukushi (K'yu-shu).

18 Watari (Wataraï)-no Sato.

19 The word means, literally, the father of an adopted child.

20 *Yakara*.

21 Inu-no Koë Yamu.

22 Funaho-no Sato.

23 Kiri-no Kuni. Corrupted to Kiï.

24 "*Sayakeshi*." The village was called Sayakè (corrupted to Sayama (Mount-Sa).

ᴬ The *Hizen-Fudoki*.

25 The meaning of the character here is uncertain.

26 These are the Chika-no Yaso-Shima (Eighty Islands of Chika), the name comprising Hirado and the Goto group, northwest of K'yushu, belonging to Hizen Province.

* See p. 87, n. 46.

27 Isafushi. A note in the *Fudoki* states that "the vulgar call the whale *isa*."

ᴬ The lost *Iki-Fudoki*.

29 Miru-kashi. The *Codium tomentosum*. The character here rendered "lady" is sometimes translated "princess," but it lacks the honorific quality of the character usually employed for the latter title.

30 The Narrative contains no other reference to this residence. It seems likely that Usa is a scribe's error for Udo, where, the *Wakan-Sanzai-Zuè*

states, this emperor had a temporary palace.
³¹ Kashiro (Kamu [Kami]-Shiro).
▲ The *Hizen-Fudoki*.
³² I.e., Tattoo (see p. 252, n. 6).
³³ As befitted a youth.
³⁴ See p. 144.
▲ Katsumada. The lost *Mimasaka-Fudoki*, quoted in the *Shirin-Saïyo-Sho*, vol. I.
³⁵ See p. 100, n. 23.
³⁶ This episode of course does not tally with the legend of his enormous stature.
³⁷ In the *Kojiki* text he calls himself here *King*-Mountain-Gate-Boy.
³⁸ Henceforth in the Narrative he is called by the name he accepted from the outlaw.
³⁹ I.e., eater (man).
⁴⁰ Sakaë-no Kori. Later corrupted to Saka-no Kori.
▲ The *Hizen-Fudoki*.
⁴² Sakashimè.
⁴³ Dr. Kurida disputes this, the popular rendition of the characters.
▲ The *Hizen-Fudoki*.
⁴⁴ Shimonoseki. A tradition says the mainland and K'yushu Island were anciently joined, there being a natural tunnel large enough to permit junks to pass.
⁴⁵ See p. 134. These two episodes were no doubt originally identical. In fact, the song assigned by the *Nihongi* to the earlier place is given by the *Kojiki* here.
⁴⁶ See p. 156. She is called in this place by her alternative name, Princess-Iho-Nono.
⁴⁷ At the Great Shrine at Isè. The record is from the *Daïjingu-Shozatsuji-Ki*, vol. I.
⁴⁸ See p. 151.
⁵¹ A descendant, presumably, of Young-Prince-Brave-Prince of Maise (see p. 117).
⁵⁵ Kurosaka-no Mikoto. He counted descent from Divine-Eight-Wells-Ears (see p. 113).
⁵⁶ Ubara.
⁵⁷ Saru-no Toki-ne-no Yama. "Monkey time" is four o'clock in the afternoon.
⁵⁸ Some texts of the *Fudoki* contain a note stating that Prince Noga was of the family of that Tribe-Master of Forehead-Ricefield (Nukata-no [or Nukatabè-no] Muraji) who figures in Ink'yo's reign (see p. 258). I regard this as a much later gloss. The character of the legend assigns it to a much earlier place in the Narrative. Probably Noga (Nuga) is a mere place name.
⁵⁹ Kata-Woka. *Kata* means one of a pair.
⁶⁰ See p. 172. These are the sole allusions to this personage in the legends. A note in the *Seïshiroku* cites an ancient Kurosaka-Village in Taga District.
⁶¹ Hitakami-no Kuni. The rendition is to say the least very doubtful. Some commentators identify the place with Mutsu.
⁶² Hatatarashi-no Kuni.

⁶³ The chronological place of this legend is uncertain. Kurida assigns it to this reign or to that of Sujin. But Mountain-Gate-Brave's activities in Michi-no-Oku at this time would seem to indicate that the event recorded took place here.
ᴀ The *Hitachi-Fudoki.*
⁶⁴ The *oni* is the Japanese demon of all sorts. This is the first mention in the Narrative of this type of evil spirit.
⁶⁶ A descendant of Sky-Great-Sun (see p. 31).
⁶⁸ This was the sword, called also "Herb-Queller," found by Brave-Swift-Impetuous-Male in the tail of the Eight-Forked-Serpent-of-Koshi (see p. 34) and given by him to Great-Sky-Shiner. It had been worshiped in the imperial palace itself up to 92 B.C., when the Shrine of Kasanui (see p. 124) was built, and had been transferred to Isè in 52 B.C.
⁷⁰ This Kami is mentioned neither by the *Kojiki* nor the *Nihongi*. He is worshiped at the Great Shrine (*Daïjingu*) at Atsuta (see p. 36, n. 20).
⁷¹ At the date of the *Kojiki's* writing, Suruga was probably a part of Sagami, which would account for the legend's location in each province. Of the name Suruga the *Manyokogi* says, "In the province are great rivers whose sound rang in all directions, from which it was probably called Shaking-River-Province (Yusuri-Kawa-no Kuni), corrupted later to Suruga." Iida Takesato gives as an alternative derivation Suruga (Smooth)-Province.
⁷² *Hi-uchi.* Whether this was the fire-drill, that has been mentioned in the earlier Narrative, or a flint-and-steel, is a bone of contention.
⁷³ Legend says the place where this occurred is near the Yaïzu Station (*yaïzu:* burnt moor) on the Tokaïdo Line of Railway, near Shizuoka. The Kusanagi Shrine at Udo-mura, near by, marks the spot. In the old tomb directly behind this, in the spring of 1916, a stone coffin, ancient jewels, swords, and pottery were unearthed.
⁷⁴ Yakizu.
⁷⁵ Teko-no Yobisaka. *Teko* was the ancient vulgar word for woman. *Yobi* (*niyobu:* to groan or *yobi:* to cry out).
ᴀ The lost *Suruga-Fudoki*, quoted in the *Shoku-Karin-R'yozaï*, vol. I. The songs are included in the *Manyoshu* Collection.
⁷⁶ Ohofu-Mura. The *Fudoki* derives the word Ohofu from *Ohihi* (*Oho-wi*).
⁷⁷ Afuga-no Mura (*afu:* to meet?).
⁷⁸ *Awabi*. The haliotis. A shellfish common to the coasts of Japan.
⁷⁹ Aïda-mura.
ʙ The *Hitachi-Fudoki.*
⁸⁰ Hashiri-mizu.
⁸¹ A popular version alleges that this was to rebuke her husband, who had said, when she declared her intention to accompany him on his expedition, that a woman's place was "on the mats" (i.e., at home).
⁸² Hisho Saïto (see his *History of Japan*) says she was drowned "because she doubted the goodness of the Kami."
⁸³ Motoöri takes this to have been an earlier name of the Kuzu tribe (see p. 97, n. 10, and p. 222). But Mountain-Gate-Brave is now in the present Hitachi Province, while the Kuzu are elsewhere mentioned as in Yamato— ten provinces away.
⁸⁴ The Narrative here credits him with what (except perhaps in the crudest

⁸⁵ Hitachi (*hitashi*).
⁸⁶ See p. 149, n. 11.
⁸⁷ Koromodè Hitashi-no Kuni. A more plausible explanation of the saying is that the dark clouds were rain clouds. The records of rainfall in the province would justify the assumption.
⁸⁸ The mythical account of the geological process in accordance with which the eastern shore of the Great Island has for centuries been rising.
⁸⁹ Mioya-no Kami. It is uncertain what deity is here intended. Even Kurida, in his commentary, hazards no guess.
⁹⁰ Fukuji-no Takè, according to the characters here used. No doubt Mount Fuji, in Suruga, is referred to.
⁹¹ Nü-namè. For the first celebration of this festival, by the Sun-Goddess, see p. 23, n. 31.
⁹² Naka-Samu-Ta-no Iratsuko. There is a place called Naka in Shimosa, Hitachi Province.
⁹³ Una-Kami-no Ajè-no Otomè.
⁹⁴ *Utagaï* (*utakagahi* [*utagaki*]). This word, whose derivation is disputed, signifies a meeting at which persons of both sexes converse in songs. These are generally of an amatory character. The term is applied also to the place at which such a gathering is held. The custom is a very ancient one, much employed in youthful courtship. It is sometimes called *Kagahi*. The earliest trace of the custom dates to the fifth century.

It was fashionable in Yur'yaku's time (459-479) at Tsuwaki-no Ichi, in Yamato, near Mount Utagaki. In that period each participant appears to have chosen the theme for his or her ode. A man began the contest by reciting his production to all, and a woman followed with hers, and so on, alternating sexes, till all had recited. Legend says the man whose verse was voted best was considered to have won the woman who was given first place, the second man the second woman, and so till all were paired.

The place preferred seems generally to have been a hill or mountain. The *Manyoshu* contains a poem entitled "A Poem Composed at Utagai on Tsukuba Mountain," and the *Settsu-Fudoki* (under the reference *Utagaki-Yama*) records: "Hahiguri-no Woka of Wotomo District has to the west Utagaki Mountain. In ancient times, men and women gathered on this mountain and made *Utagaki* (*uta-kagaï*) or song-courting, so it was named Utagaki." In later times, however, the *Utagai* was held in the capital, as appears from a reference in the *Shoku-Nihongi*: "On the first day of the second month of the sixth year of the Era of Temp'yo, the Emperor (Ninken-*Tenno*) repaired to the Shijaku Gate to observe an *Utagahi*, in which more than two hundred and forty men and women, above the fifth *hon* rank, tastefuly took part. The songs were sung in concert. . . . Among the songs were some in the Naniwa style, the Yamato style, the Asachigahara style, the Hirosè style, etc. The people of the capital were permitted to see the meeting and the men and women who sang at the time were given prizes." For a long poem sequence at a *Utagai* reported under Muretsu's reign, see p. 306. For the traditional origin of the Song-Hedge, see p. 112, n. 86.

NOTES: PAGES 179-180

⁹⁵ Dr. Kurida says, "In ancient times the southern end of Ajè Lake reached to Unakami Province and the northern end of Samuta Marsh touched Naka Province. The age of the legend can be known by these names of Naka-Samu-Ta and Unakami-no Ajè."

⁹⁶ Kiji-M'yojin. This Kami has no connection with the Cock-Pheasant mentioned on p. 58.

⁹⁷ Heso.

⁹⁸ Ohokushi (Ohokuchi).

⁹⁹ This legend was current down to the eighteenth century.

PAGES 180 - 197

¹ Taka-no Kori.
² Namegata-no Kuni.
³ Kajinashi-gawa.
ᴬ The *Hitachi-Fudoki*.
⁴ Michi-no Oku (Michinoku). This, shortened to Michi, became corrupted to Mutsu. It is the most northern province of the Great Island (Hondo).
⁵ Probably these are Emishi names. I have been unable to find any commentator who has hazarded a guess at their meaning. Their owners were not accounted Kami, though there would seem to be significance in the fact that the word Kami enters into the names only of the pair who were not put to death. The words themselves are untranslatable. The character rendered Haï (presumably phonetically) means ashes.
⁶ An *Emishi* word.
⁸ Yatsuki.
ᴬ This incident is quoted in the *K'yukisaï of* Daïzenin (Chief Priest of Tsuzuko-Wakè Shrine, Yatsukumura, Shirakawa, Mutsu Province) as related in the lost *Mutsu-Fudoki*.
⁹ From Sagami Province into Suruga Province. The present Usui Pass. The slope is today called Tsuma-goi (wife-affection). At its summit is an Inari shrine, before which superstition forbids a wedding procession to pass, lest the bride become divorced.
¹⁰ Azuma.
¹¹ A local legend of Kai Province says that on this journey he stayed awhile at Kofu. The Shrine of Saka-orè marks the spot. In it are preserved a sword, three Chinese mirrors, and an ancient tinder-bag.
¹² The Japanese word for menses is derived in the same way as the Latin and English. It is *tsuki* (*-midzu*): moon (*water*), both characters being written, but only the first (*tsuki*) being used in speaking. The polite form is *miguri*. The princess in her reply uses the double allusion to make a poetic figure.
* The *Nihongi* omits this poetic exchange entirely.
¹³ Atsusa (see p. 36, n. 20).
ᴬ The lost *Owari-Fudoki*, quoted by the *Shaku-Nihongi*, vol. VII).
¹⁴ Mt. Ibuki (4545 feet), near Nagaoka. The highest mountain of the prefecture, on the frontier between Mino and Omi Provinces. Noted for its

growth of the mugwort plant (*mogusa*), from which moxa is made. The ascent may be made from Uëno Village, three miles distant.

¹⁵ The History of Shikufu-Shima says "In the reign of the Emperor Koreï, Prince-Frost-Swift begot three children. Two of them, Blowing-Male (Kibukiwo-no Kami) and Princess-Slope-Ricefield (Sakata-Himè) went to the east of Slope-Ricefield District, of Fresh-Sea (Omi) Province, and the third, Princess-Shallow-Well, went to the north of Shallow-Well (Asawi)." Dr. Kurida identifies this Kibukiwo-no Kami with Prince-Tatami. If he is correct, Sakata-Himè is probably identical with Princess-Susashi, though the *Teïwo-Hennenki* calls her the Kami's niece.

This legend, in some accounts, is told of the two mountains Ibuki and Asawi. Indeed, sometimes Princess-Shallow-Well is called Hill-Shallow-Well (Asawi-woka).

▲ The *Teïwo-Henninki*.
¹⁶ The present Samegaï (Refreshing-Spring).
¹⁷ Aston's translation. Chamberlain translates "Rest-Wake."
¹⁸ Tagi (Taki). *Tagishi:* rudder.
¹⁹ Tsuwetsuki.
²⁰ Otsu. In Isè Province.
²¹ Mihe.
²² Nobè (Nobo-nu). In Isè Province.
²⁴ His early name (see p. 154).
²⁵ *Tokoro. Dioscorea quinqueloba.*
²⁶ The word used is *chidori:* plover, dotterel, or sandpiper. In the designation (below) of the "August-Tombs-of-the-White-Swan," however, the characters, used phonetically, read "swan" (haku-cho).
²⁷ In face of this episode, it is difficult to agree with Chamberlain, that the religious beliefs of the early Japanese, as exemplified in these legends, contained "no notion of incarnation or of transmigration."
²⁸ Vulgar legend says that when it disappeared two white flags fell from the sky at Atsuta, at the spot known as White-Bird-Mound (Shiratori), where, accordingly, his relics were interred, after his death, in Isè.
²⁹ A note in the *Fudoki* suggests the possibility that he is identical with Sacred-Quarter-Root-Brandisher (see p. 133), but the latter was put to death in a previous reign. Another note states him to be a descendant of Sky-Great-Sun (see p. 31).
³⁰ Nothing else is known of this deity.
▲ The *Izumo-Fudoki*.
³¹ See p. 174.
³² Alternative name: Princess-Younger-Princess-True-Young.
³³ His grand-niece.
³⁴ See p. 187, n. 34.
³⁶ There is a hiatus at this point in the ancient text.
▲ The *Hitachi-Fudoki*.
³⁷ See p. 155.
³⁸ See p. 119.
³⁹ It is impossible to say what this bird was. The *Nihongi* version of the legend says fish-hawk. The *Nihongi-Shiki* says osprey. The *Chiribukuro's*

comment on this is, "Has the osprey a charming voice? This seems to have been another kind of bird!"
⁴⁰ Alternative name: Bird-Bird.
⁴¹ Tori-Tori (Tottori) (see p. 145, n. 91).
ᴬ The *Chiribukuro*, vol. V.
⁴³ Ohokiri-no Sato. Later corrupted to Ohokurè-no Sato.
⁴⁴ Matokata.
ᴮ The Isè-Fudoki.
⁴⁵ Kozukè (Kami-tzu-ka-nu).
⁴⁶ Sakayama. In Harima Province.
ᴬ The *Harima-Fudoki*.
⁴⁷ Seïmu.
⁴⁸ Confirmed him in the office previously held under Keïko-*Tenno*, the preceding Emperor.
⁴⁹ I.e., east and west, and north and south (see p. 190).
⁵⁰ See p. 66.
ᴬ The *Kujiki*.
⁵¹ The characters were anciently written Spring-*Sun*-Clan (Huruhi [Kasuga] -be).
ᴮ The *Chiribukuro*, vol. III, and the *Jinten-Aïnosho*, vol. IX. The incident is told also in the *Bishu-Ki* of Sugawara Kiyokiniï.
⁵² In Yamato Province.
⁵³ Enshrined in the Ni-no Miya Hachiman (ancient Imi-no Miya) at Toyora, Nagato Province, in company with the Empress Jingu and Ojin-*Tenno*. The shrine is believed to mark the site of the ancient Palace of Toyora (*Toyo-ura:* fertile-shore). According to some authorities he is enshrined also in the Kashi-no Miya in Chikuzen Province.
⁵⁴ *Chuaï*.
⁵⁵ This prince is not mentioned in the preceding genealogy.
⁵⁶ See p. 156.
⁵⁸ The Empress Jingu (see p. 122, n. 69).
⁵⁹ She-Hwang-Ti (reigned in China, 221-209 B.C.)
ᴬ The *Seïshiroku*.
⁶⁰ This is believed to have been on the site of the present Shomen Machi.
ᴬ The *Harima-Fudoki*. The name existed previously to this, as it forms part of the title of Keïko-*Tenno's* empress (Princess-Elder-Lady-of-Wave-Hiding-of-Harima) (see p. 153).
⁶² See p. 122.
⁶³ The Kihi-no Miya record.
⁶⁴ Kagura-Zaki. On the shore of Mikata District, Wakesa Province.
⁶⁵ There is much doubt whether the character should be thus rendered, as it is by most commentators, since the legend goes back to a time anterior to the introduction of the Chinese character. The *N'yoi*-jewel (*N'yoi-Ho-ju*) is the Mani of the Buddhists and one of the Seven Treasures (*Sapta Ratna*) symbolic of the great teacher and his truth. Eitel (see *Handbook of Chinese Buddhism*) calls it "a round pearl," and Monier Williams (see *Sanskrit-English Dictionary*) "a fabulous gem, supposed to yield its possessor all desires."

B The lost *Tosa-Fudoki*, cited in the *Michiyuri-Buri* and the *Shaku-Nihongi*, vol. X.

66 According to the *Niju-Nisha-Honen*, this shrine possessed also the helmet and armor worn by Jingu on this expedition.

67 The *Niju-Nisha-Honen*, the *Shoshaji* (quoted in the *Wakun-no Shiyori*), and the *Shoken-Ko*. It is named also in R'yoshu Yoshii's shrine list of Muko District. The *Koseï-R'yogu-Ki* (1716-1735) relates that it was later kept in another shrine, especially erected for it, known as the South (Nagu) Shrine, from which it was stolen and thrown away on Mount Koya, but was later recovered. A scratch now on it was said to have been made in that time.

A The *Nihongi-Chushaku*. An ancient name of Toyora (Fertile-Shore) is Michihi (Ebb-Flow)-Island, and there is a tradition that the two tide-jewels were there preserved. Old maps show also, off the coast of Chofu, the islands of Kanju (ebb-jewel) and Manju (flow-jewel).

The *Chikushi-Do-Ki* of Soki says: "Passing the coast, I saw two islets which are called Ebb and Flow, and felt thankful to the olden time when Koreans, too, respected the country. Even now there are these two islands, Okitsu and Hiratsu, and as they preserve the two jewels of ebb and flow, they are called Michihi-no Shima, or the Islands of Ebb and Flow."

The *Usa-Hachiman-Enki* (History of the Hachiman Shrine at Usa) says: "The two jewels are kept in the Kawakami-no Miya of Saga District, in Hizen Province. The jewel-of-ebb-tide is white, but the jewel-of-flood-tide is blue. Each is five sun in length." According to the Jinmeï-Cho, the Kawakami Daïm'yojin is the deity of the Toyohimè Shrine of Saga District. There is some confusion here. Kurida speaks of "the Yotohimè Shrine in Saga District, dedicated to Toyohimè." Yotohimè (Princess-Yoto) is the alternative name of Sky-Princess (see p. 122, n. 70) younger sister of the Empress, whom the latter sent, according to one legend, to obtain the tide-jewels for her Korean expedition.

The *Shaku-Nihongi* records that a report of a violation of Uda Shrine, during the Era of Gwanr'yaku (1184-1185), stated that the jewels of flood-tide and ebb-tide were preserved there. The History of Kagoshima-Jingu, issued by its own authorities, in its section of 1916, states: "Among the treasures preserved at this shrine are two jewels called Ebb-Jewel and Flow-Jewel. They are said to be the ones used by Hiko Hohodemi-no Mikoto (Fire-Fade)."

69 Japanese commentators do not offer a satisfactory explanation of this speech.

70 Alternative name: Loyalty.

71 No doubt identical with Sky-Sun-Spear (see p. 139). Here, however, his descendant claims for him a direct celestial origin. Presumably Koma is here cited by error for Shinra (Shiragi), as Dr. Kurida supposes.

72 Possibly this is Uru-San (Renwon), cited in the later history of Japan's assaults upon Korea.

A The lost *Chikuzen-Fudoki*, quoted by the *Shaku-Nihongi*, vol. X.

73 Isoshi. Ito-Te was no doubt a native hereditary ruler. Aston quotes a Chinese traveler to Japan in the third century, who notes, "there are hereditary kings in Ito, who all own allegiance to the queen country."

A The *Harima-Fudoki*.

74 This is a pillow word (see p. XXXI). These are occasionally met with in prose as well as in poetry.

75 *The Official Guide to Eastern Asia* (prepared by the Imperial Japanese Government Railways), vol. II, pictures the Empress as making her preparations for the Korean expedition, "divining that the king of Shiragi, (Silla) was at the bottom of all the trouble in K'yushu (with the Kuma-So)." This is borne out by the legend.

78 This ignorance is difficult to reconcile with the previous Narrative. The Land of Silla had been known even to Prince-Sky-Plenty-Earth-Plenty-High-as-Sky's-Sun-Fire-Ruddy-Plenty (see p. 66). Kara had sent tribute in the reign of the Emperor Sujin (see p. 132) and from that country had come the horned-man, Tsunoga-Arashito (see p. 135) and Sky-Sun-Spear (see p. 139), each claiming to be a son of the Kara king.

79 Not the brewer to the Great Kami, mentioned on p. 127.

80 Local legend says the body was temporarily interred on a hill to the southeast of the shrine.

81 Worshiped at the shrine at Tsuruga in Echizen Province, the Kashi-no Miya at Kashiï-mura, Chikuzen Province, the Hachiman shrines at Usa in Buzen Province and Tsurugaoka, Kamakura, and the Sumiyoshi (Suminoë) shrine in Settsu Province.

82 Jingu. By the official Japanese genealogy she is counted only Regent.

83 "The Kingdom of Heaven is likened unto a man which sowed good seed in his field: but while men slept, his enemy came and sowed tares among the wheat and went his way. But when the blade was sprung up and brought forth fruit, then appeared the tares also."

84 The *Shiki* explains that rods or skewers were anciently planted in ricefields with certain incantations, to protect the property from wrongful claimants. Motoöri, less plausibly, thinks it was done with malice, to injure the owners' feet.

85 See p. 23, n. 32.

86 See pp. 108 and 195.

87 Disfigurement, by the sword, of living persons or dead bodies. Vivisection and mutilation.

88 Some render this "albinos."

89 *Kokumi*. I use *Shira-hi toko-kuni* (white-sun [day]-bed-embrace).

The inhibition is very ancient in India. See the *Prasna Upanishad:* "Day and night are Pragapati (the Lord-of-Creatures); its Day is Spirit, its Night, Matter. Those who unite in love by day waste their Spirit, but to unite in love by night is right." Brahmanism interdicts intercourse, also, on the nights of new- and full-moon. (See *Satapatha-Brahmana*, Eleventh *Kanda*, First *Adhyaya*, Eighth *Brahmana*.)

90 For example, by lightning.

91 It is interesting to note that of this list of "earth" offenses, at least two (and according to some legends three) were committed in the Sky, before the descent of the ancestral deity, by Brave-Swift-Impetuous-Male, brother of the Sun-Goddess (see pp. 22 and 23).

92 Identified with Great-Sky-Shiner.

93 It is uncertain which *Kami* is here referred to.

94 It seems likely that in this legend the names of Great-Land-Master and Eight-Fold-Thing-Sign-Master are confused (see p. 132).
95 See p. 18. These are alternative names of the three Male-Possessors.
96 *Maki. Podocarpus macrophylla.*
98 The name has no honorifics.
99 *Not* the province of that name. She is now in Chikugo Province.

PAGES 197 - 214

1 Matsura (Matsu-ura).
▲ The *Harima-Fudoki.*
2 Tamashima. Not, however, the island of the same name that she had visited previously, in Nagato Province.
3 Mezura (Mezurashiï: strange). The *Hizen-Fudoki* says this became corrupted to Matsura-no Kori.
4 Griffis asserts that to this day no males are allowed to fish at this place during this period.
▲ The lost *Buzen-Fudoki,* quoted in the *Shirin-Saïyo-Sho,* vol. I. The *Sansha-Takusen-R'yakusho* (whose authorship is unknown) gives a legend of Buzen according to which she was transported through the air to Ikeda, in that province, where on Sugiyama she prayed for the divine assistance, in response to which the Four Deva Kings, with eight white banners, descended from the Sky. The date of this text is uncertain, but it has an epilogue which is dated 1650.
5 Like a man's.
6 The *H'yobushiki.* Tanenobu supposes this to be the eastern mouth of Yobuko Harbor, where, he says, there are an Ohotomo-Ura (Great-Elbow-Pad-Beach) and a Kotomo-Ura (Small-Elbow-Pad-Beach).
B The *Hizen-Fudoki.*
7 On the Inland Sea, near Fukuyama.
8 This *Kami* cannot now be identified. The festival is cited by Yano Gendo. Dr. Yoshida says the Funatama-Jinja (Ship-Jewel-Shrine) is a subordinate shrine of that at Sumiyoshi and is now situated to the south of the main building. The *Engi-Shiki* mentions it. He identifies Ship-Jewel with the Kami Fifty-Brave (see p. 33).
▲ The lost *Chikuzen-Fudoki.*
9 Legend says that she burned a "holy war-book" and drank the ashes, with the result that the infant Ojin, her son later to be born, was at birth able to recite it wholly.
10 Mayami. The present Makura (makkura: pitchy-dark).
11 Two camphor trees now standing are said to be shoots of this tree, one in the compound of Hachiman Shrine at Kamakura in which Jingu is enshrined, and the other at Sumiyoshi shrine, in which Noble-of-Brave-Uchi (Takè-no Uchi) is worshiped. On the latter tree grows a leek-like weed called *kawanira* which is believed to creep up and down the trunk with the flow and ebb of the tide, and which is carried as a preventive of seasickness. It is said that the people of Funaki are never drowned. The present village is two *ri* from the beach. A local legend names the village of Ariho, to the

south of Funaki, as the place where the Empress made the sails for her ships.
¹² Funaki.
ᴬ The lost *Settsu-Fudoki* cited in the *Senkaku-Manyoshu*, vol. V.
¹³ The name has no honorifics.
¹⁴ This triune Kami, here viewed in his singular aspect, was, as appears in the later Narrative (see p. 206) made up of Male-Bottom-Possessor, Male-Middle-Possessor, and Male-Surface-Possessor (see p. 18).
¹⁵ Ahiko.
¹⁶ Ito.
¹⁷ Von Siebold says that in the ancient belief girdling in pregnancy was a necessary physical precaution, "by which the babe is prevented from stealing the food out of the mother's throat and so starving her to death." I have been able to find no trace of this belief.

The custom of binding is universal among all classes, and in noble families has its own peculiar observances. An English newspaper printed daily in Tok'yo, under date of March 19, 1911, reported: "The Japanese newspapers report that Princess Kitashirakawa is expecting an addition to her family early next month, and that *the ceremony of binding the obi tightly* took place on the 12th instant."
ᴮ The lost *Chikuzen-Fudoki*, cited in the *Shaku-Nihongi*, vol. XI.
¹⁸ *Miko-umi-ishi.*
¹⁹ One *kin:* one and one-third pounds avoirdupois.
ᴬ The authority for these details is the lost *Tsukushi (K'yushu)-Fudoki*. The preface to Lay 65 of the *Manyoshu* says: "On Kofu Moor, near Fukaë village, Ito District, Tsukushi Province, on a mound near the beach, are two stones, shaped like eggs, beautiful and real jewels. All who pass, officials and humble, dismount and revere them. The old say that when Princess-Long-Life-Perfect conquered Shiragi, she took these stones and put one in either sleeve to facilitate her confinement, and afterward placed them there."
²⁰ The name used here is Kuni-Katamè-no Kami (Land-Consolidating-*Kami*), a name found only in the *Harima-Fudoki*, but the phraseology used in the divine command to He- and She-Who-Invites to descend and "*consolidate the drifting earth*" makes this identification seem reasonably certain.
²¹ These are all alternative designations of the opposite land of Silla (Korea).
²² The character used in the *Usa-Hachiman-Enki* indicates that she dyed her trousers red also.
ᴮ A lost fragment of the *Harima-Fudoki*, quoted in the *Shaku-Nihongi*.
²³ *Fujishiro.*
²⁴ See p. 122.
²⁵ In this and some cognate legends he is called Sagara, the name of the Indian Naga king.
²⁶ See p. 304, n. 1.
²⁷ This dance is now unknown.
ᴬ This legend is very wide-spread, but there is no trace of it in the more ancient writings. It appears to have developed in the Hachiman propaganda of the twelfth and following centuries. Its more ornate forms are to be found in the *Gunsho-Ruiju* (*Hachiman Gudokun*) of Kwaïgen (1532) and Yoshida Kanetomo's *Hachiman Gudokun,* in the collection entitled *Zoku-*

gunshoruiju. It is not cited in the *Kinko-Shosetsu-Kaïdaï,* the *Koshiden,* the *Nihon-Shosetsu-Nemp'yo,* the *Daïnihon-Shi,* the *Kojikiden,* the *Kokoku-Kaib'yaku-Yuraï-Ki,* the *Jindaï-Maki-Koden-Kiki-Gaki,* the *Nihon-H'yaku-Sho-Den-Sho,* or the *Nihon-H'yaku-Sho-Den-Taïseï.*

²⁸ Brave-Awful-Possessing-Male (see p. 13).
²⁹ Kotoagè-no Woka.
ᴮ The *Harima-Fudoki.*
³⁰ Sukui-no Sato. Now corrupted to Suka-no Sato.
³¹ An *Emishi* word.
ᴬ The lost *Chikuzen-Fudoki,* quoted in the *Shaku-Nihongi,* vol. VI.
³² Some legends (See the *Mizu-Kagami* [1175?]) say that on her arrival off the Korean coast she took sea water in her hand and prayed to the deities of Kashima and Kasuga (see p. 90, n. 65), whereon there appeared these deities, with those of Sumiyoshi and Suwa, clad in helmets and armor. The deity of Kasuga sent the Great Kami of Kawakami to the sea palace of Sagara (one of the eight great dragon-kings) to fetch the tide-jewels. In the confusion of the original sea Kami with the dragon-king one sees the grafting of the later Buddhist theogony upon the older Shinto. There is no authority whatever for the brood of the dragon in the more ancient scriptures.
³³ There is a popular legend that Jingu, lacking fodder on this expedition, fed her horses on the seaweed *hondahara* (see p. 64, n. 9).
³⁴ This is not authentic history. Prince-Urosohorichi (Uro) was killed in 249 by an expedition sent to avenge an affront offered by him to the Empress (*Tongkam,* vol. III).
³⁵ Mr. E. H. Parker thinks these details are borrowed from the account of the taking of the Chinese capital by the founder of the Han dynasty.
³⁶ Kor'yo (Kokur'yo).
³⁷ Pékchè (Pak-jay).
³⁸ Korean records bring this date down to A.D. 346. Neither Korean nor Chinese annals record this as a successful invasion.
³⁹ See p. 194, n. 76.
⁴⁰ Iïda, discussing the etymology of this name, cites a curious legend from an ancient document of Sumiyoshi shrine according to which, when the Empress wished to delay the birth of her child, Tamomi (-Taruni) took stones, and *"crumpling the imperial trousers,* forcefully inserted them in her girdle," whence the name Tamomi (hand-crumple) (see p. 199). The same legend derives the child's name, Yahata (Hachiman) from words she used in prayer on the same occasion. Even Iïda, however, confesses himself unable to understand their meaning.
⁴¹ This, which in old histories is called Yamada-Anato, is the Sumiyoshi Aramitama-Jinja, at Kusuno, Toyohigashigami-Mura, to the west of Chofu (Fuchu). It is known as Ichi-no-Miya. Built originally by Jingu in Chikuzen Province, it was removed to its present site in Settsu, where the "tranquil spirits" of the three Kami had been enshrined by the Empress-regent according to Japanese official chronology in the third century, and by modern critical reckoning in the fourth.
⁴² *Enju.*
⁴³ Alternative name: Homuda-Lord. The Emperor Ojin.
⁴⁴ See p. 29, n. 80.

⁴⁵ Umi. One legend says the place was Karita-Village, K'yoto District, Buzen Province (The *Nihon-Shik'yo-Fuzoku-Shi*, 1902). Another locates it in Sanuki, near Hakozaki Station, "before the Hachiman Shrine, on the spot where stands the great pinetree called *Shirushi-no Matsu*." The legendary date of the shrine's foundation is 759. It is dedicated to Ojin, Jingu, and Princess-Jewel-Good (see p. 88).
⁴⁶ Umi-Nu.
⁴⁷ The *San-Kan*, the three Korean States which it is alleged were brought under subjection by Jingu's expedition, Silla (Bakan), Kudara (Benkan), and Koma (Shinkan).
⁴⁸ The *Ichiguki* and the *Wakan-Sanzaï-Zuè* give Tono. The *Engi-Shiki* gives Tsuno.
⁴⁹ This *Kami* is Great-Land-Master.
⁵⁰ The *Dazaï-Kwan-Naïshi* is disposed to identify this peak with Shinno-Zan, a mountain in Koyu District, near Mount Kirishima.
ᴬ This extraordinary legend is given in the *Chiribukuro*, vol. VII, and the *Jinten* (*Chirisoè*)-*Aïnosho*, vol. I.
⁵¹ Harihara.
⁵² See p. 75, n. 98.
ᴬ The *Harima-Fudoki*.
⁵³ The Empress' step-sons (see p. 191).
⁵⁶ In Settsu Province.
⁵⁷ The Kami who died from an injury resulting from Brave-Swift-Impetuous-Male's evil conduct (see p. 23, n. 33).
⁵⁸ See p. 21. Their "rough spirits" had already, by one account, been enshrined in Chikuzen Province (see p. 203, n. 41).
⁶² The text of these two lines is unintelligible.
⁶³ Osaka (Ofusaka). On the boundary of Yamashiro and Omi Provinces. Not the city of the same name in Settsu Province.
⁶⁴ Kurusu.
⁶⁵ Sasanami. In Omi Province. The word is thus rendered in the *Sasanami-Iri-Ayobiki* (a manuscript in the possession of the Asawi family), which quotes it from the lost *Omi-Fudoki*. Some, however, prefer to render the word "Ripples" (sazanami).
⁶⁶ *Nihodori*. Widgeon.
⁶⁷ The trio, Jingu the Empress-Regent, Noble-of-Brave-Uchi her prime minister, and the infant Ojin, are continually met with in Japanese art. An issue of Japan's bank notes carries Takè-no Uchi's picture.
⁶⁸ See p. 203.
⁶⁹ Tsushima.
⁷¹ Tsunuga.
⁷² Alternative name: Food-Wondrous-Great.
⁷³ "One account," cited in the *Nihongi* implies this. It does not appear in the Narrative, however, that the Emperor (Ojin) was ever called by the name of the Kami, and this account is opposed to all other variants of the legend.
⁷⁴ Chiyura.
⁷⁵ Prince-Little-Renowned (see p. 54).
⁷⁶ An expletive used at the end of a sentence, merely to give force.

⁷⁷ Supposed to have been a kingdom that later became a portion of the kingdom of Mimana (Imna), Korea.
⁸⁰ See p. 153.
⁸¹ Korean records assert that he was seduced into attacking Kara instead of Silla.
⁸² According to modern critics, about the year 380.
⁸³ Deified as Hachiman (Yawata), deity of war. In origin he was probably the deity Fire-Fade. This identification depends, however, on the oracle of this deity delivered centuries later than Ojin's death. In 712 the Empress Gemmeï built a shrine to him at Usa-machi, Usa District, Buzen Province, under the name Hachiman Daïjingu. Eight years later he came into prominence through his efficiency in repelling a Korean invasion. It was not till the eleventh century, however, that he was given a high rank. The Emperor Seïwa (859-876) built the second Great Shrine to him at Iwashimizu (Otoko-Yama) near K'yoto. Perhaps the most famous of his shrines in modern times is that of Tsurugaöka at Kamakura, established in the eleventh century by Minamoto Yoriyoshi (of whose family this deity was patron), and brought there in 1193 by Yoritomo. At these three shrines the Empress Jingu is also worshipped.

In ancient times soldiers commonly wore little silver swords, dedicated to him, as frontlets of their helmets.
⁸⁴ Ojin.
⁸⁵ There is a vulgar legend according to which he was born with a dragon's tail, and to hide it invented the coat-skirt (*suso*). The *Aïnosho* of the *bonzé* G'yogo relates that on one occasion his tail was pinched by a lady-in-waiting, who inadvertently closed the sliding-doors of the imperial apartment upon it.
⁸⁶ See p. 156.
⁸⁷ Aston, I think without sufficient reason, counts him and Great-Mountain identical.
⁹¹ Later to become the Emperor Nintoku (see p. 228).
⁹² First person deprecatory.
⁹³ Or Awaji (My-Shame).
⁹⁴ Not the Kami of the same name of p. 91.
⁹⁵ In later legend there is much confusion on this point. Some records even list as offspring of this union the four subsidiary shrines of Usa-Hachiman (Waka-Miya, Waka-no Tono, Urè and Kurè).
⁹⁷ Ohomi.
⁹⁸ Suzukuhi-no Oka.
⁹⁹ The derivation here is not clear. *Sega* (*segu*) means either to stimulate or to check.

PAGES 214 - 226

¹ Tanaka. The *Fudoki* text calls him Tanaka-no Kami. Magnates of Tanaka (Tanaka-no Omi) appear later in the reigns of Yomeï- and Temmu-*Tenno*, and the *Shojiroku* cites the first-named as a descendant of Noble-of-Brave-Uchi. There is no clue to the date referred to.

² Ohonori.
³ The meaning of this word is not now known.
⁴ Sasa-no Miwi.
⁵ Tachi-no Sato. This *tachi* is presumed by commentators to be written in error for *tada* (Many-Ricefields). The *Fudoki* note cities, from ancient maps of the province, a Many-Ricefields-Village and a West-Many-Ricefields-Village.
⁶ Ohoüchi (Ohochi)-no Umaya.
⁷ Kagè-Woka.
⁸ Hino-Yama.
⁹ Tsuki-Oro-Yama.
¹⁰ Kurami-Mura.
¹¹ The same syllables, written with other characters.
¹² Sashi-Nu.
¹³ Ahi-Nu.
¹⁴ Ataki-Nu.
¹⁵ Kanaya-gawa.
¹⁶ Mitachi-no Woka.
¹⁷ Ototachi-Woka.
¹⁸ Saki-me.
¹⁹ Toishi-Hori.
²⁰ Suga-Woka.
²¹ Tono-Woka.
ᴬ All of the etymologies given above are given in the *Harima-Fadoki*.
²² Some texts give Karanu (*Karu*: light?).
²³ I.e., at the imperial palace.
²⁴ Near K'yoto.
ᴮ From the lost portion of the *Harima-Fudoki*.
²⁵ Alternative names: Princess-Bridge-of-Uji; Princess-Jewel-of-Uji. The latter name is given her in the *Honcho-Jinjako*.

She is worshiped locally as a goddess of lust, and is supplicated by women for marriage. She is probably, in origin, a phallic deity. Joly says that the shrine at Uji contains phallic symbols that are now hidden from the public, but I have not seen them.

Popular modern legend counts her a deity of jealousy, the daughter of a courtier in the reign of Saga-*Tenno* (810-823) who, through prayer at Kabunè shrine to evil divinities, and by unholy incantations, was transformed into a demon and established her residence under Uji Bridge, the shrine being erected to placate her spirit. A typical form of this version is given in the *Sanshu-Meïsekishi*, vol. XV.

ᴬ The legend of Hashi-Himè (Princess-Bridge) is very old and has a hundred versions, most of them palpably constructed around the ancient poem in the *Kokinshu*:

On the narrow mat, || Spreading the sleeve of her garment,
On this very night
Princess-Bridge of Uji-town || May be awaiting me too.

There are poems concerning her also in the *Isè-Monogatari*, the *Hachidai-Shusho*, and the *Kokin-Wakashu*. Most of these versions apparently originated in the Era of Heïan, but the *Uji-Hashi-Himè-Monogatari* no doubt dates from a far earlier period. The latter, which was in existence up to the twelfth century, is cited in the *Shikiyoshu* (vol. III), the *Yakumogosho* (vol. I), and the thirteenth-century *Kenchu-Mikkan* (vol. XIV) of Fujiwara Tametsuna. In some versions she is said to have been the daughter of a court noble (kugè) of K'yoto, and a famous beauty.

[26] Worshiped with Princess-Bridge at the shrine of Uji, and supplicated in connection with divorce. In origin he, like Princess-Bridge, is probably a phallic deity. A legend cited in the *Honcho-Jinjako* states that this Kami is the spirit of Fujiwara Tadabumi (873-947), known as Uji-no Mimbuk'yo, who died of resentment at receiving no reward for his suppression of the rebellion of Taïra Masakado.

A companion deity at this shrine, whose origin and history are unknown, is the Kami Agata, especially supplicated by *geïsha* and believed to cure venereal diseases. According to some he is the spirit of Dok'yo (Yugè-no Dok'yo), a priest of the eighth century who was favored by the ex-Empress Koken, intrigued to make himself Emperor, and was exiled by Konin-*Tenno*. Others say he is the spirit of Minamoto Yorinaga.

[27] Not to be confounded with the Pleasant-to-Dwell-In (Suminoshi) in Settsu Province. He is known only in connection with the Uji Shrine, where he is confused with Kami-of-Rikuyu. One authority for the statement that the Kami of Uji Shrine is the Kami of Suminoshi is the poet R'yuen Hoki.

[28] In Yamashiro Province.

[29] He is to be regarded, no doubt, as a descendant of Prince-Wave-Swift-Brave-Furu-Bear (see p. 207, n. 60).

[31] See p. 186.

[32] Alternative name Princess-Ito.

[34] See p. 187.

[35] Alternative name King-Great-Hodo.

[37] See p. 143.

[39] These were all countries in Korea.

[40] The "Three Han" (see p. 204, n. 47).

[41] See p. 120, n. 50.

[42] It is curious to find this reference in connection with an event assigned to the third century.

[A] The *Harima-Fudoki*.

[43] See p. 119.

[45] Manè-Ko, whom the text names as ancestor, was self-slain. Noble-of-Sweet-Uchi no doubt became the slave of the head of his house.

[A] The *Harima-Fudoki*.

[46] Mura-gata.

[47] Kako.

[B] A fragment of the lost *Awaji-Fudoki*, cited in the *Ashirin-Saïyosho*.

[48] *Nunawa*, the marsh-mallow.

[49] The *Kojoki* assigns it to him.

[50] Not the Kohata of the song on p. 216.

[51] Alternative name: King-of-Great-Kuaka.

[52] Alternative names: Princess-Nagaï; Young-Kusaka-Be; Princess-Orange.

[53] Korean, Seu-Ko.

54 These teachers of the art are still worshiped, their spirits being enshrined at the supposed place of their burial.
55 See p. 115, n. 7.
56 Given also as Achiki (Ajiki) and Atogi. He is often confounded with Wan-I (below).
57 Or Wang-In.
58 See p. 211.
59 The *Rongo* (Chinese, *Lun Yu*). J'yofuku, however, by one legend, is said to have first introduced the works of Confucius (K'ung-fu-tse) into Japan, in 221 B.C.
60 I.e., manuscript volumes.
61 The *Sen-ji-Mon* (Chinese, *Ch'ien Tzu Wen*). A book composed of one thousand different characters, so disposed that each series of eight forms a complete sentence. This work was, in fact, not produced till more than two hundred years later than this time.
62 Chinese, Wu. A state of China.
63 Korean, Kung-Wol.
64 See p. 191.
65 See p. 120.
66 See p. 97, n. 10, and p. 177, n. 83.
67 See p. 9.
68 The wild goose today is not known to nest south of the 45th parallel.
69 Here occur untranslatable pillow words.
70 See p. 119, n. 36.
71 The *Kojiki* places this incident later, after Great-Wren has become the Emperor Nintoku, but I follow the older commentators, who assume that an earlier place is indicated in the expression "at last" (*tsuhi-ni*).
72 These words remain a *crux* to the commentators. Perhaps *arachishi* is an error for tarachishi, which is a pillow word (well-nigh untranslatable) of Kibi (Maise). Florenz renders, "Yield to one side (in order that) I may see my departing spouse of Kibi."
73 Of course there were no carriages in Japan at this time. The expression is borrowed from the Chinese.
74 It may be inferred from the later Narrative that he was the father of Princess-Elder.
77 Kamu-tsu-Michi.
81 *Hatori-Be*.
82 Kami-Kamo and Shimo-Kamo. These are not to be confounded with the two shrines of like names at Kamo in Yamashiro Province.
83 See p. 145.
84 See p. 116.
85 Imesaki. Mabuchi holds that Imè is for I-Be (Bowman-Clan).
86 The name has occurred before (see p. 215, n. 16).
87 The derivation here is not clear. *Ito* means "thread" or "very."
88 Kamitsukenu. This is the ancient name of the present Kozukè Province, formed (645) by combining with the ancient Kamitsukenu, the western portion of the ancient Kenu Province.
89 It is uncertain from the text whether this is to be considered a Kami in the usual sense. No doubt, however, it was locally worshiped.

⁹⁰ The allusion here is by no means clear.
⁹¹ Commentators assume a hiatus here in the ancient text which seems necessary in the light of what follows.
⁹² One *shiro*: about thirty square feet.
▲ The *Harima-Fudoki*.
⁹⁴ See p. 216, n. 22.
⁹⁵ An onomatope: "*rustle-rustle.*"
⁹⁷ Achi-no Omi, a Korean prince, descended from the Emperor Ling Ti of the Chinese dynasty of the later Han. He came to Japan in the year 289, settling in Hinosaki, Yamato. He was later called Kurando.
▲ The *Kogo-Shui*.
⁹⁸ Korean, In-Pon. Alternative name: Susukori.
⁹⁹ The name that had been given him by the Sun-Folk.

PAGES 227 - 251

² The Go here is equivalent to Wu, the Chinese dynasty previously referred to, which gave its name to one of the three great states of China in the third century, and had its capital at Nanking. Though its last sovereign had fallen long before this, the name persisted in Japanese annals, coming gradually to stand as well for later dynasties.
⁴ Korean, Sin-Cha-To.
⁵ Mikagè-no Ohe-Kami. This deity is now unknown. Iïda Takesato says the word *mikagè* signifies a hair-ornament.
⁶ A note appended to the text of the *Fudoki* attempts to explain this difficult passage by supposing them to have executed a dance similar to one that anciently formed a part of the *Taïshosaï* (the first festival of the New-Rice-Tasting following a coronation) in which chaplets or girdles of oak leaves were worn.
⁷ Toyo-no Sato.
▲ The *Harima-Fudoki*.
⁸ Munakata (see p. 33, n. 98). This three-fold deity is here spoken of collectively as a single Kami.
⁹ Nintoku.
¹⁰ See p. 212.
¹³ See p. 143.
¹⁴ *Kazura japonica*.
¹⁵ This triple adjective is perhaps the best that can be done with the much-disputed pillow word *chihayafuru*.
¹⁶ *Azusa. Rottlera japonica*.
¹⁷ *Evoynmus thunbergianus*.
¹⁸ See p. 217.
¹⁹ Those set apart for concubines.
▲ The *Seïshiroku*. This *Be* was charged with the provision of wet-nurses for the imperial princes.
²³ E. H. Parker cites these peculiarities as belonging to an earlier Liang emperor in China.

²⁴ There is an old popular song based on this incident which runs:
Takakiya-ni || Noboritè mireba,
Kemuri tatsu.
Tami-no kamado-wa || Nigiwaï-ni keri.
(To the turret high || Climb I to gaze about me.
Lo, spiralled smoke!
See how prosperously now || Grow the hearths of the people.)
²⁵ Wani-no ikè, in Kawachi Province.
²⁶ Naniwa-no Horiyè.
²⁷ Hori-ye. Motoöri identifies this with the present Ohokawa (Great-River) in Ohosa, and says the modern Horiyè is not meant.
²⁸ See p. 191.
ᴬ The Kokin-Hichu, vol. III (quoting an unnamed Fudoki).
ᴮ The lost Settsu-Fudoki, cited in the Mütsu-Michiwakè of Tachibana Moribè.
²⁹ The people who followed Yutsuki-Lord to Japan (see p. 221, n. 63). Hada: T'sin, the dynasty of She-Hwang-Ti (see p. 191, n. 59).
³¹ Alternative name: Clan-Chief-of-Skin. Hata-no Kimi (hata, skin). Evidently a descendant of Yutsuki-Lord (see p. 221). There seems to be a pun intended in this name as hata and hada are interchangeable in Japanese.
³² Tanu.
³³ Kusu-no Kori.
³⁴ Minami-Toribè-no Sato.
ᴬ The lost Yamashiro-Fudoki, quoted in the Kakaïsho, the Bungo-Fudoki, and the Chiribukuro, vol. VIII. The first gives the residence of the white-bird, and the last has a later addition as follows: "During the Era of Temp'yo (729-749, Empress Gensho) a man named Kuni, who lived in Hayami, thought it regrettable that a place should be so desolate which had been once so flourishing. So he came there and planted ricefields, but the plants withered and he was afraid and tried no more, but abandoned the place."
³⁵ Inari-no Yashiro. Florenz (Japanische Mythologie, p. 292, n. 9) renders the last syllable "man," as in hitori, futari, etc. It seems likely that this old legend had not been called to his attention.
ᴬ The Jimmeï-Cho-Tochu-Shosha-Kongen-Ki.
³⁶ Tatè-hito no Sukunè. Alternative names: Noble-of-Toda-of-Target: Ikuba: Target.
³⁷ This and the following "Magnate-of-Intelligent-Remainder" were perhaps less names than court appellations.
³⁸ Alternative name: Magnate-of-Intelligent-Remainder.
³⁹ Usu-Be (Usumè).
⁴⁰ Competent authorities identify this Kami with the earlier one of the same name (see p. 10). Here he is given the alternative name of Great-Kami-of-Carry-Across.
⁴¹ The present Settsu Province.
⁴² This line is a pillow word.
⁴⁴ Her private room.
⁴⁵ There is no satisfactory expanation of these names.
⁴⁶ See p. 6, n. 21.
⁴⁷ Yamagata. No such place is now known in Kibi (Maise).

⁴⁸ See p. 217.
⁴⁹ *Hisa-kata* (see p. 78, n. 21).
⁵⁰ It is uncertain what tree is meant. Aston's suggestion is Idzu-ki, sacred tree.
⁵¹ See p. 214.
⁵² Kurahashi-Yama, in Yamato Province.
⁵³ See p. 67, n. *.
⁵⁴ See p. 8.
⁵⁵ See p. 97, n. 11.
⁵⁶ *Kura-hito-me*.
⁵⁷ This is puzzling. Chamberlain thinks the word modernly rendered "mustard" meant anciently the aralia, which might explain this name, the aralia leaf being three-cornered. But the explanation is at best hazardous.
⁵⁸ See p. 232, n. 26.
⁵⁹ This tree is now unknown.
⁶¹ This line is an attempt at the rendition of the baffling phrase *Kimo-mukafu*, a pillow word of "heart." It has, I fear, very little to commend it. *Kimo* is the old word for intestines; the intestines of a fowl or of a small animal are still so called.
⁶² As has been said earlier, in Japanese the same word does duty for both colors (see p. 4, n. 11).
⁶³ No commentator has been able to give pronunciation or explanation of the unknown character here used. Motoöri's guess that the character means "cocoon" seems the best.
⁶⁴ See p. 226.
⁶⁶ In this incident is to be found the explanation of the herds of deer on the Island of Miyajima (Itsukushima), whose chief Shinto priest is of this Saheki family. In memory of the exile of their ancestor, these priests kill no deer, which are in consequence so tame that they run in the streets and sleep on the steps of the shrine.

A curious later variant of this legend—incidentally employed to furnish a derivation of the name Itsukushima—is given in the Nagato Text of the *Heïkè-Monogatari*, which is preserved at Amida-Ji, Shimonoseki. For Toga Moor in Settsu it gives Inami in Harima Province, for Nuta in Oki it gives Sasara-Beach, and it places the incident in the reign of the Empress Suiko (593-628). This version was written at the beginning of the Kamakura period, doubtless by some priest of the *Shingon* Sect. It is as follows:

"There was a stag on Inami Moor which belled in seven notes and the Empress desired to see it. Kuramoto of the Saheki obeyed the imperial command, and constructing a bow . . . went to Inami Moor and shot the stag and showed it to her. It was of golden hue and had five colors. Then the high officials took counsel and said, 'Of old there was a golden deer, and it was one which held authority. So that he who kills such a one cannot be without guilt.' Therefore the man was banished to Sasara-Beach in Aki Province. Perhaps from hunger, or to dissipate his ennui, he went out in a boat to fish, rowing it along the shore. Thus, one day, gazing toward the sea, he beheld nearing a large ship whose sail was scarlet, which, when it came nearer, he saw was a vase of *lapis lazuli*. It bore *goheï* and a favoring wind brought it to his boat, when there issued from the vase a lady in a court-robe who said, 'I have been in the provinces of the west, but have made this long voyage, as it is my desire to dwell here. I pray you show me this island if it be possible.' Obedient to her words, the Saheki conducted her over the Island.... Now when she viewed the scenery of Komori-Strand and Mikasa-Beach, she exclaimed, 'How lovely!' (Wherefore the place was named Lovely-Island.)"

This version states that the man built a shrine at her command and reported the occurrence to the Empress, after which he returned to the place to serve the Kami and to found the present family of Shinto priests who officiate there still. It identifies the Kami who thus appeared as the Buddhist Kwan-On. According to best authority, however, she was one of the three female children born to the Sun-Goddess in her contest with Brave-Swift-Impetuous-Male (see p. 30).

67 *Susuki*. The *Eularia japonica* or Chinese *miscanthus*.
68 Imè (umè)-nu, in Nishinari District, Settsu Province.
69 The saying is *Toga Nu-ni tateru mawoshika mo imè-no awasè-no mani*.
A The lost *Settsu-Fudoki*, cited in the *Shaku-Nihongi*, vol. XII.
70 Korean, Chyu.
71 See p. 244. Noble-of-Tsuno-of-Ki and Prince-Sotsu-of-Mulberry-Castle, here mentioned, may have been descendants of the generals of like names of the preceding century. But there are other reasons for believing there is here a confusion of chronology, due, probably, to a copyist's error, and that the episode originally belonged to an earlier place in the Narrative. According to Korean records, it did not occur till a half-century later.
72 See p. 121, n. 53.
A The *Harima-Fudoki*.
73 Aston thinks it unlikely that the Japanese had cavalry at this time. But considering the history of the nomadic peoples of western Asia, I cannot think it very improbable.
74 Modern versions of the story say he was killed by a poisoned arrow.
75 In Kagusa.
76 The great snake, which continually appears in later Japanese folklore, is called *tani*.
77 Ubè Shrine in the Village of Ko, near Tottori Castle, Tottori District, Inaba Province. The place of the shrine is called Kamreganè Mountain, and is believed to be the spot where he left the sandals. He is enshrined also in one of the temples of Sumiyoshi.
A The lost *Inaba-Fudoki*.
78 The tombs of Mountain-Gate-Brave (see p. 186). It is not clear whether the reference is to one or all of the three mounds.
79 It will be remembered that, in the preceding Narrative, the body of Mountain-Gate-Brave changed into a white swan and flew away, and only his clothing and his ceremonial hat were interred.
80 These had in charge imperial burials (see p. 150).
81 It is uncertain what this "measure" was.
82 See p. 229.
83 See p. 212.
84 See p. 101.
85 Today sakè is drunk warm.

86 See p. 207. This personage, according to the Narrative, had been generalissimo of the Empress Jingu's forces one hundred and seventy-five years previously.
87 Mozu-no Mimi.
88 But see p. 224. Presumably District-Warden was a descendant of Kamo-Lord.
89 Sawi.
90 Miyoki (*mi* [see] -*oku* [keep])-Yama.
91 Presumably a ship on which the Great Kami was temporarily enshrined.
▲ The *Harima-Fudoki*.
92 Richu.
93 Alternative name: Komotsu-of-Sanakita.
94 Hence (see p. 232) Princess-Black was his mother's aunt. She is not the same, of course, as the Princess of like name mentioned on p. 236.
95 The first Japanese record of this custom so prevalent in all Oriental countries.
96 His full brother (see p. 231).
97 See p. 127, n. 1.
98 Alternative name: Sato-Tomo.
99 Hayato. See p. 87.

PAGES 251 - 275

1 Alternative name: Sashihirè.
2 According to many legends the true wolf, though now extinct, was once common in the archipelago.
3 There are indications that a Wolf-Kami received worship. The good Brother Lourenzo, writing to his brethren in India from Miyako, February 20, 1565, records: "In another land called Vonxu (Uötsu, Etchu) live adherents of a sect, so they say, which worship the wolf. They beseech the wolf, by frequent prayer, to allow their members to be changed into wolves in the next life."
4 Ohokuchi-no Makami-no Hara. The Chinese character for wolf is rendered by Oho-Kami (Great-Kami). Dickins says "nothing is now known of this Great Kami. Later in the Narrative (see p. 316) a pair of these animals are addressed as "August Kami."
▲ An unnamed *Fudoki*, quoted in the *Makura-Kotoba-Shokumeï-Sho*.
5 See p. 249.
6 I.e. tattooed. According to the Narrative (see p. 167, n. 32) the *Emishi* had this practice. It was an ancient Chinese penalty. Until long after the Restoration Japanese criminals were tattooed for identification (see p. 270).
7 Alternative names: Lady-of-Aömi; Princess-Awo-of-Iïtoyo-of-Oshinumi; Princess-Oshinomi-Be.
8 See p. 246.
9 The three female children generated in Brave-Swift-Impetuous-Male's contest with Great-Sky-Shiner and sent down by the latter to Tsukushi (see p. 30).
10 See p. 22.
11 One of the three Imperial Treasures (see p. 72, *et seq.*).

[12] See p. 226.
[13] See p. 221.
[A] The *Kogo-Shui* and the *Shoku-in Reï*.
[15] Alternative name: Tashiraga (The *Harima-Fudoki*).
[16] Alternative name: Young-Child-of-Shima.
[17] Ohoshi. The *Nihongi* has a gloss stating that this is the only case where an emperor's personal name (which was assumed after the age of puberty and the writing of which was in ancient times forbidden) is given. Here it is said to be taken "from an old manuscript."
[18] Alternative name: Young-Child-of-Kumè.
[19] Hansho (Hanzeï).
[20] A "line" is generally counted one tenth part of the Japanese inch (*sun*). There is, however, grave doubt as to all of these ancient measures.
[22] Ink'yo.
[23] After puberty a boy's hair was dressed in man's style.
[24] See p. 221.
[25] In self-treatment for the disease from which he suffered.
[26] See p. 217.
[27] See p. 217, n. 36.
[29] Alternative name: Princess-Nakashi.
[30] Alternative name: Great-Hasè-Young-Brave. Hasè, Hatsusè. A town in Yamato Province.
[31] Heaven, Earth, Man. This is a Chinese concept.
[32] See p. 146, n. 97.
[33] This phrase has provoked much discussion. It is probably less a place-name than an appellation growing out of the trials held there.
[34] Motoöri and Iïda say *Kuka* meant stirring hot water with the hand while taking an oath. *Tachi*, according to the former, meant to go to a thing.
[35] The purpose of these is uncertain.
[36] See p. 208.
[A] The *Seïshiroku*. Unless the preceding Narrative is in error (see p. 228), the Forehead-Ricefield-Clan was already in existence. Possibly the emperor appointed him the Clan's Tribe-Master, justifying the act by this whimsical pun.
[38] Alternative names: Princess-Younger; So-to-Ori-Himè. She is not mentioned, at least under this name, in the previous list (see p. 217). The *Kojiki* identifies her with Great-Lady-of-Karu, daughter *to this* emperor; Motoöri identifies her with Lady-of-Koto-Fushi-of-Wistaria-Plain (see p. 218) his granddaughter. Aston suggests the derivation from Soto-ori (Outside-Dwell) in contradistinction to the name of her sister, Oho-Naka-tsu (Great Middle) which he elects to render "Of the Great Interior."

This Kami is widely worshiped as the Goddess of Poetry. The common people sometimes identify her with Young-Sun-Female (see p. 23) but mistakenly.
[39] Fujiwara is an ancient place name for the present Ohara-Mura (Great-Plain-Village) Takaïchi District, Yamato. This was the native place of her father, King-Prince-Kumata-Long, who was given Fujiwara for a family-name. The identity of the place is, however, in dispute, on the basis of a reference in one of the long Lays of the *Manyoshu*.

40 *Waga seko-ga* || *Kubeki yoi nari;*
Sasagami-no
Kumo-no furumaï || *Kanetè shirushi mo!*
The lines contain a suggested pun, which lies in the phonetic similarity between the word Sasagami, here a place-name used to qualify *kumo* (crab), and the word *sasagani* (crab), and in the fact that in Japan a spider is sometimes called "crablet." Presumably she saw one.
41 *Na-nori-so-mo.*
42 Presumably divination had preceded the hunt, also.
43 He-Who-Invites.
44 A popular legend identifies Naga-Zato (-mura) with the modern Nagaë (Nagago). The *Awa-no Ochiho* says that Osashi is a term for Sato-no Ama, but this is hardly credible. The *Shoku-Nihongi* mentions a certain Naga-hi, "Chief of Katsura District, Awa Province," who evidently was a native of Naga.
45 The Awa seacoast from very early times has been noted for its swimmers, and to this day the most skillful divers are to be found in Tsubakidomari-Ura of Naga District, and in Kaïbu District. The folk of the latter locality still retain in their daily vocabulary ancient words such as *kazuku* (to fish by diving) which are obsolete in other sections.
46 *Awabi. Haliotis tuberculata.*
47 A popular version of this legend says the emperor chose at random from among the pearl-divers a woman named Sasaji-Otomè to whom he swore that if she did not bring the sea-ear he would put her husband to death. She brought it, but fell dead at the emperor's feet.

In olden times the most daring divers appear to have been women. The *Engi-Shiki* speaks of marine offerings brought to the ceremony of First-Rice-Tasting from Awa Province, "gathered by ten woman-divers of Naga," and other ancient manuscripts speak of the female divers of this place. It would seem not unlikely that the vulgar legend is the older and that Osashi was a woman.
48 It is at Sato-ura, Itano District, and is locally known as Amazuka (Sea-Man-Tomb). The people of Awaji identify the tomb with one known as the Osashi-tomb at Iwaya-Ura, but the latter is plainly of later origin. There are other tombs known as Amazuka, notably two in Ohoshiro District and at Ikè-no-Tani-Mura, but the character used is that for nun, rather than for sea-man.
49 This no doubt refers to the modulation of the voice in singing.
50 "Clish-clash," an onomatope.
51 *Hydropyrum latifolium.*
52 This third line has baffled all commentators, ancient and modern.
53 This song has perhaps caused as much learned dispute as all the others in the Narrative put together. To make anything approaching coherency, the text (as it now exists) must be stretched to the breaking-point.
54 Moribè assumes this to have been a part of a ceremony, religious or magical, performed for bringing about the return of an absent one. This seems as good an explanation as any.
55 *Unemè.*
56 Anko.

⁵⁷ The *Nihongi* has a curious gloss stating that "the names of these daughters are not in any record." The *Kojiki*, however, gives three.
⁵⁸ See p. 221.
⁵⁹ See p. 265.
⁶⁰ See p. 207.
⁶¹ See p. 266. His full sister.
⁶³ An untranslatable pillow word.
⁶⁴ This is of the regular *tanka* form. For the close of her story, see p. 293.
⁶⁵ She was in fact his elder sister (see p. 265).
⁶⁶ See p. 265. The three were full brothers.
⁶⁷ Said by Confucius, in the Analects.
⁶⁸ Aston says these people, at the time the *Nihongi* was written (A.D. 720), cultivated the imperial gardens. I do not know his authority.
⁶⁹ Imaki-no Aya.
⁷⁰ Fushimi. Chamberlain surmises this to be a corruption of an original *fusè-mizu* (water-laid-on). The popular rendition "Lying-Three," however, is an error; the three years of the legend are purely coincidental, the character employed in the word being based on the radical for *to see*.
⁷¹ Sugahara. In Yamato Province.
ᴬ The *Honcho-Jinjako* of Hayashi Doshun (1583-1657). Its version says the man (Fushimi-no Okina) was a friend of G'yogi-Bosatsu, who visited him at Sugawara (Sedge-Moor) in 736. The latter was the celebrated *bonzè* of Kudaran birth, or at least descent, who first preached in Japan the doctrine of the R'yobu-Shinto, according to which the Shinto deities were regarded as manifestations (*gongen*) of Buddha or Buddhist *Bosatsu*.
⁷² Yu-r'yaku.
⁷³ See p. 252.
⁷⁵ Ogi. The *Hedysarum esculentum*.
⁷⁶ Alternative name: Naka-Chiko.
⁷⁷ See p. 254.
⁷⁸ Kariba-wi. Modern Kabawi.
⁷⁹ See p. 252.
⁸⁰ See p. 131.
⁸¹ Alternative name: Shijimi.
⁸² See p. 252.
⁸³ Asakura.
⁸⁴ *Oho-Muraji*. This term is of uncertain signification. Best authority considers it to have been a military title.
⁸⁵ Alternative name: Lord-Great-Mountain-Gate-of-White-Hair.
⁸⁶ Alternative name: Lady-of-Taku-Hata.
⁸⁷ Alternative name: Princess-Takahashi.
⁸⁸ Of her legitimacy.
⁹⁰ Korean, Kon-chi.
⁹¹ Pieces of game.
⁹² See p. 250. This would make her over seventy at this time.
⁹³ There is a village called Mitobè (Mito-Clan) in Uda District, in Yamato. The function of this Clan is not now known (see p. 148).
⁹⁴ See p. 271.

95 This is the first occurrence of this title in the Narrative. It would seem to indicate a kind of contractor.
96 Alternative name: Shikotoï.
97 Called here by her alternative name Taku-Hata (see p. 271).
98 The place of the Great Shrine of Isè (see p. 148).
99 The character used here is meaningless as rendered nowadays.

PAGES 276 - 303

1 Tani-kahi (-akaï).
2 This Kami is mentioned nowhere else in the Narrative and his paternity is given only in the *Kujiki*. It seems probable that he is to be identified with Eight-Fold-Thing-Sign-Master, grandson of Brave-Swift-Impetuous-Male.
3 The character here used is the name of a particular short form of Chinese verse for which there is no equivalent in English.
4 The *Kojiki*, notably.
5 As having given them refuge.
6 The Hall where the emperor performed the ceremony of the New-Rice-Tasting.
7 The meaning of the pillow word, thus rendered, is disputed.
8 The pillow word employed here is now unknown.
9 There are many guesses as to the meaning of this curious expression in the old texts, but none is satisfactory.
10 *Kaïko*.
11 *Ko*.
12 See p. 113, n. *.
13 The Japanese name for the realm of Wu, in China.
14 The name is so given in Iïda's *Nihonshikitsuhaku*, Vol. 3, p. 2061.
A The *Harima-Fudoki*.
15 Great-Land-Master (see p. 37). This legend is a curious one, especially in the detail of the new name given the Kami here by the emperor—which has led some commentators to consider the deity a Thunder-Kami. The identity, however, seems clear. And Great-Land-Master has once previously taken the form of a serpent (see p. 132).
16 Some popular legends say it was seventy shaku in length, others that he caught it in a bag. Illustrations of the incident rarely give the monster serpent-shape.
17 Later legend greatly elaborates this tradition. According to the *R'yo-i-ki* version, written by the *bonzè* Keïkaï (745?), the emperor, during a thunderstorm, ordered Sugaru to invite the deity to the palace, but its appearance so frightened the *Tenno* that he sent it back. On Sugaru's death the emperor ordered his tomb erected on the spot of the capture, with a stone monument inscribed, "This is the tomb of Sugaru the Thunder-Catcher." This so angered the deity that he descended in a thunderstorm and overthrew it, when the spirit of Sugaru arose and discomfited him a second time, so that the deity was unable to leave the spot for several days. Afterward a new monument was erected inscribed, "This is the tomb of Sugaru, who in life and in death caught the Thunder." For this reason the place was called Ikazuchi-no Oka (Thunder-Hill).

The *Gempeï-Seïsui-Ki* says Sugaru, entering the imperial apartments while the storm was raging, surprised the *Tenno* in intercourse with the Empress, whereon the emperor, in shame at being thus interrupted, despatched him on his difficult errand. It places the tomb between Toyora-dera and Iïoka. According to this version Sugaru summons Shinto priests and conveys the deity to the palace in a litter.

[18] Alternative name: Princess-Ke.
[19] See p. 258.
[20] In Korea.
[21] Alternative name: Iwaki.
[22] Presumably those in Kawachi as distinguished from those in Yamato Province.
[23] No doubt Silla, which lay to the eastward, is here meant.
[24] A Butcher-Clan, however, already existed (see p. 274). Possibly, however, the meaning is that its numbers were merely recruited from among the newcomers.
[25] See p. 207. Here the word has become a title.
[26] The first mention of this art.
[27] See p. 274.
[28] For the probable derivation of this place name, see p. 153, n. 44.
[29] Awi-no Hara.
[31] These Scribes were Chinese, as their names indicate.
[32] The first entrance of the Dragon into the Narrative. It is to be noted that this record was made by a Chinese brush.
[33] These were the clay objects first used at burials, according to the Narrative, in the reign of Suinin-*Tenno* (see p. 150). Legends of this class are frequent in connection with shrines. A notable one (cited in the *Junreï-Ki*) is associated with the Koëki-no Kami [Doroku-no Kami] Shrine on the border of Kiï and Izumi Provinces. According to this legend a priest, returning from a visit at Kumano, slept one night under a tree beside the shrine. In the night there appeared thirty-four horsemen, who shouted loudly, "Master! Art thou here?" at which an old man appeared and said, "My horse has injured his leg and I cannot ride him." Thereon the horsemen galloped off. At daybreak the priest, searching the shrine, found a board on which was painted a horse, and the portion that held the horse's leg was broken. He carefully mended this with cord and passed the next night under the same tree. This time at midnight, when the band of horsemen came with the summons, there appeared the same man leading a thirty-fifth horse on which he sprang and galloped off with the rest. At daybreak, as the priest lay asleep, he returned and thanked him, saying, "By your favor my horse's leg is made whole and I was able last night to discharge my office." Asked the priest, "Who were the horsemen?" Answered the old man, "They are all deities of Koëki, as am I. If we ride not to our duty we are lashed, and by your help I was able to escape the torture laid upon me."
[34] See p. 274.
[36] Alternative name: Naïta-of-Winabè.
[37] Alternative names: Uzumasa; Uzumori-Masa (see p. 289).
[38] See p. 121. In the text here he is called simply "Prince-Saö."
[39] I.e. from Kahi.

⁴⁰ According to the *Engi-Shiki-Cho*.
⁴¹ This is Female-of-Fruitful-Food (see p. 111, n. 78). Some commentators allege that the legend of her first descent, as a bird-maiden, was invented at a later time than this. If so it would point to an effort to justify the incorporation into the Isè rites of a deity originally local.
⁴² Kaminushi.
⁴³ This Kami has, of course, no connection with the sword of like name found by Brave-Swift-Impetuous-Male in the tail of the Serpent-of-Koshi (see p. 36).
⁴ The *Daïjingu-Shozatsuji-Ki, I.*
⁴⁵ He had stolen it, and to protect himself had brought about Great-Lord-of-Hatabi's death at the hands of this sovereign's elder brother, Anaho-Tenno (see p. 264).
⁴⁶ See p. 265.
⁴⁷ See p. 265.
⁴⁸ See p. 221, n. 63.
⁴⁹ The additional details are given in the *Seïshiroku*.
⁵⁰ See p. 285.
⁵¹ Kura-hito (Kurando)-Be.
⁴ The italicized portions are from the *Kogo-Shui*.
⁵³ Niye.
⁵⁴ Alternative name: *Island-Child-of-Three-Rivers-Pipe-River*. He is worshiped as the deity Urashima (Urashima-M'yojin) in Tango Province, where, local legend says, he came in the form of a crane. This province was originally a part of Tamba Province, from which it was taken in 713. Mizu-no E-no Ura-Shima-Ko (Ura [-no] Shima [-ko]). Thus the popular name, Urashima. The latter is one of the "Three Old Men" (*Sanko*), with Noble-of-Brave-Uchi and Miyura-no Osukè. The last was a warrior who fought with the Minamoto Clan against the Taïra, and who lived to the age of one hundred and six.
⁵⁵ Hiyoki. The text, however, gives the *kana* reading Heki.
⁵⁶ The divine five hues were, as a rule, white, black, red, yellow, and blue (-green).
⁵⁷ The *Nihongi* version concludes the tale from this point with this simple statement: "The child of Urashima had affection for her and wedded her, and they two entered the sea and came to the Eternal Land, where they saw the Spirits." The detail given here is from the lost *Tango-Fudoki*, quoted in the *Shaku-Nihongi*, vol. XII.
⁵⁸ There still exists at Suhara near Agematsu, a rock called Nezamè-no Toko (Bed-of-Awakening), from which legend says he angled.
⁵⁹ The text here gives him his alternative name Island-Child-of-Three-Rivers-Pipe-River.
⁶⁰ Kurida assumes this to mean "my life." The meaning, however, seems obvious enough without a strained interpretation. She meant that her desire (for him) would last forever.
⁶¹ She is worshiped, in Tango Province, as the companion deity (*M'yojin*) of Urashima-Daïm'yojin.
⁶² The characters rendered by these two expressions (*subaru-boshi* and *hiku-boshi*) stand for the constellations of the Pleiads and the Hyades. The allu-

sion shows very clear Chinese influence, as the ancient Japanese knew almost nothing of the constellations and apparently speculated little about the nightly firmament.

[63] From bashfulness.

[64] The casket is called *tamatè-bako* (jewel-hand-box).

[65] His departure had taken place in the twenty-first year of the reign of Yur'yaku-*Tenno* (478). The *Nihongi* was finished in 720, and his return must have taken place before that date, since it mentions that he reached the Eternal Land and saw the Spirits. The *Tango-Fudoki*, which gives the earliest detailed version of the entire legend, citing, however, an older version, written by the earlier governor, Umakaï, Tribe-Master of Iyobè, which Dr. Kurida believes to be one of the documents included in the *Fuso-R'yakki* of *Koën-Ajari* (Genku, known as Honen-*Shonin, c.* 1200), was in all probability written during the first half of the eighth century. An ancient gloss in the *Nihongi* text (rejected, however, by the editor of the *Shukaï* edition) speaks of the story's being "in another writing," which it would seem likely was this *Fudoki*. Moreover one of the long lays (*Suiko-Urashima-Shi wo Eïzuru-Uta*) of the ninth volume of the *Manyoshu*, compiled about 750, gives an elaborate version. All this makes incredible the statement in the *Shaku-Nihongi* (which the popular legend follows nowadays) that his return took place in the Era of *Tencho,* in the second year of the reign of Junwa-*Tenno* (826).

[66] The reading of this line is very problematical.

[67] This version, manifestly a later one, shows the grafting on the earlier tale (that of Fire-Fade) of the more modern form of the Rip Van Winkle, or Peter Klaus motive.

The tale of Urashima, or Urashima-*Taro* (-eldest son), as its hero is popularly called, is one of the oldest and most universally known in Japan. It exists in a thousand variants, in both prose and verse forms, of which the story of the *Tango-Fudoki* and the long ballad of the *Manyoshu* are the oldest extant. There is a version, also probably very ancient, in the *Otogi-Zoshi*, and a later one in the *Kokon-Chomon-Shu*. The student is referred to the *Urashima-Den* (Life of Urashima) and the *Shoku-Urashima-Den* (Additional Life of Urashima) which are both very ancient. The latter is contained in vol. CXXXV of the *Gunsho-Ruiju*, compiled by Hanawa Hokiïchi (finished in 1820).

Later popular versions substitute for the Eternal Land the sea-king's undersea palace, with all its detail.

Aston has translated into English a simpler version of the *Manyoshu* (see *Grammar of the Japanese Written Language*, Appendix, p. 17).

In a footnote in the first edition of *The Classical Poetry of the Japanese*, Chamberlain says: "Urashima's tomb, with his fishing-line, the casket given him by the maiden, and two stones said to be precious, are still shown at one of the temples in Kanagawa, near Yokohama." I have been able to find only the alleged tomb. There are other *tumuli* along the coast for which the same claim is made.

There is an Ainu variant of the tale as follows: A certain man went out in his boat to fish and was carried by a gale to an unknown Land. He found there a populous town, whose chief, an old man of divine aspect, begged him to stay for the night, promising to send him home on the morrow. He did so, and was carried back in a boat by the old chief's subjects, but on the journey was made to lie down and cover his head. When he reached his native place, he was thrown into the water, and before he came to himself, boat and men had disappeared. He had been gone a year. The chief appeared to him later in a dream, revealing himself as the king of the salmon, and required the man in future to worship him, under pain of poverty.

The story has also a number of well-developed versions in modern Japanese legend. One, which is found in Kii Province, attaches itself to a whirlpool known as Fujimaki Fuchi, in the Kumano River, east of Hommiya. The legend relates that a flute-player named Ozaki was sitting on a rock above this pool playing a secret air, when a gust of wind tore the flute from his hands and it fell into the abyss. Plunging in after it, he found at the bottom, which was spread with green mats, a beautiful woman weaving, with a kitchen-range by her side. At her solicitation he remained there three days, returning then with his recovered flute, to find his family celebrating the third anniversary of his death. It is said that a kitchen-range of stone may be discerned at the bottom of the pool. In the village near by it is believed that if its people indulge in impure life serpents will issue from the abyss and a storm will waste the countryside. Another version, of Kaï Province, is localized at the foot of Mount Kineïwa, in Kita-Tsuru District. A farmer dropped his ax into the river, and diving for it, was met by a woman of angelic beauty with whom he spent a day, and who, at his departure, gave him a magic jewel. He had been gone a year. Afterward he had only to write upon paper the name of any article he desired and, holding the jewel in his hand, throw the paper into the river, when the thing he desired appeared on its surface. He thus became rich, but the virtue of the jewel vanished when his wife unwrapped it in his absence. Prayers for rain are nowadays made at the spot, with a peculiar ceremony in which the officiating priest sets adrift one hundred short straw cords, while the villagers pour water upon branches of bamboo. The meaning of this ceremony has been lost.

A The lost *Tango-Fudoki*, quoted in the *Shaku-Nihongi*, vol. XII.
68 For the story of her affiancing, see p. 267.
69 It is difficult to account for this extended period, except on the single authority of the *Kojiki*, according to which he lived one hundred and twenty-four years.
70 Seïneï.
71 This is probably the Mound-Front-of-Tree previously met with (see p. 283). The omission of a single character (*be*) from the text would make the names identical.
72 See p. 252.
73 See p. 296.
74 *Muro* (see p. 100).
75 "It is many years since we fled," King-Little-Basket has just said to his brother. Two reigns, indeed, had elapsed meanwhile. The older commentators give much space to attempts at a reconciliation of dates which would justify the use here of this expression. But it seems more natural to count the "young children" merely local-deprecatory.
76 *Dolichos*.

77 *Etsuri.*
78 The word that forms this line (*Ina-mushiro*) is a pillow word of the word *kawa* when it means skin, since skins were in early times used to sleep upon. Here, however, the word *kawa* means river, but the pillow word is nevertheless employed, with somewhat the effect of a pun.
79 Murray hazards the guess that this song and the following chant had been known at the imperial court when the two princes were children. The personal application of most of the lines forbids this supposition, but it may quite reasonably be true of certain portions. This would explain Little-Shield's subsequent instant belief in their pretensions.
80 See p. 254.
81 This expression has by this time become conventionalized. He was not more than thirty-five years old.
82 Kenzo.
83 There seems little doubt that she ruled as Empress, but that the record was suppressed in succeeding reigns. Ban Tomonobu states in his *Hikobaë*, that she was so listed in the first draft of the *Nihongi* made in 714. Papinot gives her posthumous title as Seïteï-*Tenno*.
▲ The *Harima-Fudoki.*
84 See p. 231.
85 Alternative name: Queen-of-Wave-Swift.
86 The *Kojiki.* This, however, would make her long past the marriageable age.
87 Prince-Push-Teeth-of-Near-the-Market, who had been murdered by the emperor Great-Hasè (see p. 270).
88 See p. 269. Presumably a descendant of Noble-of-Kara-Bag.
89 They were uneven (see p. 300).
90 See p. 270.
91 His genealogy is not given in the Narrative.
92 *Euphorbia.*
93 The first mention of money in the form of coin.
94 Moon-Darkness-Possessor (see p. 19).
96 Great-Sky-Shiner.
97 Tsushima.
98 The *Lycopodium.* The word means, literally, Happiness-Plant.
▲ The *Seïshiroku.*
99 See p. 310.

PAGES 303 - 327

1 Koshi-no Michi-no Kuchi. This later became the Province of Echizen.
2 See p. 135.
3 Alternative name: Prince-Futo.
4 See p. 283.
5 Kata-woka (Kataöka).
6 Ninken. It is believed by some commentators that in the earliest texts of the *Nihongi* he was not counted in the list of sovereigns.
7 For other palaces of his, see p. 304.
8 See p. 272.

⁹ Alternative name: Princess-Middle-of-Orange.
¹⁰ Alternative names: Lady-of-Mountain-Ricefield-of-Kasuga; Princess-Great-Lady-of-Mountain-Ricefield; Princess-Akami-of-Mountain-Ricefield; Princess-Kasuga; Princess-Akami.
¹¹ See p. 270.
¹² This is probably a title used as a family name.
¹³ Korean: Sunyuki.
¹⁴ Korean: Nonyuki.
¹⁵ Muretsu.
¹⁶ *Shibi*. The *Thynnus*.
¹⁷ The first mention of a street, as distinct from a road.
¹⁸ See p. 112, n. 86.
¹⁹ The bridal enclosure.
²⁰ This song exchange is variously given, and the songs in the *Kojiki* version differ materially from these. The commentators (notably Moribè) have arbitrarily rearranged them in different order in the effort to lend coherency to a sequence which readily lends itself to a dozen interpretations, all equally unsatisfactory.
²¹ See p. 270.
²² The *Kojiki* gives this incident the earlier place.
²³ See p. 210.
²⁵ His half-sister (see p. 304).
²⁶ Aston supposes this to be an error. Kanamura had just been made Great-Tribe-Master of the imperial guard and his father Muruya had been given this office something over eighty years previously.
²⁷ Murdoch, no doubt from similarity of character, suggests that this emperor may have been identical with Yur'yaku-*Tenno*. Some Japanese commentators, who are followed by Brinkley, claim his acts to have been confused with those of the contemporaneous King Multa (Mata) of Kudara.
²⁸ If popular legend is to be credited, this Japanese Heliogabalus was murdered in the palace.
²⁹ Keïtaï.
³⁰ See pp. 171 and 190.
³¹ See p. 304. He was great-grandson of the Great-Lord whose alternative name was King-Great-Hodo (see p. 217).
³² See p. 177, n. 84.
³³ See p. 131.
³⁴ The character used here more properly means signet, and Aston questions whether a signet, which it is recorded was sent to Japan by a Chinese emperor, is here alluded to. But the context makes it reasonably sure that the Three-Great-Treasures are intended.
³⁵ Showing humbleness by taking for the time being only the least of the Three-Great-Treasures.
³⁶ Alternative names: Menoko: Iroë.
³⁸ Alternative name: Prince-Oinè-of-Magari.
³⁹ Alternative name: Prince-Himokuma-High-Ricefield.
⁴⁰ Alternative name: Princess-Youth.
⁴¹ See p. 304.
⁴² I.e. of the palace.

⁴³ In various texts Haruki is given as Hiraki or Harani.
⁴⁴ In some texts, Mariko.
⁴⁵ The *Hitachi-Fudoki*.
⁴⁷ In Mimana.
⁴⁸ Though officially reckoned as regent, she is here given the imperial character.
⁴⁹ See p. 304. She had been the half-sister and empress of the emperor Young-Wren-of-Little-Hasè (Muretsu).
⁵⁰ This line is too doubtful to hazard an interpretation.
⁵¹ For noticeably similar songs, see p. 46.
⁵² As being superior to himself. This phrase shows distinct foreign influence, as the *left* hand, anciently and modernly, is the place of honor in Japan.
⁵ᴬ The lost *Tsukushi-* and *Chikugo-Fudoki*.
⁵³ The *Shaku-Nihongi*, vol. XIII, quotes an "old legend" which declares this to be the cause of a disease peculiar to the locality.
⁵⁴ See p. 8.
⁵⁵ There is a pun here. *Kara* means hard or cruel.
⁵⁶ See p. 252.
⁵⁷ The *Kojiki* gives forty-three, the *Nihongi* eighty-two.
⁵⁸ Mishima. In Settsu Province.
⁵⁹ Ankan.
⁶⁰ He was difficult to understand.
⁶¹ Giles states that the private apartments of the empress of China were thus named in allusion to one of the Han empresses who kept by her quantities of pepper-flowers, which are noted for their fruitfulness.
⁶² Alternative name: Satoi.
⁶³ Used here in compliment, as modernly in some other eastern countries.
⁶⁴ A descendant, presumably, of the Tribe-Master Brave-Prince, mentioned on p. 274.
⁶⁵ No doubt by a scribe's error, he is here called Great-Tribe-Master of the *imperial guard*.
⁶⁶ This cattle-breeding here continued till 717.
⁶⁷ Senkwa.
⁶⁸ Two of the Three Sacred Treasures (see p. 72).
⁶⁹ See p. 304.
⁷⁰ Alternative names: King-Wiha; Mariko. The latter name had been his uncle's (see p. 321).
⁷¹ The *Hizen-Fudoki*, quoted by the *Senkaku-Manyo-Sho*, vol. V.
⁷² Hirè-Furu-Yama (*hirè*, neck-band; *furu*, wave).
⁷³ To modern Japan her name became a synonym for a faithful wife. The *Jukkunsho* gives a Chinese legend very similar to this: "There once lived a couple in China. The husband being compelled to go to the front at a great distance, the wife went as far as the north mountain of Busho to see him off, carrying her child. She wept bitterly to see him depart. He never returned, and she died where she stood with the child on her back, becoming at length petrified.... Therefore the mountain was called Bofuzan (*bo*, to desire; *fu*, husband; *zan*, mountain) and the rock was called Bofuseki (*seki*, stone)."

The same name is given to a rock on the hill called Ishikiri-Yama (Stone-

Cut-Mountain) behind the temple of Jufuku at Kamakura. It is told that the wife of Hatakeyama Shigeyasu, watching the battle (1205) between her husband's troops and those of Hojo Tokimasa, who had been sent by the *Shogun* Minamoto Yoriïyè to arrest him on a charge of treason, seeing the rout in which he was killed, was turned to this stone.

[74] The latter legend is given also by the *Yuchusho*, vol. VIII.

[A] The *Hizen-Fudoki*.

[75] Kimmeï.

[76] See p. 311.

[77] See p. 316.

[78] Alternative name: King-Yata.

[79] Korean, Kwi-Chi-Pu.

[80] Hada, T'sin.

[81] Alternative name: Great-E.

[82] Alternative names: Princess-Inamè: Princess-Imè.

[83] Her half-brother on one side and cousin on the other (see p. 324).

[84] Alternative name: Princess-Nuka-Ricefield-Clan.

[85] Alternative name: Kimi-of-Little-Elder-Sister.

[86] Alternative name: Prince-Ibaraki.

[87] Alternative name: Princess-Hasetsuka-Clan-Anaho-Clan. Under the record of this emperor the *Kojiki* text, which numbers the children as five, does not give this daughter. But it names her under the later reign of Yomeï-*Tenno*, whose Empress she became.

[88] Alternative names: King-Anaho-Clan-of-Kusa-Clan; Sumè-Irodo; Prince-Child-of-Sky-Tsuka; Sumoto. One book (cited in a gloss in the *Nihongi* text, under the later reign of Jomeï-*Tenno*) speaks of this name as indicating two separate princes, but this is no doubt a scribe's error.

[89] Alternative name: Prince-Hasè-Clan.

[90] This is the *kana* reading. The characters, according to Giles, stand for the Tungusic ancestors of the Manchu (*Su-Shen*).

[91] The Japanese rod (10 *shaku*).

[92] King Shom'yo (Korean, Myöng).

[93] S'akya-Muni (Gautama). The Buddha. The name means the S'akya (dynasty of Kabilavastu or Kabirae)-Hermit.

[94] Popular legend says there were three images given at this time, of Amida, Kwan-On, and Daïseïshi, which had originally been made by the Buddha himself from gold obtained from the palace of the sea-dragon, and had finally found their way to Korea.

[95] For this reference the student may consult Mayer's *Handbook*, p. 21.

[96] India.

[97] Later legend has it that this statue was later recovered by Honda-no Yoshimitsu, who saw its shining, and who carried it to Shinano. It was finally restored, in 1598, to its original site, at Zenkoji.

[98] Of the palace.

[99] This is a Korean name. Alternative name: Scribe-of-Ships.

¹ Ta-zu-Kahi.
² The meaning of this is not clear.
⁴ The expression is not translatable. The *Nihongi* contains a gloss which says, "Silla words whose meaning is not certainly known."
⁵ *Ohobako (obako). Plantago major.*
⁶ See p. 321.
⁷ A curious gloss, probably added to the *Nihongi* text by some commentator, says, "The iron house is in the Buddhist Temple of Choänji, but in what province this Buddhist temple is, is not known."
¹⁰ See p. 310.
¹¹ This phrase, as has been earlier noted, is conventional. Some authorities say he was eighty-one. Others say sixty-two and sixty-three.
¹² Bi-Datsu.
¹³ Not in the Korean country of that name, but in a place named after it in Japan.
¹⁴ See p. 320.
¹⁵ Alternative name: Great-Magnate-of-Island.
¹⁶ The Buddhistic *Triratna* (Buddha, the Sacred Law, and the Priesthood).
¹⁷ See p. 327.
¹⁸ Alternative name: Scribe-of-Ports.
¹⁹ Alternative name: Princess-Shitsu-Kaï-of-Uji.
²⁰ Alternative name: Otoshi-of-Unako.
²¹ Alternative names: Princess-Tamura; Princess-Nukadè-Princess.
²² Alternative name: Prince-Madè.
²³ Alternative names: Oshizaka-Oïnè-of-Prince-Man; King-Little-Maro.
²⁴ The same name as her half-sister listed above.
²⁵ Alternative name: Otoshi-of-Little-Muna-Kimi.
²⁶ Alternative name: Youth-Nakatsu-of-Kasuga.
²⁷ He became the Emperor Jomeï (Extend-Brightness), to whose reign the Narrative does not extend.
²⁸ The previous genealogies do not mention these princes.
²⁹ For her own service.
³⁰ The *Nihongi* text has "the imperial princess Uji." The incident, however, seems clearly to refer to this princess. It can scarcely have been the half-sister mentioned previously (see p. 335) whose alternative name is the same, as she married the imperial heir, Shotoku. Perhaps the two named have been confused in the genealogies.
³¹ He is not previously mentioned, at least under this name.
³² The *Nihongi* text has a gloss here which says, "These were very hairy."
³³ See p. 143.
³⁴ The Buddha-to-Come (*Maitrêya*).
³⁵ This is a Korean name.
³⁶ In every era since this time it has been the custom for each noble family to devote one daughter of the house to the religious life. The *Jodo* sect (Buddhist) maintains some fifty novices, thus contributed, in its school in K'yoto, destined to become abbesses of convents. Daughters of Prince Nijo, Viscounts Mori and Karahashi, and many other noblemen in public life have thus become *religieuses*.
³⁷ *Shari* (Sanskrit, *sarira*).

38 Noble-of-Inamè. The statue had been flung into the Naniwa (Wave-Swift) Canal (see p. 338).
39 Alternative name: Oru-Ke.
40 See p. 333, n. 16.
41 See p. 87.
42 See p. 324, n. 88.
43 Yomeï.
44 Shinto, the "Way-of-the-Deities." The first time the phrase is used in the Narrative.
45 Alternative names: Prince-Stable-Door; Prince-Fruitful-Ears-of-Stable-Door-of-Upper-Palace; Great-Law-King; King-Law-Master. This is the famous Shotoku (True-Virtue)-Taïshi (Heir-Apparent), the most talented man of his time and the real founder of Japanese Buddhism.
46 Alternative name: Hiroko.
47 Alternative name: Prince-Little-Maro.
48 Alternative name: Lady-of-Sugashiroko.
49 I.e. of the palace.
50 Prince-Hasetsuka-Clan-Anaho-Clan.
51 See p. 335.
52 This is the very ancient witchcraft of the (waxen) image. These puppets, in Japan, were later made of straw or of clay.
53 Aston thinks this reference indicates a knowledge of lacquer. But the clan is mentioned earlier. A much greater antiquity is, in fact, claimed by the Japanese for this art.
54 Alternative name: Priest-Tokusaï. A questionable gloss in the *Nihongi* text states that this man was the son of Shiba-Tatto (see p. 337).
55 *Boddhisattva*, the Buddha's attendants.
56 See p. 324.
57 Sujun.
58 See p. 336.
59 It is uncertain whether this is the Little-Maro referred to on p. 332.
60 *Celtis willdenowiana*.
61 The boy's style was called, as a *Nihongi* note states, "gourd-flower" (*hisago-hana*), and the man's style was called "roll-up" (*agè-maki*).
62 According to Hepburn, the *Rhus semialata*.
63 The four *Dêva* Kings who in Buddhism guard the four directions against *Asuras*.
64 Black was the color worn by men of no rank.
65 Commentators say that she wished to seize the family property. This seems unlikely, however. The greater part of it, land and slaves, was confiscated, and it does not appear that the Great-Magnate profited by it.
66 The Temple of Tenno-Ji at Osaka. It still stands.
67 The temple was built from the mansion's materials.
68 One *shiro*, about fifteen acres English.
69 *Oshidè*. A stamp similar to the modern rubber-stamp or seal, used to give authority to an official warrant.
70 If the characters are to be considered as used phonetically (*inu*, dog), it seems probable that this is a scribe's error, and that the personal name of this officer is not given.

71 Alternative name: Kotè-Child.
72 See p. 344. This is another officer of the same name.
73 Neither of these two wives was made empress, and Otè-Child is not mentioned by the *Kojiki*.
74 Japan's first Buddhist nun.
76 See p. 342.
77 One of the darker blots on the history of the line imperial, which regard for the latter's sacrosanct character leads Japanese commentators very generally to overlook. "In all the forty-five centuries during which Japan has passed through many vicissitudes of national existence," writes Professor Nitobè with singular forgetfulness, in *Bushido*, "no blot of the death of a Charles I or of a Louis XVI ever stained the pages of Japanese history."
78 Suiko.
79 Korean, Hye-cha.
80 A Korean name.
81 The temple which Prince-Ear-Quick-Wise-Virtue had vowed to build (see p. 344).
82 *Tera* (*dera*). The word is used for both palace and temple. In the latter sense, it is the Buddhist structure that is meant, in distinction to the Shinto shrine.
83 The name has appeared before (see p. 347) as that of a female.
84 The first mention in the Narrative of these animals.
85 Isè Sadatakè, in his *Afuhizukuri* (1779) says this deity is unknown. There is no trace of such in the Narrative, other than this mention, unless it is to be found in the legend of the *Jishin-Uwo* (Earthquake-Fish) (see p. 90, n. 71).

Aston's note to the effect that the *Shaku-Nihongi* states that in the reign of Shomu-*Tenno* (724-748) there were "shrines to the Earthquake-God in all the seven Home Provinces," perhaps was based upon a misreading of the following passage: "*Mizu noto u*: Messengers were sent to all Provinces in the Empire *to investigate Shrines which had been damaged by the earthquake,* and to offer *mitegura*."
86 See p. 349.
87 Kwal-Luk (Sozu).
90 This, erected in 604, is the present Temple of Kwor'yu-Ji (Uzumasa-Dera) in Kadono District, Yamashiro Province. It is a seat of the *Shingon* Sect.
91 All of these for sacred uses.
92 These are not, properly speaking, "laws," they are moral maxims—the first real legislation came in the "Laws of Kotoku," who reigned 646-654. Only the titles are here given.
93 Presumably matters connected with the imperial line or with the Kami.
94 A term applied to Chinese books. Some commentators, however, think it refers here to the copying of Buddhist *Sutras* (for which yellow paper was used) or to the painting of Buddhist pictures.
95 The first use of this word in the Narrative. In ancient times it was approximately equivalent to the Chinese *tael*. The *r'yo* varied greatly in later centuries.
96 Sanskrit, *Crimaladevisimhanada*.
97 Sanskrit, *Saddharma-Pundarika-Sutra*.

⁹⁸ This Clan already existed.
⁹⁹ See p. 152, n. 31.

PAGES 352 - 360

¹ This had already been constructed (see p. 132). Probably in this reign it was enlarged.
² The name of a Chinese dynasty.
³ The Chinese emperor omits from this word one of the characters used in writing his own title of emperor, to indicate the subserviency implied in the further phrasing of the letter.
⁴ These references to the weather in Chinese and in Japanese are as fully conventionalized as the English "Very truly yours."
⁵ See p. 344.
⁶ In the use of the word Sovereign a distinction is made similar to that of the Chinese letter. She herself is given the divine character, translated generally throughout this Narrative as *Sky*.
⁷ The local ruler, or commissioner.
⁸ The Japanese pronunciation. (Korean: To-Heun and Hye-Mi.)
⁹ Apparently a son of Tori, Magnate of Abè (see p. 352).
¹⁰ Probably not identical with the general of like name mentioned on p. 329, as forty-eight years elapse between the two citations.
¹¹ He is called in this place Magnate of Uchi-of-Abè.
¹² Literally, bellies.
¹³ Sanskrit, Sumêru. The great mountain that supports the Buddhist heavens.
¹⁴ Alternative name: Ugly-Maro.
¹⁵ This had been once dug in Nintoku's reign (see p. 232), but possibly required reëxcavation.
¹⁶ This island lies not far off the coast of Satsuma, in the south. It is odd that it should have been at this time accounted foreign territory.
¹⁷ Presumably one that had been struck by lightning. Among the ancient Japanese, as among many other peoples, such trees were regarded with veneration.
¹⁸ See p. 232, n. 27.
¹⁹ The first suggestions of the *kappa*, the river-haunter, which figures so largely in the folklore of Japan today.
²⁰ *Uji*. Noble houses.
²¹ The first mention in the Narrative of the use of the memorial pillar.
²² Alternative name: Governor-of-Great-Pillar.
²³ The first mention of a comet.
²⁴ Such subjects as were not slaves.
²⁵ His portrait, alleged to have been painted by himself, is to be seen at the Tenno Temple (see p. 345, n. 66).
²⁶ Heaven, Earth, and Man (see p. 257, n. 31).
²⁷ See p. 353.
²⁸ See p. 349.
²⁹ A purely religious office.
³⁰ See p. 151, n. 29.
³¹ 1 *jo*: 10 *shaku* (1 *shaku*: 11¹⁵⁄₁₆ inches, English).

ANALYSIS OF THE NARRATIVE

PAGES 387 - 434

[1] The Code of Laws promulgated in 718 indicates that a Fire-Ceremony was anciently performed annually at the four corners of the imperial palace by the diviners, but there is little doubt that it was merely incantational.

[2] Here, again, there is a shrewd suspicion that this is rather an old superstition-fragment connected with the lightning—such as in England prescribed the house-leek or "Jove's-beard," which Charlemagne, by royal edict, decreed his subjects should grow on their roofs (*et habet quisque supra domum suum Jovis barbam*).

[3] Dr. Edmund Buckley finds a hint of this in the coition-house (a corollary to the bringing-forth-house of the Narrative), considering it a necessary adjunct to the consummation of a marriage which depended on capture. This, however, is by no means an inevitable conclusion.

[4] Notably among the Kalmuks.

[5] The *couvade*, however, persists among the Ainu: "When the baby is about to be born, the father is sometimes called upon to stay at home wrapped up by the fire, or to leave the house and go to stay with some friends for a time where he has to be very quiet, as though forsooth he was ill, for six days, abstaining from *sakè* and worship. He must stay in the hut all the time, and rest by the fireside. This performance is called *yaïnunukè* (comforting or 'blessing' or resting one's self quietly). On the morning of the seventh day he is said to *shotki chupu* (fold up his bed). On this day he returns to his own hut, but even here he must abide quietly at home for another six days."—Batchelor. And from the Ainu it has crept into modern Japanese folklore.

[6] According to Howorth and Satow.

[7] "A popular device for frightening away witches and fairies was to hang bunches of garlic about the farms."—J. M. Barrie in *Auld Licht Idylls*.

[8] The necromancers of old Greece (according to Theocritus: Idyl II, *The Enchantress*) were familiar with it, and it was universal in the Europe of the middle ages. It then had many forms. King James, in his *Daemonology* (bk. II, chap. 5) writes, "the devil teacheth how to make pictures of wax or clay, that *by roasting thereof*, the person that they bear the names of may be continually melted or dried away by continual sickness." Piercing with the pin or skewer, however, was the most usual. Jane Shore in England and the Countess of Soissons in France were accused of making waxen puppets of the Duke of Gloucester and Louis XIV, respectively, and in the time of Queen Elizabeth popular belief thus explained the death of the Earl of Derby. The "Sister Helen" of Christina Rosetti has enshrined the practice in literary form. The Aymara Indian witches practice this sorcery to this day, and the *voodoo* of the West Indies and of certain sections of the United States has a recognizable form of the rite.

[9] How close is the resemblance may be seen by the Homeric line:

Chaos

Erebus (darkness) + Nyx (night)

Aether (light) + Hemera (day)

Eros (love)

Uranus (heaven) + Gaea (earth)   Pontus (sea)

Kronos (Saturn) + Rhea (Ops)   Hyperion (a Titan)

Helios (sun)   Selene (moon)   Eos (dawn)

Zeus (Jupiter)   Hera (Juno)   Pluton (Pluto)   Poseidon (Neptune)

[10] Witness the old Christmastide song (*Kolyadki*) of Carpathia:

> Once there was neither heaven nor earth,
> Heaven nor earth, but only blue sea;
> And in the midst of the sea two oaks.
> There sat there two pigeons—
> Two pigeons on the two oaks,
> And began to take council among themselves—
> To take council and to say,
> "How can we create the world?
> *Let us go to the bottom of the sea,*
> Let us bring thence fine sand,
> Fine sand and blue stone," etc.—Afanasief's Collection.

The Galacian popular legend is similar to the Russian. In the Huron version it is the muskrat which brings from the waters the bit of soil which becomes the Earth.

[11] It is common to fifty oceanic stocks, the Marshall Island version (according to Dr. Neville J. Whymant) showing greatest similarity to that of the Japanese.

[12] The student may compare the story in the *Katha Upanishad* (Muir, *Sanskrit Texts*, vol. V, p. 329).

[13] Late Rabbinical writings contain a legend of a Mohel (a circumcizer) who was summoned one winter's night by a stranger. The latter led him into the bowels of a mountain, and "after descending many flights of steps, they found themselves in a great city." In a palace there was the mother of the babe he was to circumcize. She told the Mohel that he was in the land of the Mazikin, but that she herself was human, having been stolen away when a child. She counsels him *to eat nothing there* lest he become like one of the Mazikin, and remain there forever.—Hartland, *The Science of Fairy Tales*.

[14] The Tongans say their first ancestors were deities who ate the Tonga food and thus became mortals.

[15] Saxo Grammaticus cites another example in Danish folklore.

[16] Curiously such authorities as Preller and Schwartz make Medea a goddess of the moon or of the lightning.

[17] For the Slavonic variant of this world-myth, see my "Russian Wonder-

Tales" (London, 1912): *Tzarevich Ivan, the Glowing Bird and the Grey Wolf.*

[18] In the tale as given in the "Thousand Nights and a Night," the hero thus captures the daughter of the King of T'an.

[19] In the Bulgarian tale a youth drinking from a fountain is confronted by a *Rusalka* who demands his eyes in return. He, however, seizes her by the hair, throws her across his swift steed and bears her home. There he tears off her right wing, shuts her in a coffer and makes her his wife. She bears him a son, but at the christening she refuses to dance unless her wing be restored. This is done and she flies away.

[20] For variants the student is referred to Conway's *Demonology* (1880-1881).

[21] See p. 290.

[22] Washington Irving has immortalized the Portuguese version in the "Chronicles of Wolfert's Roost and Other Papers."

[23] Aston has said, "There is no summer and winter myth in these old records and no eclipse myth." Even the rationalistic Japanese is willing to concede more. The author of the history *Kokushi-Riyaku* calls the cave-myth an account of the first solar eclipse. In this he is followed by Lord Redesdale. The whole detail of the story, however, classifies it as a version of the primal solar-myth which no myth-mass of the world is without—the eternal feud of winter and summer and the victorious return of the springtide sun.

[24] Dr. Kitto (see: *Cyclopaedia of Biblical Literature*) concludes that the later Phoenicians worshiped not the sun itself but an astral spirit within it. To the modern Chinese, similarly, the luminary has become the Sun-Governor (Tai-Yang-ti-chun) who rules men's souls.

[25] Hearn was of the opinion that the mirror invariably exposed in a Shinto shrine was not of Shinto origin, but was introduced into Japan as a Buddhist symbol of the *Shingon* Sect. This is clearly an error.

[26] The *Kokushi-Daïjiten* says it was used in the nomination of his eldest son, Prince Atsuhito, who became Daïgo-*Tenno*. The *Zoku-Koji-Dan* says it was given by Fujiwara Mototsunè, son of Nagayoshi, to Daïgo when the latter was crown-prince.

[27] I remember when Mr. Henry Satoh (who elects to spell it with the aspirate, as Mr. Ezra Pound affects to spell the *Noh* (No), a great student of swordsmithery and an authority of standing, was once much taken aback, when the late General Count Teraüchi, at that time Minister of War and later Governor-General of Korea and Premier, remarked to him (quite unjustly as it proved) at a meeting of the Sword-Society of Tok'yo, "I hear you have been recommending fine swords to foreign collectors. *I cannot approve of it!*"

[28] "*Les commentateurs disent que c'est une expression allegorique pour exprimer l'idée de l'amour et de l'attachement des deux sexes; que ces mots designent le membre viril,*" says the translator of Klaproth.

[29] From this fact Hirata argues against a phallic interpretation. But European scholars, from Aston down, do not agree with him.

[30] Dr. Edmund Buckley, in his Monograph *Phallicism in Japan* (University of Chicago Press, 1895), cites an extraordinary modern survival of a thoroughly phallic festival, held at Gwanzandaïshi Temple on Mount Hiyeï.

[31] "I have counted as many as a dozen by the roadside in a trip to Nikko. . . . Buddhist priests whom I have consulted affirm, with some warmth, that they

arose in the 'wicked time of Ashikaga,' though the majority of natives, learned and unlearned, say they are the relics of the ancient people or aborigines."—Griffis, *The Mikado's Empire*.

32 A report of Captain Luke Bickle, of the American Baptist Foreign Missionary Society, compiled from enquiries made by fifty missionaries selected for the purpose for the information of a Federated Missions Conference held in Tok'yo in 1915, states that "Phallic worship . . . is practiced in connection with many Shinto shrines."

33 The student of this subject should consult various references in Hirata Atsutanè's *Koshiden*.

34 Serpent-worship existed, according to Kromer, in Lithuania and Poland, and probably antedated the arrival of the Slavonians. The old Prussians are said to have reverenced a fiery snake which was guarded by their priests. Some authorities consider the supernatural snake an element brought into Russia by the Tatars, and certainly the "snake-country," the home of the twelve-headed-serpent, was near the Black Sea. Ferguson considers the dragon of China and Japan a survival of Turanian serpent-worship, and resemblance between certain features of the Shinto cult and that of the Dasyus will be noted in his *Tree and Serpent Worship*. But the Tatars possessed a fire-breathing snake also, which, there are other reasons for thinking, can hardly be a descendant of the Chinese dragon. I prefer to regard the winged serpent as a universal possession, linking back, it may well be, with a remote time of tenacious racial memory, of which geology has given us pregnant suggestions.

35 One must except, of course, the eating of the flesh of certain ophidians by soldiers and wrestlers, in the belief that it has the virtue of making the eater courageous. This custom—which Charlevoix, the learned Jesuit, found common in his day—is not yet dead.

36 According to Hearn it is modernly a popular belief in Izumo Province that if one kills a snake wantonly he will later find its head in his rice-box.

37 Hearn states that the fisherman who catches this reptilian messenger receives from the shrine a bag of rice. He was able to identify one which was shown him as a hydrophid of the species *Pelamis bicolor*. It is popularly called *Haku-ja* (White-Serpent) and *R'yu-ja Sama* (Lord-Serpent-of-R'yu) in allusion to the belief that it comes from the dragon-palace (R'yugo-jo). It is to be remembered that the syllable *ja* is more than "snake": it contains the idea of the supernatural.

38 Benten's white serpent is referred, by Japanese commentators who are reluctant to admit local origins, to three *sutras* which are almost certainly spurious and of Japanese workmanship. The *Shosan-Chomon-Kishu* says "Benten's original form is a serpent."

39 This is cited by Anderson, but I have not seen it.

40 According to the *Shoku-Nihongi*.

41 The Ainu give the serpent a divine origin. In heaven it was enamored of the Goddess of Fire and when the latter was sent down to earth by the creative deity, it followed her, descending in a flash of lightning.

42 See the *Jikuro-Kun* of Isè Teïjo (1715-1784), chap. III.

43 The tale is to be found in both the *Shin-Chomon-Shu* and the *Yamato-Kwäi-i-Ki*.

44 I have seen few snakes made way with in Japan. If it must be done there

are preliminary cups of *sakè* necessary to nerve the arm, and propitiatory prayers for the spirit of the slain reptile. I used to have the same experience with turtles—for a similar reason. We could never have turtle soup unless the cook was permitted to acquire for himself a sufficient degree of inebriety to enable him to strike the fatal blow.

I remember in the spring of 1917, when three hundred adders were captured by coolies in repairing a sluice gate at Inokashira, near my house in Tok'yo, the people of the place insisted upon their being set free in the hills, lest misfortune fall upon the neighborhood.

⁴⁵ The sacred tree guarded by griffins (or what-not) can be traced back to the Persian Gulf of six thousand years ago. Mrs. J. H. Philpot has pointed out its presence in the walls of St. Mark's at Venice.

⁴⁶ Modern Japanese folklore is prolific in giant trees. The locality called "Tree-Beach," on Lake Biwa in Omi Province, local legend says, is the site of a chestnut tree whose shadow covered many districts, and burrs from which fell in far-off Isè Province. The Governor tried to fell it, but the spirits of the trees and herbs round about came each night to heal the gashes of the axes. One night the hito-kusa-kazura (a kind of ivy) came with the rest, but the tree, counting it contemptible, declined its aid. To avenge the affront, the spirit of the plant appeared in a vision of the sleeping woodcutters and counselled them to burn the tree, which was successfully accomplished.

⁴⁷ Many ancient religions have employed the tree upon which gifts were hung for deity. Arabia had such a symbol, which Mahommetan tradition calls *dhât amvât* (tree-to-hang-things-on). In modern Arabia it is the date palm. In older Egypt it was the sycamore. The Siberian Yakuts nowadays hang bright trinkets on notable trees.

⁴⁸ Romulus, says Plutarch, after his victorious duel with Acron, King of the Ceninenses, "that he might perform his vow in the most acceptable manner to Jupiter . . . cut down a tall oak . . . which he trimmed to the shape of a trophy and fastened on it Acron's whole suit of armor . . . ; then he himself, girding his clothes about him and crowning his head with a laurel garland, his hair gracefully flowing, carried it erect upon his right shoulder."

⁴⁹ It (*su-jang*) was practiced in Silla (Korea) down to the sixth century, when Buddhism abolished it. At royal funerals five men and five women were interred alive. The custom, which existed in very early times in China, was abolished before Confucius and revived after his day.

⁵⁰ Presumably with their heads exposed.

⁵¹ In the same way the *ushabti* (answerer), the small images found in the graves of the Egyptian Pharaohs, took the place of the slaves that were formerly killed to accompany their royal master to the underworld; and the living virgin who was anciently thrown into the Nile at the khalig (canal)-cutting till Amr ibn el Aas conquered Egypt, became by his enlightened order the wood- or clay-puppet called modernly "The Bride Betrothed."

⁵² If Korean written records may be depended on, human sacrifice prevailed to an extraordinary degree in the ancient kingdoms of the peninsula. One instance is mentioned in which three hundred slaves had stones tied to their necks and were thrown into a river. It is related that once a year the people of Opp assembled at the bidding of the local *mootang* (divineress) to throw a beautiful virgin into a river to appease its resident deity. A certain magistrate,

in order to put a stop to this custom, attended the assembly and under the pretext that the girl selected was not sufficiently lovely, ordered the chief *mootang* to take her place. Forced into the water, she sank. He then forced others in to see what had become of their leader and they were also drowned, when the surviving *mootang* begged for their lives and offered to give up the custom.

It lasted in China, despite the disapproval of Confucius, till the seventh century and held its own among the Manchu Tatars till modern times.

53 The rite was postponed on account of the uproar raised by the people, but Kiyomori showed that he had no intention of abandoning the plan. According to some accounts his necromancer Yasuüji declared the site was over the lair of a dragon.

54 As a Kingdom Silla dates from 57 B.C.

55 It is only modernly that the name has been applied to China. In the ancient texts, however, it is sometimes employed loosely to designate the entire Korean peninsula.

56 The word Korea is derived from that of Koraï (called also Koma and Shin-Kan), one of the ancient kingdoms of the country. Koraï was founded in 37 B.C. and fell before Silla in A.D. 668. Korea did not officially receive the name of Chosen till 1392.

57 These parallels have been pointed out by Mr. S. Kanazawa (see: *The Teïkoku-Bungaku*, 1907, p. 995).

58 The *Engi-Shiki* enumerates six shrines in Izumo dedicated to Kara-Kuni Idatè.

59 He is listed by the *Shojiroku* as Korean.

60 This ancient association is reflected in numerous legends of Korea itself. One of these concerns the origin of Suk T'al, one of Silla's prime ministers. Somewhere in northwestern Japan was a kingdom known as Ta-p'a-ra, and there a woman, pregnant for seven years, brought forth an egg. The neighbors were minded to destroy it as a bad omen, but the woman wrapped it in cotton and silk, and put it in a chest and threw the latter into the sea. It drifted to the harbor of A-jin (Silla) where it was drawn ashore by a fisherwoman and found to contain a child, which she reared. Magpies followed the child wherever he went, hence his name: *Suk* (the first portion of the Chinese word for bird) and *T'al* to open. After his education was completed the boy entered the service of the famous statesman Pyo-gong, married the daughter of the king, and became at length prime minister and vice regent.

61 Modern Ung-Chhö (Bear-River), near the mouth of the Nak-Tong.

62 Some Japanese historians, hard-pressed, allege the name *Kuma-So* to have been that of a powerful chieftain ruling over H'yuga and Osumi, who rebelled against the imperial rule, and was in traitorous relations with Silla (Korea).

63 This must have resembled the Roman government of the Britons above the great wall. Silla, the most powerful of the cluster of Korean states, was never fully conquered, except in the record. Its history—by no means a collection of myths, but made up from detailed official records, and compiled under royal command by a congress of scholars, under the leadership of the great *literatus* Kim-gu Ch'il-bu, in 543 (more than 150 years before the date of the *Kojiki*)—does not even mention the Jingu expedition, which would seem inconceivable if anything approaching a real conquest of the lower peninsula

had occurred. The *Sam-guk-sa*, or *History of the Three Kingdoms*, is founded on these records, and to compare the *Kojiki* or *Nihongi* with this work is, as Hulbert has somewhere remarked, like comparing the *Niebelungenlied* with the works of Tacitus.

64 Up to the end of the ninth century the art of the archipelago was to remain almost entirely in the hands of Korean masters.

65 After the San-Kan became tributary, the Korean long-measure was imported and used in Japan under the name *koma-shaku*.

66 See the legend of the fabulous female, Si Wang Mu, and her magical peach tree whose fruit ripened once in three thousand years and bestowed thirty centuries of life upon the one who tasted it. Peach tree gum also was one of the ingredients of the Taoist elixir of life.

67 For the myth's long history before the Taoists incorporated it in their mythology the student is referred to W. Eberhard, *Lokalkulturen im alten China, Lokalkulturen des Suedens und Ostens*, Peking, 1942, pp. 272-3. Motoöri says it is the perverted form of the Japanese story *after it reached China!*

68 The myth, in its main details, belongs to the universal class. The student perhaps will be familiar with the Scandinavian variant. "They took Ymir and bore him into the middle of the yawning void, and made of him the earth: of his blood the sea and the waters; the land was made of his flesh, and the crags of his bones; gravel and stones they fashioned from his teeth and his grinders and from those bones that were broken. . . . Of the blood, which ran and welled forth freely out of his wounds, they made the sea. They took his skull also, and made of it the firmament"—Snorri Sturluson's *Prose Edda: The Beguiling of Gylfi*. The *Rig Veda* describes the creation of all things from the severed body of Purusha, and in one *Humn* (*Sanhita*. Tenth Book, Ninetieth Hymn: *Purusha Sukta*), which, however, best Sanskrit authority does not regard as of great antiquity, the Sun is born from the deity's eye.

69 Successor to Fuh Hi (Japanese, Fukki), 2737 B.C. This resemblance has been pointed out by Anderson.

70 The *Ehon-Koji-Dan*.

71 Confucius, predicting that living men would again be substituted for them, as in fact was the case later, permitted only puppets of straw. The suggestion of the clay images was made also in early Rome.

72 Hindu *toran*. Sanskrit *torana*. Akin to the Egyptian *propylon*, the Chinese *p'ai-lou* (*p'ai fang*), the Roman triumphal arch, the British lych-gate, etc. (see p. 24, n. 39).

73 Professor C. Ito finds Indian features (as well as Greek and Chinese) in the structural plan itself. This temple, near Nara, was founded in 607.

74 Fire existed in the Sky, since bonfires are used to lure the Sun-Goddess from her rock-cave.

75 "Then the Giant's dochter came to the palace where Nicht-Nought-Nothing was, and she went up into a tree to watch for him. The gardener's dochter, going to draw water in the well, saw the shadow, etc."—Lang, *Custom and Myth*, p. 91.

In the Malagasy version of the Jason myth it is the girl who hides in the tree and whose face is reflected in the well.

⁷⁶ Some (see Horiyoka Bunkichi: *A Research on the Japanese and Pan-Pacific Races*) go so far as to identify the most important Kami—even the Sun-Goddess—with those of southern origin.

⁷⁷ Aston stands alone in referring the syllable *so* to *uso* (otter), suggesting a nearer totemistic origin.

⁷⁸ "The spear used at that time, which is enshrined and called Hayakazè-no Miya, is the spirit of Yamato-Dakè-no Mikoto. The place where Hayato was killed is still called Uchiko-Bridge. The deity Yagoro is still worshiped, and his spirit is besought at various places in H'yuga and Osumi Provinces.—The *Jinja-Senshu* of Hondo Chikamitsu.

⁷⁹ The spelling is a matter of taste: Loo Choo (*Collegiate Atlas*), Lew Chew (*Colton's Atlas*), Lu-Tchu (*Chambers Encyclopedia*), Lieou-Kieou (*Abbé Grosier*). Other forms are Lieuchieux, Liquieux, Liqueo and Lexio. The islanders themselves call it Du Chu. The proper Chinese pronunciation of the word is Liu Kiu (Pekinese, Liu Chiu) but the Japanese, to whom the sounds of l (which is not in their syllabary) and r have slight distinction, would write it R'yuk'yu. Titsingh and Claproth used both forms. Hepburn, Satow and Aston have all passed their compliments apropos.

It is to be borne in mind that the Japanese do not (as do Europeans generally) count R'yk'yu as including the northern groups known as the Satsugu-Shoto (the Osumi-Shoto and Amami-Shoto) which historically have always been dependencies of southern K'yushu, but only the three southern groups of Okinawa, Miyako and Yaëyama.

⁸⁰ F. W. K. Müller, *Mythe der Kei-Insulaner und Verwandtes: Zeitschrift fur Ethnologie*, vol. 25, 1893. The tale is quoted by both Riedel and Pleyte.

⁸¹ See p. 90, n. 71.

⁸² She became wife to Count Raymond of Poitiers and built the Castle Lusinia (Lusignan), vanishing, when her husband surprised her in her bath, in her fish-form. Jean d'Arvas popularized the legend in his *Romance* (1387), versified by Conedoette (1401), and Kohler modernized it in 1895. (See his *Der Ursprung der Melusinensage*.)

⁸³ Some are disposed to identify it with the modern Fokien.

⁸⁴ There are indications—though too vague to form the basis of a hypothesis—that some of the very earliest legends may have been colored by south sea myths. Dr. D. C. Holtom has drawn attention to an old commentator's note in the *Kojiki* text, with reference to the first five deities named, to the effect that "These five are those who disconnected the Sky."

⁸⁵ Elephant remains have been found.

⁸⁶ Professor Tsuboï of Tok'yo thinks the remains of the stone age in Japan belonged to these people, though most Japanese scholars follow Professor Koganeï in ascribing them to the *Emishi*. The hills about Matsuyama, Saïtama-Ken, are honeycombed with pit-dwellings which used to be called ancient sepulchres. Dr. Tsuboï has uncovered some hundreds of these. It is an open question whether the implements, weapons and crude pottery found in them antedate the *Emishi*.

Within the last few years Professor Uchida, of the Literary College of K'yoto, unearthed in a shell-barrow on the estate of Mr. Matsuë Sojuro in Okayama Prefecture, a well-nigh perfect human skull which is believed to be a relic of this prehistoric race.

⁸⁷ Ainu legend tells also of another folk called mountain-men (*kim-un-ainu*), stronger and even hairier than themselves, who practiced cannibalism, but of these no traces remain, although some specimens, according to Chamberlain, are said to have been seen in the Teshiyo forests within the memory of men living two generations ago.

⁸⁸ This probably arose from a *Volksetymologie*, the word *koro* being mistakenly translated "burdock" (*Petasites japonica*), the Japanese *fuki*.

⁸⁹ Brinkley curtly disposes of the whole *tsuchi-gumo* question by denying that they were any different from the *Emishi*. Possibly this legend, which is quoted from the lost *Mutsu-Fudoki*, had not been brought to his attention. Incidentally, to make the distinction more obvious, the *Emishi* are in it referred to as "Ezo folk."

Of course the cave-dwelling is not direct proof, as it is a mark of many northern races on the mainland, but there is an accumulation of evidence that they were distinct.

⁹⁰ Some hold that remnants of this dwarfish race are still to be found in the Kurile Islands.

⁹¹ Hilgendorf, Doenitz and Scheube hold that the Ainu and the Japanese have a common stock. But ethnological authority groups the former with the Arctic hyperboreans of northeastern Asia. Some telltale customs such as the use of the "tump-line" for bearing burdens (common also to the Alaskan "Indians," who are as unmistakably Asiatic), the character of their wood-carving, etc., add weight to this classification. And the assertion of Ainu legend that the race's ancestors came from a snow-covered land of treeless and birdless steppes is significant of north-continental origin.

⁹² Hondo. It should be remembered that this word is a designation, not a name. The Great-Island, to the Japanese themselves, has never had a true name.

⁹³ Aston translates "local chiefs" and Chamberlain supposes the word to be a contraction of *kuni-nushi* (land-chief), which comes to the same thing. But later records make it clear that the Kuzu were a distinct tribe.

⁹⁴ Some native authorities, unwilling to admit the extent of this saturation, claim these to have been subjects of the Sun-stock who had been enslaved by the *Emishi*. Of course this has no likelihood whatever.

⁹⁵ The name anciently applied to the whole region north of Echizen, including Echizen, Etchu, Echigo, Kaga, Noto, Uzen, Ugo and the unknown territory beyond. Echigo Province still has a Koshi-*Kori* (-District) and a Koshi-Lake (Koshi-no-Mizu-Umi). The name is found also in Izumo, in the Koshi-gawa (river).

⁹⁶ "It seems equally certain," he says, "that almost all that the Japanese possess which is not of Chinese, Korean or Tartar origin, has descended from the Ainu, or has been developed or improved from an Ainu model." Certain German anthropologists also have given it as their opinion that the Ainu differ less from the Japanese than the Germans themselves from the Armenians.

⁹⁷ Even Chamberlain, who, with Batchelor, has made the most praiseworthy attempt to preserve the lore of the Ainu, is of the opinion that "like its language, it largely shows itself adopted from the Japanese"—and this because certain of its myths show resemblance to Japanese myths!

⁹⁸ Chamberlain's Collection: *Penri, the Old Chieftain of Piratori*. The legend

has several forms among the Ainu. In one variant it is the sky-lark, which the Great Deity sends. The bird played and stayed all night so that when he flew back, the deity met him "a hundred and twenty feet up" and bade him henceforth live on earth. Every summer now he flies up to the sky to protest against the sentence, whence his name, "protestant bird" (*Charange Chikap*).
99 The similarity of this word to the Japenese Kami (*Kamu*) has been noted.

PAGES 434 - 442

1 Aston has called attention to this correspondence.
2 It is interesting to note that the wry-neck, in Greek legend, exerted the same magic power (see Theocritus, Idyl II: *The Enchantress*).
3 The origin of the word Ezo (unless we suppose it a corruption of *Emisu* (barbarian) is unknown. The Ainu do not use it today. Anciently it meant any locality held by the *Emishi*. At one time it was applied to the whole northern half of the archipelago, as it is applied today, sometimes, to southern Saghalien.
4 Sayce and Wilkinson to the contrary.
5 In his *Izu-no Chi-Waki* (1851. Incomplete).
6 Later the concern of the Greek writers was to veil the earlier myth which growth of culture had made to seem blasphemous.
7 There are not lacking indications that Izumo had knowledge of the Sun-myth before its arrival with the people who claimed the Sun-Goddess as their great ancestress, and that it possessed its own lore of the "under-distant-land." Aston conjectures that Brave-Swift-Impetuous-Male was originally the moon-deity of Izumo and Moon-Darkness-Possessor the moon-deity of the Sun-Folk.
8 The question of the origin of the Sun-Folk (unless a key be found in the more abstruse calculations of ethnology or philology) will probably be disputed livelily for many a century. Various more or less serious investigators have thought them modern-Ainu, Tartar-Mongol, Malay, Turano-African, Toba-Tartar, Aztec and what-not. Macleod ventured the hypothesis that they were one of the Lost Tribes of Israel, and Kaempfer was convinced that they were among the Babel-Builders.

One of the most recent as well as the most fanciful theories, that of Mr. Jamohedff Edalgi (*Transactions of the Asiatic Society of Japan*, vol. 38, pt. II, p. 52), points to resemblances between the Japanese and Mithraic cosmogonies. According to the latter creation began with Kronos (Parsi, *Zervane Akarne*), Boundless and Infinite Time, who begot the Heaven-god and the Earth-goddess, and this couple gave birth to the deities of the ocean, forests, fecundating water, fire, wine, and the nether-world. Mithra, who can be described only as a Sun-god, was born to save the world from the scourge of the last-named and his progeny. The Mithraic Mithra, the Persian Mithra (Meter), the Hindoo Mithra the Protector and the Assyrian Mylitta are doubtless variations of the same deity, though neither the Parsis nor the ancient Zoroastrians worshiped Mithra as a god.

The ultra-fanciful point to the root recurring in the words *sube, subera, sumera, suberagi, sumeragi* (all equivalent terms signifying "under-heaven-ruler," applied indiscriminately to deities and Emperors) and would make Sumera a corruption of Semiramis—which reminds one of the argument that the Hibernian came from ancient Assyria, from the fact that the first known native king of that country (2000 B.C.?) was named Irishum. To identify the Japanese with the Assyrians and the Sun-Goddess with the Queen of Babylon is, to be sure, a *precieuse ridicule*.

The most tenable theory—one borne out by tribal customs, marriage- and burial-ceremonies, superstitions, methods of divination, language, physical measurement, and a hundred other things—places the Japanese in Doonan's "north Himalaya centre," commonly called the Altaic group. In short, he is at bottom a Ural-Tartar, cousin of the Manchu farmer, the Mongol nomad, the Korean, the Turk and the Hun.

[9] One group of scholars, represented by Dr. Tsuboï, believe they came, bringing their language with them, from southeastern Asia; another, led by C. K. Parker, count them invaders from Korea, speaking a Turco-Tartar tongue.

Chinese tradition contains several legends which account for the origin of the W*a* (Japanese) race. One traces it to a Chinese colony under Su-She (a descendant of Prince T'ai Peh of Wu) which settled in the archipelago in 219 B.C. That most popularly cited is that of the coming to the Islands of the Chinese physician J'yofuku, which event is assigned to 211 or 221 B.C. He is said to have brought with him from three hundred to three thousand followers of both sexes and to have settled at Kumano, where ancient Chinese coins are periodically unearthed. Japanese tradition credits him merely with the founding of a family in the archipelago.

An older tradition recites that the grandfather of the Emperor Buwo, first ruler of the Shu Dynasty (1120-249 B.C.) wished to bequeath the realm to a younger son and to disinherit the eldest. The younger refused the inheritance, but the eldest, who was named Taïhoku-Ki, secretly departed with his followers to the south of China, from whence he sailed to Japan, settling in H'yuga. Hence the Chinese term for the archipelago, "Kishi-Koku" (Country of the Ki Family).

Klaproth cites still another legend, according to which two elder brothers, resigning the throne to a younger, about 1280 B.C. founded a kingdom among the barbarous tribes of north China. After a history of several centuries it was conquered by its neighbors. The reigning sovereign, one Fu-sha, committed suicide, and his sons and grandsons fled by sea to Japan. The Chinese tradition places this event in 473 B.C.

[10] Modern Japan has an Awa Province in the Nankaïdo, and another in the Tokaïdo, though the etymology of the latter is less certain.

[11] Schwartz is of the belief that the Izumo legends are the "relics of an independent religion which ultimately supplied the element of hero-worship, if not ancestor-worship, in that syncretized code of religious observance later called *Kami-no Michi* (Shinto)."

[12] *Not* Brave-Swift-Impetuous-Male (as is mistakenly stated by Florenz, Murray, Brinkley and Hearn) and as might have been expected were the myth-story without some foundation in real fact.